HISTORY OF WOMEN IN THE UNITED STATES

HISTORY OF WOMEN IN THE UNITED STATES
Historical Articles on Women's Lives and Activities

Edited by Nancy F. Cott

Series ISBN 3-598-41454-4

1. Theory and Method in Women's History
   ISBN 3-598-41455-2 Part 1
   ISBN 3-598-41477-3 Part 2

2. Household Constitution and Family Relationships
   ISBN 3-598-41456-0

3. Domestic Relations and Law
   ISBN 3-598-41457-9

4. Domestic Ideology and Domestic Work
   ISBN 3-598-41458-7 Part 1
   ISBN 3-598-41475-7 Part 2

5. The Intersection of Work and Family Life
   ISBN 3-598-41459-5 Part 1
   ISBN 3-598-41476-5 Part 2

6. Working on the Land
   ISBN 3-598-41460-9

7. Industrial Wage Work
   ISBN 3-598-41461-7 Part 1
   ISBN 3-598-41693-8 Part 2

8. Professional and White-Collar Employments
   ISBN 3-598-41462-5 Part 1
   ISBN 3-598-41694-6 Part 2

9. Prostitution
   ISBN 3-598-41463-3

10. Sexuality and Sexual Behavior
    ISBN 3-598-41464-1

11. Women's Bodies: Health and Childbirth
    ISBN 3-598-41465-X

12. Education
    ISBN 3-598-41466-8

13. Religion
    ISBN 3-598-41467-6

14. Intercultural and Interracial Relations
    ISBN 3-598-41468-4

15. Women and War
    ISBN 3-598-41469-2

16. Women Together: Organizational Life
    ISBN 3-598-41470-6

17. Social and Moral Reform
    ISBN 3-598-41471-4 Part 1
    ISBN 3-598-41695-4 Part 2

18. Women and Politics
    ISBN 3-598-41472-2 Part 1
    ISBN 3-598-41697-0 Part 2

19. Woman Suffrage
    ISBN 3-598-41473-0 Part 1
    ISBN 3-598-41696-2 Part 2

20. Feminist Struggles for Sex Equality
    ISBN 3-598-41474-9

HISTORY OF WOMEN IN THE UNITED STATES
Historical Articles on Women's Lives and Activities

10. Sexuality and Sexual Behavior

Edited with an Introduction by

Nancy F. Cott
Yale University

K · G · Saur
Munich · New Providence · London · Paris · 1993

Publisher's Note
The articles and chapters which comprise this collection originally appeared in a wide variety of publications and are reproduced here in facsimile from the highest quality offprints and photocopies available. The reader will notice some occasional marginal shading and text-curl common to photocopying from tightly bound volumes. Every attempt has been made to either correct or minimize this effect.

Copyright information for articles reproduced in this collection appears at the end of this volume.

Library of Congress Cataloging-in-Publication Data
History of women in the United States : historical articles on
women's lives and activities / edited with
an introduction by Nancy F. Cott.
p. cm.
Includes bibliographical references and indexes.
Contents: 1. Theory and method in women's history -- 2. Household constitution and family relationships -- 3. Domestic relations and law -- 4. Domestic ideology and domestic work -- 5. The intersection of work and family life -- 6. Working on the land -- 7. Industrial wage work -- 8. Professional and white-collar employments -- 9. Prostitution -- 10. Sexuality and sexual behavior -- 11. Women's bodies -- 12. Education -- 13. Religion -- 14. Intercultural and interracial relations -- 15. Women and war -- 16. Women together -- 17. Social and moral reform -- 18. Women and politics -- 19. Woman suffrage -- 20. Feminist struggles for sex equality.
ISBN 3-598-41454-4 (set)
1. Women--United States--History. 2. Women--United States--Social conditions. I. Cott, Nancy F.
HQ1410.H57 1992
305.4'0973--dc20 92-16765
CIP

Die Deutsche Bibliothek - CIP - Einheitsaufnahme

History of Women in the United States: historical articles
on women's lives and activities / ed. with an introd. by Nancy F. Cott.
- Munich ; London ; New York ; Paris : Saur.
ISBN 3-598-41454-4
NE: Cott, Nancy F. (Hrsg.)
Vol. 10. sexuality and sexual behavior - (1993)
ISBN 3-598-41464-1

Printed on acid-free paper/Gedruckt auf säurefreiem Papier

Printed in the United States of America
Printed/Bound by Edwards Brothers Incorporated, Ann Arbor

ISBN 3-598-41464-1 (vol. 10)
ISBN 3-598-41454-4 (series)

Contents

CONTENTS

CONTENTS

Series Preface

In the space of one generation, women's history has become the fastest-growing area of scholarship in U.S. history. Since the resurgence of feminism in the late 1960s and 1970s, insistent questions about the historical meanings of "woman's place" have sowed and reaped a garden of scholarship. Where scholarly works used to be bare of mention of women, academic enterprise has now produced a vigorous growth of books and articles, bringing to light diverse women of every region, race, class and age. This research is marked by a renovating intent that refuses to accept as "human" history a history of men. Interest is lively and debate is stimulating and sought after: attendance at the Berkshire Conference on the History of Women rivals the size of the annual convention of the American Historical Association.

While books in women's history are daily increasing in numbers and strength, as in any fast-developing field the scholarly literature in the form of articles is most expansive and up-to-the-minute. All the history journals now publish articles on women's work, domestic settings, family relations, household matters, female politics and organizations and so forth, and new journals have sprung into being to concentrate on such topics. Women's historians publish in numerous regional and thematic history journals as well as in feminist outlets and in journals of other social science disciplines. This series brings together a collection of outstanding articles from the field, almost all written in the past twenty years and more than half published during the 1980s. It brings together, in volumes organized by topic, essays otherwise widely dispersed. These volumes reprint only articles that originally appeared in journals, not chapters of books; review articles are not included. Articles have been chosen for overall quality and for range. Each one was chosen for one or more of the following reasons: because it is the standard authority on its subject matter; represents an important statement on a topic by a recognized scholar; presages an important book to come; provides a first look at new evidence or new methods; or opens an untapped area or new controversy. Older articles have been reprinted if their data or interpretation have not been surpassed or if they marked an important stage in the historiography, even if since superseded.

The historical coverage of the series extends from the Revolutionary era to the 1960s. The articles themselves are dated from the 1940s through 1988. Volumes are organized by topic rather than time period. Within each volume, the articles are ordered chronologically (with respect to substance), so that the whole can be read as an historical overview. The only exception to this ordering principle is Volume One, on Theory and Method, in which the contents are arranged in order of publication. Within each volume there is an attempt to include articles on as diverse kinds of women as possible. None of the volume topics is regionally or racially defined; rather, all volumes are topically designed so as to afford views of women's work, family lives, and public activities which cut across races and regions. Any volume in the series stands on its own, supplying as full a treatment of a designated subject matter as the scholarly literature will provide. Several groupings of volumes also make sense; that is, volumes two through five all center around domestic and family matters; volumes five through nine consider other varieties of women's work; volumes nine through eleven concern uses and abuses of women's bodies; volumes twelve through fourteen look at major aspects of socialization; and volumes fifteen through twenty include organizational and political efforts of many sorts.

As a whole, the series displays in all its range the vitality of the field of women's history. Aside from imbuing U.S. history with new vision, scholarship in this area has informed, and should continue to inform, current public debate on issues from parental leave to the nuclear freeze. By bringing historical articles together under topical headings, these volumes both represent accurately the shape of historical controversy (or consensus) on given issues and make historians' findings most conveniently available for current reference.

Introduction

Although historians have long been interested in documenting the changing canons of sexual morality, sexuality itself—like the family—has only recently been considered susceptible of historical analysis. Historians of women have been persistent and creative in investigating past sexual behavior and its meanings as well as sexual ideology. They have questioned the common twentieth-century assumption that the history of sexual behavior is a history moving from past restriction and repression to current liberation and freedom. They have documented how important the analytical category of gender is in studying sexual behavior, that is, in pointing to the possible differences between men's and women's experience and perception of the very same sexual event or option.

For hundreds, even thousands of years, standards of sexual behavior governing same-sex and heterosexual interaction, and reproduction, have been part of human definitions of civilization and propriety. What is interesting to historians is that such standards change over time within a culture, while appearing at any given time to be unshakable. By what means, and why, do sexual standards and practices change? Moreover, what is the congruence between standards and actual practice? These kinds of questions have frequently motivated historians. Since women have been so defined by their sex—indeed, being called "the sex" during much of the nineteenth century—for historians of women probably more than for historians of men it seems necessary to pursue these questions. In examining sexual standards and behavior as on any other topic, one cardinal tenet of the new women's history is to propose women as historical actors; another is to keep in mind that gender matters in both the motivations of individual actors and the driving force of historical change. So, for instance, if standard twentieth-century interpretations of Victorian-era sexual ideology see prudery as the hallmark, and assume that men imposed on and restricted women by means of norms of chastity, the new women's history would ask what women might have seen as their own interests in "prudish" norms. Where standard interpretations of the drop (by half) in marital fertility between 1800 and 1900 would lay the cause to men's economic calculation that large numbers of children were unprofitable in an urbanizing commercializing economy, the new women's history presupposes that women's choices must have had something to do with the decline—and sets out to find what.

Besides these new approaches, different kinds of documentation have been employed. Until recently, the main sources used to document the history of sexual behavior have been retrospective reminiscences such as autobiographies and memoirs, and didactic writings by ministers, moralists, or medicine men telling people how they should act. The problem with retrospective accounts is that as times change and sexual values do, the past is rendered in light of the time of present writing, which may cause distortions. Didactic texts have an inherent defect too, in the absence of a clear relation between the sexual behavior advised and actual practices of current sexual behavior: whether the two are similar or opposite is not self-evident in the didactic text.

The new investigations bring more quantifiable data to bear. For instance, since sexuality has for the most part been connected to reproduction and contained within marriage, data on marital fertility, on rates of abortion, on divorce proceedings can be used; since sexuality has often defined the boundaries of deviance, documents from penal and reform institutions offer further quantifiable sources. On the other hand, individuals' private documents—diaries and letters—have been searched as never before for evidence about sexual beliefs and behaviors. Unlike autobiographies, these sources do not suffer from possible distortions of memory by changing times, as retrospective personal accounts are likely to.

With the use of new approaches and sources, historians have shown that the picture of the sexual past is more complicated than ever before imagined. Many people today assume that standards for women's pre-marital or extra-marital sexual activity have moved in linear fashion from tight control to relative freedom, over time. But the seventeenth-century Puritans, it now appears, gave more explicit recognition to female sexuality and female erotic drives in everyday life than did their nineteenth-century successors, the Victorians. On the other hand, much research in women's history suggests that the so-called prudery or inhibitions of the mid-nineteenth century may have been part of a complex reorientation of power within the middle-class family which benefitted women, by enabling them to regulate their husbands' sexual access to them. Such historical investigations propose that sexual leverage for women may not always be identical with emphasis on female sexual drives. Investigation of nineteenth-century mores and behavior has also suggested that the era of so-called prudery may have allowed much more leeway for emotional and sensual relations of woman to woman than our own supposedly liberated era. Carroll Smith-Rosenberg, in particular, has persuasively argued that middle-class women occupied complementary heterosexual and homosocial worlds simultaneously, and advantageously; thus Victorian sexual standards may have set up a less categorically divided and restricted spectrum of behavior from homosexual to heterosexual than we find in our own era.[1] As articles in this volume make clear, the historical evolution from Victorian standards of pure womanhood to the more sexually expressive "new woman" of the early twentieth century also included new taboos on women's same-sex intimacy. It is worth noting that where the sexual slur hurled against a woman who transgressed social norms in the nineteenth century would have been "loose" or "promiscuous," only in the twentieth century would it be "lesbian."

Many difficulties of definition, as well as problems in finding congruence between ideology, practice and feeling, hedge about the project of investigating the history of sexuality. Despite, or perhaps because of these challenges, this has been one of the most revelatory and fast-changing areas in women's history, of which the articles in this volume give an unsurpassed overview.

Notes

[1] Carroll Smith-Rosenberg, "The Female World of Love and Ritual: Relations between Women in Nineteenth-Century America," *Signs* 1 (Autumn 1975), 1-29.

Sexuality and Sexual Behavior

Daniel Scott Smith and Michael S. Hindus

Premarital Pregnancy in America 1640–1971: An Overview and Interpretation Sexual expression is a basic human drive and its control, a ubiquitous feature of all societies. Although all cultures prescribe sexual intercourse within marriage, in Western and especially American society sex has been proscribed without. Since behavior obviously does not always conform to norms, essential to uncovering the history of sex is some objective measure of the extent of non-marital intercourse. As Schumpeter once put it, "we need statistics not only for explaining things but also in order to know precisely what there is to explain."[1] Since children are a measurable, if not inevitable, result of intercourse, premarital pregnancy—operationally defined as the conception, before marriage, of the first post-maritally born child—provides an index of change in sexual behavior. This measure has the advantages of coverage (since nearly all adults marry), reliability (since the births are legitimate and more likely to be recorded than illegitimate births), objectivity (since its measurement depends on the matching of records collected for other purposes), and sensitivity to change in the underlying phenomenon (since premarital pregnancy is a relatively minor violation of the prevailing ban on non-marital intercourse).

What has to be explained in the white American premarital pregnancy record is the cyclical pattern of troughs in the seventeenth century (under 10 percent of first births) and mid-nineteenth century (about 10 percent) and peaks in the second half of the eighteenth century (about 30 percent) and in contemporary America (between 20 and 25 percent) (Fig. 1). This cycle cannot be explained away by changes in the variables intermediate between premarital coitus and

Daniel Scott Smith is Assistant Professor of History at the University of Illinois, Chicago Circle, and Associate Director of the Family History Program at the Newberry Library. Michael S. Hindus is a Fellow at the Center for the Study of Law and Society, University of California, Berkeley.

An earlier version of this analysis was presented to the annual meeting of the American Historical Association in 1971. We are indebted to John Demos, Michael Gordon, Kenneth Lockridge, Susan Norton, Edward Shorter, and Etienne van de Walle for criticism of the original paper.

1 Joseph A. Schumpeter, *History of Economic Analysis* (New York, 1954), 14. For a general introduction to the sociology of sex, see Kingsley Davis, "Sexual Behavior," in Robert K. Merton and Robert A. Nisbet (eds.), *Contemporary Social Problems* (New York, 1966; 2nd ed.), 322–372.

Fig. 1 The American Premarital Pregnancy Record

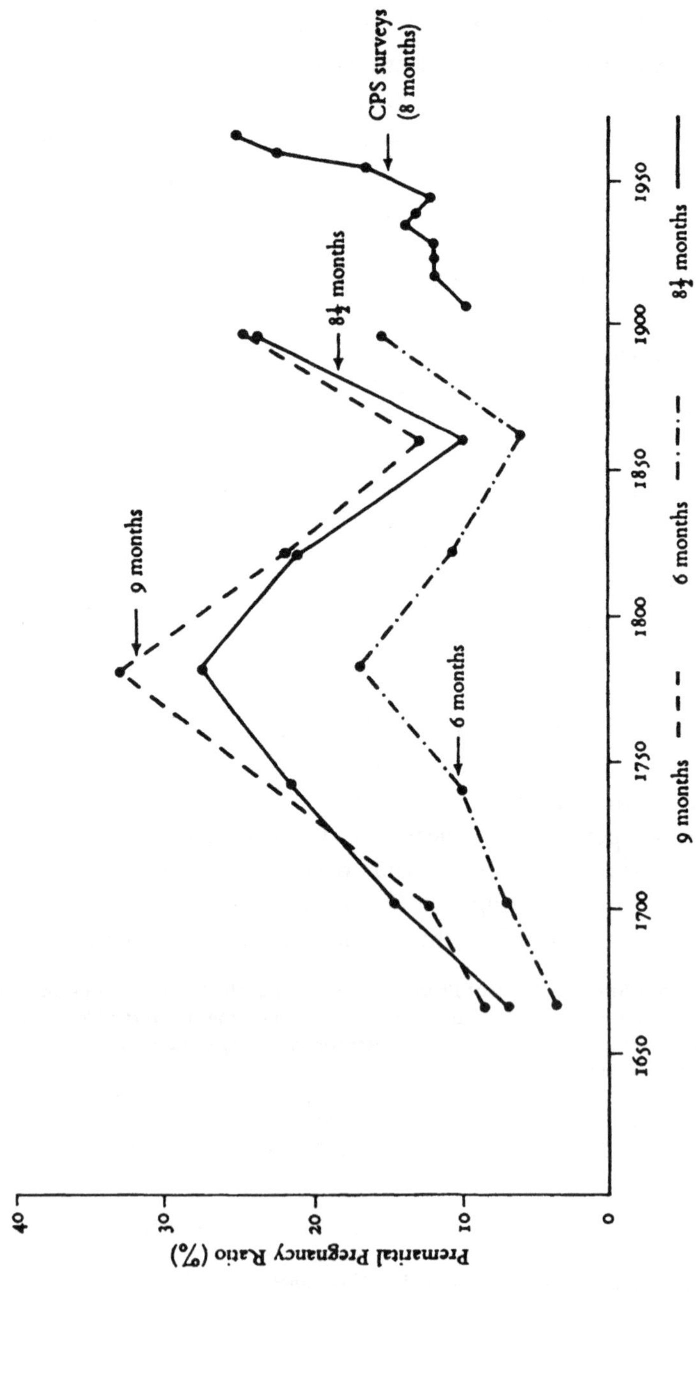

SOURCE: See Appendix I.

post-marital birth—fecundability and pregnancy wastage, contraceptive usage, induced abortion, and illegitimacy. Although these variables influence the level, we are concerned with the direction of the trend. It is unlikely that the underlying biological bases of American reproduction have varied enough to account for the magnitude and timing of the fluctuations in the premarital pregnancy ratio. Although contraceptive use obviously lowers fertility, since World War II both illegitimacy and premarital pregnancy have increased. Historically the trend in premarital pregnancy has paralleled that in illegitimacy.[2] Although the proportion of bridal pregnancies in all non-maritally conceived births is not constant over time and space, it appears to be a rule that when the overall level of non-marital conception increases, the proportion of non-marital pregnancies born outside of wedlock also rises.[3] To explain the major swings in premarital pregnancy, primary emphasis must rest on an analysis of the variation in the proportion of women who have engaged in premarital coitus. A similar long cycle also exists in West European illegitimacy and premarital pregnancy data (Fig. 2). Superficially at least the cyclical variation in premarital pregnancy is a striking regularity of early modern and modern social history.[4]

The basic strategy of this analysis is to distinguish between the periods with high ratios by comparing differentials in premarital

2 These are international phenomena; see Sidney Goldstein, "Premarital Pregnancies and Out-of-Wedlock Births in Denmark, 1950–1965," *Demography*, IV (1967), 925–936; K. G. Basavarajappa, "Pre-marital Pregnancies and Ex-Nuptial Births in Australia, 1911–66," *Australian and New Zealand Journal of Sociology*, IV (1968), 126–145; Shirley M. Hartley, "The Amazing Rise of Illegitimacy in Great Britain," *Social Forces*, XLIV (1966), 533–545; Daniel Scott Smith, "The Dating of the American Sexual Revolution: Evidence and Interpretation," in Michael Gordon (ed.), *The American Family in Social-Historical Perspective* (New York, 1973), 321–335. For the long-run European pattern see Edward Shorter, "Illegitimacy, Sexual Revolution, and Social Change in Modern Europe," *Journal of Interdisciplinary History*, II (1971), 237–272; Shorter, John Knodel, and Etienne van de Walle, "The Decline of Non-Marital Fertility in Europe, 1880–1940," *Population Studies*, XXV (1971), 375–393.

3 This rule is derived from the postwar experience of Great Britain (Hartley, "Amazing Rise," 540, Table 3), Denmark (Goldstein, "Premarital Pregnancies," 930), Australia (Basavarajappa, "Pre-marital Pregnancies," 141), and the cross-national relationship in Phillips Cutright, "Illegitimacy in the United States, 1920–1968," in Charles F. Westoff and Robert Parke, Jr. (eds.), *Demographic and Social Aspects of Population Growth* (Washington, D.C., 1972), 405.

4 The American and West European cycles are not identical. The early nineteenth-century American decline occurred a half-century or more before the corresponding downturn in Western Europe. Although a reduced incidence of premarital coitus seems central to the American decline, the use of contraception is the principal variable in the European decrease.

Fig. 2 Comparative Premarital Pregnancy Series

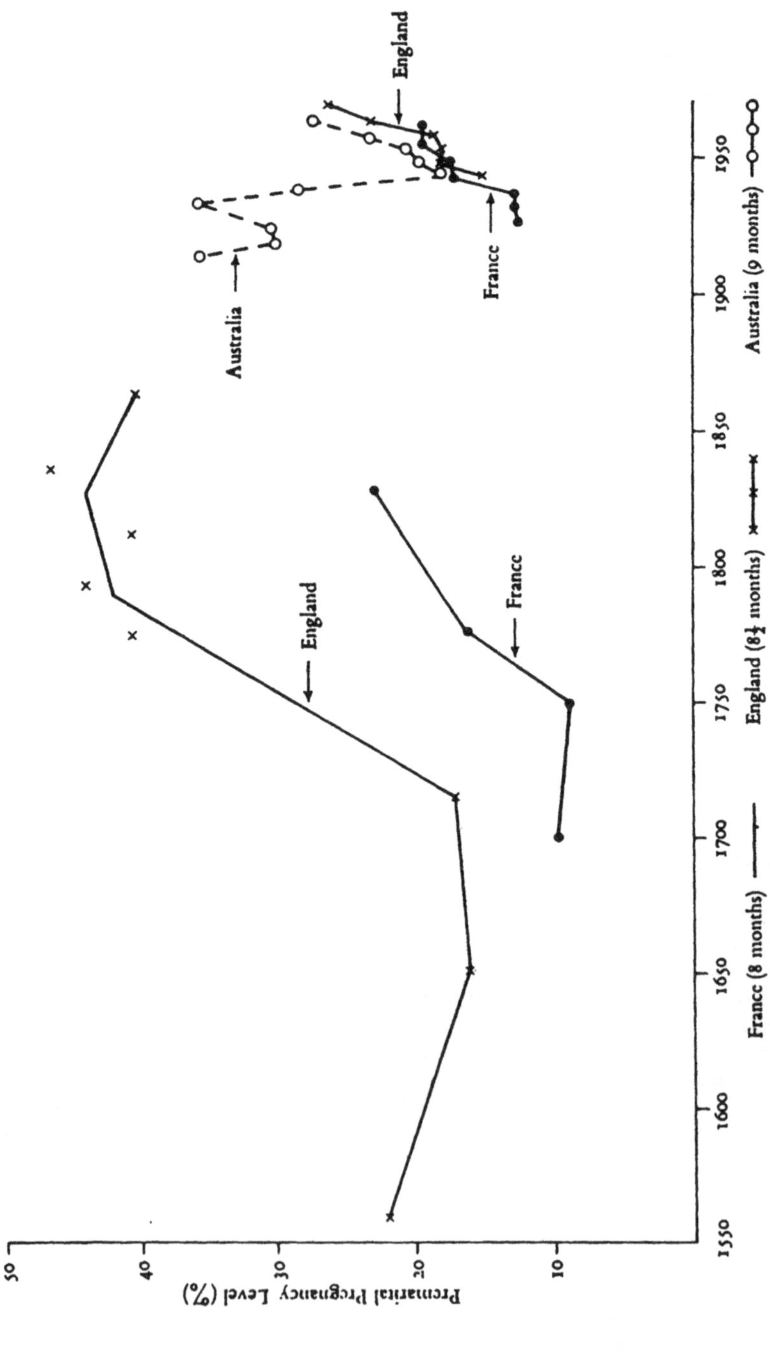

SOURCE: See Appendix II.

pregnancy between groups, and then to assess eras with lower ratios by focusing on differences in the social control of sexuality. The social relationships underlying similar premarital pregnancy levels are strikingly dissimilar. The analysis of the transitions thus concentrates on the changing relationships between sexual behavior and the social mechanisms controlling it. Throughout we will be concerned with individual behavior, the role of the family as the principal regulator of sexual expression, and the larger societal context.

PERIODS WITH HIGH RATIOS The family of orientation (family of birth) played a much more direct role in the high premarital pregnancy level of the late eighteenth century than it does in the modern peak. This contrast is apparent in the incidence of premarital pregnancy by age; the incidence by class; the relative incidence among interclass unions; and the transmission and support of the tendency toward premarital pregnancy.

Age In contrast to the relatively constant age-specific pattern among pre-industrial women, modern premarital pregnancy is increasingly concentrated among teen-agers (Table 1). Although the low teen-age rates for seventeenth-century Hingham, Massachusetts and pre-industrial West European samples may be attributed to adolescent subfecundity, the relative stability after age 20 can best be explained by the absence of a clear demarcation between youth and maturity in pre-industrial society.[5] Couples in their late 20s entered into marriage in the same social context as those marrying at an earlier age. In contemporary populations, by contrast, teen-agers do not employ contraceptives as often and as effectively as women in their 20s. Aging in modern society from 15 to 25 involves qualitative changes in the context of behavior which did not occur two centuries earlier.

Economic strata Although family income had little impact on the incidence of premarital coitus of white 15–19 year-old unmarried females surveyed in 1971, parental economic status was inversely related to the frequency of premarital pregnancy in the eighteenth-century case (Table 2). Based on a Detroit sample of 1960, parental

5 Since a low age at menarche is related to diet, particularly protein consumption, the American age historically may have been below that in Europe. For this suggestion see Peter Laslett, "Age at Menarche in Europe since the Eighteenth Century," *Journal of Interdisciplinary History*, II (1971), 236.

Table 1 Relationship of Female Age at First Marriage to Premarital Pregnancy

DESCRIPTION OF SAMPLE PLACE AND PERIOD OF MARRIAGE	AGE AT MARRIAGE OF WOMAN				
	15–19	20–24	25–29	30–34	35 AND OVER
Hingham, Mass. (rate)					
–1720	2.4 (100)	11.4 (475)	3.9 (162)[a]		
1721–1800	40.9 (100)	23.8 (58)	21.6 (53)		
1801–1840	23.9 (100)	15.5 (65)	13.5 (56)		
1841–1880	15.4 (100)	11.0 (71)	2.7 (17)		
Andover, Mass. (ratio)[1]					
1685–1744	19.0 (100)	15.8 (83)	6.7 (35)[a]		
United States (ratio)[2]					
1964–1966	29.8 (100)	14.7 (49)	5.9 (20)[a]		
Northwest France (ratio)[3]					
1670–1769	3.7 (100)	6.4 (175)	6.8 (184)	6.3 (171)	6.5 (177)
France (rate)[4]					
1925–1929	18.4 (100)	11.9 (65)	8.6 (47)	7.1 (39)	6.0 (33)
1955–1959	33.0 (100)	18.2 (55)	14.4 (44)	11.3 (34)	3.7 (11)
Australia (rate)[5]					
1911	58.8 (100)	34.5 (59)	20.3 (34)	15.2 (26)	6.8 (12)
1965	44.6 (100)	16.2 (36)	13.5 (30)	10.8 (24)	3.9 (9)

a 25 or more.

SOURCES:

1 We are indebted to Philip J. Greven, Jr. for these unpublished data.

2 Mary Grace Kovar, "Interval from First Marriage to First Birth: United States, 1964–66 Births," unpub. paper, (1970), Table A.

3 Louis Henry, "Intervalle entre le mariage," 277, Table 9.

4 Jean-Claude DeVille, *Structure*, 91, Table 35.

5 K. G. Basavarajappa, "Pre-marital Pregnancies," 143, Table A.

Table 2 Economic Status, Premarital Pregnancy in Eighteenth-Century Hingham, Mass., The United States, 1964–66, and Premarital Coital Incidence for White American 15–19 Year-Olds, 1971

DESCRIPTION OF SAMPLE	WEALTH CRITERION AND INCIDENCE OF PREMARITAL PREGNANCY IN QUINTILES					
WEALTH OF HUSBAND, HINGHAM RECONSTITUTED FAMILIES OF 1721–1800	TOP 20%	U–M 20%	M 20%	L–M 20%	POOR 20%	TOTAL
	19.8% (91)	22.5% (89)	29.1% (103)	43.8% (105)	29.2% (130)	29.3% (518)
Children of taxpayers on 1767 first parish list						
Sons	24.7% (81)	35.2% (54)	34.6% (26)	47.9% (48)	50.0% (34)	36.2% (243)
Daughters	16.4% (67)	37.3% (67)	44.2% (43)	37.8% (45)	22.2% (27)	31.3% (249)
United States, 1964–66[1]	FAMILY INCOME (IN THOUSANDS OF DOLLARS)					
	$10+	7–9.9	5–6.9	3–4.9	< 3	
	8.2%	11.5%	17.6%	23.3%	37.5%	21.6%
Premarital coital experience of unmarried white 15–19 year old females, 1971[2]	FAMILY INCOME (IN THOUSANDS OF DOLLARS)					
	$15+	10–14.9	6–9.9	3–5.9	< 3	
	25.6%	23.6%	22.1%	23.4%	28.5%	23.4%

SOURCES:

1 Kovar, "Interval from first Marriage," Table F.

2 John F. Kantner and Melvin Zelnik, "Sexual Experience of Young Unmarried Women in the United States," *Family Planning Perspectives*, IV (1972), 10–11, Tables 1, 2.

status also has relatively little effect on the frequency of premarital pregnancy.[6] Higher economic status no longer provides parents with leverage over the sexual behavior of their children.

Heterogamy In the Detroit sample, premarital pregnancy ratios were markedly higher when the wife's father was of higher status than the husband's father; pregnancies in which the male's family had higher status presumably ended in illegitimate births. Interclass marriages in Hingham show the same lower pattern of premarital pregnancy exhibited by marriages within the wealthier 40 percent of the population (Table 3). Since behavior followed the pattern of the higher status partner, parental control is more evident. The absence of a differential in interclass marriages suggests that community coercion overcame the more serious consequences of pregnancy for women. Further suggestive detail on the roles of parental and community authority is available for the reconstituted Hingham families established between 1761 and 1780. Men who married daughters of wealthier parents were penalized most by premarital pregnancy, implying that there was no necessity for the girl's father to contribute economically to a marriage that had been made inevitable by pregnancy.[7] For the children of poorer parents, premarital pregnancy seemed to have involved no economic setback. Lacking economic resources, less wealthy fathers could not restrain the sexual activity of their unmarried children.[8]

Sexually Restrictive and Permissive Groups Continuity is apparent in the institutional basis of the sexually more restrictive subculture. In both eras, religious involvement is associated with lower levels of pre-

6 Lolagene C. Coombs, Ronald Freedman, Judith Friedman, and William F. Pratt, "Premarital Pregnancy and Status before and after Marriage," *American Journal of Sociology*, LXXV (1970), 810, Table 3.

7 Premaritally pregnant couples, whose fathers both ranked in the upper 40 percent by wealth, were 1.9 quintiles lower in wealth with respect to the husband's father than couples of similar status who were not pregnant at marriage. When the husband's father was wealthy and the wife's father less so, the difference was 0.6 quintiles; in the reverse case, the premaritally pregnant were 1.5 quintiles poorer on the average. Finally, if both fathers ranked in the poorer 60 percent of the population, the premaritally pregnant were 0.4 quintiles higher in comparison with the husbands' fathers than the non-premaritally pregnant.

8 In both the eighteenth century and today, couples who had a child on the way at the wedding have lower subsequent economic status than those not pregnant at marriage (see the first and fourth row of Table 2). Curtailment of education is the major reason for the modern differential.

Table 3 Proportions Pregnant at Marriage by Status of Parents

DESCRIPTION OF SAMPLE	STATUS OF WIFE'S FATHER	STATUS OF HUSBAND'S FATHER		
Detroit marriages of 1960 (father's education)[1]		%		
		GRADE SCHOOL	HIGH SCHOOL	COLLEGE
	Grade school	16.0	16.7	16.1
	High school	17.5	20.7	16.9
	College	31.3	24.5	15.9
Hingham reconstituted families of 1761–1780 (father's wealth)		WEALTHIER 40%	POORER 60%	TOTAL
	Wealthier 40%	31.0 (29)	35.7 (14)	32.6 (43)
	Poorer 60%	33.3 (18)	50.0 (38)	44.6 (56)
	Total	31.9% (47)	44.6% (52)	39.4% (99)

[1] Coombs et al., "Premarital Pregnancy and Status," 810.

Table 4 Church Membership (1717–1786), Wealth,[1] Premarital Pregnancy Status of Parents, and Premarital Pregnancy Status of Children

CATEGORY	WEALTH STATUS WEALTHIER 40%	POORER 60%	TOTAL
Persons taxed in 1767			
One or both spouses members	9.4% (53)	32.3% (34)	18.4% (87)
Neither spouse member	27.3 (33)	35.3 (68)	32.7 (101)
Parents pregnant at marriage			
Sons			
Both or spouse member	36.4% (11)	0.0% (2)	30.8% (13)
Neither church member	25.0 (12)	46.9 (32)	40.9 (44)
Daughters			
Both or spouse member	50.0% (4)	50.0% (12)	50.0% (16)
Neither church member	40.0 (20)	69.2 (13)	51.5 (33)
Parents not pregnant at marriage			
Sons			
Both or spouse member	25.4% (63)	50.0% (20)	31.3% (83)
Neither church member	23.1 (39)	44.7 (38)	33.8 (77)
Daughters			
Both or spouse member	23.8% (63)	36.0% (25)	27.3% (88)
Neither church member	28.6 (28)	33.3 (48)	31.6 (76)

[1] Hingham first parish list of 1767.

marital sexual activity, On the Hingham first parish tax list of 1767, only 18.4 percent of the cases where the property holder or his spouse were church members involved premarital conceptions; in 30.3 percent of the cases where neither spouse was identified as a church member, there was a premarital pregnancy (Table 4, top two rows). This relationship holds, however, only for the wealthier stratum.[9] In the 1971 survey of teen-age sexual experience, females who attended church on less than three occasions in the previous month were, depending on denomination, two to three times more likely to be non-virgins than those who attended four or more times. Active religious participation is also closely related to restrictive sexual attitudes.[10]

The association of religiosity and premarital sexual restrictiveness does not automatically imply a causal relationship. In more than 80 percent of the Hingham cases from the 1767 list, church membership followed marriage, often by five or more years. Arguing from chronology, premarital pregnancy deterred religious affiliation among the wealthier rather than vice versa. Although the children of Hingham church members were less likely to be pregnant at marriage, this minor effect disappears when one controls for wealth (Table 4). Since beginning sexual intercourse and abandoning church attendance are part of a general change in life style of maturing teen-agers, the association of religiosity and premarital sexual restrictiveness in cross-sectional surveys may be largely spurious. Religion can be said to have an impact on the overall incidence of premarital sex only when it is an encompassing and controlling force in the lives of the young and not merely an option.

The more impressive relationship in Table 4 is the consistent difference between the daughters whose mothers were pregnant at marriage and those whose mothers were not. Inasmuch as there existed a sexually permissive subculture in eighteenth-century Hingham, its continuity depended on the female line and on the less wealthy section of the population. The former relationship did not pass unnoticed by

9 In the town of Groton only 11.3 percent of persons admitted to full communion between 1761 and 1775 confessed to premarital fornication while 33 percent of those owning the baptismal covenant did so. Since formal church membership is probably related to wealth, the causation here is uncertain. For the Groton figures see Henry Reed Stiles, *Bundling: Its Origins, Progress and Decline in America* (Albany, 1871), 78.

10 Kantner and Zelnik, "Sexual Experience," 16, Table 11; Ira L. Reiss, *The Social Context of Premarital Sexual Permissiveness* (New York, 1967), 42–44, 99–100.

contemporaries, as is evidenced by the subtitle and following lines of an anonymous poem published around 1785:

> Some maidens say, if through the nation,
> Bundling should quite go out of fashion,
> Courtship would lose its sweets; and they
> Could have no fun till wedding day.
> It shant be so, they rage and storm,
> And country girls in clusters swarm,
> And fly and buz like angry bees,
> And vow they'll bundle when they please.
> Some mothers too, will plead their cause,
> And give their daughters great applause,
> And tell them 'tis no sin nor shame,
> For we, your mothers did the same.[11]

In summary, intergenerational family relationships are deeply involved in the great boom of premarital pregnancy in the eighteenth century.

Premarital sexual activity in modern society is structured through the peer group and more broadly through a youth subculture, which is reinforced by age-stratified institutions such as schools and promoted by other forces such as marketing and the mass media. Although objective family background characteristics such as income, education, or religious preference have little impact on the incidence of teen-age intercourse, higher familiar status, especially parental education, is associated with the more frequent use of contraception by sexually active teen-agers.[12] Modern parents generally lack the power to be oppressive in an effective way. This absence of parental control and influence is strikingly demonstrated by the low correspondence between the political opinions of parents and children.[13] If teen-agers are not controlled by their parents, neither are they autonomous. The adolescent way station between dependent childhood and independent adulthood is characterized by an alienation but not a separation from

11 Anon., "A New Bundling Song; Or a reproof to those Young Country Women, who follow that reproachful Practice, and to their Mothers for upholding them therein," in Stiles, *Bundling*, 81–82.

12 Reiss, *Social Context*, 171–180; James J. Teevan, Jr., "Reference Groups and Premarital Sexual Behavior," *Journal of Marriage and the Family*, XXXIV (1972), 283–291; Kantner and Zelnik, "Sexual Experience," Tables 2, 3, 4, 10; "Contraception and Pregnancy: Experience of Young Unmarried Women in the United States," *Family Planning Perspectives*, V (1973), 21–35, esp. Tables 2, 3, 9.

13 See the summary article by R. W. Connell, "Political Socialization in the American Family: The Evidence Re-Examined," *Public Opinion Quarterly*, XXXVI (1972), 322–333. The median correlation in a range of studies was only 0.2.

parental values and culture. Survey research suggests that premarital coitus is directly related to the extent of this estrangement.[14] Although the modern family fails to restrict successfully the sexual activity of children, it and the other institutions involving youth limit the possibilities of a rational separation of sex and procreation.

PERIODS WITH LOW RATIOS Just as the peaks in premarital pregnancy when examined in detail reflect quite different underlying patterns, so the troughs of the seventeenth and nineteenth centuries result from different systems of control. Although a sexually repressive ideology characterized both centuries, the emphasis in the Puritan seventeenth century was on external controls, while internal control or self-repression was the central feature of Victorian morality. Premarital sexual restraint was possible both in the seventeenth-century community and in nineteenth-century society, but not during the transition. Maintenance of morality, however, shifted from direct to indirect, from being based primarily on social control to resting principally on socialization.

The importance of external controls in the seventeenth century may be readily demonstrated. Premarital pregnancy ratios were low not just in North America but in England and France as well. English premarital pregnancy, for example, was 26 percent below the sixteenth-century figure, and illegitimacy ratios between 1651 and 1720 were less than half of those prevailing between 1581 and 1630 and from 1741 to 1820. English North America shared the organized religious intensity that pervaded Western Europe during the seventeenth century.[15] With a premarital pregnancy level less than half that of England, mid-seventeenth-century New England, as Governor Bradford of Plymouth was "verily persuaded," was a society "with not more evils in this kind [sexual deviation], nor nothing near so many by proportion as in other places; but they are here more discovered and seen and made public by due search, inquisition and due punishment; for the churches look narrowly to their members, and the magistrates over all, more

14 For example, 43.4 percent of white 15–19 year-old females who "strongly agreed" with the statement, "I don't confide very much in my parents," had had intercourse, while only 13.5 percent of those who strongly disagreed were not virgins (Kantner and Zelnik, "Sexual Experience," 15, Table 9).

15 For English bridal pregnancy data, see Appendix II. For illegitimacy trends see Peter Laslett, *The World We Have Lost* (London, 1971; 2nd ed.), 142. John Bossy, "The Counter-Reformation and the People of Catholic Europe," *Past & Present*, XLVII (1970), 51–70.

strictly than in other places."[16] Instead of the Puritans becoming "inured to sexual offenses, because there were so many," as Morgan puts it, they prosecuted their comparatively few sexual offenders vigorously. Morgan was right in his now classic reading of the court records, however, when he emphasized the calm, matter-of-fact approach of the Puritans toward even the most extreme manifestations of sexual deviance. Although this composure had its roots in the theological belief in original sin, the elaborate structure of social repression maintained by the Puritans suggests that they did not expect the population at large to have internalized sexual control. Broadly speaking, Puritanism may be characterized as a communal response to the strains accompanying the disintegration of the bases of medieval society.[17]

Nineteenth-century morality was forged in a new social matrix and constructed with different materials. The reappearance of premarital sexual restraint in the nineteenth century was based on the autonomy of the young adult and the incorporation of the groups tending toward premarital pregnancy into a new social order. By the early nineteenth century, people were generally independent in life at a younger age than ever before.[18] Although there were objective changes, such as the economic shift from the apprentice to the wage system and the substitution of boarding for service as the transitional living arrangement for young people, most significant was the social acceptance of youthful autonomy.

The new independence of nineteenth-century youth was recognized in various ways. The practical impact of the introduction of universal male suffrage was not so much the enfranchisement of a permanent proletariat as the granting of political rights to young adults. Proponents of manhood suffrage presented their arguments in terms of the reality of allowing young men the political autonomy commensurate with their social and economic status.[19] During and after the

16 William Bradford (ed. Samuel Eliot Morison), *Of Plymouth Plantation, 1620–1647* (New York, 1959), 317.

17 Edmund S. Morgan, "The Puritans and Sex," *New England Quarterly*, XV (1942), 595; Michael Walzer, "Puritanism as a Revolutionary Ideology," *History and Theory*, III (1961), 59–90.

18 Joseph F. Kett, "Growing Up in Rural New England, 1800–1840," in Tamara K. Hareven (ed.), *Anonymous Americans* (Englewood Cliffs, N.J., 1971), 9–10. For the comments of European travelers on the freedom of antebellum youth, see Frank F. Furstenberg, Jr., "Industrialization and the American Family: A Look Backward," *American Sociological Review*, XXXI (1966), 329–330, 335.

19 For examples of this argument, see Chilton Williamson, *American Suffrage from Property to Democracy* (Princeton, 1960), 139, 147, 171, 177, 187–188, 195.

Second Great Awakening, religious conversion became a common experience for teen-agers. Not unrelated to early religious involvement is the fact that youths began to play important roles in reform movements.[20]

The early nineteenth century also witnessed the social incorporation of the groups previously prone to premarital pregnancy. The erosion of the social base of the sexually permissive segment of the population was partly the result of a dramatic expansion of religious participation. Estimated formal church membership in America tripled from 7 to 23 percent between 1800 and 1860.[21] With younger conversion, religion could have a more effective impact on premarital sexual choices. The concomitant splintering of American Protestantism meant that each stratum had one or more denominations tailored to its particular condition and needs. Although denominations differed in social base and religious style, the regulation of individual morality was a central concern of nineteenth-century Protestantism.[22] Although seventeenth-century Puritanism stressed external controls, antebellum religious enthusiasm rejected Calvinist determinism in favor of free will doctrines. The basic social support of nineteenth-century sexual restraint—religion—rested on the centrality of autonomy and individual choice. Finally, nineteenth-century Protestantism incorporated women, the apparent source of the intergenerational transmission of premarital pregnancy in the eighteenth century, into the social order. If women did not entirely dominate religion symbolically and organizationally in the nineteenth century, the churches did provide an important outlet for a wide range of female needs.[23] A more active part of the churches, nineteenth-century women absorbed the message of sexual restraint more completely.

Since the supporting social restraints involved voluntary action, the new anti-sexual ideology of the nineteenth century was necessarily more total than the Puritan hostility to non-marital sexual expression.

20 Joseph F. Kett, "Adolescence and Youth in Nineteenth-Century America, "*Journal of Interdisciplinary History*, II (1971), 289–291; Lois W. Banner, "Religion and Reform in the Early Republic: The Role of Youth," *American Quarterly*, XXIII (1971), 677–695.

21 N. J. Demerath III, "Trends and Anti-Trends in Religious Change," in Eleanor B. Sheldon and Wilbert E. Moore (eds.), *Indicators of Social Change: Concepts and Measurements* (New York, 1968), 353.

22 Timothy L. Smith, *Revivalism and Social Reform* (New York, 1965), esp. 33–44, 148–162. See also Alexis de Tocqueville (ed. Phillips Bradley), *Democracy in America* (New York, 1945), I, 313–318.

23 Barbara Welter, "The Feminization of American Religion: 1800–1860," in William L. O'Neill (ed.), *Insights and Parallels: Problems and Issues of American Social History* (Minneapolis, 1973), 305–332.

Intellectually intertwined with the entire system of liberal bourgeois ideology, Victorian morality was more than a functional system for the control of premarital sexual behavior. The exaggerated aversion to masturbation, for example, is inexplicable if the system were merely designed to prevent premarital pregnancy.[24] Victorian morality was relevant to the immediate needs and social position of both young men and women. Tocqueville emphasized the free marriage market as the structural determinant of the high degree of sexual restraint among young American women. "No girl," observed the aristocratic visitor, "then believes that she cannot become the wife of the man who loves her, and this renders all breaches of morality before marriage very uncommon."[25] Since women were on their own in the marriage market but lacked economic resources thereafter, Victorian morality raised the price of sex and thus substantially increased the bargaining power of both single and married women.[26]

Because sexual restraint was compatible with the norms of thrift and abstinence required of the upwardly striving young capitalist. the morality advantageous to women also appealed to the rationality, if not the passion, of males. The early age of independence from the family of orientation prepared young middle-class men not for early marriage but for a period of capital accumulation and entry into a career, the two prerequisites to marriage. Having internalized the mechanism of deferred gratification in terms of his economic life, the nineteenth-century American male would not risk the consequences of a marriage precipitated by a premarital pregnancy. Although not every man was making it in nineteenth-century America, more and more were caught up in the competition. Most importantly, the obstacles to advancement in society were seen as within the capacity of the individual to overcome.

THE TRANSITIONS AND THEIR IMPLICATIONS Have basic American institutions changed gradually and easily? Have the external forms

24 Peter Cominos, "Late Victorian Sexual Respectability and the Social System," *International Review of Social History*, VIII (1963), 18–48, 216–250; Steven Willner Nissenbaum, "Careful Love: Sylvester Graham and the Emergence of Victorian Sexual Theory in America, 1830–1840," unpub. Ph.D. diss. (University of Wisconsin, 1968), 3–32.

25 Tocqueville, *Democracy*, II, 216; generally, 215–221.

26 For a more extended discussion of the role of nineteenth-century women in promoting Victorian morality, see Daniel Scott Smith, "Family Limitation, Sexual Control and Domestic Feminism in Victorian America," *Feminist Studies*, I (1973), 40–57.

of control been painlessly modified to conform to new or more freely expressed desires of individuals? Or did "crises" arise in the older social arrangements before new patterns of behavior appeared? With more than three centuries of data on the key aspect of human behavior which is under examination here, some insights are possible concerning this fundamental problem in American history. Since two thirds of white women were not pregnant at marriage throughout the course of American history, continuity in the efficacy of control is obviously apparent. Yet, since premarital pregnancy is at least a mild form of deviancy, the magnitude of the cyclical fluctuation is impressive. Our contention is that rising premarital pregnancy is a manifestation of a collision between an unchanging and increasingly antiquated family structure and a pattern of individual behavior which is more a part of the past than a harbinger of the future. The downturn in premarital pregnancy follows as a necessary but not sufficient consequence of a transformation in the family's role as a regulator of the sexual behavior of the young. Neither the old institutional pattern of control nor the rebellion against it can predict the subsequent sexual behavior of the young. The sexual revolutionaries of the eighteenth century, if the premarital procreators may be so labeled, were obviously not the vanguard of a sexually liberated nineteenth century.

The increase in premarital pregnancy in late seventeenth-century New England provides empirical evidence for the notion of the declension of Puritanism from a "golden age." At first the authorities attempted to maintain their vigilance in the face of increased sexual deviance (Table 5). As late as the 1670s, at least by a rough estimate of the number of premarital pregnancies in Essex County, well over half of the guilty couples were being convicted.[27] Before any marked socio-economic change occurred in New England, cracks surfaced in the sexually repressive order. During the last third of the century punishment declined from corporal to monetary, and individuals were given the choice between fines or whippings.[28] Although illegitimacy

27 Direct matching of premarital pregnancy cases from the vital records to prosecutions in court records yields a similar estimate. Three of five couples in Ipswich (1657–1682), and three of five in Hingham (1670–1682) with a birth within six complete months of marriage were found in the published court records.

28 See Table 5. Even with this amelioration in penalties, punishment and prosecution were more severe in New England than in English church courts. See Ronald A. Marchant, *The Church under the Law: Justice, Administration and Discipline in the Diocese of York, 1560–1640* (Cambridge, 1969), 27, 215–219, 240–243; George Elliott Howard, *A History of Matrimonial Institutions* (Chicago, 1904), II, 180–200.

Table 5. Crime and Punishment for Fornication in Essex County, Massachusetts, 1643–1682

CONVICTIONS	1643–1652	1653–1667	1668–1682	TOTAL
Married couples	4	19	85	108
(known early birth)	3	3	13	19
Women only	6	30	69	105
(known pregnancy)	2	18	38	58
Men only	4	22	46	72
(bastardy cases)	2	7	26	35
Total incidences[a]	11	54	161	226
Mean population[b]	4,100	6,000	11,000	
Incidence rate (per 1000 per decade)	2.7	6.0	9.8	
KNOWN PUNISHMENTS				
fine	5	22	66	93
whipping	4	27	17	48
whipping or fine	2	8	95	105
child support only	1	22	17	40
other	2	2	1	5
Total known	14	81	196	291

ESTIMATE OF PERCENTAGE OF PREMARITAL PREGNANCIES CONVICTED:

MARRIED COUPLES CONVICTED, 1671–80	POPULATION ESTIMATE	MARRIAGE RATE[c]	PREGNANCIES EXPECTED[d]	PERCENT CONVICTED
65	11,000	12/1000	106	61%

a The total of incidences is obtained by adding the number of married couples convicted, the number of single women convicted, and the small number of single men (thirteen for the forty year period) who were prosecuted without a partner being arraigned.
b From William I. Davisson, "Essex County Wealth Trends," *Essex Institute Historical Collections*, CIII (1967), 292.
c From Susan Norton, "Population Growth in Colonial America: A Study of Ipswich, Massachusetts," *Population Studies*, XXV (1971), 451.
d Premarital pregnancy ratio of 8% based on three Essex County towns—Ipswich (7.3% before 1700), Salem (8.2%, 1671–1700), and Topsfield (7.7%, 1660–1679). To be conservative, a nine-month standard was used.

prosecutions continued after 1700, civil punishment for premarital pregnancy gradually disappeared. Although the churches then picked up the burden of repression by requiring confessions for baptism and admission, individuals, typically, were ready to join only after their premarital experience had passed. As premarital pregnancy continued to increase during the eighteenth century, the churches dropped or diluted the confession requirement.[29] In short, the severity of active social repression is inversely related over time to the level of premarital pregnancy.

The removal of the communal controls of Puritanism left exposed a set of traditional relationships. Although pressures in the direction of the substantive autonomy of youth may have been inherent in the American wilderness from the beginning, environmental forces were more than blunted by traditional familial, social, and ideological arrangements. Nearly a century passed before the customary high male age at marriage was lowered. Other indices of traditionalism in family patterns persisted well past the middle of the eighteenth century.[30] Even the modernity of the influential *Some Thoughts Concerning Education* may be questioned.[31] Although Locke stressed affection between mature sons and their fathers (who handily reserved the right to disinherit), the psychological basis for this rational relationship developed in the context of a severe, but not total, crushing of the son's will as an infant. "Fear and awe," proclaimed Locke to fathers, "ought to give you the first power over their minds," and thus compliance "will seem natural to them."[32]

Alternative explanations do not account adequately for the transition to higher premarital pregnancy levels in the eighteenth century. Premarital sex was never normatively approved, even during engagement. Most premaritally pregnant couples (from two thirds to three fourths of those marrying in Hingham between 1741 and 1780) were also pregnant at the time of legal engagement—the filing of the intention to marry.[33] On the other hand, over 40 percent of women not

29 Emil Oberholzer, Jr., *Delinquent Saints: Disciplinary Action in the Early Congregational Churches of Massachusetts* (New York, 1956), 136.

30 Philip J. Greven, Jr., *Four Generations: Population, Land, and Family in Colonial Andover, Massachusetts* (Ithaca, 1970); Daniel Scott Smith, "The Demographic History of Colonial New England," *Journal of Economic History*, XXXII (1972), 176–180; *idem*, "Parental Power and Marriage Patterns: An Analysis of Historical Trends in Hingham, Massachusetts," *Journal of Marriage and the Family*, XXXV (1973), 419–428.

31 For the mixture of patriarchalism and consent in Locke, see Gordon J. Schochet, "The Family and the Origins of the State," in John W. Yolton (ed.), *John Locke: Problems and Perspectives* (Cambridge, 1969), 81–98; M. Seliger, *The Liberal Politics of John Locke* (New York, 1968), 209–226.

32 John Locke, *Some Thoughts Concerning Education* in James E. Axtell (ed.), *The Educational Writings of John Locke* (Cambridge, 1968), 146–147. In the introduction to his recent documentary collection (*Childrearing Concepts, 1620–1860* [Itasca, Ill., 1973], 1–6), Greven stresses the continuity of repressive ideas until the 1820s and 1830s.

33 Of the thirty-six children born within 4 complete months of marriage, thirty-three (91.7%) were born within 8½ months of the intention to marry; of the thirty-seven born in the fifth and sixth month after marriage, twenty-nine (78.4%) were born within

pregnant at marriage had been legally engaged for three months or longer. If betrothal licence is an unsatisfactory explanation, the custom of bundling is even less adequate. Although an environmental explanation (cold weather and poorly heated houses) has been seriously advanced, the low seventeenth-century incidence of premarital pregnancy and its seasonal pattern contradict this argument. Premarital conceptions occurred year-round with a slight bulge during the warmer months.[34] Bundling was an eighteenth-century compromise between persistent parental control and the pressures of the young to subvert traditional familial authority.

As a system with contradictory elements, eighteenth-century courtship was not dominated by the newer theme of romantic love. If interpersonal affection and attraction—resulting in premarital pregnancy—had been replacing the old criteria of property and status in mate selection, then one would expect that "love matches" would be more heterogamous than "property matches." To the contrary, however, premaritally pregnant couples were as similar in wealth origins as non-pregnant couples.[35] The eighteenth-century surge in premarital pregnancy did involve a revolt of the young, but it was constrained within the framework of traditional motivation. The generational interpretation is not, of course, new. Eilert Sundt, the most astute observer of courtship practices in nineteenth-century rural Europe, saw the phenomenon as "a form of protest against inordinate parental authority; its decline was in part explained by the moderating of familial controls which young people sought to subvert."[36] And an

---

8½ months of the intention; of the thirty-eight born between the beginning of the seventh and 8½ months of marriage, only thirteen (34.2%) were born within 8½ months of the intention. Overall, 67.6% of the births within 8½ months of marriage came within 8½ months of the intention, and 73.9% were born within 9 months of the intention.

34 Stiles, *Bundling*, 53. Of premarital conceptions in Hingham between 1721 and 1800, 27.2%, 26.5%, 23.1%, and 23.1% (N = 147) occurred respectively in the quarters April–June, July–Sept., Oct.–Dec., and Jan.–March. Post-marital first conceptions (N = 363) were distributed in the same quarters as follows—19.0%, 21.5%, 26.7%, and 32.8%.

35 Comparing the wealth of the wife's father and the husband's father in Hingham reconstituted marriages between 1761 and 1780, we find no difference between the relative origins of the pregnant and nonpregnant couples. (Gamma for the pregnant couples was 0.70 (N = 39) and 0.69 (N = 60) for the nonpregnant).

36 Arthur Hillman, "Eilert Sundt: Pioneer Student of Family and Culture," in Thomas D. Eliot et al. (eds.), *Norway's Families* (Philadelphia, 1960), 40. On the work of Sundt, see Michael Drake, *Population and Society in Norway, 1735–1865* (Cambridge, 1969), 19–29.

Anglican polemicist in 1763 anticipated Sundt's conclusion. "Among dissenters, when a married pair happen to have a child born too soon after marriage," he noted, "they do not repent but if they were again in the same circumstances, they would do the same again, because otherwise they could not obtain their parent's consent to marry."[37]

The transference of this generational conflict to the political domain during the pre-Revolutionary crisis with Great Britain was not, as two scholars have recently maintained, because the contractual, Lockean, and republican nature of the family was a settled issue in everyday experience. Rather, power relationships within the family were being challenged, and the very ambiguity of the relationship between parents and children heightened the salience of the familial analogy for the parallel struggle that was developing between the colonies and the mother country.[38] Nor did the leaders of the resistance to England wish to incite a revolution in the family. For example, among the other evils which Jefferson cited in the preamble to the Virginia bill to abolish entail was that this custom "sometimes does injury to the morals of youth, by rendering them independent of, and disobedient to their parents."[39] The Revolution did signal, however, a general shift from passive to active consent on the part of the people; although an analogy is necessarily vague, it is not unreasonable to assume that a similar shift occurred in intergenerational relations. By the 1830s this new republican consensus on the family was firmly established. The father, according to Tocqueville, "exercised no other power than that which is granted to the affection and experience of age. . . . . The master and the constituted ruler have vanished, the father remains."[40] The sexual expression underlying the eighteenth-century peak in premarital pregnancy was a product of a situation of profound social disequilibrium, not an end in itself. Once the familial and social context had altered, sexual restrictiveness reappeared.

37 John Beach, *A Friendly Expostulation with all persons concern'd in publishing a late Pamphlet, Entitled, The real Advantages which Ministers and People may enjoy, especially in the Colonies, by conforming to the Church of England* (New York, 1763), 38. (We are indebted to Samuel Haber for this reference.)

38 Edwin G. Burrows and Michael Wallace, "The American Revolution: The Ideology and Psychology of National Liberation," *Perspectives in American History*, VI (1972), 167–306, esp. 255–267.

39 Paul Leicester Ford (ed.), *The Works of Thomas Jefferson* (New York, 1904), II, 269.

40 Tocqueville, *Democracy*, II, 205–206, and generally Ch. 8 "Influence of Democracy on the Family,"202–208

The crisis in traditional family structure was resolved by a republican solution—the acceptance of the maturity of young adults. Men and women in the nineteenth century responded to the risks of premarital freedom by constraining their sexual drives. Yet, the ideology of the participant-run courtship system emphasized romantic affection and love. Although elaborate dichotomies between pure love and evil sex were developed, the potential for premarital sexual intimacy was built into the Victorian system of courtship. As the Victorian cultural synthesis collapsed in the late nineteenth and twentieth centuries, the dominant themes in premarital sexuality continued to be commitment, love, and marriage. For the young adults who had become autonomous as a result of the transformation in age roles in the family a century earlier, higher rates of sexual intercourse did not produce proportional increases in premarital pregnancy. Contraception made possible the temporary separation of sex and procreation. Teen-agers, on the other hand, remained psychologically enmeshed in but not controlled by their families of orientation. With the extension of schooling in the twentieth century, the trend toward youthful autonomy perhaps has been reversed.

The dependence-independence ambivalence is crucial in the explanation of the high premarital pregnancy ratios of contemporary teen-agers. With an estimated decline in the age of menarche of 2.5 to 3.3 years during the twentieth century, American females are biologically mature earlier but socially immature as long or longer than in the nineteenth century.[41] Not independent in society (and therefore not responsible for the consequences of their actions), teen-aged girls accept the risk of pregnancy rather than consciously separate sexual intercourse from procreation. The rational use of contraception requires a teen-aged girl to adopt a self-definition inconsistent with her own assumptions.[42] The "problem," then, is not an absence of "morality" among teen-agers, but rather the persistence of a morality based on the sexual restraint of women presumed to be independent and responsible. In modern America, teen-age sexual behavior is

41 J. M. Tanner, "Earlier Maturation in Man," *Scientific American*, CCXVIII (Jan. 1968), 24–27.

42 For example, roughly two thirds of 13–19 year olds agreed with statement, "If a girl uses birth control pills or other methods of contraception, it makes it seem as if she were *planning* to have sex" (Robert C. Sorenson, *Adolescent Sexuality in Contemporary America* [New York, 1973], 408, Table 185). Both the responses and the use of italics in the question convey the implicit values.

guided neither by the old standard of prohibition nor by a new one of rational expressiveness.[43]

SUMMARY The historical variation in premarital pregnancy in America suggests a notable absence of a Malthusian constancy of passion. Sexual restraint before marriage typified eras in which intergenerational relationships were well defined, in which extrafamilial institutions reinforced familial controls, and in which the population was relatively well integrated into the central structure of values. Conversely, premarital sexual activity has been more prevalent when there was more ambiguity and uncertainty in the parent-child relationship, when the social supports of morality were weakened or not appropriate to the current realities of coming of age, and when there emerged a segment of the population outside the mainstream of the culture. Discontinuity is the central fact of the premarital pregnancy record. In this important area of behavior, American history has not been a "seamless web." The transitions, furthermore, have not involved the simple triumph of new behavioral patterns over outmoded institutions of control. During the crisis periods the actions of the "rebels" appear, ironically, to be well integrated into the old regime of sexuality and its control.

Perhaps the cycle in premarital pregnancy should not surprise social historians. It fits two well-known models of the discontinuities of modern history—the cultural and the structural stages. The first perspective is the familiar Puritan-Enlightenment-Victorian-Post-modern organization of the four centuries of American cultural history. The latter and more interesting model involves a sequence of equilibrium-shock-adjustment-new equilibrium. In this perspective, the eighteenth-century surge in premarital pregnancy is related to the disintegration of the traditional, well-integrated rural community and to the beginnings of economic and social modernization. Once the crisis of transition to modern society had passed, premarital pregnancy began to decrease. Expectations among individuals and groups were once again predictable, and the various parts of the social system

43 The sex education debate is revealing in this context. Both sides in the controversy oppose sexual autonomy for teen-agers. Although the opponents see it as a threat to parental authority, the supporters perceive it as a supplement to parental authority by presenting sex in a wider matrix of adult values. For an amusing and perceptive account of the struggle, see Mary Breasted, *Oh! Sex Education* (New York, 1970).

meshed together.[44] Contemporary Western societies also appear to be in a similar transitional phase. The proliferation of transitional terms, e.g., post-industrial, post-modern, post-Protestant, suggests an awareness that a social order is dead but a new one is not yet definable.

What, then, of the future of premarital pregnancy and sexuality? If sexuality and procreation do become separated in the future through the universal acceptance and use of contraception and abortion in premarital relations, and if teen-agers emerge as an autonomous age group in society, then premarital pregnancy will obviously decline. Whether sexuality will continue within the romantic boundaries of love and relatively permanent commitment between individuals or jump to the utopian sexuality envisioned by Herbert Marcuse and Wilhelm Reich is more problematic. Alterations in the social control of sexuality historically have had unanticipated consequences for sexual behavior. Thus the future qualitative meaning of sexuality cannot be categorized as either romantic or utopian. Evidence exists that the structural basis for such an option is being constructed at present. The eighteen-year-olds' vote, for example, is a symbolic recognition of a younger age at maturity. Less symbolic but more to the point at issue here is the sharp drop from 68 percent of Americans in 1969 to only 48 percent in 1973 who think that "it is wrong for people to have sex relations before marriage."[45] If the analysis in this essay has validity, such a redefinition of the family and age groups in society has a clear historical precedent.

44 Examples of the use of this model are numerous. See Charles Tilly, "Collective Violence in European Perspective," in Hugh Davis Graham and Ted Robert Gurr (eds.), *The History of Violence in America* (New York, 1969), 4–44, esp. 21–33; E. J. Hobsbawm, "Economic Fluctuations and Some Social Movements since 1800," in his *Laboring Men* (New York, 1967), 148–184, esp. 153–157. For the framework applied to the family, see Shorter, "Illegitimacy, Sexual Revolution, and Social Change"; Neil Smelser, *Social Change in the Industrial Revolution* (Chicago, 1959); Smith, "Parental Power and Marriage Patterns."

45 Gallup poll for national sample reported in the *Hartford Courant*, 12 Aug. 1973, 24. The trend toward a complete separation of premarital sex and conception is apparent in Western Europe. Between the mid-1960s and c. 1970 the premarital pregnancy rate increased in only one of nine countries examined in a recent study; during the first half of the 1960s, however, the rate increased in seven of the nine countries. See France Prioux-Marchal, "Les Conceptions Prénuptiales en Europe Occidentale Depuis 1955," *Population*, XXIX (1974), 63, Table 1.

APPENDIX I

Summary

PERIOD	UNDER 6 MONTHS		UNDER 8½ MONTHS		UNDER 9 MONTHS	
	%	N	%	N	%	N
–1680	3.3	511	6.8	511	8.1	663
1681–1720	6.7	445	14.1	518	12.1	1156
1721–1760	9.9	881	21.2	1146	22.5	1442
1761–1800	16.7	970	27.2	1266	33.0	1097
1801–1840	10.3	573	17.7	815	23.7	616
1841–1880	5.8	572	9.6	467	12.6	572
1881–1910	15.1	119	23.3	232	24.4	119

Individual Studies: For the efficient display of the maximum detail, the data are reported in the following order: sample description, marriage period, percent of marriages linked to first births, number matched, percentage born under 6, 8½, and 9 months.

Hingham, Massachusetts: reconstitution study (non-native-born excluded in the nineteenth century).

	%		%	%	%
1641–1660	n.a.	33	0.0	0.0	0.0
1661–1680	n.a.	80	5.0	11.2	11.2
1681–1700	n.a.	86	3.5	12.8	18.6
1701–1720	69	109	7.3	13.8	17.4
1721–1740	67	172	11.6	22.7	27.3
1741–1760	65	212	13.2	31.2	38.2
1761–1780	64	200	19.0	33.5	36.5
1781–1800	55	204	21.0	32.8	39.1
1801–1820	58	215	14.9	24.6	28.4
1821–1840	61	276	7.3	16.0	20.3
1841–1860	n.a.	235	4.7	8.5	10.2
1861–1880	n.a.	145	9.0	16.0	16.5

Watertown, Massachusetts: genealogy.

	%		%	%	%
–1660	n.a.	9	0.0	11.1	11.1
1661–1680	n.a.	35	0.0	8.6	8.6
1681–1700	n.a.	44	6.8	9.1	13.6
1701–1720	n.a.	76	7.9	19.8	25.1
1721–1740	n.a.	96	4.2	18.7	25.8
1741–1760	n.a.	110	10.9	21.8	23.6
1761–1780	n.a.	112	15.2	24.1	29.4
1781–1800	n.a.	111	15.3	26.1	32.5

Dedham, Massachusetts: vital record study.

	%		%	%	%
1662–1669	84	21	4.8	4.8	4.8
1671–1680	67	36	2.8	8.5	11.1
1760–1770	43	73	19.2	30.1	32.9

Topsfield, Massachusetts: vital record study.

	%		%	%	%
1660–1679	n.a.	13	7.7	7.7	7.7
1680–1699	n.a.	44	2.3	4.5	6.8
1738–1740	n.a.	25	12.0	24.0	24.0

Andover, Massachusetts: Greven, *Four Generations,* 113. (The figure for 1731–1749 comes from unpublished data kindly furnished by Greven.)

	%				%
1655–1674	41	21	—	—	0.0
1675–1699	55	64	—	—	12.5
1700–1730	41	115	—	—	11.5
1731–1749	8	29	—	—	17.3

Hollis, New Hampshire: vital record study.

	%		%	%	%
1741–1760	n.a.	39	2.6	12.8	17.9
1761–1780	n.a.	84	13.1	26.2	29.8
1781–1800	n.a.	57	10.5	31.6	35.1

Coventry, Connecticut: vital record study; Cheryl Krajcik, "The Trend in Premarital Pregnancy Ratios in Mansfield 1700–1849 and Coventry, 1711–1840," unpub. undergraduate sociology paper (University of Connecticut, 1972). We are indebted to the author and to Michael Gordon for this reference.

	%				%
1711–1740	n.a.	84	—	—	20.2
1741–1770	n.a.	179	—	—	23.5
1771–1800	n.a.	104	—	—	25.0
1801–1840	n.a.	43	—	—	4.6

Mansfield, Connecticut: vital record study; Phyllis Schneider, "Premarital Pregnancy in Mansfield, Connecticut, 1700–1849," unpub. undergraduate sociology paper (University of Connecticut, 1972.) We are indebted to the author and to Michael Gordon for this reference.

	%				%
1700–1739	n.a.	73	—	—	12.3
1740–1769	n.a.	265	—	—	19.2

	%				%
1770–1799	n.a.	296	—	—	20.6
1800–1819	n.a.	154	—	—	12.3
1820–1849	n.a.	88	—	—	5.7

Christ Church Parish, Middlesex County, Virginia: vital record study of marriages and baptisms.

	%		%	%	%
1720–1736	64	191	9.4	15.2	16.8

Kingston Parish, Gloucester County, Virginia: vital record study of marriages and baptisms, letters A–I.

	%		%	%	%
1749–1760	n.a.	36	2.8	13.9	13.9
1761–1770	n.a.	66	12.1	22.7	24.2
1771–1780	n.a.	63	12.7	25.4	30.1
1749–1780	64	165	10.3	21.8	24.2

Bergen, New Jersey: Reformed Dutch Church, vital record study of marriages and baptisms.

	%		%	%	%
1665–1680	64	18	0.0	5.6	5.6
1681–1700	55	31	19.4	19.4	19.4
1701–1720	47	16	18.7	25.0	25.0

New Paltz, New York: Reformed Dutch Church, vital record study of marriages and baptisms.

	%		%	%	%
1801–1803 } 1808–1812 }	37	82	8.5	28.0	33.0

Boston, Massachusetts: vital record study.

	%		%	%	%
1651–1655	62	84	3.6	6.0	14.3
1690, 1692	52	39	0.0	17.9	23.1

Ipswich, Massachusetts: reconstitution; Susan Norton, "Population Growth in Colonial America: A Study of Ipswich, Massachusetts," *Population Studies*, XXV (1971), 636; (1650–1687 from our own study).

	%		%	%	%
–1700	n.a.	68	—	—	7.3
1701–1725	n.a.	143	—	—	5.6
1726–1750	n.a.	100	—	—	6.3
1650–1687	76	182	3.8	6.0	8.2

Bristol, Rhode Island: vital record study; John Demos, "Families in Colonial Bristol, Rhode Island: An Exercise in Historical Demography," *William and Mary Quarterly*, XXV (1968), 56.

	%				%
1680–1700	c.33	19	—	—	0.0
1700–1720	c.14	8	—	—	0.0
1720–1740	c.40	42	—	—	10.0
1740–1760	c.23	35	—	—	49.0
1760–1780	c.14	23	—	—	44.0

Salem, Massachusetts: reconstitution (based on unpublished data kindly supplied by James Somerville).

	%				%
1651–1670	n.a.	131	—	—	5.3
1671–1700	n.a.	123	—	—	8.2
1701–1730	n.a.	239	—	—	5.8
1731–1770	n.a.	176	—	—	12.5

Lexington, Massachusetts: vital record study.

	%		%	%	%
1854–1866	n.a.	56	3.6	3.6	12.5
1885–1895	n.a.	119	15.1	19.3	24.4

Willimantic, Connecticut: vital record study; John P. Sade, "Premarital Conception and Social Change in Willimantic, Connecticut, 1850–1910," unpub. undergraduate history paper (University of Connecticut, 1973). We are indebted to Sade for these data.

	%				%
1850, 1870	26	31	—	—	19.3
1890	48	41	—	—	31.7
1910	46	72	—	—	25.0

Washentaw County, Michigan: vital record study. Data for 1867–1870 and 1886–1890 include Ann Arbor and Ypsilanti only. Overall, 34.2% of marriages were linked to births (Samuel Gorsline and Harold Smith, "A Study of Premarital Pregnancy in Washentaw County, 1867–1900," unpub. undergraduate history paper [University of Michigan, 1972]). We are indebted to the authors and to Kenneth Lockridge for these data.)

			%		%
1867–1870 } 1876–1880 }	—	136	5.1	—	11.8
1886–1890 } 1896–1900 }	—	162	8.0	—	16.0

Utah County, Utah, vital record study. Percent born within 196 and 251 days of all first births coming in first 48 months of marriage; 1670 cases. Harold T. Christensen, "The Time between Marriage of Parents and the Birth of Their First Children: Utah County, Utah," *American Journal of Sociology*, XLIV (1939), 521.

	196 days (%)	251 days (%)
1905–1907	11.9	20.1
1913–1915	14.8	29.1
1921–1923	9.6	20.4
1929–1931	8.0	19.3

Tippecanoe County, Indiana: vital record study. Percent born within 196 and 251 days of all first births coming within the first 48 months of marriage. Harold T. Christensen and Olive P. Bowden, "Studies in Child-Spacing, II: The Time-Interval between Marriage of Parents and Birth of Their First Child, Tippecanoe County, Indiana," *Social Forces*, XXXI (1953), 348.

	%		196 days (%)	251 days (%)
1919–1921	39	487	11.9	19.6
1929–1931	28	352	14.8	28.2
1939–1941	37	692	9.8	20.0

Defiance County, Ohio: vital record study. Percent born within 196 days of marriage of those births coming within first 48 months of marriage. Harold T. Christensen, "Child-Spacing Analysis via Record Linkage: New Data plus a Summing Up from Earlier Reports," *Marriage and Family Living*, XXXV (1963), 275.

	%
1918–1922	10.9
1929–1931	14.1
1939–1942	6.9

Wood County, Ohio: vital record study; Samuel H. Lowrie, "Early Marriage, Premarital Pregnancy and Associated Factors," *Journal of Marriage and the Family*, XXVII (1965), 50.

		195 days (%)	265 days (%)
1957–1962	1,850	9.3	18.8

Massachusetts: vital record study. Elizabeth Murphy Whelan, "The Temporal Relationship of Marriage, Conception, and Birth in Massachusetts," *Demography*, IX (1972), 404.

	196 days (%)	265 days (%)
1966–1968	17.8	29.0

National surveys: See the discussion and data in Smith, "Dating of the American Sexual Revolution," 323–327.

APPENDIX II

I. *France* (within 7 complete months of marriage):

PLACE	SOURCE	PERIOD	RATIO (%)
A. *Before the second half of the eighteenth century:*			
Sainghin-en-Mélantois	5	1690–1769	15.2
Boulay	15	before 1749	9.1
Boulay (7 surrounding villages)	16	before 1760	8.6
Crulai	11	1674–1742	2.8
Meulan	19	1660–1739	7.7
Troarn	2	1661–1740	12.0
Tamerville	28	1624–1740	10.1
Tourouvre	4	before 1750	3.0
Bayeux	8	1600–1699	8.3
Lourmarin	24	1681–1750	15.1
Sérignan	22	1716–1750	20.0
Northwest France	13	1670–1769	5.8
Southwest France	14	1720–1769	6.4
Total of 13 samples			9.5
B. *Encompassing the mid-eighteenth century:*			
Saint-Méen	1	1720–1792	8.9
Bayeux	8	1700–1780	11.3
Blere	20	1677–1788	4.0
Bessin, three villages	8	1686–1792	17.1
Bas-Quercy	27	1700–1792	4.8
Saint-Agnan	17	1730–1792	9.1
Ingouville	26	1730–1770	14.7
Rumont	23	1720–1790	9.0
Tonnerrois	7	1720–1800	7.8
Villedieu-les Poëles	18	1711–1790	2.6
Saint-Pierre-Eglise	21	1657–1790	9.0
Total of 11 samples			8.9
C. *Second half of the eighteenth century:*			
Tamerville	28	1741–1790	20.0
Tourouvre	4	after 1750	10.0
Meulan	19	1740–1789	11.8
Lourmarin	24	1751–1800	18.1
Boulay	15	1750–1809	12.3
Boulay (7 surrounding villages)	16	1760–1799	7.4

PLACE	SOURCE	PERIOD	RATIO (%)
C. *Second half of the eighteenth century* (continued):			
Sainghin-en-Mélantois	5	1770–1799	15.8
Troarn	2	1741–1780	13.7
Saint-Auban	1	1749–1789	4.3
Bilhères	9	1740–1819	10.3
Ile-de-France	10	1740–1799	14.0
Sotteville-les-Rouen	12	1760–1790	30.2
Châtillon-sur-Seine	3	1772–1805	15.8
Southwest France	14	1770–1789	12.1
Serignan	22	1751–1792	40.9
Total of 15 samples			17.4
D. *First half of the nineteenth century:*			
Sainghin-en-Mélantois	5	1800–1849	50.5
Boulay	15	1810–	28.5
Boulay (7 surrounding villages)	16	1800–1862	18.3
Meulan	19	1790–1839	23.6
Bilhères	9	1820–1859	2.8
Lourmarin	24	1801–1830	23.9
Southwest France	14	1790–1819	11.2
Total of 7 samples			22.7
E. *Twentieth Century* (within 7 complete months per 100 marriages; sample of 240,000 families in the 1962 census):			
France	6	1925–1929	12.3
		1930–1934	12.6
		1935–1939	12.6
		1940–1944	17.0
		1945–1949	17.2
		1950–1954	19.4
		1955–1959	19.5
		1960–1961	19.3

SOURCES

(1) Yves Blayo, "Trois paroisses d'Ille-et-Villaine," *Annales de démographic historique*, VI (1969), 206.

(2) Michel Bouvet and Pierre-Marie Bourdin, "A travers la Normandie des XVIIe et XVIIIe siècles," *Cahier des Annales de Normandie*, VI (1968), 191–202.

(3) Antoinette Chamoux and Cécile Dauphin, "La Contraception avant la Révolution francaise: L'exemple de Châtillon-sur-Seine," *Annales: E.S.C.*, XXIV (1969), 680.

(4) Hubert Charbonneau, *Tourouvre-au-Perche aux XVIIe et XVIIIe siècles: Etude de démographie historique* (Paris, 1969), 142.
(5) Raymond Deniel and Louis Henry, "La population d'un village du Nord de la France, Sainghin-en-Mélantois, de 1665 a 1851," *Population*, XX (1965), 581.
(6) Jean-Claude Deville, *Structure des Familles* (Paris, 1972), 91.
(7) D. Dinet, "Quatre paroisses du Tonnerrois," *Annales de démographie historique*, VI (1969), 80.
(8) Mohamed El Kordi, *Bayeux aux XVIIe et XVIIIe siècles: Contribution à l'histoire urbaine de la France* (Paris, 1970), 91.
(9) Michel Fresel-Lozey, *Histoire démographique d'un village en Béarn: Bilheres-d'Ossau* (Bordeaux, 1969), 142.
(10) Jean Ganiage, *Trois villages d'Ile-de-France au XVIIIe siècle* (Paris, 1963), 92.
(11) Etienne Gautier and Louis Henry, *La population de Crulai, paroisse normande* (Paris, 1958), 257–264.
(12) Pierre Girard, "Aperçus de la démographie de Sotteville-les-Rouen vers la fin du XVIIIe siècle," *Population*, XIV (1959), 494.
(13) Louis Henry, "Intervalle entre le mariage et la première naissance. Erreurs et corrections," *ibid.*, XXVIII (1973), 263.
(14) Louis Henry, "La fécondité des mariages dans le quart sud-ouest de la France de 1720 a 1829," *Annales: E.S.C.*, XXVII (1972), 998.
(15) J. Houdaille, "La population de Boulay (Moselle) avant 1850," *Population*, XXII (1967), 1075.
(16) Jacques Houdaille, "La population de sept villages des environs de Boulay (Moselle) aux XVIIIe et XIXe siècles," *ibid.*, XXVI (1971), 1063.
(17) Jacques Houdaille, "Un village du Morvan: Saint-Agnan," *ibid.*, XVI (1961), 304.
(18) Marie-Hélène Jouan, "Les originalités démographiques d'un bourg artisan normand au XVIIIe siècle: Villedieu-les-Poeles (1711–1790)," *Annales de démographie historique*, VI (1969), 107.
(19) Marcel Lachiver, *La population de Meulan du XVIIe au XIXe siècle (vers 1600–1850)* (Paris, 1969), 175.
(20) Marcel Lachiver, "Une étude et quelques equisses," *Annales de démographie historique*, VI (1969), 220.
(21) Jacques Lelong, "Saint-Pierre-Eglise, 1657–1790," *ibid.*, 131.
(22) Alain Molinier, "Une paroisse du Bas-Languedoc, Sérignan, 1650–1792," *Mémoires de la société archéologique de Montpellier*, XII (1968), 164.
(23) Patrice Robert, "Rumont (1720–1790)," *Annales de démographie historique*, VI (1969), 36.
(24) Thomas F. Sheppard, *Lourmarin in the Eighteenth Century: A Study of a French Village* (Baltimore, 1971), 41.
(25) Edward Shorter, "Female Emancipation, Birth Control, and Fertility

in European History," *American Historical Review*, LXXVIII (1973), 638–639.
(26) Michel Terrisse, "Un faubourg du Havre: Ingouville," *Population*, XVI (1961), 286.
(27) Pierre Valmary, *Familles paysannes au XVIII° siècle en Bas-Quercy* (Paris, 1965), 93.
(28) Phillipe Wiel, "Une grosse paroisse du Cotentin aux XVII° et XVIII° siècles," *Annales de démographie historique*, VI (1969), 161.

II. *Australia* (nine-month standard):

MARRIAGE PERIOD	PREMARITAL PREGNANCY INDEX	
	% OF MARRIAGES	% OF FIRST BIRTHS
1911–1915	29.1	35.0
1916–1920	25.2	29.9
1921–1925	25.0	29.8
1926–1930	26.7	32.5
1931–1935	26.4	35.1
1936–1940	19.3	27.7
1941–1945	13.8	17.9
1946–1950	16.7	19.2
1951–1955	18.1	20.2
1956–1960	21.9	23.2
1961–1965	23.6	28.3

SOURCE: Basavarajappa, "Pre-marital Pregnancies," 143, Table A; 145, Table C.

III. *Great Britain*

A. *England:* non-random sample of printed parish records; marriages traced to birth or baptism within 8½ months.

PERIOD	% MATCHED	NO. MATCHED	% PREGNANT
1500s	46	164	22.6
1600s	44	275	15.6
Late 1600s to 1749	50	199	17.6
1750 to c. 1800	50	713	40.2
1800 to 1819	43	388	40.2
1820 to 1843	45	95	46.3

SOURCE: P. E. H. Hair, "Bridal Pregnancy in Rural England in Earlier Centuries," *Population Studies*, XX (1966), 241–242.

III. (continued):

B. *England:* same description as above.

PERIOD	% MATCHED	NO. MATCHED	% PREGNANT
1500s	52	301	21.3
1600s	41	328	16.5
Late 1600s to 1749	42	79	16.5
1750 to 1836	48	288	43.4
1837 to 1887	52	50	40.0

SOURCE: P. E. H. Hair, "Bridal Pregnancy in Earlier Rural England Further Examined," *Population Studies*, XXIV (1970), 60.

C. *England and Wales:* To 1951, an interval of 8½ months was used; after 1951, 8 months.

	PREMARITAL PREGNANCY INDEX	
MARRIAGE PERIOD	% OF MARRIAGES	% OF LEGITIMATE FIRST BIRTHS
1941–1945	11.7	14.5
1946–1950	14.5	18.0
1951–1955	12.9	18.0
1956–1960	14.6	18.8
1961–1965	18.3	23.0
1966–1968	18.6	26.0

SOURCE: Great Britain, General Register Office, *The Registrar General's Statistical Review of England and Wales for the year 1968, Part II* (London, 1969), 192, Table UU; 12, Table Cl.

Passionlessness: An Interpretation of Victorian Sexual Ideology, 1790–1850

Nancy F. Cott

In 1903 Havelock Ellis announced that the notion of women's sexual "anaesthesia," as he called it, was a nineteenth-century creation. He had researched literary and medical sources from ancient Greece to early modern Europe and discovered, to his own amazement, that women had generally been thought to desire and enjoy sexual relations more than men.[1] Ellis and his contemporaries initially sought the source of the idea that women lacked sexual passion in the generations immediately preceding their own. The late nineteenth century was an era of contention over female sexuality, physiology, health, dress, and exercise, and one in which medical opinion had become an authoritative sector of public opinion. Since investigators have found rich documentation on these controversies, particularly in medical sources, they have been little induced to look beyond them. Until quite recently, historians tended not only to follow Ellis's chronological bias but, like him, to associate the idea that women lacked sexual passion with social repression and dysfunction. Now that attitude has been challenged by the possibility that nineteenth-century sexual ideology held some definite advantages for women, and by the claim that ideology reflected or influenced behavior far less than had been thought.[2]

I am grateful to the friends who have kindly read and criticized one or another version of this essay over the past several years. I would especially like to thank Sacvan Bercovitch, Mari Jo Buhle, Laurie Crumpacker, John Demos, David B. Davis, Ellen Dubois, David H. Fischer, Linda Gordon, James R. Green, Jean Humez, Janet W. James, Carol Karlsen, Ann Margolis, Michael McGiffert, Mary Beth Norton, and Kathryn Kish Sklar. In addition, the anonymous readers were exceptionally helpful in bringing the essay to its final form.

1. Havelock Ellis, *Studies in the Psychology of Sex*, 2d ed., rev. (1903; Philadelphia: F. A. Davis Co., 1913), 3:193–94.

2. On the former challenge, see Carroll Smith-Rosenberg, "Beauty, the Beast, and the Militant Woman," *American Quarterly* 23 (1971): 562–84, and "The Female World of Love

[*Signs: Journal of Women in Culture and Society*, 1978, vol. 4, no. 2]

A full appraisal of the idea that women lacked sexual passion requires an investigation of its origins. My purpose is to offer a hypothesis, if not a proven case, regarding the initiation and reception of that central tenet of Victorian sexual ideology which I call "passionlessness." I use the term to convey the view that women lacked sexual aggressiveness, that their sexual appetites contributed a very minor part (if any at all) to their motivations, that lustfulness was simply uncharacteristic. The concept of passionlessness represented a cluster of ideas about the comparative weight of woman's carnal nature and her moral nature; it indicated more about drives and temperament than about actions and is to be understood more metaphorically than literally.

Obviously, a single conception of women's sexuality never wholly prevails. Western civilization up to the eighteenth century, as Ellis discovered, accentuated women's concupiscence: a fifteenth-century witch-hunters' guide warned, for instance, that "carnal lust . . . in women is insatiable."[3] But the Christian belief system that called unsanctified earthly women the devil's agents allowed, on the other hand, that women who embodied God's grace were more spiritual, hence less susceptible to carnal passion, than men. Nineteenth-century views of female sexuality

---

and Ritual," *Signs* 1 (1975): 1–29; Linda Gordon, "Voluntary Motherhood: The Beginnings of Feminist Birth Control Ideology in the U.S.," in *Clio's Consciousness Raised,* ed. Mary Hartman and Lois Banner (New York: Harper Torchbook, 1974), and *Woman's Body, Woman's Right* (New York: Grossman Publishers, 1976); John S. Haller, Jr., and Robin M. Haller, *The Physician and Sexuality in Victorian America* (Urbana: University of Illinois Press, 1974), esp. p. xii; Daniel Scott Smith, "Family Limitation, Sexual Control and Domestic Feminism in Victorian America," in Hartman and Banner; and Randall Collins, "A Conflict Theory of Sexual Stratification," *Social Problems* 19 (Summer 1971): 7, 13–19. The latter point has been raised most recently by Carl N. Degler, "What Ought to Be and What Was: Women's Sexuality in the Nineteenth Century," *American Historical Review* 79 (December 1974): 1467–90. Historians' focus on the later part of the nineteenth century in discussions of sexual ideology is evident in Haller and Haller's and Degler's works as well as in Peter T. Cominos, "Innocent Femina Sensualis in Unconscious Conflict," in *Suffer and Be Still,* ed. Martha Vicinus (Bloomington: University of Indiana Press, 1972), and "Late Victorian Sexual Respectability and the Social System," *International Review of Social History* 8 (1963): 18–48, 216–50; Nathan G. Hale, Jr., *Freud and the Americans* (New York: Oxford University Press, 1971); and Charles E. Rosenberg and Carroll Smith-Rosenberg, "The Female Animal: Medical and Biological Views of Woman in Nineteenth-Century America," *Journal of American History* 60 (September 1973): 332–56. Daniel Scott Smith, "The Dating of the American Sexual Revolution: Evidence and Interpretation," in *The American Family in Social-Historical Perspective*, ed. Michael Gordon (New York: St. Martin's Press, 1974), pp. 328–32, and Michael Gordon, "From an Unfortunate Necessity to a Cult of Mutual Orgasm: Sex in Marital Education Literature, 1830–1940," in *Studies in the Sociology of Sex*, ed. James Henslin (New York: Appleton-Century-Crofts, Inc., 1971), note conflict and change in sexual opinion in the last third of the century.

3. Quoted from *Malleus Maleficarum* in Deirdre English and Barbara English, *Witches, Midwives and Nurses: A History of Women Healers* (Oyster Bay, N.Y.: Glassmountain Pamphlets, 1972), p. 10. I remain indebted to Eleanor McLaughlin for conversations, at Wellesley in 1974, about medieval views of women and passionlessness.

were also double edged: notions of women's inherent licentiousness persisted, to be wielded against women manifesting any form of deviance under the reign of passionlessness. Acknowledging that notions of women's sexuality are never monolithic, I would nonetheless emphasize that there was a traditionally dominant Anglo-American definition of women as *especially* sexual which was reversed and transformed between the seventeenth and the nineteenth centuries into the view that women (although still primarily identified by their female gender) were *less* carnal and lustful than men.

The following pages focus on early appearances of the idea of female passionlessness, discuss its social context, and analyze if and why it was acceptable, especially to women. The documents in this test case are limited to New England; to apply the interpretive paradigm to literate, Protestant, middle-class women elsewhere would require further testing. I have looked to women's public and private writings in order to put the women involved in the forefront and prevent viewing them as passive recipients of changing ideas. My other sources are largely didactic and popular works, especially religious ones, which influenced women. Most of what is known about sexual ideology before the twentieth century comes from "prescriptive" sources—those manuals, essays, and books that tried to establish norms of behavior. Although religious views, expressed in sermons and tracts, were the most direct and commanding "prescriptions" from the seventeenth through the early nineteenth centuries, they have not been so finely combed for evidence of sexual norms as has been medical advice, a comparable source of "prescriptions" for the later nineteenth century.[4] Religious opinion is particularly relevant to this inquiry because of the churches' hold on the female population. Women became a majority in the Protestant churches of America in the mid-seventeenth century and continued to increase their numerical predominance until, by the mid-nineteenth century, "Christian" values and virtues and "female" values and virtues were almost identical.[5] In my view, the ideology of passionlessness was tied to the rise of evangelical religion between the 1790s and the 1830s. Physicians' adoption of passionlessness was a second wave, so to speak, beginning at mid-century. By the time that physicians took up the question of passionlessness and attempted to reduce the concept to "scien-

4. Historians have noted that doctors took over the advisory role of ministers in the late nineteenth century (see Haller and Haller, pp. x–xi; Gordon, *Woman's Body*, p. 170; Barbara Sicherman, "The Uses of Diagnosis: Doctors, Patients, and Neurasthenia," *Journal of the History of Medicine and Allied Sciences* 32 [January 1977]: 53–54). The new function of doctors as spiritual counselors highlights the shift of moral authority from religion to science during the course of the century.

5. See Barbara Welter, "The Feminization of American Religion," in Hartman and Banner; and Nancy F. Cott, *The Bonds of Womanhood: 'Woman's Sphere' in New England, 1780–1835* (New Haven, Conn.: Yale University Press, 1977), chap. 4.

tific" and somatic quantities the idea had been diffused through the spiritual realm and had already engendered its own opposition.[6]

* * *

Early American prescriptive and legal documents suggest that the New England colonists expected women's sexual appetites to be comparable with men's, if not greater.[7] Calvinists assumed that men and women in their "fallen" state were equally licentious, that sexual drives were natural and God-given in both sexes, and had their proper outlet in marriage. If anything, the daughters of Eve were considered more prone to excess of passion because their rational control was seen as weaker. And yet it was objectionable for women to exercise the sexual initiative; regardless of women's sexual drives, the religious and social context required female subordination. Puritan theology weakened but did not destroy the double standard of sexual morality. In colonial law, for example, fornication was punished equally in either sex, but adultery was defined by the participation of a married women. A married man did not commit adultery but fornication—unless he took up with another man's wife. In Massachusetts until the Revolutionary period, a wife's adultery was always cause for her husband to divorce her, but wives had little success in freeing themselves from unfaithful husbands. Men also won suits to recover "damages" from their wives' lovers.[8] As Keith Thomas has put it, such suits reflected the underlying tenet of the double standard: "the view that men have property in women and that the value of this property is immeasurably diminished if the woman at any time has sexual relations with anyone other than her husband."[9] There was vast potential for sexual exploitation in a society in which women's sexual nature was considered primary and their social au-

6. Degler, pp. 1469–79, cites numerous conflicts within medical opinion. Physicians were never of one mind, and the British physician William Acton, who announced in the 1850s that "the majority of women . . . are not very much troubled with sexual feeling of any kind," represented one end of the range of opinion (see Gordon, "From an Unfortunate Necessity," pp. 57–58).

7. See Edmund Morgan, "The Puritans and Sex," *New England Quarterly* 15 (1942): 592–93, and *The Puritan Family*, rev. ed. (New York: Harper Torchbooks, 1966), pp. 37–42; and Otho T. Beall, Jr., "Aristotle's Masterpiece in America: A Landmark in the Folklore of Medicine," *William and Mary Quarterly*, 3d ser. 20 (1963): 216–20.

8. George E. Howard, *A History of Matrimonial Institutions* (1904; New York: Humanities Press, 1964), 2:169–70, 173, 331, 348, 351, 354; John P. Demos, *A Little Commonwealth* (New York: Oxford University Press, 1970), pp. 96–97; Nancy F. Cott, "Eighteenth-Century Family and Social Life Revealed in Massachusetts Divorce Records," *Journal of Social History* 10 (Fall 1976): 34–35, and "Divorce and the Changing Status of Women in Eighteenth-Century Massachusetts," *William and Mary Quarterly*, 3d ser. 33 (October 1976): 586–614.

9. Keith Thomas, "The Double Standard," *Journal of the History of Ideas* 20 (1959): 210.

tonomy was slight.[10] The physical and biological consequences of sexual adventure also burdened women more heavily than men in an era lacking effective means to prevent conception or infection.

In the second century of colonial settlement one finds many more numerous prescriptions for the role of women. The reasons for this increase are diverse: new class concern for standards of distinction and taste, the spread of literacy, the growth of printing and journalism, and "enlightened" interest in reformulating social systems and personal relations in "natural," "rational," rather than scriptural, terms. Britain led in discussions of female character and place, setting sex-role conventions for the literate audience.[11] Since British social ideals became more influential in the mid-eighteenth century with the decline in Puritanism, the diffusion of Protestant energies, and the growth of an affluent urban class in the colonies, British "prescriptions" must be taken into consideration. At least three phases of British opinion contributed to the development of the idea of passionlessness. In the beginning of the century when spokesmen for the new professional and commercial middle class began explicitly to oppose aristocratic pretension, vanity, and libertinism, reforming writers such as Daniel Defoe, Jeremy Collier, Richard Steele, and Samuel Richardson portrayed sexual promiscuity as one of those aristocratic excesses that threatened middle-class virtue and domestic security. Their kind of propriety led to an ideal of sexual self-control, verbal prudery, and opposition to the double standard of sexual morality (for the sake of purity for men rather than justice for women). Due to their influence, in part, "the eighteenth century witnessed a redefinition of virtue in primarily sexual terms," Ian Watt has pointed out. By elevating sexual control highest among human virtues the middle-class moralists made female chastity the archetype for human morality.[12]

10. See Morgan, "Puritans and Sex," pp. 594–600, for examples.

11. On the sex-role distinctions employed in British and American writings, see Mary S. Benson, *Women in Eighteenth-Century America* (New York: Columbia University Press, 1935), pp. 37–39. Frank L. Mott notes, in his *History of American Magazines, 1741–1850* (Cambridge, Mass.: Belknap Press, 1957), pp. 64–65, that titles such as "Advice to the Fair" and "Counsel upon Female Virtues" became "sickeningly frequent" in the last quarter of the eighteenth century.

12. Ian Watt, "The New Woman: Samuel Richardson's Pamela," in *The Family: Its Structure and Functions*, ed. Rose L. Coser (New York: St. Martin's Press, 1964), pp. 281–82. On the rise of middle-class morality, see also Watt, pp. 286–88; Thomas, p. 204; Gordon Rattray Taylor, *The Angel-Makers: A Study in the Psychological Origins of Historical Change, 1750–1850* (London: William Heinemann, 1958), pp. 12–24; Christopher Hill, "Clarissa Harlowe and Her Times," *Essays in Criticism* 5 (1955): 320. Samuel Richardson's *Pamela* (1742) first portrayed a heroine whose delicacy verged on passionlessness. On the American attention paid to these British moralists and novelists, see Lawrence A. Cremin, *American Education: The Colonial Experience* (New York: Harper Torchbooks, 1970), pp. 366–67,

Out of the upper class came a different prescriptive genre, the etiquette manual. The ones most available to middle-class women in America, such as George Savile's *A Lady's New Year's Gift* or John Gregory's *A Father Legacy to His Daughters*, consistently held that woman was made for man's pleasure and service; woman was strong only insofar as she could use her own weakness to manipulate the opposite sex (within the bounds of social propriety).[13] These authors advised a great deal of restraint and affectation (not to mention deception) in women's behavior. At the same time, modesty and demureness took center stage among the female virtues enshrined. According to Keith Thomas, the idea of passionlessness emerged in this context as an extension of the ideal of chastity needed to protect men's property rights in women; it was a reification in "nature" of the double standard.[14] Yet it must be objected that in the nineteenth century women who believed in passionlessness usually rejected the double standard of sexual morality. Modesty was the quintessential female virtue in works such as Gregory's, but, amid the manipulative and affected tactics advised, it connoted only demure behavior—a good act—not, necessarily, passionlessness. Indeed, the underlying theme that women had to appeal to men turned modesty into a sexual ploy, emphasizing women's sex objectification.[15] John Gregory did hint that sexual desire was weaker in women, with their "superior delicacy," than in men. He was sure that nature had assigned to wives rather than husbands the "reserve" which would prevent "sati-

---

371; Benson, p. 46; and Robert Palfrey Utter and Gwendolyn B. Needham, *Pamela's Daughters* (New York: Macmillan Publishing Co., 1936).

13. [George Savile, Marquis of Halifax], *The Lady's New Year's Gift, or, Advice to a Daughter* (London: Randal Taylor, 1688); Dr. [John] Gregory, *A Father's Legacy to His Daughters* (London: J. Sharpe, 1822). James Fordyce, *Sermons to Young Women*, new ed. (Philadelphia: Thomas Dobson, 1787), should be grouped with these although it was not an etiquette book in the traditional sense. Savile's book, which went through fifteen British editions, circulated in the colonies during the first two-thirds of the eighteenth century. Fordyce's work was first published in England in 1765 and was reprinted in America by 1787; it was then frequently excerpted in magazines and reprinted in entirety. Gregory's appeared in England in 1774, was published in Philadelphia the following year, and had sixteen more editions in the United States before 1794 plus selections in compilations and serials. Editions continued to appear into the nineteenth century. See Julia C. Spruill, *Woman's Life and Work in the Southern Colonies* (1935; New York: W. W. Norton & Co., 1969), pp. 215–25, and Benson, pp. 60–61, on the circulation of these books. Direct evidence of Gregory's readership in America appears in the manuscript diaries of Ruth Henshaw of Leicester, Mass., July 1, 1792, and Sally Ripley of Greenfield, Mass., December 1, 1799, both in the collection of the American Antiquarian Society, Worcester, Mass. American essayists frequently echoed the themes of the British didactic works (see, e.g., *Gentleman's and Lady's Town and Country Magazine* [Boston] 1 [May 1784]: 28; and Noah Webster's *American Magazine* [1788], quoted in Mott, p. 64).

14. Thomas, p. 214.

15. The eighteenth-century prescriptive work which made the connection between modesty and sexual ploy most obvious was Rousseau's *Emile* (1762), book 5, on the character of the ideal woman.

ety and disgust" in marital relations.[16] But not until a third phase at the close of the century did emphasis move implacably from modesty to passionlessness, under the Evangelical aegis.

The British Evangelicals were conservative reformers horrified at the French Revolution and its "godlessness"; they worked to regenerate Protestantism in order to secure social and political order. Like earlier middle-class moralists, the Evangelicals opposed aristocratic blasphemies and profligacy, cherished family life, and advocated chastity and prudence in both sexes. Because they observed women's greater piety, and hoped that women would influence men and the next generation, they focused much of their proselytizing zeal on women. In contrast to earlier eighteenth-century didacts, they harped on the theme that women were made for God's purposes, not man's. Thomas Gisborne, for example, clearly considered women moral beings responsible for themselves and to society. His call for self-conscious moral integrity on women's part directly opposed Gregory's insinuations about the shaping of women's behavior to men's tastes; he objected that such behavior was "not discretion, but art. It is dissimulation, it is deliberate imposition."[17] Evangelical works of the 1790s argued that aristocratic models of vanity, artifice, and irreligion had undermined and corrupted women's valuable potential. They claimed that female piety and sincerity would bring "effectual reformation . . . in every department of society," because "all virtues, all vices, and all characters are intimately connected with the manners, principles, and dispositions of our women."[18] The Evangelicals transformed the truism of etiquette books, that individual women influenced individual men's manners, into the proposition that the collective influence of women was an agency of moral reform.

More to the point, the Evangelicals linked moral agency to female character with a supporting link to passionlessness. Their insistence on sincerity or "simplicity," accompanying their emphasis on women's moral potential, caused them to imply that women were virtuous by nature. Continuing to stress the female virtue of modesty, Evangelicals could not (in contrast to Gregory) allow that modesty was a behavior

16. Gregory, pp. 11, 36, 72, 83.

17. Thomas Gisborne, *An Enquiry into the Duties of the Female Sex* (London; reprint ed. Philadelphia: J. Humphreys, 1798), pp. 2–3, 187, 193. On the British Evangelicals, see Charles I. Foster, *An Errand of Mercy: The Evangelical United Front, 1790–1837* (Chapel Hill: University of North Carolina Press, 1960); and M. G. Jones, *Hannah More* (Cambridge: Cambridge University Press, 1952).

18. Quotations from *Female Tuition, or, An Address to Mothers, on the Education of Daughters* (London: J. Murray, 1784), preface, and p. 34; see also pp. 2–3, 42–47; and Gisborne, chaps. 2, 4, 7, 9; *The Female Aegis* (London: J. Ginger, 1798) an anonymous plagiarism of Gisborne's book; Thomas Branagan, *The Excellency of the Female Character Vindicated* (1807; Harrisburg, Pa.: Francis Wyeth, 1828), chap. 2; Hannah More, *Strictures on the Modern System of Female Education*, 9th ed. (1799; London: T. Cadell & W. Davies, 1801), 1:70–72, 75–79, 111–12, 256–57.

assumed to suit society's conventions and men's preferences. If women were to act modest and sexually passive, and also act without affectation, then, logically, they must be passionless. Gisborne said women had "quicker feelings of native delicacy, and a stronger sense of shame" than men. The anonymous author of *Female Tuition* claimed the female sex was "naturally attached to purity."[19]

Hannah More's work perfected the transformation of woman's image from sexual to moral being. Her *Strictures on the Modern System of Female Education* called for the rescue of religion and morality and located her constituency among her own sex. She detailed further than any predecessor the power that women could command, first making clear that this was power derived from their moral and spiritual endowment, not from their winning or endearing (sexual) ways. "It is humbling to reflect," More began her *Strictures,* "that in those countries in which fondness for the mere persons of women is carried to the highest excess, *they are slaves;* and that their moral and intellectual degradation increases in direct proportion to the adoration which is paid to mere external charms."[20] More offered a resounding alternative to the idea that women were made for men's pleasure—but at the price of a new level of self-control. Since she believed that human nature was corrupt, her educational program consisted of repression as much as enhancement.[21] Her outlook revealed to women a source of power (in moral influence) and an independence of men (through reliance on God) in a female world view that inspired and compelled women throughout the nineteenth century.[22] In her refusal to see women as childish and affec-

19. Gisborne, p. 183; *Female Tuition*, p. 243. On "simplicity" see, e.g., Gisborne, pp. 104–11, 187, 193; *Female Tuition*, p. 112–75.

20. More, 1:3 (quotation) and passim. Her *Strictures* followed upon her two other successful critiques of aristocratic manners, *Thoughts on the Importance of the Manners of the Great* (1788) and *An Estimate of the Religion of the Fashionable World* (1790) (see Jones, n. 17 above, on her life and work).

21. *Strictures*, see esp. pp. 17–18, 29, 32–33, 137–38, 154–55.

22. During the first several decades of the nineteenth century all sorts of literate women—farm-bred daughters, society girls, schoolteachers, and matrons, from rural towns to commercial seaports—read and quoted Hannah More. For examples see *The Writings of Nancy Maria Hyde* (Norwich, Conn.: Russell Hubbard, 1816), diary entry for June 14, 1812; manuscript journal of Margaret Searle, August 22, 1812, Curson Family Papers, Houghton Library, Harvard University; manuscript book of extracts of Lucinda Read, 1815–16, Massachusettes Historical Society, Boston; manuscript journal of Mehitable May Dawes, June 12, 1815, May-Goddard Papers, Schlesinger Library, Radcliffe College. Jones, p. 193, states that More's novel *Coelebs in Search of a Wife* (which personified her ideals for female character) sold out thirty editions in the United States between 1808 and 1834. The British visitor Harriet Martineau was mightily impressed, in the 1830s, with the impact More had on American women; her comments and others are cited by Keith Melder, "Ladies Bountiful," *New York History* 48 (July 1967): 233–34, 254n. Jill K. Conway assembles other evidence of More's wide-ranging influence on American women in "Evangelical Protestantism and Its Influence on Women in North America, 1790–1860" (paper read at the American Historical Association Convention, New Orleans, December 1972).

tedly weak beings, designed only "to gratify the appetite of man, or to be the upper servant," she agreed with her contemporary, Mary Wollstonecraft. Despite the spectrum of difference between More and Wollstonecraft in politics and personal behavior, they both abhorred "libertine notions of beauty" and "weak elegancy of mind" in women, wished to emphasize women's moral and intellectual powers rather than their "mere animal" capacities, and expected reformed women to reform the world.[23] Their two critiques rose from shared indignation that women were degraded by their sexual characterization.

* * *

The new focus on moral rather than sexual determinants of female character in didactic works at the end of the eighteenth century required a reversal in Protestant views of women. In Puritan ideology, earthly women were the inheritors of Eve's legacy of moral danger. By the mid-eighteenth century, however, New England ministers had discarded similes to Eve, probably in deference to their predominantly female congregations, and portrayed women as more sensitive to the call of religion than men.[24] Nineteenth-century Protestantism relied on women for its prime exemplars and symbols. Between 1790 and 1820 particularly, as an evangelical united front spread across the United States and Britain, the clergy intensified their emphasis on women as crucial advocates of religion.[25] Evangelical Protestants constantly reiterated the theme that Christianity had raised women from slaves in status to moral and intellectual beings.[26] The tacit condition for that elevation was the suppression of female sexuality. Christian women were "exalted above human nature, raised to that of angels"; proper understanding of the gospel enabled women to dismiss the earthly pride or sensuality that subjected them to men's whims.[27] The clergy thus renewed and generalized the idea that women under God's grace were more pure than men, and they expected not merely the souls but the bodies of women to corroborate that claim.

The pastors had a double purpose in training their eyes on the moral rather than the sexual aspect of woman's being. It enabled them to welcome women as worthy allies and agents of Protestantism, which

23. Mary Wollstonecraft, *A Vindication of the Rights of Women* (1792), ed. Charles W. Hagelman, Jr. (New York: W. W. Norton & Co., 1967), pp. 34–35, 49–72, 77, 84, 91–92, 191–92, 206–10.

24. Lonna Myers Malmsheimer, "New England Funeral Sermons and Changing Attitudes toward Women, 1692–1792" (Ph.D. diss., University of Minnesota, 1973), esp. pp. 178–79.

25. See Cott, *Bonds of Womanhood*, pp. 128–35, 146–48; Foster, pp. 92–100, 115–32.

26. See Cott, p. 130.

27. *The Female Friend, or, the Duties of Christian Virgins* (Baltimore: H. S. Keatinge, 1809), pp. 40–42; Samuel Worcester, *Female Love to Christ* (Salem, Mass.: Pool & Palfrey, 1809), pp. 12–13.

seemed more and more essential as men's religious commitment dissipated. Second, a world view in which woman's sexual nature was shadowed behind her moral and spiritual endowment eclipsed her primitive and original power over men, the power of her sexuality.[28] The evangelical view, by concentrating on women's spiritual nature, simultaneously elevated women as moral and intellectual beings and disarmed them of their sexual power. Passionlessness was on the other side of the coin which paid, so to speak, for women's admission to moral equality.

The correlation between passionlessness and a distinctly improved view of women's character and social purpose begins to suggest the appeal of the concept to women. By replacing sexual with moral motives and determinants, the ideology of passionlessness favored women's power and self-respect. It reversed the tradition of Christian mistrust based on women's sexual treacherousness. It elevated women above the weakness of animal nature, stressing instead that they were "formed for exalted purity, felicity, and glory."[29] It postulated that woman's influence was not ensnaring but disinterested. It routed women out of the cul-de-sac of education for attractiveness, thus allowing more intellectual breadth.[30] To women who wanted means of self-preservation and self-control, this view of female nature may well have appealed, as Hannah More's views appealed. It remains to be seen in what social circumstances such views came to the fore.

* * *

There was extraordinary turbulence in sexual patterns and definitions in the late eighteenth century. The traditional system under which parents exercised authority over their children's marriage choices was breaking down.[31] This change might seem to imply greater freedom for youth of both sexes in choosing their spouses. Since men conventionally exercised the sexual/marital initiative, however, the demise of parental control probably meant a relative decline in the leverage available to marriageable women, who no longer had their parents operating openly on their behalf and could not assume that role themselves. Eliza Southgate, an articulate and well-to-do eighteen-year-old of Maine, remarked in 1800 that women sensed their "inequality of

28. See Karen Horney, "The Dread of Woman," *International Journal of Psychoanalysis* 13 (1932): 348–60; and H. R. Hays, *The Dangerous Sex: The Myth of Feminine Evil* (New York: Putnam Books, 1966).

29. Worcester, pp. 12–13.

30. Cf. Emma Willard's protest, in her *Plan for Improving Female Education* (1819; reprint ed., Middlebury, Vt.: Middlebury College, 1918), pp. 14–15, that current female education was far too attuned to pleasing the opposite sex.

31. Daniel Scott Smith, "Parental Power and Marriage Patterns—an Analysis of Historical Trends in Hingham, Massachusetts," *Journal of Marriage and the Family* 35 (1973): 326.

privilege" most grievously "in the liberty of choosing a partner in marriage; true, we have the liberty of refusing those we don't like, but not of selecting those we do."[32] Owing primarily to the changing sex ratio, the average age at which women first married rose from a low of about twenty years in the early colonies to about twenty-three by the Revolutionary period, while men's age at first marriage fell slightly. The proportion of women who never married rose appreciably in the same period, and the remarriage rate of widows dropped. One might interpret these statistics favorably to mean that "those who wed may have taken longer to consider the implications of such actions and the alternatives," or even that it was now "possible for unmarried men and women to find a satisfying role."[33] But since marriage was the principal means women had of supporting themselves, one could argue that the number of desperate and exploitable women multiplied. While marriage was the likeliest source for economic security for a woman, marital subjection remained the living symbol of women's general subjection to men. In Abigail Adams's famous request to her husband John in 1776 to "remember the ladies," her central complaint was not women's political disenfranchisement but husbands' legal exercise of "unlimited power" over their wives. Turning Revolutionary rhetoric to marital relations, Abigail reminded John that "all men would be tyrants if they could," and urged that a new law code "put it out of the power of the vicious and lawless to use us with cruelty and indignity with impunity."[34] Her objections evoke the double spectres, of sharper victimization or greater equity, borne before women's eyes during these Revolutionary years. Did women's marital status trouble her because it had become, of late, more abject, or because some hints of improvement in women's marital power precipitated her demand for further change?

During the same decades, the prebridal pregnancy rate rose dramatically. At peak years between 1760 and 1800, one-third to one-half of all recorded legitimate first births were the result of premarital sexual intercourse in several New England towns where the same measure was one-tenth or one-twentieth in the seventeenth century.[35] Again, numerous and contradictory interpretations can be drawn from these figures.

32. Eliza Southgate to Moses Porter, 1800, reprinted in *A Girl's Life Eighty Years Ago*, ed. Clarence Cook (New York: Scribner's, 1887).

33. Robert V. Wells, "Quaker Marriage Patterns in a Colonial Perspective," *William and Mary Quarterly*, 3d ser. 29 (1972): 437–39 (quotations); and Daniel Scott Smith, personal communication. Wells's figures for the proportion of women never marrying, and for remarriage of widows, are based on a New Jersey population; those on age at marriage reflect both the New England and the middle colonies population.

34. Abigail Adams to John Adams, March 31, 1776, reprinted in *The Feminist Papers*, ed. Alice Rossi (New York: Bantam Books, 1974), pp. 10–11.

35. Daniel Scott Smith and Michael S. Hindus, "Premarital Pregnancy in America: An Overview and Interpretation," *Journal of Interdisciplinary History* 6 (1975): 537–71; cf. David H. Flaherty, "Law and the Enforcement of Morals in Early America," *Perspectives in American History* 5 (1971): 246–47.

The increase in prebridal pregnancy could be ascribed to a general increase in premarital sexual activity, which in itself could possibly represent greater individual and sexual freedom for both sexes, or just as possibly indicate greater vulnerability and exploitation of women. Or, premarital sexual activity could have remained constant but have led more frequently to marriage and legitimation.[36] The continued reign of a double standard of sexual morality made it unlikely that sexual "freedom" came without cost to women. A content analysis of nine New England magazines between 1777 and 1794 has shown that characters in both fiction and nonfiction regularly advocated punishment or ostracism for the male partner in illicit sex and sympathy for the female as the victim of force or misguided ignorance. In actual portrayals of illicit sexual encounters, however, the males involved escaped scot-free and the women almost always suffered punishment or ostracism.[37] On this injustice the young wife of a lawyer in Haverhill, Massachusetts, reflected in 1802: "Man boasts superior strength of mind, I would have him prove it, by avoiding or conquering temptation; but man disgraces his godlike reason, and yields to a thousand follies, to give them no harsher name—and passes through the world in high repute, such conduct would blast the reputation of poor weak woman. . . . 'tis an unrighteous custom, which gives such license to our lords of the creation." She was not alone in protesting men's combination of sexual license with their claim to righteous social power. On the eve of her marriage, Sarah Connell of Concord, New Hampshire, lamented a local instance of seduction and betrayal, empathizing with the many unprotected girls who had "fallen victim to the baseness of those who call themselves lords of the Creation."[38]

The sexual exploitation possible in contemporary disruption of marital and sexual patterns was probably more obvious to women because of heightened expectations on their part. The clergy, adopting a more positive image of women in their sermons, no longer presented marriage as a hierarchical relationship but stressed that women were complementary, and piously influential, marriage partners. The rhetoric of the American Revolution glorified women's role further by connecting it with the success of the national experiment. In an abrupt reversal

36. If premarital sexual activity remained constant while bridal pregnancy increased then illegitimate births would have decreased. This is unlikely. Although the figures for illegitimacy in early America are not known, as Smith and Hindus point out, illegitimacy and bridal pregnancy usually rise and fall together. Another factor affecting the rise and fall of bridal pregnancy is nutrition, but Smith and Hindus tend to discount its relevance in this case.

37. Herman R. Lantz et al., "Preindustrial Patterns in the Colonial Family in America: A Content Analysis of Colonial Magazines," *American Sociological Review* 33 (1968): 422–23.

38. Manuscript diary of Mary Orne Tucker, May 7, 1802, James Duncan Phillips Library, Essex Institute, Salem, Mass.; Sarah Connell to Susan Kittredge, March 13, 1810, in *Diary of Sarah Connell Ayer* (Portland, Me.: n. p., 1910), pp. 372–73.

in 1773, Massachusetts women were victorious if they petitioned their governor and council for divorce on account of their husbands' adulteries; and women's overall success in obtaining divorce was almost equal to men's in the decade after 1776.[39] If not the most isolated farmers' wives, then literate women, living in populated areas sharing in the commerce of goods and ideas, were particularly likely to anticipate better treatment.[40]

A vision of sexual equity arising from awareness of sexual injustice brought feminist writers into the open during the same years. Judith Sargent Murray of Gloucester, Massachusetts, began criticizing female education in the 1770s, anticipating the themes of More and Wollstonecraft. Under the pseudonym "Constantia" she argued that men's presumed superiority in rationality was due to their superior education and continued advantages, not to any inherent preeminence. She demanded that women have opportunity to cultivate other means than sexual attraction. Pointing out that the typical upbringing of girls trivialized their minds and made them rely on physical beauty, she urged women to develop aspirations, a "reverence of self," moral and intellectual integrity, and the capacity for self-fulfillment.[41] Constantia put her hopes in the female academies springing up. Another pseudonymous feminist, an "aged matron" of Connecticut who published *The Female Advocate* in 1801, wished to disabuse the world of the idea that woman was inferior to man or made for men's uses. God and Nature, she claimed, had given the two sexes "equality of talents, of genius, of morals, as well as intellectual worth," and only male arrogance had invaded that equality. Men had deprived women of education and experience while they themselves "engross[ed] all the emoluments, offices, honors and merits, of church and state." In her eyes the sexual double standard epitomized male usurpation of power, because it allowed a man to flaunt the arts of seduction without losing public esteem while it condemned a woman forever if she once succumbed to a deceiver. *The Female Advocate*'s images of women's powerlessness and vulnerability contrasted with its portrayal of men's aggrandizement of power and seductive wiles. Yet its author

39. Malmsheimer, pp. 138–79; Gordon S. Wood, *The Creation of the American Republic* (New York: W. W. Norton & Co., 1969), pp. 65–70, 123–24; Cott, "Divorce and the Changing Status of Women."

40. Kenneth R. Lockridge, *Literacy in Colonial New England* (New York: W. W. Norton & Co., 1974), pp. 38–42, 57–58, estimates that half of New England women were literate in the 1780s (see also Cott, "Divorce and the Changing Status of Women," pp. 595–96; and Richard D. Brown, "The Emergence of Urban Society in Rural Massachusetts, 1760–1830," *Journal of American History* 61 [June 1974: 29–51]).

41. Constantia, "On the Equality of the Sexes," *Massachusetts Magazine* 2 (March 1790): 32–35, reprinted in Aileen S. Kraditor, ed., *Up from the Pedestal* (Chicago: Quadrangle Books, 1968), pp. 31–33; "Desultory Thoughts upon the Utility of Encouraging a Degree of Self-complacency, Especially in Female Bosoms," *Gentleman's and Lady's Town and Country Magazine* 1 (October 1784): 251–53.

was optimistic that "well informed mind[s]" would be "the mean of enabling us [women] to possess some command over ourselves."[42]

Polite ladies' magazines, which first appeared in the 1780s with the growth of a literate female audience, unintentionally paraded the contemporary controversy over sexual definitions. They celebrated female intellectual accomplishments and aimed not to cater to homemakers' tastes but to "improve and amuse" ladies' minds. In this "polite" entertainment, the subjects of fornication, prostitution, adultery, seduction, and betrayal were legion.[43] By and large, the stories and essays in these magazines broadcast the view that women's modus operandi was sexual, and consisted in manipulating men. But they also gave the impression that women met victimization and downfall more often than they gained influence and happiness through the solicitation of men's passions. The sexual definition of women could undermine their control of encounters with men, as Patty Rogers, a young woman of Exeter, New Hampshire, discovered for herself and confided to her diary.[44] Some writers in ladies' magazines were restless or indignant with the sexual characterization of women. A "Fragment on Prostitutes" argued that so-called women of pleasure were really women of grief and suffering, who had been betrayed by their seducers and abandoned by unsympathetic kin. The author railed against the injustice of prostitutes being punished by laws made by men, their seducers.[45] Another author, opposing "what is called Amiable Weakness in women," asserted that women deserved the chance to cultivate their knowledge, intelligence, and self-discipline, because they were moral beings and not merely decorative objects or household drudges. A serious "Scheme for Increasing the Power of the Ladies" called on women to end the double standard by refusing to tolerate fashionable "rakes"; like Hannah More, the writer emphasized that it was up to women to reverse their complaisance with and degradation under the existing code. Sarah Connell concluded her account of her acquaintance's seduction with similar sentiment: "Did every virtuous female show her detestation of the libertine by wholly renouncing his society, there would be a much smaller number of them."[46]

42. *The Female Advocate*, Written by a Lady (New Haven, Conn.: Thomas Green & Son, 1801), pp. 6, 13–17, 22, 27–28.

43. My discussion is based on *Gentleman's and Lady's Town and Country Magazine*, Boston, 1784; *Gentleman's and Ladies' Town and Country Magazine*, Boston, 1789–90; *Lady's Magazine and Repository of Entertaining Knowledge*, Philadelphia, 1792–93; *Lady* [sic] *and Gentleman's Pocket Magazine of Literary and Polite Amusement*, New York, 1796; *Ladies' Museum*, Philadelphia, 1800–1801; *Lady's Magazine and Musical Repository*, New York, 1801; *Ladies' Monitor*, New York, 1801–2; *Ladies' Miscellany, or the Weekly Visitor*, New York, 1802–5; *Ladies' Visitor*, Boston, 1806–7; *Ladies' Weekly Miscellany*, New York, 1805–8.

44. Manuscript diary of Polly [Patty] Rogers, August 4, September 14, September 21, 1785, in the collection of the American Antiquarian Society.

45. *Weekly Visitor*, vol. 2 (January 21, 1804).

46. *Lady and Gentleman's Pocket Magazine* (October 1796), pp. 174–79; *Lady's Magazine* (June 1792); *Diary of Sarah Connell Ayer*, p. 373.

Only a handful of New England women at this time questioned the political inequities of their situation, but sexual and marital subjection—unequal sexual prerogatives—seem to have rankled a much larger population. As *The Female Advocate* pointed out, women had to conform to male tastes and wait to be chosen but resist seduction or suffer ostracism for capitulating; men, meanwhile, were free to take the first step, practice flattery, and escape the consequences of illicit sexual relations. In sexual encounters women had more than an even chance to lose, whether by censure under the double standard, unwanted pregnancy and health problems, or ill-fated marriage. In this perspective, women might hail passionlessness as a way to assert control in the sexual arena—even if that "control" consisted in denial. Some scholars have claimed that women adhered to the ideology of passionlessness to bolster their position in a disadvantageous marriage market, that is, to play "hard to get" with conviction.[47] More essentially, passionlessness served women's larger interests by downplaying altogether their sexual characterization, which was the cause of their exclusion from significant "human" (i.e., male) pursuits.[48] The positive contribution of passionlessness was to replace that sexual/carnal characterization of women with a spiritual/moral one, allowing women to develop their human faculties and their self-esteem. The belief that women lacked carnal motivation was the cornerstone of the argument for women's moral superiority, used to enhance women's status and widen their opportunities in the nineteenth century. Furthermore, acceptance of the idea of passionlessness created sexual solidarity among women; it allowed women to consider their love relationships with one another of higher character than heterosexual relationships because they excluded (male) carnal passion. "I do not believe that men can ever feel so pure an enthusiasm for women as we can feel for one another," Catherine Sedgwick recorded in her diary of 1834, upon meeting Fanny Kemble, "—ours is nearest to the love of angels."[49] "Love is spiritual, only passion is sexual," Mary Grew wrote at the end of the century to vindicate her intense and enduring friendship with Margaret Burleigh. That sense of the angelic or spiritual aspect of female love ennobled the experience of sisterhood which was central to the lives of nineteenth-century women and to the early wom-

47. See D. S. Smith (n. 2 above), pp. 129–31; Collins (n. 2 above), pp. 7, 13–19; Watt (n. 12 above).

48. Cf. Harriot Hunt's defensive line of argument in her application for admission to the Harvard Medical School in 1850: "In opening your doors to woman, it is mind that will enter the lecture room, it is intelligence that will ask for food; sex will never be felt where science leads for the atmosphere of thought will be around every lecture" (quoted in Mary Roth Walsh, *Doctors Wanted: No Women Need Apply* [New Haven, Conn.: Yale University Press, 1977], p. 31).

49. Manuscript diary of Catherine Maria Sedgwick, May 16, 1834, Massachusetts Historical Society, Boston.

an's rights movement.[50] Women considered passionlessness an important shared trait which distinguished them favorably from men.[51]

It must not be assumed that women who internalized the concept of passionlessness necessarily shunned marriage. The pervasive ideology of romantic love, and also the evangelical conflation of the qualities of earthly and spiritual love, bridged the gap and refuted the ostensible contradiction between passionlessness and marriage. On a practical level, belief in female passionlessness could aid a woman to limit sexual intercourse within marriage and thus limit family size. Daniel Scott Smith has postulated a direct relation between women's exertion of that sort of power within the family, which he calls "domestic feminism," and the decline of the birthrate during the nineteenth century.[52] The conviction and the demand that it was woman's right to control reproduction, advocated by health reformers in the 1850s and promulgated in the movement for"voluntary motherhood" in subsequent decades, depended on the ideology of female passionlessness. Linda Gordon has shown the feminist basis of the argument for voluntary motherhood in the claim that women had the right to refuse their husbands' sexual demands, despite the legal and customary requirements of submission to marital "duty."[53]

The degree to which a woman might incorporate the idea of passionlessness is revealed in an 1845 letter of Harriet Beecher Stowe to her husband. Responding to his revelations about "licentiousness" on the part of certain clergymen, she wrote: "What terrible temptations lie in the way of your sex—till now I never realized it—for tho I did love you with an almost insane love before I married you I never knew yet or felt the pulsation which showed me that I could be tempted in that way—there never was a moment when I felt anything by which you could have drawn me astray—for I loved you as I now love God. . . ."[54] Angelina Grimké's passionless attitude was a feminist affirmation of woman's dignity in revulsion from male sexual domination. To the man who would become her husband she revealed her judgment "that men in general, the vast majority, believe most seriously that women were made to gratify their animal appetites, *expressly* to minister to their pleasure—yea

50. Mary Grew to Isabel Howland, April 27, 1892, quoted in Carroll Smith-Rosenberg, "The Female World of Love and Ritual," p. 27, an essay which describes in rich detail female friendships during the nineteenth century. See also Cott, *Bonds of Womanhood*, chap. 5.

51. At the end of her life Sarah Grimké opined to Elizabeth Smith Miller that "the sexual passion in man is ten times stronger than in woman," and that woman was innately man's superior (quoted in Ronald G. Walters, "The Erotic South: Civilization and Sexuality in American Abolitionism," *American Quarterly* 25 [May 1973]: 196).

52. See Smith (n. 2 above).

53. Gordon, *Woman's Body*, p. 103.

54. Quoted in Edmund Wilson, *Patriotic Gore* (New York: Oxford University Press, 1966), p. 22. I am indebted to Kathryn Kish Sklar for bringing this letter to my attention.

Christian men too." She continued: "My soul abhors such a base letting down of the high dignity of my nature as a woman. How I have feared the possibility of ever being married to one who regarded *this* as the *end*—the great design of marriage. In truth I may say that I never was reconciled to the compound [relat]ions of marriage until I read Combe on the Constitution of man this winter."[55]

Yet a belief so at odds with the traditional appreciation of female sexuality, and one which seems to mid-twentieth-century sensibilities so patently counterproductive, so symbolic of the repression and subordination of women, cannot be interpreted simply. Historians' frequent assumption that men devised the ideology of female passionlessness to serve their own interests—"to help gentlemen cope with the problem of controlling their own sexuality"—is partial (in both senses of the word) but not illogical.[56] An ideal of male continence, of virtuous and willed repression of existing carnal desires (as distinct from passionlessness, which implied absence of carnal motivation), figures in nineteenth-century directions for men's respectability and achievement in the bustling new world of industrial capitalism.[57] In one aspect, female passionlessness was a keystone in men's construction of their own self-control. But Howard Gadlin has underlined the paradox of the ideology, as well as reason for its diffusion and rootedness, in his remark that "the nineteenth-century double standard was the vehicle for a desexualization desired by both men and women for opposing purposes. Men wanted to desexualize relationships to maintain their domination; women wanted to desexualize relationships to limit male domination."[58]

Both women's participation in the creation of Victorian sexual standards and the place of passionlessness in the vanguard of feminist thought deserve more recognition. The serviceability of passionlessness to women in gaining social and familial power should be acknowledged as a primary reason that the ideology was quickly and widely accepted. Yet feminists were the first to question and oppose the ideology once it was entrenched. When prudery became confused with passionlessness, it undermined women physically and psychologically by restricting their knowledge of their own sexual functioning. From the first, women health reformers and moral reformers rejected this injurious implication

55. Angelina Grimké to Theodore Dwight Weld, March 4, 1838, in *Letters of Theodore Dwight Weld, Angelina Grimké Weld, and Sarah Grimké*, ed. Gilbert Barnes and D. L. Dumond (New York: D. Appleton-Century, 1934), 2:587. "Combe" is the Scottish phrenologist Andrew Combe.

56. Cominos (n. 2 above), p. 162 and passim.

57. See Charles E. Rosenberg, "Sexuality, Class and Role in Nineteenth-Century America," *American Quarterly* 25 (1973): 131–53; and Stephen Nissenbaum, "Sex, Reform, and Social Change, 1830–1840" (paper delivered at the annual meeting of the Organization of American Historians, Washington, D.C., April 6, 1972).

58. Howard Gadlin, "Private Lives and Public Order: A Critical View of the History of Intimate Relations in the U.S.," *Massachusetts Review* 17 (Summer 1976): 318.

while fostering the positive meanings of passionlessness.[59] Feminist opposition arose when the medical establishment adopted passionlessness and moved the grounds for judging the concept from the spiritual to the somatic. When female passionlessness came to be insisted upon literally, more than one woman reacted as Rebecca Harding Davis did: "In these rough and tumble days, we'd better give [women] their places as flesh and blood, with exactly the same wants and passions as men." Mary Gove Nichols claimed: "A healthy and loving woman is impelled to material union as surely, often as strongly, as man. . . . The apathy of the sexual instinct is caused by the enslaved and unhealthy condition in which she lives."[60] Several woman's rights activists of the later part of the century, including Isabella Beecher Hooker, Alice Stockham, and Elizabeth Cady Stanton, discussed among themselves their belief in the existence and legitimacy of female sexual drives, even while the movement of which they were part banked on women's superior morality and maternal instinct as chief supports.[61] Consistent with the general conflicts and contradictions in sexual ideology after 1860, feminists perceived oppression in prudery while clinging to the promises that passionlessness held out.

The ideology of passionlessness, conceived as self-preservation and social advancement for women, created its own contradictions: on the one hand, by exaggerating sexual propriety so far as to immobilize women and, on the other, by allowing claims of women's moral influence to obfuscate the need for other sources of power. The assertion of moral integrity within passionlessness had allowed women to retrieve their identity from a trough of sexual vulnerability and dependence. The concept could not assure women full autonomy—but what transformation in sexual ideology alone could have done so?

American Studies Program
Yale University

59. See Catharine E. Beecher, *Letters to the People on Health and Happiness* (New York: Harper & Bros., 1855); Smith-Rosenberg, "Beauty, the Beast," p. 571; Walsh, pp. 40–41.

60. Rebecca Harding Davis, "Paul Blecker," *Atlantic Monthly* (June/July 1863), quoted in introduction by Tillie Olsen to Davis's *Life in the Iron Mills* (New York: Feminist Press, 1972), p. 168n; Mary Gove Nichols (with T. L. Nichols), *Marriage; Its History, Character and Results* . . . (New York: T. L. Nichols, 1854), quoted in Nancy F. Cott, ed., *Root of Bitterness*, (New York: E. P. Dutton & Co., 1972), p. 286. Cf. Elizabeth Cady Stanton's response to Walt Whitman's poem "There Is a Woman Waiting for Me" in her diary of 1883: "Whitman seems to understand everything in nature but woman. . . . He speaks as if the female must be forced to the creative act, apparently ignorant of the great natural fact that a healthy woman has as much passion as a man, that she needs nothing stronger than the law of attraction to draw her to the male" (quoted in *Feminist Papers*, p. 393).

61. Gordon, *Woman's Body*, pp. 98–100, 183.

The Female World of Love and Ritual: Relations between Women in Nineteenth-Century America

Carroll Smith-Rosenberg

The female friendship of the nineteenth century, the long-lived, intimate, loving friendship between two women, is an excellent example of the type of historical phenomena which most historians know something about, which few have thought much about, and which virtually no one has written about.[1] It is one aspect of the female experience which consciously or unconsciously we have chosen to ignore. Yet an abundance of manuscript evidence suggests that eighteenth- and nineteenth-century women routinely formed emotional ties with other women. Such deeply felt, same-sex friendships were casually accepted in American society. Indeed, from at least the late eighteenth through the mid-nineteenth century, a female world of varied and yet highly structured relationships

Research for this paper was supported in part by a grant from the Grant Foundation, New York, and by National Institutes of Health trainee grant 5 FO3 HD48800-03. I would like to thank several scholars for their assistance and criticism in preparing this paper: Erving Goffman, Roy Schafer, Charles E. Rosenberg, Cynthia Secor, Anthony Wallace. Judy Breault, who has just completed a biography of an important and introspective nineteenth-century feminist, Emily Howland, served as a research assistant for this paper and her knowledge of nineteenth-century family structure and religious history proved invaluable.

1. The most notable exception to this rule is now eleven years old: William R. Taylor and Christopher Lasch, "Two 'Kindred Spirits': Sorority and Family in New England, 1839–1846," *New England Quarterly* 36 (1963): 25–41. Taylor has made a valuable contribution to the history of women and the history of the family with his concept of "sororial" relations. I do not, however, accept the Taylor-Lasch thesis that female friendships developed in the mid-nineteenth century because of geographic mobility and the breakup of the colonial family. I have found these friendships as frequently in the eighteenth century as in the nineteenth and would hypothesize that the geographic mobility of the mid-nineteenth century eroded them as it did so many other traditional social institutions. Helen Vendler (*Review of Notable American Women, 1607–1950*, ed. Edward James and Janet James, *New York Times*) [November 5, 1972]: sec. 7) points out the significance of these friendships.

[*Signs: Journal of Women in Culture and Society* 1975, vol. 1, no. 1] appears to have been an essential aspect of American society. These relationships ranged from the supportive love of sisters, through the enthusiasms of adolescent girls, to sensual avowals of love by mature women. It was a world in which men made but a shadowy appearance.[2]

Defining and analyzing same-sex relationships involves the historian in deeply problematical questions of method and interpretation. This is especially true since historians, influenced by Freud's libidinal theory, have discussed these relationships almost exclusively within the context of individual psychosexual developments or, to be more explicit, psychopathology.[3] Seeing same-sex relationships in terms of a dichotomy between normal and abnormal, they have sought the origins of such apparent deviance in childhood or adolescent trauma and detected the symptoms of "latent" homosexuality in the lives of both those who later became "overtly" homosexual and those who did not. Yet theories concerning the nature and origins of same-sex relationships are frequently contradictory or based on questionable or arbitrary data. In recent years such hypotheses have been subjected to criticism both from within and without the psychological professions. Historians who seek to work within a psychological framework, therefore, are faced with two hard questions: Do sound psychodynamic theories concerning the nature and origins of same-sex relationships exist? If so, does the historical datum exist which would permit the use of such dynamic models?

I would like to suggest an alternative approach to female friendships—one which would view them within a cultural and social setting rather than from an exclusively individual psychosexual perspective. Only by thus altering our approach will we be in the position to evaluate the appropriateness of particular dynamic interpretations. Intimate friendships between men and men and women and women ex-

2. I do not wish to deny the importance of women's relations with particular men. Obviously, women were close to brothers, husbands, fathers, and sons. However, there is evidence that despite such closeness relationships between men and women differed in both emotional texture and frequency from those between women. Women's relations with each other, although they played a central role in the American family and American society, have been so seldom examined either by general social historians or by historians of the family that I wish in this article simply to examine their nature and analyze their implications for our understanding of social relations and social structure. I have discussed some aspects of male-female relationships in two articles: "Puberty to Menopause: The Cycle of Femininity in Nineteenth-Century America," *Feminist Studies* 1 (1973): 58–72, and, with Charles Rosenberg, "The Female Animal: Medical and Biological Views of Women in 19th Century America," *Journal of American History* 59 (1973): 331–56.

3. See Freud's classic paper on homosexuality, "Three Essays on the Theory of Sexuality," in *The Standard Edition of the Complete Psychological Works of Sigmund Freud*, trans. James Strachey (London: Hogarth Press, 1953), 7:135–72. The essays originally appeared in 1905. Prof. Roy Shafer, Department of Psychiatry, Yale University, has pointed out that Freud's view of sexual behavior was strongly influenced by nineteenth-century evolutionary thought. Within Freud's schema, genital heterosexuality marked the height of human development (Schafer, "Problems in Freud's Psychology of Women," *Journal of the American Psychoanalytic Association* 22 [1974]: 459–85).

isted in a larger world of social relations and social values. To interpret such friendships more fully they must be related to the structure of the American family and to the nature of sex-role divisions and of male-female relations both within the family and in society generally. The female friendship must not be seen in isolation; it must be analyzed as one aspect of women's overall relations with one another. The ties between mothers and daughters, sisters, female cousins and friends, at all stages of the female life cycle constitute the most suggestive framework for the historian to begin an analysis of intimacy and affection between women. Such an analysis would not only emphasize general cultural patterns rather than the internal dynamics of a particular family or childhood; it would shift the focus of the study from a concern with deviance to that of defining configurations of legitimate behavioral norms and options.[4]

This analysis will be based upon the correspondence and diaries of women and men in thirty-five families between the 1760s and the 1880s. These families, though limited in number, represented a broad range of the American middle class, from hard-pressed pioneer families and orphaned girls to daughters of the intellectual and social elite. It includes families from most geographic regions, rural and urban, and a spectrum of Protestant denominations ranging from Mormon to orthodox Quaker. Although scarcely a comprehensive sample of America's increasingly heterogeneous population, it does, I believe, reflect accurately the literate middle class to which the historian working with letters and diaries is necessarily bound. It has involved an analysis of many thousands of letters written to women friends, kin, husbands, brothers, and children at every period of life from adolescence to old age. Some collections encompass virtually entire life spans; one contains over 100,000 letters as well as diaries and account books. It is my contention that an analysis of women's private letters and diaries which were never intended to be published permits the historian to explore a very private world of emotional realities central both to women's lives and to the middle-class family in nineteenth-century America.[5]

The question of female friendships is peculiarly elusive; we know so little or perhaps have forgotten so much. An intriguing and almost alien form of human relationship, they flourished in a different social structure and amidst different sexual norms. Before attempting to reconstruct their social setting, therefore, it might be best first to describe two not atypical friendships. These two friendships, intense, loving, and

4. For a novel and most important exposition of one theory of behavioral norms and options and its application to the study of human sexuality, see Charles Rosenberg, "Sexuality, Class and Role," *American Quarterly* 25 (1973): 131–53.

5. See, e.g., the letters of Peggy Emlen to Sally Logan, 1768–72, Wells Morris Collection, Box 1, Historical Society of Pennsylvania; and the Eleanor Parke Custis Lewis Letters, Historical Society of Pennsylvania, Philadelphia.

openly avowed, began during the women's adolescence and, despite subsequent marriages and geographic separation, continued throughout their lives. For nearly half a century these women played a central emotional role in each other's lives, writing time and again of their love and of the pain of separation. Paradoxically to twentieth-century minds, their love appears to have been both sensual and platonic.

Sarah Butler Wister first met Jeannie Field Musgrove while vacationing with her family at Stockbridge, Massachusetts, in the summer of 1849.[6] Jeannie was then sixteen, Sarah fourteen. During two subsequent years spent together in boarding school, they formed a deep and intimate friendship. Sarah began to keep a bouquet of flowers before Jeannie's portrait and wrote complaining of the intensity and anguish of her affection.[7] Both young women assumed nom de plumes, Jeannie a female name, Sarah a male one; they would use these secret names into old age.[8] They frequently commented on the nature of their affection: "If the day should come," Sarah wrote Jeannie in the spring of 1861, "when you failed me either through your fault or my own, I would forswear all human friendship, thenceforth." A few months later Jeannie commented: "Gratitude is a word I should never use toward you. It is perhaps a misfortune of such intimacy and love that it makes one regard all kindness as a matter of course, as one has always found it, as natural as the embrace in meeting."[9]

Sarah's marriage altered neither the frequency of their correspondence nor their desire to be together. In 1864, when twenty-nine, married, and a mother, Sarah wrote to Jeannie: "I shall be entirely alone [this coming week]. I can give you no idea how desperately I shall want you. . . ." After one such visit Jeannie, then a spinster in New York, echoed Sarah's longing: "Dear darling Sarah! How I love you & how happy I have been! You are the joy of my life. . . . I cannot tell you how much happiness you gave me, nor how constantly it is all in my thoughts. . . . My darling how I long for the time when I shall see you. . . ." After another visit Jeannie wrote: "I want you to tell me in your next letter, to assure me, that I am your dearest. . . . I do not doubt you, & I am not jealous but I long to hear you say it once more & it seems already a long

6. Sarah Butler Wister was the daughter of Fanny Kemble and Pierce Butler. In 1859 she married a Philadelphia physician, Owen Wister. The novelist Owen Wister is her son. Jeannie Field Musgrove was the half-orphaned daughter of constitutional lawyer and New York Republican politician David Dudley Field. Their correspondence (1855–98) is in the Sarah Butler Wister Papers, Wister Family Papers, Historical Society of Pennsylvania.

7. Sarah Butler, Butler Place, S.C., to Jeannie Field, New York, September 14, 1855.

8. See, e.g., Sarah Butler Wister, Germantown, Pa., to Jeannie Field, New York, September 25, 1862, October 21, 1863; or Jeannie Field, New York, to Sarah Butler Wister, Germantown, July 3, 1861, January 23 and July 12, 1863.

9. Sarah Butler Wister, Germantown, to Jeannie Field, New York, June 5, 1861, February 29, 1864; Jeannie Field to Sarah Butler Wister November 22, 1861, January 4 and June 14, 1863.

time since your voice fell on my ear. So just fill a quarter page with caresses & expressions of endearment. Your silly Angelina." Jeannie ended one letter: "Goodbye my dearest, dearest lover—ever your own Angelina." And another, "I will go to bed . . . [though] I could write all night—A thousand kisses—I love you with my whole soul—your Angelina."

When Jeannie finally married in 1870 at the age of thirty-seven, Sarah underwent a period of extreme anxiety. Two days before Jeannie's marriage Sarah, then in London, wrote desperately: "Dearest darling—How incessantly have I thought of you these eight days—all today—the entire uncertainty, the distance, the long silence—are all new features in my separation from you, grevious to be borne. . . . Oh Jeannie. I have thought & thought & yearned over you these two days. Are you married I wonder? My dearest love to you wherever and *who*ever you are."[10] Like many other women in this collection of thirty-five families, marriage brought Sarah and Jeannie physical separation; it did not cause emotional distance. Although at first they may have wondered how marriage would affect their relationship, their affection remained unabated throughout their lives, underscored by their loneliness and their desire to be together.[11]

During the same years that Jeannie and Sarah wrote of their love and need for each other, two slightly younger women began a similar odyssey of love, dependence and—ultimately—physical, though not emotional, separation. Molly and Helena met in 1868 while both attended the Cooper Institute School of Design for Women in New York City. For several years these young women studied and explored the city together, visited each other's families, and formed part of a social network of other artistic young women. Gradually, over the years, their initial friendship deepened into a close intimate bond which continued throughout their lives. The tone in the letters which Molly wrote to Helena changed over these years from "My dear Helena," and signed "your attached friend," to "My dearest Helena," "My Dearest," "My Beloved," and signed "Thine always" or "thine Molly."[12]

10. Sarah Butler Wister, London, to Jeannie Field Musgrove, New York, June 18 and August 3, 1870.

11. See, e.g., two of Sarah's letters to Jeannie: December 21, 1873, July 16, 1878.

12. This is the 1868–1920 correspondence between Mary Hallock Foote and Helena, a New York friend (the Mary Hallock Foote Papers are in the Manuscript Division, Stanford University). Wallace E. Stegner has written a fictionalized biography of Mary Hallock Foote (*Angle of Repose* [Garden City, N.Y.: Doubleday & Co., 1971]). See, as well, her autobiography: Mary Hallock Foote, *A Victorian Gentlewoman in the Far West: The Reminiscences of Mary Hallock Foote*, ed. Rodman W. Paul (San Marino, Calif.: Huntington Library, 1972). In many ways these letters are typical of those women wrote to other women. Women frequently began letters to each other with salutations such as "Dearest." "My Most Beloved," "You Darling Girl," and signed them "tenderly" or "to my dear dear sweet friend, good-bye." Without the least self-consciousness, one woman in her frequent letters to a female friend referred to her husband as "my other love." She was by no means

The letters they wrote to each other during these first five years permit us to reconstruct something of their relationship together. As Molly wrote in one early letter:

> I have not said to you in so many or so few words that I was happy with you during those few so incredibly short weeks but surely you do not need words to tell you what you must know. Those two or three days so dark without, so bright with firelight and contentment within I shall always remember as proof that, for a time, at least—I fancy for quite a long time—we might be sufficient for each other. We know that we can amuse each other for many idle hours together and now we know that we can also work together. And that means much, don't you think so?

She ended: "I shall return in a few days. Imagine yourself kissed many times by one who loved you so dearly."

The intensity and even physical nature of Molly's love was echoed in many of the letters she wrote during the next few years, as, for instance in this short thank-you note for a small present: "Imagine yourself kissed a dozen times my darling. Perhaps it is well for you that we are far

---

unique. See, e.g., Annie to Charlene Van Vleck Anderson, Appleton, Wis., June 10, 1871, Anderson Family Papers, Manuscript Division, Stanford University; Maggie to Emily Howland, Philadelphia, July 12, 1851, Howland Family Papers, Phoebe King Collection, Friends Historical Library, Swarthmore College; Mary Jane Burleigh to Emily Howland, Sherwood, N.Y., March 27, 1872, Howland Family Papers, Sophia Smith Collection, Smith College; Mary Black Couper to Sophia Madeleine DuPont, Wilmington, Del.: n.d. [1834] (two letters), Samuel Francis DuPont Papers, Eleutherian Mills Foundation, Wilmington, Del.; Phoebe Middleton, Concordiville, Pa., to Martha Jefferis, Chester County, Pa., February 22, 1848; and see in general the correspondence (1838–49) between Rebecca Biddle of Philadelphia and Martha Jefferis, Chester County, Pa., Jefferis Family Correspondence, Chester County Historical Society, West Chester, Pa.; Phoebe Bradford Diary, June 7 and July 13, 1832, Historical Society of Pennsylvania; Sarah Alden Ripley, to Abba Allyn, Boston, n.d. [1818–20], and Sarah Alden Ripley to Sophia Bradford, November 30, 1854, in the Sarah Alden Ripley Correspondence, Schlesinger Library, Radcliffe College; Fanny Canby Ferris to Anne Biddle, Philadelphia, October 11 and November 19, 1811, December 26, 1813, Fanny Canby to Mary Canby, May 27, 1801, Mary R. Garrigues to Mary Canby, five letters n.d., [1802–8], Anne Biddle to Mary Canby, two letters n.d., May 16, July 13, and November 24, 1806, June 14, 1807, June 5, 1808, Anne Sterling Biddle Family Papers, Friends Historical Society, Swarthmore College; Harriet Manigault Wilcox Diary, August 7, 1814, Historical Society of Pennsylvania. See as well the correspondence between Harriet Manigault Wilcox's mother, Mrs. Gabriel Manigault, Philadelphia, and Mrs. Henry Middleton, Charleston, S.C., between 1810 and 1830, Cadwalader Collection, J. Francis Fisher Section, Historical Society of Pennsylvania. The basis and nature of such friendships can be seen in the comments of Sarah Alden Ripley to her sister-in-law and long-time friend, Sophia Bradford: "Hearing that you are not well reminds me of what it would be to lose your loving society. We have kept step together through a long piece of road in the weary journey of life. We have loved the same beings and wept together over their graves" (Mrs. O. J. Wister and Miss Agnes Irwin, eds., *Worthy Women of Our First Century* [Philadelphia: J. B. Lippincott & Co., 1877] p. 195).

apart. You might find my thanks so expressed rather overpowering. I have that delightful feeling that it doesn't matter much what I say or how I say it, since we shall meet so soon and forget in that moment that we were ever separated. . . . I shall see you soon and be content."[13]

At the end of the fifth year, however, several crises occurred. The relationship, at least in its intense form, ended, though Molly and Helena continued an intimate and complex relationship for the next half-century. The exact nature of these crises is not completely clear, but it seems to have involved Molly's decision not to live with Helena, as they had originally planned, but to remain at home because of parental insistence. Molly was now in her late twenties. Helena responded with anger and Molly became frantic at the thought that Helena would break off their relationship. Though she wrote distraught letters and made despairing attempts to see Helena, the relationship never regained its former ardor—possibly because Molly had a male suitor.[14] Within six months Helena had decided to marry a man who was, coincidentally, Molly's friend and publisher. Two years later Molly herself finally married. The letters toward the end of this period discuss the transition both women made to having male lovers—Molly spending much time reassuring Helena, who seemed depressed about the end of their relationship and with her forthcoming marriage.[15]

It is clearly difficult from a distance of 100 years and from a post-Freudian cultural perspective to decipher the complexities of Molly and Helena's relationship. Certainly Molly and Helena were lovers —emotionally if not physically. The emotional intensity and pathos of their love becomes apparent in several letters Molly wrote Helena during their crisis: "I wanted so to put my arms round my girl of all the girls in the world and tell her . . . I love her as wives do love their husbands, as *friends* who have taken each other for life—and believe in her as I believe in my God. . . . If I didn't love you do you suppose I'd care about anything or have ridiculous notions and panics and behave like an old fool who ought to know better. I'm going to hang on to your skirts. . . . You can't get away from [my] love." Or as she wrote after Helena's decision to marry: "You know dear Helena, I really was in love with you. It was a passion such as I had never known until I saw you. I don't think it was the noblest way to love you." The theme of intense female love was one Molly again expressed in a letter she wrote to the man Helena was to marry: "Do you know sir, that until you came along I believe that she loved me almost as girls love their lovers. *I know I loved her so.* Don't you

13. Mary Hallock [Foote] to Helena, n.d. [1869–70], n.d. [1871–72], Folder 1, Mary Hallock Foote Letters, Manuscript Division, Stanford University.

14. Mary Hallock [Foote] to Helena, September 15 and 23, 1873, n.d. [October 1873], October 12, 1873.

15. Mary Hallock [Foote] to Helena, n.d. [January 1874], n.d. [Spring 1874]

wonder that I can stand the sight of you." This was in a letter congratulating them on their forthcoming marriage.[16]

The essential question is not whether these women had genital contact and can therefore be defined as heterosexual or homosexual. The twentieth-century tendency to view human love and sexuality within a dichotomized universe of deviance and normality, genitality and platonic love, is alien to the emotions and attitudes of the nineteenth century and fundamentally distorts the nature of these women's emotional interaction. These letters are significant because they force us to place such female love in a particular historical context. There is every indication that these four women, their husbands and families—all eminently respectable and socially conservative—considered such love both socially acceptable and fully compatible with heterosexual marriage. Emotionally and cognitively, their heterosocial and their homosocial worlds were complementary.

One could argue, on the other hand, that these letters were but an example of the romantic rhetoric with which the nineteenth century surrounded the concept of friendship. Yet they possess an emotional intensity and a sensual and physical explicitness that is difficult to dismiss. Jeannie longed to hold Sarah in her arms; Molly mourned her physical isolation from Helena. Molly's love and devotion to Helena, the emotions that bound Jeannie and Sarah together, while perhaps a phenomenon of nineteenth-century society were not the less real for their Victorian origins. A survey of the correspondence and diaries of eighteenth- and nineteenth-century women indicates that Molly, Jeannie, and Sarah represented one very real behavioral and emotional option socially available to nineteenth-century women.

This is not to argue that individual needs, personalities, and family dynamics did not have a significant role in determining the nature of particular relationships. But the scholar must ask if it is historically possible and, if possible, important, to study the intensely individual aspects of psychosexual dynamics. Is it not the historian's first task to explore the social structure and the world view which made intense and sometimes sensual female love both a possible and an acceptable emotional option? From such a social perspective a new and quite different series of questions suggests itself. What emotional function did such female love serve? What was its place within the hetero- and homosocial worlds which women jointly inhabited? Did a spectrum of love-object choices

16. Mary Hallock [Foote] to Helena, September 23, 1873; Mary Hallock [Foote] to Richard, December 13, 1873. Molly's and Helena's relationship continued for the rest of their lives. Molly's letters are filled with tender and intimate references, as when she wrote, twenty years later and from 2,000 miles away: "It isn't because you are good that I love you—but for the essence of you which is like perfume" (n.d. [1890s?]).

exist in the nineteenth century across which some individuals, at least, were capable of moving? Without attempting to answer these questions it will be difficult to understand either nineteenth-century sexuality or the nineteenth-century family.

Several factors in American society between the mid-eighteenth and the mid-nineteenth centuries may well have permitted women to form a variety of close emotional relationships with other women. American society was characterized in large part by rigid gender-role differentiation within the family and within society as a whole, leading to the emotional segregation of women and men. The roles of daughter and mother shaded imperceptibly and ineluctably into each other, while the biological realities of frequent pregnancies, childbirth, nursing, and menopause bound women together in physical and emotional intimacy. It was within just such a social framework, I would argue, that a specifically female world did indeed develop, a world built around a generic and unself-conscious pattern of single-sex or homosocial networks. These supportive networks were institutionalized in social conventions or rituals which accompanied virtually every important event in a woman's life, from birth to death. Such female relationships were frequently supported and paralleled by severe social restrictions on intimacy between young men and women. Within such a world of emotional richness and complexity devotion to and love of other women became a plausible and socially accepted form of human interaction.

An abundance of printed and manuscript sources exists to support such a hypothesis. Etiquette books, advice books on child rearing, religious sermons, guides to young men and young women, medical texts, and school curricula all suggest that late eighteenth- and most nineteenth-century Americans assumed the existence of a world composed of distinctly male and female spheres, spheres determined by the immutable laws of God and nature.[17] The unpublished letters and diaries of Americans during this same period concur, detailing the existence of sexually segregated worlds inhabited by human beings with different values, expectations, and personalities. Contacts between men and women frequently partook of a formality and stiffness quite alien to twentieth-century America and which today we tend to define as "Victorian." Women, however, did not form an isolated and oppressed subcategory in male society. Their letters and diaries indicate that women's sphere had an essential integrity and dignity that grew out of women's

17. I am in the midst of a larger study of adult gender-roles and gender-role socialization in America, 1785–1895. For a discussion of social attitudes toward appropriate male and female roles, see Barbara Welter, "The Cult of True Womanhood: 1820–1860," *American Quarterly* 18 (Summer 1966): 151–74; Ann Firor Scott, *The Southern Lady: From Pedestal to Politics, 1830–1930* (Chicago: University of Chicago Press, 1970), chaps. 1–2; Smith-Rosenberg and Rosenberg.

shared experiences and mutual affection and that, despite the profound changes which affected American social structure and institutions between the 1760s and the 1870s, retained a constancy and predictability. The ways in which women thought of and interacted with each other remained unchanged. Continuity, not discontinuity, characterized this female world. Molly Hallock's and Jeannie Fields's words, emotions, and experiences have direct parallels in the 1760s and the 1790s.[18] There are indications in contemporary sociological and psychological literature that female closeness and support networks have continued into the twentieth century—not only among ethnic and working-class groups but even among the middle class.[19]

Most eighteenth- and nineteenth-century women lived within a world bounded by home, church, and the institution of visiting—that endless trooping of women to each others' homes for social purposes. It was a world inhabited by children and by other women.[20] Women helped each other with domestic chores and in times of sickness, sorrow, or trouble. Entire days, even weeks, might be spent almost exclusively with other women.[21] Urban and town women could devote virtually every day to visits, teas, or shopping trips with other women. Rural women developed a pattern of more extended visits that lasted weeks and sometimes months, at times even dislodging husbands from their beds and bedrooms so that dear friends might spend every hour of every day together.[22] When husbands traveled, wives routinely moved in with other women, invited women friends to teas and suppers, sat together sharing and comparing the letters they had received from other close

18. See, e.g., the letters of Peggy Emlen to Sally Logan, 1768–72, Wells Morris Collection, Box 1, Historical Society of Pennsylvania; and the Eleanor Parke Custis Lewis Letters, Historical Society of Pennsylvania.

19. See esp. Elizabeth Botts, *Family and Social Network* (London: Tavistock Publications, 1957); Michael Young and Peter Willmott, *Family and Kinship in East London*, rev. ed. (Baltimore: Penguin Books, 1964).

20. This pattern seemed to cross class barriers. A letter that an Irish domestic wrote in the 1830s contains seventeen separate references to women and but only seven to men, most of whom were relatives and two of whom were infant brothers living with her mother and mentioned in relation to her mother (Ann McGrann, Philadelphia, to Sophie M. DuPont, Philadelphia, July 3, 1834, Sophie Madeleine DuPont Letters, Eleutherian Mills Foundation).

21. Harriett Manigault Diary, June 28, 1814, and passim; Jeannie Field, New York, to Sarah Butler Wister, Germantown, April 19, 1863; Phoebe Bradford Diary, Janurary 30, February 19, March 4, August 11, and October 14, 1832, Historical Society of Pennsylvania; Sophie M. DuPont, Brandywine, to Henry DuPont, Germantown, July 9, 1827, Eleutherian Mills Foundation.

22. Martha Jefferis to Anne Jefferis Sheppard, July 9, 1843; Anne Jefferis Sheppard to Martha Jefferis, June 28, 1846; Anne Sterling Biddle Papers, passim, Biddle Family Papers, Friends Historical Society, Swarthmore College; Eleanor Parke Custis Lewis, Virginia, to Elizabeth Bordley Gibson, Philadelphia, November 24 and December 4, 1820, November 6, 1821.

women friends. Secrets were exchanged and cherished, and the husband's return at times viewed with some ambivalence.[23]

Summer vacations were frequently organized to permit old friends to meet at water spas or share a country home. In 1848, for example, a young matron wrote cheerfully to her husband about the delightful time she was having with five close women friends whom she had invited to spend the summer with her; he remained at home alone to face the heat of Philadelphia and a cholera epidemic.[24] Some ninety years earlier, two young Quaker girls commented upon the vacation their aunt had taken alone with another woman; their remarks were openly envious and tell us something of the emotional quality of these friendships: "I hear Aunt is gone with the Friend and wont be back for two weeks, fine times indeed I think the old friends had, taking their pleasure about the country . . . and have the advantage of that fine woman's conversation and instruction, while we poor young girls must spend all spring at home. . . . What a disappointment that we are not together. . . ."[25]

Friends did not form isolated dyads but were normally part of highly integrated networks. Knowing each other, perhaps related to each other, they played a central role in holding communities and kin systems together. Especially when families became geographically mobile women's long visits to each other and their frequent letters filled with discussions of marriages and births, illness and deaths, descriptions of growing children, and reminiscences of times and people past provided an important sense of continuity in a rapidly changing society.[26] Central to this female world was an inner core of kin. The ties between sisters, first cousins, aunts, and nieces provided the underlying structure upon which groups of friends and their network of female relatives clustered. Although most of the women within this sample would appear to be living within isolated nuclear families, the emotional ties between nonresidential kin were deep and binding and provided one of the fundamental existential realities of women's lives.[27] Twenty years after

23. Phoebe Bradford Diary, January 13, November 16–19, 1832, April 26 and May 7, 1833; Abigail Brackett Lyman to Mrs. Catling, Litchfield, Conn., May 3, 1801, collection in private hands; Martha Jefferis to Anne Jefferis Sheppard, August 28, 1845.

24. Lisa Mitchell Diary, 1860s, passim, Manuscript Division, Tulane University; Eleanor Parke Custis Lewis to Elizabeth Bordley [Gibson] February 5, 1822; Jeannie McCall, Cedar Park, to Peter McCall, Philadelphia, June 30, 1849, McCall Section, Cadwalader Collection, Historical Society of Pennsylvania.

25. Peggy Emlen to Sally Logan, May 3, 1769.

26. For a prime example of this type of letter, see Eleanor Parke Custis Lewis to Elizabeth Bordley Gibson, passim, or Fanny Canby to Mary Canby, Philadelphia, May 27, 1801; or Sophie M. DuPont, Brandywine, to Henry DuPont, Germantown, February 4, 1832.

27. Place of residence is not the only variable significant in characterizing family structure. Strong emotional ties and frequent visiting and correspondence can unite

Parke Lewis Butler moved with her husband to Louisiana, she sent her two daughters back to Virginia to attend school, live with their grandmother and aunt, and be integrated back into Virginia society.[28] The constant letters between Maria Inskeep and Fanny Hampton, sisters separated in their early twenties when Maria moved with her husband from New Jersey to Louisiana, held their families together, making it possible for their daughters to feel a part of their cousins' network of friends and interests.[29] The Ripley daughters, growing up in western Massachusetts in the early 1800s, spent months each year with their mother's sister and her family in distant Boston; these female cousins and their network of friends exchanged gossip-filled letters and gradually formed deeply loving and dependent ties.[30]

Women frequently spent their days within the social confines of such extended families. Sisters-in-law visited each other and, in some families, seemed to spend more time with each other than with their husbands. First cousins cared for each other's babies—for weeks or even months in times of sickness or childbirth. Sisters helped each other with housework, shopped and sewed for each other. Geographic separation was borne with difficulty. A sister's absence for even a week or two could cause loneliness and depression and would be bridged by frequent letters. Sibling rivalry was hardly unknown, but with separation or illness the theme of deep affection and dependency reemerged.[31]

---

families that do not live under one roof. Demographic studies based on household structure alone fail to reflect such emotional and even economic ties between families.

28. Eleanor Parke Custis Lewis to Elizabeth Bordley Gibson, April 20 and September 25, 1848.

29. Maria Inskeep to Fanny Hampton Correspondence, 1823–60, Inskeep Collection, Tulane University Library.

30. Eunice Callender, Boston, to Sarah Ripley [Stearns], September 24 and October 29, 1803, February 16, 1805, April 29 and October 9, 1806, May 26, 1810.

31. Sophie DuPont filled her letters to her younger brother Henry (with whom she had been assigned to correspond while he was at boarding school) with accounts of family visiting (see, e.g., December 13, 1827, January 10 and March 9, 1828, February 4 and March 10, 1832; also Sophie M. DuPont to Victorine DuPont Bauday, September 26 and December 4, 1827, February 22, 1828; Sophie M. DuPont, Brandywine, to Clementina B. Smith, Philadelphia, January 15, 1830; Eleuthera DuPont, Brandywine, to Victorine DuPont Bauday, Philadelphia, April 17, 1821, October 20, 1826; Evelina DuPont [Biderman] to Victorine DuPont Bauday, October 18, 1816). Other examples, from the Historical Society of Pennsylvania, are Harriet Manigault [Wilcox] Diary, August 17, September 8, October 19 and 22, December 22, 1814; Jane Zook, Westtown School, Chester County, Pa., to Mary Zook, November 13, December 7 and 11, 1870, February 26, 1871; Eleanor Parke Custis [Lewis] to Elizabeth Bordley [Gibson], March 30, 1796, February 7 and March 20, 1798; Jeannie McCall to Peter McCall, Philadelphia, November 12, 1847; Mary B. Ashew Diary, July 11 and 13, August 17, Summer and October 1858, and, from a private collection, Edith Jefferis to Anne Jefferis Sheppard, November 1841, April 5, 1842; Abigail Brackett Lyman, Northampton, Mass., to Mrs. Catling, Litchfield, Conn., May 13, 1801; Abigail Brackett Lyman, Northampton, to Mary Lord, August 11, 1800. Mary Hallock Foote vacationed with her sister, her sister's children, her aunt, and a female cousin in the

Sisterly bonds continued across a lifetime. In her old age a rural Quaker matron, Martha Jefferis, wrote to her daughter Anne concerning her own half-sister, Phoebe: "In sister Phoebe I have a real friend—she studies my comfort and waits on me like a child. . . . She is exceedingly kind and this to all other homes (set aside yours) I would prefer—it is next to being with a daughter." Phoebe's own letters confirmed Martha's evaluation of her feelings. "Thou knowest my dear sister," Phoebe wrote, "there is no one . . . that exactly feels [for] thee as I do, for I think without boasting I can truly say that my desire is for thee."[32]

Such women, whether friends or relatives, assumed an emotional centrality in each others' lives. In their diaries and letters they wrote of the joy and contentment they felt in each others' company, their sense of isolation and despair when apart. The regularity of their correspondence underlines the sincerity of their words. Women named their daughters after one another and sought to integrate dear friends into their lives after marriage.[33] As one young bride wrote to an old friend shortly after her marriage: "I want to see you and talk with you and feel that we are united by the same bonds of sympathy and congeniality as ever."[34] After years of friendship one aging woman wrote of another: "Time cannot destroy the fascination of her manner . . . her voice is music to the ear. . . ."[35] Women made elaborate presents for each other, ranging from the Quakers' frugal pies and breads to painted velvet bags and phantom bouquets.[36] When a friend died, their grief was deeply felt. Martha Jefferis was unable to write to her daughter for three weeks because of the sorrow she felt at the death of a dear friend. Such distress was not unusual. A generation earlier a young Massachusetts farm woman filled pages of her diary with her grief at the death of her "dearest friend" and transcribed the letters of condolence other women

---

summer of 1874; cousins frequently visited the Hallock farm in Milton, N.Y. In later years Molly and her sister Bessie set up a joint household in Boise, Idaho (Mary Hallock Foote to Helena, July [1874?] and passim). Jeannie Field, after initially disliking her sister-in-law, Laura, became very close to her, calling her "my little sister" and at times spending virtually every day with her (Jeannie Field [Musgrove] New York, to Sarah Butler Wister, Germantown, March 1, 8, and 15, and May 9, 1863).

32. Martha Jefferis to Anne Jefferis Sheppard, January 12, 1845; Phoebe Middleton to Martha Jefferis, February 22, 1848. A number of other women remained close to sisters and sisters-in-law across a long lifetime (Phoebe Bradford Diary, June 7, 1832, and Sarah Alden Ripley to Sophia Bradford, cited in Wister and Irwin, p. 195).

33. Rebecca Biddle to Martha Jefferis, 1838–49, passim; Martha Jefferis to Anne Jefferis Sheppard, July 6, 1846; Anne Jefferis Sheppard to Rachael Jefferis, January 16, 1865; Sarah Foulke Farquhar [Emlen] Diary, September 22, 1813, Friends Historical Library, Swarthmore College; Mary Garrigues to Mary Canby [Biddle], 1802–8, passim; Anne Biddle to Mary Canby [Biddle], May 16, July 13, and November 24, 1806, June 14, 1807, June 5, 1808.

34. Sarah Alden Ripley to Abba Allyn, n.d., Schlesinger Library.

35. Phoebe Bradford Diary, July 13, 1832.

36. Mary Hallock [Foote] to Helena, December 23 [1868 or 1869]; Phoebe Bradford Diary, December 8, 1832; Martha Jefferis and Anne Jefferis Sheppard letters, passim.

sent her. She marked the anniversary of Rachel's death each year in her diary, contrasting her faithfulness with that of Rachel's husband who had soon remarried.[37]

These female friendships served a number of emotional functions. Within this secure and empathetic world women could share sorrows, anxieties, and joys, confident that other women had experienced similar emotions. One mid-nineteenth-century rural matron in a letter to her daughter discussed this particular aspect of women's friendships: "To have such a friend as thyself to look to and sympathize with her—and enter into all her little needs and in whose bosom she could with freedom pour forth her joys and sorrows—such a friend would very much relieve the tedium of many a wearisome hour. . . ." A generation later Molly more informally underscored the importance of this same function in a letter to Helena: "Suppose I come down . . . [and] spend Sunday with you quietly," she wrote Helena ". . . that means talking all the time until you are relieved of all your latest troubles, and I of mine. . . ."[38] These were frequently troubles that apparently no man could understand. When Anne Jefferis Sheppard was first married, she and her older sister Edith (who then lived with Anne) wrote in detail to their mother of the severe depression and anxiety which they experienced. Moses Sheppard, Anne's husband, added cheerful postscripts to the sisters' letters—which he had clearly not read—remarking on Anne's and Edith's contentment. Theirs was an emotional world to which he had little access.[39]

This was, as well, a female world in which hostility and criticism of other women were discouraged, and thus a milieu in which women could develop a sense of inner security and self-esteem. As one young woman wrote to her mother's longtime friend: "I cannot sufficiently thank you for the kind unvaried affection & indulgence you have ever shown and expressed both by words and actions for me. . . . Happy would it be did all the world view me as you do, through the medium of kindness and forbearance."[40] They valued each other. Women, who had little status or power in the larger world of male concerns, possessed status and power in the lives and worlds of other women.[41]

37. Martha Jefferis to Anne Jefferis Sheppard, August 3, 1849; Sarah Ripley [Stearns] Diary, November 12, 1808, January 8, 1811. An interesting note of hostility or rivalry is present in Sarah Ripley's diary entry. Sarah evidently deeply resented the husband's rapid remarriage.

38. Martha Jefferis to Edith Jefferis, March 15, 1841; Mary Hallock Foote to Helena, n.d. [1874–75?]; see also Jeannie Field, New York, to Sarah Butler Wister, Germantown, May 5, 1863, Emily Howland Diary, December 1879, Howland Family Papers.

39. Anne Jefferis Sheppard to Martha Jefferis, September 29, 1841.

40. Frances Parke Lewis to Elizabeth Bordley Gibson, April 29, 1821.

41. Mary Jane Burleigh, Mount Pleasant, S.C., to Emily Howland, Sherwood N.Y., March 27, 1872, Howland Family Papers; Emily Howland Diary, September 16, 1879, January 21 and 23, 1880; Mary Black Couper, New Castle, Del., to Sophie M. DuPont, Brandywine, April 7, 1834

An intimate mother-daughter relationship lay at the heart of this female world. The diaries and letters of both mothers and daughters attest to their closeness and mutual emotional dependency. Daughters routinely discussed their mother's health and activities with their own friends, expressed anxiety in cases of their mother's ill health and concern for her cares.[42] Expressions of hostility which we would today consider routine on the part of both mothers and daughters seem to have been uncommon indeed. On the contrary, this sample of families indicates that the normal relationship between mother and daughter was one of sympathy and understanding.[43] Only sickness or great geographic distance was allowed to cause extended separation. When marriage did result in such separation, both viewed the distance between them with distress.[44] Something of this sympathy and love between

42. Harriet Manigault Diary, August 15, 21, and 23, 1814 Historical Society of Pennsylvania; Polly [Simmons] to Sophie Madeleine DuPont, February 1822; Sophie Madeleine DuPont to Victorine Bauday, December 4, 1827; Sophie Madeleine DuPont to Clementina Beach Smith, July 24, 1828, August 19, 1829; Clementina Beach Smith to Sophie Madeleine DuPont, April 29, 1831; Mary Black Couper to Sophie Madeleine DuPont, December 24, 1828, July 21, 1834. This pattern appears to have crossed class lines. When a former Sunday school student of Sophie DuPont's (and the daughter of a worker in her father's factory) wrote to Sophie she discussed her mother's health and activities quite naturally (Ann McGrann to Sophie Madeleine DuPont, August 25, 1832; see also Elizabeth Bordley to Martha, n.d. [1797], Eleanor Parke Custis [Lewis] to Elizabeth Bordley [Gibson], May 13, 1796, July 1, 1798; Peggy Emlen to Sally Logan, January 8, 1786. All but the Emlen/Logan letters are in the Eleanor Parke Custis Lewis Correspondence, Historical Society of Pennsylvania).

43. Mrs. S. S. Dalton, "Autobiography," (Circle Valley, Utah, 1876), pp. 21–22, Bancroft Library, University of California, Berkeley; Sarah Foulke Emlen Diary, April 1809; Louisa G. Van Vleck, Appleton, Wis., to Charlena Van Vleck Anderson, Göttingen, n.d. [1875], Harriet Manigault Diary, August 16, 1814, July 14, 1815; Sarah Alden Ripley to Sophy Fisher [early 1860s], quoted in Wister and Irwin (n. 12 above), p. 212. The Jefferis family papers are filled with empathetic letters between Martha and her daughters, Anne and Edith. See, e.g., Martha Jefferis to Edith Jefferis, December 26, 1836, March 11, 1837, March 15, 1841; Anne Jefferis Sheppard to Martha Jefferis, March 17, 1841, January 17, 1847; Martha Jefferis to Anne Jefferis Sheppard, April 17, 1848, April 30, 1849. A representative letter is this of March 9, 1837 from Edith to Martha: "My heart can fully respond to the language of my own precious Mother, that absence has not diminished our affection for each other, but has, if possible, strengthened the bonds that have united us together & I have had to remark how we had been permitted to mingle in sweet fellowship and haye been strengthened to bear one another's burdens. . . ."

44. Abigail Brackett Lyman, Boston, to Mrs. Abigail Brackett (daughter to mother), n.d. [1797], June 3, 1800; Sarah Alden Ripley wrote weekly to her daughter, Sophy Ripley Fisher, after the latter's marriage (Sarah Alden Ripley Correspondence, passim); Phoebe Bradford Diary, February 25, 1833, passim, 1832–33; Louisa G. Van Vleck to Charlena Van Vleck Anderson, December 15, 1873, July 4, August 15 and 29, September 19, and November 9, 1875. Eleanor Parke Custis Lewis's long correspondence with Elizabeth Bordley Gibson contains evidence of her anxiety at leaving her foster mother's home at various times during her adolescence and at her marriage, and her own longing for her daughters, both of whom had married and moved to Louisiana (Eleanor Parke Custis [Lewis] to Elizabeth Bordley [Gibson], October 13, 1795, November 4, 1799, passim, 1820s and 1830s). Anne Jefferis Sheppard experienced a great deal of anxiety on moving two

mothers and daughters is evident in a letter Sarah Alden Ripley, at age sixty-nine, wrote her youngest and recently married daughter: "You do not know how much I miss you, not only when I struggle in and out of my mortal envelop and pump my nightly potation and no longer pour into your sympathizing ear my senile gossip, but all the day I muse away, since the sound of your voice no longer rouses me to sympathy with your joys or sorrows. . . . You cannot know how much I miss your affectionate demonstrations."[45] A dozen aging mothers in this sample of over thirty families echoed her sentiments.

Central to these mother-daughter relations is what might be described as an apprenticeship system. In those families where the daughter followed the mother into a life of traditional domesticity, mothers and other older women carefully trained daughters in the arts of housewifery and motherhood. Such training undoubtedly occurred throughout a girl's childhood but became more systematized, almost ritualistic, in the years following the end of her formal education and before her marriage. At this time a girl either returned home from boarding school or no longer divided her time between home and school. Rather, she devoted her energies on two tasks: mastering new domestic skills and participating in the visiting and social activities necessary to finding a husband. Under the careful supervision of their mothers and of older female relatives, such late-adolescent girls temporarily took over the household management from their mothers, tended their young nieces and nephews, and helped in childbirth, nursing, and weaning. Such experiences tied the generations together in shared skills and emotional interaction.[46]

---

days' journey from her mother at the time of her marriage. This loneliness and sense of isolation persisted through her marriage until, finally a widow, she returned to live with her mother (Anne Jefferis Sheppard to Martha Jefferis, April 1841, October 16, 1842, April 2, May 22, and October 12, 1844, September 3, 1845, January 17, 1847, May 16, June 3, and October 31, 1849; Anne Jefferis Sheppard to Susanna Lightfoot, March 23, 1845, and to Joshua Jefferis, May 14, 1854). Daughters evidently frequently slept with their mothers—into adulthood (Harriet Manigault [Wilcox] Diary, February 19, 1815; Eleanor Parke Custis Lewis to Elizabeth Bordley Gibson, October 10, 1832). Daughters also frequently asked mothers to live with them and professed delight when they did so. See, e.g., Sarah Alden Ripley's comments to George Simmons, October 6, 1844, in Wister and Irwin, p. 185: "It is no longer 'Mother and Charles came out one day and returned the next,' for mother is one of us: she has entered the penetratice, been initiated into the mystery of the household gods, . . . Her divertissement is to mend the stockings . . . whiten sheets and napkins, . . . and take a stroll at evening with me to talk of our children, to compare our experiences, what we have learned and what we have suffered, and, last of all, to complete with pears and melons the cheerful circle about the solar lamp. . . ." We did find a few exceptions to this mother-daughter felicity (M.B. Ashew Diary, November 19, 1857, April 10 and May 17, 1858). Sarah Foulke Emlen was at first very hostile to her stepmother (Sarah Foulke Emlen Diary, August 9, 1807), but they later developed a warm supportive relationship.

45. Sarah Alden Ripley to Sophy Thayer, n.d. [1861].

46. Mary Hallock Foote to Helena [winter 1873] (no. 52); Jossie, Stevens Point, Wis., to Charlena Van Vleck [Anderson], Appleton, Wis., October 24, 1870; Pollie Chandler,

Daughters were born into a female world. Their mother's life expectations and sympathetic network of friends and relations were among the first realities in the life of the developing child. As long as the mother's domestic role remained relatively stable and few viable alternatives competed with it, daughters tended to accept their mother's world and to turn automatically to other women for support and intimacy. It was within this closed and intimate female world that the young girl grew toward womanhood.

One could speculate at length concerning the absence of that mother-daughter hostility today considered almost inevitable to an adolescent's struggle for autonomy and self-identity. It is possible that taboos against female aggression and hostility were sufficiently strong to repress even that between mothers and their adolescent daughters. Yet these letters seem so alive and the interest of daughters in their mothers' affairs so vital and genuine that it is difficult to interpret their closeness exclusively in terms of repression and denial. The functional bonds that held mothers and daughters together in a world that permitted few alternatives to domesticity might well have created a source of mutuality and trust absent in societies where greater options were available for daughters than for mothers. Furthermore, the extended female network—a daughter's close ties with her own older sisters, cousins, and aunts—may well have permitted a diffusion and a relaxation of mother-daughter identification and so have aided a daughter in her struggle for identity and autonomy. None of these explanations are mutually exclusive; all may well have interacted to produce the degree of empathy evident in those letters and diaries.

At some point in adolescence, the young girl began to move outside the matrix of her mother's support group to develop a network of her own. Among the middle class, at least, this transition toward what was at the same time both a limited autonomy and a repetition of her mother's life seemed to have most frequently coincided with a girl's going to school. Indeed education appears to have played a crucial role in the lives of most of the families in this study. Attending school for a few months, for a year, or longer, was common even among daughters of relatively poor families, while middle-class girls routinely spent at least a

---

Green Bay, Wis., to Charlena Van Vleck [Anderson], Appleton, n.d. [1870]; Eleuthera DuPont to Sophie DuPont, September 5, 1829; Sophie DuPont to Eleuthera DuPont, December 1827; Sophie DuPont to Victorine Bauday, December 4, 1827; Mary Gilpin to Sophie DuPont, September 26, 1827; Sarah Ripley Stearns Diary, April 2, 1809; Jeannie McCall to Peter McCall, October 27 [late 1840s]. Eleanor Parke Custis Lewis's correspondence with Elizabeth Bordley Gibson describes such an apprenticeship system over two generations—that of her childhood and that of her daughters. Indeed Eleanor Lewis's own apprenticeship was quite formal. She was deliberately separated from her foster mother in order to spend a winter of domesticity with her married sisters and her remarried mother. It was clearly felt that her foster mother's (Martha Washington) home at the nation's capital was not an appropriate place to develop domestic talents (October 13, 1795, March 30, May 13, and [summer] 1796, March 18 and April 27, 1797, October 1827).

year in boarding school.[47] These school years ordinarily marked a girl's first separation from home. They served to wean the daughter from her home, to train her in the essential social graces, and, ultimately, to help introduce her into the marriage market. It was not infrequently a trying emotional experience for both mother and daughter.[48]

In this process of leaving one home and adjusting to another, the mother's friends and relatives played a key transitional role. Such older women routinely accepted the role of foster mother; they supervised the young girl's deportment, monitored her health and introduced her to their own network of female friends and kin.[49] Not infrequently women, friends from their own school years, arranged to send their daughters to the same school so that the girls might form bonds paralleling those their mothers had made. For years Molly and Helena wrote of their daughters' meeting and worried over each others' children. When Molly finally brought her daughter east to school, their first act on reaching New York was to meet Helena and her daughters. Elizabeth Bordley Gibson virtually adopted the daughters of her school chum, Eleanor Custis Lewis. The Lewis daughters soon began to write Elizabeth Gibson letters

47. Education was not limited to the daughters of the well-to-do. Sarah Foulke Emlen, the daughter of an Ohio Valley frontier farmer, for instance, attended day school for several years during the early 1800s. Sarah Ripley Stearns, the daughter of a shopkeeper in Greenfield, Mass., attended a boarding school for but three months, yet the experience seemed very important to her. Mrs. S. S. Dalton, a Mormon woman from Utah, attended a series of poor country schools and greatly valued her opportunity, though she also expressed a great deal of guilt for the sacrifices her mother made to make her education possible (Sarah Foulke Emlen Journal, Sarah Ripley Stearns Diary, Mrs. S. S. Dalton, "Autobiography").

48. Maria Revere to her mother [Mrs. Paul Revere], June 13, 1801, Paul Revere Papers, Massachusetts Historical Society. In a letter to Elizabeth Bordley Gibson, March 28, 1847, Eleanor Parke Custis Lewis from Virginia discussed the anxiety her daughter felt when her granddaughters left home to go to boarding school. Eleuthera DuPont was very homesick when away at school in Philadelphia in the early 1820s (Eleuthera DuPont, Philadelphia, to Victorine Bauday, Wilmington, Del., April 7, 1821; Eleuthera DuPont to Sophie Madeleine DuPont, Wilmington Del., February and April 3, 1821).

49. Elizabeth Bordley Gibson, a Philadelphia matron, played such a role for the daughters and nieces of her lifelong friend, Eleanor Parke Custis Lewis, a Virginia planter's wife (Eleanor Parke Custis Lewis to Elizabeth Bordley Gibson, January 29, 1833, March 19, 1826, and passim through the collection). The wife of Thomas Gurney Smith played a similar role for Sophie and Eleuthera DuPont (see, e.g. Eleuthera DuPont to Sophie Madeleine DuPont, May 22, 1825; Rest Cope to Philema P. Swayne [niece] West Town School, Chester County, Pa., April 8, 1829, Friends Historical Library, Swarthmore College). For a view of such a social pattern over three generations, see the letters and diaries of three generations of Manigault women in Philadelphia: Mrs. Gabrielle Manigault, her daughter, Harriet Manigault Wilcox, and granddaughter, Charlotte Wilcox McCall. Unfortunately the papers of the three women are not in one family collection (Mrs. Henry Middleton, Charleston, S.C., to Mrs. Gabrielle Manigault, n.d. [mid 1800s] Harriet Manigault Diary, vol. 1; December 1, 1813, June 28, 1814; Charlotte Wilcox McCall Diary, vol. 1, 1842, passim. All in Historical Society of Philadelphia).

with the salutation "Dearest Mama." Eleuthera DuPont, attending boarding school in Philadelphia at roughly the same time as the Lewis girls, developed a parallel relationship with her mother's friend, Elizabeth McKie Smith. Eleuthera went to the same school and became a close friend of the Smith girls and eventually married their first cousin. During this period she routinely called Mrs. Smith "Mother." Indeed Eleuthera so internalized the sense of having two mothers that she casually wrote her sisters of her "Mamma's" visits at her "mother's" house —that is at Mrs. Smith's.[50]

Even more important to this process of maturation than their mother's friends were the female friends young women made at school. Young girls helped each other overcome homesickness and endure the crises of adolescence. They gossiped about beaux, incorporated each other into their own kinship systems, and attended and gave teas and balls together. Older girls in boarding school "adopted" younger ones, who called them "Mother."[51] Dear friends might indeed continue this pattern of adoption and mothering throughout their lives; one woman might routinely assume the nurturing role of pseudomother, the other the dependency role of daughter. The pseudomother performed for the other woman all the services which we normally associate with mothers; she went to absurd lengths to purchase items her "daughter" could have obtained from other sources, gave advice and functioned as an idealized figure in her "daughter's" imagination. Helena played such a role for Molly, as did Sarah for Jeannie. Elizabeth Bordley Gibson bought almost all Eleanor Parke Custis Lewis's necessities—from shoes and corset covers to bedding and harp strings—and sent them from Philadelphia to Virginia, a procedure that sometimes took months. Eleanor frequently asked Elizabeth to take back her purchases, have them redone, and argue with shopkeepers about prices. These were favors automatically asked and complied with. Anne Jefferis Sheppard made the analogy very explicitly in a letter to her own mother written shortly after Anne's marriage, when she was feeling depressed about their separation: "Mary

50. Frances Parke Lewis, Woodlawn, Va., to Elizabeth Bordley Gibson, Philadelphia, April 11, 1821, Lewis Correspondence; Eleuthera DuPont, Philadelphia, to Victorine DuPont Bauday, Brandywine, December 8, 1821, January 31, 1822; Eleuthera DuPont, Brandywine, to Margaretta Lammont [DuPont], Philadelphia, May 1823.

51. Sarah Ripley Stearns Diary, March 9 and 25, 1810; Peggy Emlen to Sally Logan, March and July 4, 1769; Harriet Manigault [Wilcox] Diary, vol. 1, December 1, 1813, June 28 and September 18, 1814, August 10, 1815; Charlotte Wilcox McCall Diary, 1842, passim; Fanny Canby to Mary Canby, May 27, 1801, March 17, 1804; Deborah Cope, West Town School, to Rest Cope, Philadelphia, July 9, 1828, Chester County Historical Society, West Chester, Pa.; Anne Zook, West Town School, to Mary Zook, Philadelphia, January 30, 1866, Chester County Historical Society, West Chester, Pa.; Mary Gilpin to Sophie Madeleine DuPont, February 25, 1829; Eleanor Parke Custis [Lewis] to Elizabeth Bordley [Gibson], April 27, July 2, and September 8, 1797, June 30, 1799, December 29, 1820: Frances Parke Lewis to Elizabeth Bordley Gibson, December 20, 1820.

Paulen is truly kind, almost acts the part of a mother and trys to aid and *comfort me*, and also to *lighten my new cares.*"[52]

A comparison of the references to men and women in these young women's letters is striking. Boys were obviously indispensable to the elaborate courtship ritual girls engaged in. In these teenage letters and diaries, however, boys appear distant and warded off—an effect produced both by the girl's sense of bonding and by a highly developed and deprecatory whimsy. Girls joked among themselves about the conceit, poor looks or affectations of suitors. Rarely, especially in the eighteenth and early nineteenth centuries, were favorable remarks exchanged. Indeed, while hostility and criticism of other women were so rare as to seem almost tabooed, young women permitted themselves to express a great deal of hostility toward peer-group men.[53] When unacceptable suitors appeared, girls might even band together to harass them. When one such unfortunate came to court Sophie DuPont she hid in her room, first sending her sister Eleuthera to entertain him and then dispatching a number of urgent notes to her neighboring sister-in-law, cousins, and a visiting friend who all came to Sophie's support. A wild female romp ensued, ending only when Sophie banged into a door, lacerated her nose, and retired, with her female cohorts, to bed. Her brother and the presumably disconcerted suitor were left alone. These were not the antics of teenagers but of women in their early and mid-twenties.[54]

Even if young men were acceptable suitors, girls referred to them formally and obliquely: "The last week I received the unexpected intelligence of the arrival of a friend in Boston," Sarah Ripley wrote in her diary of the young man to whom she had been engaged for years and whom she would shortly marry. Harriet Manigault assiduously kept a lively and gossipy diary during the three years preceding her marriage, yet did not once comment upon her own engagement nor indeed make any personal references to her fiance—who was never identified as such but always referred to as Mr. Wilcox.[55] The point is not that these young women were hostile to young men. Far from it; they sought marriage and domesticity. Yet in these letters and diaries men appear as an other or out group, segregated into different schools, supported by their own male network of friends and kin, socialized to different be-

52. Anne Jefferis Sheppard to Martha Jefferis, March 17, 1841.

53. Peggy Emlen to Sally Logan, March 1769, Mount Vernon, Va.; Eleanor Parke Custis [Lewis] to Elizabeth Bordley [Gibson], Philadelphia, April 27, 1797, June 30, 1799; Jeannie Field, New York, to Sarah Butler Wister, Germantown, July 3, 1861, January 16, 1863, Harriet Manigault Diary, August 3 and 11–13, 1814; Eunice Callender, Boston, to Sarah Ripley [Stearns], Greenfield, May 4, 1809. I found one exception to this inhibition of female hostility. This was the diary of Charlotte Wilcox McCall, Philadelphia (see, e.g., her March 23, 1842 entry).

54. Sophie M. DuPont and Eleuthera DuPont, Brandywine, to Victorine DuPont Bauday, Philadelphia, January 25, 1832.

55. Sarah Ripley [Stearns] Diary and Harriet Manigault Diary, passim.

havior, and coached to a proper formality in courtship behavior. As a consequence, relations between young women and men frequently lacked the spontaneity and emotional intimacy that characterized the young girls' ties to each other.

Indeed, in sharp contrast to their distant relations with boys, young women's relations with each other were close, often frolicsome, and surprisingly long lasting and devoted. They wrote secret missives to each other, spent long solitary days with each other, curled up together in bed at night to whisper fantasies and secrets.[56] In 1862 one young woman in her early twenties described one such scene to an absent friend: "I have sat up to midnight listening to the confidences of Constance Kinney, whose heart was opened by that most charming of all situations, a seat on a bedside late at night, when all the household are asleep & only oneself & one's confidante survive in wakefulness. So she has told me all her loves and tried to get some confidences in return but being five or six years older than she, I know better. . . ."[57] Elizabeth Bordley and Nelly Parke Custis, teenagers in Philadelphia in the 1790s, routinely secreted themselves until late each night in Nelly's attic, where they each wrote a novel about the other.[58] Quite a few young women kept diaries, and it was a sign of special friendship to show their diaries to each other. The emotional quality of such exchanges emerges from the comments of one young girl who grew up along the Ohio frontier:

> Sisters CW and RT keep diaries & allow me the inestimable pleasure of reading them and in turn they see mine—but O shame covers my face when I think of it; theirs is so much better than mine, that every time. Then I think well now I *will* burn mine but upon second thought it would deprive me the pleasure of reading theirs, for I esteem it a very great privilege indeed, as well as very improving, as we lay our hearts open to each other, it heightens our love & helps to cherish & keep alive that sweet soothing friendship and endears us to each other by that soft attraction.[59]

56. Sophie Madeleine DuPont to Eleuthera DuPont, December 1827; Clementina Beach Smith to Sophie Madeleine DuPont, December 26, 1828; Sarah Faulke Emlen Diary, July 21, 1808, March 30, 1809; Annie Hethroe, Ellington, Wis., to Charlena Van Vleck [Anderson], Appleton, Wis., April 23, 1865; Frances Parke Lewis, Woodlawn, Va., to Elizabeth Bordley [Gibson], Philadelphia, December 20, 1820; Fanny Ferris to Debby Ferris, West Town School, Chester County, Pa., May 29, 1826. An excellent example of the warmth of women's comments about each other and the reserved nature of their references to men are seen in two entries in Sarah Ripley Stearn's diary. On January 8, 1811 she commented about a young woman friend: "The amiable Mrs. White of Princeton . . . one of the loveliest most interesting creatures I ever knew, young fair and blooming . . . beloved by everyone . . . formed to please & to charm. . . ." She referred to the man she ultimately married always as "my friend" or "a friend" (February 2 or April 23, 1810).

57. Jeannie Field, New York, to Sarah Butler Wister, Germantown, April 6, 1862.

58. Elizabeth Bordley Gibson, introductory statement to the Eleanor Parke Custis Lewis Letters [1850s], Historical Society of Pennsylvania.

59. Sarah Foulke [Emlen] Diary, March 30, 1809.

Girls routinely slept together, kissed and hugged each other. Indeed, while waltzing with young men scandalized the otherwise flighty and highly fashionable Harriet Manigault, she considered waltzing with other young women not only acceptable but pleasant.[60]

Marriage followed adolescence. With increasing frequency in the nineteenth century, marriage involved a girl's traumatic removal from her mother and her mother's network. It involved, as well, adjustment to a husband, who, because he was male came to marriage with both a different world view and vastly different experiences. Not surprisingly, marriage was an event surrounded with supportive, almost ritualistic, practices. (Weddings are one of the last female rituals remaining in twentieth-century America.) Young women routinely spent the months preceding their marriage almost exclusively with other women—at neighborhood sewing bees and quilting parties or in a round of visits to geographically distant friends and relatives. Ostensibly they went to receive assistance in the practical preparations for their new home—sewing and quilting a trousseau and linen—but of equal importance, they appear to have gained emotional support and reassurance. Sarah Ripley spent over a month with friends and relatives in Boston and Hingham before her wedding; Parke Custis Lewis exchanged visits with her aunts and first cousins throughout Virginia.[61] Anne Jefferis, who married with some hesitation, spent virtually half a year in endless visiting with cousins, aunts, and friends. Despite their reassurance and support, however, she would not marry Moses Sheppard until her sister Edith and her cousin Rebecca moved into the groom's home, met his friends, and explored his personality.[62] The wedding did not take place until Edith wrote to Anne: "I can say in truth I am entirely willing thou shouldst follow him even away in the Jersey sands believing if thou are not happy in thy future home it will not be any fault on his part. . . ."[63]

Sisters, cousins, and friends frequently accompanied newlyweds on their wedding night and wedding trip, which often involved additional family visiting. Such extensive visits presumably served to wean the daughter from her family of origin. As such they often contained a note of ambivalence. Nelly Custis, for example, reported homesickness and loneliness on her wedding trip. "I left my Beloved and revered Grandmamma with sincere regret," she wrote Elizabeth Bordley. "It was sometime before I could feel reconciled to traveling without her." Perhaps

60. Harriet Manigault Diary, May 26, 1815.

61. Sarah Ripley [Stearns] Diary, May 17 and October 2, 1812; Eleanor Parke Custis Lewis to Elizabeth Bordley Gibson, April 23, 1826; Rebecca Ralston, Philadelphia, to Victorine DuPont [Bauday], Brandywine, September 27, 1813.

62. Anne Jefferis to Martha Jefferis, November 22 and 27, 1840, January 13 and March 17, 1841; Edith Jefferis, Greenwich, N.J., to Anne Jefferis, Philadelphia, January 31, February 6 and February 1841.

63. Edith Jefferis to Anne Jefferis, January 31, 1841.

they also functioned to reassure the young woman herself, and her friends and kin, that though marriage might alter it would not destroy old bonds of intimacy and familiarity.[64]

Married life, too, was structured about a host of female rituals. Childbirth, especially the birth of the first child, became virtually a *rite de passage*, with a lengthy seclusion of the woman before and after delivery, severe restrictions on her activities, and finally a dramatic reemergence.[65] This seclusion was supervised by mothers, sisters, and loving friends. Nursing and weaning involved the advice and assistance of female friends and relatives. So did miscarriage.[66] Death, like birth, was structured around elaborate unisexed rituals. When Nelly Parke Custis Lewis rushed to nurse her daughter who was critically ill while away at school, Nelly received support, not from her husband, who remained on their plantation, but from her old school friend, Elizabeth Bordley. Elizabeth aided Nelly in caring for her dying daughter, cared for Nelly's other children, played a major role in the elaborate funeral arrangements (which the father did not attend), and frequently visited the girl's grave at the mother's request. For years Elizabeth continued to be the confidante of Nelly's anguished recollections of her lost daughter.

64. Eleanor Parke Custis Lewis to Elizabeth Bordley, November 4, 1799. Eleanor and her daughter Parke experienced similar sorrow and anxiety when Parke married and moved to Cincinnati (Eleanor Parke Custis Lewis to Elizabeth Bordley Gibson, April 23, 1826). Helena DeKay visited Mary Hallock the month before her marriage; Mary Hallock was an attendant at the wedding; Helena again visited Molly about three weeks after her marriage; and then Molly went with Helena and spent a week with Helena and Richard in their new apartment (Mary Hallock [Foote] to Helena DeKay Gilder [Spring 1874] (no. 61), May 10, 1874 [May 1874], June 14, 1874 [Summer 1874]. See also Anne Biddle, Philadelphia, to Clement Biddle (brother), Wilmington, March 12 and May 27, 1827; Eunice Callender, Boston, to Sarah Ripley [Stearns], Greenfield, Mass., August 3, 1807, January 26, 1808; Victorine DuPont Bauday, Philadelphia, to Evelina DuPont [Biderman], Brandywine, November 25 and 26, December 1, 1813; Peggy Emlen to Sally Logan, n.d. [1769–70?]; Jeannie Field, New York, to Sarah Butler Wister, Germantown, July 3, 1861).

65. Mary Hallock to Helena DeKay Gilder [1876] (no. 81); n.d. (no. 83), March 3, 1884; Mary Ashew Diary, vol. 2, September–January, 1860; Louisa Van Vleck to Charlena Van Vleck Anderson, n.d. [1875]; Sophie DuPont to Henry DuPont, July 24, 1827; Benjamin Ferris to William Canby, February 13, 1805; Benjamin Ferris to Mary Canby Biddle, December 20, 1825; Anne Jefferis Sheppard to Martha Jefferis, September 15, 1884; Martha Jefferis to Anne Jefferis Sheppard, July 4, 1843, May 5, 1844, May 3, 1847, July 17, 1849; Jeannie McCall to Peter McCall, November 26, 1847, n.d. [late 1840s]. A graphic description of the ritual surrounding a first birth is found in Abigail Lyman's letter to her husband Erastus Lyman, October 18, 1810.

66. Fanny Ferris to Anne Biddle, November 19, 1811; Eleanor Parke Custis Lewis to Elizabeth Bordley Gibson, November 4, 1799, April 27, 1827; Martha Jefferis to Anne Jefferis Sheppard, January 31, 1843, April 4, 1844; Martha Jefferis to Phoebe Sharpless Middleton, June 4, 1846; Anne Jefferis Sheppard to Martha Jefferis, August 20, 1843, February 12, 1844; Maria Inskeep, New Orleans, to Mrs. Fanny G. Hampton, Bridgeton, N.J., September 22, 1848; Benjamin Ferris to Mary Canby, February 14, 1805; Fanny Ferris to Mary Canby [Biddle], December 2, 1816.

These memories, Nelly's letters make clear, were for Elizabeth alone. "Mr. L. knows nothing of this," was a frequent comment.[67] Virtually every collection of letters and diaries in my sample contained evidence of women turning to each other for comfort when facing the frequent and unavoidable deaths of the eighteenth and nineteenth centuries.[68] While mourning for her father's death, Sophie DuPont received elaborate letters and visits of condolence—all from women. No man wrote or visited Sophie to offer sympathy at her father's death.[69] Among rural Pennsylvania Quakers, death and mourning rituals assumed an even more extreme same-sex form, with men or women largely barred from the deathbeds of the other sex. Women relatives and friends slept with the dying woman, nursed her, and prepared her body for burial.[70]

Eighteenth- and nineteenth-century women thus lived in emotional proximity to each other. Friendships and intimacies followed the biological ebb and flow of women's lives. Marriage and pregnancy, childbirth and weaning, sickness and death involved physical and psychic trauma which comfort and sympathy made easier to bear. Intense bonds of love and intimacy bound together those women who, offering each other aid and sympathy, shared such stressful moments.

These bonds were often physical as well as emotional. An undeniably romantic and even sensual note frequently marked female relationships. This theme, significant throughout the stages of a woman's life, surfaced first during adolescence. As one teenager from a struggling pioneer family in the Ohio Valley wrote in her diary in 1808: "I laid with

67. Eleanor Parke Custis Lewis to Elizabeth Bordley Gibson, October–November 1820, passim.

68. Emily Howland to Hannah, September 30, 1866; Emily Howland Diary, February 8, 11, and 27, 1880; Phoebe Brandford Diary, April 12 and 13, and August 4, 1833; Eunice Callender, Boston, to Sarah Ripley [Stearns], Greenwich, Mass., September 11, 1802, August 26, 1810; Mrs. H. Middleton, Charleston, to Mrs. Gabrielle Manigault, Philadelphia, n.d. [mid 1800s]; Mrs. H. C. Paul to Mrs. Jeannie McCall, Philadelphia, n.d. [1840s]; Sarah Butler Wister, Germantown, to Jeannie Field [Musgrove], New York, April 22, 1864; Jeannie Field [Musgrove] to Sarah Butler Wister, August 25, 1861, July 6, 1862; S. B. Raudolph to Elizabeth Bordley [Gibson], n.d. [1790s]. For an example of similar letters between men, see Henry Wright to Peter McCall, December 10, 1852; Charles McCall to Peter McCall, January 4, 1860, March 22, 1864; R. Mercer to Peter McCall, November 29, 1872.

69. Mary Black [Couper] to Sophie Madeleine DuPont, February 1827, [November 1, 1834], November 12, 1834, two letters [late November 1834]; Eliza Schlatter to Sophie Madeleine DuPont, November 2, 1834.

70. For a few of the references to death rituals in the Jefferis papers see: Martha Jefferis to Anne Jefferis Sheppard, September 28, 1843, August 21 and September 25, 1844, January 11, 1846, summer 1848, passim; Anne Jefferis Sheppard to Martha Jefferis, August 20, 1843; Anne Jefferis Sheppard to Rachel Jefferis, March 17, 1863, February 9, 1868. For other Quaker families, see Rachel Biddle to Anne Biddle, July 23, 1854; Sarah Foulke Farquhar [Emlen] Diary, April 30, 1811, February 14, 1812; Fanny Ferris to Mary Canby, August 31, 1810. This is not to argue that men and women did not mourn together. Yet in many families women aided and comforted women and men, men. The same-sex death ritual was one emotional option available to nineteenth-century Americans.

my dear R[ebecca] and a glorious good talk we had until about 4[A.M.]—O how hard I do *love* her. . . ."[71] Only a few years later Bostonian Eunice Callender carved her initials and Sarah Ripley's into a favorite tree, along with a pledge of eternal love, and then waited breathlessly for Sarah to discover and respond to her declaration of affection. The response appears to have been affirmative.[72] A half-century later urbane and sophisticated Katherine Wharton commented upon meeting an old school chum: "She was a great pet of mine at school & I thought as I watched her light figure how often I had held her in my arms—how dear she had once been to me." Katie maintained a long intimate friendship with another girl. When a young man began to court this friend seriously, Katie commented in her diary that she had never realized "how deeply I loved Eng and how fully." She wrote over and over again in that entry: "Indeed I love her!" and only with great reluctance left the city that summer since it meant also leaving Eng with Eng's new suitor.[73]

Peggy Emlen, a Quaker adolescent in Philadelphia in the 1760s, expressed similar feelings about her first cousin, Sally Logan. The girls sent love poems to each other (not unlike the ones Elizabeth Bordley wrote to Nellie Custis a generation later), took long solitary walks together, and even haunted the empty house of the other when one was out of town. Indeed Sally's absences from Philadelphia caused Peggy acute unhappiness. So strong were Peggy's feelings that her brothers began to tease her about her affection for Sally and threatened to steal Sally's letters, much to both girls' alarm. In one letter that Peggy wrote the absent Sally she elaborately described the depth and nature of her feelings: "I have not words to express my impatience to see My Dear Cousin, what would I not give just now for an hours sweet conversation with her, it seems as if I had a thousand things to say to thee, yet when I see thee, everything will be forgot thro' joy. . . . I have a very great friendship for several Girls yet it dont give me so much uneasiness at being absent from them as from thee. . . . [Let us] go and spend a day down at our place together and there unmolested enjoy each others company."[74]

Sarah Alden Ripley, a young, highly educated women, formed a similar intense relationship, in this instance with a woman somewhat older than herself. The immediate bond of friendship rested on their atypically intense scholarly interests, but it soon involved strong emotions, at least on Sarah's part. "Friendship," she wrote Mary Emerson, "is fast twining about her willing captive the silken hands of dependence, a

71. Sarah Foulke [Emlen] Diary, December 29, 1808.

72. Eunice Callender, Boston, to Sarah Ripley [Stearns] Greenfield, Mass., May 24, 1803.

73. Katherine Johnstone Brinley [Wharton] Journal, April 26, May 30, and May 29, 1856, Historical Society of Pennsylvania.

74. A series of roughly fourteen letters written by Peggy Emlen to Sally Logan (1768–71) has been preserved in the Wells Morris Collection, Box 1, Historical Society of Pennsylvania (see esp. May 3 and July 4, 1769, January 8, 1768).

dependence so sweet who would renounce it for the apathy of self-sufficiency?" Subsequent letters became far more emotional, almost conspiratorial. Mary visited Sarah secretly in her room, or the two women crept away from family and friends to meet in a nearby woods. Sarah became jealous of Mary's other young woman friends. Mary's trips away from Boston also thrust Sarah into periods of anguished depression. Interestingly, the letters detailing their love were not destroyed but were preserved and even reprinted in a eulogistic biography of Sarah Alden Ripley.[75]

Tender letters between adolescent women, confessions of loneliness and emotional dependency, were not peculiar to Sarah Alden, Peggy Emlen, or Katie Wharton. They are found throughout the letters of the thirty-five families studied. They have, of course, their parallel today in the musings of many female adolescents. Yet these eighteenth- and nineteenth-century friendships lasted with undiminished, indeed often increased, intensity throughout the women's lives. Sarah Alden Ripley's first child was named after Mary Emerson. Nelly Custis Lewis's love for and dependence on Elizabeth Bordley Gibson only increased after her marriage. Eunice Callender remained enamored of her cousin Sarah Ripley for years and rejected as impossible the suggestion by another woman that their love might some day fade away.[76] Sophie DuPont and her childhood friend, Clementina Smith, exchanged letters filled with love and dependency for forty years while another dear friend, Mary Black Couper, wrote of dreaming that she, Sophie, and her husband were all united in one marriage. Mary's letters to Sophie are filled with avowals of love and indications of ambivalence toward her own husband. Eliza Schlatter, another of Sophie's intimate friends, wrote to her at a time of crisis: "I wish I could be with you present in the body as well as the mind & heart—I would turn your *good husband out of bed*—and snuggle into you and we would have a long talk like old times in Pine St.—I want to tell you so many things that are not *writable*. . . ."[77]

75. The Sarah Alden Ripley Collection, the Arthur M. Schlesinger, Sr., Library, Radcliffe College, contains a number of Sarah Alden Ripley's letters to Mary Emerson. Most of these are undated, but they extend over a number of years and contain letters written both before and after Sarah's marriage. The eulogistic biographical sketch appeared in Wister and Irwin (n. 12 above). It should be noted that Sarah Butler Wister was one of the editors who sensitively selected Sarah's letters.

76. See Sarah Alden Ripley to Mary Emerson, November 19, 1823. Sarah Alden Ripley routinely, and one must assume ritualistically, read Mary Emerson's letters to her infant daughter, Mary. Eleanor Parke Custis Lewis reported doing the same with Elizabeth Bordley Gibson's letters, passim. Eunice Callender, Boston, to Sarah Ripley [Stearns], October 19, 1808.

77. Mary Black Couper to Sophie M. DuPont, March 5, 1832. The Clementina Smith–Sophie DuPont correspondence of 1,678 letters is in the Sophie DuPont Correspondence. The quotation is from Eliza Schlatter, Mount Holly, N.J., to Sophie DuPont, Brandywine, August 24, 1834. I am indebted to Anthony Wallace for informing me about this collection.

Such mutual dependency and deep affection is a central existential reality coloring the world of supportive networks and rituals. In the case of Katie, Sophie, or Eunice—as with Molly, Jeannie, and Sarah—their need for closeness and support merged with more intense demands for a love which was at the same time both emotional and sensual. Perhaps the most explicit statement concerning women's lifelong friendships appeared in the letter abolitionist and reformer Mary Grew wrote about the same time, referring to her own love for her dear friend and lifelong companion, Margaret Burleigh. Grew wrote, in response to a letter of condolence from another women on Burleigh's death: "Your words respecting my beloved friend touch me deeply. Evidently . . . you comprehend and appreciate, as few persons do . . . the nature of the relation which existed, which exists, between her and myself. Her only surviving niece . . . also does. To me it seems to have been a closer union than that of most marriages. We know there have been other such between two men and also between two women. And why should there not be. Love is spiritual, only passion is sexual."[78]

How then can we ultimately interpret these long-lived intimate female relationships and integrate them into our understanding of Victorian sexuality? Their ambivalent and romantic rhetoric presents us with an ultimate puzzle: the relationship along the spectrum of human emotions between love, sensuality, and sexuality.

One is tempted, as I have remarked, to compare Molly, Peggy, or Sophie's relationships with the friendships adolescent girls in the twentieth century routinely form—close friendships of great emotional intensity. Helena Deutsch and Clara Thompson have both described these friendships as emotionally necessary to a girl's psychosexual development. But, they warn, such friendships might shade into adolescent and postadolescent homosexuality.[79]

It is possible to speculate that in the twentieth century a number of cultural taboos evolved to cut short the homosocial ties of girlhood and to impel the emerging women of thirteen or fourteen toward heterosexual relationships. In contrast, nineteenth-century American society did not taboo close female relationships but rather recognized them as a socially viable form of human contact—and, as such, acceptable throughout a woman's life. Indeed it was not these homosocial ties that were inhibited but rather heterosexual leanings. While closeness, freedom of emotional expression, and uninhibited physical contact charac-

78. Mary Grew, Providence, R.I., to Isabel Howland, Sherwood, N.Y., April 27, 1892, Howland Correspondence, Sophia Smith Collection, Smith College.

79. Helena Deutsch, *Psychology of Women* (New York: Grune & Stratton, 1944), vol. 1, chaps. 1–3; Clara Thompson, *On Women*, ed. Maurice Green (New York: New American Library, 1971).

terized women's relationships with each other, the opposite was frequently true of male-female relationships. One could thus argue that within such a world of female support, intimacy, and ritual it was only to be expected that adult women would turn trustingly and lovingly to each other. It was a behavior they had observed and learned since childhood. A different type of emotional landscape existed in the nineteenth century, one in which Molly and Helena's love became a natural development.

Of perhaps equal significance are the implications we can garner from this framework for the understanding of heterosexual marriages in the nineteenth century. If men and women grew up as they did in relatively homogeneous and segregated sexual groups, then marriage represented a major problem in adjustment. From this perspective we could interpret much of the emotional stiffness and distance that we associate with Victorian marriage as a structural consequence of contemporary sex-role differentiation and gender-role socialization. With marriage both women and men had to adjust to life with a person who was, in essence, a member of an alien group.

I have thus far substituted a cultural or psychosocial for a psychosexual interpretation of women's emotional bonding. But there are psychosexual implications in this model which I think it only fair to make more explicit. Despite Sigmund Freud's insistence on the bisexuality of us all or the recent American Psychiatric Association decision on homosexuality, many psychiatrists today tend explicitly or implicitly to view homosexuality as a totally alien or pathological behavior—as totally unlike heterosexuality. I suspect that in essence they may have adopted an explanatory model similar to the one used in discussing schizophrenia. As a psychiatrist can speak of schizophrenia and of a borderline schizophrenic personality as both ultimately and fundamentally different from a normal or neurotic personality, so they also think of both homosexuality and latent homosexuality as states totally different from heterosexuality. With this rapidly dichotomous model of assumption, "latent homosexuality" becomes the indication of a disease in progress—seeds of a pathology which belie the reality of an individual's heterosexuality.

Yet at the same time we are well aware that cultural values can effect choices in the gender of a person's sexual partner. We, for instance, do not necessarily consider homosexual-object choice among men in prison, on shipboard or in boarding schools a necessary indication of pathology. I would urge that we expand this relativistic model and hypothesize that a number of cultures might well tolerate or even encourage diversity in sexual and nonsexual relations. Based on my research into this nineteenth-century world of female intimacy, I would further suggest that rather than seeing a gulf between the normal and the abnormal we view sexual and emotional impulses as part of a continuum or spectrum of affect gradations strongly effected by cultural norms and arrangements, a continuum influenced in part by observed and thus learned behavior. At one end of the continuum lies committed heterosexuality, at the other uncompromising homosexuality; between, a wide latitude of emotions and sexual feelings. Certain cultures and environments permit individuals a great deal of freedom in moving across this spectrum. I would like to suggest that the nineteenth century was such a cultural environment. That is, the supposedly repressive and destructive Victorian sexual ethos, may have been more flexible and responsive to the needs of particular individuals than those of mid-twentieth century.

University of Pennsylvania

What Ought To Be and What Was: Women's Sexuality in the Nineteenth Century

CARL N. DEGLER

As EVERY SCHOOLGIRL KNOWS, the nineteenth century was afraid of sex, particularly when it manifested itself in women. Captain Marryat, in his travels in the United States, told of some American women so refined that they objected to the word "leg," preferring instead the more decorous "limb." Marryat also reported seeing this delicacy carried to extremes in a girls' school where a school mistress, in the interest of protecting the modesty of her charges, had dressed all four "limbs" of the piano "in modest little trousers with frills at the bottom of them!"[1] Women's alleged lack of passion was epitomized, too, in the story of the English mother who was asked by her daughter before her marriage how she ought to behave on her wedding night. "Lie still and think of the Empire," the mother advised.

This view of Victorian attitudes toward sexuality is captured in more than stories. Steven Marcus, writing about the attitudes of English Victorians toward sexuality, and Nathan Hale, Jr., summarizing the attitudes of Americans on the same subject, both quote at length from Dr. William Acton's *Functions and Disorders of the Reproductive Organs*, which went through several editions in England and the United States during the middle years of the nineteenth century.[2] Acton's book was undoubtedly one of the most widely quoted sexual-advice books in the English-speaking world. The book summed up the medical literature on women's sexuality by saying that "the majority of women (happily for them) are not very much troubled with sexual feelings of any kind. What men are habitually, women are only ex-

1 Captain Frederick Marryat, *A Diary in America, with Remarks on Its Institutions* (London, 1839), 2: 244–47. The story of the trousers on piano legs is taken seriously in John Duffy, "Masturbation and Clitoridectomy: A Nineteenth Century View," *Journal of the American Medical Association*, 186 (1963): 246; G. Rattray Taylor, *Sex in History* (New York, 1954), 203; and Peter T. Cominus, "Innocent Femina Sensualis in Unconscious Conflict," in Martha Vicinus, ed., *Suffer and Be Still: Women in the Victorian Age* (Bloomington, 1972), 157.

2 William Acton, *The Functions and Disorders of the Reproductive Organs in Youth, in Adult Age, and in Advanced Life: Considered in Their Physiological, Social, and Psychological Relations* (1857; 2d ed., London, 1858; expanded American ed., Philadelphia, 1865). For references to Acton's writings, see Steven Marcus, *The Other Victorians: A Study of Sexuality and Pornography in Mid-Nineteenth-Century England* (New York, 1966), ch. 1; and Nathan G. Hale, Jr., *Freud and the Americans: The Beginnings of Psychoanalysis in the United States, 1876–1917* (New York, 1971), 36–37.

ceptionally."[3] Theophilus Parvin, an American doctor, told his medical class in 1883, "I do not believe one bride in a hundred, of delicate, educated, sensitive women, accepts matrimony from any desire for sexual gratification; when she thinks of this at all, it is with shrinking, or even with horror, rather than with desire."[4]

Modern writers on the sexual life of women in the nineteenth century have echoed these contemporary descriptions. "For the sexual act was associated by many wives only with a duty," writes Walter Houghton, "and by most husbands with a necessary if pleasurable yielding to one's baser nature; by few, therefore, with any innocent and joyful experience."[5] Writing about late-nineteenth-century America, David Kennedy quotes approvingly from Viola Klein when she writes that "in the whole Western world during the nineteenth century and at the beginning of the twentieth century it would have been not only scandalous to admit the existence of a strong sex urge in women, but it would have been contrary to all observation."[6] Nathan Hale, Jr. sums up his review of the sexual-advice literature at the turn of the century with a similar conclusion: "Many women came to regard marriage as little better than legalized prostitution. Sexual passion became associated almost exclusively with the male, with prostitutes, and women of the lower classes."[7] Most recently Ben Barker-Benfield has argued that male doctors were so convinced that women had no sexual interest that when it manifested itself drastic measures were taken to subdue it, including excision of the sexual organs. "Defining the absence of sexual desire in women as normal, doctors came to see its presence as disease. . . . Sexual appetite was a male quality (to be properly channelled of course). If a woman showed it, she resembled a man."[8]

[3] Acton, *Functions and Disorders* (1865), 133.

[4] Theophilus Parvin, "Hygiene of the Sexual Functions," *New Orleans Medical and Surgical Journal*, n.s. 11 (1883–84): 607. Parvin also quotes at length from Acton's book.

[5] Walter E. Houghton, *The Victorian Frame of Mind, 1830–1870* (New Haven, 1957), 353. Marcus presents a portrait of Victorian attitudes toward sex similar to that of Houghton, but he disclaims to be talking about behavior: "We need not pause to discuss the degree of truth or falsehood in these assertions. What is of more immediate concern is that these assertions indicate a system of beliefs." *Other Victorians*, 32. Yet it is not clear what point there is in detailing a system of beliefs unless it has some behavioral consequences. Peter T. Cominos also relies upon Acton, in "Late Victorian Sexual Respectability and the Social System," *International Review of Social History*, 8 (1963): 18–48, 217–50. E. M. Sigsworth and T. J. Wyke doubt the pervasiveness in Victorian England of Acton's conception of women's sexuality. They write: "Victorian opinion on the innate sexuality of women was cloudy and divided"—a view about which more will be said in this article. "A Study of Victorian Prostitution and Venereal Disease," in Vicinus, *Suffer and Be Still*, 83.

[6] Viola Klein, *The Feminine Character: History of an Ideology* (1946; reprint, Urbana, 1972), 85, as quoted in David M. Kennedy, *Birth Control in America: The Career of Margaret Sanger* (New Haven, 1970), 56–57.

[7] Hale, *Freud and the Americans*, 31. Elsewhere Hale sums up the medical view as he sees it: "By 1906 . . . some physicians regarded the asexual female as the norm: 'It may be offered that the sexual appetite in the majority of American females is evoked only by the purest love. In many the appetite never asserts itself and, indeed, the only impulse thereto is in the desire to gratify the object of affection'" (pp. 39–40; quotation from Ferdinand C. Valentine, "Education in Sexual Subjects," *New York Medical Journal*, Feb. 10, 1906, p. 276).

[8] Ben Barker-Benfield, "The Spermatic Economy: A Nineteenth Century View of Sexuality," *Feminist Studies*, 1 (1972): 54.

Despite the apparent agreement between the nineteenth-century medical writers and modern students of the period, it is far from clear that there was in the nineteenth century a consensus on the subject of women's sexuality or that women were in fact inhibited from acknowledging their sexual feelings. In examining these two issues I shall be concerned with an admittedly limited yet significant population, namely, women of the urban middle class in the United States. This was the class to which the popular medical-advice books, of which William Acton's volume was a prime example, were directed. It is principally the women of this class upon whom historians' generalizations about women's lives in the nineteenth century are based. And though these women were not a numerical majority of the sex, they undoubtedly set the tone and provided the models for most women. The sources drawn upon are principally the popular and professional medical literature concerned with women and a hitherto undiscovered survey of married women's sexual attitudes and practices that was begun in the 1890s by Dr. Clelia D. Mosher.

LET ME BEGIN with the first question or issue. Was William Acton representative of medical writers when he contended that women were essentially without sexual passion? Rather serious doubts arise as soon as one looks into the medical literature, popular as well as professional, where it was recognized that the sex drive was so strong in woman that to deny it might well compromise her health. Dr. Charles Taylor, writing in 1882, said, "It is not a matter of indifference whether a woman live [*sic*] a single or a married life. . . . I do not for one moment wish to be understood as believing that an unmarried woman cannot exist in perfect health for I know she can. But the point is, that *she must take pains for it*." For if the generative organs are not used, then "some other demand for the unemployed functions, must be established. Accumulated force must find an outlet, or disturbance first and weakness ultimately results." His recommendation was muscular exercise and education for usefulness. He also described cases of women who had denied their sexuality and even experienced orgasms without knowing it. Some women, he added, ended up, as a result, with impairment of movement or other physical symptoms.[9]

Other writers on medical matters were even more direct in testifying to the presence of sexual feelings in women. "Passion absolutely necessary in woman," wrote Orson S. Fowler, the phrenologist, in 1870. "Amativeness is created in the female head as universally as in the male. . . . That female passion exists, is as obvious as that the sun shines," he wrote. Without woman's passion, he contended, a fulfilled love could not occur.[10] Both sexes enjoy the

[9] Charles Fayette Taylor, "Effect on Women of Imperfect Hygiene of the Sexual Function," *American Journal of Obstetrics*, 15 (1882): 175–76, 168–71, italics in original.

[10] Orson S. Fowler, *Sexual Science; Including Manhood, Womanhood, and Their Mutual Interrelations, etc. . . . as Taught by Phrenology* (Philadelphia, 1870), 680.

sexual embrace, asserted Henry Chevasse, another popular medical writer, in 1871, but among human beings, as among the animals in general, he continued, "the male is more ardent and fierce, and . . . the desires of the female never reach that hight [*sic*] as to impel her to the commission of crime." Woman's pleasure, though it may be "less acute," is longer lasting than man's, Chevasse said. R. T. Trall, also a popular medical writer, counseled in a similar vein. "Whatever may be the object of sexual intercourse," he wrote, "whether intended as a love embrace merely, or as a generative act, it is very clear that it should be as pleasurable as possible to *both parties*."[11]

If one can judge the popularity of a guide for women by the number of its editions, then Dr. George Napheys's *The Physical Life of Woman: Advice to the Maiden, Wife, and Mother* (1869) must have been one of the leaders. Within two weeks of publication it went into a second printing, and within two years 60,000 copies were in print. Napheys was a well-known Philadelphia physician. Women, he wrote, quoting an unnamed "distinguished medical writer," are divided into three classes. The first consists of those who have no sexual feelings, and it is the smallest group. The second is larger and is comprised of those who have "strong passion." The third is made up of "the vast majority of women, in whom the sexual appetite is as moderate as all other appetites." He went on to make his point quite clear. "It is a false notion and contrary to nature that this passion in a woman is a derogation to her sex. The science of physiology indicates most clearly its propriety and dignity." He then proceeded to denounce those wives who "plume themselves on their repugnance or their distaste for their conjugal obligations." Napheys also contended that authorities agree that "conception is more assured when the two individuals who co-operate in it participate at the same time in the transports of which it is the fruit." Napheys probably had no sound reason for this point, but the accuracy of his statement is immaterial. What is of moment is that as an adviser to women he was clearly convinced that women possessed sexual feelings, which ought to be cultivated rather than suppressed. Concerning sexual relations during pregnancy he wrote, "There is no reason why passions should not be gratified in moderation and with caution during the whole period of pregnancy." And since his book is directed to women, there is no question that the passion he is talking about here is that of women.[12]

In 1878 Dr. Ely Van de Warker of Syracuse, a fellow of the American Gynecological Society, described sexual passion in women as "the analogue of the subjective copulative sensations of man, and that the acme of the sexual orgasm in woman is the sensory equivalent of emission in man, observ-

11 P. Henry Chevasse, *Physical Life of Man and Woman: or, Advice to Both Sexes* (1866; reprint, New York, 1897), 291–92; quotation from Trall in Michael Gordon, "From an Unfortunate Necessity to a Cult of Mutual Orgasm: Sex in American Marital Education Literature, 1830–1940," in James M. Henslin, ed., *Studies in the Sociology of Sex* (New York, 1971), 58, my italics.

12 George H. Napheys, *The Physical Life of Woman: Advice to the Maiden, Wife, and Mother* (1869; Philadelphia, 1871), 74–75, 180.

ing the distinction necessarily implied between the sexes—that in woman it is psychic and subjective, and that in man it has also a physical element and is objective," that is, it is accompanied by seminal emission. The principal purpose of Van de Warker's article was to deplore the fact that some women lacked sexual feeling, a state which he called "female impotency."[13] What is striking about his article is that he obviously considered such lack of feeling in women abnormal and worthy of medical attention, just as impotency in a man would cause medical concern.

Van de Warker's remarks, as well as his use of the word, make it evident that physicians were well aware that normal women experienced orgasms. Lest there be any doubt that their meaning of the word was the same as ours today, let me quote from a physician in 1883 who described in some detail woman's sexual response. He began by describing the preparatory stage, which, he said,

> may be reached by any means, bodily or mental, which, in the opposite sex, cause erection. Following upon this, then, is a stage of pleasurable excitement, gradually increasing and culminating in an acme of excitement, which may be called the stage of consummation, and the analogue of which in the male is emission. This is followed in both sexes by a degree of nervous prostration, less marked, however, in the female, and . . . by a relief to the general congestion of all the genital organs which has existed, and perhaps increased, from the beginning of the preparatory stage.[14]

All of this evidence, it seems to me, shows that there was a significant body of opinion and information quite different from that advanced on women's sexuality by William Acton and others of his outlook.-Now it might be asked how widespread was this counter-Acton point of view? Was it not confined primarily to physicians writing for other physicians? Not at all. Napheys, Chevasse, and Fowler, to name three, were all writing their books for the large lay public that was interested in sexual matters. As we have seen, many of these marriage manuals, particularly Napheys's and Fowler's, were printed in several large editions.

Yet, in the end, there is a certain undeniable inconclusiveness in simply raising up one collection of writers against another, even if their existence does make the issue an open one, rather than the closed one that so many secondary writers have made it. It suggests, at the very least, that there was a sharp difference of medical opinion, rather than a consensus, on the nature of women's sexual feelings and needs. In fact there is some reason to believe, as we shall see, that the so-called Victorian conception of women's sexuality was more that of an ideology seeking to be established than the prevalent view or practice of even middle-class women, especially as there is a substantial amount of nineteenth-century writing about women that assumes

13 Ely Van de Warker, "Impotency in Women," *American Journal of Obstetrics*, 11 (1878): 47.

14 J. Milne Chapman, "On Masturbation as an Etiological Factor in the Production of Gynic Diseases," *American Journal of Obstetrics*, 16 (1883): 454.

the existence of strong sexual feelings in women. One of the historian's recognized difficulties in showing, through quotations from writers who assert a particular outlook, that a social attitude prevailed in the past is that one always wonders how representative and how self-serving the examples or quotations are. This is especially true in this case where medical opinion can be found on both sides of the question. When writers, however, assume the attitude in question to be prevalent while they are intent upon writing about something else, then one is not so dependent upon the tyranny of numbers in quoting from sources. For behind the assumption of prevalence lie many examples, so to speak. Such testimony, moreover, is unintended and therefore not self-serving. This kind of evidence, furthermore, helps us to answer the second question—to what extent were women in the nineteenth century inhibited from expressing their sexual feelings? For in assuming that women had sexual feelings, these writers are offering clear, if unintended, testimony to women's sexuality.

Medical writers like Acton may have asserted that women did not possess sexual feelings, but there were many doctors who clearly assumed not only that such feelings existed but that the repression of them caused illness. One medical man, for example, writing in 1877, traced a cause of insanity in women to the onset of sexuality. "Sexual development initiates new and extraordinary physical changes," he pointed out. "The erotic and sexual impulse is awakened."[15] Another, writing ten years later, asserted that some of women's illnesses were due to a denial of sexual satisfaction. "Females feel often that they are not appreciated," wrote Dr. William McLaury in a medical journal, "that they have no one to confide in; then they become morose, angular, and disagreeable as a result of continual disappointment to their social and sexual longings. Even those married may become the victims of sexual starvation when the parties are mentally, magnetically, and physically antagonistic."[16] Henry Chevasse, writing for a popular audience, was also impressed by the need for sexual outlets for women. There may be some individuals "of phlegmatic temperament," he conceded, who are not injured by celibacy, but "absolute continence in the sanguine and ardent disposition predisposes to the gravest maladies." His listing of the resulting maladies, of which nymphomania was one, makes it clear that he was referring to women as well as men. These maladies, he went on, "are born as well of extreme restraint as of extreme excess. . . . Females seem to suffer even more than males . . . perhaps because their continence is more complete." (Presumably he was referring here to the absence of nocturnal emissions in women.) As a result, he continued, nunneries were notorious as places of fanaticism. "Hence the old proverb, 'The convent and the confessional are the cradles of hysteria and nymphomania.' "[17]

15 Montrose S. Pallen, "Some Suggestions with Regard to the Insanities of Females," *American Journal of Obstetrics*, 10 (1877): 209.

16 William M. McLaury, "Remarks on the Relation of the Menstruation to the Sexual Functions," *American Journal of Obstetrics*, 20 (1887): 161.

17 Chevasse, *Physical Life of Man and Woman*, 372–73.

To Dr. Van de Warker women's sexuality was so obvious that he assumed men required it in order to achieve full sexual satisfaction for themselves. In marriage, he wrote, the husband

> not only demands pleasure and satisfaction for himself, but he requires something much more difficult to give—the appearance, if not the real existence, of satisfaction and pleasure in the object of his attentions. Unhappiness and suspicion are often the result of the absence of this pleasure [in women], and are sure to work to the material disadvantage of the weaker party. To show that this is really the case, I need but to remind physicians how often they are approached by husbands upon this subject; yet further, how often the coldness and indifference of wives are alleged as the excuse for conjugal infidelity.[18]

What is striking in this passage is that husbands complained to doctors about their wives' coldness, a fact that makes it quite evident that passion in wives was not only desired by men, but expected—why, otherwise, would they complain of its lack? Van de Warker, it is worth pointing out, was writing for his fellow physicians, who were in a position to verify his assertions from their own experience with patients.

Van de Warker's explanation for "impotency" in women is revealing, too. Ascribing it to "sexual incompatibility," he went on to say that "so far as my own observation extends, the husband is generally at fault. The more common cause is acute sexual irritability on the part of the husband."[19] Dr. William Goodell, writing in 1887, also asserted that mutual pleasure was essential to successful marital intercourse. In Goodell's mind, as in Van de Warker's, that meant men must recognize women's interests and sexual rhythm. "Destroy the reciprocity of the union," Goodell cautioned, "and marriage is no longer an equal partnership, but a sensual usurpation on the one side and a loathing submission on the other."[20] Another medical writer who also acknowledged women's pleasure in the sex act made the same point as Goodell and Van de Warker. Men must not force themselves upon women or "overpersuade, but await the wife's invitation at this time [during ovulation], when her husband is a hero in her eyes." In this way the husband "would enjoy more and suffer less," the physician predicted.[21] These writers, in short, were not only testifying to their knowledge that women possessed sexual feelings, they were also explaining how those feelings were sometimes denied legitimate satisfaction by inept husbands.

The assumption that women had sexual feelings which required satisfaction also comes through in the course of discussions about contraception. Generally, physicians and other writers on this subject in the nineteenth century strongly opposed contraception, though all recognized that it was

18 Van de Warker, "Impotency in Women," 38–39.

19 *Ibid.*, 41. Today the complaint is called premature ejaculation.

20 William Goodell, *Lessons in Gynecology* (Philadelphia, 1887), 567, as quoted in Hale, *Freud and the Americans*, 40.

21 McLaury, "Remarks on the Relation of the Menstruation," 161.

widely practiced. One of the methods in common use was *coitus interruptus*, or withdrawal by the male prior to ejaculation. This method was condemned for a variety of reasons, but for our purposes it is significant that among the objections was its harmful effects upon women. This method, wrote Henry Chevasse, is "attended with disastrous consequences, most particularly to the female, whose nervous system suffers from ungratified excitement."[22] Dr. John Harvey Kellogg, a popular writer on medical matters, also warned against the method because of its effects upon women. He quoted at length from a French authority. Whenever this method is practiced, the authority wrote, all of women's genital organs "enter into a state of orgasm, a storm which is not appeased by the natural crisis; a nervous super excitation persists" after the act. The authority then compared the unreleased tension to that evoked in presenting food to a "famished man" and then snatching it away. "The sensibilities of the womb and the entire reproductive system are teased to no purpose." It is evident that in the minds of both writers women were assumed to have sexual feelings that were normally aroused during sexual intercourse.[23] Dr. August Gardner, writing in 1870 also for a popular audience, quoted from the same French authority and for the same purpose as Kellogg.[24]

Anyone who has looked into the sexual history of the nineteenth century is immediately struck by the deep and anxious concern physicians as well as other people felt about masturbation. Although it is often thought that boys were the principal objects of that concern, the fact is that girls were just as much fretted about. That there were such concerns about girls' masturbating is in itself a sign and measure of the recognition of sexual feelings in women. In fact in 1871 one popular medical writer on women defined masturbation as "the mechanical irritation of the sexual organs in order to excite the same voluptuous sensations attendant upon natural intercourse."[25] Mary Wood-Allen, a leader in the Women's Christian Temperance Union and a writer of advice books for young women, had no doubt that girls could be led into self-abuse. Even girls who would not use any mechanical means "to arouse sexual desire," she pointed out, nevertheless permitted themselves to fantasize or to have mental images that "arouse the spasmodic feelings of sexual pleasure."[26] Indeed from Wood-Allen's book one receives the message that women's sexual feelings were not only present but dangerously easy to arouse.

Discussion about masturbation in women reveals in another way how widely accepted was the idea that women possessed sexual desires. One physician, in the course of an article on the subject, said that the worst thing about masturbation in women was that a climax and resolution of

[22] Chevasse, *Physical Life of Man and Woman*, 424–25.

[23] John Harvey Kellogg, *Plain Facts for Old and Young* (1879; Burlington, Iowa, 1881), 252.

[24] Augustus K. Gardner, *Conjugal Sins against the Laws of Life and Health and Their Effects upon the Father, Mother, and Child* (New York, 1870), 98.

[25] Chevasse, *Physical Life of Man and Woman*, 33.

[26] Mary Wood-Allen, *What a Young Woman Ought to Know* (Philadelphia, 1905), 155.

tension were generally not achieved; hence the vice was persisted in. In response another doctor agreed that masturbation indeed gave rise to all the physical harm alleged in the article. But he disagreed with the assertion that in a woman sexual excitation could stop short of orgasm. "A commencement of the act, either of masturbation or coition," the letter writer contended, "*naturally* leads to its consummation, viz., an orgasm." Furthermore, he persisted, if "in the *healthy* female, an orgasm is not produced in the act of coition, she is not satisfied, and either will continue the act herself or with her coadjutor till such consummation does take place."[27]

Women's sexuality is also assumed in another class of medical-concerns. When Dr. J. Marion Sims, the "founding father" of American gynecology, published *Clinical Notes on Uterine Surgery* in 1866, conception was only dimly understood. In explaining how it took place Sims revealed, in passing, that most people took for granted that women experienced sexual feelings. "It is the vulgar opinion, and the opinion of many savants," Sims remarked, "that, to ensure conception, sexual intercourse should be performed with a certain degree of completeness, that would give an exhaustive satisfaction to both parties at the same moment." This sounds like twentieth-century ideas on optimum sexual performance, for Sims then went on to note, again in passing, that husbands and wives strove for such simultaneity and were unhappy when they failed to have simultaneous orgasms. "How often do we hear husbands complain of coldness on the part of the wives; and attribute to this the failure to procreate. And sometimes wives are disposed to think, though they never complain, that the fault lies with the hasty ejaculation of the husband."[28] Sims's point, of course, was that conception did not depend upon either sexual arousal or satisfaction in the woman. The important point for us, however, is that Sims, the medical readers he was addressing, and the patients he treated, all believed women were naturally capable of sexual feelings. Napheys in his popular book of advice for women also alluded to the prevalent idea that conception and pleasure were connected. He said that many people erroneously believed that conception could be known from the "more than ordinary degree of pleasure" on the part of the woman during the sexual act.[29]

In the course of discussing other kinds of women's illnesses, physicians often made it clear that they not only recognized the existence of sexual feelings in women but expected them in normal women. As we have observed already, Dr. Van de Warker considered the lack of sexual feelings in a woman as an abnormality to be cured. He called such women "impotent," just as one would denominate a man who failed to have adequate sexual responses.

[27] Chapman, "On Masturbation"; letter from S. E. McCully, *American Journal of Obstetrics*, 16 (1883): 844, my italics.

[28] James Marion Sims, *Clinical Notes on Uterine Surgery* (London, 1866), 369.

[29] Napheys, *Physical Life of Woman*, 104–05. This belief, which other writers also speak of, may well have affected some women's attitudes toward orgasm, for if a woman, under this view, could repress pleasure or climax, conception could be prevented.

To Van de Warker, women had to learn how to dislike sex; enjoyment of it was natural.[30] Napheys, too, saw frigidity as abnormal; its removal, he thought, was "so desirable."[31] One physician in 1882, in discussing a case of excessive masturbation, wrote that during an examination his female patient experienced "the most intense orgasm that I have ever witnessed,"[32] implying that he had witnessed others. Another physician listed among the pathological symptoms of one patient "an absence of all sexual desire"[33]—as if its presence were the normal condition of a woman. One medical doctor, in trying to show how intense was the pain a married patient experienced during intercourse, said that both partners had given up sexual relations "although both had unusually violent animal passions."[34] In arguing against birth control Dr. August Gardner told of a wife who, fearing pregnancy since she had borne seven children in seven years, was "otherwise very ardent."[35]

During the 1880s and 1890s, as surgeons became more skillful and antisepsis made abdominal operations safer, a number of doctors sought to alleviate otherwise incurable or obscure pelvic pains and nervous conditions in women through the removal of ovaries. This medical development is a complex one, especially as to the attitudes it might reveal on the part of doctors and society in general. This is not the place to pursue that question, however. It serves to explain, though, why ovariodectomies were a subject of considerable interest among gynecologists. One consequence of that interest was a report in 1890 by a surgeon who had removed forty-six pairs of ovaries. Significantly, he related that "the sexual instinct was always preserved. Three patients, virginal before operation, married later and lived in happy wedlock. The passions persist particularly when the operation is performed early on young persons," he concluded.[36] For us the significance of this report is not whether it is accurate; in fact I suspect that it is not. For as Dr. Van de Warker remarked on a different occasion, many women who suffered the pain or nervousness that caused them to submit to the operation in the first place probably had never felt any sexual pleasure. Consequently, to ask them after the operation whether there was any diminution in sexual feeling generally brought a denial. Moreover, the removal of the ovaries may well have reduced or eliminated hormonal secretions that may contribute to normal sexual feelings in women. In short, the physician's

30 Van de Warker, "Impotency in Women," 39.

31 Napheys, *Physical Life of Woman*, 86.

32 Horatio R. Bigelow, "Aggravated Instance of Masturbation in the Female." *American Journal of Obstetrics*, 15 (1882): 437.

33 "A Case of Excision of Both Ovaries for Fibrous Tumors of the Uterus, and a Case of Excision of the Left Ovary for Chronic Oöphoritis and Displacement," reported by Dr. E. H. Trenholme in *Canada Lancet*, July 1876, *American Journal of Obstetrics*, 9 (1876–77): 703.

34 "Case of Vaginismus," reported by Dr. George Pepper, *American Journal of Obstetrics*, 3 (1871): 322–24.

35 Gardner, *Conjugal Sins*, 97.

36 Summary of paper by Dr. Keppler, "The Sexual Life of the Female after Castration," given at the 10th International Medical Congress, *American Journal of Obstetrics*, 23 (1890): 1155–56.

report suffers from his clear wish to put his series of operations in a good light. But that very wish is revealing, for what it tells us is that women were expected to have sexual feelings and it was undesirable for a surgeon or, presumably, anyone else, to eliminate or even reduce those feelings.

IN THE LIGHT of the foregoing it is difficult to accept the view that women were generally seen in the nineteenth century as without sexual feelings or drives. The question then arises as to how this widely accepted historical interpretation got established? Part of the reason, undoubtedly, is the result of the general reticence of the nineteenth century in regard to sex. The excessive gentility of the middle class has been read by historians as a sign of hostility toward sexuality, particularly in women. The whole cult of the home and women's allegedly exalted place in it was easily translated by some historians into an antisexual attitude.[37] But a good part of the explanation must also be attributable to the simple failure on the part of historians to survey fully the extant sources. The kind of statements quoted from medical writers in this article, for example, was either overlooked or ignored. Another important part of the explanation is that the sources that were surveyed and quoted were taken to be descriptive of the sexual ideology of the time when in fact they were part of an effort by some other medical writers to establish an ideology, not to delineate an already accepted one. In other words, the medical literature that was emphasized by Steven Marcus, Oscar Handlin, or Nathan Hale, Jr. was really normative or prescriptive rather than descriptive.

This misinterpretation was easy enough to make since much nineteenth-century medical literature was often descriptive in form even though in fact it was seeking to set a new standard of sexual behavior. Sometimes, however, the normative concerns and purposes showed through the ostensible description. A close reading, for example, of William Acton's second edition of *The Functions and Disorders of the Reproductive Organs* reveals in several places his desire to establish a new and presumably "higher" standard of sexual attitude and behavior. After pointing out that publicists strongly condemn sexual relations outside marriage, he asks, "But should we stop there? I think not. The audience should be informed that, in the present state of society, the sexual appetites must not be fostered; and experience teaches those who have had the largest means of information on the matter, that self-control must be exercised." So far, he continues, no one has "dared publicly to advocate . . . this necessary regulation of the sexual feelings or training to continence." Or later, when he discusses women in par-

[37] Not all historians, it should be noted, have assumed that nineteenth-century concerns about sex meant hostility toward women's sexuality. In tracing the history of the social-purity movement after 1870, David J. Pivar is careful to distinguish between a concern with the exploitation of women's sexuality and an opposition to women's sexual feelings. See his *Purity Crusade, Sexual Morality, and Social Control: 1868–1900* (Westport, 1973).

ticular, it is evident that he is arguing for a special attitude, not merely describing common practice. "The *best* mothers, wives, and managers of households know little or nothing of sexual indulgence. Love of home, children, and domestic duties are the only passions they feel," he writes.[38]

American writers of the time who followed the lead of Acton as well as quoting him display a similar mixture of prescription and description. Take Dr. John Kellogg's *Plain Facts for Old and Young*, which sold over 300,000 copies by 1910 and went through five editions. Kellogg, like Acton, made it clear that he thought sex was too dominant in the thoughts of people. As we look around us today, he wrote, "it would appear that the opportunity for sensual gratification has come to be, in the world at large, the chief attraction between the sexes. If to these observations," he continued, "we add the filthy disclosures constantly made in police court and scandal suits, we have a powerful confirmation of the opinion."[39] It was this excess that he warns against, drawing upon quotations from Acton to support his arguments. He is at pains to show, too, that continence, especially in men, is not deleterious to health, as some contended. He admits that the medical profession is not in agreement on the amount of sexual indulgence permitted in marriage. "A very few hold that the sexual act should never be indulged except for the purpose of reproduction, and then only at periods when reproduction will be possible. Others, while equally opposed to the excesses . . . limit indulgence to the number of months in the year." Human beings, he advised, should take their cue from animals, who have intercourse only for procreation and then at widely spaced intervals. Instead of heeding this counsel, he writes, loosely quoting from Acton, "the lengths to which married people carry excesses is perfectly astonishing."[40]

Kellogg's reference to the behavior of animals as a worthy guideline for human behavior was echoed by other writers who sought to control sexuality. William Acton and Orson S. Fowler, for example, also used that standard of sexual behavior. Kellogg even went so far as to make an overt defense of the analogy. He carefully explained to his readers that in the modern age of biology these analogies were extremely helpful in getting at nature's purpose. "It is by this method of investigation," he remarked, "that most of the important truths of physiology have been developed; and the plan is universally acknowledged to be a proper and logical one." Then he launched into a condemnation of those men who use their wives as harlots, "having no other end but pleasure." For it was clear that among animals the end was reproduction only and then only at those one or two times a year when reproduction was possible. But by the time Kellogg reached the place in his book where he defended the analogy with animals he had already revealed

38 Acton, *Functions and Disorders* (1858), 8–9; (1865), 134, my italics.

39 Kellogg, *Plain Facts*, 178. Hale gives the figures on Kellogg's sales in *Freud and the Americans*, 37.

40 Kellogg, *Plain Facts*, 206, 209, 247, 225–26. Kellogg also quoted Acton.

that his purpose in invoking the analogy was reformist and normative, not simply scientific and logical. For in the early pages of his book, in making a different normative point—the need to protect children from premature sexuality—he told of a parent whose adolescent children often played games in the nude. When admonished for permitting this practice, the parent replied that it was only natural. "Perfectly harmless; just like little pigs!" Kellogg quoted the parent as saying. Kellogg's comment, however, was quite different from that which he would advise later in his book: "as though pigs were models for human beings!"[41]

In the end Kellogg himself virtually admitted that his "plain facts" were hardly facts at all, but prescriptions and hopes. "There will be many," he wrote, "the vast majority, perhaps, who will not bring their minds to accept the truth which nature seems to teach, which would confine sexual acts to reproduction wholly." And so he was prepared to offer a compromise, that is, a method of contraception. It was not a very effective method, as he admitted—the so-called safe period—but again what is important is his frank recognition that only a minority among his readers confined their sexual activities to reproduction and that he hoped he would be able to induce more to do so.[42]

It would be a mistake, in short, to accept the prescriptive or normative literature, like that of Acton, Kellogg, and others,[43] as revealing very much about sexual behavior in the Victorian era. It may be possible to derive a sexual ideology from such writers, but it is a mistake to assume that the ideology thus delineated is either characteristic of the society or reflective of behavior. On the contrary, it is the argument of this article that the attitudes and behavior of middle-class women were only peripherally affected by that ideology. Not only did many medical writers, as we have seen, encourage women to express their sexuality, but there is a further, even more persuasive reason for believing that the prescriptive literature is not a reliable guide to either the sexual behavior or the attitudes of middle-class women. It is the testimony of women themselves.

ANY SYSTEMATIC KNOWLEDGE of the sexual habits of women is a relatively recent historical acquisition, confined to the surveys of women made in the 1920s and 1930s and culminating in the well-known Kinsey report.[44] Until

[41] *Ibid.*, 217, 221–25, 118.

[42] *Ibid.*, 265–66.

[43] It is true that some of the advice and medical literature that recognized women's sexual feelings and from which I have been quoting was also prescriptive rather than merely descriptive. But for convenience and economy of words in subsequent pages when I refer to "prescriptive or normative literature" I mean only that which minimized or denied women's sexuality.

[44] Among the largest and most significant of such surveys were Katharine B. Davis, *Factors in the Sex Life of Twenty-two Hundred Women* (New York, 1929); Robert Latou Dickinson and Lura Beam, *A Thousand Marriages: A Medical Study of Sex Adjustment* (Baltimore, 1931); and Alfred C. Kinsey *et al.*, *Sexual Behavior in the Human Female* (Philadelphia, 1953). The first

recently no even slightly comparable body of evidence for nineteenth-century women was known to exist. In the Stanford University Archives, however, are questionnaires completed by a group of women testifying to their sexual habits. The questionnaires are part of the papers of Dr. Clelia Duel Mosher (1863–1940), a physician at Stanford University and a pioneer in the study of women's sexuality. Mosher began her work on the sexual habits of married women when she was a student at the University of Wisconsin prior to 1892. That year she transferred for her senior year to Stanford, where she received an A.B. degree in 1893 and an M.A. in 1894. In 1900 she earned an M.D. degree from Johns Hopkins University. After a decade of private practice she joined the Stanford faculty as a member of the department of hygiene and medical adviser to women students. Her published work dealt with the physical capabilities of women; she was a well-known advocate of physical exercise for women. Mosher's questionnaires are carefully arranged and bound in volume 10 of her unpublished work, "Hygiene and Physiology of Women." Mosher, however, apparently never drew more than a few impressionistic conclusions from the highly revealing questionnaires. She did not even publish the fact of their existence, and so far as can be ascertained no use has heretofore been made of this manuscript source. Yet the amount and kind of information on sexual habits and attitudes of married women in the late nineteenth century contained in these questionnaires are unique.

The project, which spanned some twenty years, was begun at the University of Wisconsin when Mosher was a student of biology in the early 1890s. She designed the questionnaire when asked to address the Mother's Club at the university on the subject of marriage. In later years she added to her cases and used the information when giving advice to women about sexual and hygienic matters.[45] This initiative, as well as the kind of questions she asked, reveals that Mosher was far ahead of her time. She amassed information on women's sexuality that none of the many nineteenth-century writers on the subject studied in any systematic way at all.

The questionnaire itself is quite lengthy, comprising twenty-five questions, each one of which is divided into several parts. Much of the questionnaire, it is true, is taken up with ascertaining facts about the parents and even the grandparents of the respondents, but over half of the questions deal directly with women's sexual behavior and attitudes.[46] The informa-

---

chapter of Robert Latou Dickinson and Lura Beam, *The Single Woman* (Baltimore, 1934), concerns the sexual life of working girls in the 1890s, but it is based on forty-six cases, the typical patient being born "soon after 1870." I am indebted to David M. Kennedy of Stanford University for this reference.

[45] Mosher, "Hygiene and Physiology of Women," 10: xv, Mosher Papers, Stanford University Archives.

[46] The principal questions dealing with women's sexual habits are: number of conceptions; number of conceptions by choice and by accident; frequency of intercourse; whether intercourse is participated in during pregnancy; whether intercourse is "agreeable"; whether an orgasm occurs; what effects from orgasm, or from failure to have one; purpose of intercourse; the ideal

tion contained in the questionnaires not only supports the interpretation of women's sexuality that already has been drawn from the published literature, both lay and medical, but it also provides us with a means of measuring the degree to which the prescriptive marriage literature affected women's sexual behavior.

Since the evidence in this questionnaire, which I call the Mosher Survey, has never been used before, it is first worthwhile to examine the social background of the women who answered the questionnaires. All told there are forty-six useable questionnaires, but since two of the questionnaires seem to have been filled out by the same woman at an interval of twenty-three years, the number of women actually surveyed is forty-five.[47] In the aggregates that follow I have counted only forty-five questionnaires. The questionnaires, it ought to be said, were not administered at the same time, but at three different periods at least; moreover the date of administration of nine questionnaires cannot be ascertained. Of those that do provide that information, seventeen were completed before 1900, fourteen were filled out between 1913 and 1917, and five were answered in 1920.

More important than the date of administration of the questionnaires are the birth dates of the respondents. All but one of the forty-four women who provided their dates of birth were born before 1890. In fact thirty-three, or seventy per cent of the whole group, were born before 1870. And of these, seventeen, or slightly over half, were born before the Civil War. For comparative purposes it might be noted that in Alfred Kinsey's survey

---

habit of sexual relations; whether there is desire for intercourse other than during pregnancy; whether contraception is used and method employed; whether wife sleeps in same bed with husband; knowledge of sexual physiology prior to marriage; and the character of menses: age of onset, pain, and amount.

[47] The small number of women queried in the Mosher Survey may cause some readers to discount almost entirely the significance of any conclusions drawn from it. While such a response may be understandable as a first reaction, in the end I think it would be unwise. So far as I know, this is the only survey of sexual attitudes and practices in the nineteenth century; historians' standard conception of women's sexual practices and attitudes in the nineteenth century has been derived from no previous survey at all. Certainly the systematic questioning of forty-five women at considerable length and their rationales for their answers ought to be at least as significant in shaping historians' conceptions of women's sexuality as the scraps of information from interested writers at the time, novels, and recollections, which have been the bases of our traditional picture of women's sexual attitudes and behavior in the nineteenth century. It is true that we do not know at the present time who these women were or how random their selection was. But there seems little reason to believe that the women were specially chosen by Mosher, if only because the purpose of the original questionnaire as well as the use of the information gained from it were to help her in advising women students. Moreover, as an unmarried woman herself, it is very likely that the information from the questionnaires was Mosher's most valuable source of knowledge on women's sexuality. It is probably true, given the general reluctance of nineteenth-century people to discuss sex, that some women whom Mosher approached refused to answer the questionnaire. But it is worth recalling that the value even of modern sex surveys, including Kinsey's, has been questioned on the grounds that the respondents were largely self-selected. Obviously the Mosher Survey is not the final word on the sexual behavior and attitudes of women in the nineteenth century. But at the same time it ought not to be rejected because of its limited size; that would be applying a methodological standard quite inappropriate for a sensitive subject in which the evidence is always limited and fugitive.

of women's sexuality the earliest cohort of respondents was only born in the 1890s. In short, the attitudes and practices to which the great majority of the women in the Mosher Survey testify were those of women who grew up and married within the nineteenth century, regardless of when they may have completed the questionnaires.

An important consideration in evaluating the responses, of course, is the social origins of the women. From what class did they come, and from what sections of the country? The questionnaire, fortunately, provides some information here, but not with as much precision as one might like. Since the great majority of the respondents attended college or a normal school (thirty-four out of forty-five, with the education of three unknown), it is evident that the group is not representative of the population of the United States as a whole. The remainder of the group attended secondary school, either public or private, a pattern that is again not representative of a general population in which only a tiny minority of young people attended secondary school. But for purposes of evaluating the impact of the prescriptive or marital-advice literature upon American women this group is quite appropriate. For inasmuch as their educational background identifies them as middle- or upper-class women, it can be said that they were precisely those persons to whom that advisory literature was directed and upon whom its effects ought to be most evident.

In geographical origin the respondents to the Mosher Survey seem to be somewhat more representative, if the location of parents, birthplaces, and colleges attended can be taken as a measure, albeit impressionistic, of geographical distribution. Unfortunately there is no other systematic or more reliable information on this subject. The colleges attended, for example, are located in the Northeast (Cornell [6], Smith, Wellesley, and Vassar [2]), in the Middle West (Ripon, Iowa State University, and Indiana), and in the Far West (Stanford [9], the University of California, and the University of the Pacific). The South is not represented at all among the colleges attended.

Although the emphasis upon prestigious colleges might make one think that these were women of the upper or even leisure class, rather than simply middle class, a further piece of information suggests that in fact they were not. One of the questions asked concerned working experience prior to marriage. Although seven of the respondents provided no data at all on this point, and eight reported that they had married immediately after completing their education, thirty of the women reported that they had worked prior to marriage. As a side light on the opportunities available to highly educated women in the late nineteenth century, it is worth adding that twenty-seven of the thirty worked as teachers. On the basis of their working experience it seems reasonable to conclude that the respondents were principally middle- or upper-middle-class women rather than members of a leisure class.

Despite the high level of education of these women, they confessed to having a pretty poor knowledge, by modern standards, of sexual physiology before marriage. Only eleven said that they had much knowledge on that subject, obtained from female relatives, books, or courses in college, while another thirteen said that they had some knowledge. The remainder—slightly over half—reported that they had very little or no knowledge. No guidelines were given in the questionnaire for estimating the amount of knowledge. The looseness of the definition is shown by the fact that three of the respondents who said that they had no knowledge at all named books on women's physiology that they had read. From other titles mentioned in passing it is clear that a number of these women had direct acquaintance with the prescriptive and advisory literature of the time. How did it affect their behavior? Did they repress their sexual impulses or deny them, as some of the prescriptive literature advised? Were they in fact without sexual desire? Or were they motivated toward personal sexual satisfaction as the medical literature quoted in this article advised?

The Mosher Survey provides a considerable amount of evidence to answer these and other questions. To begin with, thirty-five of the forty-five women testified that they felt desire for sexual intercourse independent of their husband's interest, while nine said they never or rarely felt any such desire. What is more striking, however, is the number who testified to orgasmic experience. According to the standard view of women's sexuality in the nineteenth century, women were not expected to feel desire and certainly not to experience an orgasm. Yet it is striking that in constructing the questionnaire Dr. Mosher asked not only whether the respondents experienced an orgasm during intercourse but whether "you *always* have a venereal orgasm?" (my italics). Although that form of the question makes quite clear Mosher's own assumption that female orgasms were to be expected, it unfortunately confuses the meaning of the responses. (Incidentally, only two of the forty-five respondents failed to answer this question.) Five of the women, for instance, responded "no" without further comment. Given the wording of the question, however, that negative could have meant "not always, but almost always" as well as "never" or any response in between these extremes. The ambiguity is further heightened when it is recognized that in answer to another question, three of the five negatives said that they had felt sexual desire, while a fourth said "sometimes but not often," and the fifth said sex was "usually a nuisance." Luckily, however, most of the women who responded to the question concerning orgasm made more precise answers. The great majority of them said that they had experienced orgasms. The complete pattern of responses is set forth in table 1.

In sum, thirty-four of the women experienced orgasm, with the possibility that the figure might be as high as thirty-seven if those who reported "no" but said they had felt sexual desire are categorized as "sometimes." (Interestingly enough, of nine women out of the forty-five who said they had never felt any sexual desire, seven said that they had experienced orgasms.) Moreover, sixteen or almost half of those who experienced orgasms did so either

TABLE 1. RESPONSE TO THE QUERY: "DO YOU ALWAYS HAVE A VENEREAL ORGASM?"

Response	*Number*	*Percentage*
No Response	2	4.4%
"No" with No Further Comment	5	11.1%
"Always"	9	20.0%
"Usually"	7	15.5%
"Sometimes," "Not Always," or "No" with Instances	18	40.0%
"Once" or "Never"	4	8.8%

"always" or "usually." As we have seen, in the whole group of forty-five, all but two responded to the question asking if an orgasm was always experienced. Of those forty-three, thirty-four were born before 1875. Five answered "no" to that question without any further comment. One other woman responded "never," and two others said "once or twice." If the "noes" and the "never" are taken together, the proportion of women born before 1875 who experienced at least one orgasm is eighty-two per cent. If the "noes" are taken to mean "sometimes" or "once or twice," as they might well be, given the wording of the question, then the proportion rises to ninety-five per cent. For comparative purposes the figures for twentieth-century women provided in Kinsey's study are given in table 2. Kinsey's proportions are arranged by age group and chronological period; hence they are not strictly comparable with those derived from Mosher's data. But the comparison is still suggestive, even when made with the women in the age group 26–30.[48]

TABLE 2. PERCENTAGE OF WOMEN EXPERIENCING ORGASM DURING INTERCOURSE
(by decade of birth)

Women Born	*Ages 21–25*	*Ages 26–30*
Before 1900	72%	80%
1900–09	80%	86%
1910–19	87%	91%
1920X29	89%	93%

SOURCE: Alfred C. Kinsey *et al.*, *Sexual Behavior in the Human Female* (Philadelphia, 1953), 397, table 97.

[48] A comparison of the sexual responses of the older and younger women in the Mosher Survey did not reveal any greater interest in sex among the younger group, but the numbers involved were too small to be significant. The responses of fourteen women born before 1860 were compared with those of the eight women born after 1875. On the other hand, if the responses to the questions about desire for sex and about orgasmic experience are categorized by date at which the questionnaire was completed, regardless of the age of the respondent, there is a slight, if somewhat ambiguous, difference between the earlier and later respondents. Seventeen women completed the questionnaire before 1900; nineteen did so after 1912. Thirteen of the seventeen completed before 1900 responded to the question of whether they had experienced orgasm; four of the thirteen said they had not. Eighteen of the nineteen who completed the questionnaire after 1912 answered that question; only one out of eighteen failed to experience

MUCH MORE INTERESTING and valuable than the bare statistics are the comments or rationales furnished by the women, which provide an insight into the sexual attitudes of middle-class women. As one might expect in a population by its own admission poorly informed on sexual physiology, the sexual adjustment of some of these women left something to be desired. Mosher, for example, in one of her few efforts at drawing conclusions from the Survey, pointed out that sexual maladjustment within marriage sometimes began with the first intercourse. "The woman comes to this new experience of life often with no knowledge. The woman while she may give mental consent often shrinks physically." From her studies Mosher had also come to recognize that women's "slower time reaction" in reaching full sexual excitement was a source of maladjustment between husband and wife that could kill off or reduce sexual feelings in some women. Women, she recognized, because of their slower timing were left without "the normal physical response. This leaves organs of women over congested."[49] At least one of her respondents reported that for years intercourse was distasteful to her because of her "slow reaction," but "orgasm [occurs] if time is taken." On the other hand, the respondent continued, "when no orgasm, [she] took days to recover."[50] Another woman spoke of the absence of an orgasm during intercourse as "bad, even disastrous, nerve-wracking—unbalancing, if such conditions continue for any length of time." Still a third woman, presumably referring to the differences in the sexual rhythms of men and women, said, "Men have not been properly trained." One of the women in the Mosher Survey testified in another way to her recognition of the differences in the sexuality of men and women. "Every wife submits when perhaps she is not in the mood," she wrote, "but I can see no bad effect. It is as if it had not been. But my husband was absolutely considerate. I do not think I could endure a man who forced it." And her response to a question about the effects of an orgasm upon her corroborate her remark: "a general sense of well being, contentment and regard for husband. This is true Doctor," she earnestly wrote.[51]

Mosher's probing of the attitudes of women toward their sexuality went beyond asking about orgasms. Several of her questions sought to elicit the

an orgasm. In themselves these data suggest that women who answered the questionnaire in the twentieth century achieved somewhat more satisfaction in their sexual experience than those who completed the questionnaire in the nineteenth century. But when a similar division by century is made of the questionnaires in regard to another question, that conclusion is not so clear. One of the questions asked whether the respondent felt sexual desire. Fourteen women answered the question prior to 1900, of whom only two said they had failed to feel desire. But of the sixteen who responded to the same question after 1912, three said they lacked any feeling of desire. Here the proportion of sexuality was higher among the nineteenth- than the twentieth-century respondents.

49 Mosher, "Hygiene and Physiology of Women," 10: 1. Twelve of the women were asked how soon after marriage they engaged in intercourse. Six said within the first three days, while six said from ten days to a year after the ceremony.

50 *Ibid.*, case no. 51. The case numbers have been assigned by Mosher herself and appear on each page of each questionnaire. Hereafter the citation of cases will carry only "Hygiene and Physiology of Women" and case number.

51 *Ibid.*, case nos. 47, 40, 41.

reactions of women to sexual intercourse. What is the purpose of sex, she asked? Is it a necessity for a man or for a woman? Is it for pleasure, or is it for reproduction?[52] Only two of the women failed to respond in some fashion to these questions. Nine thought sex was a necessity for men, while thirteen thought it was a necessity for both men and women. Fifteen of the respondents thought it was not a necessity for either sex. Twenty-four of the forty-five thought that it was a pleasure for both sexes, while only one thought it was exclusively a pleasure for men. Given the view generally held about sexual attitudes in the nineteenth century, it comes as something of a surprise to find that only thirty marked "reproduction" as the primary purpose of sex. In fact, as we shall see in a moment, some of the women thought reproduction was not as important a justification for intercourse as love.

As one might expect, this particular series of questions was usually answered with a good deal of explanation. One woman who emphasized reproduction as the principal justification took the opportunity to condemn those couples she apparently had heard of who did not want children. "I cannot recognize as true marriage that relation unaccompanied by a strong desire for children." She thought it was close to "legalized prostitution." She admitted that because of her love for her husband she "cultivated the passion to effect the 'compromise' in this direction that must come in every other [area] when people marry." She went on to say that she did not experience orgasm until the fifth or sixth year of her marriage and that even at the time of her response to the questionnaire—the early 1890s—she still did not reach a sexual climax half of the time. A second woman was also apparently out of phase with her husband's sexual interests, for she thought a woman's needs for sex occurred "half as often as a man's." It is revealing of her own feelings that though she said "half as often," the figures she used to illustrate her point—twice a week for a man and twice a month for a woman —are actually in the ratio of one to four rather than of one to two as she said. Her true attitude was also summed up in the remark that since she was always in good health and intercourse "did not hurt me, . . . I always meant to be obliging."[53]

But, as the earlier statistical breakdown makes evident, the women who only tolerated intercourse were in a decided minority. A frank and sometimes enthusiastic acceptance of sexual relations was the response from most of the women. Sexual intercourse "makes more normal people," said a woman born in 1857. She was not even sure that children were necessary to justify sexual relations within marriage. "Even if there are no children, men love their wives more if they continue this relation, and the highest devotion is based upon it, a very beautiful thing, and I am glad nature gave it to us."

[52] Since each respondent could legitimately answer "yes" to all three suggested justifications for sexual relations, the totals here can go beyond forty-five, though not all questions were always answered.

[53] *Ibid.*, case nos. 24, 19.

Since marriage should bring two people close together, said one woman born in 1855, sexual intercourse is the means that achieves that end. "Living relations have a right to exist between married people and these cannot exist in perfection without sexual intercourse to a moderate degree. This is the result of my experience," she added. A woman born in 1864 described sexual relations as "the gratification of a normal healthy appetite." The only respondent who was divorced and remarried testified in 1913 that at age fifty-three "my passionate feeling has declined somewhat and the orgasm does not always occur," but intercourse, she went on, was still "agreeable" to her.[54]

Several of the women even went so far as to reject reproduction as sufficient justification for sex. Said one woman, "I consider this appetite as ranking with other natural appetites and like them to be indulged legitimately and temperately; I consider it illegitimate to risk bringing children into the world under any but most favorable circumstances." This woman was born before the Compromise of 1850 and made her comment after she had been married ten years. Another woman, also born a decade before the Civil War, denied that reproduction "alone warrants it at all; I think it is only warranted as an expression of true and passionate love. This is the prime condition for a happy conception, I fancy." To her, too, the pleasure derived from sexual intercourse was "not sensual pleasure, but the pleasure of love."[55]

A third woman born before 1861 doubted that sex was a necessity in the same sense as food or drink, but she had no doubt that "the desire of both husband and wife for this expression of their union seems to me the first and highest reason for intercourse. The desire for offspring is a secondary, incidental, although entirely worthy motive but could never to me make intercourse right unless the mutual desire were also present." She saw a clear conflict between the pleasure of intercourse and reproduction. "My husband and I," she said in 1893,

> believe in intercourse for its own sake—we wish it for ourselves and spiritually miss it, rather than physically, when it does not occur, because it is the highest, most sacred expression of our oneness. On the other hand, even a slight risk of pregnancy, and then we deny ourselves the intercourse, feeling all the time that we are losing that which keeps us closest to each other.[56]

Another woman, in describing the ideal of sexual relations, said that she did not want intercourse to occur at any time when conception was likely, for conception should not occur by accident. Instead it ought to be the result of

> deliberate design on both sides in time and circumstances most favorable physically and spiritually for the accomplishment of an immensely important act. It

[54] *Ibid.*, case nos. 41, 18, 2. It is worth noting that here, as elsewhere in the survey, no mention was made of religious reasons for or against intercourse. These women had almost entirely secularized their sexual ideology.

[55] *Ibid.*, case nos. 14, 12.

[56] *Ibid.*, case no. 15.

amounts to separating times and objects of intercourse into (a) that of expression of love between man and woman (that act is frequently simply the extreme caress of love's passion, which it would be a pity to limit . . . to once in two or three years) and (b) that of carrying on a share in the perpetuation of the race, which should be done carefully and prayerfully.[57]

It seems evident that among these women sexual relations were neither rejected nor engaged in with distaste or reluctance. In fact for them sexual expression was a part of healthy living and frequently a joy. Certainly the prescriptive literature that denigrated sexual feelings or expression among women cannot be read as descriptive of the behavior or attitude of these women. Nevertheless this is not quite the same as saying that the marriage handbooks had no effect at all. To be sure, there is no evidence that the great majority of women in the Mosher Survey felt guilty about indulging in sex because of what they were told in the prescriptive literature. But in two cases that literature seems to have left feelings of guilt. One woman said that sexual relations were "apparently a necessity for the *average* person" and that it was "only [the] superior individuals" who could be "independent of sex relations with no evident ill-results." To her, as to St. Paul and some of the marriage-advice books, it was better to indulge than to burn, but it was evidently even better to be free from burning from the beginning. A more blatant sign of guilt over sex came from the testimony of a woman who quite frankly thought the pleasure of sex was a justification for intercourse, but, she added "not necessarily a legitimate one."[58]

Dr. Mosher herself obliquely testified to the effects of the prescriptive literature. She attributed the difficulties some women experienced in reaching orgasm to the fact that "training has instilled the idea that any physical response is coarse, common and immodest which inhibits [women's] proper part in this relation."[59] That was the same point that some of the medical writers in the nineteenth century had made in explaining the coldness of some women toward their husbands.

The advice literature, for men as well as for women, generally warned

[57] *Ibid.*, case no. 22.

[58] *Ibid.*, case nos. 47, 30. Marcus found a comparable example of guilt arising out of the prescriptive literature against masturbation. In discussing the Victorian sexual autobiography *My Secret Life,* Marcus observes that the anonymous author gave full credence to the dangers described in the literature, yet he masturbated nonetheless. After doing so, however, the anonymous author reported he suffered from depression, guilt, fatigue, and general feelings of debilitation though he felt none of these symptoms after sexual intercourse. Marcus ascribes these feelings to an internalizing of social attitudes, presumably derived from the prescriptive literature against masturbation. *Other Victorians,* 112. It is significant, however, that the prescriptions did not stop the practice. Why it did not stop is suggested by a more recent study of sexual behavior. Masters and Johnson report that most of their male subjects still believed the old tales of physical and psychical harm from masturbation, especially from "excessive" activity, but none of them desisted from the practice. The authors point out that no matter how active a subject was in this respect, he always defined "excessive" as more active than his own practice. William H. Masters and Virginia E. Johnson, *Human Sexual Response* (Boston, 1966), 201–02.

[59] Mosher, "Hygiene and Physiology of Women," 10: 1.

against excessive sexual activity.[60] This emphasis upon limits is reflected in the remarks of some of the women in the Mosher Survey. One woman said, for example, that "the pleasure is sufficient warrant" for sexual relations, but only if "people are extremely moderate and do not allow it to injure their health or degrade their best feelings toward each other." Another woman had concluded that "to the man and woman married from love," sexual intercourse "may be used temperately as one of the highest manifestations of love granted us by our Creator." A third woman who had no doubt that sexual relations were "necessary to marital happiness," nonetheless said she believed "in temperance in it."[61] But temperance, another one of the women in the Mosher Survey reminds us, should not be confused with repugnance or distaste. Although this respondent did not think the ideal sexual relation should occur more often than once a month, she did think it ought to take place "during the menstrual period . . . and in the daylight." The fact is that this woman, in answer to other questions, indicated that she experienced sexual desire about once a week, but with greatest intensity "before and during menses." She was, in short, restricting her own ideal to what she considered an acceptable frequency of indulgence. Her description of her feelings after orgasm suggests where she learned that limits on frequency might be desirable or expected: "Very sleepy and comfortable. No disgust, as I have heard it described."[62]

THIS EXAMINATION OF THE LITERATURE, the popular advice books, and particularly the Mosher Survey makes clear that historians are ill-advised to rely upon the marital-advice books as descriptions either of the sexual behavior of women or of general attitudes toward women's sexuality. It is true that a literature as admittedly popular as much of the prescriptive or normative literature was could be expected to have some effect upon behavior as well as attitudes. But those effects were severely limited. Most people apparently did not follow the prescriptions laid down by the marriage and advice manuals. Indeed some undoubtedly found that advice wrong or misleading when measured against experience. Through some error or accident the same woman was apparently interviewed twice in the Mosher Survey, twenty-three years apart. As a result we can compare her attitudes at the beginning of her marriage in 1896 and her attitude in 1920. After one year of marriage she thought that sexual relations ought to be confined to reproduction only, but

[60] Hale cites sources ranging in origin from 1830 to 1910 on the concern for conserving sexual energy. *Freud and the Americans*, 35. Oscar Handlin sums up the advice in this fashion: "Abstinence, repression, and self-restraint thus were the law; and violations were punished by the most hideous natural consequences, described in considerable graphic detail." Handlin's conclusion, however, that the readers of that literature "were overwhelmed by the guilt and shame the necessities of self-control imposed," seems unwarranted on the basis of present evidence. *Race and Nationality in American Life* (Garden City, 1957), 122–23.

[61] Mosher, "Hygiene and Physiology of Women," case nos. 33, 10, 13.

[62] *Ibid.*, case no. 11.

when asked the same question in 1920, she said that intercourse ought not to be confined to reproduction, though she thought it should be indulged in only when not pressed with work and when there was time for pleasure.[63] Another woman in the Mosher Survey changed her mind about sexual relations even earlier in her sexual life. She said,

> My ideas as to the reason for [intercourse] have changed materially from what they were before marriage. I then thought reproduction was the only object and that once brought about, intercourse should cease. But in my experience the habitual bodily expression of love has a deep psychological effect in making possible complete mental sympathy, and perfecting the spiritual union that must be the lasting "marriage" after the passion of love has passed away with years.

These remarks were made in 1897 by a woman of thirty after one year of marriage.[64]

Her comments make clear once again that historians need to recognize that the attitudes of ordinary people are quite capable of resisting efforts to reshape or alter them. That there was an effort to deny women's sexual feelings and to deny them legitimate expression cannot be doubted in the light of the books written then and later about the Victorian conception of sexuality. But the many writings by medical men who spoke in a contrary vein and the Mosher Survey should make us doubt that the ideology was actually put into practice by most men or women of the nineteenth century, even among the middle class, though it was to this class in particular that the admonitions and ideology were directed. The women who responded to Dr. Mosher's questions were certainly middle- and upper-middle-class women, but they were, as a group, neither sexless nor hostile to sexual feelings. The great majority of them, after all, experienced orgasm as well as sexual desire. Their behavior in the face of the antisexual ideology pressed upon them at the time offers testimony to the truth of Alex Comfort's comment that "the astounding resilience of human commonsense against the anxiety makers is one of the really cheering aspects of history."[65]

[63] *Ibid.*, case nos. 30, 33. Mosher gives no indication that she knew the two questionnaires were from the same person.

[64] *Ibid.*, case no. 22.

[65] Alex Comfort, *The Anxiety Makers: Some Curious Preoccupations of the Medical Profession* (London, 1967), 113.

Private Lives and Public Order: A Critical View of the History of Intimate Relations in the U.S. *by Howard Gadlin*

HISTORY CAUTIONS against a naive acceptance of announcements of sexual liberation and the death of the family. What appears to be the disintegration of a past mode of relationship is often only a transformation of that mode. Interpersonal relations, since they develop more slowly and in response to the economic and social realities that dominate them, come eventually to be appropriate to the social conditions in which we exist, so what appears to be a liberation from past oppression is often only a transformation of that oppression.

It is the thesis here that both the repression of sexuality in the nineteenth century and the liberation of sexuality in the twentieth century are related to the more general changes in the meaning and function of the family and interpersonal relations necessitated by the development of industrial capitalism and the growth of urban centers since the nineteenth century. Whereas earlier the family had been the center of interrelated social institutions, now it had become a weak connecting link between newly differentiated public and private realms of social life. Precisely as it "decreased" in social importance, the family now "increased" in psychological significance. Within these developments the significance of sexuality has been drastically transformed; whereas its repression was necessitated by the sundering of the public from the private, its liberation can be seen as a requisite for their reintegration under terms that do not threaten the foundations of advanced industrial capitalism. To examine these transformations I will look at four historical epochs which appear to mark significant stages in the metamorphosis of the United States from a traditional rural to a modern urban industrial society, and which are notable for strikingly different attitudes toward sexuality: the colonial (mid-1600's), the Jacksonian (1825–40), the second decade of the twentieth century, and the contemporary period (post 1950).

For colonial Americans, personal life was embedded within public existence. One's personal space was located within a clearly articulated and relatively stable social structure. Personal life was not private life. Personal identity and social stability were directly and mutually interdependent. The household, under the guidance and surveillance of the community, served a multiplicity of religious, social, economic, and educational functions. What we call interpersonal relations took place within the performance of these functions, not separated from them. Intervention in malfunctioning families was expected and generally accepted. If a married person ran off with someone else, he or she would be punished and placed back within his or her "rightful" home. Even within one's own home personal privacy was rare because families were large and homes small; most of the few rooms there were, were multipurpose.

Yet despite the physical intimacy imposed by living conditions, even the closest of relationships was formal to a degree we would find not only awkward but contradictory to intimacy. In relationships between men and women this formality reflected a social context of paternal authoritarianism, misogyny, and a fundamentalist Christian distrust of uncontrolled earthly pleasures and human passion. In such a context love was not the basis for a relationship, but the result of it. It was a duty to love one's spouse, and failure to do so was seen as disobedience of God. Of course, since the family was the core institution of colonial life, love and affection were important, not as ends in themselves, but as a support for social stability.

In addition, since feeling and emotion were understood as basically anti-social, they were seen as requiring "governance" by placement within boundaries drawn by reason and shaped by the will. Thus, even in matters of love, affections were commanded to act according to the choices of reason. It was not on the basis of having established a promising relationship that one decided to marry, but on the basis of being ready to marry that one went out to find a mate. Being ready to marry meant being ready to assume financial independence and full social responsibility within the community.

But with all the emphasis on directing passion and feeling within the bounds of reason, people in colonial society do not seem to have believed they could alter the *nature* of basic feelings or impulses. As famous as the puritans were for their restrictions of sexuality, their efforts went primarily toward the control of behavior rather than the manipulation and shaping of impulse. The colonial attitude toward the impulses they sought to curb through restrictions on behavior was highly ambivalent. On the one hand man's basic nature was seen as depraved; on the other hand, that depravity was accepted as natural. Within that framework, sexual feeling was acknowledged as natural, and even sexual pleasure could be accepted as good, within limits. The limits were clear: sexual behavior was sanctioned only within marriage. Sexual intimacy outside of marriage was anti-social and necessitated punishment. But when sexual pleasure occurred within marriage it was treated as any other earthly delight, acceptable so long as it was kept within the bounds of social responsibility and order.

In the nineteenth century this all changed. Rapid industrialization and the growth of urban centers transformed the social structure that had provided the context of social and personal life. The home ceased to be the center of all social existence; the family ceased to be a productive unit. People's lives were divided between their work and their homes. For the individual, this separation of the public from the private leads to a great expansion of personal consciousness. Contemporary forms of interpersonal intimacy emerge with the self-conscious bourgeois individual whose life is torn between the separated worlds of work and home. Indeed, one could almost say the social changes in the early decades of the nineteenth century created personal identity, and it is only along with the personal that it becomes necessary to speak of the "interpersonal." Individualism and intimacy are the Siamese twins of modernization.

When work is moved outside of the home and the people with whom one works are no longer the people with whom one lives, there develop two fundamentally separate types of relationships. These relationships are defined within the boundaries of the separate institutions in which they occur; the dynamic of these relationships is determined by the functions of the institutions. Since the functions are different, a conflict between the styles of relationships required by the work place and home life is structured into the lives of all persons. These separate spheres of existence require different and often incompatible feelings, expectations, attitudes, interests and behavior. Evidence of the conflict between the personal characteristics required by the separate domains of work and home can be seen in the advice given to their clients by phrenologists, nineteenth-century predecessors of today's psychological testers and counselors. For example Orson Fowler's analysis presented to an Edgar Hopkins contained the following:

> can manage work very well, are very reserved, need thawing out; Lack hope, must undertake more . . .
>
> have too much kindness, must be more selfish, trust people too much, don't endorse . . . need the softening influence of a woman, will be fond of traveling and always good in it. Very much need training from the female sex. Select for a wife a girl who compliments, could not endure a scold . . . your distinguishing trait will be good sound judgment . . . will succeed as a coal dealer.[1]

Clearly, those traits appropriate to success in the business world were generally incompatible with close personal relationships—restricted kindness, increased selfishness and heightened distrust of others hardly are promotive of deep romantic love and sustained intimacy. The situation is further complicated by the fact that within developing industrial capitalism, the public sphere dominates the private. Consequently, occupational demands came to determine and shape the course of development of home life and intimate relationships. Much of the differentiation of roles that was a part of the changes of the

---

[1] This is taken from the handwritten inscription by Fowler in a copy of *The New Illustrated Self-Instructor in Phrenology and Physiology* (New York, 1859). My thanks to Steve Nissenbaum for drawing my attention to this copy, and for his inspiration in the conception of this paper.

nineteenth century was in direct response to the requisites of the work place and the reactions of people to those requisites. Because the quality and tone of existence in the work place were out of the direct or even indirect control of the great majority of people, personal existence became the province in which they could exercise their will and hope for some respite from the strains and deprecations of the world of work.

The popular literature of the time is filled with articles, advice, and stories glorifying the family and the home as a utopian retreat. These words from an article entitled "Home" in an 1830 edition of *Ladies* Magazine capture quite well the popular middle-class opinion of the time:

> We go forth into the world, amidst scenes of business and of pleasure; we mix with the gay and the thoughtless, we join the busy crowd, and the *heart* is sensible to a desolation of feeling: we behold every principle of justice and of honor, and even the dictates of common honesty disregarded, and the delicacy of our moral sense is wounded; we see the general good sacrificed to the advancement of personal interest; and we turn from such scenes, with a painful sensation, almost believing that virtue has deserted the abodes of men; again, we look to the *sanctuary* of *home:* there sympathy, honor, virtue, are assembled; there the eye may kindle with intelligence, and receive an answering glance; there disinterested love, is ready to sacrifice everything at the altar of affection.[2]

Of course we cannot take such a passage as an accurate description of the facts of domestic life. In fact, such glowing terms were necessitated to counteract the gloomy situation of the family at the time. The early 1800's produced an extraordinary increase in desertion rates, sufficient to warrant the granting of a special legal status to abandoned wives. It would seem that the problems city life imposed upon the individual were equally problems for the couple.

In Jacksonian America both personal identity and interpersonal relations were in crisis. Large numbers of people were

---

[2] Kirk Jeffrey, "The Family as Utopian Retreat from the City," pp. 21–41, Sallie Tessele, ed., *The Family, Communes and Utopian Societies* (New York: Harper & Row, 1972).

living in urban settings for which they had not, nor could they have, been prepared. Steve Nissenbaum, a contemporary historian, has described the situation of the person as follows:

They were on their own, then in mind and body. Reared as most of them must have been on farms and in small towns, they had been forced to leave by the pressures of population increase, insufficient or inadequate land, and competition from cheaper markets . . . What loomed before them was not just a bleak future, but an *unknowable* future—and a far wider range of options than their parents had ever known, and for which nobody was equipped to prepare them. To remain at home might be to face a vicious circle of impoverishment; but to leave . . . actually created more problems than it solved: it introduced social arrangements, life-styles, daily routines, that were at the very least unsettling. Neighbors were unfamiliar; the new communities were often demographically skewed; the seasonal cycle of seed-time and harvest no longer served to regulate the rhythm of their lives; even their *bodies*, which had served to confirm their identity through the physical labor imposed by farm work, were useless and "alien" to the kind of activities demanded of them in colleges or cities. In such places people lived *in* their bodies, not *by* them, and indeed, those bodies—if not subdued—would themselves be part of the larger pattern of unpredictability and disorder in their lives.[3]

It is as if there were an epidemic of identity crises, one that intensified as traditional institutions continued to be inappropriate to the uncertainties in peoples' lives. In colonial America, it often appeared that personal privacy was feared by society. In Jacksonian America, with the individual suddenly "free" of constant surveillance, personal privacy, at least initially, seemed a threat to personal identity. No longer under the watchful eye of others, freed from the controlling influences of community shame and public punishment, people must have panicked over the flood of unchecked impulse which suddenly became their own responsibility. The following statement, written in 1833 by a New York City carpenter reflecting

[3] Steve Nissenbaum, "Sex, Reform, and Social Change, 1830–1840," paper presented to American Historical Association, 1972.

on his first experiences on his own, is representative of the response many people had to urban life:

> I became excessively nervous, so that I was continually full of apprehensions of danger, afraid of everything, and starting with alarm at almost everything. If anything came upon me suddenly, it affected me very much . . . I often became so much embarrassed and confused, that I would lose the power of speech; and frequently, when in conversation, I used suddenly to lose my thoughts in the midst of a sentence, and totally forgot what I was talking about . . . When out from home I was often attacked with these turns in the street, and became so much confused and bewildered, that it was with great difficulty that I could find my way to my house. . . .[4]

The dilemma of these people, it seems, is that at the same time that they were threatened from within by their own impulses, they were also isolated from the very people from whom they had come to expect not only restraint and control, but warmth, intimacy, and in general the gratification of emotional needs. There were, of course, a variety of ways in which people attempted to satisfy these needs. Phrenology, special diets, sexual restraint, regimented living arrangements—all can be shown to have shared an emphasis on providing self-government, where once the family and community had reigned. For many, of course, it was to marriage that they turned. An institution rooted in the traditions of the communities they had left behind, marriage must have promised people to re-establish that link with society that had been so abruptly severed. At the same time it offered some of the emotional satisfactions people needed with heightened urgency in the tough, uncaring environs of the city. Particularly given the anonymity of the city, the possibility of being known must have seemed very attractive. Disconnected from the network of social relationships that characterized the colonial period, people were dependent upon each other for a depth and range of companionship that previously was provided by a diversity of people within community life.

---

[4] *Ibid.*, p. 11.

Cut off from this social support and restraint, couples had to generate the bases of their relationships from within the dynamic of their relationship and their personal feelings. In colonial America, relationships had provided the obligation of feeling; in the Jacksonian period, feeling came to provide the reason for relationships. When feeling was gone, the relationship might end. The early nineteenth-century glorification of romantic love, particularly in popular literature, was one major indicator of the new legitimacy of subjectivity. Still, it must be recognized that just as the colonial emphasis of the obligation to love acknowledged the tensions created by the intense intimacy of daily life, so we must suspect that the Jacksonians glorified the feelings of love when the conditions of daily existence made such feelings problematical.

We have seen that the idea of the home as utopian retreat was founded directly on the uncontrollable frustrations and indignities of the work world. At the same time, to become the person who could "succeed" (survive) at work required becoming a person in many ways incapable of warm and passionate intimate relationships. Given the intransigence of the public sphere, relations in the private domain were transformed so as to allow some degree of individual integrity and personal satisfaction to persons who needed to direct most of their energies to economic success. It was primarily through desexualization that this was accomplished.

In the Jacksonian era, not only was sexual behavior severely restricted but sexual impulses were repressed as well. Colonial Americans had acknowledged sexual feelings as natural and restricted sexual behavior to marriage where it did not threaten social cohesion. And sodomy, which was seen as beyond the limits of sociality, was punishable by death.

Jacksonian Americans attempted to control the sexual impulses themselves. In so doing they transformed the nature and meaning of sexuality. Whereas sexual relations had previously been seen as naturally directed at obtaining sexual pleasure, they were now understood as legitimate only as an expression of warmth and intimacy, the ultimate indicator of a deep spiritual bond between people. All sexual release became suspect, and there emerged an extensive popular literature and active social campaigns against masturbation, prostitution, and all forms of "excessive" sexuality. It was not simply prudery that motivated these attacks on sexuality. Consider, for example, the following description of orgasm in the writings of Sylvester Graham, a major figure in the sex reform movement, and manager of highly regimented boarding houses in which young men overwhelmed by the complications and ambiguities of urban life could find some structure around which to rebuild their lives. Graham wrote:

> The convulsive paroxysms attending venereal indulgence, are connected with the most intense excitement, and cause the most powerful agitation to the whole system that it is ever subject to. The brain, stomach, heart, lungs, liver, skin, and the other organs, feel it sweeping over them with the violence of a tornado. The powerfully excited and convulsed heart drives the blood, in fearful congestion, to the principal viscera,—producing oppression, irritation, debility, rupture, inflammation, and sometimes disorganization;—and this violent paroxysm is generally succeeded by great exhaustion, relaxation, lassitude, and even protraction.[5]

Hardly an experience one would strive to obtain.

Even the phrenologists, for the time among the most accepting of sexuality and sexual pleasure, argued against sexual gratification as an end in itself, separated from "virtuous love and wedlock." One of Fowler's works was entitled

AMATIVENESS
or
EVILS AND REMEDIES
of
Excessive and Perverted Sexuality:
including
Warning and Advice
to the
Married and Single[6]

---

[5] *Ibid.*, p. 6.
[6] Orson S. Fowler, *Amativeness* etc. (New York: Fowler & Wells, 1840).

This work was a supplement to *Love and Parentage* in which Fowler had written:

> Let the libertine revel in his lustful, and therefore comparatively tasteless, pleasures, so soon to become the gall of bitterness to his innermost soul! Let the abandoned prostitute herself for gold—for a *living* even—but while the world stands, will the bed of lust be comparatively insipid . . . besides ultimately torturing the body and polluting the soul! Mistaken they, who expect happiness in either promiscuous indulgence or unbridled licentiousness . . . How completely foolish the sensualist! Blasting the *very* pleasure he seeks! Bartering the most luxurious apple of paradise for the green, bitter, and poisonous grape of lust![7]

He then went on to explain how only by the cooperation of amativeness with the intellect and moral sentiment could one rise above carnality, be consonant with one's true nature, and achieve the spiritual love that constituted real happiness.

Finally, examination of the sexual radicals of the period, the communards and free love advocates, shows that even in rejecting monogamous marriage these non-conformists shared with the larger society a distrust of carnal sexuality. By no means were these people advocates or practitioners of orgiastic sexuality. Typically, sexual relations were carefully regulated and controlled, often towards the same goal—the maintenance of love and spiritual intimacy between people—that the dominant morality advocated. The non-conformists argued that monogamous marriage was incompatible with sustained intimacy. Their sexual practices, however, mirrored the general dichotomy between spiritual and physical love. In the Oneida community, for example, John Humphrey Noyes advocated "male continence" as the proper form of sexual intercourse. In this technique the partners were motionless and they never, except when reproducing, achieved orgasm. Nissenbaum relates how Noyes justified this curious mixture of free love between consenting partners and restraint from sexual pleasure. Noyes distinguished between "amative" and "propagative" sexual

---

[7] Orson S. Fowler, *Love and Parentage*, 12th ed. (New York: Fowler & Wells, 1846), p. 82.

acts, the first performed by the "organs of love or union" the second by the "organs of reproduction and procreation." If sexual intercourse were limited to the "conjunction of the organs of union" then "sexual intercourse becomes a purely social affair, the same in kind with other modes of kindly communion." Noyes went so far as to show that physical pleasure was a component of procreation not "union." This followed from the "fact" that:

> The discharge of the semen and the pleasure connected with it, is not essentially social, since it can be produced in solitude . . . The pleasure of the act is not produced by contact and interchange of life with the female, but by the action of the seminal fluid on the internal nerves of the male organ.[8]

Even in free love, then, spiritual intimacy was the proper goal of sexual relations.

Thus far, we have focused on the problems these changes created within the newly emergent private sphere. However, the separation of the public from the private was no less a threat to social cohesion than it was to individual integrity and interpersonal intimacy. Urban industrial development demanded strong and autonomous individuals and contained, self-sustaining couples. But these autonomous individuals, because of the enormous energies they directed toward the maintenance of personal identity, were less susceptible to social sanctions and collective concerns than their colonial predecessors. Similarly, couples cut off from networks of families and friends and tied by individualized emotional bonds as well as role expectations, were directed toward personal welfare and private satisfactions to an unprecedented degree. Ironically, then, the emergence and development of an autonomous economic sphere which itself disrupts traditional social stability, is dependent upon conditions of personal and interpersonal identity which are themselves additionally threatening to social cohesion. At the same

[8] Quoted in Rosabeth Moss Kanter, *Commitment and Community* (Cambridge, Mass.: Harvard University Press, 1972), p. 27.

time, since personal identity is necessarily bound up with social structure, the integrity of individual identity is threatened by the very terms of its own constitution.

From this perspective the near obsession with masturbation in the early nineteenth century makes a good deal of sense. In many ways masturbation is the epitome of autonomous individuality. The masturbator is an eroticized caricature of the self-sufficient person. Victorian Americans condemned masturbation as self-abuse. Our analysis suggests that they feared it as self-love. Suddenly there appeared in the 1830's a widely read literature warning against the harmful effects of onanism. Books such as *Solitary Vice Considered* made clear that both physical and mental health were endangered by masturbation. The notion of masturbation insanity was prevalent, and mechanical devices designed to prevent children from in any way manipulating their genitals became popular. The campaign against masturbation then can be seen as serving the needs of both personal identity and social cohesion. Refraining from masturbation serves to control those impulses whose release threatens the person, and simultaneously functions as a form of self-control that can substitute for the shattered external controls that previously guaranteed social cohesion. It could therefore be surmised that at least for Jacksonian Americans the strong ego was not an unambiguous evil. On the one hand, persons with strengthened individual egos threatened social cohesion to the extent that such persons were less responsible to others. Fowler's advice to Hopkins that he be less trusting, etc. confirms this. At the same time, people reared within the strong community responsibility traditions of pre-industrial America, and consequently dependent upon external rather than self-control, were lacking the ego-strength required to be sufficiently self-denying to function effectively in the development of the autonomous economic sphere. This is a consequence of the fact that the demands of social cohesion and the demands of economic development were often contradictory. From the perspective developed here, the repression of masturbation in the early nineteenth century appears as an understandable response to new personal and social dilemmas.

Self-sustaining couples present an even greater threat to "aggregate maintenance" than do autonomous individuals. Speaking from a psychoanalytic perspective Philip Slater has observed:

> An intimate dyadic relationship always threatens to shortcircuit the libidinal network of the community and drain off its source of sustenance. The needs binding the individual to collectivities and reinforcing his allegiance thereto are not satisfied in the dyadic relationship, and the libido attached to these collectivities and diffused through their component members is drawn back and invested in the dyad.[9]

We have already seen how in Jacksonian America the couple was released from the control and support of the larger social community, and how this created problems for interpersonal intimacy as well as personal identity. When we examine this phenomenon with Slater's optic, we see again that economic development creates the conditions that could potentially disrupt the social cohesion upon which further economic development must be dependent. When public and private life are divorced there exists a need for an institution(s) that satisfies the unmet personal needs exacerbated by capitalism. These needs must be satisfied without threatening social dissolution as does dyadic withdrawal. Ideally such an institution should also serve the needs for personal identity. The trick was to locate individuals within intimate relationships that did not completely destroy the fragile but increasingly resilient boundaries of self-identity while simultaneously tying such intimate relationships back into the needs of the developing social system rather than the pleasures and satisfactions of the dyad. In many respects the emotionally based but sexually monogamous and de-eroticized marriages of Jacksonian America were ideally suited to these purposes.

The literature of the Jacksonian period is filled with references to the special importance of marriage and the family in determining the quality of social life. Crime, delinquency,

---

[9] Philip Slater, "On Social Regression," *American Sociological Review*, 38 (1963), 339–363.

poverty, and insanity were all linked to inadequacies of the family. Similarly, the well-ordered family was credited for economic success, social stability, and moral propriety. Kanter's analysis, in *Commitment and Community*, of the communal movement of the period can be taken as further demonstration of a generalized concern with social cohesion and uncertainty about the family's ability to create and sustain social order and community. Certainly the repression of sexuality—the psychological core of Victorian morality—was perfectly consonant with the need to establish a new base for the integration of the family with society. At the same time, desexualization probably served the needs of personal identity, not only through the process of impulse control, but additionally by limiting the fusion which often accompanies intensified dyadic intimacy. Colonial Americans, although lacking sharply individualized identities, were not so threatened by fusion because of the diffusion of "libido" throughout a multiplicity of relations. The separation of public and private spheres places opposing pressures on individual identity. Economic conditions were now favorable to autonomous individuals, while the intensified and expanded demands of the interpersonal subverted that autonomy and pushed toward fusion. Desexualization placed some limits on that fusion, and therefore shored up the shaky identities of persons who had to fit together in many more ways than had couples earlier.

However, desexualization proceeded differently in men than in women. Victorian morality was constituted around a double standard for men and women. The base of this double standard was the redefinition of women as non-sexual beings. William Sanger, a respected physician, stated the dominant viewpoint as follows:

> But it must be repeated and most decidedly, that without . . . stimulating cause (such as destitution, drink, or seduction and abandonment) the full force of sexual desire is seldom known to a virtuous woman. In the male sex, nature has provided a more susceptible organization than in the females.[10]

---

[10] Milton Rugoff, *Prudery and Passion* (New York: Putnam, 1971), p. 46.

At the same time women were seen as innocent, the civilizing force juxtaposed against man's more animal nature; women's sexual transgressions were condemned more severely than those of men. Clearly, it was the desexualization that was new, not the unequal criteria against which men and women were judged.

The double standard is typically understood as a simple extension of male domination. I would like to suggest, rather, that the nineteenth-century double standard was the vehicle for a desexualization desired by both men and women for opposing purposes. Men wanted to desexualize relationships to maintain their domination; women wanted to desexualize relationships to limit male domination. The relationship of desexualization to domination can best be understood in terms of the finer differentiation of sex roles in the nineteenth century.

The development of industry created a sexual division of labor that mirrored the essential features of the separation of the public from the private. Women were located in the private realm, men in the public. When work left the home, so did men. Women were left behind managing the affairs of the home and caring for and raising the children. It is in the 1830's that books giving advice on "domestic economy" and child-rearing principles became popular. It was only in the 1800's that children began to come under the authority of women. Until the nineteenth century, children, although cared for by women, were seen as under the authority of the man; and women, no matter who was judged to be at fault, never received custody of children in cases of divorce. In the nineteenth century women's energies were directed, with unprecedented intensity, toward the raising of their children. Simultaneously, men's energies were directed toward the development of autonomy and the achievement of economic success. Recall the concern of Jacksonian men with the preservation of energy, equation of loss of sperm with debility and the glorification of spiritual love. Perhaps separating sexual from emotional love allowed men to "reinvest" their "unspent" sexual energies (the nineteenth-century euphemism for orgasm is "spend") in the world of work. However, simply pulling back from sexuality would have created additional problems for men because, traditionally, sexuality and domination had been fused. A unilateral rejection of sexuality would have been tantamount to abdication of male authority. Hence, the only way to preserve male domination while still reducing the pressures of sexual expectations was to redefine women as asexual creatures, or at least as less sexual than men.

Ironically, such a redefinition of the sexual nature of women was compatible with the attempts of early nineteenth-century women to curb male authority and redefine sexual roles. Carroll Smith-Rosenberg suggests that many of the women participants in the moral reform movement were responding to the position of women in Jacksonian America and against male domination. Women

> . . . had few rights and little power. Their role in society was passive and sharply limited. Women were . . . denied formal education . . . [seen as] . . . inadequate to sustained intellectual effort . . . denied the vote . . . Professional roles . . . were closed to women . . . Most economic alternatives to marriage . . . were closed to women. Their property rights were still restricted and females were generally considered to be the legal wards of either the state or of their nearest male relative.[11]

She suggests

> . . . such women channeled frustration, anger and a compensatory sense of superior righteousness into the reform movement. . . .[12]

Smith-Rosenberg goes on to discuss the way in which the moral reform movement attacked the double standard by demanding equal treatment of men and women. However, while attacking the double standard, the women of the moral reform movement exploited and accepted the image it presented of woman

---

[11] Carroll Smith-Rosenberg, "Beauty, the Beast and the Militant Woman: A Case Study in Sex Roles and Social Stress in Jacksonian America," *American Quarterly* (1973), pp. 562–584, p. 563.

[12] *Ibid.*, p. 564.

as asexual innocent. The *Advocate*, the weekly of the Female Moral Reform Society,

> entertained several primary assumptions concerning the nature of human sexuality. Perhaps most central was the conviction that women felt little sexual desire; they were in almost every instance induced to violate the Seventh Commandment by lascivious men who craftily manipulated not their sensuality, but rather the female's trusting and affectionate nature. A woman acted out of romantic love, not carnal desire; she was innocent and defenseless, gentle and passive . . . The male lecher on the other hand was a creature controlled by base sexual drives which he neither could or would control. He was . . . powerful and decisive; unwilling . . . to curb his own willfulness, he callously used it to coerce the more passive and submissive female.[13]

Whatever their intent, the moral reformers' demand for desexualization meshed well with the needs of Jacksonian men to limit their investment in intimate relations and maintain their domination. Simultaneously, this desexualization of the husband-wife relation probably allowed for the redirection of women's repressed sexual energies to the relationship with her children. Since at the same time, desexualization also served the male and female need for impulse control and also was compatible with the socially needed limitations on dyadic withdrawal, we can see Victorian morality as a quite creative response to social conditions.

By the end of the century, however, the altered social patterns which the Victorians had taken to be signs of the disintegration of the family were recognized as indicators of adjustment to the living conditions associated with urban life and industrial development. The problems which were unprecedented traumas for the first generations of urban pioneers were familiar difficulties for many early twentieth-century city dwellers. Attitudes and ideas were catching up with a reality which had formed in the early twentieth century; various institutions such as compulsory education, modifications in child-

---

[13] *Ibid.*, p. 571.

rearing practices, and reductions in family size had resulted in more autonomous and individuated persons, and intensified expectations of personal fulfillment within relationships based on mutual interest and attraction. For women this required a degree of cultivation and education previously denied them, and resulted in a heightened self-consciousness. Very quickly questions of personal identity and self-actualization became public issues; feminist critics in politicizing women's private problems had focused on the impoverishment of personal life. They asked, in the most general sense, if and how social relations and self-fulfillment were connected. They raised the question about the compatibility of interpersonal intimacy and self-fulfillment. Such critical questions had the potential to expand into a general critique of social relations and the social structure. The critical thrust of these questions was circumvented by a reduction in the opposition between the public and the private, by de-privatizing personal identity.

When people's personal needs can be aligned with the priorities of economic development, demands for personal fulfillment can support the dominant social order. Social cohesion is then served rather than threatened by personal fulfillment. Feminists experienced the need to redefine personal identity, but business dominated the process of redefinition.

The progressive era saw the sudden spread of enormously popular advice to the love-lorn column. ***True Story Magazine*** and a variety of imitations along with developing radio and movie industries both reflected and created public interest in personal accounts of private experiences. It was not only by transforming personal problems to commercial products and public entertainment that the larger social order reasserted its control of personal life. Personal fulfillment itself was equated with consumption.

As the economy which had undermined the productive role of the house and family in society continued to expand, it transformed the nature of domestic life as well. The period between 1914 and 1924 saw huge increases in the sale of canned goods, and comparable increases in the use of commercial laundries.

At the same time, the number of appliances such as electric irons, washing machines, and vacuum cleaners doubled and tripled. There were large economic stakes in keeping women at home, and magazines such as *Good Housekeeping*, and *Harper's Bazaar* as well as the advertising industry and the Home Economist movement combined to create the image of homemaking as a profession; by 1920 the woman did not have to step outside her door to be an administrator or an executive; her house was a plant with its equipment, and she was the director of personnel.

The fulfillment that was available for the woman who accepted marriage was that of a consumer, cut off from direct spontaneous action in the world. It was a curious fulfillment, based on the denial of self as actor, and the deception that consuming was acting. The more radical feminists, such as Charlotte Perkins Gilman and Olive Schreiner, decried this development towards what they called "parasitism." They called on women to give up the luxuries and leisure of consumerism. Clearly, for both feminists and non-feminists, fulfillment was represented in the new expectations women could hold for their lives and the new demands they might place on relationships. It was the definition of that fulfillment and the content of those expectations that separated feminists from non-feminists.

It was not only around the issue of consumerism that questions about the fulfillment of the new woman arose. One of the most striking features of the second decade of the twentieth century was the re-emergence of the sexuality which had been so thoroughly repressed throughout the Victorian era. Civilized morality required a denial of sexual feelings as well as restrictions on sexual behavior. When the feminists raised questions about the degree to which sex dominated all aspects of social life they were referring to gender, not erotic sexuality. It is particularly interesting, then, that it was precisely when women had begun to question the overriding social significance of gender that their erotic sexuality was rediscovered, encouraged, and developed. Women changed drastically, in appearance and behavior. Between the years 1913 and 1928 the amount of material needed for an average dress decreased from 19¼ yards to 7 yards. Just an examination of the styles of dress alone would show the changes from restraint to release. There were equally striking changes in sexual behavior. One of the first studies of sexual behavior found that women before the turn of the century had much less sexual experience (both pre- and post-marriage) than did those women born after. These results were later confirmed in Kinsey's report that almost all the increase in frequency of sexual behavior of women occurred between 1916 and 1930.

A multiplicity of factors, too numerous to integrate into this discussion, went into the re-emergence of female sexuality and the legitimization of sexual pleasure. Among these was psychoanalysis. Freud had visited America in 1909 and his impact was tremendous, coming as he did in the midst of great uncertainty about sex roles and sexuality. Although there is often a great disparity between Freud's writings and the psychoanalytic literature that became popular in the United States, both formal psychoanalytic works and the popularized psychoanalysis of the "new psychology" converged on the conclusion that the repression of sexual impulses was "bad." In liberating erotic sexuality at a time when the question of self-fulfillment loomed large in the consciousness of both critics and defenders of the social order, psychoanalysis facilitated the equation of sexual gratification with sexual fulfillment.

As popularly interpreted, Freudian psychology provided an answer to the question of "what was the nature of the female personality?" Women were passive and irrational, their nature grounded in sexually-bound, instinctually determined psychological needs. In this way psychoanalytic thought, however incorrectly understood, allowed for an updating of the female personality through the emergence of sexuality and a continuation of the notion of a biologically-based woman's nature. Simultaneously this change preserved the balance of power between men and women without too severely threatening social cohesion. Women were free to seek fulfillment, so long as it was within the boundaries of their sexuality. The flapper that emerged in the 1920's confirmed her self-worth in her value as a sexual object.

It must also be mentioned that the re-emergence of sexuality also served the larger economic needs to transform the home to a self-conscious center of consumption. Slater reminds us that Freud had said

> Two people coming together for the purpose of sexual satisfaction, in so far as they seek solitude, are making a demonstration against . . . the group feeling . . .[14]

There developed after World War I new modes in advertising, as the advertisement came not only to inform people of product availability, but also to create and manipulate product needs. Modern advertising attempted to equate product consumption with self-fulfillment, and one of the major manipulations with which this equation was created was the eroticization of commodities. The emerging advertising industry borrowed many of its ideas, and bought many of its personnel, from the ranks of the psychological professions. In this way, the sexuality that surfaced early in the twentieth century did not remain the possession of the couples who experienced it. Sexuality rather rapidly became public property, and served to undercut the accentuated threat of dyadic withdrawal that was represented by sexual intimacy.

Of course it is necessary to recognize that there is a great difference between the release of sexuality and the fulfillment of its potentiality. We know now how far from satisfactory were those newly legitimized sexual relations. We know too that attitudes and values change slowly, and that even as sexual behavior had changed, people were not always easy with even their own behaviors. Nonetheless, these changes are significant ones, and they prepare us for an examination of our own time.

However one interprets the developments of the progressive era, questions about the nature and possibilities of self-fulfill-

---

[14] Slater, *op. cit.*, p. 351.

ment could not be fully answered before sexuality itself was legitimized within relationships. If we see as one of the results of the last 50 years the legitimization of sexuality, we can understand somewhat better how we have returned to the question of the relationship between intimacy and self-fulfillment. In a certain sense then, we can say that sexuality has been "liberated" in that 1) it can be rather openly acknowledged and valued; and 2) it no longer seems confined to the sanctioned relationship of marriage. It is not enough, however, to observe that sexuality is "liberated." We need to ask as well "how has it been liberated?" and "toward what ends?" Let us briefly retrace the history of this "liberation."

In the nineteenth century emotional intimacy was severed from sexual pleasure. Sexual intercourse was accepted as an expression of and means to emotional intimacy. By itself, sexual pleasure was seen as demeaning the love between two people. Beginning in the early years of the twentieth century, sexual pleasure was readmitted to meaningful intimate relationships, and accepted as a part of that intimacy. Specifically, sexual pleasure was accepted as an aspect of self-fulfillment and self-fulfillment acknowledged as an acceptable purpose of intimate relationships. In turn, these relationships had to function to satisfy people for whom the notion of self-fulfillment had been greatly expanded. However, sexual intercourse was still taken as an indicator of emotional intimacy. Consequently, once sexual pleasure was legitimized, sexual intercourse took on more emotional significance in relationships and sexual pleasure became the indicator of emotional intimacy.

Consider the way in which the so-called recent liberation of sexuality has proceeded; primarily by again separating sexual pleasure from emotional intimacy, by lessening the importance of sexual relations. Almost all of the practices by which sexuality is brought into so-called open-relationships depend on limiting the emotional meaning of sexuality in both the primary and secondary relationships. While sexuality is made to mean less in relationships, it is still taken as a measure of self-fulfillment and advocated as the means to such.

Think also of the terms in which sexuality has been "liberated"—primarily by transforming that sexuality, once it is severed from social relations, into a technological skill. Thus we develop manuals to teach sexual techniques; and therapeutic programs to reeducate those whose technical training was inadequate. It is not only sexuality which is so transformed—sensitivity and encounter groups, human relations training, and other institutions have also developed. These too can be seen as an extension of the reduction of the interpersonal to the technological. These too remove emotionality from the social relations in which it originates and relocate it in the realm of skill.

One needs to question how, if sexuality is accepted because its significance is reduced, it can serve as a means of self-fulfillment? And if it does so function, who are the selves for whom such sexuality is self-fulfilling? Are they persons who see and experience themselves as conglomerates of technical skills, obtaining satisfaction in the proficiency of their performance? Certainly one might question whether these changes are rightly called "liberation."

Slater cites Alexander's remark that:

> *the erotic value of an action is inversely related to the degree to which it loses the freedom of choice and becomes coordinated* and subordinated to other functions and becomes a part of an organized system, of a goal structure.[15]

One fears that the seeming "liberation" of sexuality has occurred because sex has become coordinated and subordinated to that organized system, and a part of the goal structure of the most recent developments of corporate capitalism. Among those goals is the re-integration of the public and the private. At that level of abstraction, this goal neither threatens nor supports the social structure. It can be held by both critics and supporters of this system. The significant issue is on what terms this re-integration will take place. If the terms by which we under-

---

[15] *Ibid.*, p. 350.

stand both our personal identities and our most intimate relationships become the terms of the technological economy that dominates our lives, then we will participate, as have numerous generations before us, in making ourselves over into the beings that system needs us to be. In *Group Psychology and the Analysis of the Ego*, Freud remarked:

> The more they are in love, the more completely they suffice for each other . . . Even in a person who has in other respects become absorbed in a group the *directly sexual tendencies preserve a little of his individual activity*.[16]

Perhaps sexuality and emotionality are "defused" by removing them from their organic base in social relations and relocating them in the repertoire of individual technical skills. This is not to argue against teaching people about sexuality and sexual technique. There are ways in which technical training is potentially liberating. But technical training, by itself, severed from social relations, directs people toward performance not fulfillment. Once sexual relations become performances sexuality no longer threatens to promote dyadic withdrawal. Rather, in Alexander's words, sexual behavior "becomes coordinated and subordinated to other functions." If this analysis is correct it suggests that sexuality will lose its "erotic value" and the "sexual tendencies" will be unable to preserve individuality. Rather, sexual activity will become a means of reabsorbing the person into the group. This analysis complements Marcuse's discussion of the effects of the sexualization of the work world, a phenomenon he designates as repressive desublimation.

> It has often been noted that advanced industrial civilization operates with a greater degree of sexual freedom—"operates" in the sense that the latter becomes a market value and a factor of social mores. Without ceasing to be an instrument of labor the body is allowed to exhibit its sexual features in the everyday work world and in work relations . .

---

[16] *Ibid.*, p. 351.

> The sexy office and sales girls, the handsome, virile junior executive and floor walker are highly marketable commodities . . .[17]

There are other ways as well in which the criteria and values of the economic sphere permeate the interpersonal and personal under the guise of liberation. Consider the conception of intimate relationships represented by the modern "personalized" marriage contract. Jan Dizard has observed how the increasingly common practice of writing specific contracts for marriages, while it appears to make explicit the rights and obligations, duties and expectations of the "partners," represents a further incursion of the values and conceptions of the business world into the interpersonal.[18] Contracts are necessary in the business world, because the parties must assume each other interested in and motivated by self-interest in the most narrow sense of that term. Presumably a business relationship progresses so long as it continues to serve the narrow self-interest of the marriage "partners." One might wonder whether such an orientation to marriage precludes the possibility of a love based upon "unselfish" love. Some might argue that the historical record provides ample reason to distrust the "costs" of interpersonal intimacy, particularly for women. Still it hardly seems that the writing of contracts has made the business world a model to emulate for personal relationships.

The analysis developed here suggests that we should return to the questions raised by the early feminists: how are we to define self-fulfillment? what is the relationship between intimacy and self-fulfillment? These are, of course, enormous questions. They are anchored in our conception of the person and our beliefs about social relations. I suspect we still think of the person as indivisible, we still imagine fulfillment as occurring in spite of rather than through social relations. I believe our culture creates persons for whom what appears as self-actualization and genuinely satisfying relationships with others are incompatible. This was recognized many years ago

---

[17] Herbert Marcuse, *One Dimensional Man* (Boston: Beacon, 1964), p. 74.
[18] Jan Dizard, personal communication.

by Karen Horney, when she spoke of the "neurotic personality of our time." By this she meant

> not only . . . that there are neurotic persons having essential peculiarities in common, but also that these basic similarities are essentially produced by the difficulties existing in our time and culture.[19]

She went on to discuss how, because of systematic features of our culture

> the great majority of us have to struggle with problems of competition, fears of failure, emotional isolation, distrust of others and of our own selves . . .[20]

One of the main features of the personality who emerged from the struggle with these problems was the "neurotic need for affection."

> We all want to be liked and to feel appreciated, but in neurotic persons the dependence on affection or approval is disproportionate to the real significance which other persons have for their lives. Although we all wish to be liked by persons of whom we are fond, in neurotics there is an indiscriminate hunger for appreciation or affection, regardless of whether they care for the person concerned or whether the judgment of that person has any meaning for them . . . there is a marked contradiction between their wish for affection and their own capacity for feeling or giving it.[21]

In the context established here, we could reinterpret the neurotic need for affection as the modal response to the "competition, fears of failure, emotional isolation, distrust of others, and our own selves." In other words, from this reading it would appear that we have asked more of relationships than they can give. This is precisely what defines a neurotic response. We were attempting to satisfy in personal relationships needs that did not originate in and could not be satisfied by those

[19] Karen Horney, *The Neurotic Personality of Our Time* (New York: Norton, 1937), p. 34.

[20] *Ibid.*

[21] *Ibid.*, p. 36-37.

relationships. Relationships so burdened, necessarily fail, and in failing they exacerbate the sense of emotional isolation, distrust of others and ourselves, etc., from which people seek release and relief. From this perspective the tendency today to make relationships "mean" less can be seen as a "more realistic" assessment of the potentialities of interpersonal intimacy. However, this overlooks the fact that the demands that had been placed on intimate relationships were themselves important and legitimate demands; it was only inappropriate to expect that they could be met by love and intimacy. It appears that the direction in which we are moving today means abandoning those demands and settling for less, for what we can get. What we can get are commodities and we have moved toward a new form of consumerism in which the products consumed are other persons who are appreciated in terms of their ability to satisfy our fragmented needs. The personal sections of our newspapers and periodicals are filled with advertisements for these commodities. Computer matching, mate swapping, and "sensitivity" weekends all participate in this transformation of persons into commodities. In this way we come also to ask too little of social relations. Ultimately I think we must turn to a restructuring of society. The needs that have led us to ask both too much and too little of social relations have not disappeared, nor will they. Clearly, a social structure does not guarantee the actualization of persons. Certainly the elimination of economic and sexual inequality, the abolition of alienated labor is not the same as satisfying, passionate, and loving relations. But I cannot believe that such relations are possible between people who are not free to be equals.

☆

WOMEN'S LIFE IN UTOPIA: THE SHAKER EXPERIMENT IN SEXUAL EQUALITY REAPPRAISED — 1810 TO 1860

D'ANN CAMPBELL

"SOMETHING very essential is missing in our studies of communes and communities," complained the sociologist Jessie Bernard, who noted that researchers must "discover or uncover the *female* structure."[1] Why is this structure so vital? The answer may be two-fold. First, such information can broaden, deepen or complete our sketches of the communitarian experiment. Scholars have traditionally interpreted these societies primarily from male source materials. We can now reanalyze these histories on the basis of their two constantly interacting constituents: men and women. Second, after gaining an improved concept of the communitarian lifestyle, we can more accurately portray the needs, interests, and contradictions of American society during the antebellum period. As Paul Conkin has explained, a utopian society "usually reflects, in reverse, the dominant fears of an individual or an age." As other historians have suggested, radical movements "by the very fact of their effort to break free of convention [are] particularly accurate reflectors of the larger social contours of their days . . . here lies their greatest value to historians."[2] Are these claims justified? Will an examination of the role of women in these experiments yield essential information on the nature of communal experiments, as well as on the internal stresses of the larger American society? By focusing on unused manuscript materials of women participants in one communal experiment, this essay may answer these questions.

[1] Speech by Jessie Bernard, Conference on Communes, Northern Illinois University, April 8, 1975.

[2] Paul K. Conkin, *Two Paths to Utopia* (Lincoln, Nebraska, 1964), v; Aileen Kraditor, "American Radical Historians on Their Heritage," *Past and Present*, LXVI, 142-143 (Aug., 1972); both quoted in Paul Boyer, "A Joyful Noyes: Reassessing America's Utopian Tradition," *Reviews in American History*, III, 27 (March, 1975).

The Shaker experiment—founded and perfected in the New England area—serves as a logical, data-rich, starting point. It was the largest and most permanent of the early nineteenth-century religious communal groups, reaching its apogee from 1810 to 1860, and leaving behind voluminous records, letters, and diaries. Moreover, Shaker communities are the best examples of utopian designs reflecting sexual equality. They were founded by Mother Ann Lee, the only woman to pioneer an American religious communal experiment that lasted longer than one generation.[3] Specific questions to be addressed to Shaker literature include: How did the political, economic, demographic, and social structures of the Shaker society reflect their doctrine of sexual equality? What were the social and economic backgrounds of the Shaker women? Finally, what may have enticed them to join and remain in such an experiment?

A dual system of government with half the offices filled by women, the other half by men, served as the cornerstone of the Shaker system because Shakers believed that God embodied both male and female elements. Just as Christ had incarnated the male principle of the Godhead, "Mother" Ann Lee had been chosen to embody the female principle to serve as God's second representative on Earth. Mother Ann's message was that since the Deity had forgiven both Adam and Eve and their earthly descendants, men and women must now be united and treated equally in the sight of God.[4] A summary

[3] For a list of "successful communal settlements" during the nineteenth century see Rosabeth Moss Kanter, *Commitment and Community* (Cambridge, 1972).

[4] Frederick W. Evans, *Shakers: Compendium of the Origin, History, Principles, Rules, and Regulations, Government, and Doctrines of the United Society of Believers in Christ's Second Appearing* (New York, 1859), 23, 103, 107; Calvin Green and Seth Y. Wells, Editors, *A Brief Exposition of the Established Principles and Regulations of the United Society of Believers Called Shakers* (Albany, 1834), 22, 31, 38, 51; Marguerite F. Melcher, *The Shaker Adventure* (Cleveland, 1941), 10; see also: Edward D. Andrews, *The People Called Shakers* (New York, 1963) or any of his other books on Shakers; John Humphrey Noyes, *History of American Socialisms* (New York, 1870); J. P. MacLean, *Shakers of Ohio* (Columbus, 1907); Mary L. Richmond, *Shaker Literature, A Bibliography* (Hancock, Mass., 1977).

view of the Shaker governmental institutions illustrates the genuineness of this professed doctrine of sexual equality. Guiding all eighteen communities was the Ministry composed of two men and two women selected for life. All Shakers were consulted concerning major changes of policy, but one of the four ministers, at times a woman, at other times a man, had the ultimate voice.

Consistent with Shaker teachings, each family or settlement employed both sexes as leaders: Elders and Eldresses oversaw spiritual affairs on local levels, Deacons and Deaconesses guarded temporal concerns, and a board of Trustees managed finances. In short, Shaker men and women occupied a variety of positions in their hierarchical structure. Not all had equal power; spiritual development, not gender, was the basis for distinction. Under this arrangement, some women rapidly developed administrative skills and became charismatic leaders. For example, Mother Ann Lee founded and directed the movement, and Mother Lucy Wright served as its presiding genius during the Shakers' golden period of expansion in the early nineteenth century.

While the Shaker political creed gave women an equal voice with men, it was not designed to appeal exclusively to women. Had this been so, Shaker women could have formed a convent and existed in a solitary retreat on the borders of the larger society. Shaker doctrines, however, preached salvation for both men and women, and for all persons adopting the Shaker creed. Furthermore, if the Shakers had wanted to favor women they might have apportioned offices on the basis of the female-male membership ratio. Since more women than men joined the Shaker sect throughout its existence, women would have occupied more positions, double or triple the number held by men. Had this been the practice, men would probably have felt uncomfortable, left, or refused to join the movement. To prevent this, the Shakers engineered a "male quota system," although it was never so-called. Half the offices were reserved for men despite the fact that males were always a minority in the membership.

A separate but equal philosophy also characterized Shaker economics. Work done by either sex was not ranked as superior or more important than the other, although these celibates felt it was dangerous for men and women to work in close proximity. Journalist Charles Nordhoff asked a Shaker man if women were allowed to work as blacksmiths. "No," he answered, "because this would bring men and women into relations we do not think wise." By implication, this Shaker did not think women incapable of becoming good blacksmiths. The separation was based on moral rather than upon ethical or economic grounds.[5]

Unlike contemporary accounts by Shaker men, many women's diaries outlined in minute detail the activities of the *entire* community. One feminine diarist recorded a week's activities: "The men butchered four beef creatures and commenced thrashing. . . . Young boys began school. . . . cooking shifts rotated and most women began the fall cleaning. . . . The aged sisters at the East shop commenced spinning the mops . . . the young sisters at the new shop set up their two wheels. . . ."[6] Efficiency of labor-saving measures dominated the assignments. Men did the heavy work even in the domestic quarters, and undertook duties usually assigned to women such as picking fruit or carding wool during rainy weather or odd times before meals.[7] Such actions indicate that Shakers were more concerned with getting the work done than with worrying about which jobs were reserved for men and which for women. On the whole, however, women performed tasks

[5] Charles Nordhoff, *The Communistic Societies of the United States* (New York, 1875), 166.

[6] Journals and diaries of the Shakers are found in the Shaker MSS Collection, Western Reserve Historical Society, Cleveland, Ohio (listed in Kermit Pike, *A Guide to Shaker Manuscripts* [Cleveland, 1974]) hereafter referred to as Shaker MSS followed by series and volume number. See Shaker MSS, V, B, Crossman journal (no. 143); see also Hampton journal (no. 263); no. 41 Susan H. Myrick's journal (Harvard, 1834-1842); nos. 44-46 Grove B. Blanchard's journal (Harvard, 1836-1844); no. 50 Harvard Sisters' journal (Harvard, 1840-1844); no. 127 Annie William's journal (Mt. Lebanon, 1832-1855); no. 231 Church Family's daily record (Union Village, 1805-1896).

[7] Shaker MSS, V, B, Church Family diary (no. 33).

inside the communal household and men outside. Jobs were often rotated.[8]

What is described above is a preindustrial nineteenth-century household economy. The division of labor was traditional, because the Shakers did not have to allocate fifty percent of their blacksmith, carpenter or field jobs to women to achieve equal status for them, as some twentieth-century feminists insist is necessary. The point is that on the basis of their religious doctrines and government structure, Shaker women were considered on equal terms with men. Shakers could thus arrange for women to perform the tasks for which they had been trained or were best equipped physically to do. For the Shakers, equality for women did not mean "doing what men do."

Shakers believed that abolishing nuclear families and forbidding sexual relations were essential to the integrity of their creed. In the traditional family the husband acted as if he "owned" his wife. Indeed during the early and mid-nineteenth century, women have been classified as "overgrown children" or "perpetual wards," first of their fathers and later of their husbands.[9] According to Shaker doctrine, both feelings of superiority and possessiveness by men, and of inferiority and submissiveness by women must be overcome to achieve salvation.

In addition, Shakers maintained that sexual intercourse,

[8] For excellent source materials on Shaker men and women and their work, see Series V, B volumes, especially no. 28, no. 29, Sister Polly Lee's journal (Groveland, 1843-1871); no. 50 Sisters of Harvard journal (Harvard, 1840-1844); no. 92 memoranda kept by an unidentified sister (Mt. Lebanon, 1835, 1836); no. 93, no. 94 Elizabeth Lovegrove's journal (Mt. Lebanon, 1827); no. 128 Betsy Bates' journal (Mt. Lebanon, 1833-1835); no. 134 Betsy Crosmann's journal (Mt. Lebanon, 1848-1872); no. 158 Unidentified Sister's journal (Mt. Lebanon, 1860-1866); no. 263 Emily Hampton's journal (Union Village, 1851). See also Edward D. and Faith Andrews, *Work and Worship: The Economic Order of the Shakers* (Greenwich, 1974), 109-136.

[9] Sarah Margaret (Fuller) Ossoli, *Women in the Nineteenth Century and Kindred Papers Relating to the Sphere, Condition and Duties of Women* (Boston, 1893), 72-73; Eleanor Flexner, *Century of Struggle* (New York, 1959), 7; see Nancy F. Cott, *The Bonds of Womanhood: "Woman's Sphere" in New England, 1780-1835* (New Haven, 1977).

even when sanctified by marriage, was the main root of evil. Mother Ann's heavenly inspired instructions on how to avoid this primal sin were to abolish traditional marriage and deny any sexual congress.[10] Mother Ann had personal as well as scriptural sanctions for their abandonment. Fearing childbirth, she remembered so great was her anguish that bloody sweat pressed through the pores of her skin, tears flowed down her cheeks until the skin cleaved off and she wrung her hands until the blood gushed from under her nails.[11] Even worse, after such suffering Mother Ann lost all of her four children at birth or during infancy. Scarred by her ordeals, it was not surprising that Mother Ann concluded that as long as women engaged in sexual relations, their lives would be punctuated by physical pain and the threat of imminent death for themselves and their children.

The appeal of Shaker life for women of childbearing and child-rearing ages is revealed by an examination of the demographic composition of these communities. Shaker settlements averaged a 2:1 female to male sex ratio but ranged from nearly 1:1 to as great as 5:1 ratios. Specific age data calculated from an analysis of nine Shaker communities using the 1810, 1830, and 1850 manuscript censuses give a much more graphic and accurate picture of the settlements' makeup. Shaker men and women have been divided into categories of younger (under 20), years of childbearing and child rearing (20-45) and older (over 45). The sexes were approximately equal in the under-20 age group, but in the 20-45 grouping—the main years of childbearing and child rearing—women predominated by 2 to 1 or even 3 to 1 ratios. In the oldest group, ages 45 and up, the ratios continued to be predominately female, but not by quite so large a ratio.[12]

10 Calvin Green and Seth Wells, *Summary View of the Millennial Church* (Albany, 1848), 107.

11 Andrews, *Shakers*, 8.

12 United States Census of Population, Manuscript returns for 1810, 1830, 1850. For 1810 Enfield, N. H.; Canterbury, N. H.; Hancock, Mass.; Tyringham, Mass. For 1830 Watervliet, N. Y.; South Union, Ky. For 1850 Mt. Lebanon, N. Y.; Hancock, Mass.; South Union, Ky.; Enfield, N. H.; Union Village, Ohio;

To see how the Shakers contrasted demographically with their neighbors, one region, Upstate New York and one county, Logan County, Kentucky, were compared with the Shaker settlements in the area. In Upstate New York (with the Shaker settlement figures included), women comprised 48 to 49 percent of the entire population. In the Shaker settlement of Watervliet, women made up the majority of the population in all three life-cycle stages and ranged from 59 percent of the youth and 60 percent of the old to a high of 65 percent in the middle grouping.

The substantially larger proportion of women in the Shaker settlements than in nearby areas is also illustrated by comparing the 1830 ratios of women in the South Union settlement with those in all of Logan County, Kentucky. In Logan County (with the Shaker settlement figures included) women made up 49 percent of the population. In contrast, women comprised 58 percent of the Shaker settlement population. More specifically, women constituted 52 percent of the younger, 62 percent of the heavy childbearing and child-rearing class, and 57 percent of the older members. Twenty years later, Shaker women constituted 48 percent of the younger members (down a bit from 52 percent), 63 percent of the older members (up 1 percent) and 77 percent of the middle-aged members, a sharp jump of 15 percent in the largest group which gave the community a three-to-one women-to-men ratio in this potentially most fertile category.

While a detailed analysis of all Shaker settlements over the century is needed, this sampling indicates a significant demographic pattern differing from the surrounding communities, counties, even regions, and which varied by birth cohorts or generations. The significant female bulge in the child-rearing group would argue that the Shaker colonies were a haven for

---

Watervliet, N. Y. The female proportion in sample Shaker communities was, for the under 20 group, 45 percent in 1810, 56 percent in 1830 and 48 percent in 1850. For the 20-44 group, the proportions were 65 percent, 63 percent, and 57 percent, respectively. For the over 45 group, the rates were 57 percent, 59 percent, and 59 percent.

women who preferred celibacy to traditional marriage and its concomitant dangers to their own lives and to their possible offspring.

Although much has been made of the Shaker spirit of Christian brotherhood, little or nothing has been written about Shaker sisterhood, which also developed by separating the sexes. Actually sisterhood was an integral part of both the Shaker and the larger American society. As Carroll Smith-Rosenberg recently demonstrated, "devotion to and love of other women became a plausible and socially accepted form of interaction in the nineteenth century" stimulated in part by "rigid gender-role differentiation within the family and within society as a whole."[13] Smith-Rosenberg argues that marriage caused high levels of intense anxiety for many women. Perhaps the large number of women joining the Shakers at the time they would traditionally be raising a family reflected this inability for some women to make necessary adjustments to the married state.

If Smith-Rosenberg is correct in believing that a "specifically female world did indeed develop, a world built around a generic and unself-conscious pattern of single-sex or homosocial network," then the Shaker settlements with their rigid separation of the sexes should present primary examples of such female structures.[14] Diaries of Shaker women were filled with such sentiments for their fellow women within each settlement and for women in other settlements. Visits as well as correspondence were recorded as frequent and rewarding. In one sister's record of a week's visitation schedule, "Sister Harriet comes here, Elder Sister Hannah goes to the second order. . . . Four sisters and brothers go to New York. . . . Sisters Ann, Prudence, and Florinda and three girls call here and then go to the other families. . . . Sisters Caroline and Marcia came down

[13] Carroll Smith-Rosenberg, "The Female World of Love and Ritual; Relations between Women in Nineteenth Century America," *Signs, Journal of Women in Culture and Society*, I, 9 (Autumn, 1975).

[14] Smith-Rosenberg, 1, 9, 20, 21, 28.

to help weave carpets."[15] Women corresponded with their new friends, exchanging such comments as "I was so excited to have visited with you," or "thank you so much on behalf of all your Hancock sisters." They also exchanged presents and cherished their attachments. Some visits were remembered for decades—at least one visit for over fifty years by both the surviving hosts and guests.[16] Whether these attachments were physical or not is difficult to document. Although there are extensive denunciations of heterosexual love, I have not encountered a single explicit reference to or condemnation of homosexual behavior. However, as Smith-Rosenberg pointed out, physical or nonphysical but very deep attachments between women were generally "socially acceptable."[17] The private accounts by Shaker women helped recreate an atmosphere of excitement, vivacity, and closeness of community members which has been largely missing in the published accounts. Most important, since so much human warmth and exchange of information were generated by these visits, Shaker sisterhood must have substantially strengthened the Shaker network and have helped the separate settlements maintain a unity of human affection and purpose.

The sexes were not always separated, since religious festivals and nightly gatherings were attended by both sexes. Cross-community occasions were made possible by extended traveling of mixed Shaker groups. As one Shaker woman described these visits, "Brothers Daniel and John visited the brethern while we visited the sisters . . . then we changed . . . we had a

[15] Shaker MSS, VI, B, Crossman journal (no. 143); see also Church Family diary (no. 33), Sisters of Harvard journal (no. 50), Bates journal (no. 128), Hampton journal (no. 263), no. 2 "Journal of what took place on December 25th" (Alfred, 1845), no. 13 Anna Grange's journal (Enfield, Conn., 1842-1885), no. 24, no. 25 Daily journal of Mary Dryer (Groveland, 1839-1846), no. 39 Lucy Ann Hammond's journal (Harvard, 1830), no. 141 Prudence Merrell and Eliza Sharp's account of a journey west (Mt. Lebanon, 1847), no. 346 Polly J. Reed's journal (Watervliet, N. Y., 1876).

[16] Shaker MSS, V, B, December 25th journal (no. 2), Hammon journal (no. 39).

[17] Smith-Rosenberg, "Female World," 1, 8, 24.

very good time." Another remembered that "after breakfast Brother Rufus came to see me, he was very free, and talked about the brethern and sisters at Harvard."[18] Shaker men and women often traveled together by horseback, sleighs, or by coach for longer journeys. This is not to suggest, however, that Shaker men and women were constantly commingling, but rather that our portrait of a complete division between the sexes—except for the famous after-dinner conversation period—needs reexamination. In addition, male and female friendships, deep as well as superficial, were integral parts of Shaker society.

While we have already suggested some religious and personal reasons why women might have wanted to join the Shakers, exact motivations are difficult to pinpoint. What is needed for an improved understanding of the phenomena is a series of studies of the Shaker converts. My collection of biographical information taken from testimonial accounts of eighty-five women living between the 1820's and 1840's in Shaker settlements[19] illuminates their needs, interests, and probably their motivations for joining the Shakers.

Like many religiously oriented people, a search for eternal salvation was the reason most often listed for joining the Shaker settlements. Many of these women had previous religious training and strict moral upbringings. In fact, most joined the Shakers after attending one of their revivals and deciding that they wanted to be among the saved. As one convert explained, "When I came to the age of adult years, I found myself in a miserable situation, lost from God by reason

18 Shaker MSS, V, B, no. 30 Cynthia Dryer's journal (Groveland, 1846-1850); see also, Hammond journal (no. 39), Sisters of Harvard journal (no. 50), Williams journal (no. 127), Crossman journal (no. 143), and Hampton journal (no. 263).

19 All Shaker women who could be identified from the journals, diaries, and testimonies and had some basic biographical or autobiographical information given for them were used for my analysis. The names and information gained about these women are contained in the following series, volumes, and folders. Shaker MSS, VI, A, folders no. 2, no. 4, no. 5, no. 6, no. 7, no. 9, no. 11; VI, B, no. 13, no. 19, no. 39, no. 49, no. 52; plus all women's diaries and journals listed above under series V, B.

of sin and knew no way to find union and acceptance with him." Another confessed, "When I was about eighteen years old my trouble of mind increased to such a degree that I could not rest nights." And a third stated, "Previous to my coming among the Believers [Shakers], my mind was often powerfully wrought upon the spirit of conviction, and I would go away by myself and kneel and cry to God to teach me how to be good."[20] This girl joined the Shakers shortly after her tenth birthday. Because of their intense religious feelings, these women wanted to devote their lives to achieving salvation. Since the Shakers emphasized religious training, their communities offered excellent preparatory retreats for such spiritually minded girls with or without their parents, and young women with or without their husbands. Although most of them joined their parents or their husbands, at least one-third broke familial ties to follow the Shaker creed.

Whatever its importance, religious motivations alone cannot fully explain why these women joined the Shaker movement rather than the multitude of other religious groups also promising salvation. This was an evangelical age with all varieties of religious sects promising almost immediate salvation. Perhaps it was also usual for the masses of people to phrase unconsciously their motivations in religious terms.

Consequently, we must attempt to probe deeper into the common backgrounds, letters, and diaries to find other possible motivations. Fortunately, available materials provide information which can help to indicate other reasons for joining and remaining Shakers.

The women converts shared common economic and social backgrounds. They came from generally large families of six to ten children which were headed by farmers, artisans or backwoods storekeepers. To keep the family solvent any "excess" daughters—not absolutely necessary to perform household tasks—were commonly sent out to other families. One

[20] Shaker MSS, V, A, folder no. 4, testimonies of Mehetable Farrington and Anna Cogswell (Hancock, 1827, 1849); folder no. 11, testimony of Lucy Myrick (Watervliet, 1816-1871).

woman remembered that at age nine, "I was put out to strangers, where I suffered many hardships and by unkind dealings I lost my health. . . ."[21] Indeed, more than one-fourth of the women surveyed had been "bound out" or served similar apprenticeships. About half of the families of the women studied joined the Shakers as a unit, quite frequently with many young children, some mere babies.

It was probably a great relief to converts to realize that their children would be fed and clothed until they reached adulthood even if the parents died. One Shaker sister remembered that her parents joined when she was only three and both died before she turned eight. As she explained, "Here I have lived ever since and have found kind, loving friends who have ever been ready to help me in time of need, yet truly I have found parents in the gospel."[22] Perhaps economic security was as much if not more of a factor than eternal salvation in these women's and their families' decisions to adopt and maintain the Shaker creed.

Not only were many of these nineteenth-century families financially insecure but many were unstable. Upon the death of one or both parents, a family might completely disintegrate. Just over half of the women surveyed came from such broken homes. In general, if the father died and if a Shaker settlement was nearby, the widowed mother might bring her children "amongst the people of God."[23] If the mother died, the father was more likely to leave some of the children with relatives or neighbors. If neglected or ill-treated, these children might eventually end up in a Shaker settlement. A third factor, a search for an emotionally stable, socially, economically, and culturally supportive environment to serve as a substitute for the typical nuclear family life-style, brought women to the

[21] Shaker MSS, VI, A, folder no. 2 testimony of Cilenda Wardwell (Enfield, Conn., 1816, 1843); folder no. 11 testimony by Abigail Worster (Watervliet, 1816-1871).

[22] Shaker MSS, VI, A, folder no. 2, testimony of Betsey Haskell (Enfield, Conn., 1843).

[23] Shaker MSS, VI, B, no. 49, testimony of Sarah Pool (Pleasant Hill, Ky., 1841).

Shaker settlements either as bereaved mothers or fatherless girls.

By providing an extended family network for members of broken families, the Shakers appealed to more than a small minority of women and their children. It has been estimated that only one Massachusetts female in five born in the early or mid-nineteenth century completed a "typical" or "preferred" life cycle (marrying, having children, and surviving jointly with her husband to age fifty-five).[24] This pattern was probably characteristic of the region of Shaker settlements from New Hampshire to Kentucky. Men as well as women lived broken life-cycle patterns. A sampling of seventy-five autobiographical male accounts from the 1820's and 1840's demonstrates that most Shaker men were also from broken families.[25]

Because little is actually known about the daily life of ordinary families before 1850, it is difficult at this stage of the investigation to do more than surmise about the alternatives open to members of broken families besides joining the Shakers. Undoubtedly most depended upon their relatives. Perhaps those who joined were isolated geographically or emotionally from their kinfolk. Before the 1840's Shaker communities functioned as community orphanages, and later as old people's homes. Although the first orphanages were then being established, old people's homes were rare until after the Civil War.[26] Since a large number of Shaker converts came from broken homes, we should try to see if they had any kin in the area by attempting to link surnames from the surrounding communities. Such a study will be a time-consuming process. The place of birth, information provided by the 1850 federal

[24] Peter R. Uhlenberg, "A Study of Cohort Life Cycles: Cohorts of Native Born Massachusetts Women, 1830-1920," *Population Studies* (1969), 415.

[25] The seventy-five Shaker men used for this experiment and the basic biographical or autobiographical information about them are contained in Shaker MSS, VI, A, folders no. 2, no. 4, no. 5, no. 11, and VI, B, no. 49, no. 52.

[26] David J. Rothman, *The Discovery of the Asylum: Social Order and Disorder in the New Republic* (Boston, 1971), 206, 207. See also Homer Folks, *The Care of Destitute, Neglected and Delinquent Children* (Albany, N. Y., 1900), 30-36.

manuscript census, shows that men and women from widely dispersed places had come together in Shaker communities.

Not all visitors to the Shakers were convinced that the Shaker life-style offered a utopia for its female members. One such skeptical soul, Abigail Alcott, concluded after visiting a Shaker community in the 1840's that "There is servitude somewhere, I have no doubt. There is a fat sleek comfortable look about the men, and among the women there is a stiff awkward reserve that belongs to neither sublime resignation nor divine hope."[27] However, the journals, diaries, letters, and other accounts left by Shaker women seem to refute Alcott's observations.

In summary, women joined the Shakers to satisfy the basic needs unfullfilled by their own families and communities, especially stability, security, and a promise of eternal salvation. Fear of sexual relations and possible consequences for both the women and their offspring must have also played an important, but an almost impossible to document, role in these women's decisions. A brief review of the childhood of Rhoda Blake illustrates how interrelated these motivations could be. Born in 1808, at Savoy, Massachusetts, Rhoda was the child of a second marriage of her father and mother, each with two children when they married. They proceeded to have eight more children of whom only four survived infancy. To supplement the family income, the girls learned to weave but in 1811 when the local cotton factories switched to power looms and "we were thrown out of that line of employment. . . . Father tried farming. . . . Mother tried managing a hotel and restaurant." In 1816 a religious revival excited their community. The family, curious about the Shakers, visited them and left impressed. "Father decided to finish the harvest and unite with the Believers." Unfortunately he was "killed in an accident soon after." His wife, Olive, settled the estate and decided to join the extended Shaker family, bringing with her the unmarried children. About twelve years old at this time,

[27] Abigail Alcott, Diary, July 2, 1843 quoted in O. Shepard, *Journal of Bronson Alcott* (Boston, 1938), 153.

Rhoda joined the Shakers and remained with them until her death in 1891, presumably without much regret for missing the normal cycle of sexuality, childbearing, and child rearing.[28] This example portrays the intermeshing of social, economic, and religious factors which in individual cases may defy both ranking and differentiation, but which when studied from a group perspective, can be used by the historian to understand women like Rhoda. These materials also highlight the economic insecurity, family instability, and precariousness of life during the early and mid-nineteenth century.

Because Shakers firmly adhered to the doctrines of celibacy, they were constantly forced to recruit new members from outside their ranks. As long as nondenominational revivals inspired thousands of persons, the Shakers could convert likely subjects. After 1838, however, the Shakers developed their separate revivals based on spiritualism, cutting themselves off from the general evangelistic movement. These revivals were led by adolescent girls, apparently those most fearful of the family roles traditional society had in store for them. After the mid-1840's the Shaker revivals burned themselves out; thereafter the communities began to lose hold of the orphans and children in their care. Only a small proportion of such children remained in the community. The younger generation of Shakers, without firsthand experience of the spiritualist revival, became alienated from their foster families. Collapse was inevitable; Shakerism by the 1850's had become an old people's religion, a religion of remembrance of bygone glory and excitement. It was the adolescents who joined in the last great upsurge of the revivals in the 1840's that kept the Shaker society functioning, at least partially, until the turn of the century and beyond.

However transitory Shaker society was, it does provide an historical American example in which women functioned as the political, economic, and social equals of men. They did so in a nonauthoritarian society inspired by religious ethics

[28] Shaker MSS, VI, B, no. 3, Rhoda Blake, [a sketch of her life, experience and recollections, copied and amended by A. G. Hollister, 1904].

whose chief instrument in arriving at its main goal was the overturning of marriage, one of society's oldest and most venerated institutions, and by the attempted abolition of one of the strongest drives, sexual intercourse. In the light of society's current search for new standards of intersexual relations, an appreciation of the Shaker contribution that goes beyond their marvelous furniture would illuminate the benefits and the costs of true equality.

SEX AND SELF-CONTROL: MIDDLE-CLASS COURTSHIP IN AMERICA, 1770-1870

Ellen K. Rothman

In February 1834, during his last winter at Brown, Elias Nason wrote to his sweetheart Mira Bigelow, at home in Massachusetts: "My college life is well nigh over." Like so many educated young men in the early Republic, his immediate plans led to teaching. "I think I shall take a school in Grafton when I leave here," he announced, and he hoped that marriage to Mira would soon follow. "Can you come to me?" he asked. "How I hope you will . . . Why how happily we would live together. To *see* & *hear* & *touch* each other every day — And tell our joys & sorrows to each other — and to make things *comfortable*." In the future Elias envisioned, he and Mira would enjoy emotional and physical intimacy; they would be both mates and friends. During their two-year courtship, they had already developed "a multitude of associations." Elias mused, "My heart loves to dwell on the scenes that we have passed together — all the *walks* and *kisses* and *larks* and *sings* and *thoughts* and *meetings* and *partings* and *clingings*."[1]

Elias Nason's rhapsody on his and Mira's past and his anticipation of their future capture the quality of early nineteenth-century courtship. Young middle-class men and women possessed a degree of autonomy and privacy that allowed them to develop genuine closeness in their relationships with one another. Believing that candor was both a sign of and a safeguard for intimacy, they felt free to express their feelings openly in what they said and how they behaved. One kind of behavior in particular concerns us here: sex. Separating sexual behavior from the ideas and feelings that stimulate and are stimulated by it is unfortunate but necessary. A short essay could not possibly do justice to the total experience of intimacy — its psychological, attitudinal, and affective dimensions.[2] What follows, therefore, focuses on the behavioral — especially sexual — aspects of courtship.

The evidence is drawn from correspondence, diaries, and other personal documents generated by 160 middle-class men and women, living east of the Mississippi and north of the Mason Dixon line, who reached courting age in the century after 1770.[3] Although they had greater opportunity for education, professional achievement, and material security than most young Americans in the nineteenth century, they did not enjoy the wealth or status of the elite. Many, it is true, went on to careers in public life, a few even to fame and fortune, but at the time of courtship such distinctions lay in the future. These were middle-class youths without the resources of the rich or the disadvantages of the poor. Some left only occasional clues to courtship — callers received, walks taken, visits exchanged — while others recorded their feelings and activities in detail. Those who wrote explicitly about sex were unusual, but we have no reason to believe that their experiences were exceptional.

At the outset, we need to resolve two problems of definition. Certain behavior would have been considered sexual in the nineteenth century and is easily categorized as such today. However, many other acts, and many of the images associated with romantic love, would have had a different meaning for the men and women recording them than they do for us reading those records. They were not sexual in the sense that they led to coitus (although sometimes they did), but they involved the physical expression of affection. In this study, sexual refers to any physical intimacy between a man and a woman and to the feelings and fantasies aroused by that intimacy.

We also need a working definition — and a social context — for courtship. Webster's offers us "social activities leading to engagement and marriage." Sometimes a walk in the woods ended with a proposal, sometimes with an embrace, sometimes with nothing more than a casual parting. Do we consider it courtship? Men and women of the early Republic would have called it courting but not courtship. Only the latter implied a progression towards marriage. The verb "to court" was used more broadly to describe socializing between unmarried men and women. Thus, the term courtship is used here only in reference to activities that were *expected* to lead to marriage; those of a more casual or communal nature are called courting.

There was a wide range of activities that led to marriage only in the sense of bringing potential partners together. In school and church, in field and factory, at dances and parties, middle-class young women and men shared the tasks and pleasures of daily life. They did so with a freedom that contradicts our old stereotypes of Victorian courtship as well as newer theories of sexual segregation.[4] Even as gender role distinctions sharpened in the course of the nineteenth century, young unmarried men and women remained relatively unconstrained by them. It was the "home" and the "world" that defined the proper spheres for Victorian women and men, but most single women were not yet responsible for a home nor were most young men completely on their own in the world. Marital status was, after all, critical to the fulfillment of expectations for True Womanhood. Young *unmarried* men and women were able to move more freely — and perhaps experiment with greater closeness — than their married elders.[5]

At the end of the eighteenth and the beginning of the nineteenth centuries, gender roles still reflected a division of labor more than of "spheres;" women in the dairy and men in the flax barn had not yet become "True Women" protecting the "home" while their men folk faced the "world." By the time they were teenagers, young people were semidependent members of their parents' households; they made their own decisions about work, education, and religion, within limits defined by the resources and values of their family and community.[6] They encountered each other in meeting, schoolroom, and shop; they met on the lanes and commons of the village and in the houses of neighbors and kin. Young men and women born in the years after Independence enjoyed a high level of self-determination. This meant not only that they were free to choose their own mates but that they socialized with little parental supervision.

In groups they went berrying, riding, picnicking; they sang and danced together at parties, balls, and at the singing and dancing schools that were popular in small towns and villages. Although these events were often group affairs, twosomes were not discouraged. A young man and woman who were interested in each other could spend time alone as well as in the company of friends and relations. They were allowed to go off walking or riding together, to sit alone in the parlor late at night, and to make unchaperoned visits to family and friends. David Shepard, Jr., for example, was living on his parents' farm in Chester, Massachusetts in 1798, the year he turned twenty-one. His affections belonged to Ellen Savage, a young woman whom he favored with invitations to balls, poetic verses, and stolen looks in church. David had never declared an intention to marry Ellen; even so, the two of them freely exchanged letters, thoughts, and caresses. His journal is full of entries like these:

> Sunday 27 May . . . proceeded on down to Capt. Plum's where I found my girl — passed the time here till about two . . . then walked home with my Ellen, where I found the little bed room empty and a good fire, by which I spent the evening sweetly with my little girl — gave her the fictitious letter I wrote.
>
> Wednesday 4 July . . . In the course of the P.M. & evening had opportunity & danced several times with my little Ellen . . . between one & two sat out to see my little partner home. We both being well mounted on one horse as I had purposely started before the others, that I might have the company of my little girl to myself.[7]

The absence of parents from the scenes of David and Ellen's courting exemplifies the low level of parental surveillance and intervention that middle-class couples experienced throughout the 1770-1870 period. In some cases, parents made little or no effort to oversee their children's courting behavior; in others, the family took active steps to give a young couple privacy. Sometimes this meant that family members went out for a walk or early to bed when a suitor came to call. Since in most houses the parlor was the only space considered appropriate for courting activities, this was often the only way a couple could visit alone without going out themselves. Mary Guion, a rural New Yorker, reported in her diary a typical visit from her suitor Samuel Brown in 1807: "After tea Samuel came here we were all reading in the Parlor when he came but they [her family] soon all took a walk but him who chose to stay with me, we read, sung, and discoursed . . . till they returned."[8]

On occasion, it was the couple rather than the family who left the room but this raised issues of propriety. Mary Guion described her discomfort during another visit from Samuel Brown:

> I was showing him some things and as I went to put them in the beadroom[sic], he followed me in and we sat there by the window by the light only of the full moon, but that act I very much disapprove. When he first went in he asked me how long he [might] stay not more than tenn minutes said I. Ah ten o'clock said he, that will do very well and I am almost ashamed to own we sat there til twelve and there was company in the Parlour all the time.[9]

Mary "disapproved" and was "almost ashamed" of Samuel's actions and her response to them, but there is no evidence that her parents condemned, or even commented on, the couple's behavior. References to parental interference with the conduct of their children's courtship are extremely rare. The only case in the sample of a parent actively expressing disapproval of courtship behavior is one where the behavior itself was unusual; it is worth looking at in detail.

For much of 1860 Lester Ward, a young wheelwright in the small town of Towanda, Pennsylvania, courted a woman whom he referred to simply as "the girl." (Only after their marriage does she begin to appear in his diary as Lizzie.) On the first Sunday in November, Lester paid a visit to Lizzie Vought.

> I found the family as usual seated around the warm and crackling fire with every indication of comfort and relief. Sarah [Lizzie's sister] did not go to bed until ten o'clock, after which my beloved and I went down, made a fire, and sat down to talk and kiss and embrace and bathe in love . . .[10]

Lester's visits — and his sexual relationship with Lizzie — continued, but by the following summer Mrs. Vought's opposition was aroused. He reported a confrontation which took place after he and Lizzie had watched together at a neighbor's deathbed:

> I accompanied the girl home, and she insisted on my staying there and getting a little sleep, but she came into my room to give me my socks and to kiss me a little, and her mother found us there and she said several things concerning us which made me angry and I got up and soon left the house. I shall never spend another night there.

This episode did not, however, mark the end of Lester and Lizzie's nighttime intimacies nor was it the last time Mrs. Vought tried to intercede. In April 1862 Lester reported: "Her mother gave me an invitation to discontinue my visits but I do not know that I shall accept. She is angry with the girl, and with me also, I think." A week later, he believed "the affair with her mother is cleared up," but shortly thereafter, when Lizzie was ill, he noted in his diary: "Her mother was very angry with me because I sat down on the girl's bed yesterday. That made me miserable."[11]

Mrs. Vought's anger in this situation is striking for two reasons: first, because parents rarely became so directly involved in their children's courtship; and second, because the intimacy between Lizzie and Lester apparently developed unchecked for two years before encountering any parental opposition. It is difficult to believe that Lizzie's parents were completely unaware of what was going on in their own house. When Lester Ward was first courting Lizzie, he was disturbed by rumours about her sister Sarah's moral character, so it is possible that the standards in the Vought family were looser than most of their neighbors'. However, given Mrs. Vought's eventual disapproval, it is clear that she did *have* standards for her daughter's behavior. The laxity and inconsistency with which she enforced them reflects a strong bias in the culture against parental interference in courtship and in favor of autonomy and privacy for courting couples.[12]

Any remnants of the "parental-run marriage system" that had prevailed until the middle of the eighteenth century had disappeared. The few middle-class parents who tried to control their children's courtships were considered to be misguided. A young Maine lawyer expressed the popular nineteenth-century view: "As a general rule no good comes from opposition. In affairs of love, young people's hearts are generally much wiser than old people's heads." Children who allowed their parents to influence the course of their courtship were weak and irresponsible. "A man that is not capable of managing his love affairs without the assistance of friends," one midwesterner declared, "is not fit to be married at all, and he who will permit himself to be dictated [to] is worse yet."[13]

Young people did not expect to have to struggle for control over the daily events of courtship. They were entitled to it, but they also believed they should deserve it. Augusta Hubbard, an eighteen year old Upstate New Yorker, was grateful that her parents respected her autonomy in her dealings with young men. "I am glad," she noted in an 1860 diary entry, that

> my parents dare trust me as much as they do — I know if they were in the habit of acting as if they suspected me — I should be sly — deceitful and very obstinant. And lovers more than all others I think ought not to be opposed in such a way as parents often treat their children, if they wish to have them act with any moderation.[14]

Augusta's closing comment, "I think if my father was like some I have heard of, I should be as wild as their daughters are," suggests that there were parents who sought to control their children's courtship behavior, but they were greatly outnumbered by people like the Hubbards who gave their children almost complete freedom. Augusta's diary for the summer of 1867 records many occasions on which she and her suitor Frank Blakeslee were left on their own. For example:

> June 30 Sunday . . . We all (the young folks) went to shaker meeting at Mount Morriss — had a pleasant ride. F[rank] and I spent a pleasant afternoon in the orchard & we sat on the steps to visit during the even except we went upstairs to pray. July 15 Monday . . . Frank came this eve. We spent the evening in the graveyard alone.[15]

The important thing is not that Augusta and Frank were praying while Lester and Lizzie were petting — most couples probably did neither during their time alone together — but that they all enjoyed the autonomy and privacy to develop relationships that were sexually and emotionally intimate.

In their fantasies, young couples revealed the physical power of the tie between them. Separated lovers evoked the past and anticipated the future with images of sexual intimacy. Alexander Hamilton Rice, a student at Union College, looked forward to his reunion with Augusta McKim this way: "O happy hours when I may *once more* encircle within these arms the dearest object of my love — when I shall again feel the pressure of that 'aching head' which will delight to recline upon my bosom, when I may *again* press to my heart which palpitates with the purest affection the loved one who has so long shared its undivided devotion."[16]

Sometimes, the fantasies were more explicit. Lawrence Chamberlain, a divinity student whose relationship with his financée Fannie Adams was sexually charged, recounted a dream which he himself understood to be about the dangers of intimacy.

> I dreamed last night that my F--- had a little "gold.---" tossing him up in her arms and playing with him. I was very jealous, for she would not let me take him at all and I was so unreasonable as to imagine I had as much right to him as she. But there wasn't any *quarrel*. I wish I could tell you my feelings when I looked upon those two . . . Only I remember my starting when I thought that my F---. was not F---***** yet. After that I dreamed something else, which if it had been carried much farther, I am afraid would have made the two dreams come in rather an inverted order.[17]

Men were not the only ones to record fantasies of sexual closeness. Mary Butterfield told her fiancé Champion Chase, "In fancy my arms have been around you & myself clasped to that dear 'home' of mine your own loving heart & I have kissed you again & again & felt your cheek resting against mine & your fond embrace so vividly that I could scarce believe it was not real." Throughout the period, couples remembered partings in terms of the kisses exchanged, and they envisioned meetings that would allow unembarrassed embraces. Elizabeth Prentiss hoped there would "be nobody within two miles" of her meeting with her returning suitor. "Suppose you stop in some out of the way place just of town, and let me trot out there to see you?" she playfully proposed.[18]

Although during weeks and months of separation, men and women allowed themselves fantasies of sexual union and reunion, their behavior when together might well have been more restrained and controlled. Fantasies of sexual expression need not, of course, reflect sexual freedom in reality. Yet middle-class courting couples in the New Republic felt comfortable with a wide range of sexual activities, a range that narrowed as the nineteenth century went on. Evidence of sexual behavior between 1770 and 1820 is relatively limited.[19] What there is indicates that sexual boundaries between unmarried men and women were loosely drawn and crossed with relative ease. Mary Beth Norton argues that because eighteenth-century women who "engaged in premarital sex, or who were merely suspected of having done so, had greatly greatly lessened their chances for a good marriage . . . many genteel women adhered carefully to strict standards of behavior." Outside of "genteel" circles, standards — or at least adherence to them — may not have been so strict. The second half of the eighteenth century was, after all, marked by a rise in the ratio of bridal pregnancy until it peaked at close to thirty percent in the 1770s and 1780s. This was the period when a young man like David Shepard, Jr. thought nothing of going into a bedroom where his cousin and confidante Polly Austin was asleep and "spending a few minutes in hugging and kissing" her or of "hugging, talking to, and sometimes kissing my sweet girl" during walks with Ellen Savage.[20]

Transgressions often met with nothing more serious than a scolding. One evening in 1807, Samuel Brown arrived early to escort Mary Guion to a dance; he entered the room where she was dressing. She recorded the incident in her diary:

> "Polly," said he, advancing towards me, "Don't you want me to help you dress?" I felt rather confused, and gave him a very abrupt answer. "No," said I, "and you may just march out." He stood and laughed at me some time and then went into the Parlour.

If the offense was more flagrant, it could provoke a harsher response. During a visit in 1785, a young man she called "Philamon" put his hand on Patty Rogers's breast; afterwards she reported:

> In the course of the evening he took some liberties that would not have been *strictly* decent had they come to light — It gave me *pain* — Surely thought I he must have mistaken my Character — Don't you hate me said I? I hate you? Because you treated me Ill ass [sic] you thot me a bad girl.

Patty worred that her suitor would think her "a bad girl;" she directed her disapproval not at him but inward at herself and was not so much outraged by his behavior as she was ashamed of her own.[21]

As a woman, Patty Rogers held herself responsible for maintaining the sexual boundaries in a relationship with a man. She was more vulnerable than he to the consequences of sexual actions, more likely to be stranded outside the pale of propriety. There was nothing new about this; it expressed an age-old "double-standard." What was new in the late eighteenth century was the proposition that woman had the inclination as well as the obligation to control sexuality. Nancy Cott has shown that "there was a traditionally dominant Anglo-American definition of woman as *especially* sexual which was reversed and transformed between the seventeenth and the nineteenth centuries into the view that women . . . were *less* carnal and lustful than men." A relatively literate woman like Patty Rogers might have been among the first to internalize what would become "the central tenet of Victorian sexual ideology" — female passionlessness.[22]

If Patty Rogers and her suitor read the medical and advice literature of their day, they would have found a more accepting view of male sexuality. According to Charles Rosenberg, "authorities of the eighteenth and early nineteenth centuries routinely indicted 'sexual excess;' yet their injunctions have a calm, even bland tone. These writers accepted sexual activity after puberty as both normal and necessary." It was only during the second quarter of the nineteenth century that "the ritualized prudence of these traditional admonitions became sharpened and applied far more frequently, while for some authors sexuality began to assume an absolutely negative tone."[23]

The emergence of what Rosenberg calls the ideal of the "Christian gentleman" who was "continually testing his manliness in the fire of self-denial" together with the ideology of female passionlessness dominated public discourse on sexuality from the 1830s on. But what effect did these ideas have on individual behavior? Rosenberg concluded that nineteenth-century Americans "clearly regarded overt sexuality, especially in women, as part of a life style demeaning to middle-class status. Virtue and self-denial . . . could be embraced by any man who so willed." But *were* they? For their part, women, Cott suggests, might "hail passionlessness as a way to assert control in the sexual arena."[24] But *did* they? To answer these questions, we need to reconstruct the sexual experiences and attitudes of individual men and women. This is possible beginning in the 1830s, when the evidence allows us to explore the sexual dimension both of casual courting and of the more intimate relationships that followed.

The second quarter of the nineteenth century was marked by the "reappearance of premarital sexual restraint" and by a decline in the bridal pregnancy ratio. After the "extraordinary turbulence in sexual patterns and definitions" and the related rise in prenuptial conceptions, boundaries began to tighten.[25] A wide range of sexual behavior remained an accepted — and expected — part of middle-class courtship, but such behavior was subject to more and more careful self-regulation. Romantic love was defined to include sexual attraction and gratification but to exclude coitus between unmarried couples. What happened might be thought of as the "invention of petting," or the removal of intercourse from premarital sex. Coitus was placed on its own continuum rather than at the far end of one that began with hand-holding in church. This meant the posting of intercourse as not only "off limits" but as an altogether separate terrain, accessible only to married people. There were, of course, couples who failed to observe those limits; for them crossing the boundary line was a risk, albeit one they were willing to take.

For the great majority of Americans who stayed within the limits, great latitude in behavior was allowed. Coquetry and seduction were, of course, condemned, but flirtation and sexual playfulness characterized much male-female interaction. An exchange between two New England college students in the early 1830s reveals the sexual nature of courting. When Elias Nason encouraged his friend Charles Everett to "let the girls alone," Charles assured him: "I have done so, as yet that is. I have not shocked their modesty by putting my hands where they should not be, but once this vacation or rather twice." The first time was on an overnight visit to Pawtucket, Rhode Island; he reported: "I felt *of a leg there*, a most glorious pretty girl. She was an old acquaintance but some parts of her were new to me." His second lapse occurred in church: "Sitting beside a young lady . . . I passed my hand through the armholes of her and my cloak and had a very interesting meeting, but she, owing to my *feeling so affectionately*, told me to take it out, but I consoled her and *felt on* til meeting was done." Charles Everett instructed Elias Nason to return the letter if it was illegible or burn it if it was not, but his embarrassment was mixed with a large measure of male pride in his accomplishments; whatever discomfort he felt was in the *telling* rather than the *doing*.[26]

Literary historian Ernest Earnest discovered a similar pattern in the diaries he studied. He believed that a Litchfield law student's reports of girls who were "kissable," of "near being swallowed at the kissing bout" and of being "all but kissed to death" were typical of the middle decades of the nineteenth century. He suggested that into the 1860s young men and women continued to express affection sexually. In New Jersey in 1861, John Henry Smith noted in his diary: "Came up with Lizzie Green. I don't know how many kisses I had that evening.

was almost smothered with the sweet things." Lizzie Green was far from unique; two days later, John Henry reported, "'Escourted' two girls to a Mrs. Norwood's where they played cards and ate chestnuts. Miss Albert gave me a sweet kiss before I was aware of the fact; went home with my lady. She too gave me a farewell salute."[27]

Such physical contact between young people was not limited to the citified eastern seaboard. In Ohio, for example, John Ballard teased his sixteen year old sister Mary because she "was so obstinate and unyielding to the oft-repeated efforts of the young men to get a *sweet kiss* from [her] lips." Mary replied: "I look with contempt on such things and especially on little girls having beaux." In Indiana, a young Quaker Emma Hadley told her cousin: "I have no 'Beau' to while away the Sabbath eve or I would not be writing to thee." Emma was ambivalent about what she was missing, which she described in this verse:

> The boys they go courting they dress very fine
> To keep the girls up 'tis all their design
> They will hug them & kiss them & flatter & lie
> And keep the girls up till they are ready to die.

She asked: "Isn't that nearly true?" and added: "I don't want thee to think I have lost confidence in all the young gents."[28]

Although Mary Ballard and Emma Hadley viewed young men as sexual aggressors, there is ample evidence that young men were often willing participants in the sexual "play" that was common in courting. When Mary Ballard was no longer a little girl but a twenty-eight year old woman, she was hardly "obstinate and unyielding." After what he considered "the happiest night of [his] life," her fiancé William Ross wrote, "We were too happy last night to part. You came very near pursuading me to stay all night. I assure you I left very reluctantly." Charles Everett reported to Elias Nason that the young woman he had "fondled" on his visit to Pawtucket "told me that she should know I was a collegian, because I took such measures to please her." And John Henry Smith certainly seemed to accept rather than extort kisses from the young women he encountered a generation later.[29]

In more serious relationships, a woman's sexual responsiveness could cause conflict. Mira Bigelow, the young woman in Elias Nason's life, expressed her sexual feelings openly. "I sincerely regret not kissing you more that day I came down," she wrote at the beginning of one separation. She and Elias were often apart and Mira looked forward to their reunions this way:

> O! I do really want to kiss you . . . How I should like to be in that old parlor with you . . . I hope there will be a carpet on the floor for it seems you intend to act worse that you ever did before by your letter . . . but I shall humbly submit to my fate and willingly too, to speak candidly.

Mira was "willing," but she was given to second thoughts. Elias described her ambivalence on one occasion:

> My how you did act when I was at home. To say you "don't care" [illeg.] that's the rub — Why, Mi, what a girl you are! I can't but laugh to think how perfectly indifferent you would be and in a moment clinging around me would say "Oh do do" — For *shame* on you Mira Ann Bigelow — And then to say I never will again and the very next night . . .[30]

Elias was teasing in his judgment of Mira's behavior; he found her inconsistency more amusing than incriminating. He was less sure about his own conduct. He made no secret of his desire for Mira. "Oh Mi how intensely do I long to see you — to *feel* you — to put these very hands that hold this pen upon you. Yes in your bosom — that soft delicious bosom . . . I shall tear you to pieces." Elias was not afraid to admit, "I cannot restrain my passions when I see my own loved girl," but he believed that they *should* be restrained. "How is it, Mi, that you can bear so much from me? How can you *love* me after *all*?" In the absence of his own powers of self-control, he relied on her: "My passions are terrible and none but you could master them. And you forgive me all and love me still."[31] Both Mira and Elias expected that Mira would restrain her own feelings as well as her suitor's, but neither made an effort to *deny* those feelings.

A couple whose courtship took place fifteen years later was even more sexually intimate. In 1845, while clerking in a law office in Buffalo, New York, Champion Chase met Mary Butterfield. Her family was soon to emigrate to Wisconsin and in the summer of 1846, after they had known each other for a year, Mary and Champion became engaged. During the next two years, Mary lived with her family in Racine, while Champion moved from one part of Wisconsin to another, lecturing on phrenology until he established himself in business.

From the beginning, their relationship involved those forms of touching and kissing so common to mid-nineteenth-century courtship. During a visit in January 1848, they seem to have entered into new — and perhaps forbidden — territory. The next morning, "after sleeping three or four hours" in the Racine Hotel, Champion exclaimed that he "never had such a living joyous time before." For Mary it was not so simple. In a painfully honest letter, she described her feelings:

> I did not feel so quiet a part of the time last night as I appeared & you supposed. Although I love you dearly & trust you so perfectly that I am perfectly willing & glad to make you happy by those favors which no one else in the wide world could obtain, yet even towards you I can not at once resign all the feelings which nature and education have fixed in my mind — I was glad afterwards when you seemed so sincerely pleased & happy — so *satisfied* with *me*.[32]

For a week or two after this episode, Champion addressed his letters to Mary, "Dear Wife." Only one of Mary's letters, two months later, began "My dear Husband," but much of her correspondence after the January visit dealt with the question of how soon they could be married. It is possible to conclude from all this that Mary Butterfield and Champion Chase had intercourse on that night in Racine, but the correspondence offers no direct evidence. What seems certain is that their behavior that night was *more intimate* than any they had engaged in before and brought them much closer in their own minds to marriage.

During the next months, there was no retreat from whatever had taken place in January. Champion's letters closed with statements such as "Ah, if I could get at you just now there would be some aching lips I guess before I should get through," and Mary's fantasies were equally erotic:

> I always laugh when I think of those kisses upon your neck, they used to amuse me so. It was half mischief that prompted them but I loved them because they were half denied. My lips are growing too heavy there are so many kisses accumulated there.

If either had doubts, they did not admit them. In March, Champion told Mary:

> How I love to have you write me so frankly about your feelings and reflections upon our late intimacy . . . You have reason to put confidence in these loving impulses of ours dearest . . . They are our best indices surely and I am perfectly satisfied that however intimate we might permit ourselves to be, *they* would not permit us to be too much so.[33]

For her part, Mary Butterfield celebrated what she had learned — that she was "endowed with every womanly attribute in perfectness & beauty." Her passion unsettled her, but it did not unsex her. She assured her fiancé, "The knowledge has no base effect upon me. I am . . . *proud* that I can give myself to you as I am . . . I *am* a woman now." Mary's affirmation of her womanhood through sexuality suggests that although "nature and education" might point to passionlessness, experience could tell a different tale. "You have lifted a veil which concealed from me many beautiful paths of happiness & which taught me joys & blessings I had never dreamed of," she told Champion.[34]

Mary's first response, however, had been less positive. She confessed to Champion that during their January encounter in Racine, she "felt strongly inclined to turn or fly away and hide [her] face in some corner." But she did not. "*I shut my eyes* and was a good, quiet little Fron [her nickname], was I not?" Other women were more active participants from the outset. Lizzie Vought, for example, was as interested as Lester Ward in the sexual explorations that characterized their courtship. On a typical visit, Lester reported, "She looked at me so gently and spoke so tenderly. 'I love you,' she said kissing me on the mouth, 'I love this mouth, I love these dear eyes, I love this head' and a thousand other little caressing pet names."[35]

Since we must rely on Lester Ward for our picture of Lizzie Vought, we cannot know for certain whether she was indeed as sexually free as she appears here and elsewhere in her lover's dairy. Perhaps Lester failed to record her protestations or self-doubts or perhaps she hesitated to express them, but this seems unlikely. On the one occasion when Lizzie admitted, "I am afraid I am doing something I shouldn't in putting my hand on your bare breast," Lester found the "tenderness and humility" of her remark endearing. It apparently generated no guilt or conflict in either of them.[36]

Things were less harmonious between Annie Cox and Winan Allen, another couple courting in the 1860s. They met in 1861 when Winan was a student at the University of Wisconsin in Madison, Annie's home town. In 1862, Winan, a Copperhead Democrat, left Wisconsin for the University of Michigan where he struggled to finish his education and evade the draft. He spent part of the summer of 1863 doing agricultural day labor, the rest of it living with the Coxes in Madison. It appears that at least once during that extended visit, Annie and Winan, in Lester Ward's words, "tasted the joys of love and happiness which only belong to married life."[37] But for Annie, the taste was bitter.

In response to a letter that does not survive, she explained how she viewed their actions:

> When temptation to wrong suggested itself from natural passions and opportunity, 'twas my mission to have been *fine*, giving you a kind refusal and leading your mind away and beyond. In the first instance, I failed in the full possession of my reason & judgment thus giving strength to your desire and weakening my better nature. We made firm resolves and the next opportunity showed how they were kept . . .

Winan's passions were "natural" — for a man; as a woman, Annie should have acted on "reason & judgment." When she "reviewed [her] conduct," she concluded: "God only knows how I detested myself. You meanwhile," she assured her fiancé, "kept your old standing place in my estimation."[38]

Annie did not absolve Winan of all responsibility. "I own I think you to blame in some degree. That is, for not accepting my first denial," but in a postscript the next day, she added: "We have both done wrong. I have done much the greater because I should have acted the part of a true, noble, Christian woman." Although hers was the greater wrong, his was the greater loss. "If I have not injured you dear one, fear not for me," she wrote. "'Tis only for you I weep for the sorrow I have caused when you think of me." She herself did "not feel, strange as it may seem, any the less pure *now*." She declared to Winan: "I shall stand at the altar with you, only humble and for that reason better . . . . I know this experience will be for my good, though it would have been better if it could never happen [sic]."[39]

But it *had* happened, and Annie's ultimate response was to retreat sexually. "Let it all pass," she told Winan, and apparently on subsequent visits they did not repeat their indiscretions of the summer of 1863. Only in the months before their marriage did they return to the subject. Then Winan wondered if Annie did "not judge a little harshly of the past? *Whom* could you have confided in more securely than me?" he asked. "Do you know of any with whom judgment would have had greater control?"[40] Winan Allen was willing to admit that self-control cost him an effort. He could compare himself with other members of his sex, among whom sexual discipline was assumed to be lacking, and claim credit for his own attempt – regardless of the results. It was an occasion for self-congratulation.

Annie, on the other hand, expected self-control of herself. "I should have made my Christian principles guide and restrain me in all things," she said.[41] His role was to accept, hers to enforce, restraint. But was this the restraining influence of propriety or of passionlessness? More than Mira Bigelow, Mary Butterfield, or Lizzie Vought, Annie Cox can be said to have denied her sexual feelings; yet she did not use passionlessness to assert control of her relationship with Winan Allen. The issue was her failure to restrain *his* sexual feelings, rather than the absence of of her own. Her implicit message of reproof to Winan was "You are too passionate" – not "I have no passion."

Winan Allen gave himself credit for being an unusually self-controlled male, but did he view Annie as an exception among her sex? If he was *more* in control of himself than most men, was she *less* in control of herself than most women? Was her disclaimer of pleasure in their sexual activities what he expected of a woman? The Cox-Allen manuscripts leave these questions unanswered, but we do know that other men of Winan Allen's generation expected and encouraged the women in their lives to express affection sexually. A New England mechanic wrote his absent fiancée, "No doubt you often think it would be pleasant to have a young man by your side, with your hand in his; or perhaps with his arm twined fondly around your neck . . . I presume that you have the same feelings I often have." Lawrence Chamberlain was more insistent:

> It might make a person a little angry for a woman to *try* to ignore the fact that she was not above human passion & susceptibilities . . . a warm blooded girl come & lie in a warm blooded man's bosom & think that he will not "touch" her ever? Why, leave a girl to her own way about it & my word for it, she wouldn't lie still a great while without *extending* her *acquaintance*, I know that.[42]

Lawrence was prepared to defer to his fiancée on sexual matters. "*Your will shall be my law*," he promised her, but he wanted her to admit that "it was a matter requiring as much self-denial on [her] part as on [his]." Will Adkinson, an Indiana lawyer, took a similar stand. He told Lu Burlingame he thought of her "not as an angel but as a women . . . [his] equal with flesh and blood, with magnetism, electricity, passion." These men ignored or internalized incompletely the view that "women lacked carnal motivation." But what about the women themselves? Did they use "passionlessness as a way to assert control in the sexual arena?"[43] Were Lawrence Chamberlain and Will Adkinson responding to — and assailing — a position of self-conscious female passionlessness?

In the case of Will Adkinson's relationship with Lu Burlingame, we are able to suggest an answer. Will and Lu lived in the small Indiana town of Moore's Hill. In 1870, when both were twenty-three, they became engaged. The following year Will was practicing law in a town twenty miles from Moore's Hill. Most Saturdays, he came by train to visit Lu. They referred to these visits as their "talks," but it seems clear that they involved something more intimate than conversation. When the interaction produced enough conflict for Lu to want to break their engagement, Will revealed that he had waged a campaign to develop what he called the "passional elements" in her nature.

"I don't believe," he wrote, "there has been or is or will be a time when you are folded in my arms . . . when you can be cold indifferent negative towards me." He admitted, "In the effort to tempt you and draw out this part of your nature . . . I was excited beyond my control." The effort had not been completely in vain. "I learned to hunger for your tender words & caresses . . . the pressure of your lips," Lu conceded, "but I never wanted extremes." In her view, the ideal woman was "strong & perfectly developed in body, brain & heart, & crowns her womanhood with capable, healthy, glad wifehood & motherhood," but she was adamant that "all women were not intended to be mothers." Lu claimed that if she "were a wife, & fully competent and *wanted* to be a mother," the sex act would be "the most sacred & perfect expression of love possible." However, in her own case, an unspecified "physical derangement" interfered.[44] In her assertion of passionlessness, Lu Burlingame presented herself as an exception; passionlessness was a complaint but not an inborn trait of her sex. If she "lacked carnal motivation," it was because of the weakness of her constitution rather than the strength of her character, the result of an "affliction" rather than of woman's moral superiority.

Perhaps Lu Burlingame felt too guilty about her own complicity — her failure in fact to *be* passionless — to assume the mantle of moral superiority. Instead, she focused on a physical condition that disabled her from participating in full sexual activity and maternity. It may also have been the case that female passionlessness was simply too bitter a pill for women to ask men to swallow. If Lu's passionlessness was an affliction, there was always the hope that it could be cured. She held out to Will the possibility that she might "grow stronger & more as you wish," which obviously meant more sexually passionate.[45]

Although Lu and Will, like the other couples discussed above, believed that self-control came more easily to women than to men, they considered it a necessity for both. This raises the question of why Victorian sexual ideology extolled female *passionlessness* rather than self-control. Why was continence — "virtuous and willed repression of existing carnal desires" — not sufficient demonstration of woman's moral and intellectual strength? Nancy Cott observed that older "notions of women's inherent licentiousness persisted, to be wielded against women manifesting any form of deviance under the reign of passionlessness."[46] I would suggest that passionlessness was itself tied to the earlier view of woman as a sexually dangerous being who could not be trusted to *control* her feelings: they had to be *denied*. Yet the women themselves, and the men they loved, expected not denial but restraint. However attractive as an ideology, in practice passionlessness created more problems than it solved.[47]

Perhaps that helps explain why in the late nineteenth century many medical writers (and some feminists) advanced a more positive view of female sexuality than the one espoused by William Acton and other proponents of female passionlessness. Carl Degler has found "a substantial amount of nineteenth-century writing about women that assumes the existence of strong sexual feelings" and that encourages women to express them.[48] All of the authorities whom Degler cites were writing *after* 1870. Post-war medical opinion, and sexual ideology, were divided into two camps: the "idealists" who defined woman as a sexually pure, morally superior creature, and the "realists" who concluded — as much from observation as theory — that women as well as men experienced and acted on sexual feelings. After fifty years as "the central tenet of Victorian sexual ideology," female passionlessness still failed to describe behavior. A significant number of medical experts rejected it; ordinary men and women who resisted it could find their view affirmed in the medical literature.

The alternative was not, of course, a world in which sexuality was unleashed. Indeed, the recognition of female sexual passion made self-control all the more important. Couples who did not deny the existence of powerful sexual feelings might have had a greater need for self-control than those who subscribed to passionlessness. Sexual passion might be natural, but excess was still dangerous. If this was true for married couples, it was doubly so for men and women during courtship. Evidence in an on-going study of middle-class American courtship suggests that after the Civil War sexual boundaries were tightened further. Premarital sexual restraint was no longer the result of a struggle but represented a common assumption — and a norm — of middle-class courtship. The early nineteenth century's "invention of petting" was modified and replaced by a much narrower definition of acceptable behavior.[49]

More research is needed before we will know how widespread those patterns were. That they were not evenly distributed throughout American society is evident in the rising premarital pregnancy ratio; clearly, sexual self-control was limited to certain groups of people, to precisely those most likely to read and respond to prescriptive advice.[50] But changes in behavior and shifts in ideology cannot be reduced to cause and effect; this look at the century after 1770 reminds us that the relationship is a complex and ever-changing one.

American History Workshop, Boston Ellen K. Rothman

FOOTNOTES

1. Elias Nason to Mira Bigelow, Feb. 23, 1834, Elias Nason Papers, American Antiquarian Society.

2. These aspects of courtship are discussed at length in my doctoral thesis, "'Intimate Acquaintance': Courtship and the Transition to Marriage in America, 1770-1900." Brandeis, 1980.

3. Of these 160 individuals, thirty percent courted between 1770 and 1820, seventy percent between 1820 and 1870. Sixty-two percent lived in New England, fifteen percent in the Midwest, and twenty-three percent in the Mid-Atlantic states. Twenty percent lived in large cities such as Boston or Philadelphia, while thirty percent lived in smaller cities and large towns such as Bangor, New Bedford, or Indianapolis. Half lived on farms and in country villages. Of the women courting between 1820 and 1870, forty percent had some education

beyond grade school, and about ten percent are known to have been employed before marriage, mostly as schoolteachers. Almost half of the men were either preparing for or pursuing careers in the ministry, law or medicine.

4. The findings of this study suggest the need for revision in Carroll Smith-Rosenberg's theory that "American society was characterized in large part by rigid gender-role differentiation within the family and within society as a whole, leading to the emotional segregation of women and men." At least during the years just before marriage, distance between men and women was much less than Smith-Rosenberg and other more traditional scholars suggest. There is no sign of the "severe social restrictions on intimacy between young men and women" that she argues existed. Her picture of men "as an other or out group, segregated into different schools, supported by their own male network of friends and kin, socialized to different behavior and coached to a proper formality in courtship behavior" may be more accurate for the eighteenth century but even then, it is at best an exaggeration of the middle-class pattern. See "The Female World of Love and Ritual: Relations Between Women in Nineteenth-Century America," *Signs*, 1:1, p. 9, 21.

5. See Nancy F. Cott, *Bonds of Womanhood: Woman's Sphere in New England, 1780-1835* (New Haven, 1977); Mary P. Ryan, "American Society and the Cult of Domesticity, 1830-1860" (unpublished Ph.D. dissertation, University of California at Santa Barbara, 1971); Barbara Welter, "The Cult of True Womanhood" in *Dimity Convictions* (Athens, Ohio, 1976).

6. Joseph Kett, *Rites of Passage: Adolescence in America, 1790 to the Present* (New York, 1977), pp. 14-31.

7. David Shepard, Jr., Diary, May 27, July 4, 1798 in *The Chester and Westfield, Mass. Diaries*, ed. by Alexander G. Rose III (Baltimore, 1975), pp. 159-60, 183-85. The fact that David Shepard wrote his diary in a Latin-based code may help explain its slightly salacious, and unusually explicit, tone.

8. Mary Guion, Diary, June 20, 1807, The New-York Historical Society. Although young women spent a great deal of their lives in the kitchen, courtship seems to have been associated almost exclusively with the parlor. It is not difficult to imagine a young man venturing into the kitchen or buttery to keep a young woman company while she shelled peas or made pies, but such scenes were either too ordinary or somehow too embarrassing to be mentioned in letters or diaries.

9. Mary Guion, Diary, June 20, 1807.

10. Lester Ward, Diary, Nov. 6, 1860 in *Young Ward's Diary*, ed. by Bernhard J. Stern (New York, 1935).

11. Lester Ward, Diary, Nov. 6, 1860, July 16, 1861, April 13 and 27, 1862.

12. The only indication we have of Lizzie's father's reaction is this entry in Lester's diary: "Her father growled a little, and I am determined not to go back before the end of two weeks." Feb. 24, 1861.

13. Daniel Scott Smith, "Parental Power and Marriage Patterns: An Analysis of Historical Trends in Hingham, Mass." *Journal of Marriage and the Family* (1973): p. 426; Henry Poor to Mary Pierce, Jan. 26, 1840, Poor Family Papers, fol. 100, Schlesinger Library, Radcliffe College; Champion S. Chase to Mary Butterfield, May 12, 1846, Champion S. Chase Papers, Yale University Library. See also Marcia [Northy] to Martha Boody, Oct. 23, 1837, Northy Papers, Box 12, fol. 2, Essex Institute, James Duncan Phillips Library.

14. Augusta Hubbard, Diary, July 27, 1860, private collection.

15. *Ibid.*; June 30 and July 16, 1867.

16. Alexander Hamilton Rice to Augusta E. McKim, Aug. 29, 1842, Alexander Hamilton Rice Papers, Massachusetts Historical Society.

17. Lawrence Chamberlain to Fannie Adams, Oct. 31, 1852, Chamberlain Papers, Schlesinger Library, Radcliffe College.

18. Mary Butterfield to Champion S. Chase, Dec. 27, 1847. Elizabeth Prentiss to George Prentiss, Feb. 22, 1843 in Elizabeth Prentiss, *Life and Letters* (New York, 1882).

19. The relative silence on sexual matters among the 1770-1820 courting cohorts may in part reflect the fact that the pre-1820 group represents a more elite socio-economic stratum than the one that followed. The sons and daughters of the wealthy may have observed a set of conventions that inhibited the discussion of sexual feelings or behavior in diaries and letters, or they may have actually *been* more restrained in their premarital conduct than their less privileged contemporaries. Both of these explanations are supported by other evidence. The first is consistent with Herman Lantz, et. al.'s finding of "sexual conservatism" in the magazines read by upper status groups in the 1776-1794 period. [See Herman Lantz, et.al., "Pre-Industrial Patterns in the Colonial Family in America: A Content Analysis of Colonial Magazines," *American Sociological Review* 33 (June 1968), 423]. The second fits with Smith and Hindus's argument that there was "a sexually permissive subculture" the continuity of which "depended on the female line and on the less wealthy section of the population." [See Daniel Scott Smith and Michael Hindus, "Premarital Pregnancy in America, 1640-1971: An Overview and Interpretation," *Journal of Interdisciplinary History* 4 (Spring 1975), 547]. It is also possible that the paucity of data on the earlier period reflects, at least in part, the collecting biases of historical societies and libraries with strong colonial holdings. Their collections tend to focus on the careers of *men* in politics, the ministry, or the law, and to be weak in the kinds of personal documents in which sexual references are most likely to be found.

20. Mary Beth Norton, *Liberty's Daughters: The Revolutionary Experience of American Women* (Boston, 1980), p. 53; Smith and Hindus, "Overview," 538; David Shepard, Jr., Diary, May 27 and June 12, 1798, pp. 155-56, 169-70.

21. Mary Guion, Diary, Sept. 4, 1807; Patty Rogers, Diary, quoted in Norton, *Liberty's Daughters*, p. 53.

22. Nancy F. Cott, "Passionlessness: An Interpretation of Victorian Sexual Ideology, 1790-1850;" *Signs* (1978): 220-221. Carl Degler places the change somewhat later, during the 1840s and 1850s when he believes "a whole new literature on sexual behavior came forward, in which women's sexuality was either played down or virtually denied." See *At Odds: Women and the Family in America from the Revolution to the Present* (New York, 1980), p. 253.

23. Charles Rosenberg, "Sexuality, Class and Role in Nineteenth-Century America," *American Quarterly* 25 (May 1973), 135.

24. *Ibid*, p. 139, 143; Cott, "Passionlessness," 233.

25. Smith and Hindus, "Premarital Pregnancy," 550; Cott, "Passionlessness," 228. Howard Gadlin has argued that Jacksonian Americans had "de-eroticized marriages." Based on data from unmarried people, this study cannot speak directly to that question. However, it does strongly suggest that during the stage of the life cycle when conjugal relationships were being formed, sex was an important part of male-female interaction. (See Howard Gadlin, "Private Lives and Public Order: A Critical View of the History of Intimate Relations in the United States," *Massachusetts Review* 17 (1976).

26. Charles Everett to Elias Nason, May 5, 1833, Elias Nason Papers, Box 1, fol.1.

27. Ernest Earnest, *The American Eve in Fact and Fiction, 1774-1914* (Champaign-Urbana, 1974), pp. 72, 74.

28. Mary Ballard to John Ballard, May 14, 1846, Mary P. Ballard Letters, Box 1, fol. 1, Western Reserve Historical Society; Emma Hadley to Miriam Green, Dec. 27, 1863, Miriam Green Papers, Indiana Historical Society.

29. William Ross to Mary Ballard, Aug. 22, 1858, Box 1, fol. 1; Charles Everett to Elias Nason, May 5, 1833. Also, see Alexander Hamilton Rice to Augusta E. McKim, Aug. 19, 1842; Mary E. Thorn to James W. White, May 22, 1850, White Papers, Historical Society of Western Pennsylvania. For one unusually undemonstrative woman, see John Patch to Margaret Poor, June 21, 1846, John Patch-Margaret Poor Correspondence, Essex Institute, James Duncan Phillips Library.

30. Mira Bigelow to Elias Nason, Oct. 21, 1831; Elias to Mira, Jan. 19, 1833, Box 1, fol. 1.

31. Elias Nason to Mira Bigelow, Jan. 19, 1833.

32. Mary Butterfield to Champion S. Chase, Jan. 11, 1848, Box 8, fol. 163; Mary to Champion, March 25, 1848, Box 2, fol. 20; Champion to Mary, March 25, 1848, Box 8, fol. 167.

34. Mary Butterfield to Champion Chase, March 17, 1848, Box 2, fol. 20.

35. Mary Butterfield to Champion Chase, Jan. 3, 1848, Box 1, 1, fol. 18; Lester Ward, Diary, Oct. 21, 1860.

36. Lester Ward, Diary, Oct. 21, 1860.

37. Lester Ward, Diary, Oct. 25, 1861.

38. Annie Cox to Winan Allen, Oct. 20, 1863, Cox-Allen Papers, Newberry Library.

39. *Ibid.*

40. Winan Allen to Annie Cox, March 1, 1865.

41. Annie Cox to Winan Allen, Oct. 20, 1863.

42. Samuel Kingman to Emily Brooks, Jan. 25, 1853, in "Pennings from the Past: The Growth of a Nineteenth-Century Relationship," ed. by Jane Walter (Honors Thesis, College of Holy Cross, 1979), p. 142; Lawrence Chamberlain to Fannie Adams, n.d. [1852].

43. Lawrence Chamberlain to Fannie Adams, n.d. [1852]. Will Adkinson to Lu Burlingame, July 1, 1871, Florence Burlingame Adkinson Papers, Schlesinger Library, Radcliffe College; Cott, "Passionlessness," 233.

44. Will Adkinson to Lu Burlingame, July 8 and 19, 1871; Lu to Will, July 24 and August 13, 1871. Apparently, Lu discussed her physical condition with Will face-to-face; the correspondence contains no explanation of its nature or cause.

45. Lu Burlingame to Will Adkinson, April 9, 1872.

46. Cott, "Passionlessness," 235, 221.

47. Cott points out how "the ideology of passionlessness... created its own contradictions: on the one hand, by exaggerating sexual propriety so far as to immobilize women and, on the other, by allowing claims of women's moral influence to obfuscate the need for other sources of power." ("Passionlessness," 236) These contradictions affected women's personal relationships as well as their role in society.

48. Carl Degler, "What Ought to Be and What Was: Women's Sexuality in the Nineteenth Century," *American Historical Review* 79 (1974): 1472, 1479.

49. The 1870-1900 pattern is discussed in "Intimate Acquaintance," pp. 176-181.

50. The rising premarital pregnancy ratio may in fact offer one explanation for increasingly tight sexual control in middle-class courtship: As the sexual behavior of some women loosened, young middle-class women may have felt more pressure to affirm their status by raising their standards. Charles Rosenberg explores this line of argument in terms of middle-class men in "Sexuality, Class and Role," 149.

SEEKING ECSTASY ON THE BATTLEFIELD: DANGER AND PLEASURE IN NINETEENTH-CENTURY FEMINIST SEXUAL THOUGHT

ELLEN CAROL DUBOIS AND LINDA GORDON

It is often alleged that female sexuality is a more complex matter than men's, and, if so, a major reason is that sex spells potential danger as well as pleasure for women. A feminist politics about sex, therefore, if it is to be credible as well as hopeful, must seek both to protect women from sexual danger and to encourage their pursuit of sexual pleasure.

This complex understanding of female sexuality has not always characterized the feminist movement. In general feminists inherit two conflicting traditions in their approach to sex. The strongest tradition, virtually unchallenged in the mainstream women's rights movement of the nineteenth century, addressed primarily the dangers and few of the possibilities of sex. Another perspective, much less developed despite some eloquent spokeswomen by the early twentieth century, encouraged women to leap, adventurous and carefree, into sexual liaisons, but it failed to offer a critique of the male construction of the sexual experience available to most women. It is no use to label one side feminist and the other antifeminist, to argue by name-calling. We cannot move ahead unless we grasp that both traditions are part of our feminism.

Neither feminist tradition is adequate to our needs today. Both were thoroughly heterosexist in their assumptions of what sex is. Even the nineteenth-century women who experienced intense emotional and physical relationships with each other did not incorporate these into their definition of what was sexual. Certainly women had relationships with other women that included powerful sexual components, but the feminists who are the subject of this paper did not theorize these relationships as sexual.[1] Furthermore, both feminist lines of thought—that emphasizing danger and that emphasizing pleasure—were often moralistic.

Feminist Studies 9, no. 1 (Spring 1983). © by Feminist Studies, Inc.

They condemned those whose sexual behavior deviated from their standards, not only sexually exploitive men but also women who did not conform.

Still, without an appreciation of these legacies and the processes of thought and experience that produced them, we cannot have much historical insight into our own concerns. Without a history, political movements like ours swing back and forth endlessly, reacting to earlier mistakes and overreacting in compensation, unable to incorporate previous insights and transcend previous limitations. Today we observe some of that pendulum-like motion. In reaction to the profound disappointments of what has passed for "sexual liberation," some feminists are replicating an earlier tradition, focusing exclusively on danger and advocating what we believe to be a conservative sexual politics.

We use a label like "conservative" cautiously. Such terms, like "left" and "right," come to us from class politics. When applied to sex and gender, they fit less comfortably. The oppressions of women, the repressions of sex, are so many and so complex, by virtue of their location in the most intimate corners of life, coexisting even with love, that it is not always obvious in which direction a better world lies. We use the term "conservatism" to characterize strategies that accept existing power relations. We are suggesting that even feminist reform programs can be conservative in some respects if they accept male dominance while trying to elevate women's "status" within it. In this case, we believe that the nineteenth-century feminist mainstream accepted women's sexual powerlessness with men as inevitable, even as it sought to protect women from its worst consequences. Its appraisal of women's sexual victimization was not, on balance, offset by recognition of women's potential for sexual activity and enjoyment. We think our judgment will be justified by the historical description which follows. Through that description we hope to show, too, that despite the stubborn continuities of women's sexual oppression, there have also been momentous changes in the last 150 years, changes that require different strategies today.

The feminist movement has played an important role in organizing and even creating women's sense of sexual danger in the last 150 years. In that movement, two themes more than others have encapsulated and symbolized women's fears: prostitution and rape. There is a certain parallel construction between the nineteenth-century focus on prostitution and the modern emphasis on rape as the quintessential sexual terror. It is remarkable, in fact, how little emphasis nineteenth-century feminists placed on rape per se. It is as if the norms of legal sexual intercourse were in themselves so objectionable that rape did not seem that much worse! Instead feminists used prostitution as the leading symbol of male sexual coercion. While rape is an episode, prostitution suggests a condition that takes hold of a woman for a long time—possibly for life—difficult to escape. The symbolic emphasis in prostitution is on ownership, possession, purchase by men, while in rape it is on pure violence. Rape can happen to any woman, while prostitution involves the separation of women into the good and the bad, a division with class implications, as we shall see, even when the division is blamed on men.

Lest it seem trivializing to the real sufferings of women as prostitutes or rape victims to treat experiences as symbols or metaphors, let us emphasize again our subject: we are looking at how feminists conceptualized different sexual dangers, as a means of organizing *resistance* to sexual oppression. We want to look at how these feminist strategies changed, so that we can examine historically how we conduct feminist campaigns around sexual issues today.

In different periods, feminists emphasized different aspects of prostitution. In the 1860s and 1870s, for example, they focused on the economic pressures forcing women into sexual commerce, while in the Progressive Era their primary theme was "white slavery," the physical coercion of women into the trade. Despite these shifts, however, aspects of their approach to prostitution were consistent. First, they exaggerated its magnitude.[2] They did so because their definition of prostitute included virtually all women who engaged in casual sex, whether or not they were paid. Second, feminists consistently exaggerated the coerciveness of prostitution. In their eagerness to identify the social structural forces encouraging prostitution, they denied the prostitute any role other than that of passive victim. They insisted that the women involved were sexual innocents, helpless young women who "fell" into illicit sex. They assumed that prostitution was so degrading that no woman could freely choose it, not even with the relative degree of freedom with which she could choose to be a wife or a wage earner. Thus the "fallen woman" was always viewed as a direct victim, not only of male dominance in general, but of kidnapping, sexual imprisonment, starvation, and/or seduction in particular.[3] These attitudes toward prostitution were not exclusive to feminists, but were also part of the ideological outlook of many male reformers, including some antifeminists. Our point here, however, is that feminists not only failed to challenge this oversimplified and condescending explanation of prostitution, but also made it central to their understanding of women's oppression.

The feminists' exclusive emphasis on the victimization of the prostitute ultimately prevented their transcending a sexual morality dividing women into the good and the bad.[4] They wanted to rescue women from prostitution, and to admit prostitution's victims into the salvation of good womanhood; but they clung fast to the idea that some kinds of sex were inherently criminal, and they were confounded by the existence of unrepentant whores. Furthermore, their equation of prostitution with any illicit sex indicates that a crucial element of their fear was loss of respectability. The power of prostitution rested on the common understanding that once a woman had sex outside of marriage she was "ruined," and would become a prostitute sooner or later. This potential loss of respectability was not imaginary, but a real, material process with sanctions that varied by culture and class. For middle-class and many white working-class women, the loss of purity—we would call it, getting a bad reputation— damaged prospects for marriage. It led to a total loss of control over one's own sexuality, as once "used" by a man, women became free game for that entire sex.

Maintaining respectability was an especially severe problem for black women, fighting to free their entire race from a slave heritage that tended to place them at the disposal of white men's sexual demands. Thus the black women's movement conducted a particularly militant campaign for respectability, often making black feminists spokespeople for prudery in their communities.[5] White feminists assimilated the horror of black slavery to their fears of prostitution. They understood the sexual tyranny of slavery as central, and as a form of prostitution; among their most powerful antislavery writings were images of beautiful, pure black womanhood defiled; and white feminist abolitionists found it difficult to accept the possibility of willing sex between black women and white men.[6]

The fear of prostitution represented also a fear of direct physical violence, but in a displaced manner. In the nineteenth century, as today, women encountered sexual and nonsexual violence most often at home. Rape in marriage was no crime, not even generally disapproved; wifebeating was only marginally criminal. Incest was common enough to require skepticism about the idea that it was tabooed. Although feminists occasionally organized against domestic violence, they did not make it the object of a sustained campaign, largely because they were unable to challenge the family politically.[7] The focus on prostitution was a focus on extrafamilial violence. Nineteenth-century feminists came closer to intrafamily matters in the temperance campaign. Their criticisms of drinking were laced through with imagery of the bestial, violent quality of male sexuality, but blaming alcohol also allowed a displacement of focus, an avoidance of criticizing men and marriage directly.[8]

Certain dangers in marriage had to be faced. One was venereal disease, and this too was assimilated to the central imagery of prostitution, for men who patronized prostitutes could then transmit disease to their wives. In keeping with the division of women between good and bad, feminists implicitly considered prostitution as the source of venereal disease. The communicability and incurability of these diseases proved to them that absolute monogamy was women's only source of safety amid the sexual dangers.[9] (One is reminded of conservative response to herpes today.) Feminists also opposed the sexual demands of self-centered husbands on their wives, which law and convention obligated women to meet. But instead of protesting "marital rape," as we do, they criticized what they called "legalized prostitution" in marriage.[10]

Sex posed another serious danger in marriage—unwanted conception. Given the equation of sex with intercourse, and the lack of access to reliable contraception, desire to control conceptions often resulted in the antisexual attitudes of women.[11] Despite a great reverence for motherhood, an unexpected pregnancy was often threatening. For poor women, for virtually all black women, having children meant introducing them into social and economic circumstances where their safety and well-being could not be guaranteed. Even for prosperous women, mothers' economic dependence on men was extreme. Single motherhood was an extremely difficult situation in the absence of any regular welfare or childcare provisions. Mothers were frequently forced to remain with abusive men for fear of losing their children. Indeed, prostitution was sometimes seen as an option for a single mother, for at least she could do it while she remained at home with her children![12] A bitter irony surrounds the place of motherhood in the sexual system of nineteenth-century feminism: clearly it was women's greatest joy and source of dignity; for many women it was what made sexual intercourse acceptable. But at the same time motherhood was the last straw in enforcing women's subordination to men, the factor that finally prevented many from seeking independence. What was conceived as women's greatest virtue, their passionate and self-sacrificing commitment to their children, their capacity for love itself, was a leading factor in their victimization.

Of the many factors constructing the feminist fear of prostitution perhaps none is so hard for contemporary feminists to understand as religion. But we would miss the dilemma that these women faced in dealing with sex if we did not thoroughly appreciate their religious culture. Those actively rebelling against established religion were as influenced by it as the dutiful church members or Christian reform activists. All had been raised on the concept of sin, especially sexual sin. They all shared the view that there could be high and low pleasures, and the guilt they felt about indulging in the low was not just psychological self-doubt. It was a sense of self-violation, of violation of the source of their dignity.[13]

We are arguing here that the feminist understanding of sexual danger, expressed so poignantly in the fear of prostitution, must be seen as part of a sexual system in which they were participants, sometimes willing and sometimes unwilling, sometimes conscious and sometimes unaware.[14] Their very resistance often drew them into accomodation with aspects of this oppressive system. What is surprising is the extent of resistance that actually challenged this sexual system. Some women labelled "loose," who might or might not have been prostitutes, rejected the notion that their disreputable sexual behavior was something to be ashamed of or something that had been forced upon them.[15] There were young sexual "delinquents" who took pleasure and pride in their rebellion.[16] There were women who passed as men in order to seize male sexual (and other) prerogatives, and to take other women as wives.[17] Even respectable, middle-class married women had orgasms more than they were supposed to. One survey had 40 percent of women reporting orgasms occasionally, 20 percent frequently, and 40 percent never, proportions which may not be so different than those among women today.[18] About the present, it is angering that so many women do not experience orgasm; about the past, it is impressive—and analytically important—that so many women did. In other words, our nineteenth-century legacy is one of resistance to sexual repression as well as victimization by it.

Despite resistance, the weight of the nineteenth-century feminist concern was with protection from danger. This approach, usually known as "social purity," reflected an experienced reality and was overwhelmingly protectionist in its emphasis.

The major target of the feminist social purity advocates was the double standard. Their attack on it had, in turn, two aspects: seeking greater safety for women and more penalties for men. Their object was to achieve a set of controls over sexuality, structured through the family, enforced through law and/or social morality, which would render sex, if not safe, at least a decent, calculable risk for women. Social purity feminists railed against male sexual privileges, against the vileness of male drunkenness and lust, and they sought with every means at their disposal to increase the costs attached to such indulgences.[19]

The most positive achievements of social purity feminism were in the homes and communities of the middle-class women most likely to be its advocates. Here, efforts to make marriage laws more egalitarian, upgrade women's property rights, and improve women's educational and professional opportunities altered the balance of power between wife and husband. Social purity thought emphasized the importance of consensual sex for women, and insisted that even married women should not be coerced into any sexual activities they did not choose freely; inasmuch as they believed that sexual drive and initiative were primarily male, they understood this as women's right to say no. Through organizations like the Women's Christian Temperance Union, feminists propagandized for these standards, with tirades against the threat to civilization caused by immorality, and with energetic moral and sex education programs.[20] And they succeeded in changing culture and consciousness. Without knowing precisely how much peoples' lives conformed to this standard, we can say that the ideal of marital mutuality and a woman's right to say no were absorbed into middle-class culture by the turn of the century. There is mounting evidence that, for reasons not yet clear, immigrant and poor women did not establish the same standards of marital mutuality, but fought for power within their families differently, by accepting certain patriarchal prerogatives while asserting their power as mothers and housewives.[21]

The negative consequences of social purity's single-minded focus on sexual danger come into focus when we look at their vigorous campaign against prostitution. Over time the repressive tendencies of this campaign overwhelmed its liberatory aspects and threw a pall over feminism's whole approach to sexuality. The beginning of women's reform work on prostitution in the early nineteenth century was a big step forward in the development of feminism. That "respectable" women took the risk of reaching out, across a veritable gulf of sexual sin, to women stigmatized as whores, was a declaration of female collectivity that transcended class and moralistic divisions. The reformers visited and talked with prostitutes, conducted public discussion of the issue, and established homes into which prostitutes could "escape." In doing so they were opening a crack in the wall of sexual "innocence" that would eventually widen into an escape route for women of their class as well. The attitudes that we today perceive as a patronizing desire to "help," were initially a challenge to the punitive and woman-hating morality that made sexual "ruin" a permanent and irredeemable condition for women.[22]

In the 1860s and 1870s feminists reactivated themselves into a militant and successful campaign to halt government regulation of prostitution. The system of regulation, already in existence in France and parts of England, forced women alleged to be prostitutes to submit to vaginal examinations and licensing; its purpose was to allow men to have sex with prostitutes without the risk of venereal disease. Feminist opposition drew not only from their anger at men who bought female flesh, but also reaffirmed their identification with prostitutes' victimization. Feminists asserted that all women, even prostitutes, had a right to the integrity of their own bodies.[23]

But, after a relatively easy victory over government regulation, social purity feminists began to press for the abolition of prostitution itself. They sponsored legislation to increase the criminal penalties for men clients, while continuing to express sympathy with the "victimized" women. The catch was that the prostitutes had to agree that they were victims. The "white slavery" interpretation of prostitution—that prostitutes had been forced into the business—allowed feminists to see themselves as rescuers of slaves.[24] But if the prostitutes were not contrite, or denied the immorality of their actions, they lost their claim to the aid and sympathy of the reformers. "The big sisters of the world [want the] chance to protect the little and weaker sisters, by surrounding them with the right laws for them to obey for their own good," one feminist explained, unwittingly capturing the repressive character of this "sisterhood."[25] The class nature of American society encouraged these middle-class feminists to conduct their challenge to the double standard through other women's lives, and to focus their anger on men other than their own husbands and fathers.

Another attack on prostitution which sometimes turned into an attack on women was the campaign to raise the age of sexual consent.[26] In many states in the nineteenth century this had been as low as nine or ten years for girls. The feminist goals were to deny the white slavers their younger victims, to extend sexual protection to girls, and to provide punishments for male assailants. Like most of these feminist sexual causes this one had in it a radical moment: it communicated an accurate critique of the limitations of "consent" by women in a male-dominated society. Yet by late in the century, when urban life and the presence of millions of young working girls changed the shape of family and generational relations, age-of-consent legislation explicitly denied women the right to heterosexual activity until they were adults, or—and note that this qualification applied at any age—married. In fostering this hostility to girls' sexual activity, the feminists colluded in the labeling of a new class of female offenders: teenage sex delinquents. Sex delinquency was soon the largest category within which young women were sent to reformatories.[27] These moralistic reformers, some of them feminists, allowed the criminal justice system to take over the task of disciplining teenage girls to conform to respectable morality.

This inability to see anything in prostitution but male tyranny and/or economic oppression affected not only "bad" women, but the "good" ones as well. Feminists' refusal to engage in a concrete examination of the actuality of prostitution was of a piece with their inability to look without panic at any form of sexual nonconformity. We do not suggest that prostitutes were necessarily freer than other women sexually. Our point is that feminists remained committed to the containment of female sexuality within heterosexual marriage, despite the relative sexual repressiveness that marriage meant for women at that time.[28] "Are our girls to be [as] free to please themselves by indulging in the loveless gratification of every instinct . . . and passion as our boys?" the social purity feminist Frances Willard asked her audience in 1891; and we can imagine that they answered with a resounding "No!"[29]

Feminist politics about sex became more conservative in the period up to World War I because women's aspirations and possibilities outstripped the feminist orthodoxy. Growing feminist organizational strength, and the ability to influence legislation, combined with the class and racial elitism of the world in which the feminists moved, further strengthened their conservative political tendencies. Social purity feminists not only accepted a confining sexual morality for women, but they also excluded from their sisterhood women who did not or could not go along. The prostitute remained, for all their sympathy for her, the leading symbol of the woman excluded, not only from male-bestowed privilege, but also from the women's community.[30]

Yet, just as there was behavioral resistance to the sexually repressive culture of the nineteenth century, so too there was political resistance within the women's movement. Although a decidedly minority viewpoint, a thin but continuous stream of feminists insisted that increased sexual activity was not incompatible with women's dignity and might even be in women's interests. We refer to this as the "pro-sex" tendency within the feminist tradition. It began with the free love and utopian movements of the 1820s through the 1840s. These radicals challenged the identification of sexual desire as masculine; and even though they remained for the most part advocates of the strictest monogamy, they challenged the coercive family and legal marriage as the channels for sexuality.[31] In the 1870s the free lover Victoria Woodhull appeared as a spokesperson from within the women's movement, idealizing as "true love" sex that involved mutual desire and orgasms for both parties.[32] At the same time Elizabeth Cady Stanton, a revered, if maverick, heroine, also asserted women's sexual desires.[33] In the 1880s and 1890s a few extremely visionary free love feminists began to formulate the outlines of a sexuality not organized around the male orgasm. Alice Stockham, a physician and suffragist, condemned the "ordinary, hasty and spasmodic mode of cohabitation . . . in which the wife is a passive party" and envisioned instead a union in which "the desires and pleasure of the wife calls forth the desire and pleasure of the husband."[34] Still, on the whole these nineteenth-century feminists were only relatively "pro-sex," and most of them shared with social purity advocates a belief in the need to control, contain, and harness physiological sex expression to "higher" ends. Furthermore, even this limited sex-radical tradition was so marginal to American feminism that when the twentieth-century feminist Margaret Sanger searched for a more positive attitude to sex, she had to go to Europe to find it.

The only issue within mainstream nineteenth-century feminism where "pro-sex" ideas had a significant impact was divorce. Led by Cady Stanton, some feminists argued that the right to divorce and *then to remarry*—for that was the crucial element, the right to another sexual relationship after leaving a first—was a freedom important enough to women to risk granting it to men as well. Still, most feminists took a strict social purity line and opposed divorce for fear it would weaken marriage and expose women to even greater sexual danger.[35]

Ironically, one sexual reform strongly supported by social purity advocates became the vehicle by which a new generation of feminists began to break with the social purity tradition. This was birth control.[36] Nineteenth-century feminists had argued this as "voluntary motherhood," the right of women to refuse intercourse with their husbands if they did not want to conceive. Voluntary motherhood was a brilliant tactic because it insinuated a rejection of men's sexual domination into a politics of defending and improving motherhood. Consistent with its social purity orientation, voluntary motherhood advocates rejected contraception as a form of birth control for fear it would allow men to force even more sex upon their wives and to indulge in extramarital sex with even greater impunity. In the early twentieth century, by contrast, an insurgent feminist support for contraception arose, insisting that sexual abstinence was an unnecessary price for women to pay for reproductive self-determination, and that sexual indulgence in the pursuit of pleasure was good for women.

That this new generation of feminists could break with social purity was possible in part because they were no longer controlled by their fear of becoming, or being labeled, prostitutes. They no longer saw the prostitute as only a victim; they began to break the association between sexual desire and prostitution. Indeed they embraced and romanticized sexual daring of all sorts.[37] The specter of the white slaver no longer haunted them, and they were willing to take risks. They ventured unchaperoned into theaters and bars, lived without families in big cities, and moved about the city to discover the lives of those across class and race boundaries where their mothers would not have gone. Some of their names you recognize—Emma Goldman, Margaret Sanger, Crystal Eastman, Elizabeth Gurley Flynn, even Louise Bryant—but there were many many more. Above all they asserted a woman's right to be sexual. They slept with men without marrying. They took multiple lovers. They became single mothers. Some of them had explicitly sexual relationships with other women, although a subsequent repression of evidence, along with their own silences about homosexuality, make it hard for us to uncover this aspect of their sexual lives.[38]

In many ways these women were beginning to explore a sexual world which we are determined to occupy. But as pioneers they could explore only part of it and they did not imagine changing its overall boundaries. Even when it contradicted their own experience, they continued to accept a male and heterosexual definition of the "sex act." They were, so to speak, upwardly mobile, and they wanted integration into the sexual world as defined by men. The man's orgasm remained the central event, although now it was preferable if a woman had one at the same time; stimulation other than intercourse was considered foreplay; masturbation was unhealthy. And sex, all the more desirable now because of the transcendent possibilities they attributed to it, remained bound up with the structure of gender: it could only happen between a man and a woman.[39] These feminists criticized male dominance in the labor force and in the public arena, but they did not seem to notice how it shaped sex. They fought for women's freedom, but they rarely criticized men.

Once the organized women's rights movement began to fade, women who advocated this "pro-sex" politics were more and more alienated from a larger community of women; they seemed to feel that to enter the world of sex, they had to travel alone and leave other women behind. This rejection of women occurred both because the dominant tradition of feminism was so antisexual, and because their own understanding of sex was so heterosexual. They were part of a generation that branded intense female friendships as adolescent.[40] The tragedy was that in rejecting a community of women which they experienced as constricting and repressive, they left behind their feminist heritage.

At the same time these pioneering sex radicals offer us a positive legacy in their willingness to take risks. It would be easier if we could progress toward sexual liberation without sufferings, if we could resolve the tension between seeking pleasure and avoiding danger by some simple policy; but we cannot. We must conduct our sexual politics in the real world. For women this is like advancing across a mined field. Looking only to your feet to avoid the mines means missing the horizon, and the vision of why the advance is worthwhile; but if you only see the future possibilities you may blow yourself up.

If this is warlike imagery, it is not bravado. The dangers are substantial, women are assaulted and killed. But each act of violence against women would be multiplied in its effect if it prevented us from seeing where we have won victories, and if it induced us to resign ourselves to restriction of our sexual lives and constriction of our public activities.

Seen in this light, the contemporary focus on rape and other sexual violence against women represents an advance over the earlier campaign against prostitution. Through this new conceptualization of the problem of sexual danger, feminists have rejected the victim blaming that was inherent in the notion of the "fallen woman"; we know that any of us can be raped. Our critique of sexual violence is an institutional analysis of the whole system of male supremacy which attempts to show the commonalities of women, as potential agents as well as victims. Thus the campaign against rape comes out of our strength as well as our victimization. Whether the actual incidence of rape has increased or decreased, the feminist offensive against it represents an escalation of our demands for freedom. We have redefined rape to include many sexual encounters that nineteenth-century feminists would have considered mere seduction, and for which they might have held the woman responsible; we have included in our definition of rape what was once normal marital intercourse. We have denied impunity to any men: we will bring charges against boyfriends, fathers, and teachers; we will label as sexual harassment what was once the ordinary banter of males asserting their dominance. We declare our right—still contested, viciously—to safety not only in our homes but in the streets. We *all* intend to be streetwalkers.

It is vital to strategy building to know when we are winning and when losing, and where. Failing to claim and take pride in our victories leads to the false conclusion that nothing has changed. When the campaign against rape is fought as if we were the eternal, unchanged victims of male sexuality, we run the risk of reentering the kind of social purity world view that so limited the nineteenth-century feminist vision.[41] It is important to offer our comprehensive critique of misogyny, violence, and male dominance without ceding the arena of sexuality itself to the men, as the nineteenth-century feminists did.

We have tried to show that social purity politics, although an understandable reaction to women's nineteenth-century experience, was a limited and limiting vision for women. Thus we called it conservative. Today, there seems to be a revival of social purity politics within feminism, and it is concern about this tendency that motivates us in recalling its history. As in the nineteenth-century, there is today a feminist attack on pornography and sexual "perversion" in our time, which fails to distinguish its politics from a conservative and antifeminist version of social purity, the Moral Majority and "family protection movement." The increasing tendency to focus almost exclusively on sex as the primary arena of women's exploitation, and to attribute women's sexual victimization to some violent essence labeled "male sexuality" is even more conservative today, because our situation as women has changed so radically. Modern social purists point to one set of changes. The rise of sexual consumerism, and the growing power of the mass media to enforce conformity to sexual norms are debilitating for women's sexual freedom. As feminists, we are learning to be suspicious of a sexual politics that simply calls for "doing your own thing," and to ask whether women's desires are represented in these visions of sexual "freedom." We must not make the same mistake as the early twentieth-century sexual libertarians who believed that ending sexual inhibition in itself could save women. Instead, we have to continue to analyze how male supremacy and other forms of domination shape what we think of as "free" sexuality.

But there have been liberating developments as well, that we can ill afford to ignore. Women have possibilities for sexual subjectivity and self-creation today that did not exist in the past. We have a vision of sexuality that is not exclusively heterosexual, nor tied to reproduction. We have a much better physiological understanding of sexual feeling, and a vision of ungendered parenting. We have several strong intellectual traditions for understanding the psychological and social formation of sexuality. Perhaps most important, we have today at least a chance at economic independence, the necessary material condition for women's sexual liberation. Finally, we have something women have never enjoyed before—a feminist past, a history of 150 years of feminist theory and praxis in the area of sexuality. This is a resource too precious to squander by not learning it, in all its complexity.

NOTES

Since this paper grew out of material we have been thinking about for years, our intellectual debts are literally innumerable. For specific critical comments on this paper we want to thank Ann Ferguson, Vivian Gornick, Amber Hollibaugh, Jill Lewis, Cora Kaplan, Esther Newton, Ann Snitow, Carol Vance, Judith R. Walkowitz, and Marilyn B. Young. About this paper we need to add, more than ever, that we alone are responsible for our conclusions. This paper was originally written for the Ninth Barnard Conference on the Scholar and the Feminist, April 1982, New York City.

1. These "homosocial" relationships are documented and analyzed in Lillian S. Faderman, *Surpassing the Love of Men: Romantic Friendship and Love between Women from the Renaissance to the Present* (New York: William Morrow & Co., 1981); Carroll Smith-Rosenberg, "The Female World of Love and Ritual: Relations between Women in Nineteenth-Century America," *Signs*, 1 (Autumn 1975): 1-29; Blanche Wiesen Cook, "Female Support Networks and Political Activism: Lillian Wald, Crystal Eastman, Emma Goldman," *Chrysalis* 3 (1977): 43-61.

We distinguish here between behavior recognized as sexual by its actors and behavior not so recognized, aware that some historians will not agree. Furthermore, we are also emphasizing the importance of conscious sexual thought, theorizing and politicizing for the feminist effort to transform women's sexual experience. We do so aware that, in the past decade, in an exciting renaissance of feminist historical scholarship, women's history scholars have chosen to focus more on behavior and culture than on political ideology. In the history of American feminism, for reasons that are undoubtedly important to explore, the initial focus for explicitly sexual politics was on the relations between women and men. The history and chronology of feminist conceptualization of what we today call lesbianism is different and we do not address it here, but Carroll Smith-Rosenberg and Esther Newton do so in their paper, "The Mythic Lesbian and the New Woman: Power, Sexuality and Legitimacy," delivered at the "Fifth Berkshire Conference on the History of Women," June 1981, Poughkeepsie, New York.

2. For instance, in 1913, a suffrage newspaper estimated that there were 15,000 to 20,000 prostitutes in New York City, who serviced 150,000 to 225,000 male customers daily; this would work out to roughly 1 out of every 100 females in all five boroughs and 1 out of every 10 males. See *Women's Political World*, (2 June 1913), 7. Using a more precise definition of prostitution, for example, women who supported themselves solely by commercial sex, a member of New York City's Vice Commission estimated less than one-half that number (Frederick Whitten to Mary Sumner Boyd, 17 March 1916, National American Woman Suffrage Association Collection, New York Public Library).

3. The historical literature on nineteenth-century and early twentieth-century reformers' views of prostitution is extensive. The best recent study is Judith R. Walkowitz, *Prostitution and Victorian Society: Women, Class, and the State* (Cambridge: Cambridge University Press, 1980); much less aware of issues concerning gender, see

Mark Connelly, *Response to Prostitution in the Progressive Era* (Chapel Hill: University of North Carolina Press, 1980).

4. Marian S. Goldman, *Gold Diggers and Silver Miners: Prostitution and Social Life on the Comstock Lode* (Ann Arbor: University of Michigan Press, 1981), chap. 7. Also see Elizabeth Jameson, "Imperfect Unions: Class and Gender in Cripple Creek, 1894-1904," in *Class, Sex, and the Woman Worker*, ed. Milton Cantor and Bruce Laurie (Westport, Conn.: Greenwood, 1977).

5. *Black Women in White America: A Documentary History*, ed. Gerda Lerner (New York: Pantheon, 1972), 150-72; Cynthia Neverdon-Morton, "The Black Woman's Struggle for Equality in the South, 1895-1925," in *The Afro-American Woman: Struggle and Images*, ed. Sharon Harley and Rosalyn Terborg-Penn (Port Washington: Kennikat, 1978), 55-56.

After attending the 1914 convention of the National Association of Colored Women, white feminist Zona Gale wrote of black women's effort to work "against the traffic in women (which I hope I shall never again call the 'white slave' traffic)." See *Life and Labor* "National Association of Colored Women's Biennial," 4 (September 1914): 264.

6. For examples of feminist abolitionists' focus on sexual abuse in their attacks on slavery, see Lydia Maria Child, "Appeal in Favor of That Class of Americans Called Africans," in *America Through Women's Eyes*, ed. Mary R. Beard (New York: MacMillan, 1933), 164; and Elizabeth Cady Stanton, "Speech to the [1860] Anniversary of the American Anti-Slavery Society," in *Elizabeth Cady Stanton-Susan B. Anthony: Correspondence, Writings, Speeches*, ed. Ellen C. DuBois (New York: Schocken, 1981), 84.

The reluctance of white feminist abolitionists to acknowledge the possibility of affection and/or voluntary sex between black women and white men can be seen in the initial response of Angelina and Sarah Grimke to the discovery that their brother had fathered a child by a slave woman. They assumed that Thomas Grimke had raped the woman, but their nephew Archibald, who had been raised as a slave, objected that this was untrue and cast his parents and the circumstances of his birth in a sordid light.

7. Linda Gordon, *Woman's Body, Woman's Right: A Social History of Birth Control in America* (New York: Viking, 1976), chaps. 5 and 6; William L. O'Neill, *Everyone Was Brave: A History of Feminism in America* (Chicago: Quadrangle, 1971).

8. Barbara Leslie Epstein, *The Politics of Domesticity: Women, Evangelism, and Temperance in Nineteenth-Century America* (Middletown: Wesleyan University Press, 1981), 100-14; Ruth Bordin, *Woman and Temperance: The Quest for Power and Liberty, 1873-1900* (Philadelphia: Temple University Press, 1981), 7, 26.

9. Walkowitz, chap. 3; Gordon, *Woman's Body, Woman's Right*, 106; E.M. Sigsworth and T.J. Wyke, "A Study in Victorian Prostitution and Venereal Disease," in *Suffer and Be Still: Women in the Victorian Age*, ed. Martha Vicinus (Bloomington: Indiana University Press, 1972); Connelly, chap. 4.

10. For example see Elizabeth Cady Stanton, "Speech to the McFarland-Richardson Protest Meeting," 1869 in *Elizabeth Cady Stanton, Susan B. Anthony*, 129; Clara Cleghorne Hoffman, "Social Purity," and Lucinda B. Chandler, "Marriage Reform," in *Report of the International Council of Women* (Washington, D.C.: R.H. Darby, 1888), 283, 285.

11. See Gordon, chap. 5, "Voluntary Motherhood."

12. Evidence of these problems abounds in case records of social service agencies used by Linda Gordon in her research on family violence, and in her paper, "Child-saving and the Single Mother: A View from the Perspective of the Massachusetts Society for the Prevention of Cruelty to Children, 1880-1920."

13. For an exceptionally good account of the religious culture of nineteenth-century

women and the conflicts it generated, see Kathryn Kish Sklar, *Catherine Beecher: A Study in American Domesticity* (New Haven: Yale University Press, 1973); the major nineteenth-century feminist opponent of women's religious traditions was Elizabeth Cady Stanton; see *Elizabeth Cady Stanton, Susan B. Anthony,* pt. 3.

14. In taking this approach, we are drawing on two recent schools of historical interpretation: feminist historians, for instance, Nancy Cott, Gerda Lerner, and Ann Douglas, who emphasize the role of women as active agents of cultural change, but who have concentrated on domesticity rather than sexuality; and male theorists of sexuality, notably Michele Foucault, who regard sexuality as a socially constructed, historically specific cultural system, but leave women out of their accounts.

15. Ruth Rosen, and Sue Davison, eds., *The Maimie Papers,* (Old Westbury, N.Y.: Feminist Press, 1977).

16. Estelle B. Freedman, *Their Sisters' Keepers: Women's Prison Reform in America, 1830-1930* (Ann Arbor: University of Michigan Press, 1981); Rosalind Rosenberg, *Beyond Separate Spheres: Intellectual Roots of Modern Feminism* (New Haven: Yale University Press, 1982), chap. 5 and p. 228. Sheldon Glueck and Eleanor T. Glueck, *Five Hundred Delinquent Women* (New York: Alfred A. Knopf, 1934), chap. 5; Mabel Ruth Fernald et al., *A Study of Women Delinquents in New York State* (New York: Century, 1920), chap. 12.

17. Jonathan Katz, *Gay American History: Lesbians and Gay Men in American History* (New York: Crowell, 1976), pt. 3; Erna O. Hellerstein et al., eds, *Victorian Women: A Documentary Account of Women's Lives in Nineteenth-Century England, France, and the United States* (Stanford: Stanford University Press, 1981), 185-89.

18. Carl Degler, *At Odds: Women and the Family in America from the Revolution to the Present* (New York: Oxford, 1980), 262-63. Beatrice Campbell, "Feminist Sexual Politics: Now You See It, Now You Don't," *Feminist Review* no. 5 (1981): 1-18. For a contemporary assessment of women's orgasms, see Shere Hite, *The Hite Report: A Nationwide Study on Female Sexuality* (New York: MacMillan, 1976). Despite conceptual problems, Hite's study points to women's continuing problems with having orgasms, at least in partnered sex.

19. David J. Pivar, *Purity Crusade: Sexual Morality and Social Control, 1868-1900* (Westport, Conn.: Greenwood, 1973); Degler, chap. 12; Walkowitz, chap. 12; Gordon, chap. 6; Social Purity Session, *Report of the International Council of Women,* 251-84.

20. Epstein, 125-37; Bordin, chap. 6.

21. For a good summary of black and immigrant family life, in contrast to middle-class families, see Degler, chap. 4 and passim. For specific evidence of poor women's weaker marital position vis-à-vis their husbands' sexual demands, see Eli S. Zaretsky, "Female Sexuality and the Catholic Confessional," Special Issue on Women—Sex and Sexuality, *Signs* 6 (Autumn 1980): 176-84; and Ruth Hall, ed., *Dear Dr. Stopes: Sex in the 1920s,* (New York: Penguin, 1978), chaps. 1 ("The Lower Classes") and 2 ("The Upper Classes"). Note that we deliberately avoid expressing this difference as a contrast between middle- and working-class families. We suspect that greater male sexual dominance is not so much a matter of proletarian experience as it is of peasant authoritarian background and women's extreme economic dependence.

22. Carroll Smith-Rosenberg, "Beauty, the Beast, and the Militant Woman: A Case Study in Sex Roles and Social Stress in Jacksonian America," *American Quarterly* 23 (October 1971): 562-84; Mary P. Ryan, "Power of Women's Networks: A Case Study of Female Moral Reform in Antebellum America," *Feminist Studies* 5 (Spring 1979): 66-85; Barbara Berg, *The Remembered Gate: Origins of American Feminism* (New York: Oxford, 1978).

23. Walkowitz, pt. 2; Pivar, chap. 2; Degler, 284-88; John Burnham, "Medical Inspection of Prostitutes in America in the Nineteenth Century: St. Louis Experiment and its Sequel," *Bulletin of the History of Medicine* 45 (May-June 1971): 203-18.

24. Connelly, chap. 6; Pivar, 135-39; Walkowitz, epilogue; Deborah Gorham, "'The Maiden Tribute of Modern Babylon' Re-Examined: Child Prostitution and the Idea of Childhood in Late Victorian England," *Victorian Studies* 21 (Spring 1978): 353-79; Mari Jo Buhle, *Women and American Socialism, 1870-1920* (Urbana: University of Illinois Press, 1981), 253-56.

25. Jeanette Young Norton, "Women Builders of Civilization," *Women's Political World*, 1 September 1913, 5.

26. On efforts to raise the age of consent, see Pivar, 139-46; Degler, 288-89; Gorham; Michael Pearson, *The Age of Consent: Victorian Prostitution and its Enemies* (London: Newton Abbot, David and Charles, 1972).

27. Steven Schlossman and Stephanie Wallach, "The Crime of Precocious Sexuality: Female Juvenile Delinquency in the Progressive Era," *Harvard Educational Review* 48 (February 1978): 65-94; Steven Schlossman, *Love and the American Delinquent* (Chicago: University of Chicago Press, 1977); William I. Thomas, *The Unadjusted Girl, with Cases and Standpoint for Behavior Analysis* (Boston: Little, Brown, 1923).

28. Leslie Fishbein, "Harlot or Heroine? Changing Views of Prostitution, 1870-1920," *Historian* 43 (December 1980): 23-35.

29. Quoted in Pivar, 157.

30. This is one of the themes in *The Maimie Papers.* Wrote sometime prostitute Maimie Pinzer, "I would like to have women friends—but I can't have . . . I dreaded [they] would find out, perhaps inadvertently, something about me, and perhaps cut me, and I couldn't stand that," (p. 10).

31. On the free love movement in general, see Taylor Stoehr, *Free Love in America: A Documentary History* (New York: AMS Press, 1979); Hal D. Sears, *The Sex Radicals: Free Love in High Victorian America* (Lawrence, Kans.: Regents Press of Kansas, 1977); Gordon, chaps. 5 and 6; Mary S. Marsh, *Anarchist Women, 1870-1920* (Philadelphia: Temple University Press, 1981), chap. 4; William Leach, *True Love and Perfect Union: Feminist Reform of Sex and Society* (New York: Basic Books, 1981), 82-83 and passim. We use the term "pro-sex" provisionally, in lieu of a more precise term which is yet to emerge.

32. Victoria C. Woodhull, *Tried as by Fire: Or, the True and the False Socially: An Oration* (New York: Woodhull & Claflin, 1874).

33. *Elizabeth Cady Stanton, Susan B. Anthony,* 94-98 and 185-87.

34. Alice Stockham, *Karezza: Ethics of Marriage* (Chicago: Alice B. Stockham, 1897), 22.

35. William L. O'Neill, *Divorce in the Progressive Era* (New York: Franklin Watts, 1973); *Elizabeth Cady Stanton, Susan B. Anthony,* passim.; Leach, passim.

36. Gordon, chap. 5; James Reed, *From Private Vice to Public Virtue: The Birth Control Movement and American Society Since 1830* (New York: Basic Books, 1978).

37. Caroline Ware, *Greenwich Village, 1920-1930* (Boston: Houghton Mifflin, 1935); Floyd Dell, *Love in Greenwich Village* (New York: George H. Doran, 1926); Rheta Childe Dorr, *A Woman of Fifty* (New York: Funk & Wagnalls, 1924); Judith Schwarz, *Radical Feminists of Heterodoxy, Greenwich Village, 1912-1940* (Lebanon, N.H.: New Victoria Publishers, 1982); Buhle, 257-68; Gordon, 189-99.

38. For lesbianism among the Greenwich Village feminists see Schwarz, 30-31 and 67-72. Also see Marion K. Sanders, *Dorothy Thompson: A Legend in Her Time* (Boston: Houghton Mifflin, 1973). Emma Goldman's relationship with Almeda Sperry is discussed in Katz, pp. 523-29. Elizabeth Gurley Flynn's long relationship with the pioneering

lesbian, Marie Equi, is traced in Rosalyn F. Baxandall's introduction, "Selected Writings of Elizabeth Gurley Flynn, unpublished manuscript; there is also some suggestion that Flynn gave lesbianism a positive treatment in her original draft of *The Alderson Story: My Life as a Political Prisoner* (New York: International Publishers, 1972) but that Communist party officials insisted that she rewrite the material and make her portrait more judgmental and negative (Baxandall, private communication to authors, 1982). The larger issue of repression of evidence of lesbianism is considered in Blanche Wiesen Cook, "The Historical Denial of Lesbianism," *Radical History Review* 5 (Spring/Summer 1979): 55-60.

39. Gordon, 359-80; note the *new* insistence on the importance of the vagina, replacing an older recognition of the role of the clitoris in women's experience of orgasm.

40. Faderman, pts. 2 and 3; Christina Simmons, "Compassionate Marriage and the Lesbian Threat," Special Issue on Lesbian History, *Frontiers* 4 (Fall 1979): 54-59; Nancy Sahli, "Smashing: Women's Friendships Before the Fall," *Chrysalis* 8 (Summer 1979): 17-27.

41. For a major modern feminist study of rape, extremely important to our movement but marred by its ahistorical assumptions, see Susan Brownmiller, *Against Our Will: Men, Women, and Rape* (New York: Simon & Schuster, 1975).

"LIVING THE PRINCIPLE" OF PLURAL MARRIAGE: MORMON WOMEN, UTOPIA, AND FEMALE SEXUALITY IN THE NINETEENTH CENTURY

JULIE DUNFEY

> I could not listen to the sermon for looking at those wretched and deluded women, who first enslaved by this atrocious fanaticism, were then swayed at the will of their prophet. I asked myself what new principle of mental magnetism or psychology could fully explain their submission and his power.
>
> *Harper's Weekly*, 10 Oct. 1857

The role of women in Mormonism was the subject of intense controversy in the nineteenth century, usually eliciting emotional responses about the enslavement or delusion of women who would participate in a plural marriage. Non-Mormons associated female members of the Latter-day Saints Church first and foremost with polygamy, a radical, and to most Americans an unacceptable, innovation in sexual roles. Polygamy ran counter to the larger society's monogamous ideal; female participation in the "degradation" of plural marriage was comprehensible only as a consequence of fanaticism or mental magnetism. But Mormon women were articulate defenders of their religion, polygamy, and a wide range of women's causes, including suffrage. Their contribution to the settling of the frontier was encouraged and acknowledged by the church leadership. Their public and private writings reveal them to be neither enslaved nor deluded, but faithful to their religion and concerned with Victorian notions of propriety. Yet their marriage arrangements were at odds with the larger society. What prompted women to accept such a departure from Victorian sexual mores?

The rearrangement of sexual roles in polygamy provoked conflicting emotions in Mormon women, but those who remained in

Feminist Studies 10, no. 3 (Fall 1984). © by Feminist Studies, Inc.

the church perceived their role in terms of their religious and ideological commitment to a utopian society. Having removed themselves from the mainstream of society to become Latter-day Saints, Mormon women were then called upon to forego the conventional arrangements of monogamy for polygamy. All Latter-day Saints women had to come to terms with the possibility of being a plural wife and many had to put it into practice.[1] The women in this study migrated to Utah without prior knowledge of polygamy, or, in one case, were born into the church. Thus, these women had to confront the issue in the context of their faith. Although the power of religion may explain the large issue of how women raised with the conventional ideal of the monogamous family and its sexual roles were able to accept polygamy, how they "lived the principle" remains an unexplored issue. That it was a women's issue is evident from the number of popular novels written by non-Mormon women about the degradation of their sisters in Mormonism.[2] Mormon women's defenses of plural marriage were as vehement as the antipolygamy novels were inflammatory. For Latter-day Saints women, as for gentile women, questions about marriage arrangements were fraught with implications about women's position in society, and, implicitly, female sexuality.

In the middle years of the nineteenth century, women's role in society was prescribed by domesticity. The domestic ideal dictated that a woman's life be built around her husband and children in the private sphere of the home, where the wife and mother provided a refuge from the public sphere of men. Women were expected to be the keepers of tradition and the upholders of morality. "Angel of the home," pure and spiritual, the ideal woman provided stability in a rapidly changing society. Further, women's role took on a special meaning on the frontier, as a civilizing mission. Several historical interpretations of sexual ideologies which fostered a "cult of true womanhood" and exalted the passionlessness qualities of women have maintained that such sexual roles worked to the elevation of women's position, by granting women a degree of autonomy and a sense of self-interest, and perhaps some control over their fertility.[3] Certainly women who rejected the role assigned them by society were considered noxious. For most Americans, Mormon polygamy threatened these standards of behavior and the special status accorded women as wives and mothers. But Mormon women argued that the role their church assigned them was not degraded. The sources available from nineteenth-century Mormon women, diaries and letters, the journal the *Woman's Exponent,* and public defenses of plural marriage, reflect the importance of issues involving sex, marriage, and the home for all women, and reveal the ambivalence in nineteenth-century sexual ideology and behavior. In particular, the question of how Mormon women reconciled their conventional expectations of monogamy with their experience of polygamy raises issues about the social control of sex, reproductive versus erotic sexuality, and the relative benefits accruing to both genders from particular sexual standards.

To understand how the principle of plural marriage shaped Mormon women's lives, it is necessary to understand the utopian origins of the Latter-day Saints church. The founding of the church and the subsequent settlement of Utah were one of many nineteenth-century efforts to create a new society in response to perceived social disorder. The Church of Jesus Christ of Latter-day Saints was founded by a charismatic prophet and drew its members from the mainstream of American religions. The Mormon utopian vision was formed by a desire to restore individual and community order and by a belief that all could be part of the immediate building of Zion on earth. Self-control and self-denial for the good of the group were integral parts of life; most Mormons eventually gave up their homes to settle the Utah desert. In the doctrine of plural marriage, sexuality emerged as the fundamental link between control of the individual and control of the group. In rejecting the monogamous ideal of the larger society for the "patriarchal" marriage of the Old Testament, the church was able to shape the intimate lives of its members. Polygamy became a social duty, as well as the way to salvation. Plural marriage was practiced by the most respected male members of the church; indeed having more than one wife was a prerequisite for advancement in the church hierarchy. Plural wives gained status and salvation through their association with church leaders, but only the first wife had any status, legal or otherwise, in the larger society, a situation that was clear in the difficulties encountered by apostate women.

Faithful Mormon women understood polygamy to be a principled religious practice with biblical precedent, but the initial reactions of early converts to the church in the 1840s and early 1850s reflect the conflict women felt between their upbringing and their faith. In the journals and letters of the first pioneers, a noticeable pattern emerges in reaction to the idea of plural marriage: initial offense and refusal, followed by careful consideration of the character of the male leaders, and occasionally a reported vision releasing them from doubt. When the prophet Joseph Smith introduced the subject to Mary Ann Price in Nauvoo, Illinois, where the Saints had gathered in the late 1830s, she "resisted it with every argument I could command," because with her "tradition, it was most repulsive to my feelings and I could not reconcile it with the purity of the Gospel of Christ." She was twenty-four and had left her home to become a Mormon. She refused to become church elder Orson Hyde's second wife. He married another, and in the meantime she tried "to learn the character of the leading men, for I sincerely hoped they were men of God." She became Hyde's third wife when she was convinced he was "a conscientious, upright, and noble man."[4] Martha Spence, a self-termed old maid in her late thirties who had joined the Saints against the advice of friends in Canada and New York, had her first acquaintance with the doctrine of plural marriage when she was three hundred miles from Salt Lake City, camped at Sweetwater (Wyoming territory) in the Rocky Mountains. She met Sarah Lawrence, an unhappy plural wife: "Some knowledge imparted was calculated to make me feel sober and [the] light heartedness and buoyancy of spirits I have been want to feel will have to be given up for a variety of perplexities." She continued towards Salt Lake City, reconsidering her judgment in embracing Mormonism "against the dictates of my best and dearest friends," and confiding to her diary: "What have I not enjoyed except a wedded life and its consequent happiness. And that is now the most dreaded thought." She became the third wife of Joseph Heywood shortly after she arrived in Utah, reassured by her assessment that she was among "the best men on Earth." Clearly the idea of being a plural wife produced enormous strain between a woman's idea of what was right and the religion for which she had often left home.[5]

The prospect of sharing a husband sexually was as difficult to accept, if not more so, for women who were already married. Janet Snyder and her family had converted to the church and left their home in upstate New York to join the Saints. She met her future husband in Nauvoo and married him in 1842, when she was nineteen. When her husband brought up the subject of polygamy, Mrs. Richards told him that it was "repugnant to her idea of virtue." Because she had strong feelings on the subject, her husband did not mention it again for three years, at which time she reported having a vision in which Joseph Smith appeared to her and she realized her religious duty. Other women reported having visions relating to polygamy, a fact noteworthy not because of the numbers who reported it, but because of the indication of tension in the few who did. In addition, Jane Snyder Richards's husband told her that he would not practice polygamy "if he did not think she would love his wives as much as he himself," which reassured her that "his love was not lustful, that he married simply because his religion demanded it." The experiences of pioneer women point to the difficulty they had accepting a practice at odds with social mores, as well as to the strength of their faith and the importance of their view of Mormon men in acquiescing in the practice.[6]

But having accepted the principle of plural marriage as a religious duty, how did Mormon women "live the principle"? With church removal to Utah and public announcement of the doctrine in 1852, the practice became more widespread and came under increasing attack by non-Mormons. Mormon women responded with vehement defenses of their church in letters and pamphlets, and the establishment of a twice-monthly journal in 1872, the *Woman's Exponent,* which had for its motto: "It is better to represent ourselves than to be misrepresented by others." As Mormons, they had removed themselves from the larger society to build Zion on earth, and as women they had removed themselves by rejecting the monogamous ideal and the sexual standards which granted women special status as wives and mothers. Female Saints sought to explain the principle in terms that went beyond blind obedience, by linking the practice to the utopian mission of the church. As the editors of the *Woman's Exponent* expressed it: "The women of Utah. . .are engaged in the practical solution of some of the greatest social and moral problems of the age."[7]

In public defense of polygamy, Mormon women pointed to the corruption of Gentile society from which they had removed themselves to create a new society patterned upon relationships which would restore order: "The 'Mormons' sought in coming here and reclaiming a desolate wilderness, by the grace of God and under his direction, to found a social system that should preclude all possibility of conditions such as they exist in the world, at the present time," wrote the editor of the *Woman's Exponent*. The *Woman's Exponent* and pamphlets distributed in defense of plural marriage cited stories of infanticide, alcoholic and abusive husbands, desertion, divorce, and prostitution as evidence of the corruption of the larger society. A return to the patriarchal marriage system of the Bible would purify corrupt society. If the principle of plural marriage was carried out in its "perfection," it would "reconcile and harmonize all animate nature." Polygamy would strengthen the human family because every woman would be able to marry a worthy man able to support her, and no woman would have to become a prostitute. Men would not have to resort to prostitutes for they would have legitimate alternative sexual outlets. Thus did Mormon women argue that "no state or condition of society is so well calculated to foster purity and social advancement as the doctrine and practice of plural wives," and thus did they portray themselves as "practically solving the questions which will result in a more complete purity of life."[8]

Perhaps because of the portrayal of Mormon women by the larger society as little better than subjugated prostitutes, or perhaps because of their own need to reassure themselves that polygamy was a principled undertaking, female Saints found it important to explain their motives and to argue that plural marriage worked toward the elevation of women's position. In speaking of their mothers, the pioneer women, the editors of the *Woman's Exponent* wrote: "They were most of them daughters of the Puritans, girls born, reared and educated in New England, brought up to look with horror upon any breach of decorum or propriety." And to their daughters, the *Woman's Exponent* said: "We mothers have been willing to lay aside our preconceived notions, training and moral education. . .that our daughters might be nobler, purer, better," not, the writer emphasized, "for pleasure, happiness or enjoyment here." Patriarchal marriage required great self-sacrifice, "laying aside selfishness and becoming endowed with that nobility of character, which will grasp the higher good for the larger number." No woman who was not "innately pure and strictly virtuous and moral" would "live in polygamy for any length of time." In fact, women had been specifically chosen for this task because "God knew that women were better prepared than men to keep this holy law and that there were more devotional women than men." Women were capable of holding themselves above "the touch or embrace of impurity," because of course, women did not have to experience sex erotically in order to reproduce, as men did.[9]

Just as the ideology of the larger society stressed the pure and passionless qualities of the ideal woman in contrast to the lust of man, so too did Mormon women see themselves as curbing the passion of depraved men. Female Latter-day Saints also saw their honorable and proper roles as wives and mothers, but they argued that injustice was built into monogamy, an attitude which hinged on their view of men. If most men were depraved and most women pure and lacking in passion, it followed that there were not enough good men to marry all the good women and thus allow them to fulfill their proper sphere. As Helen Mar Whitney said: "It is useless to try to shut our eyes to the fact that real men are rare, especially as have souls sufficiently large to take upon themselves the responsibilities of families."[10] Lucinda Lee Dalton was more forthright about the injustice of the situation: "Since undeniably there are vastly more good women than good men on the earth, who would dare decide that it would not be better for all potent custom to allow two or more of these good women, to marry one good man, than to condemn them, whether they would or not, either to live single or to wed a man a thousand fathoms beneath them?"[11]

Mormon women were unhappy with a double standard of behavior over which they had no control. How, Helen Mar Whitney wondered, could woman fulfill "her proper sphere, which seems a favorite theme for men to harp upon, never thinking that through their own course, thousands of women are denied their privilege"?[12] The "course" of men was a frequent theme in the *Woman's Exponent*. After leading lives of "intemperance and ludness [sic] for years then they seek fair, young, pure virgin forms for their wives." On another occasion, the editor related an incident which illustrated the "grave injustice of society in the treatment of men and women who may have fallen in evil ways." The son brought home a "hard" friend and the females in the family were expected to be polite to him. In retaliation, the mother brought home a "fallen woman," and the male members of the family were scandalized when the women in their family associated with her. The moral of the story was that men should "shun the male sinners with equal horror to that which they expect their wives, sisters and daughters to shun the female sinner." In "A Mormon Woman's View of Marriage," the writer asserted that men, who were unwholesome and dissipate, unfit to become fathers, not only married, but insisted on marrying chaste women. "Yet society. . .gives millions of women no choice but to marry such men or become single." Men were transgressors, but monogamy degraded women who were forced to marry beneath them, or worse, to remain single and not fulfill their proper sphere as wives and mothers.[13]

Women then were always the potential victims of male sexuality, and in this fact Mormon women located the ills of the society from which they had removed themselves: "See the misery and degradation which is so fast increasing year by year, and then reflect if there is not something needed to allay the wicked practice of men, which is the primal cause, and their victims women." The *Woman's Exponent* applauded the introduction of a bill in the Missouri legislature which would have made seduction a crime. As long as women could be victimized by male sexuality, "so long will women remain at a discount." Lucinda Lee Dalton declared that there was "not a spark of justice," in the situation, a proposition with which many non-Mormon women would have agreed, but unlike many women in the larger society, Mormon women did not see the solution in a single standard of sexual behavior.[14]

The constitution and character of men and the consequences of uncontrolled male sexuality for women and society were the fundamental issues determining women's position, according to Mormon women. Belinda Marden Pratt wrote to her sister in New Hampshire in 1854 that nature had "constituted the female differently from the male and for a different purpose." Woman's strength was "periodic," to be given to the nourishment of children, but "not so with man, he has no such drawback upon his strength," a condition which led to "abominable excesses," and to unlawful outlets for his sexuality. Polygamy, however, would correct the situation. Instead of taking a mistress and degrading a woman in a "secret and lawless" way, "the law of God would have given her to him as an honorable wife." In other words, polygamy would institutionalize "natural" law and a double standard of sexuality. Such social control was the key to women's attaining their "true" position: "The door would be open to form the endearing relationships of wife and mother."[15] In a letter to the editor of the *Woman's Exponent,* Mrs. A. Randal was more explicit in explaining how polygamy worked to the advantage of women, "Do not our children have the privilege of acknowledging their fathers, and fathers their children, honorably sustaining them?"[16] Polygamy meant male responsibility for the consequences of male sexuality.

Furthermore, polygamy contributed to the identification of sex with procreation, while acknowledging and containing the troubling potential of the erotic. Certainly female Saints recognized a sexuality not linked to reproduction through their frequent references to fallen women, mistresses, prostitutes, and the necessity of alternative sexual outlets for men. But the security and status of their position, in the church and in society, were linked to their reproductive capacity and to their virtue. The great object of marriage relations, Belinda Marden Pratt wrote, was the multiplying of the species: "Indulgence should not be merely for pleasure or wanton desires, but mainly for the purpose of procreation." Mormon women were especially concerned about the effects of intercourse when a woman was pregnant. A woman should refrain from intercourse during pregnancy because "her heart should be pure, her thoughts and affections chaste, her mind calm, her passions without excitement."[17] The editor of the *Woman's Exponent* was explicit about the consequences of intercourse while pregnant: men "entail upon their posterity such appetites and passions, as no amount of self-denial, or discipline on the part of the mothers, or after cultivation can ever wholly obliterate." The statement expresses the author's repugnance at uncontrolled male sexuality and the female's helplessness to control it, no matter how virtuous she might be. The problem lay with the "improper, unjust, and unholy marriage regulations."[18] Polygamy thus provided "legitimate" outlets for men; Mormon women often pointed to the fact that there were no houses of ill-repute in Salt Lake City. According to Belinda Marden Pratt, women would be "honorable wives of virtuous men, and mothers of faithful, virtuous, healthy, and vigorous children."[19]

The arguments focusing on male depravity and female purity and passionlessness, with the consequent degradation of women, were closely linked to a fear of disease and eugenic control. Uncontrolled male sexuality, in other words, had dire consequences not only for women, but also for society as a whole. Young men in large cities sowing their wild oats, the *Woman's Exponent* said, were "sowing a harvest that is to produce a crop of evils, disease, shattered constitutions, ruined fortunes, (and) blighted reputations." As Belinda Marden Pratt argued, the problem was with men: a plurality of husbands "would work unto death and not life, or, in plain language, it would multiply disease instead of children." Or as the *Woman's Exponent* argued, polygamy was in "strict accordance with the laws of life and health, not only for the present, but more especially future generations." Monogamy, because it forced good women to marry bad men, produced tainted offspring. The *Woman's Exponent* provided a metaphor to illustrate its point: "For though the wife be purity itself, if the father is wicked and corrupt, [he] contaminate[s] the fountains of life. . .the taint is there and impregnates those who partake. Grapes are not produced from thorns, nor figs from thistles." Plural marriage, however, allowed women to share the few good men. (Indeed some eugenic control was achieved since the church hierarchy had to approve plural marriages.) Mormon women maintained the result was healthy children. Polygamy was given for the "regeneration of mankind," Mary J. Tanner explained in a letter; "there are no healthier, no better developed children."[20]

The contention that polygamy produced healthier, better children brought the argument in favor of plural marriage back to the utopian mission of the Latter-day Saints Church. In the development of that argument, female Saints elaborated the determinants of women's position as wives and mothers by linking women's degradation to uncontrolled male sexuality and women's elevation to the social control of sex, specifically identifying sex with procreation, and by containing the troubling potential of the erotic. Historians have argued that nineteenth-century sexual ideologies that minimized female sexuality granted women some control over their fertility and a certain degree of autonomy, as well as an elevated place in society which contributed to their self-consciousness as women.[21] Mormon women's fertility levels were higher than average.[22] Female Saints demonstrated self-consciousness as women in defense of their religion's practice of polygamy, and the circumstances of both polygamy and the frontier contributed to a certain degree of autonomy: women were often left alone to raise their families, and the church hierarchy encouraged women's economic participation in the settling of Utah, and supported women's suffrage. But to what extent could women use a repressive sexual ideology to their benefit?

The practice of plural marriage had emotional costs for women. Publicly, female Saints would admit that it was a "trial." As Mary Isabella Hayes Horne said, "It is a great trial of feelings"; for Helen Whitney, "the severest of [my] life." Privately, the trials were made explicit, and women found a certain amount of compensation in their children and in sisterhood. Mary Ann Hafen cried on the way to her wedding because she knew the first wife objected to the marriage. When Annie Clark Tanner sat down alone to her wedding supper of bread and milk after her husband

and his first wife had left her, she said to her family, "The experience wasn't half bad." But when Mr. Tanner failed to keep his appointment to see her two weeks later, "I was so disappointed that it seemed to me that the very angels wept with me." In time, she remarked, "I learned to steel myself against disappointment." Similar advice was exchanged among women. Jane Snyder Richards remembered another woman advising her "to make herself happy whether her husband was with her or not, not to think about it, where he was or who he was with, and that she would outgrow all the troubles she met at the outset." Sarah A. Cooke was advised "to simply be indifferent to my husband if I would be happy."[23]

Steeling one's self against disappointment, outgrowing troubles, and being indifferent meant divesting the marital relationship of any emotional need or desire beyond friendship. As one first wife wrote to a childhood friend on the day of her husband's third marriage: "My heart aches to think I have not the same love as the third wife, but I console myself with thinking that it will subside into affection, the same as it is with me." The woman who counseled Sarah A. Cooke said she put aside any thought about what her husband was doing when he was away from her, and when he came home: "[I] was as pleased to see him as [I] was pleased to see any friend." Jane Snyder Richards outgrew her troubles by often forgetting her husband was at home and she "even sat down at meals forgetting to call him." She felt badly when such things happened, but contended that he was more necessary to her in her earlier life.[24]

To whom did female Saints turn for emotional outlet? Women turned to their children, and often to other women, in compensation. Given a choice between being with her husband in England for three years or with her baby and the other wives in Salt Lake City, Jane Snyder Richards chose Salt Lake City. Martha Spence Heywood, Annie Clark Tanner, and Ellen Clawson reported mitigation of acute loneliness with the arrival of children. Martha Spence Heywood lived alone in a sparse settlement in southern Utah; Annie Clark Tanner lived underground alone (so her husband would not be arrested for polygamy), and was constantly moving; Ellen Clawson lived with her husband and his wives in Salt Lake City. But each woman expressed the same sentiment as Ellen Clawson did, when speaking of her six-month-old baby: "She is so much company for me while her father is gone I don't know how I should live without her." And when her husband's second wife died during their migration to Utah, Jane Snyder Richards wrote: "I felt I could not have it so, then I should be entirely alone." Annie Clark Tanner expressed unguarded joy in the companionship of her husband's third wife, as did Ellen Clawson with her husband's second wife. Occasionally, the sisterhood was literal, as when Jane Snyder Richards's sister's husband deserted her and Mrs. Richards encouraged her husband to marry her sister, in order to be near and assist her.[25]

But the company of children and other women notwithstanding, Mormon women themselves indicated that there were limits to the benefits one could obtain from plural marriage in exchange for the cost, at least on this earth. It was a "martyr's crown." Women in the nineteenth century may have been able to benefit from the minimization of their sexuality in the forms of autonomy, control over fertility, and moral superiority over depraved men. But as institutionalized by the Latter-day Saints, the feminine ideal and the double standard of sexual behavior had few benefits for women. Female Saints' diaries and letters reveal the difficulty and sadness of "living the principle." As Martha Spence Heywood said, "Tis rather trying to a woman's feelings not to be acknowledged by the man she has given herself to and desires with all her heart." Mormon women's public explanation elaborated the tensions of the larger society's sexual ideology and behavior in order to explain the increase of male sexual privileges at the expense of females and the social control of sex to contain eroticism. Mormon women, however, hoped for the benefits of plural marriage in another world. As Lucinda Lee Dalton said: "Only for the sake of its expected joys in eternity, could I endure its trials through time."[26]

Such sentiments suggest that the inflammatory novels written by non-Mormon women were right in one sense: Mormon women endured; they did not revel in polygamy. But the sources available from nineteenth-century Latter-day Saints women do not reveal them to be as deluded or degraded as the novels would portray them. Mormon women were articulate defenders of the social control of sex sanctioned by their church, and in terms easily understood by the larger society. As the arguments about female purity, male depravity, social disease, and disorder demonstrate, Mormon women perceived their church to be removing them from a hypocritical society in which erotic and nonprocreative sex was increasingly apparent, if not accepted. According to Mormon women such a situation had already eroded women's traditional role in the home. Mormon polygamy attempted to incorporate and control erotic potential in men's lives, while maintaining the total identification of sex with procreation, and thus women's role, in women's lives. Perhaps this is what non-Mormon women found so objectionable—not just a loss of influence in their exalted roles as wives and mothers, but the development and sanctioning of male sexuality at the expense of female sexuality, but not at the expense of female reproductive risks. And perhaps this is what the "trials" experienced by Mormon women, so articulate and outspoken in defense of plural marriage, reveal: a society increasingly ambivalent about its sexual mores and at odds with the possibilities of nonprocreative sexuality for both women and men.

NOTES

Harper's Weekly quote taken from Davis Bitton and Gary L. Bunker, "Double Jeopardy: Visual Images of Mormon Women to 1914," *Utah Historical Quarterly* 46 (Spring 1978): 192.

1. Estimates vary on the percentage of the Mormon population participating in plural marriage, with 5 and 20 percent constituting the lower and upper limits for men between 1852 and 1890, when the practice was discontinued. Figures on the number of women involved are harder to come by because only the first wife was recognized legally and recorded as such. See Stanley S. Ivins, "Notes on Mormon Polygamy," *Western Humanities Review* 10 (Summer 1956): 230; and Dean L. May "People on the Mormon Frontier: Kanab's Families of 1874," *Journal of Family History* 1 (Winter 1976): 172.
2. For examples of these novels, see Orvilla S. Belisle, *The Prophets; or, Mormonism Unveiled* (Philadelphia: William White Smith, 1855); A. Jennie Bartlett Switzer, *Elder Northfield's Home; or, Sacrificed on the Mormon Altar: A Story of the Blighting Curse of Polygamy* (New York: J. Howard Brown Co., 1882).
3. Barbara Welter, "The Cult of True Womanhood: 1820-1860," *American Quarterly* 18 (1966): 151-74; Nancy F. Cott, "Passionlessness: An Interpretation of Victorian Sexual Ideology, 1790-1850," *Signs* 4 (Winter 1978): 219-36; and Carl N. Degler, *At Odds: Women and the Family in America from the Revolution to the Present* (New York: Oxford University Press, 1980), esp. chap. 11.
4. Mary Ann Price Hyde, Autobiography, 1884, the Bancroft Library, University of California, Berkeley (hereafter cited as Bancroft), PF 25: 2-3.
5. Juanita Brooks, ed., *Not By Bread Alone: The Journal of Martha Spence Heywood, 1850-56,* (Salt Lake City: Utah Historical Society, 1978), 15.
6. Jane Snyder Richards, "The Inner Facts of Social Life in Utah," 1880, Bancroft, PF 2: 1. See also Mary Isabella Hayes Horne, "Migration and Settlement of the Latter-day Saints," 1884, Bancroft, PF 24: 34, 18.
7. The *Woman's Exponent* 1 (31 Jan. 1884): 136. The paper was edited, published, and distributed by women from 1872 to 1914, with subscriptions varying from 1,000 to 3,000. It was sustained by its subscriptions, but enjoyed church approval, publishing

articles ranging from women's suffrage and various reforms to household hints and fiction. See Carol Cornwall Madsen, "Remember the Women of Zion: A Study of the Editorial Content of the *Woman's Exponent*, A Mormon Women's Journal" (master's thesis, University of Utah, 1977), 4-14; and Sherilyn Bennion Cox, "The *Woman's Exponent:* Forty Years of Speaking for Women," *Utah Historical Quarterly* 44 (Summer 1976), 222-39, for additional history and details of the paper.

8. *Woman's Exponent:* "A Plea for Utah," vol. 10 (1 Dec. 1881): 100; "No Surplus Women, " vol. 5 (1 Feb. 1877): 131; "Letter to the Editor from A. M. Jones," vol. 1 (1 Apr. 1873): 167; and "Patriarchal Marriage," vol. 6 (15 Aug. 1877): 44.

9. *Woman's Exponent:* "Why, Ah! Why," vol. 8 (30 Sept. 1874): 67; "Something to Live For," vol. 3 (1 Dec. 1874): 100-1; "A Plea for Utah," 100; "Why, Ah! Why," 67; "A Mormon Woman's View of Marriage," vol. 6, (1 Sept. 1877): 54; and "No Surplus Women," 139.

10. Helen Mar Whitney, "Plural Marriage, As Taught By the Prophet Joseph" (Salt Lake City: Juvenile Instructor Office, 1882), 47-48.

11. Lucinda Lee Dalton, Autobiography, Bancroft, PF 20: 8-9.

12. Helen Mar Whitney, "Why We Practice Plural Marriage, by a Mormon Wife and Mother" (Salt Lake City: Juvenile Instructor Office, 1884), 7.

13. *Woman's Exponent:* vol. 1 (15 May 1873): 188; vol. 1 (31 Jan. 1873): 132-33; and "A Mormon Woman's View of Marriage," 54.

14. *Woman's Exponent:* vol. 10 (1 Dec. 1881): 100; vol. 1 (15 Feb. 1873): 139; "No Surplus Women," 139; and Dalton MS, 8-9.

15. Belinda Marden Pratt, "Defense of Polygamy by a Lady in Utah, in a Letter to her Sister in New Hampshire, Salt Lake City, January 12, 1854," reprinted in *City of Saints* by Richard J. Burton (New York: Alfred Knopf), 489, 488, 490.

16. "Letter to the Editor from Mrs. A. Randal of Spanish Fork," *Woman's Exponent* 1 (1 May 1873): 179.

17. Pratt MS, 487.

18. "A Mormon Woman's View of Marriage," 54.

19. Margaret Thompson McMeans Smoot, "Experiences of a Mormon Wife," Bancroft, PF 5: 9; and Pratt MS, 489-90, 487.

20. *Woman's Exponent* vol. 1 (15 May 1873): 188; Pratt MS, 488; "The Position of Utah," *Woman's Exponent* vol. 10 (1 Jan. 1882): 116; *Woman's Exponent* vol. 6 (1 Sept. 1877): 54; Mary J. Tanner to Mrs. H. H. Bancroft," 24 Oct. 1880. Bancroft, PF 12 #4: 5. See also Whitney, "Why We Practice Plural Marriage," 54; and Smoot MS, 8.

21. See Welter, Cott, and Degler.

22. James E. Smith and Philip Kunz, "Polygamy and Fertility in Nineteenth-Century America," *Population Studies* 30 (1976): 465-580.

23. Horne MS, 34; Whitney, "Why We Practice Plural Marriage," 23; Mary Ann Hafen, "Recollections of a Handcart Pioneer," in *Let Them Speak for Themselves: Women in the American West, 1849-1900*, ed. Christine Fischer (Hamden, Conn.: Archon Books, 1977); 101-2; Annie Clark Tanner, *A Mormon Mother: An Autobiography* (Salt Lake City: University of Utah Press, 1969), 66-67, 68-69; Richards, "Inner Facts of Social Life in Utah," 18; and Sarah A. Cooke, "Theatrical and Social Affairs in Utah," 1884, Bancroft, PF 19: 6.

24. Samuel George Ellsworth, ed., *Dear Ellen: Two Mormon Women and Their Letters*, (Salt Lake City: University of Utah Press, 1974), 33; Cooke MS, 61; and Richards, "Inner Facts of Social Life in Utah," 13-14.

25. Jane Snyder Richards, "Reminisces," 1880, Bancroft PF 4: 41; *Journal of Martha Spence Heywood*, 76; Ellsworth, 42; Richards, "Reminisces," 27; Tanner, 131-32; Ellsworth, 25; and Richards, "Reminisces," 38.

26. Cooke MS, 5; *Journal of Martha Spence Heywood*, 50; and Dalton MS, 19.

FALLEN WOMEN: THE INMATES OF THE MAGDALEN SOCIETY ASYLUM OF PHILADELPHIA, 1836-1908

Steven Ruggles

This paper is a case study of the records of 2000 inmates of the Magdalen Society Asylum of Philadelphia between 1836 and 1908. It describes long-term changes in the characteristics of the inmates, the methods of reforming them, the effectiveness of those methods, and official asylum policies. The goals are twofold: first, to test historical theories regarding the evolution of asylums in the nineteenth century, and second, to evaluate the effects on the Magdalen Society of changes in Victorian attitudes to sexuality and prostitution and of changes in the social and institutional environment of Philadelphia.

The Magdalen Society Asylum of Philadelphia was the first association in America devoted to the reform of prostitutes. By isolating fallen women from their former associations and exposing them to a strict regimen of prayer and piecework, the subscribers hoped "to be instrumental in recovering to honest rank in life those unhappy females, who, in an unguarded hour, have been robbed of their innocence, and sunk into wretchedness and guilt."[1] The records of the asylum are particularly appropriate for the present purpose, since they provide data over a broad period (1836-1908) and highly detailed information — including some on the fate of the inmates after they left the asylum — for the period of greatest change, 1878-1908.[2] In addition, the records are remarkably complete and readily quantifiable.

A recurring theme in the recent literature on nineteenth century asylums is the shift from rehabilitation in the first half of the century to purely custodial functions after the Civil War. In the process, asylums became increasingly regimented, enforcing an exacting daily routine, strict discipline and uniform procedures for all inmates.[3]

For the most part, historical investigations of asylums have relied on statements made by their supporters and administrators. However, the statements of reformers may bear little relation to the actual operation of the asylums. In some cases, spokesmen for asylums were actually ignorant of conditions in their institutions, and they frequently indulged in wishful thinking. Furthermore, there were often conscious attempts to conceal the real operation of institutions, for the sake of public approval and funding. If we wish to go beyond an intellectual history of the ideology of asylums, we must look at what asylums actually did rather than just what they said they were doing. The differences between the theory and practice of asylums can lend insight into the constraints under which they labored.

In order to test whether the Magdalen Asylum changed from rehabilitative to custodial functions, it is necessary to use sources which reveal the day-to-day treatment of the inmates and the effectiveness of the asylum in modifying their behavior. The various registers of admissions and departures for the Magdalen Asylum, the reports of the Visiting Committee, and the matron's diaries of daily events provide considerable detail about the inmates, especially after 1878.[4] They allow analysis of admissions policies, treatment of inmates, the failure rate of the asylum and characteristics of the inmates. In addition to these materials, the

Annual Reports and weekly minutes of meetings of the Board of Managers were used as sources for information on policy decisions.

There are reasons to expect significant differences between asylums for prostitutes and other kinds of asylums. Despite official hostility, prostitution flourished in the nineteenth century, possibly to a greater extent than before or since.[5] Although they saw it as a threat to social morality and masculine energy, many Victorians also thought prostitution was necessary. Thus, the policy towards prostitution vacillated between regulation and reform.[6] This paper argues that the ambivalence of the Victorians towards prostitution contributed to significant differences between the evolution of asylums for the control of prostitutes and those for other deviant and dependent populations.

The body of this paper consists of two parts. The first section describes the long-term shifts in the characteristics of the inmates of the Magdalen Asylum, changes in their treatment, the relative success of the asylum in achieving its goal of reform in different periods, and changes in asylum policy. The second section assesses the relative importance of various internal and external factors in producing the major changes in the asylum. A brief conclusion suggests some broader hypotheses and directions for future research.

Evolution of the Magdalen Society Asylum

In its early years, the Magdalen Society Asylum functioned as a refuge, open to even the most hardened prostitutes. Most of these stayed only a few days or a few weeks, just "long enough to get reclothed and recuperated."[7] But if the asylum was a refuge, it was one of last resort. The inmates were constantly being "deeply impressed with their guilt in the eyes of their maker."[8] Conditions were spartan, and the inmates worked long hours for their keep. It seems that only the naive and the desperate could be persuaded to commit themselves. In the early period, the Magdalen Asylum seems to have specialized in the latter: "the family was composed almost exclusively of the illiterate and the depraved," who were "always alternating between the Prison Alms House and places of licentiousness."[9] The asylum met with little success in its attempts at rehabilitation in this period.[10] The early *Annual Reports* were often optimistic, but since they were primarily vehicles for the solicitation of funds, they could not very well admit that the asylum served no other purpose than to scold some of the most miserable of society's cast-offs.

During the 1850s, the Board of Managers attempted some fundamental changes of asylum policy. They searched for women "whose early opportunities for improvement were superior to those who preceded them."[11] They attempted to recruit women who were younger, better educated, less corrupt, and of a higher social class. At the same time, the managers decided that itinerant Magdalens should be discouraged, and all should be urged to stay for one year.[12] However, it appears that these policies had little effect until after 1877, when Miss Anna MacDonald died, ending her 40 year tenure as matron of the asylum. Under her successor, Elizabeth T. Freeberger, the asylum was transformed from a refuge for prostitutes into a home for wayward girls. Shortly after Freeberger was appointed, a "change in the rules regulating the family" was announced, which asserted that "those of advanced sinful life, whose confirmed habits of intemperance, and other contaminating vices, unfit them for companionship with younger and more hopeful inmates" would no longer be admitted.[13] Within a year, it became a rule to stay in the asylum for twelve months.[14] This time, the policies were actually followed.[15]

Changes also took place in the treatment of the Magdalens. No longer did the managers insist that "whatever shall tend to . . . give them confidence in their resolution of amendment must be avoided."[16] The rhetoric of damnation and pollution virtually disappeared, and the atmosphere apparently became less repressive. Before 1850, one of the chief concerns of the Visiting Committee was the prevention of escape. They were constantly "securing the fence" or "disposing of the articles in the yard so as to preclude their being used to facilitate . . . a departure from the house."[17] Nevertheless, even after the fence was enlarged from 11 feet to 13 feet high, the Magdalens continued to "elope" over it in alarming numbers. By the 1890s, escape was almost unheard of. The attempt to produce overwhelming guilt was replaced by a new concern with maintaining the cheerfulness of the "family." Pleasurable evening entertainments became the rule, such as ice cream and cake or viewing a magic lantern.[18] Under Matron Freeberger, the severest punishment was locking up on bread and water. While previously only religious speakers had been allowed, concerts and poetry readings were now given at the asylum, as well as lectures on such secular topics as travel, microscopy, and physiology.[19]

For the period after 1877, detailed information on the characteristics of the inmates survives. These data indicate that between 1878 and the latter part of the 1890s, there was a dramatic shift towards inmates that were young, Protestant, rural-born, and never previously employed. For the most part, these trends reversed slightly during the twentieth century.

Table 1 shows the changing age structure of the inmate population between 1878 and 1910. The percentage of women 21 or older dropped from 52.6% in 1878-82 to 5.1% around the turn of the century, while the percentage 25 or over dropped from 30.7% to zero. At the same time, the Magdalens became more homogeneous in terms of age, as the standard deviation fell from 6.63 to 1.76 years.

TABLE 1
Age Distributions of Inmates of the Magdalen Society
(Percentages)

			Period				
Age	*1878 to 1882*	*1883 to 1887*	*1888 to 1892*	*1893 to 1897*	*1898 to 1902*	*1903 to 1909*	*Total*
Under 16	8.8	12.8	28.6	29.1	23.5	30.9	22.1
17-20	37.6	68.2	64.3	64.8	71.3	59.6	60.9
21-24	22.9	12.0	4.8	4.9	5.1	7.8	9.8
25 and over	30.7	7.0	2.3	1.2	—	2.1	7.2
Total	100.0	100.0	100.0	100.0	100.0	100.0	100.0
Number of cases	170	217	168	165	136	230	186
Mean age	21.7	18.3	16.9	16.6	16.8	16.7	17.8
Standard deviation	6.6	4.4	2.4	2.0	1.8	2.3	4.1

Equally striking is the change in the religion of the inmates. The asylum was always predominantly Protestant, but in the years from 1878 to 1882, 23.5% of entering inmates were Catholic. The representation of Catholics dropped steadily over the next two decades, until it reached a low of 1.9% in 1893-7. By 1903-9, the percentage had recovered to 7.4%.[20]

The most important change in the birthplaces of the inmates was a decline in the percentage of inmates born in Philadelphia, Camden, and New York, and a corresponding increase in the percentage born in rural Pennsylvania, New England, and the West. The percentage born in Philadelphia dropped from 51.7% in 1878-82 to 31.8% in 1898-1902, while the percentage born elsewhere in Pennsylvania increased from 13.8% in 1878-82 to 42.6% in 1903-08. During this period the percentage of foreign-born inmates fell from 20.6% to 7.4%. Most of this change was due to a fall in the percentage of German and Irish inmates, from 12.5% to 2.0%.

We can get some indication of the ethnicity of native-born inmates through analysis of surnames. Of course, this is only a rough guide since many names were anglicized. The percentage of native-born inmates with Scottish and Irish names was approximately the same as the percentage of inmates actually born in those countries in all periods. However, the percentage with German surnames increased from 1.8% in 1878-82 to a high of 11.5% in 1893-7.[21]

There was also considerable change in the previous employment of the Magdalens. In 1878-82, 60.6% of the entering inmates had been employed in some sort of job, but by 1898-1902, this had fallen to only 5%. Within the group that had previously held jobs, there was a general shift towards the more skilled occupations. Both trends reversed after 1902.

These data indicate that the policy adopted in the 1850s excluding older, more corrupt prostitutes did not become really effective until the 1880s and the 1890s. The same can be said for the rule which required inmates to remain in the asylum for a full year, as shown in Tables 2 and 3. These tables are shown separately because they are based on data compiled by different matrons using different procedures, and are therefore not strictly comparable.[22] The reasons why the policies first promoted in the 1850s were actually applied only in the 1880s and the 1890s are explored later in this paper.

TABLE 2
Distribution of Duration of Stay, 1836-1877
(% of Total Admissions)

Duration of Stay	*1836-1847*	*1848-1857*	*1868-1877*
Under 1 month	60.5	20.1	5.2
1 month	4.5	12.0	11.9
2-3 months	7.3	12.9	17.6
4-5 months	3.4	6.3	12.0
6-10 months	3.2	5.1	10.4
11 months	0.6	1.2	2.8
12 months	0.6	1.5	2.0
13 months	0.3	0.3	1.6
14-23 months	2.0	5.1	4.0
24 or more months	1.7	3.0	1.6
Unknown	16.2	32.4	31.1
Total	100.0	100.0	100.0
Number of cases	357	333	251
Mean	2.2	5.1	5.9
Median	0.7	1.2	3.0

TABLE 3
Distribution of Duration of Stay, 1878-1908
(% of Total Admissions)

Duration of Stay	*1878 to 1882*	*1883 to 1887*	*1888 to 1892*	*1893 to 1897*	*1898 to 1902*	*1903 to 1908*
Under 1 month	19.5	13.1	8.4	9.1	10.0	16.8
1 month	12.8	8.9	6.0	2.4	10.7	8.9
2-3 months	15.2	12.6	7.2	4.2	8.6	9.4
4-5 months	7.3	11.3	6.0	3.0	2.8	5.6
6-10 months	22.0	11.7	9.8	0.0	3.5	9.0
11 months	1.8	6.6	1.8	2.4	1.4	2.2
12 months	9.1	27.2	33.1	48.2	50.7	26.3
13 months	2.4	2.8	6.0	5.5	2.9	4.5
14-23 months	8.7	4.2	12.6	10.6	5.7	12.3
24 or more months	1.2	1.4	9.6	14.0	3.6	5.0
Total	100.0	100.0	100.0	100.0	100.0	100.0
Number of cases	164	213	166	164	140	179
Mean	6.0	7.3	10.8	12.4	9.2	8.9
Median	3.8	6.9	11.3	11.6	11.3	8.1

It is clear that the Magdalen Society Asylum did not have an increase in the proportion of dangerous and chronic cases, as historians have postulated for other kinds of asylums. On the contrary, there was a pronounced trend in the opposite direction. However, the argument that asylums in the late nineteenth century increasingly stressed regimentation and uniformity is entirely consistent with the evidence of duration of stay and other characteristics of the Magdalen Society inmates.

As the Magdalen Society Asylum became more selective, relaxed its emphasis on personal guilt and salvation, and standardized in some respects the treatment of the inmates, its rate of failure diminished. The destinations of the Magdalens are shown in Tables 4 and 5. Again, we must be cautious in making comparisons between these two tables, since they are based on data compiled by different matrons and the classification is subjective. The percentage of inmates who left to go to their families, a job, friends, or husband increased from 21.6% in 1836-47 to 86.3% in 1893-97, while the percentage sent to almshouse, or who escaped, were dismissed for improper conduct, left at their own request, or died declined from 56.1% to 1.2%.[23] There are data on recidivism for the period after 1878. The percentage of inmates who returned to the asylum declined from 18.6% in 1878-82 to 3.6% in 1893-97.

The best evidence on the effectiveness of the asylum is data on 137 inmates who were subsequently married. The rhetoric of the Board of Managers often cited marriages as the ultimate goal of reform. The fact that an inmate was listed as married indicates not only that she found a husband, but also that she at least indirectly maintained contact with the matron who recorded the information. Unfortunately, the information on marriage was recorded only during the 1880s, so long-term changes in the rate of marriage cannot be measured. However, the information can be used to identify which characteristics of inmates were associated with subsequent marriage.

TABLE 4
Destinations and Reasons for Departure of Magdalen Society Inmates, 1836-1877
(Percentage distributions)

	1836 to 1847	*1848 to 1857*	*1858 to 1867*	*1868 to 1877*
Family	0.9	0.4	0.9	0.0
Husband	2.6	0.4	0.9	0.0
Service	12.1	4.3	19.8	32.2
Other employment	0.0	0.7	0.0	0.0
Hospital	0.9	0.4	0.9	2.5
Alms House	18.1	8.6	1.8	2.5
Own request	13.8	25.4	7.2	21.5
Friends	6.0	13.7	18.9	21.5
Dismissed for improper conduct	16.4	18.0	10.8	12.8
Escaped	5.2	3.2	2.7	1.6
Died in asylum	2.6	3.2	2.7	1.6
Other	0.0	1.2	0.0	0.0
Unknown	21.5	20.5	33.3	3.7
Total	100.0	100.0	100.0	100.0
Number of cases	116	278	111	242

TABLE 5
Destinations and Reasons for Departure of Magdalen Society Inmates, 1878-1908
(Percentage distributions)

	1878 to 1882	*1883 to 1887*	*1888 to 1892*	*1893 to 1897*	*1898 to 1902*	*1903 to 1908*
Family	14.0	52.4	54.9	72.8	58.4	57.5
Husband	1.7	1.4	1.8	1.2	0.0	1.0
Service	19.3	10.1	17.1	11.1	4.5	11.6
Hospital etc.*	9.4	6.9	6.0	5.4	4.3	6.5
Other institution	8.1	9.0	10.5	7.8	9.7	13.3
Own request	12.3	6.7	2.4	1.2	0.6	1.0
Friends	4.1	2.4	1.8	0.6	1.1	1.4
Dismissed for improper conduct	7.6	3.8	0.6	0.0	2.2	0.5
Escaped	5.8	4.3	4.3	0.0	0.6	2.9
Died in asylum	0.6	0.0	0.0	0.0	0.0	0.5
Unknown	12.9	1.0	0.0	0.0	18.5	1.5
Total	100.0	100.0	100.0	100.0	100.0	100.0
Number of cases	170	217	168	165	136	230

*Blockley Hosptial, State Hospital, Philadelphia Hospital, Home for Consumptives, Went home due to illness, Maternity Hospital, Orthopedic Hospital.

The inmates listed as "married" tended to have all the characteristics that the Magdalen Society was selecting for. Relative to other inmates of the same period, those who subsequently married were more often young, Protestant and rural born. Furthermore, they tended to remain in the asylum for exactly the prescribed one year, and when they left they more frequently returned to their families.[24]

Causes of the Transformation

The transformation of the Magdalen Asylum raises several questions. Why did the asylum adopt a policy of admitting only the least corrupt of fallen women, while other kinds of asylums seem to have admitted more and more chronic cases? Why did they develop more uniform and even regimented standards of admission and procedures for handling the inmates, as reflected in the twelve-month rule? Why, after these policies were first announced in the 1850s, was the asylum unable to carry them out until the 1890s? Why did the asylum reduce its emphasis on personal guilt and salvation, and adopt less harsh modes of persuasion? Perhaps most importantly, why did the Magdalen Asylum have greater success in reforming its inmates towards the end of the century, while some other types of asylums seem to have had less?

It is easiest to explain why the policies of admitting only comparatively innocent prostitutes and requiring them to stay for a year were not carried out for many years after they were supposed to be in effect. The minutes of the Board of Managers state repeatedly and explicitly that the asylum had great trouble finding women willing to enter the asylum, and so they had to take anyone they could get, no matter how corrupt or unwilling to stay for a year.[25] In 1856, the Managers attempted

> "to call to the attention of those who might be called a better class (who have not yet been so deeply steeped in crime) by the pastoral visits of ministers and by properly authorized agents who in their dwellings as well as by the wayside handed them tracts well adapted to arouse the wanderers, loudly appealing to them to foresake their ways of sin."[26]

However, as late as 1875, Matron MacDonald excused her unfilled beds because "it is proper to state that all efforts to gather in a larger number have been unavailing."[27] The population of the asylum increased somewhat during the Civil War and during depressions, but under Matron MacDonald it was never maintained at capacity for more than a few months. Prior to 1878, there was significant seasonal fluctuation in the population of the asylum; on the average it was 8 to 15 percent larger in the winter than the summer, which suggests that the institution was used as a casual refuge from the weather. After 1878, there was no significant seasonal variation at all. However, it was not until 1887 that the Board of Managers first complained that suitable applicants had been rejected for lack of space.[28] On three occasions, data on rejected applicants were provided in the annual reports, and these statistics are given in Table 6. Since it covers only three isolated years, this evidence is not by itself conclusive, but it illustrates a sequence of events indicated by other evidence.

How was the asylum able to increase the applications of less hardened and more pliable prostitutes? In part, this may have resulted from the increasing number of prostitutes in the city. It seems that prostitution expanded in the late nineteenth century, but even if the rate actually remained constant, the growing population of the city would have led to a rise in absolute numbers of prostitutes.[29] At the same time, conditions within the asylum became more attractive to prospective inmates as the managers relaxed their determination to "exclude indulgence."

TABLE 6
Reasons for Rejection of Applicants to the Magdalen Society Asylum (Percentage distributions)

	1882	*1883*	*1893*
No room to accommodate	—	—	41.1
Too old	34.9	29.5	11.0
Pregnant	32.5	35.1	11.0
Not really fallen	32.5	36.4	—
Incorrigible, feeble minded, or otherwise unsuitable	—	—	37.0
Total	100.0	100.0	100.0
Number of cases	43	44	73

Source: *Annual Reports* for 1883, 1884, 1894.

While these factors undoubtedly contributed to the supply of inmates, there was another development that was probably even more important. Prior to the incumbency of Matron Freeberger, it seems that virtually all of the inmates either brought themselves or were actively recruited from the streets and brothels, although a few were sent by the police. After 1878 the asylum developed ties with other institutions which supplied the kind of innocent inmates they were looking for. During the first decade of Freeberger's tenure, 5 such institutions referred inmates to the asylum; by the turn of the century, this had grown to 25.[30] The Society for the Prevention of Cruelty to Children supplied by far the greatest number of inmates. The source of referral of inmates was regularly recorded after 1887, and these data are presented in Table 7.

TABLE 7
Source of Referral of Magdalen Society Inmates (Percentage distributions)

	1888 to 1892	*1893 to 1897*	*1898 to 1902*	*1903 to 1907*
Society for the Prevention of Cruelty to Children	35.5	65.2	42.1	20.1
Police, etc.*	21.1	7.9	22.1	22.3
Family	22.9	15.9	22.1	22.4
Other institutions	9.7	8.6	11.6	31.9
Brought herself	4.8	1.8	0.0	2.7
Unknown	6.0	0.6	2.1	1.1
Total	100.0	100.0	100.0	100.0
Number of cases	168	165	140	230

*Mr. Camp, Prison Agent; Detective Almingdinger; Detective Fenstermacher; Officer; Magistrate; Station House; House of Corrections.

The alleviation of oppressive conditions within the asylum and its integration into networks of exchange with other institutions may have been a consequence of the change of matrons. The personalities of the matrons are obscure, but there are indications that Miss MacDonald was especially strict and orthodox.[31] It seems that Matron Freeberger, who was a generation younger, was less sternly puritanical and put energy into recruitment. In any case, the quantitative evidence clearly indicates that the changes accelerated after Freeberger was appointed.

Whether it was because of the increased number of prostitutes in Philadelphia, the amelioration of conditions within the asylum, the growth of institutions concerned with saving wayward girls from the path of wickedness, or Matron Freeberger, there can be little doubt that the growth in the numbers of applicants was crucial to the increased selectivity of the Magdalen Asylum. It is quite plausible that all four factors contributed to the change.[32]

While it is fairly easy to understand why the Magdalen Society was unable to carry out its intended policies until the 1890s, it is more complicated to explain why they adopted the policies in the first place. The increasing preference for young, uncorrupted inmates is the opposite of the trend towards the admission of more chronic cases by other types of institutions.[33] However, these other institutions — especially insane asylums — were either public or were increasingly dependent on public funding. Because of this, they were frequently required to accept anyone. Many institutions were required to care for wards of the State and persons committed to asylums by the courts. These involuntary committals often involved more radical deviance. In other words, other institutions took more chronic cases not because they wanted to but because they were forced to do so. Little information survives concerning the finances of the Magdalen Society, but it is near certainty that all of their subscribers were private.

Beyond finances and control, there are things that set the Magdalen Society apart from other asylums. As suggested earlier, there are intrinsic differences between prostitution and other forms of social deviance. No Victorian would have argued that the services of the insane, the criminal, or paupers were necessary, but they raised this very argument with regard to prostitution. Nor was it considered necessary to lock up prostitutes for the protection of society. As long as they were fairly discreet, prostitutes could be ignored, and if they acted offensively, they could be treated as criminals. There were alternative strategies for attacking prostitution, besides incarcerating the prostitutes. In particular, one could discourage the customers, or attack third parties involved in the business, such as pimps, madams, and dance halls.[34]

At the same time, the Victorians were uniquely preoccupied and threatened by sexuality. Most threatening of all was the sexual woman, since she had the power to drain men's vital energies.[35] The control of women in Victorian America required their de-sexing. The restoration of prostitutes to the path of virtue was one aspect of this control.

On balance, however, the Victorian attitude to prostitutes was ambivalent. They were a greater threat than other deviants, but towards the end of the nineteenth century they were increasingly seen as a necessary evil. Before mid-century, reformers frequently saw the abolition of prostitution as their ultimate goal. Shortly afterwards, however, this attitude began to be challenged by the view that prostitution was a permanent feature of society and should be legalized and regulated.[36] One could not eliminate the social evil, but one could ameliorate its effects.

It was during this period — the second half of the century — that the Magdalen Society abandoned its attempt to rehabilitate hardened prostitutes and focused its attention on saving wayward girls "not yet steeped in sin." They may have adopted this course in part because of their almost complete failure in their former role, but the decision was undoubtedly reinforced by the growing feeling that prostitution was inevitable. The "lowest of the low" were generally beyond rescue, and even if they could be saved, others would come along to take their place.

The policies of the Magdalen Society seem to reflect the changing interpretation of the causes of prostitution. Robert Riegle has persuasively argued that there was a shift away from religious interpretations of prostitution which stressed moral failure and personal salvation. The decline of puritan Calvinism diminished the stress on individual guilt and personal responsibility. Instead, prostitution was explained in terms of social and economic deprivation.[37]

As long as the causes of prostitution lay with the individual, then it could be eliminated if only all of the fallen women could be redeemed; every time the Magdalen Society rescued an "unhappy female," prostitution was diminished. On the other hand, if prostitution was caused by such things as poverty and alcohol, its cure was obviously beyond the meager resources of the asylum.

The changing policies of the Magdalen Asylum in the 1850s are entirely consistent with this interpretation. As we have seen, the early stress on personal discipline, guilt, and salvation was replaced by a less repressive atmosphere. If the early environment of the prostitute was the cause of her downfall, then one would need only to alter her environment in order to rescue her. Thus the asylum attempted to recreate the atmosphere of the healthy and happy family.[38]

As individual responsibility became less important, the treatment of the Magdalens became less individualized. The standardization of duration of stay in the Magdalen Society Asylum is probably indicative of a tendency towards standardization of all features of the inmates' lives. This standardization would provide stability, security, and regularity — the antithesis of the environmental sources of corruption. Of course, to some extent, standardized procedures may simply be a function of the age of an institution; with increasing experience the matrons and board of directors might learn which methods of treatment are most convenient and effective.

The new practices of the Magdalen Society were probably both more convenient and more effective. Surely it must have been more convenient for the matron to regulate a group of young, naive women than to attempt to control a diverse, dissatisfied and largely unrepentant group of prostitutes, most of whom were there only for food and shelter. If the wardens of asylums for the chronically insane could have transformed their institutions into homes for the moderately neurotic, they probably would have done so. They could not, because of legal, financial, and societal pressures. There were not such pressures on the Magdalen Asylum, because it was a private organization and society did not demand that prostitutes, like the insane or the criminal, be incarcerated.

The effectiveness of the new procedures of the Magdalen Society is suggested by the increased success of their attempts at reform. Of course, this may be simply a result of increased selectivity. As the Magdalen Society Asylum was transformed from a refuge for prostitutes into a home for wayward girls, it is to be expected that fewer departing inmates would have returned to the streets. Furthermore, as the managers repeatedly argued, the older, more experienced prostitutes who initially made up a large proportion of the inmate population may have had a corrupting influence on those who were younger and comparatively innocent.[39]

In addition to the effects of greater selectivity, the success of the asylum may have been improved because of the adoption of more effective methods of rehabilitation. As the emphasis on profound guilt diminished, the inmates were increasingly allowed small pleasures and rewards. Thus, the original strategy of negative reinforcement was supplemented by positive encouragement.

In summary, the actions of the Magdalen Society were severely constrained by external structural factors. In particular, the asylum was unable to carry out its policies of selectivity and standardization because of a shortage in the supply of suitable applicants. However, if we wish to understand the sources of those policy changes, we must look to changes in theories on the source of prostitution and the reform of prostitutes. Ultimately, the causes of the transformation of the Magdalen Society Asylum seem to lie with the liberalization of religion and a new "scientific" orientation toward social problems, which viewed deviance as a consequence of environmental factors.

As described earlier, most of the long-term trends in the Magdalen Asylum reversed after 1900. The inmates became older, more often Catholic, and more often previously employed; the mean duration of stay declined, while the variance increased; referrals from the SPCC declined; recidivism went up; and the percentage of inmates departing to family, employment, or friends declined dramatically. During this period, the quality of the records deteriorated. The entries provide less detail, and the handwriting is often difficult to decipher. After 1908, the entries are too irregular to permit systematic analysis. In 1916 the remanants of the asylum were absorbed by the White Williams Foundation.[40]

The decline of the asylum may have resulted from financial problems. In 1899, an "appeal for funds" was circulated which suggested that the shortfall of income had reached a critical stage.[41] On top of this, Matron Freeberger was growing old, and the energy she devoted to searching out suitable inmates may have flagged. Perhaps the role of the Magdalen Asylum was taken over by other institutions, especially those with public funding. On the other hand, it is quite likely that the Magdalen Asylum deteriorated because of declining private interest in the reform of prostitutes.

Conclusion

Between the 1850s and the 1890s, the Magdalen Society changed from a refuge for hardened prostitutes into a home for wayward girls. During the same period, the treatment of the inmates became less harsh and oppressive, but the standards governing admissions and departures became more rigid and uniform. The basis for the transformation can be traced to policy changes formulated during the late 1840s and the 1850s, which seem to stem from broader changes in theories of deviance and reform. However, it was not until the 1880s and 1890s that the changes were successfully implemented, because before then the asylum was unable to recruit a sufficient number of innocent and pliable fallen women.

It could be easily argued that the Magdalen Society Asylum is unimportant; it never had a significant effect on prostitution in Philadelphia, and it warrants only a footnote in the history of moral reform.[42] Nevertheless, this case study has some important lessons for the investigation of the development of asylums in the nineteenth century. In particular, it provides a vivid illustration of the contrast between policy and practice in institutions. If the quantitative evidence had not been available, it would have seemed that the period of greatest selectivity and uniformity in the Magdalen Asylum was the 1850s, since that is when these policies were promoted most vociferously. The delay of forty years in the effective application of these policies provides considerable insight into the workings of this kind of asylum.

More generally, the evidence from the Magdalen Society Asylum highlights the variety of patterns of institutional development in the nineteenth century. Most of the nineteenth century institutions that have been studied to date were substantially larger than the Magdalen Society Asylum, and they frequently were publicly funded. Unlike these asylums, the Magdalen Society did not undergo a shift from rehabilatative functions to purely custodial ones. I suspect this reflects basic differences in the nature of the organizations. There existed, probably, a social structure of institutions; small private ones at one pole and large public ones at the other. No single model of institutional development is appropriate to all of these.

The evolution of each asylum depends on its particular circumstances, such as whether it was publicly or privately funded, its physical and social location, its age, its intended function, and the personal idiosyncrasies of its managers. Nevertheless, we may be able to detect some general trends common to virtually all asylums. I suspect that a trend towards regimentation is one of these, but abandonment of attempts to rehabilitate is not. However, such monolithic generalizations may be premature.

Future research should make as much use as possible of the records of individual inmates of asylums if we are interested in more than an intellectual history of institutional theory. However, case studies will not be sufficient. In order to understand the evolution of institutions, we must begin to study the interrelationships between them.[43] Institutions influence each other both because of the direct transfer of inmates and because the managers are aware of each other's methods and policies. As more and more institutional files are converted to machine-readable form we will be better able to analyze the flows of inmates between institutions.

The study of the ways in which Victorian society dealt with its deviant and dependent populations has the potential to yield great insight into both the Victorian mind and the evolution of modern public policies. We should focus on the social and economic constraints faced by different kinds of institutions, and on the emergence of institutional networks in the late nineteenth century. In the long run, the most interesting questions may concern the effects of asylums on their inmates, and on society generally. The Magdalen Society Asylum appears to have had little effect on either prostitution or society. However, it is clear that other institutions — such as prisons — did have an effect, although frequently not the intended one. As we begin to analyze the case histories so carefully compiled by Victorians and Progressives, we will be better able to understand the real impact of asylums.

University of Pennsylvania
Department of History
Philadelphia, PA 19104

Steven Ruggles

FOOTNOTES

My thanks to Michael B. Katz, Carroll Smith-Rosenberg, Marcia Carlisle, Walter Licht, Patricia Ruggles, Nancy D. Ruggles, Erica Flapan, and Miriam King for their helpful comments and advice.

1. *The Constitution of the Magdalen Society of Philadelphia* (Philadelphia, 1909), p. 3. Details of the history and operation of the asylum can be found in N.K. Teeters, *They Were in Prison*

(Philadelphia, 1937) pp. 266-69; *A Concise Account of the Magdalen Society Asylum* (Philadelphia, 1847); the *Annual Reports of the Board of Managers of Magdalen Society of Philadelphia* for 1819, 1820, 1901; *Annual Report of the White-Williams Foundation, 1917;* and a brief history handwritten in the front of the "Register of Admissions and Discharges, 1878-1908."

2. The quantitative evidence was derived from a variety of sources. All of the micro-level quantitative data on prostitutes for the period 1836-1877 was taken from the "registers of admissions and departures" for those years. Only limited data are available in this period: date of arrival, date of departure, duration of stay, and reason for departure or destination. During the period 1858-1862, the completeness and accuracy of the data deteriorated badly. Between 1878 and 1908 far better data are available. A main register provides all the information of the earlier period, plus information on age, birthplace, occupation, and the dates of arrival and departure for up to four re-entries. After 1885, the same register provides the source of referral of each inmate, and during the period 1908-09 it also gives detailed information on the parents of the inmates. A supplemental register of arrivals gives information on the religion of the inmates, and a separate register of departures distinguishes inmates who were subsequently married, and gives the destination or reason for departure for second, third, and fourth departures. Finally, missing data was frequently located in the matron's "diaries of daily events." All of these records are located in the Pennsylvania Historical Society.

3. David Rothman, *The Discovery of the Asylum: Social Order and Disorder in the New Republic* (Boston, 1971) pp. 206-295; Gerald Grob, *Mental Institutions in America: Social Policy to 1875* (New York, 1977) pp. 257-342; Paul Boyer, *Urban Masses and Moral Order in America 1820-1920* (Cambridge, Mass., 1978) pp. 94-96, 102; Peter L. Tyor and Jamil S. Zainaldin, "Asylum and Society: an Approach to Industrial Change," *Journal of Social History* 13 (1979): 23-48. Historians have offered a variety of explanations for the shift from rehabilitative to custodial functions. For example, Grob, Rothman, and Tyor and Zainalden attribute the shift to changes in the inmate population. Asylums, they argue, were originally intended for the care of short-term, curable cases, but either because of internal or external pressures they increasingly were forced to admit the most troublesome, dangerous, and chronic cases. Tyor and Zainalden, *op. cit.* pp. 23-48, explain the transition from rehabilitation to custody in terms of the professionalization of institutional leadership, the increasing scale of asylums, and, most importantly, the shift from private to public control of many institutions. Public control frequently meant not only that legislatures held the purse-strings, but also that the courts could dictate admissions. They further suggest that because of common internal changes, most institutions in the nineteenth century followed an organic, sequential pattern of development. Also see Christopher Lasch, *The World of Nations: Reflections on American History, Politics, and Culture* (New York, 1973) Ch. 1. Others stress external factors, including immigration, economic growth, and demographic change, all of which increased social dislocation and led to a decline in traditional means of social control. As preceived deviance grew and the old fashioned means of controlling it diminished, institutions were called upon to bridge the gap. However, when the demands on asylums grew, their inability to reform became more glaring. The regimentation of asylums and their retreat from the goal of rehabilitation was therefore a pragmatic response to conditions beyond their control. See Rothman, *op. cit.* pp. 265-295. On the need for institutions to exert social control, see Michel Foucault, *Discipline and Punish. The Birth of the Prison* trans. Allen Sheridan (New York, 1977) *passim.*

4. See note 2.

5. Vern Bullough, *The History of Prostitution* (New Hyde Park, N.Y., 1975) pp. 187-198, 215; E. Woolston, *Prostitution in the U.S. Prior to the Entrance of the U.S. into the World War* (1921) pp. 3-38; A. Corbin, *Les Filles de Noce: misère sexuelle et prostitution: 19e 20e siècles* (Paris, 1978).

6. On this conflict and attempts to regulate prostitution, see David Pivar, *Purity Crusade: Sexual Morality and Social Control 1868-1900* (Westport, Conn., 1973) pp. 18, 32, 34, 83-85); R.R. Wagner, "Virtue Against Vice: A Study of Moral Reformers and Prostitution in the Progressive Era," Ph.D. dissertation, Univ. of Wis., 1971; Roy Lubove, "The Progressive and the Prostitute," *The Historian* 24 (1962): 308-330; John C. Burnham, "The Medical Inspection of Prostitutes in the Nineteenth Century," *Bulletin of the History of Medicine* 45 (1971): 203-18; John C. Burnham, "The Social Evil Ordinance — A Social Experiment in Nineteenth Century St. Louis," *Bulletin of the Missouri Historical Society* 27 (1971): 203-207; Boyer, *op. cit.* p. 192; Robert Riegle, "Changing American Attitudes Toward Prostitution, 1800-1900," *Journal of the History of Ideas* 29 (1968): 446.

7. *Annual Reports* (1891) p. 14; (1833) p. 6; (1873) p. 1; (1874) pp. 8-9; "Minutes of the weekly visiting committee," Feb. 10, 1852; "Weekly minutes of the Board of Managers," Feb. 10, 1852, p. 47.

8. "Minutes of the weekly meetings of the Board of Managers," Mar. 6, 1859, p. 234. In the earlier period, guilt, pollution, degradation and self-denial were constantly stressed, e.g., *A Concise Account of the Magdalen Asylum* (1847) p. 7; *Annual Reports*, (1831) p. 4; "Minutes of the weekly visiting committee," Feb. 5, 1818; *Annual Reports* (1835) p. 5. My thanks to Marcia Carlisle for the latter citations.

9. "Minutes of the weekly meetings of the Board of Managers," (1856) p. 123. This document goes on to attribute the increase in prostitution to "Pic-Nics, . . . which have so increased in latter years."

10. See Table 4, below. Evidently the Magdalens were often out of control until the appointment of the firm Matron MacDonald in 1835; see "Minutes of the weekly meetings of the Board of Managers," Dec. 7, 1819.

11. *Annual Reports*, (1855) pp. 3-4; (1854) p. 10. The preference for youth began as early as 1845; *Annual Reports*, (1845) pp. 4-5. The fact that this policy was adopted this early was pointed out to me by Marcia Carlisle.

12. "Minutes of the weekly meetings of the Board of Managers," May 10, 1855.

13. *Annual Reports*, (1878) p. 14. "More hopeful" sometimes meant not being a prostitute at all. On several occasions, the main register indicates that an inmate had simply been "ruined" by beau or employer. (Main register, Nov. 1883, Lucy Simkins Curry, Feb. 1877, p. 2; Aug. 1885, p. 97). Although the definition of prostitutes was more flexible in the nineteenth century than today, and prostitution was less professionalized, some inmates clearly had no claim to the title. However, the matron continued to reject applicants — and dismiss those already admitted — if it was discovered that they were "not really fallen," at least until 1883; see Table 6.

14. "Diaries of Daily Events," July 8, 1879. It appears that there was some controversy between the subscribers who felt that all repentant inmates should be accepted and the Board of Managers who favored a more restrictive policy. As late as 1882, when a woman was rejected on the grounds that she was too corrupt to be saved, this policy provoked some protests. In their *Annual Report*, the Board of Managers wrote, "without any reference to the specific merits of the case, we may be allowed to say, that there are often valid reasons for refusing promiscuous applications by a public institution; of which only itself can be the judge." *Annual Reports* (1882) pp. 9-10.

15. Evidence that policy was actually followed appears in the *Annual Reports* (1892) p. 9-10, 14. "Diaries of daily events," July 1, 1882; Aug. 10, 1882; Oct. 19, 1882; Apr. 9, 1883; July 4, 1883; Feb. 14, 1884; May 1, 1884; May 26, 1884; July 16, 1884.

16. "Minutes of the weekly meetings of the Board of Managers," Mar. 6, 1850, p. 234.

17. "Minutes of the weekly visiting committee," July 4, 1824; also "Minutes of the weekly meetings of the Board of Managers," Sept. 2, 1823, Jan. 11, 1808, Mar. 6, 1850; *A Concise Account of the Magdalen Asylum* (1847). These sources sometimes indicate that inmates were detained against their will; however, Marcia Carlisle's close reading of these materials has shown that it was official asylum policy that inmates could come and go at their own discretion, as the managers pointedly noted on several occasions (*Annual Reports* 1851, p. 17). The Magdalen Society had no legal authority to detain inmates. However, if they never did so one wonders why they found it necessary to put up a 13-foot fence and lock everyone up at night.

18. "Diaries of Daily Events," May 24, 1882.

19. *Ibid.* July 24, 1886; *Annual Reports* (1891) p. 14.

20. The percentage of Jews followed exactly the opposite trend; the first, "Rachel the Jewess," was admitted in 1883, and 14 more were admitted in the next 20 years. Rachel had been converted to Christ and saved, so Matron Freeberger was encouraged to repeat her experiment. "Diaries of Daily Events," Jan. 1, 1884.

21. The declining percentage of foreign born may be a function of declining age, since the young are always more likely to be native born. The increase in second generation Germans and the decline in second generation Scots occured immediately after the change from Matron MacDonald — who was presumably of Scottish ancestry — to Matron Freeberger — who was probably of German descent. This may not have been a coincidence.

22. Table 2 is based on registers compiled by Matron MacDonald, while Table 3 is based on the registers of Matron Freeberger. The data for 1858-1867 are not shown, because there were too much missing data to yield meaningful results. The fact that there were no missing data at all after 1877 must be attributed to the greater care with which Matron Freeberger recorded arrivals and departures. In Table 2, the missing data may have resulted in a downward bias in duration of stay. Upon the departure of an inmate, the matron had to go searching through the register of admissions, find the entry for the Magdalen in question, and note the date and reason for departure next to the date of entry. If she could not find the record of admission, or if she did not want to leaf through dozens of pages, she could make a new entry and just record the information on departure. The latter practice accounts for most of the missing data in Table 2. If an inmate had registered only days or weeks before, the entry would be comparatively easy for the matron to find. Therefore, it is likely that many of the missing cases stayed longer than a month.

23. The data in Table 4 were recorded by Matron MacDonald, while those in Table 5 were recorded by Freeberger. Because the categories are subjective and are not mutually exclusive, the two tables are not strictly comparable. Differences of judgment may help to explain the discontinuities before and after 1878. However, there is evidence to suggest that the period immediately after Freeberger's appointment was somewhat chaotic. (The "Minutes of the Weekly Meetings of the Board of Managers," 1878, describe a "stampede of inmates over the wall, and various other incidents of defiance, including indecent exposure of some of the inmates in front of the windows). Placement with families, as opposed to placement in service, was a deliberate policy change. See the "Minutes of the Annual Meeting of the Board of Managers" in "Minutes of the Weekly Minutes of the Board of Managers" (1896) p. 233.

24. Those listed as "married" were young (under 19), Protestant, and born outside of Philadelphia, New York, and Camden 42% more frequently than those who were not, when we standardize for change over time; they stayed in the asylum exactly one year 95% more often, and returned to their families 65% more often.

25. "Minutes of the weekly meetings of the Board of Managers," Feb. 10, 1852, p. 47; *Annual Report*, (1833) p. 6; (1872) p. 6; (1875) p. 6.

26. "Minutes of the weekly meetings of the Board of Managers," (1856) p. 123. They had attempted to recruit additional inmates on several previous ocasions. See *Annual Reports*, (1835) p. 5; (1847) p. 8; "Minutes of the weekly meetings of the Board of Managers," Nov. 12, 1850, Feb. 12, 1850.

27. *Annual Reports* (1875) p. 6.

28. *Annual Reports* (1887) p. 12.

29. See note 5.

30. The growth of institutions was so great that some inmates spent more time shuttling between them than as prostitutes. See, for example, the case of Maggie Smith, "Diaries of Daily Events," July 16, 1879. The proliferation of other institutions may have had other effects on asylum policy. It is possible that as the number of institutions grew, each took on a more specialized role. However, it appears that many of the newer organizations — such as the SPCC, the Children's Aid Society, Friends' Home for Children, and the New Jersey Children's Home Society — were devoted to the protection of children from the start, and their functions must have overlapped with the new role of the Magdalen Asylum. Even if specialization was simply a function of the growth in the number of institutions, that does not explain why the Magdalen Society sought the particular niche that it did.

31. She was described by Matron Freeberger (apparently) as a woman of "fervid piety and systematic mind" (handwritten history — see note 1.) Although she seems to have gotten on with the Managers well enough, her relationship with the inmates seem rather strained.

32. The changing characteristics of the inmate population cannot be ascribed to changes in the population of prostitutes generally. Three surveys of prostitutes were taken in 1859 and 1912 in New York and Philadelphia. These surveys are reproduced in William W. Sanger, *The History of Prostitution: its Extent, Causes, and Effects Throughout the World* (New York, 1939) esp. pp. 452, 545, 456, 460; George J. Kneeland, *Commercialized Vice in New York City* (New York, 1913) pp. 216, 232, 245, 215, 198, 229, 243; Vice Commision of Phildelphia, *Report on Existing Conditions with Recommendations to the Honorable Rudolph Blankenburg, Mayor of Philadelphia* (Philadelphia, 1913) pp. 84, 85, 98, 99. Also, see Egal Feldman, "Prostitution, the Alien Woman, and the Progressive Imagination," for discussion of the changing ethnicity of prostitutes. *American Quarterly* 19 (1967): 192-206. While these data are far from unimpeachable, they provide a rough guide to the characteristics of non-institutionalized prostitutes. In all three cases, the mean age was about 24 years. Furthermore, there appears to have been a decrease in the percentage of prostitutes who were rural-born between 1858 and 1912. In all periods, the Magdalen Society prostitutes seem to have been younger and more often Protestant than those "in life."

33. See note 4.

34. Such strategies were increasingly followed after mid-century; see Lubove, *op. cit.* 308-330; Riegle, *op. cit.* 437-452. Estelle Freedman argues that deviance of women was perceived fundamentally differently from that of men; see *Their Sister's Keepers: Women's Prison Reform in America, 1830-1930* (Ann Arbor, 1981) pp. 41, 52-57.

35. See Walter Houghton, *The Victorian Frame of Mind 1830-1870* (New Haven, 1957) pp. 348-393; W. Barker-Benfield, "The Spermatic Economy" in Michael Gordon (ed.), *The American Family in Social-Historical Perspective* (New York, 1978) 2nd Ed., 374-402; Carl Degler, "What Ought to Have Been and What Was," also in Gordon, 403-435; Peter Cominos, "Late Victorian Sexual Respectability and the Social System," *International*

Review of Social History 8 (1963): 18-40, 216-250; Michel Foucault, *The History of Sexuality* (New York, 1978); Keith Thomas, "The Double Standard," *Journal of the History of Ideas* 20 (1959): 195-216; Stephen Marcus, *op. cit.;* Margaret Wyman, "The Rise of the Fallen Woman," *American Quarterly* 3 (1951): 167-177.

36. Actually, the situation is somewhat more complex. Demands for the regulation of prostitution put forth by physicians, military officials, and some politicians were countered by the demands of social purity advocates and feminist reformers for the eradication of prostitution through the imposition of a single, chaste standard of sexual morality. See Judith Walkowitz, *Prostitution and Victorian Society: Women, Class, and the State* (Cambridge, 1980). Also, see note 6.

37. Riegle, *op. cit.*, pp. 437-52; Freedman, *op. cit.*, pp. 40, 42-43, 110-116.

38. The Magdalens are usually referred to as the 'family' in the diaries of daily events. Paradoxically, the ideological changes of the 1850s did not really affect the composition of the asylum until the 1870s, when it seems that the environmentalist philosophy may have been on the wane. Evidence from a variety of sources suggests that the 1870s were a period of renewed emphasis on individualistic definitions of deviance and dependence, this time based on theories of heredity rather than on personal salvation; see Charles Rosenberg, "The Bitter Fruit: heredity, disease, and social thought," *Perspectives in American History* 8 (1974): 189-235; Michael B. Katz, *The Irony of Early School Reform: Educational Innovation in Mid-Nineteenth Century Massachusetts* (Cambridge, Mass., 1968) pp. 207-8, 180-83; David Brion Davis, *Homicide in American Fiction 1798-1865: A Study in Social Values* (Ithaca, 1957) p. 82; Norman Dain, *Concepts of Insanity in the United States, 1789-1865* (New Brunswick, 1965) p. 110. A change in explanations for deviance could easily be reconciled with increased selectivity, however. If deviance was genetically determined, then hardened prostitutes were incapable of reform regardless of environmental influences. Thus, only 'deserving' women — those who were not really professional prostitutes at all — had any hope of being saved.

39. The managers stated in 1882: "To admit to an asylum of juvenile Magdalens, . . . the most dissoulute and depraved women, where they must necessarily mingle with the younger and the less guilty, would be to corrupt the former, without much hope of reclaiming the latter. In the intimacy of the family, the vicious women will take pleasure in detailing to her [fellow] inmates all her wicked experiences; even boastfully magnifying her vile conquests, to add interest to her story." *Annual Report* pp. 9-10.

40. *Annual Report of the White-Williams Foundation* (1917).

41. *Magdalen Society of Philadelphia: Circular* (1899).

42. In a city with thousands of prostitutes, the asylum usually held no more than a few dozen, and in 72 years, only 2000 were admitted. In the early years, most of these stayed in the asylum only a short time period before "returning to their old haunts," *Annual Reports* (1878), p. 6. When the asylum finally was able to lower its rate of failure, its inmates no longer came directly from the street, but were transferred from other institutions such as the SPCC or the Children's Aid Society. Given that they were no longer active prostitutes, it is possible that most of these wayward girls would not have returned to a life of sin even if they had never been to the asylum. If the asylum had virtually no effect, then we can eliminate all functional explanations for its existence. It was established as a means of controlling women, but it didn't work. To regard the asylum as a useful and necessary agency of social control would be a gross misinterpretation.

43. The course of the Magdalen Asylum was profoundly affected by the SPCC, and its policies were probably significantly affected by other institutions that were devoted to the reform of prostitutes; see note 31. There may have been a direct effect of other asylums.

Marcia Carlisle, who is writing her dissertation on ideology and moral reform in Philadelphia, argues that the policies of the Magdalen Asylum were reformed after the late 1840s because of criticism from a new organization, the Rosine Society. However, if the policy changes of the 1850s were inspired by the Rosines, one would have expected the Magdalen Asylum to loosen, rather than tighten, its standards for admission, since the Rosine Home was evidently more egalitarian in its early years. What may be more important is Carlisle's finding that the Rosine Home, like the Magdalen Asylum, increasingly preferred to admit younger and less corrupt prostitutes as time went on. This suggests that we should look for explanations that are applicable to both organizations. See Carlisle's unpublished paper, "The Boundaries of Sisterhood: An Essay on Class and Gender in 19th Century America," esp. pp. 21-34. Also, see Carlisle's dissertation, "Prostitutes and Their Reformers in Nineteenth Century Philadelphia," Ph.D. dissertation, Rutgers University, 1982, pp. 125-27.

"RUINED" GIRLS: CHANGING COMMUNITY RESPONSES TO ILLEGITIMACY IN UPSTATE NEW YORK, 1890-1920

Joan Jacobs Brumberg

Shortly after supper, on the evening of March 22, 1898, a girl calling herself "Minnie Evans" complained that she had a headache and asked to be excused from evening prayers on that account. "Minnie Evans" was eighteen years old, unmarried, and the mother of an infant girl named Helen. Only a week before, "Minnie" had given birth in a large frame house at 905 College Avenue in Elmira, generally known as the Anchorage, a home for "wayward and erring girls" supported by a regional network of New York State chapters of the Women's Christian Temperance Union (WCTU). Although daily prayers were generally compulsory in this evangelical environment, the young woman's delicate post-partum condition allowed absence from the central religious ritual of Anchorage life. When her request for rest and time to nurse her baby was honored, she retired to her single room, snatched up her daughter and an empty satchel, and fled the home out the back door and over a fence, leaving approximately a dozen other girls praying in the front parlor.

On admission to the Anchorage, "Minnie Evans" confessed that she was pregnant and that she faced life alone on the street because she had no family. Allegedly, only an aunt, to whom she wrote her whereabouts, cared anything at all for her. In fact, the aunt was her mother, Etta Baker Mayers, the wife of the owner of a small cigar factory in Addison, New York, a town of approximately 2000 people lying thirty miles west of Elmira. The pregnant, 5'2" girl – whose real name was Nettie Mayers – came to the Anchorage alone in her ninth month without the knowledge of her father, Joseph, who later claimed that he thought she was in Rochester "for the purpose of having an operation performed for the removal of a tumor." The Mayers family, which also included a twenty year old daughter, Bessie, was Presbyterian and they were well-respected in the community. Despite this essentially middle-class family constellation, Nettie Mayers managed to become pregnant in adolescence.

The girl's sexual indiscretion and pregnancy eventually became a matter of public concern. After escaping the protection and the insularity of the Anchorage, Nettie Mayers bought a ticket on a train leaving Elmira for Addison at 9:10 p.m.; observers later reported that as she waited for the train in the Erie depot, dressed in a long black coat and hat, she slept fitfully but held tightly to a large satchel. Upon arrival in her hometown, en route to her parents' home, Nettie nursed her babe, and then, threw it off the Addison Bridge into the rushing waters of the Canisteo River. She returned home immediately where she took to her bed, visibly distressed, incoherent, and according to her father, "highly excited and comatose at the same time." The parents told officials that the girl's sleep was punctuated only by random cries of "Did you bring my baby?" as she appeared to search frantically for something in the bed linen. A telegram from Nettie's mother to the Anchorage, informing them of the girl's whereabouts, unlocked the mystery of "Minnie Evans'" identity and history. The Elmira police, following on the report of a missing inmate and her child, sent investigators directly to the troubled family in Addison. Both the unexplained disappearance of the infant and the parents' report of the girl's behavior since the night of March 22 pointed to the criminal act of infanticide.

As a result, the Chief of Police in Elmira and the district attornies of Chemung and Steuben County became involved. Although they were able to secure a bedside confession from the girl, the infant's body was never recovered, confounding a criminal prosecution. Joseph Mayers, the father, perceiving that there was an alternative to prison, quickly arranged for medical examination of his daughter by two local physicians. By March 25, Nettie Mayers was declared insane and committed to the state mental asylum at Ovid. The *Elmira Daily Gazette* noted frankly that insanity "has been accepted as a solution of the case and has made an explanation for the actions of the young girl." The journal of the Anchorage's matron, however, noted something else: that "the father said it cost him $500 to settle."[1]

The dramatic case of Nettie Mayers raises a number of important but unanswered questions about the manner in which young women and their families negotiated the crisis posed by an out-of-wedlock pregnancy. The desperation that fueled Nettie Mayers' response and that fostered her parents' veil of ignorance (or their deceit) reappears in other families in less severe but equally painful stories. Young women commonly abandoned babies, aborted them, and gave them up for adoption while families were torn asunder by the anguish that out-of-wedlock pregnancy created. In the late 19th century, the unwed mother and her child were actors in a particularly acute social drama that involved lovers, peers, family and community. In this respect, homes like the Anchorage played an important mediating role, their very presence suggesting an alternative for those pregnant and unmarried women who might have chosen more traditional means of coping with unwanted children: abortion, abandonment, or infanticide.[2]

Building on the work of Robert Wells and Maris Vinovskis, this paper argues that by the late 19th century illegitimacy became a traumatic event which it was not in the eighteenth and early nineteenth century. However, while out-of-wedlock pregnancy presented an enormous threat to the aspirations of Victorian middle-class families, it was handled – at least until 1920 – on a relatively *ad hoc* basis, relying in large part on private networks and organizations in the sphere of women. Beginning in the 1890s, middle-class women operating in the context of evangelicalism and social purity reform, began to offer a rudimentary but important form of social service to younger women who were pregnant and unmarried. At this point in time, in small Upstate towns and villages, sexuality remained a community concern and had not, yet, been designated a strictly private or individual matter. Women's particular interest in the problem of illegitimacy was born of many factors: empathy, a sense of community responsibility, class orientation, religious fervor, an awareness of the sexual double standard, and knowledge of the exigencies of economic life for unmarried women. The particularly dramatic illegitimacy episodes of this period, captured in the case of Nettie Mayers and in the well-known fiction of Theodore Dreiser, suggested that for Victorian women melodrama was not always disconnected from their reality. In many ways, the late nineteenth century drama of "ruined" girls served middle-class women as both prescription and critique.

In a recent study of the demographic history of adolescent pregnancy and childbearing, Maris Vinovskis has demonstrated that tolerance for sexual activity in the young changes over time. Vinovskis argues that in Colonial America there were no particular liabilities attached to sexual activity or childbearing among adolescents so long as sexual activity resulted in marriage. In the 17th century, the central preoccupation was extramarital sexuality and little distinction was drawn among bastardy, adultery, premarital pregnancy, and premarital intercourse: all were brought into court as fornication. By the 18th century, these offenses were differentiated but not by age. Rather, an exclusive concern with bastardy indicates that anxiety about economic responsibility for illegitimate children was paramount in shaping the Colonial legal and moral order.[3]

By the close of the nineteenth century, illegitimacy posed difficult problems not only for the girl, but for families and communities at most levels of society. For the unmarried mother, emotions of disappointment, betrayal, and embarrassment combined with real fear about the future. For communities, identification of an out-of-wedlock pregnancy immediately raised a potential problem of long-term economic support; by the laws of the State of New York, county superintendents of the poor were mandated to provide for bastard children and indigent mothers. Although the legal apparatus was in place to compel putative fathers to admit paternity and support their child, establishing filiation was a difficult, time-consuming, and costly business which girls and their families generally wished to avoid.[4] For most families, an out-of-wedlock pregnancy was regarded as a mark of shame which constituted a symbolic affront to patriarchal authority and standards of kinship organization. Moreover, the bastard child represented an unanticipated economic drain on family resources. Among the propertied classes, bastard children complicated delicate issues of intergenerational inheritance. For adult middle-class women, particularly those involved in the interlocking causes of evangelical religion, temperance, and social purity, the very presence of illegitimacy in the community demonstrated the continuing hegemony of the sexual double standard. And, for clergymen, educators, and physicians, when illegitimacy reared its ugly head, it forced recognition of two equally alarming, but inter-related facts of life: that sexuality did, indeed, occur outside of marriage as well as in youth.

By the late nineteenth century, American society had dropped its tolerance for any kind of premarital sexuality and began to proscribe adolescent sexuality in particular. In fact, illegitimate pregnancy in adolescence became a traumatic event. The Victorian abhorrence for premarital sexuality is well known because the pervasive advice literature of the period abounds with examples of how Victorian moralists and pedagogues worked to make both heterosexuality and autoeroticism seem dangerous. The message to young women was unambiguous: those who wished to proceed to the "hymeneal altar" had to preserve their virginal physiology by rejecting premarital intercourse.[5] Intercourse among the engaged simply was not presented as a viable option. Added to the general message about premarital chastity, there was a concern for physical and emotional readiness that was not present in Colonial times.

For three discrete groups, religious women, social purity reformers, and doctors, the age of the sexual initiate became a salient consideration. After 1870, the women's foreign missionary crusade presented as proof of "heathen" debasement the low age of sexual initiation among non-Christians; this crucial tidbit of ethnographic evidence was designed to stimulate evangelical giving, particularly among women.[6] Medical men were also prone to give advice on the appropriate age to marry and begin sexual intercourse; late 19th century physicians generally proscribed marriage for girls before age twenty because they believed their pelvic development was incomplete until then.[7] The notion that marriage should not occur at the onset of menarche was also promulgated in popular women's periodicals. For example, Edward Curtis Bok, editor of the *Ladies' Home Journal*, dismissed the "primitive idea" that "with the dawn of sex consciousness" mating should occur.[8] These social and medical ideals actually came together in the 1880s in the Social Purity drive to raise the age of consent, a favorite cause of the WCTU which encapsulated in a single legislative campaign a powerful assault on the sexual abuses of adult men and a commitment to the protection of American girls. In 1887, New York State raised the age of consent from 10 to 16 years of age; Elmira's Helen L. Bullock, who led the effort to establish the Anchorage, was active in that campaign and served as national chair of the WCTU's Social Purity Department.[9] In sum, the notion of female adolescence as a hiatus free from the burdens of adult sexual life was central to the depiction of Victorian girlhood. The ability of a family to delay the full implications of a daughter's menstruation, that is her marriage and motherhood, was a source of pride, and probably, middle-class self-definition.[10]

The intensity of middle-class distaste for girlhood sexuality was coupled, however, with changing social experiences and the emergence of romantic love as a singularly important source of female identity. In post-Civil War America, the evolution of youth organizations and the growth of the public high school inevitably freed young women from some of their family ties and domestic centeredness.[11] A wider, easier, and more leisured association with peers outside the family meant greater opportunity to "fall in love" or, at least, to think about it. For young women coming of age in the 1880s and 1890s, love could easily be viewed as a requirement for adult female status. According to the prescriptive formula of the day, adult women's lives moved in a "natural" sequence from romantic love to marriage, the centerpiece of female existence. Then, as now, naive young women assumed an inevitability to this sequence that is belied by social facts. However, by 1904 G. Stanley Hall was making romantic love a characteristic of normal female adolescent development.[12] Thus, Victorian girls were expected to find love and be loving within specific behavioral limits. Where love led to a marriage sanctioned by parents, the young woman was promised the social status of adulthood. But, where love was unrequited, frustrated, or inappropriate (and when it failed to eventuate in marriage), female identity was regarded as truncated or spoiled. These ideas, rooted in what William Goode has called the "love pattern" of the culture, gave the social drama of illegitimacy an urgency that was reflected in vernacular language.[13]

Popular use of the term "ruined" to describe a young woman who was both unmarried and pregnant conveyed the ostracism and the economic liabilities attached to out-of-wedlock pregnancy in Victorian America. Because the concept was so embedded in the culture, the term was pervasive throughout the case histories I describe. Girls, parents, and Anchorage officials commonly used the term: as a descriptive adjective (a "ruined" girl), as a verb ("he ruined her"), and as a noun ("the cause of my ruin" or "he accomplished her ruin"). In the latter usage, as a noun, "ruin" denoted a state of being that implied intentionality on the part of the male. "Ruined" meant to be less than physically perfect, to be non-virginal and without an intact hymen. It also suggested something about the future, about truncated marital and educational opportunities – a liability that would be particularly deadly to the economic and social aspirations of the Victorian middle-class family. Because premarital pregnancy so clearly undermined the social status of Victorian women, the fear of being "ruined" had particular efficacy in families that aspired to any kind of social or economic mobility. In this sense, "ruined" carried a robust prescriptive message.

In labeling the sexually active girl "ruined," Victorian society marked her as a deviant, someone whose unacceptable behavior moved her outside the boundaries of the social system. Deviants, as Kai Erikson argues, often serve a didactic purpose in that they establish the behavioral parameters within which people must function.[14] Consequently, the social isolation illegitimacy implied was a common theme in the popular moralistic fiction of the 19th century. Literary portrayals incorporated both the vernacular usage of the term "ruined" and were structured around the emotional angst suffered by women who bore children out-of-wedlock.[15]

For the historian, systematic assessment of the long-term psychological consequences of illegitimacy is extremely difficult. Unmarried mothers sought anonymity more than most people did: many changed their locations and their names intentionally or they eventually married, virtually disappearing from the documentary record. Thus, what we confront in the historical investigation of illegitimacy is the code of silence that surrounded the issue in real life. Unmarried pregnant girls were encouraged by the very women who protected them to pursue life-long silence about this aspect of their autobiography. Dr. Kate Waller Barrett, a founder of the national Florence Crittenton maternity home movement, wrote: "We try to impress upon our girls the fact that they must not discuss their fall with anyone; that if someone should ask them anything in regard to their past life they should say with quiet dignity: 'I have had a great deal of trouble in my life and it only brings up painful memories to discuss the subject.'"[16] So, too, at the Anchorage the surnames of girls were known only to the staff, a kind of secrecy that demonstrated respect for the reputation of patriarchically organized families.

As a consequence of the Victorian code of silence, bastardy became by the 1890s less of a public or community affair and more of a private family agony. However, the case records considered here do reveal the persistence, into the first decade of this century, of an older view of sexuality as a community concern rather than as a strictly private matter. The self-confident middle-class matrons of the WCTU created the Anchorage precisely because they saw collective, voluntary action as a means to mitigate the excruciating predicament of the pregnant but unmarried girl.

"Betrayal" and Adolescent Motherhood

As part of the larger story of the evolving concept and consequences of illegitimacy in American society, this study focuses on responses to out-of-wedlock pregnancy among women in Upstate New York between 1890 and 1907. In general, two common concerns in previous historiography are avoided: that is, determining the causes of illegitimacy or taking measurements of its frequency.[17] Rather, I have looked for ways to assess the consequences of out-of-wedlock pregnancy in the lives of adolescent girls as well as the level of family and community involvement in determining the resolution of individual cases. The primary historical method has been the reconstruction and analysis of sixty-one cases involving young women who were between the ages of thirteen and twenty-one when they experienced pregnancy outside of marriage. The sixty-one cases are drawn from the population of a single New York State institution, the Anchorage. While the mandate of that institution was inclusive rather than exclusive, it could physically hold no more than twenty girls at any one time. No claims, then, are made for the representativeness of the sample.

As demonstrated below, the institution did maintain its own informal referral service, based in WCTU chapters across the state of New York. The WCTU net was cast in such a way that it seemed to encircle farm and working girls with respectable connections. However, it also offered services to a small group of middle-class girls, who came directly from high school with parental support, and a number of women who were sufficiently dispossessed to arrive in the company of the County Overseer of the Poor after a stint in the county poorhouse. Undoubtedly, some cases of illegitimate birth in the region went unnoticed because the young woman and her child could be absorbed into either a family or a subculture where the absence of a legal spouse/father carried no particular social or economic liability. Borrowing from Peter Laslett, there is some evidence of a "bastardy prone subsociety" in rural Upstate New York in this period.[18] At least two of the sixty-one unwed mothers considered here were themselves born out of wedlock; both cases came from the same rural village and were, apparently, native born. A limit of the Anchorage study is that it captures only the anxieties and experiences of those women and girls who regarded pregnancy outside of marriage with some degree of alarm. However, while Victorianism is best understood as a pluralistic model (as demonstrated in important work by Steven Marcus and Peter Cominos nearly two decades ago), certain subcultures with more power and autonomy are more pervasive in terms of their ideology.[19] In late nineteenth century America, particularly in the small towns and villages of Upstate New York, standards of respectability were set, by and large, by the middle class. Thus, as middle-class women sought ways to extend aid to "the fallen" they may also have exacerbated and spread the social stigma of that condition as part of their class prerogative.

On the issue of cause, my experience with the Anchorage records confirms the essential accuracy of the "failed" courtship hypothesis associated with European studies by Peter Laslett, Joan Scott and Louise Tilly, Cissie Fairchild, John Gillis and Judith Walkowitz.[20] In the same way that 60% of the bastard bearing women in 17th century Somerset explained their situation to English Justices of the Peace in terms of broken marriage promises, young women in Upstate New York in the 1890s told the admitting officials at the Anchorage of failed courtships, generally with young unmarried men of approximately their own age.[21] The persistent use of the phrase "betrayed under promise of marriage" conveys a great deal about the dashed expectations of girls and their psychological orientation at the time they became sexually active.[22] Based on recent portraits of American working-class women by Leslie Woodcock Tentler and Faye Dudden, it seems that marriage was a central enticement for beginning sexual intercourse, particularly among poor girls who faced frustrating and low paying work.[23] Thus, the preponderance of working girls at the Anchorage and their apparent vulnerability to sexual seduction may be more a function of a particular psychological dynamic (i.e., the expectation of finding security in marriage) than the result of exploitation by lascivious employers.

Underlying my treatment of the issue is the assumption that illegitimacy is a dilemma generated and enforced by human society, in effect, a socially constructed status like slavery or bankruptcy.[24] Illegitimacy is not simply a statistical phenomenon or a measure of sexuality outside of marriage. In this sense, I have tried to redress the balance of previous work in this area: by restoring people and their emotions to the quantitative profiles generated by historical demographers. Illegitimacy is, after all, a social, economic, legal, and religious construction of enormous complexity and, as such, its definition and handling reveal a great deal about a culture.

Rescuing "The Fallen"

By the late 1890s, the city of Elmira, New York, had earned a national and regional reputation as both an economic and cultural center. With a population of over 30,000 Elmira was serviced by over sixty passenger trains a day, making it something of a railroad hub for a large region encompassing parts of both New York State and north-central Pennsylvania. Building on the city's recognized role in moving goods and men south to Civil War battlefields, local boosters advertised their town in glossy promotional materials as "the Queen City of the Southern Tier" and they touted its scenic parks and cultural advantages. Elmira also housed one of the premier women's colleges in the land and had a fully developed system of parochial education built around a number of ethnic churches. In effect it was the kind of city to which young women might be drawn for entertainments; for work in burgeoning industries, hotels, and stores; for the opportunity to meet young railroad men; for education at the high school, commercial, or collegiate levels; or for anonymity when they found themselves "in trouble."

Elmira's Women's Christian Temperance Union (WCTU) was the crucial linchpin in developing a local institution to serve girls in need. In Elmira the link between evangelical associations of women and "preventive work" among girls was absolutely clear. By 1880, Elmira's affluent Protestant churches housed all the major women's foreign missionary societies. The first Chemung County chapter of the WCTU was established in Elmira in 1886; auxiliaries in surrounding towns soon followed, ringing the city. As a result of the national WCTU's interest in prison work and their larger crusade to establish female care for women prisoners, the Elmira Central Chapter of the WCTU secured the appointment in 1889 of the city's first police matron, Esther D. Wilkins, the sister of the mayor and the wife of a carpenter.[25] In the same spirit, the Elmira Central Chapter approached the "women of the various church missionary societies" to form Elmira's Women's Council for the Uplifting of Women. Both the impulse and the rhetoric were strictly evangelical; middle-class Protestants in Elmira obviously found something of an analogue to heathen degradation in some of the troubling life experiences faced by American girls. The old "Mission to Fallen Girls," traditionally a ward in a hospital operated by a state charities system, or the unsystematic Magdalen Society efforts to convert urban prostitutes, seemed somehow inadequate to contemporary problems of behavior and illegitimate births among the current generation of young women.[26] Moreover, the older efforts failed to promote adoption of a single code of morality equally binding for women and men.[27]

Consequently, Elmira's female leadership was activitated by the cause of saving "girls" within an institution. In 1890, Elmira women opened the Anchorage, a "protective and rescue home" in the heart of a respectable residential neighborhood. The constituency for the home was described as girls who had "fallen or who were in circumstances that might lead to their fall from want of employment, from destitution, or from evil associates."[28] In this respect, the Anchorage was an effort to reach across age and class lines to assist younger women who were perceived as mistreated by men. In a region where WCTU activities filled the front pages of local newspapers, the "rescue home" in Elmira drew attention and financial support from numerous local chapters of the organization. In March, 1898, for example, the *Addison Advertiser* gave prominent coverage to the county's semi-annual WCTU convention, involving fifty-four women delegates who represented over ten times as many members. At this meeting in the tiny community of Wayland, the delegates authorized "special work for the Anchorage in Elmira" and pledges were given for an amount adequate to build a "Steuben County room at that place." Similarly, readers of the *Yates County Chronicle* heard regularly about WCTU "tea meetings" for the "benefit of the Rescue Home for girls."[29]

By word of mouth and by identification in the local newspapers, women and girls throughout the state learned about the existence of the Anchorage, its program, and its staff of women physicians.[30] Where to have an illegitimate baby if you could not have it at home was a crucial problem; the region had few hospitals and these differed with respect to their tolerance for young women who had no husbands.[31] Consequently, the Anchorage was something of a beacon to those who faced the frightening possibility of being on their own at the time of delivery. The fact that 97% of the Anchorage's unmarried mothers were experiencing pregnancy and parturition for the first time explains why they constituted a relatively desperate and docile population, willing to tolerate the exigencies of moral rehabilitation in exchange for their physical care.[32]

Within an intensely evangelical framework, a modicum of respect for cultural pluralism was maintained at the Anchorage. Both Catholic and Jewish girls were admitted. Although the majority of the inmates (70%) were native born, some came from Irish and German Catholic families residing in Elmira rather than in rural towns and villages. (Between 1890 and 1907, there was only one admission of a Jewish girl.) Since the Anchorage was avowedly a Protestant home, the moral rehabilitation program including daily Bible and prayer meeting, posed problems for girls of non-Protestant background. Some Catholics were articulate about their religious identity and, as a consequence, used the Anchorage in a very circumspect manner, as simply a way-station on the road to a more hospitable Catholic charitable environment in Buffalo or in New York City. Babies were, after all, a religious issue in the context of a culturally diverse society and births raised thorny problems about baptism, naming, and circumcision; adoption posed questions about upbringing and future religious training. When babies born to Catholic mothers died at the Anchorage, arrangements were made for burial in the Catholic cemetery in conjunction with the services of local priests. Whatever tolerance the Anchorage maintained for the wishes of committed Catholics, it went hand-in-hand with a perpetual interest in dissuading or converting those girls who were ambivalent or less than loyal to the Mother Church. For example, the matron wrote proudly of eighteen year old Mary McGuire: "She became convinced she could not live a conscientious Christian life as a Roman Catholic and after due deliberation she joined the First Methodist Church on Baldwin Street." Still other Catholic girls moved out of the church, through marriage, into the Protestant denominations.[33]

In nineteenth-century evangelical women's culture, particularly in the small towns and villages of rural New York State, both the women's foreign missionary crusade and the WCTU played a preeminent role in the organization of female lives at the local level. This influence extended beyond the common fare of meetings and study groups to direct intervention in the lives of girls in a moment of enormous personal crisis. More than 70% of the escorts who accompanied pregnant girls to the Anchorage had WCTU connections. This kind of intervention was regarded as a service to the girl and her family as well as a help to the community. In this sense, the WCTU acted as a resource for unmarried pregnant girls on a statewide basis much in the manner of an established welfare agency. In their handling of this highly charged emotional issue, the WCTU local (or certain women in it) took on the role of moral arbiter for the community, explaining, in part, the strength of socially conservative pro-family women's movements in the late nineteenth century. To a surprising degree, local WCTU representatives reinforced traditional community mores and concerns at the same time that they pursued female advocacy and the demise of the sexual double standard. Their ability to achieve this integration of roles prompts us to look more closely at the principles by which they operated.

At the outset it is important to note that admission to the Anchorage constituted tacit acknowledgement that marriage would not occur, at least with the male responsible for the problematic pregnancy. In this sense, the Anchorage was a placement of last resort for those girls who could not or did not want to resolve their difficulty through marriage. Most young women, either in truth or as a way of eliciting sympathy, explained their situation as a form of male "betrayal." Consequently, WCTU locals and their representatives clearly preferred a marital resolution both as a form of justice and because it solved future problems of child support. Moreover, where a local girl went to the Anchorage it generally required some degree of fund-raising by the WCTU auxiliary. When Ida May Roderbaugh, 20, went alone to the Anchorage in 1905, without the recommendation of her Halsey Valley local, women in her home community were annoyed that the Elmira Chapter granted her admission. The matron's journal reported: "When the WCTU of Halsey Valley learned that we had taken her, they thought it very unwise for they said the man who was the cause of all her trouble should have married her."[34]

Women in the local community were clearly critical of the Anchorage's rescue mission when and if it foreclosed their efforts to promote a marriage. In their role as marriage "brokers" or "enforcers," the thrust of WCTU activity was to mediate situations where local girls became pregnant by identifiable and suitable local men. In the case of May Roderbaugh, the putative father was John Hutt, 27, the son of a farm laborer. May was the daughter of a poor but "good" family disrupted by the death of her mother. As a result, she boarded in the village in the home of an older brother, a school teacher. Community residents knew that May and John has been "keeping company" for at least four years. "Under promise of marriage" intercourse was evidently begun: in

1903 or 1904, May experienced either a spontaneous or an induced abortion. In 1905, she became pregnant again and, this time, faced the prospect of illegitimacy. When John Hutt made no move to marry her, she left Halsey Valley, on her own, in her fifth month. The town's WCTU chapter regarded May's institutionalization as a mistake because they perceived John Hutt as an appropriate husband for the girl.

Despite the bias for a conjugal resolution, the WCTU did not promote marriage at any cost. Rather, the marital imperative was tempered by cultural ideas about appropriateness, particularly with respect to class and age. Age was a relevant but largely unspoken consideration in determining how unmarried pregnant girls were handled and whether or not the family or community supported a "shot gun marriage." In the community at large, adolescent motherhood was certainly not the norm: only 10% of the female population of Chemung County aged 13-21 was married. Married girls under the age of 18 constituted only 1% of the girls in the 13-21 age group. Consequently, the community maintained certain expectations about what constituted an acceptable age for motherhood even among the community of deviant girls. At the Anchorage, 68% of the unmarried mothers were between the ages of 16 and 20, confirming what Judith Walkowitz and Ruth Rosen found in their studies of prostitution: that for those women who became sexually active before marriage, intercourse generally began at about age sixteen.[35]

Among WCTU women, the prospect of pregnancy and motherhood under 18 usually generated enormous distaste, invoking bleak images of "girl life" among the heathen.[36] In 1906, the situation of a thirteen year old farm girl from Athens, Pennsylvania, prompted the Anchorage leadership to renege on an institutional decision to deny admission to inmates from other states for anything but extremely short stays. This "New York Only" policy was justified by the fact that the Anchorage received cash payments for girls who came to them from within the New York State system of county poorhouses. Yet, in 1906, they admitted Dora Barrett, the daughter of a "shiftless" Pennsylvania farm family, because they considered her case particularly grevious.[37]

Thirteen year old Dora Barrett became pregnant by an unidentified farm hand whom her father compelled her to marry. Immediately after the marriage, the reluctant groom ran away. The child was born in Pennsylvania and left there for adoption before Dora was removed from her home and brought to the Anchorage in March 1906 by her aunt, a Mrs. Kirk from Smithfield, Pennsylvania. Mrs. Kirk, who had WCTU connections, considered Dora's situation intolerable. Apparently, she contacted the state (Pennsylvania) WCTU, traveled 150 miles from Smithfield to Athens, separated Dora from the baby, and had the marriage annulled before bringing the youngster to the Anchorage. Because the Anchorage was the maternity shelter closest to the girl's home, the Pennsylvania WCTU asked their "sisters" in Elmira for assistance in this unusual case involving a thirteen year old. Dora Barrett was received "as a special favor to the Penn Unions," wrote the admitting matron. Obviously, WCTU women in Pennsylvania and in New York regarded the girl's protection from a prurient and premature marriage as justification for an adjustment in institutional rules.

Although WCTU intervention undoubtedly included some obsessive preaching about morality, the Anchorage case records actually underscore the practical economic side of their involvement with out-of-wedlock pregnancies. These women demonstrated rather clearly that they were alert to the economic exigencies of the day and aware of the legal difficulties involved in exacting support from putative fathers. As a result, the Anchorage women had to develop a vocabulary for dealing with men on the move. High rates of male (and female) transiency, generated by the search for work had consequences for heterosexual relations, particularly among the working class. Many men who were transient and without resources were identified in the matron's journal with only a generic description: "clerk," "farm hand," "street car employee." These were men who simply could not be pursued fruitfully for their responsibility in a pregnancy or for their financial support.[38] In this sense, the WCTU served working-class girls least effectively in that lower expectations about the "responsibility" of males in the working class probably meant less zealous pursuit of them and, consequently, higher rates of out-of-wedlock births. In Britain, one analyst reports that "the second half of the 19th century was a succession of field days for the young man who could persuade the working class girl that he was single and ready to marry . . ."[39] Pathbreaking mobility studies by Stephan Thernstrom surely suggest that high rates of male transiency may be part of both the experience and the perception of an illegitimacy problem in late 19th century America as well.[40]

By contrast, where paternity was clear and the male's economic resources sufficient to justify payment, the WCTU could engineer financial settlements. Support that continued after confinement was not, however, encouraged since it smacked of something else: a girl did not want to become "kept" in the manner described by Theodore Dreiser in *Jennie Gerhardt*. Thus, financial arrangements had to be resolved quickly at the point of the girl's admission or, at least, before the baby was born. This kind of settlement happened only occasionally but when it did there was a clear presumption that the male's economic resources justified the resolution.

In the situation of Mildred Millville, the daughter of a Schuyler County farmer, the economic status of her sexual partner shaped the WCTU's intervention. Millville who was 21, came to the Anchorage in December 1903, when she was seven months pregnant, accompanied by Dr. W.H. Beach of Odessa, Schuyler County. Mildred's parents were "good people" who, like Dr. Beach, attended the Methodist Episcopal Church in the village of Catherine. Her seducer was Grove Tyron, 25, the son of a local merchant and hotel owner. Dr. Beach and others found Mildred's condition surprising because of her parents' respectability and her own upright reputation. The matron's journal noted that Mildred Millville had been well regarded in her home community for her "pure moral character" and her diligence. Apparently, she was "sought after by farmer's wives to help them as she was a strong girl physically and . . . an excellent worker." In time, Mildred Millville was enticed, by the promise of more money, away from the seasonal rhythms of helping farm women into a wage-earning situation, as a domestic, in a local hotel. There she met the owner's son, Grove, described by the matron at the Anchorage as a "shrewd wily scamp" who set about "to accomplish her ruin."[41]

For reasons left unstated in the written record, Millville and Tyron were not to marry. We might speculate, however, that Tyron's father saw no particular merit in having his only child marry a diligent but coarse farmer's daughter doing domestic work in his hotel. For the families of propertied young men, resolution through marriage could be highly problematic since it opened the possibility of unwelcome intrusions on both the family's economic interests and its social status. Moreover, a marriage that came too early in a young man's life might stymie aspirations and block a career.[42] We have no way of knowing how Mildred Millville felt about the possibility of marriage to Grove Tyron; perhaps she saw him for what the record suggests he was, "a masher," who would not make a good husband. Perhaps she held out a hope that he would marry her, saving her from a life of continued hard work on the farm.

The Millville-Tyron relationship was ultimately resolved with a financial settlement rather than a marriage; in that settlement, Grove Tyron admitted his paternity. Although the name of the individual who initiated the settlement is unclear, it is relevant to point out that the Millville-Tyron agreement was surrounded by local professionals – Dr. W.H. Beach who brought the girl to Elmira and an unnamed attorney from Montour

Falls. The structure of the payments made by Grove Tyron reveal who the interested parties were. In acknowledgement of his role in the ruin of a popular local girl, Tyron paid over to his lawyer the sum of $100 to be divided up in the following manner: $50 to the WCTU's Anchorage for Mildred's care; $10 for the attending physician in Elmira; $15 for Dr. Beach for "his trouble;" $10 for the lawyer; and $15 for Mildred when she left the Anchorage. Whether or not the financial settlement eased a girl's pain, it allowed vigilant locals to rationalize that the responsible male had, at least, "paid his due."[43]

The prominent role of WCTU women in arbitrating the economic responsibilities of illegitimacy within the community should not obscure the extent to which out-of-wedlock pregnancy was also a private family issue. Most girls did not come to the Anchorage alone; of those who did, it is significant that they were all at least eighteen years of age – suggesting that the very youngest girls were under someone's supervision. Not surprisingly, where girls were accompanied to the Anchorage by family members (26%) mothers and aunts were the primary escorts.[44] However, an examination of the family backgrounds of the 61 pregnant girls at the Anchorage does indicate that at least 44 percent came from families that experienced an essential form of disruption, that is the death or desertion of one or more parents. Of these, 78 percent were without mothers meaning that their biological mother was dead or incapacitated through insanity or chronic intemperance. This "mother deficit" may reflect the bias of the Anchorage staff in favor of seeking out and admitting "worthy" girls whose hapless situation could be explained as a function of environmental deprivation rather than innate moral depravity. A mother was, ideally, the best monitor and guide of heterosexuality in girlhood and a young woman's best protection against the experience of "betrayal." Clearly the "mother deficit" implies an emotional rather than an economic liability.[45]

Among girls eighteen or over who came to the Anchorage alone, three different but not altogether exclusive predicaments appear to prevail, each related to the issue of family. First, a young woman came alone because she was already on her own, trying to make a living in one of the ways single women did: as a domestic servant in a private household, hotel, or health-care institution; as a laundress or seamstress; as a teacher; or as a prostitute. Somewhere between 20 and 25 percent of the unmarried pregnant women at the Anchorage entered from domestic service but their employers generally were not the putative fathers. Generally, their sexual relationships were characterized by age and class endogamy. For example, nineteen-year-old Rosalind Lockhart from Victor entered the Anchorage pregnant in 1905 after a term of service in Rochester where she worked as a "housemaid and as a nurse," probably assisting in a family sickroom. Lockhart had family of her own but they were not interested in her: her mother was dead, her father "a drunkard," her two older brothers had "no sense of responsibility to her." In Rochester she was "ruined by a young man working in one of the hotels" in that city, but his identity was undisclosed. There were always, however, some relationships that were highly problematic because of a differential in status. For example, twenty year old Matilda Hochmeyer, a domestic servant and the daughter of an Ithaca cigar maker, became sexually involved with an aspiring young professional, James Hillard, a medical student at Cornell, whom she met through her employment in a professor's home. When the "ambitious" young woman, whom the matron described as "wanting to make something of herself more than a mere house servant," informed Hillard of her condition, he callously "told her it was her own fault, that a woman ought to know enough to take care of herself." Hillard conveniently left Ithaca at that point, for Rochester, and work in a hospital.[46]

Only about 3 percent of the young women who entered the Anchorage on account of pregnancy included prostitution or commercial sex in their background, a figure which could be shaped by the applicants' sense of what the Anchorage's admitting officer wanted to hear. Yet, it makes little sense to conclude that there was an operative bias against the admission of young prostitutes. Rather, in the evangelical psychology of moral rehabilitation the admission of a prostitute and the chance to effect her reform provided the classic opportunity to demonstrate the meliorative powers of a Christian environment. Among evangelical women, religious belief encouraged mental pictures (or fantasies) that included the projection of their own role as reformer of fallen women. Precisely because religiously inspired women operated with the model of Christ's charity to the harlot fully in mind, there was unlikely to be institutional prejudice against prostitutes unless they were diseased.[47] "Though your sins be as scarlet so they shall be as white as the snow," adorned the 1900 annual report of the Anchorage.[48] However, pregnant prostitutes may well have avoided the Anchorage because they rejected moral rehabilitation and had their own functional support community among those in "the life."[49]

Girls whose families were embarrassed or infuriated by their condition constituted a second group of Anchorage inmates who came alone to the shelter. When pregnancy occurred in unmarried daughters, some parents reacted with sorrow, anger, or both. Mothers, in particular, were described as "wild with grief" or "heartbroken" over their daughters' condition. In 1886, a grandmother of an illegitimate child allegedly murdered the infant born to her daughter "who had not loved wisely."[50] In other cases, parents – mothers as well as fathers – became enraged and hostile toward the pregnant girl, forcing her, either physically or as a condition of emotional survival, to leave the family. In 1893, the mother of Charlotte Baker in the village of Watkins would not allow her eighteen-year-old daughter to remain with the family after her pregnancy, the result of a relationship with the hired man, became known: "she being pregnant . . . it was impossible for her mother to keep her at home." In 1905, Emily Saunders, a pregnant fifteen-year-old, was driven from her Big Flats home "when her mother learned the facts." The father of sixteen-year-old Hilda Bock, from Canaan Four Corners, Columbia County, became "so enraged that he threatened to throw her out doors."[51] Familial ostracism, which was not uncommon, added greatly to the difficulty of the girl's already ambiguous situation vis-a-vis her sexual partner, her relationship with friends and neighbors, and her precarious future. Moreover, familial ostracism underscores the extent to which a premarital pregnancy threatened the status of an entire family.

In the third group, the girl and her family were enmeshed in a web of secrecy and self-deception. Many girls who came alone to the Anchorage, particularly the 85 percent who came after their sixth month experienced an anxious period of uncertainty as to their actual condition and, then, months of cautious calculation to determine an approximate delivery date. Information about duration of pregnancy and its "presumptive, probable, and positive signs" was readily available in obstetrical texts and guidebooks for physicians, for nurses, and for lay use.[52] Yet, with surprising regularity girls claimed uncertainty as to the extent of the pregnancy and, typically, one or more parents claimed they did not know about their daughter's condition – despite close proximity in the same household where the signs of pregnancy were hard to avoid. Given the timing of Anchorage admissions one is forced to ask whether it was really possible to conceal from one's family all the physical changes that had occurred by the third trimester of pregnancy? Did parents really *not* know? Or was the description of unsuspecting parents an expression of wishful thinking (on the part of a guilt-ridden girl) or an act (on the part of parents)? Undoubtedly, there were girls in the New York region like twenty year old Evelyn Stewart from Northfield, Maine:

when Evelyn entered a Boston hospital in October 1873 she was "laced very tightly and wore a firm bandage about the abdomen to hide her condition."[53] Yet, camouflage through clothing seems an unlikely explanation since fashions of the day accentuated rather than finessed the waistline.[54] Moreover, many of the young women in question probably owned no more than a change or two of clothing and were forced to expand physically within the limits of their meager wardrobes. In other words, most could not easily generate special maternity outfits to disguise their condition.

Consequently, it seems logical to conclude that denial was a primary mechanism for coping within the Victorian family wherever there was a great deal of emotional confusion or trauma attached to an out-of-wedlock pregnancy. Plainly, some young women never gave up the hope that they would be married before the baby was born. Families and girls tended to procrastinate, and come to the Anchorage remarkably late in pregnancy only after overt physiological changes forced recognition that a delivery must be reckoned with. A young woman admitted to the Anchorage in her seventh month explained to the admitting matron that she came to the home only "when her condition became so apparent there was no possibility of concealing it any longer."[55] Until that point, many girls and their parents did not discuss what was actually going on. Reports of parents and employers who "did not know" about rather advanced and obvious pregnancies probably means that there was no confrontation or open discourse about issues of love, intimacy and trust which surrounded this personal and family crisis. With this scenario in mind it is easier to make sense of the following cases. Despite the fact that she lived at home, eighteen-year-old Martha Bossert claimed that her mother was "not aware of her condition" though she was in the seventh month of her pregnancy by a twenty-two-year-old bookkeeper in the Erie Freight office. Similarly, Cynthia Brown reported that her mother "didn't know until the last minute" of her impending motherhood. And, finaly, there was Lila Stone, a student at the Mansfield State Normal School, who apparently attended classes into her sixth month and, then, in September 1903, came to the Anchorage undetected from the home where she worked for her room and board up until three weeks before she delivered a baby girl.[56]

If some parents and employers chose not to look, others constructed alternative medical rationales to explain gross changes in their daughters' physiology and/or energy level. Recall that Nettie Mayers' father thought she was in Rochester for removal of a tumor, probably a polite euphemism for a gynecological problem. Similarly, in the case of Margaret Asgood, a twenty-one year old seamstress who worked alongside her widowed mother, the record states that Mrs. Asgood "knew nothing" of her daughter's condition and "supposed she was in the hospital to receive treatment for rheumatism" when she gave birth.[57]

The fact that families were apt to intentionally mask a girl's condition prompted the Anchorage leadership to take a strident position on the business of their acting as a cover. The WCTU clearly believed that social status should not act as a cloak for sin. Anchorage literature proclaimed, as a counter to those moralists who saw the fledgling institution as a promoter of impurity: "We never receive girls simply to hide their shame although often offered large sums to do this."[58] The implication was that while the institution strove to be discrete, it did not intend to serve the needs of wealthy families (or men) seeking anonymity for daughters (or lovers). Although the records do not include any offers by the wealthy to "buy" a place at the Anchorage, it would be incorrect to conclude that the institution served only the poor. There was that population of young women (8%) who came to the Anchorage directly from high school, suggesting that, in some cases, middle-class parents preferred temporary institutionalization: as a way of mediating public disclosure of the girl's condition or as a device for heading off an unwise marriage that threatened family resources or the girl's long-term future.[59]

The problem was, however, that short terms (in and out to deliver, give the baby up for adoption, and return home on the pretext of "visiting Aunt Sally") were made difficult by the institution's evangelical imperative to reform, not simply service, the girl. Anchorage rules required a period of residency longer than a normal social visit: "No girl can enter this institution who will not promise to remain for training and instruction as long as the trustees think it for her good as this institution is especially to reform and save, not to encourage sin."[60] Consequently, the average stay among the pregnant population was 20 months, a period that needed accounting for. Yet, the Anchorage interlude clearly allowed some young women the opportunity to retreat from their aborted role as wife and mother and gave their families time to reconstruct shattered social relations in the community. Some middle-class girls were even able to return home and reintegrate themselves into their local peer group, restoring some semblance of girlish innocence. Obviously, reintegration into respectable small town society was easiest after the birth of a stillborn child or after an adoption. For example, when twenty year old Lillian Van der Mayer lost her baby in a fire at the Anchorage, the girl told the matron with relief: "Maybe it is for the best. I think it a judgement on me, but I can go home to my mother now and she will never know my disgrace." After giving up her infant to the care of a county orphanage, nineteen year old Florence Hibbings returned home to Avoca. The matron's journal aptly captured what middle-class parents considered the best resolution: "Florence is at home with her parents doing nicely. Her misfortune is not known to the world."[61]

Recovery from the multiple crises posed by an unmarried pregnancy was possible so long as the birth remained covert and the baby properly disposed of. A proper disposition meant adoption – either through a private family or through a welfare agency, generally a county orphanage. The promise of social regeneration or, at least, the opportunity to escape the overt symbol of her "ruin" was offered every young woman who gave up her child. Told upon entry to the Anchorage that her behavior had robbed her child of "an honest birth and an unsullied name" and that the child was now "handicapped in the battle of life," many girls saw adoption as the only responsible corrective.[62] And, for WCTU women in upstate New York, community aversion to taking on long-term support of illegitimate children worked against retention as did their own ability to make placements in "good Christian homes." In effect, the WCTU appeared to be able to intersect with what many have been a middle-class market for children.[63] Consequently, the imperative for adoption was strong and the institutional records confirm that fact: of 32 babies born alive at the Anchorage between 1890 and 1907, 69 percent were adopted; 31 percent were kept by their mothers. Placing out of illegitimate children, without a legally binding contract, was also a common option.[64]

A closer look at the disposition of the Anchorage babies confirms that the mother's age and corresponding work options influenced the resolution of these cases. Among girls under sixteen, 80 percent gave their infants up for adoption; among 16 to 18 year olds, 78 percent of their infants were adopted; and among girls over 18, 62 percent chose the adoptive resolution. A declining preference for separation from the child reflected the economic and social reality of the day: among unmarried women with children, older women had a better chance to find work and make a life of their own with the child, however marginal their income.

To the middle class sponsors of the Anchorage, domestic service appeared to offer the "ruined" girl her best opportunity because it combined wage earning with a supervised middle-class environment. Service was, until 1920, the single largest category of female employment in the United States.[65] At the home in Elmira, WCTU women affirmed that hard domestic work was, in and of itself, a therapeutic regime. It was as if scrubbing "helped a girl work off her sin" or that laundry was a "means of grace." Few in this time period stopped to consider how the emphasis on homemaking and domestic work was a "taunting reminder" to the girl of "the very thing she had failed to achieve – love, her own home and marriage."[66] Obviously, the public (and WCTU women) expected these drudgeries to be part of the rehabilitation of the "ruined." At least 40 percent of the unwed mothers were placed out of the institution into service, for the first time, in the homes of WCTU members and their friends. Thus, for a significant number of the pregnant girls, the Anchorage interlude provided food, shelter, medical services, and moral education but, at the same time, reduced them, formally, to the status of servant.

In families and communities across the State of New York, women wearing the imprimatur of the Women's Christian Temperance Union stepped in to provide a form of assistance, a self-defined "rescue mission" to the pregnant and unmarried who had no place to go. Both familial ostracism and a declining preference for absorption of illegitimate children into the mother's family suggest that in Victorian America the unmarried mother and her child were an intolerable reminder of parental failure as well as a dysfunctional form of family membership. Unmarried mothers and their children were not easily absorbed into respectable small town society where social life outside the home was organized around age-graded voluntary and benevolent groups in the shadow of the Christian churches. An unmarried mother with an infant child might stay at home a great deal, but not for a lifetime. Family strategies for economic advancement and consolidation did not include the cost of sheltering and educating another generation, a project, which, by the 1890s, was increasingly extended and expensive. In this way, the heightened Victorian sensitivity to illegitimacy was part and parcel of the same economic and ideological ethos that was limiting family size even among families that were legally constituted.[67]

* * *

By the 1890s, institutionalization and middle-class adoption were emerging as modern management techniques for handling the crisis of out-of-wedlock pregnancy. For this reason, the story of Nettie Mayers attracted enormous attention in the region because it seems so atavistic. Homes like the Anchorage, supported and staffed by evangelical Protestant women, were intended to reduce the chaos, insecurity, and brutality that illegitimacy could generate. Moreover, the Anchorage helped to relieve the financial and supervisory burdens of the County Overseers of the Poor. However, just as illegitimacy was being organized for the first time it was also becoming a particularly dread and damaging form of social deviance for young women and their families. Consequently, people in the Upstate region plainly understood and resonated to the shame and the anguish of the Mayers family.

In the public's willingness to accept the physicians' resolution of the problem, the Mayers case foreshadowed events to come, e.g., the medicalization of illegitimacy by 1920. By 1920, physicians and social workers joined hands to define illegitimacy as a national social problem requiring a professional curative. Whether or not this new public concern was the result of a real or, simply, a perceived escalation in illegitimacy as a result of World War I was questionable then, as it is now.[68] Recognizing that the war brought enormous social and economic dislocation as well as an increased role for the federal government in shaping the lives of its people, Emma O. Lundberg, Director of the Social Service Division, U.S. Children's Bureau, explained to the National Conference on Charities in 1920 that there were "cycles of special interest and emphasis" in social work. Lundberg identified the cause of the moment: "We are now in a period of special concern . . . [with] the protection of children born out of wedlock."[69]

In effect, the illegitimacy problem hooked its wagon to the star of state and federal child welfare reform: children, not unmarried mothers, were the focus of Progressive reformers who lobbied everywhere for legislative protections for the child born out-of-wedlock. When Progressives spoke in favor of doing something about illegitimacy they offered little in the way of a program for the desolate and stigmatized mother. In 1920, Ada Eliot Sheffield, President of Boston's Conference on Illegitimacy, admitted that it was a "futile attempt" to remove the stigma assigned to the mother, given "our present sex ideals," and she called the old adage, "Women soiled is women spoiled," a bit of "compressed social wisdom."[70] Conflicted about the unmarried mother and how society could treat her fairly without devaluing monogamy, Progressive reformers recognized a distinction between "deserved" and "undeserved" social stigma; the latter, they suggested accompanied the illegitimate *child*. Consequently, they pushed for: uniform birth registration; establishing methods for the adjudication of paternity and for reporting illegitimate births to administrative agencies; entitling children to inheritance and their father's name; and establishing state supervision over the business of adoption and guardianship. Additionally, Lundberg urged that the state license and supervise all private maternity hospitals and shelters like the Anchorage, as well as "child-helping" and "child-placing" agencies.[71]

Those Progressive era doctors who became involved in the illegitimacy issue always began by citing statistics on infant mortality among children born out-of-wedlock.[72] Infant mortality among the illegitimate was presented as two to three times what it was among the legitimate. In 1920, Dr. George W. Kosmak, Chairman of the Committee on Obstetrical Care of Unmarried Mothers, explained the data by the fact that "obstetric care given to unmarried mothers is not on a par with that extended to those legitimately pregnant."[73] In other words, Progressive physicians argued, quite persuasively, for uniform medical care for all pregnant women be they married or not. In this respect, the physicians represented an egalitarian and humane influence in the handling of the unmarried mother.[74]

At the same time, the provision of uniform care for married and unmarried mothers implied that only obstetricians – not midwives and certainly not untrained volunteer women in maternity shelters – manage the birth process. Kosmak's 1920 address was explicit about his program for revamping the older, indigenous, volunteer maternity shelter. In addition to objections to "improper discipline" in these homes, Kosmack observed "insufficient medical care" which he suggested, contributed to high infant death. "A campaign of education must be waged," he argued, "which will convince the managers of the responsibility that rests upon them as regards the necessary professional care of their inmates and that the sheltering mantle of charitable secrecy must not be allowed to interfere with the application of appropriate medical observation and care." Beyond convincing the shelter managers (inevitably women) of the efficacy of professionally administered prenatal and postnatal care, Kosmack called for the introduction and continued presence of the physician (generally male) in the daily environment of the institutional home: "The responsibility which attaches to every maternity home to maintain the physical as well as the moral well being of its inmates calls for the appointment of an attending obstetrician in each instance, to whom all inmates should be referred on admission for general examination and diagnosis and who shall maintain a close supervision of the patients during their stay in the institution. It is only by this means," Kosmack concluded, "that the morbidity and mortality among these institutions can be kept down."[75]

Thus, by the force of statistical arguments about infant mortality and through the rise of social services and the growing authority of medicine, the care of illegitimacy was moved, by 1920, out of the world of women into the medical domain of the therapeutic state.[76] This is not to suggest that illegitimate births took place after 1920 only in hospitals; the well-known Florence Crittenton chain, a nationwide network of maternity shelters, continued to serve a portion of the pregnant and unmarried population in their respective urban locations but they were subject to the Progressive pressures just described; in particular, Progressivism required that evangelically-oriented matrons be replaced by professional social workers with psychiatric expertise.[77] Other institutional and economic developments contributed as well to the decline of the traditional female mode of handling the problem of out-of-wedlock pregnancy and birth. An increasing number of hospitals staffed by physicians seeking experiences with parturient women probably tempered policies of exclusion, making hospitals a wider option for the "illegitimately pregnant." Equally important, the decline, by 1920, of domestic service as the largest source of female employment signified the emergence of wider options in women's work, as clerks in the commercial sector and in federal and state government and as workers in industry as well. Preparing a girl for a life in "service," which had been the primary placement out of the early maternity shelters, was no longer adequate in the view of professional social workers.[78] Vocational education became the perceived route to an improved station in life for those in the working and lower middle class. Reflecting this new pedagogical orientation, the Anchorage (noting that there were now "other places" for unmarried mothers to go) dropped its services to pregnant girls entirely in 1907 and changed its mandate and its name to the Helen L. Bullock Industrial School for Girls, an institution for the vocational training of young women 12 to 16 years old.[79] Finally, the nature of community life itself underwent important transformations by 1920. Late 19th century illegitimacy dramas, like that of Nettie Mayers, took place in a society undergoing a transition from the mores of a small scale community to the conditions of a more impersonal and class-divided social order. Characterized by a rich network of female associations and a ritualistic process of separating out and, then, reintegrating the "ruined" girl, the Anchorage interlude represents a sense of collective female responsibility on the local level which distinguishes this moment in time before either professionalism or institutionalization came to predominate. The "protection and rescue" of one generation of women by another was interdicted by the nature of Progressive reform.

Cornell University
Ithaca, NY 14853

Joan Jacobs Brumberg

FOOTNOTES

The author is indebted to G. David Brumberg, Faye Dudden, Glen Elder, John Gillis, Linda Gordon, Joseph Kett, Nancy Tomes and Robert Wells for their helpful criticism of earlier versions of this paper. The 1982-83 Fellows of the Charles Warren Center, Harvard University, also provided insightful comments. Funds to support research on this paper were supplied by the New York State College of Human Ecology, Cornell University.

With the exception of those cases reported in newspapers, the names of individuals have been changed.

1. Although Nettie Mayers never revealed the identity of her sexual partner, interested locals speculated about two different putative fathers. First, that the person responsible for her condition was a young Canisteo man seen with her at a fireman's convention in Hammondsport the preceeding summer. Second, that a young Addison resident was the father but that the parents, who had "higher social aspirations for their daughter," rejected his offer to marry her before her condition became apparent.

Reconstruction of the narrative history of Nettie Mayers is drawn from the Matron's journal of the Anchorage (AMJ), 93; Willard State Hospital Admissions report #8421; *Elmira Daily Gazette and Free Press* (March 23, 1898), 5; *ibid.* (March 24, 1898), 5; *ibid.* (March 25, 1898), 5; *ibid.* (March 29, 1898), 5; *Elmira Daily Advertiser* (March 24, 1898), p. 7; *ibid.* (March 26, 1898), 9; *ibid.* (March 30, 1898), 9; *Addison Advertiser* (March 24, 1898), 5; *ibid.* (March 31, 1898), 5; *ibid.* (May 19, 1898), 5; *Corning Journal* (March 24, 1898), 3; R.G. Dunn Records, Baker Library, v. 36, 227; "Biography of Joseph Mayer," Office of The Town Historian, Addison, New York; 1892 Addison Census; Steuben County Surrogate's Wills #3642.

2. By all accounts, 19th century maternity shelters routinely dealt with abandoned newborns, a telling symbol of the desparation of the unmarried mother. AMJ #11, *Yates County Chronicle LXXVII:18* (June 6, 1900), 3; *Elmira Daily Gazette and Free Press* (March 19, 1898), 5. In the effort to avoid the worst implications of abandonment the New York Foundling Asylum always maintained a "receiving basket" at its entrance door so that unmarried mothers could deposit unwanted babies and safely rid themselves of the "badge of shame." Both the maternity shelter and the "receiving basket" were regarded as practical innovations since "frequently the only other recourse for the unmarried mother was abandonment or infanticide." See Sarah Boudin Edlin, *The Unmarried Mother in Our Society* (New York, 1954), 36.

For an historical analysis of infanticide, see Peter C. Hoffer and N.E.H. Hull, *Murdering Mothers: Infanticide in England and New England, 1558-1803* (New York, 1981); on abortion, see *Abortion in America* (New York, 1979). According to Mohr, by the 1890s abortion was increasingly a tool of middle class married women acting to control their reproductive lives and limit the size of their families. Moreover, girls may have been less likely to try abortion in the 1890s because the laws were increasingly restrictive and abortions cost money, oftentimes beyond the reach of the younger women who was alone in her difficulty.

3. Maris Vinovskis, "An Epidemic of Adolescent Pregnancy? Some Historical Considerations," *Journal of Family History* VI:2 (1981): 205-230; "Adolescent Sexuality, Pregnancy and Childbearing in Early America: Some Preliminary Speculations," Paper presented at Social Science Research Council Conference on "School Age Pregnancies and Parenthood," Baltimore, Md., May 23-26, 1982. Vinovskis is quick to point out that the Colonial inattention to age can not be explained by early marriages: rather, the age at marriage was relatively high and marriages by teenagers were not the norm.

4. See Montgomery Throop, ed., *Revised Statutes of the State of New York* IV (Albany, 1889), 2211-2215; Robert C. Cumming and Robert B. Gilbert, *State of New York: The Poor, Insanity and State Charities Laws* (Albany, 1897), 52-88; *The Consolidated Laws of the State of New York* VII (Albany, 1909), 2882-2885.

5. See for example, Martin Luther Holbrook, *Physical, Intellectual and Moral Advantages of Chastity* (New York, 1894); John Harvey Kellogg, *Man the Masterpiece* (Des Moines, Iowa, 1886); Mary Wood-Allen, *What A Young Girl Ought To Know* (Philadelphia, 1905); William M. Thayer, *Womanhood: Hints and Helps For Young Women* (New York, 1895); John W. Kramer, *The Right Road* (New York, 1891).

6. See Joan Jacobs Brumberg, "Zenanas and Girlless Villages: The Ethnology of American Evangelical Women, 1870-1910," *Journal of American History* 69:2 (1982): 363-66.

7. See George H. Napheys, *The Physical Life of Woman* (Toronto, 1875), 46-48, 67.

8. *Ladies Home Journal* (April, 1910), 5.

9. See David J. Pivar, *Purity Crusade, Sexual Morality, and Social Control* (Westport, Conn., 1973), 104-106, 140-146; Ruth Bordin, *Woman and Temperancce – The Quest for Power and Liberty, 1873-1900* (Philadelphia, 1981), 110-111; Frances Graham and Georgeanna Gardner, *Two Decades: A History of the First Twenty Years Work by the WCTU* (Oswego, 1884), 43; *Union Signal* (July 9-16, 1927), 425. The effort to raise the marriage age, generally a Progressive Era

reform, built on these earlier notions about age and sexuality emanating from 19th century women's culture and Social Purity work. On the issue of marriage age see Pivar, 139-146; Mary E. Richmond and Fred S. Hall, *Child Marriages* (New York, 1925); Women's Protective Association of Cleveland, *School Girl Brides: A Study of the Ohio Marriage Laws Relating to Minors* (Cleveland, 1926); Arthur W. Towne, "Young Girl Marriages in Criminal and Juvenile Courts," *Journal of Social Hygiene* 8 (July 1922): 287-90.

10. The elaborate iconography of girlhood that developed around the turn of the century, including visual representations by Charles Dana Gibson and Howard Chandler Christy, poetry by James Whitcomb Riley, serialized novels, popular songs, and college humor were all tied to the notion that American girls were unencumbered by their sexuality. The author is at work on a study of this aspect of "The Iconography of Girlhood in Victorian America."

11. In "Sex and Self Control: Middle Class Courtship in America, 1770-1870," *Journal of Social History* 15:3 (1982), Ellen Rothman argues that 19th century middle class youth had greater opportunities for heterosexual intimacy than heretofore thought. See also Joseph Kett, *Rites of Passage* (New York, 1977), Chapter 7.

12. G. Stanley Hall, *Adolescence* (New York, 1905), II, 220-26.

13. See William Goode, "The Theoretical Importance of Love," *American Sociological Review* XXIV (1959); 38-47. Also relevant is Ann Swidler, "Love and Adulthood in American Culture," in *Themes of Work and Love in Adulthood*, ed. Neil Smelser and Erik Erikson (Cambridge, Mass., 1980), 120-145. On the changing definition of adult female identity and its relation to the "love complex," I am indebted to John Gillis for suggestions and for his astute commentary on an earlier version of this paper.

14. Kai Erikson, "Notes on the Sociology of Deviance," *Social Problems* 9:4 (1962): 307; *Wayward Puritans* (New York, 1966).

15. See Caroline Corbin's popular novel, *A Woman's Secret* (Chicago, 1867), for a classic example of how suffering, as a result of disgrace, was assumed as a psychological dimension of the illegitimacy experience. Theodore Dreiser in *Jenny Gerhardt* developed the same convention: the unwed mother who struggled over her lifetime with the loneliness and the social ostracism that her status implied. Dreiser wrote three important novels dealing with the theme of sexual nonconformity in young women: *Sister Carrie* (New York, 1900); *Jennie Gerhardt* (New York, 1911); *An American Tragedy* (New York, 1925).

On "disgrace" in the family characterized by illegitmacy, see Ernest W. Burgess, *The Family* (New York, 1953), 186-188, 549-551 and Frank Furstenberg, *Unplanned Parenthood* (New York, 1976).

16. Kate Waller Barrett, *Some Practical Suggestions on the Conduct of a Rescue Home* (New York, 1974), 45. At the Anchorage a girl was considered a trouble maker "by talking of her condition to the younger girls." AMJ, #174. The Annual Report for 1900 states that girls were "not allowed to speak of their past lives except to the superintendent or officers."

17. See Daniel Scott Smith and Michael S. Hindus, "Premarital Pregnancy in America, 1640-1971: An Overview and Interpretation," *Journal of Interdisciplinary History*, V:4 (1975): 537-570. In this pioneering monograph that charts the course of premarital pregnancy in the U.S., Smith and Hindus contend that bridal pregnancy and illegitimacy are positively correlated, providing a general index of sexual behavior. See also Daniel Scott Smith, "The Long Cycle in American Illegitimacy & Prenuptial Pregnancy" in eds. Peter Laslett et al., *Bastardy and Its Comparative History* (Cambridge, 1980), 362-378. Lawrence Stone in *The Family, Sex, and Marriage in England 1500-1800* (New York: 1979), 388-89 suggests that in the period 1500-1800 illegitimacy and premarital pregnancy present different analytical problems; Robert Wells, "Illegitimacy and Bridal Pregnancy in Colonial America," in Laslett, *Bastardy*. . ., 349-361, distinguishes between the two forms of prenuptial conception and points to the fact that the evidence for bridal pregnancy is "fuller and probably more accurate."

The amount of illegitimacy in the period between the Civil War and World War I is extremely difficult to determine. Smith says that the recording of illegitimacy in America is so "problematic" that it is "doubtful whether scholars will ever be very certain concerning the magnitude of the phenomenon." (Smith, "The Long Cycle...," 373). The business of documenting illegitimate births in this period is problematic as a result of these facts: 19th century Protestant churches were not vigilant on this issue and did not keep records; registration of births was not required in New York State until 1914; and out-of-wedlock pregnancies were surrounded by an aura of shame which tended towards non-disclosure. However, projections by Smith, Wells, and other suggest the following: that illegitimacy, like bridal pregnancy, began to increase after the Civil War into the early years of the 20th century; the illegitimacy ratio (calculated on the basis of all babies born) went up simply because there were fewer births, due to declining marital fertility and an increasing number of never-married women.

18. Peter Laslett, "The Bastardy Prone Sub-Society," in eds. Laslett et al., *Bastardy*, 217-440. According to Laslett, a bastardy prone sub-society consisted "in a series of bastard producing women, living in the same locality, whose activities persisted over several generations and who tended to be related by kinship or marriage."

19. On the existence of several Victorian subcultures at the same time, see Steven Marcus, *The Other Victorians: A Study of Sexuality and Pornography in Mid Nineteenth Century England* (New York, 1966); Peter T. Cominos, "Late Victorian Sexual Respectability and the Social System," *International Review of Social History 8* (1963): 18-48, 216-250; Brian Harrison, "Underneath the Victorians," *Victorian Studies 10* (1967); F.B. Smith, "Sexuality in Britain, 1800-1900: Some Suggested Revisions," in *A Widening Sphere: Changing Roles of Victorian Women*, ed. Martha Vicinus (Bloomington, 1977), 182-98.

On the regularities and variations among cultures with respect to illegitimacy, see Harold T. Christensen, "Cultural Relativism and Premarital Sex Norms," *American Sociological Review* 25:1 (1960): 31-39.

20. See Peter Laslett, "Introduction," in Laslett, ed., *Bastardy*---, 57, 92, 108 for a statement of the disappointed courtship hypothesis. For explanations of the apparent rise in illegitimacy in late 18th and early 19th century Europe see Edward Shorter, "Illegitimacy, Sexual Revolution, and Social Change in Modern Europe," *Journal of Interdisciplinary History II* (1971): 237-272; "Capitalism, Culture, and Sexuality: Some Competing Models," *Social Science Quarterly* LII (1972): 338-356; "Female Emancipation, Birth Control, and Fertility in European History," *American Historical Review* LXXVIII (1973): 605-640; *The Making of the Modern Family* (New York, 1975); Louise A. Tilly, Joan W. Scott, and Miriam Cohen, "Women's Work and European Fertility Patterns," *Journal of Interdisciplinary History* VI (1976): 447-476; Tilly and Scott, "Women's Work in Nineteenth Century Europe," *Comparative Studies in Society and History* XVII (1975): 55-58; Stone, *Family, Sex, and Marriage*, 395-402. A study by John Gillis of the relationship between 19th century domestic service and illegitimacy in London, pointed to the particular vulnerability of certain groups by demonstrating how social and economic relationships shape an individual's options in the marriage market. John R. Gillis, "Servants, Sexual Relations, and the Risks of Illegitimacy in London, 1801-1900," *Feminist Studies* 5:1 (1979): 142-169. In *Prostitution and Victorian Society: Woman, class, and the state* (Cambridge, 1980), Judith Walkowitz argues, on the basis of a comparative study of two British industrial centers, that premarital sexual activity with a steady lover was more likely to culminate in marriage where employment was stable for both men and women. In other words 19th century business cycles and the structure of employment significantly affected an individual's ability to legitimatize his or her sexual activity through marriage. For historians of the 19th century United States, this is a particularly suggestive but, as yet, untested formulation.

21. Case records included in the matron's journal are roughly equivalent to the depositions taken by 17th century English officials and the *déclarations de grossesse* required by French law in the 18th century. See G.R. Quaife, *Wanton Wenches and Wayward Wives* (New Brunswick, 1979), 59; Susan D. Amussen "Governors and Governed: Class and Gender Relations in English Villages, 1590-1725," unpublished Ph.D. dissertation, Brown University, 1982; Cissie Fairchilds, "Female

Sexual Attitudes and The Rise of Illegitimacy: A Case Study," *Journal of Interdisciplinary History* VIII:4 (1978): 627-667. Narrative case histories were taken by the matron, superintendent, or her assistants and generally included the young woman's age, her hometown, her family background, and the circumstances by which she came to the Anchorage. In 26% of the cases the putative father is named. Unlike the French records, however, the case histories do not provide a great deal of intimate detail: the circumstances under which a couple met are not generally described nor is the place of first intercourse. In the Elmira institution, relationships characterized by inequalities of status are not common; there are few stories of seductions by men of higher status offering money or gifts of food as in Fairchild's materials. Rather, marriage seems to have been the central enticement for beginning sexual intercourse. This is in keeping with the interpretation offered by Tilly, Scott, and Cohen as well as Tentler and Dudden. See footnote 23 below.

22. See AMJ, #151, 208, 142, 128, 127, 143, 119, 136, 125, 192, 185, 169, 140, 191, 191A, 153, 155 for cases where term "betrayed" and "ruined" are used.

23. See Leslie Woodcock Tentler, *Wage Earning Women* (New York, 1979) and Faye Dudden, *Serving Women: Household Service in Nineteenth Century America* (Middletown, Conn., 1983). A study of bridal pregnancy in Ashford, Kent, in the period 1840-1870 confirms the fact that physical intimacy accompanied the expectation rather than the act of marriage. See Carol G. Pearce, "Some Aspects of Fertility in a mid-Victorian Community," *Local Population Studies 10* (1973): 25-29. Two interesting comments on the American working class girl's particular vulnerability to sexual seduction in the 1890s are in H. Hatch, "Illegitimacy," *Medical Mirror* VII (June, 1896): 267 and Henry Seidel Canby, "Sex and Marriage in the Nineties," *Harpers Magazine* 169 (Sept. 1934): 427.

24. Jenny Teichman, *Illegitimacy: An Examination of Bastardy* (Ithaca, New York, 1982) is the best recent discussion of the complex social, legal, and economic meanings of the legitimacy/illegitimacy distinction. Teichman's book deals with the history of the concept in Britain but not in the United States and stresses the extent to which illegitimacy is a socially constructed as opposed to a natural category. Teichman, a philosopher, is indebted for the thrust of this argument to Kingsley Davis, "Illegitimacy and the Social Structure," *American Journal of Sociology* LV (1939-40): 215 ff. who first presented a functional analysis of the role the legitimacy/illegitimacy distinction played in modern society. See also Bronislaw Malinwoski, "Kinship," *Encyclopedia Brittannica* Vol. XIII (14th edition) (London, 1929), 403 ff and Derek Gill, *Illegitimacy, Sexuality, and The Status of Women* (Oxford, 1977). The earliest attempts in English language social science to assess the relative causes of illegitimacy are: Albert Leffingwell, *Illegitimacy and the Influences of Seasons Upon Conduct* (London, 1918), and Percy Kammerer, *The Unmarried Mother* (London, 1918).

25. In so doing, Elmira joined at least a dozen other cities in the 1880s which gave to police matrons the supervision of women and girls in jails, detention homes, or hospitals. On the police matron movement see Estelle Freedman, *Their Sisters Keepers: Women's Prison Reform in America, 1830-1930* (Ann Arbor, 1981), 61 and Chloe Owings, *Women Police: A Study of the Development and Status of The Women Police Movement* (New York, 1925), 95-99.

26. Antebellum city mission movements established refuges and shelters for fallen women and prostitutes in cities like New York and Philadelphia. On the New York Magdalen Society see Pivar, 26-27 and Carroll Smith-Rosenberg, *Religion and the Rise of the City: The New York City Mission Movement* (Ithaca, 1971), 97-124.

27. Readers of the WCTU's *Union Signal* were made acutely aware that impure males were treated as if nothing were amiss, while ruined girls were isolated and scorned. See for example *Union Signal*, June 3, 1893, 91.

28. 1900 Annual Report; *Elmira Sunday Telegram* (May 2, 1971), 24.
The Anchorage should be seen as part of the larger movement for "protective and rescue"

work among girls that characterizes the period between 1870 and World War I. The WCTU began "rescue work" in 1876 but shifted largely to a preventive emphasis according to Pivar, 85. In 1899, the WCTU had "rescue" homes in at least 6 cities. See Charlton Edholm, *Traffic in Girls and Work of Rescue Missions* (Chicago, 1899). The best known rescue or maternity shelter was the National Association of Florence Crittenton homes, founded in 1883 as a mission in New York's "red light" district. Under the leadership of Dr. Kate Waller Barrett, the Crittenton movement grew to over fifty homes and in 1898 was chartered by Congress; the evangelical religious imperative for conversion of prostitutes was transformed under Barrett's direction to a residential and maternity care program for girls with a strong vocational emphasis. Local initiatives, such as Elmira's Anchorage, were inspired by and sometimes absorbed by the Crittenton organization which had significant funding from Charles Crittenton until 1909. For an overview of the history of the institutional response to the pregnant and unmarried, see Michael W. Sedlak, "Young Women and the City: Adolescent Deviance and the Transformation of Educational Policy, 1870-1960," *History of Education Quarterly* 23:1 (1983): 1-28. Also relevant are Carol L. Urness, "Kate Waller Barrett," *Notable American Women* I (Cambridge, Mass., 1977), 97-99; Otto Wilson, *Fifty Year's Work with Girls* (New York, 1933); Charles N. Crittenton, *The Brother of Girls* (Chicago, 1910).

29. *Addison Advertiser* (March 31, 1898), 6; *Yates County Chronicle* LXXVII:19 (1900): 1.

30. Women physicians in Elmira who provided maternity care were Dr. Mary Potts, Dr. Anna M. Stuart, Dr. Delphine Butcher-Smith, and Dr. Jessie L. Herrick.

31. At the time of this writing, I have been unable to ascertain the pattern of policies in regional hospitals with respect to out-of-wedlock births. According to Janet Bogdan, a Ph.D. candidate at Syracuse University studying 19th century childbirth, the New York Lying-In Hospital required a marriage certificate as did Boston Lying-In. This situation, however, tends to describe hospitals at mid century.

32. This paper will not discuss life inside the Anchorage and the "exigencies of moral rehabilitation" in great detail. However, it is important to remember that evangelical pedagogy offered each girl the opportunity to recast her life and compensate for her sin rather than ever truly erase it. The underlying assumption of the institution was that the girl and her future child were marked and that isolation from the world in a moral institution might head off the worst aspects of the social stigma. The best discussion of a related but not altogether similar institutional environment at the Lancaster School for Girls is Barbara M. Brenzel, *Daughters of The State: A Social Portrait of the First American Reform School for Girls in North America, 1856-1905* (Cambridge, 1983).

33. AMJ, #136, #15.

34. AMJ, #191.

35. Walkowitz, 17-18; Ruth Rosen, *The Lost Sisterhood: Prostitution in America, 1900-1918* (Baltimore, 1982), 144. Both Walkowitz and Rosen confirm that women began prostitution in Britain and the U.S. in their late teens. According to Walkowitz, unwed mothers in Britain appear to be older and be drawn primarily from the population of servants; Walkowitz discredits the idea that unwed mothers and prostitutes were from the same population group. Insofar as we can generalize from the Anchorage records, in the United States unwed mothers appear to be younger (16-20) and more heterogeneous in terms of class. The assumption that illegitimacy was both cause and consequence of prostitution pervades the 19th Century Social Purity leadership. See David J. Pivar, *Purity Crusade, Sexuality, Morality, and Social Control* (Westport, Conn., 1973).

36. Brumberg, 360-71.

37. AMJ, #104, #199.

38. In 26% of the cases fathers are actually named; in 30% they are designated by a generic identification. My explanation for the rationale of naming/non-naming is based on my understanding of the institutional interest in putative fathers. If, for example, a girl came to the Anchorage via the poor house, the father was never named since it was already clear that he could not be held responsible for support. On the other hand, girls who came with a local WCTU escort generated more detailed narrative histories and, in that case, the father or a generic identification was more likely to be included.

There are still other ways to account for inconsistent naming of men: some sexual partners could have been so casual they were unknown or paternity was questionable where a young woman had multiple partners. Still another scenario might be that no name signified a closed-mouthed young woman, loyally protecting the reputation of the man she loved or feared. Protection of the reputation of married men could provide one portion of an explanation of those records which include no male name. Yet, the stories told by the girls do not suggest that the putative fathers were generally married men.

On the unmarried father and folkways governing his "identification" see Clark Vincent, "Unmarried Fathers and the Mores: 'Sexual Exploiter' as An Ex Post Facto Label," *American Sociological Review* 25:1 (1960): 40-48. Also relevant are Samuel Futterman and Jean B. Livermore, "Putative Fathers," *Journal of Social Casework* 28 (1947): 174-178; Ruth Reed, "Unmarried Fathers," in *The Illegitimate Family in New York City* (New York, 1934): Norman Reider, "The Unmarried Father," *American Journal of Orthopsychiatry* 18 (April, 1948): 230-37.

39. Ronald Pearsall, *The Worm in the Bud: The World of Victorian Sexuality* (New York, 1983), 165.

40. Stephan Thernstrom, *Poverty and Progress: Social Mobility in a Nineteenth Century City* (Cambridge, 1964); *The Other Bostonians: Poverty and Progress in the American Metropolis* (Cambridge, 1973).

41. AMJ, #155. See Dudden, Chapter 1, on "helping."

42. Gillis, 163, discusses the implications of premature marriage for men of the lower middle class.

43. Another Anchorage case that involved an out-of-court financial settlement is #143 involving Estella Soper whose "seducer" paid $60 in installments directly to the Anchorage. In this case, the girl came to Elmira from Waverly under the supervision of Mrs. J.W. Knapp of the WCTU local. New York State Law allowed County Overseers of the Poor to arrange such "compromises" with the putative father.

44. I have no way of determining if the aunts were sister to the girl's mother or father although I suspect the former based on the matrifocal orientation of 19th century women's culture. See Marilyn Ferris Motz, "True Sisterhood: The Female Family in Nineteenth Century Michigan," unpublished Ph.D. dissertation, University of Michigan, 1981 and Ellen M. Henrotin, "The Social Status of American Women," in Kate Baym Martin and Ellen M. Henrotin, *The Social Status of European and American Women* (Chicago, 1887), 38.

45. Motherlessness has also been identified as an important factor in the sexual abuse of children. See David Finkelhor, *Sexually Victimized Children* (New York, 1979). Although it is "tricky business" to link illegitimacy historically to any particular family pathology, the evidence does seem to point in the following direction: that among young women undergoing the particular developmental strains of adolescence, the absence of mother may be critical in terms of sex-role identification, in terms of supervision, and in terms simply of love and nurturance. Where the "mother deficit" was complicated by poverty, paternal indifference and/or brutality, or unhappy relationships with resident employers, girls may have begun premarital activity in the hope of a functional outcome: marriage and removal from an unpleasant situation. In this sense, girlhood sexual activity should be linked to the female adolescent's well-known capacity for "idealization," that is to fantasize and to project herself into sentimental but culturally-mandated scenarios of marriage and motherhood.

A relevant study of the socialization of female adolescents is Elizabeth Douvan and Joseph Adelson, *The Adolescent Experience* (New York, 1966) which posits that between 18 and 21 the female sense of self is less clearly defined as she waits until marriage to provide a context for her life. In the area of adolescent cognitive development, the Piagetian theory of formal operations means that the individual is now able to project situations different than his/her own and, consequently, try on alternative identities. See Jean Piaget, *The Moral Judgement of the Child* (New York, 1965). Thus, both social setting and cognitive skills point the female adolescent in a particular direction: thinking about marriage.

46. AMJ, #180, #185.

47. Unmarried mothers with venereal disease (6% of the Anchorage's pregnant population) were quickly removed from the Anchorage and sent to other locations: a hospital in Canandaigua, the Crittenton home in New York City, or the Salvation Army home in Buffalo. For the social history of syphilis in this period see Allan Brandt, *No Magic Bullet: A Social History of Venereal Disease in the United States, 1880-1980*, (New York, 1985).

48. Rosen, 63-66; 86-110.

50. New York *Times* (April 17, 1886) 1:5.

51. AMJ, #54, #188, #208.

52. See Charles Jewett, *Outlines of Pregnancy* (Philadelphia, 1894), 65-67; Dr. E. Verrier, *Practical Manual of Obstetrics* (New York, 1884), 44-46, 56-58; Dr. A. Charpentier, *Cyclopedia of Obstetrics and Gynecology* (New York, 1887), 263-265; Joseph Brown, *A Nurse's Handbook of Obstetrics* (Philadelphia, 1903), 98-104.

53. Records, New England Hospital for Women, 1873, #89.

54. For examples of the Victorian "hour glass" silhouette see *Vogue* 5:1 (January 3, 1895), 4; 8:2 (October 8, 1898), 7; T.S. Sozinskey, *The Culture of Beauty* (New York, 1877): On the changing physical configuration of American women, see Lois Banner, *American Beauty* (New York, 1983).

55. AMJ, #185.

56. AMJ, #61; #95; #154.

57. AMJ, #90.

58. *Anchorage Annual Report*, 1900 and 1907, 3.

59. In these middle-class cases (N = 5), defined by high school attendance, the records indicate that courtship and mate selection were a primary arena for conflict between girls and their parents. In middle and upper class families children's choices with respect to marital partners were linked to both the transfer of property and the maintenance of status. See Goode, 38. For an excellent statement about the "romantic" but "sexless" companionship of middle-class youth in this period, see Henry Seidel Canby, "Sex and Marriage in the Nineties," *Harpers Magazine* 169 (Sept. 1934); 427-436, Canby's retrospective evaluation of the situation as "a golden age of free companionship" without amorous or erotic content suggests how devastating out-of-wedlock pregnancy must have been in middle-class society.

60. *Anchorage Annual Report*, 1900, 3.

61. AMJ, #140; *Elmira Sunday Telegram* (May 2, 1971); AMJ, #85.

62. Barrett, 45.

63. The market for children may have been a consequence of declining fertility in the American middle class. See Jamiel Zainalden, "Child Exchange in Boston: The Origins of Modern Adoption, 1851-1900," unpublished dissertation, University of Chicago, 1976. Zainalden argues that adoptions became less familial and more anonymous by 1900; by 1900, infants of both sexes (as opposed to male children 3-10 years in an earlier period) were the primary constituency for adoption. In his study of Boston, the number of illegitimate children among the adopted increased significantly by the end of the century.

64. The tendency to adoption reported here does not mesh with Michael Sedlak's study of the institutional response to unmarried pregnant women in the Crittenton homes of the Midwest (see footnote 28 above). Sedlak characterizes the period 1870-1930 as "Evangelism and the Maternal Bond" and argues that Crittenton homes pushed for the retention of babies by the mother as a way of insuring the mother's moral rehabilitation through nurturance.

65. Joseph A. Hill, ed., *Women in Gainful Occupations, 1870 to 1920* (U.S. Department of Commerce: Washington, D.C.) Census Monograph IX (1929), 36-39.

66. Boudin, a socialist and a Jew, discusses these elements of the psychology of work in the typical Christian maternity shelter, 51-55. On illegitimacy and domestic service see Dudden, 214-217. On vocational training for domestic service in a 19th century reform school, see Brenzel, 197, 202-203, 209-11.

67. On the declining fertility of American women see Robert V. Wells, "Family History and Demographic Transition," *Journal of Social History* (1975): 1-19; "Quaker Marriage Patterns in a Colonial Perspective," *William and Mary Quarterly* 3rd Series, 29 (1972): 439-41; Richard Easterlin, "Factors in the Decline of Farm Family Fertility in the United States: Some Preliminary Research Results," *Journal of American History* 63 (1976): 600-612; Carl Degler, *At Odds: Women and the Family in America From the Revolution to the Present* (New York, 1980), 178-209.

68. See Emma O. Lundberg, "The Illegitimate Child and War Conditions," *American Journal of Physical Anthropology*, 1:3 (1918): 339-352, for a discussion of the consequences of World War I on European and American rates of illegitimacy. Because the requirement of birth registration varied by state and was not included in the federal compilation of vital statistics until 1933, it is extremely difficult to ascertain the war's true impact. Whatever the overall rate of illegitimacy, it is certainly true that the language of the reformers and their goals and methods depend on their perception of the extent of the problem.

69. Emma O. Lundberg, "Progress Toward Better Laws for the Protection of Children Born Out of Wedlock," *Proceedings of the National Conference of Social Work* (1920): 111.

70. Ada Eliot Sheffield, "The Nature of the Stigma Upon the Unmarried Mother and Her Child," *Proceedings of the National Conference of Social Work* (1920): 119-120.

71. See Lundberg, 113-115, for a prototypical discussion of Progressive reforms in this area. For a model of social case work investigation of the unmarried mother see Mary Richmond's classic *Social Diagnosis* (New York, 1917), 413-20, and Amey Eaton Watson, "The Illegitimate Family," *Annals of American Academy of Political and Social Science*, 77 (May 1918): 103-106.

72. Physicians were long associated with child saving. Prior to 1900, medical journals reveal that when doctors addressed the problems created by out of wedlock pregnancy they directed their attention to foundlings, to the proper care of deserted infants. By 1926, the medical, social, and psychological problems of illegitimacy constitute major entries. See the *Index Catalogues of the Library of the Surgeon General's Office. U.S. Army* (Washington, D.C.) Series I (1884), Series II (1902), Series III (1926).

73. George W. Kosmak, "Committee on Obstetrical Care of Unmarried Mothers," *Proceedings of the National Conference on Social Work* (1920): 116.

74. Some Progressive physicians, then, were willing to treat any pregnant woman, even the venereally diseased, and urged other hospitals and doctors to do so. See footnote 47 above.

75. *Ibid.*, See also Foster S. Kellog, "Illegitimacy from the Standpoint of the Physician," *Boston Medical and Surgical Journal* CLXXXII:8 (1920): 191-193. Kosmak's recommendations for upgrading the medical care of the "illegitimately pregnant" were designed to "go hand in hand with the development of the sociological features of the problem." In the Progressive Era, reformers and physicians associated illegitimacy with two particular social problems: juvenile delinquency and feeblemindedness. Both were, allegedly, spawned by it in a continuous chain. In the management of both problems, Kosmak urged the employment of a psychiatrist. Kosmak, 118; Lundberg (1920), 112. Increasingly, after 1920, psychiatry took on these issues. Preliminary work by Nancy Tomes has established how psychiatry transformed female adolescent sexual activity and, hence, out-of-wedlock pregnancy into a psychological issue of "maladjustment." Nancy Tomes, "Dynamic Psychiatry and the Female Adolescent," unpublished paper delivered at the Organization of American Historians Meeting, April, 1983.

76. Christopher Lasch, *Haven in a Heartless World* (New York, 1977) links this vast army of professional "help providers" to the rise of the "therapeutic state."

77. Michael Sedlak, "The Education of 'Girls with Special Needs,' 1865-1972: The Impact of Public Policy on Young Women," unpublished paper (1981), 27. Sedlak provides a thorough description of the changing institutional history of the Crittenton homes.

78. *Ibid.*, 36.

79. The change in institutional direction was explained in this way: that the board felt its "greatest hope" lay in the education and industrial training of "innocent" rather than "fallen" girls. The 1911 report indicated that "experience" taught the board that there were two distinct classes of girls and that it was best to separate them. By 1911, the board felt "there are many rescue homes where mothers and children are cared for. . .but there was no place for the young girl who had not fallen." This probably is a reference to the Crittenton chain. Moreover, the board realized that placement at the Anchorage stigmatized girls: "if [a girl] was in. . .the rescue home with the unwed mother, immediately she was counted as one who was immoral and she felt she had little opportunity to secure the confidence of people when it was known she had been in the Anchorage." After 1907, the Anchorage only took 12-16 year olds who had not been "immoral," were not "mentally deficient," and whose homes had been "broken up and their natural protectors taken from them by death or strong drink."

The Awesome Power of Sex: The Polemical Campaign Against Mormon Polygamy

Charles A. Cannon

The author is a research fellow at the Center of Military History, Washington, D.C.

DURING THE SECOND HALF of the nineteenth century, when Americans of social conscience were confronted with the issue of Mormon polygamy, most of them responded with an immediate, indignant, and negative response. A characteristic reaction was that of the Reverend L. H. Chamberlain, who in 1882 wrote that the sins of polygamy outweighed the combined immorality of the whole nation outside the Utah Territory. Polygamy's criminality, he said, was "simply monumental." "Our utmost offences against chastity and marriage," he insisted, "are as nothing when put beside it."[1] President Grover Cleveland, in his first annual message to Congress, identified the central values of American civilzation and, in so doing, carefully eliminated the Mormons from his national vision. "The strength, the perpetuity, and the destiny of the nation," he said, "rests upon our homes, established by the law of God, guarded by parental care, regulated by parental authority, and sanctified by parental love." But this glorious vision of national destiny growing out of the enclave of domestic harmony was marred by one deviant group in American society. "These homes," he said, "are not the homes of polygamy."[2]

1 Rev. L. T. Chamberlain, *Mormonism and Polygamy* (Published privately, Feb. 19, 1882), 11.

2 As quoted in William Alexander Linn, *The Story of the Mormons* (New York, 1902), 588–589.

What was so odious about the institution? What rendered any comparison of American society to that institution unthinkable? And how did the Mormon polygamists come to be excluded from the national cult of domesticity? Like their President, most Americans looked upon the family as the core of civilization. Polygamy threatened not only sexual ethics and values, but also the institutional order that rested on those values. The very existence of polygamy demonstrated that monogamy was not the inevitable form of family life in Victorian America. Since the social order was thought to rest on monogamy, this alternative was an intolerable challenge. If only because it challenged proper sexual and familial relations, polygamy had to be condemned in the most explicit terms available. Americans who were ordinarily reluctant to talk about sex in anything but the most familiar euphemisms were able to overcome these inhibitions when they discussed the despised institution of Mormon polygamy.

The purpose of this paper is to examine the polemical literature directed against Mormon polygamy with the aim of exploring popular attitudes towards sex in America. The descriptions of polygamy's sensual excesses in this literature—often a caricature of the reality—reveal much about America's attitudes towards sex and the relationship of sex to family life. Because the condemnation of polygamy presented a rare opportunity to speak freely about sex, the polemical literature offers a unique insight into the Victorian mind. The critics of Mormon polygamy often revealed more about their own attitudes towards sex than they did about the institution of polygamy. The myths concerning Mormon polygamy that emerge from the polemical literature are far more useful for an exploration of popular sexual values than for defining Mormon practices or beliefs.

The literature emerging from the crusade against Mormon polygamy can be said to be representative of American thought because it spanned several decades and engaged the interest of a large number of Americans. When the Republicans argued in their platform of 1856 that it was "both the right and imperative duty of Congress to prohibit in the territories those twin relics of barbarism—Polygamy and Slavery," they initiated a thirty-year political campaign against the Mormons.[3] From the first public admission of the practice by Brigham Young in 1852 until the official Mormon manifesto disavowing the practice in 1890, polygamy was an object of public concern.

Discussion of polygamy was not, however, confined to the halls of Congress. Public interest in the practice was reflected in frequent articles in national periodicals. Most national magazines carried numerous reports on the Mormons, and polygamy was the most common theme in this literature.[4] Of the fifty novels written about the Mormons in the nineteenth century, most were concerned at least in part with the practice of polygamy and many went through several editions.[5] Further evidence of the widespread public concern with polygamy were the countless tracts and sermons on polygamy distributed in the late nineteenth century.

Discussion of the "Mormon problem" was conducted on at least three levels: the economic-political-constitutional level; the theological level; and the moral level.[6] It was at the third level that the

---

[3] Richard D. Poll, "The Mormon Question Enters National Politics, 1850–1856," *Utah Historical Quarterly*, XXV (1957), 117–131. The political campaign against the Mormons included the "Utah Expedition" of 1857 and a series of congressional acts between 1862 and 1887. For an account of the Utah expedition, see Norman F. Furniss, *The Mormon Conflict, 1850–1859* (New Haven, 1960). The political aspects of the campaign have been explored in detail in, for example, Mark Cannon, "The Mormon Issue in Congress, 1872–1882" (Ph.D. dissertation, University of California, Berkeley, 1948).

[4] For the content and frequency of articles on Mormon polygamy in the national periodicals, see Richard O. Cowan, "Mormonism in National Periodicals" (Ph.D. dissertation, Stanford University, 1961), 25–30, and Appendix. Other recent studies of periodical literature on the Mormons confirm Cowan's findings on the importance of the polygamy issue. These include Dennis L. Lythgoe, "The Changing Image of Mormonism in Periodical Literature, 1830–1969" (Ph.D. dissertation, University of Utah, 1969); and Jan Shipps's content analysis presented to the 1973 Annual Meeting of the Organization of American Historians, "From Satyr to Saint: American Attitudes toward the Mormons, 1860–1960."

[5] Leonard J. Arrington and Jon Haupt, "Intolerable Zion: The Image of Mormonism in Nineteenth Century American Literature," *Western Humanities Review*, XXII (1968), 243–260. Eighteen of the fifty works cited by Arrington and Haupt went through more than one edition, and fourteen of those went through more than three editions.

[6] Most of the historical scholarship on Mormon polygamy deals with the legal-political struggle. The constitutional issues are set out in Orma Linford, "The Mormons and the Law: The Polygamy Cases" (Ph.D. dissertation, University of Wisconsin, 1964). Relations between the federal government and the Mormons are explained in

critics of Mormon polygamy were most candid about sex and the family. Although at times there was enormous confusion and intermixing of these levels of argument, it was the moral critic who revealed most about himself and his society. While the political struggle between federal authority and Mormon "theocracy" produced a substantial literature, the focus of this article is on the moral critics of polygamy.

Discussion of the family in America was carried on with an intense seriousness in the latter half of the nineteenth century. There was a general belief that the enclave of private family life was essential to the growth of the republic, and that it was in this enclave that the individual found true satisfaction and fulfillment. Americans agreed that the home could and should be made a heaven on earth.[7] In his inaugural address, President James A. Garfield argued that the protection of conventional family relations was an important goal of his administration. Speaking directly on the Mormon question, he insisted that it was the "duty of Congress, while respecting to the uttermost the conscientious convictions and religious scruples of every citizen," to prohibit within its jurisdiction all criminal practices, "especially of that class which destroy the family relations and endanger social order."[8]

Klaus J. Hansen, *Quest for Empire: the Political Kingdom of God and the Council of Fifty in Mormon History* (East Lansing, Mich., 1967); and Gustive O. Larsen, *The "Americanization" of Utah for Statehood* (San Marino, Calif., 1971). Henry J. Wolfinger will make a significant contribution to the literature on the political-legal struggle if he is able to deal with the questions he raises in his review essay, "An Irrepressible Conflict," *Dialogue*, VI (1971), 124–131. He is presently working on a dissertation at Princeton University.

Despite the scholarly interest in the "Mormon question," the only serious treatment of the moral critics of polygamy is found in the work of Kimball Young and David Brion Davis. Kimball Young's *Isn't One Wife Enough?* (New York, 1954) is a sociological analysis of the impact of polygamy on the institutions of marriage and family in the Mormon community, but the introductory chapter, "The Mormon Chamber of Horrors: The Gentile Looks at Polygamy," provides an overview of the moral-religious critique of polygamy. Young categorizes the various non-Mormon responses to polygamy, but he does not make much of an effort to explore the implications of this material for American sexual values. David Brion Davis's "Some Themes of Counter-Subversion: An Analysis of Anti-Masonic, Anti-Catholic, and Anti-Mormon Literature," *Mississippi Valley Historical Review*, XLVII (1960–1961), 205–224, deals with the process of projection in more detail, but his primary interest in the evidence is to show how Americans sought unity and meaning in their own lives by attacking the alleged conspiracies of others.

7 Kirk Jeffrey, Jr., "The Family as Utopian Retreat from the City: The Nineteenth-Century Contribution," *Soundings*, LV (1972), 21–41.

8 James D. Richardson, ed., *Messages and Papers of the Presidents* (10 vols., Washington, D. C., 1897), VII, 11.

Why did Americans believe that polygamy threatened the social order? Civilization was perceived as a fragile structure. The morality that stood at the heart of civilization and held it together was believed to be based on man's ability to control desire. And the most disruptive of all man's desires was his wild sexual impulse. Americans feared that any relaxation of sexual standards would lead to a complete breakdown of the civilized order. Once polygamy had liberated man's base sexual desires from the normal restraints of civilization, they argued, he would be completely alienated from morality and virtue. He would be consumed by unrestrained sensuality.

The theme of unrestrained sensuality was often explicit and always implicit in the arguments brought to bear on the question of polygamy. To a people who had come to see a strict Christian monogamy as the foundation of civilization, the idea that a man might share his bed with more than one wife was shocking, and that a man might do so with impunity and with the sanction of his church was an evil too great to be tolerated. A report to the Cincinnati Methodist Conference in 1884 spelled out the evils of the system: "Mormonism is not a religion. It is a crime.... It is not a religious superstition but a system of masked sensuality, and hence subversive of every principle of morality, and abhorrent to every feeling of virtue...." The correlation between sexuality and morality was unmistakable. Once a man had capitulated to unrestrained sensuality he had forfeited his ability to act morally. The report recognized that the "infernal scheme" of the Mormons was "partly mercenary" and "partly political," but at its heart the system was "chiefly licentious."[9] Mrs. Thomas Fitch insisted that the system was nothing more than "organized indulgence," an attempt to "religionize sensuousness."[10]

Although the image of Mormon sensuality was common throughout the polemical literature on Mormon polygamy, there was little evidence to support this charge in Mormon practice. Non-Mormons understood neither the Mormon view of sexuality in the larger scheme of eternity nor their numerous restrictions defining their sexual ethics and specific daily practices. While many Americans considered the sexual impulse to be alien and disruptive, Mormon

[9] As quoted in Young, *Isn't One Wife Enough?*, 4.

[10] Mrs. Thomas Fitch, "The Mohamet of the West," *Overland Monthly*, VII (1871), 236–237.

theologians argued that sexuality was as much a part of man's potentially divine nature as was charity or benevolence. Orson Pratt raised the question of whether sexual love would "exist in the eternal worlds after the resurrection," and then went on to answer that not only would sexual love exist, but that men would enjoy it even more than they did on earth.[11] Brigham Young echoed these sentiments when he promised that those receiving exaltation would "have the power then of propagating their species in spirit."[12]

Despite the fact that Mormons viewed man's sexuality and his divine potential as a unity rather than a duality, it is important to note the limits they imposed on the role of sex in marriage. The union of the sexes after the resurrection, argued Parley Pratt, was "mainly for the purpose of renewing and continuing the work of procreation." Brigham Young explained that polygamy was instituted so "that the noble spirits which are waiting for tabernacles might be brought forth."[13] The Mormons differentiated between sexual intercourse in marriage, which they considered a divine institution, and adultery, which they believed was a sin second only to murder. Brigham Young maintained that he would rather follow his daughter to the grave than suffer her "to be polluted through the corruptions of wicked men"; and another Mormon leader warned that some men brought premature decay on themselves by "the too frequent use of sexual intercourse."[14] Thus, while Mormon ideas may have been subversive of America's concept of sexuality, the day-to-day sexual ethics of Mormons were at least not unlike those of other Americans.[15]

Still, there was an important difference between Mormon and gentile conceptions of sexuality. While Mormons saw procreation as the most important aspect of the sexual relationship, they went beyond this concept to argue that sexuality, within the marriage relationship, was not only necessary but divine. "The object of the union of the sexes is the propagation of their species," wrote Parley

11 Orson Pratt, *The Bible and Polygamy* (Salt Lake City, 1877), 75.

12 *Journal of Discourses* (26 vols., Liverpool, England, 1854–1886), VI, 275.

13 Parley P. Pratt, *Key to the Science of Theology* (5th ed., Salt Lake City, 1891), 180; *Journal of Discourses*, IV, 56.

14 *Journal of Discourses*, II, 322; Young, *Isn't One Wife Enough?*, 186.

15 "Actually Mormon polygamy soon became as formalized, as limited by taboos and as respectable within its own terms as monogamy." Milton Rugoff, *Prudery and Passion* (New York, 1971), 198–199.

Pratt, "also for mutual affection, and the cultivation of those eternal principles of never ending charity and benevolence, which are inspired by the Eternal Spirit; also for mutual comfort and assistance in this world of toil and sorrow, and for mutual duties toward their offspring."[16]

Within the context of polygamous marriage the Mormons adhered to a standard of sexual behavior that was in some respects as strict as that of their critics. Nevertheless, commentators continued to insist that the Mormons had taken a natural human impulse and debased it by "making mere animals of themselves." They had cast man down from the intellectual sphere in which God had placed him "to a level with the brutes."[17] This distorted picture of polygamy suggests, on the one hand, an intense fear of sexuality among the anti-polygamists. One may ask, on the other hand, why the critics described the sexual immorality of the Mormons in such detail and with such apparent relish? The manner of handling the theme of sexuality that shaped the anti-polygamy critique reveals an ambivalence in Victorian America. One sees a constant fluctuation between fear of sexuality and a fascination with the Mormons' purported sensual excesses. True, sensuality was always condemned in the literature, but the critics seem to have been alternating between a pious desire to eliminate sexuality entirely and a desire to dwell on sexual themes in great detail.

How can one account for the disjunction between relatively strict Mormon practices and the myth of Mormon lust and debauchery found in the polemical literature? If there was little basis for the exaggerated descriptions of Mormon sensuality, what does this tell us about the anti-polygamists and their readers? Uncertain of the ability of their own social institutions to control sexuality, the anti-polygamists were convinced that any deviation from sexual norms must produce a reign of lust and debauchery. A society that believes that the social order rests on man's ability to control sexual desire cannot tolerate what seems to be an alternative to and an implied criticism of its sexual ethics. The crusade to purge American society of the alleged sexual excesses of polygamy was not merely a campaign for Christian virtue; it was also essential for the preservation

---

16 Pratt, *Key to Theology*, 173.

17 Jules Remy and Julius Brenchley, *A Journey to Great-Salt-Lake-City* (2 vols., London, 1861), II, 172.

of the community's confidence in itself. In a community where repression and sexual frustration were common, an alternative that seemed freer was dangerous. Such a community had to suppress its doubts by eliminating those experiments which threatened conventional sexual relations.

Fear of sexuality was the dominant theme in the anti-polygamy literature, and lust was the great enemy of the domestic order, the cornerstone of American civilization. Lust had no place in the ideal marriage. The sexual drives of the husband were perceived as a threat to the purity of his wife and the stability of his home. The husband was to exercise a continual self-restraint in order to allow his wife's mild influence to save them both. One incident of sexual indulgence per lunar month, according to William Alcott in his *Physiology of Marriage,* was "all that the best health of the parties" could possibly require. Abstinence, repression, and self-restraint were the law.[18]

J. H. Beadle, editor of the *Salt Lake Reporter* and one of the most vigorous critics of polygamy, explained his own view of the role of sex in marriage. The sexual impulse, he said, had three manifestations and three objects to fulfill: first and lowest, the desire that the male has for the female, common to both man and the brutes, had for its object simple reproduction. Second, there was the companionship, society, and love of a conjugal partner; its object was the founding of families and the establishment of communities. Finally, there was the love that a man had in common with the angels: "a high and most holy affection, a pure regard for what is pure, a silent adoration for that which is divine in the human; its exercise and reward alike are in a complete intercommunion of soul and interchange of pure affection."[19]

Beadle was apparently trying to insulate the "highest" form of the sexual impulse from any implication that it contained animal or brute instincts. Like most anti-polygamists he saw the physical aspect of marriage as little more than an animal necessity. The ideal "sexual" relationship for them involved no physical contact at all.

---

18 Jeffrey, "The Family as Utopian Retreat," 33; Oscar Handlin, *Race and Nationality in American Life* (Garden City, New York, 1957), 118–123; William A. Alcott, *The Physiology of Marriage* (Boston, 1855), *passim.*

19 J. H. Beadle, *Life in Utah* (Philadelphia, 1870), 355–356. Beadle wrote his book as a first-hand exposé of the "mysteries and crimes" of Mormonism.

Of course, this ideal was far more extreme than the reality of most marriage relationships in the 1870s and 1880s, but it appears that the fear of or guilt over sexuality was so intense as to render unthinkable any suggestion that sexuality might be an important part of marriage.

Having defined sexuality as subhuman or brutish, the critics relegated the Mormon polygamist to the lower levels of sensual existence. Because the polygamist acknowledged only the reproductive aspect of the sexual impulse, he was, according to Beadle, "but one-third married."[20] In addition, Beadle argued that, because the second and third "higher" forms of non-physical, sexual fulfillment could be achieved only in the union of one man with one wife, they were beyond the reach of the polygamist.

The fear of sexuality so dominant in the literature, complemented by a fascination with the sensual evils of the system, suggests that American men were jealous of the polygamist's extended sexual opportunities. One ex-Mormon, who claimed to have had a different wife for each night of the week, complained of the "conjugal drudgery" he had been "compelled to perform."[21] Did this arouse pity or envy? Did women indulge in fantasies about the alleged sexual potency of the polygamist? The obviously alarmist statement that a "woman's health, and even life, are not weighed in the balance against the polygamist's desires" may have served only to stimulate in the reader the unacknowledged desire for sexual excitement.[22]

Anti-polygamists took advantage of every opportunity to discuss the variety of sexual experiences supposedly available to the Mormons. The opportunities for the male under polygamy were obvious, but the critics cited several alleged arrangements whereby women also enjoyed varied sexual experiences. A largely fanciful system of free love through the trading of wives was described by Mormon critic Alfreda Eva Bell in 1855. Mormon women, she said, after living with one husband were requested to move on from one to another until they had sampled all.[23] Beadle described an "almost

20 *Ibid.*, 357.

21 Falstaff (pseud.), "A Year Among the Mormons," *Red, White & Blue*, III (1856), 1–3.

22 Mrs. Jennie Anderson Froiseth, ed., *The Women of Mormonism* (Detroit, Mich., 1882), 193.

23 Alfreda Eva Bell, *Boadicea, the Mormon Wife: Life Scenes in Utah* (Baltimore, 1855), 32–34, 54.

incredible reign of lust and fanaticism." Not only did Mormons take many wives, he said, but easy divorce created a system of organized promiscuity known as "going the rounds."[24] Easy divorce and husband-trading were largely fantasies on the part of the critics. Mormon authorities looked upon divorce as domestic failure and made it difficult to obtain.[25] The extensive discussion of sexual variety under Mormon polygamy suggests that the anti-polygamists took some pleasure in describing this particular "evil" of the system. The line between disgust and envy in the literature is sometimes difficult to draw.

Unrestrained sensual pleasure may have been a sure sign of degradation, but there was a certain admiration mixed with the shock of J. H. Beadle when he revealed the contents of a secret set of phrenological charts. They demonstrated, he said, that on a scale of "amativeness" or "sexual passion" running from one to twelve, Joseph Smith's head was recorded at eleven: "Very full!"[26] The sexual abilities and appetites of the Mormon polygamist were given recognition by one woman writer who maintained that the wife of a polygamist was reduced to a "mere animal or machine." The woman under polygamy "no longer lives; she simply exists, to be used by and to serve the foul purposes of, a licentious, beastly man."[27] The theme of envy was, of course, never explicit in the literature. Nevertheless, an anonymous female observer also revealed a certain fascination beneath horror in describing excessive Mormon sensuality: "There were a few intelligent countenances interspersed with sly cunning and disgusting sensuality, in both male and female. . . ."[28]

The trace of hidden envy that lay beneath the suggestion that polygamy was simply degradation points to areas of frustration and tension in American society. According to the moral ideal, sexuality had only a minor role to play in family life. The extensive description of sexual powers and "free love" opportunities, however, sug-

---

24 Beadle, *Life in Utah*, 339–350.

25 Brigham Young frequently argued against divorce. "By seeking to cast off her husband," he argued on one occasion, a woman "casts a dark shade upon his path. . . ." *Journal of Discourses*, VII, 280.

26 Beadle, *Life in Utah*, 339–350.

27 Froiseth, *Women of Mormonism*, 333.

28 "Life Among the Mormons," *Putnam's Monthly*, VI (Oct. 1855), 377.

gests that the sexual drives of the Americans writing these articles, and perhaps those of their readers, were not so much repressed as simply inhibited. Unacceptable desires that were denied direct satisfaction elsewhere were left to operate in the area of intense moral indignation. The American of the late nineteenth century could find temporary escape from his own frustration and tension by projecting his sexual fantasies onto the Mormon polygamist at the same time that he was supposedly rooting out a great social evil. The ideal Victorian sought to preserve the sanctity and purity of marriage by campaigning against the sexual excesses of others.

The most popular form of anti-polygamy literature in the nineteenth century was the novel. All but five of the fifty novels on Mormonism published in the nineteenth century were hostile to the religion; many of them give the impression that they were designed, at least in part, as vehicles of erotic fantasy.[29] Combinations of piety and suggestiveness could, apparently, be read in good conscience by Americans, because they exposed and condemned a social evil.

By far the most popular anti-polygamy novel was Maria Ward's *Female Life Among the Mormons* which sold 40,000 copies in only a few weeks after its publication in 1855. It was translated into four foreign languages, and printed under various titles until as late as 1913.[30] This most popular work on polygamy was also the most violent and explicitly erotic. It tells one more about the sexual fantasies of the author than the realities of Mormon polygamy. There were countless episodes of women being tortured in the most bizarre fashion:

> One poor woman, who had told an emigrant, in the hearing of a Mormon elder, that polygamy was a system of abominations, and who repeated a few of her troubles and sufferings, was taken one night when she stepped out for water, gagged, carried a mile into the woods, stripped nude, tied to a tree, and scourged till the blood ran from her wounds to the ground. . . .[31]

---

[29] Arrington and Haupt, "Intolerable Zion," 243–260. There is some difficulty in distinguishing fiction from nonfiction in the polemical literature. For example, Maria Ward's *Female Life Among the Mormons* claims to be a "Narrative of Many Year's Personal Experience," but Arrington and Haupt have placed it on their list of fictional accounts because there are frequent errors of chronology and geography within the text.

[30] Arrington and Haupt, "Intolerable Zion," 253.

[31] Maria Ward (pseud.), *Female Life Among the Mormons* (New York, 1856), 429.

The theme of nudity was common in the polemical literature, and the naked human body seems to have produced an acute anxiety in Victorian readers. The disgust for the naked body reached its peak in the late nineteenth century.[32] It may well have been related to the general ambivalence towards sexuality that has already been identified in the anti-polygamists. Mrs. Mary Ettie Smith apparently felt justified in describing the washing and anointing temple ceremonies of the Mormons because she was exposing the evils of polygamy, and she most likely would not have mentioned nudity in any other context. Her description of the details, however, suggests more fascination than disgust.[33]

Sadism was also a frequent theme in the literature. In addition to the woman who was "scourged till the blood ran from her wounds to the ground" in the passage above, Maria Ward included in the pages of her bestseller graphic descriptions of women being tortured with red-hot irons, with tomahawks, with whips, and with ice. It is unlikely that Americans acknowledged or even understood that the infliction of pain upon a love object might be an abnormal but not uncommon means of obtaining sexual release, but the wide sales of this novel can be accounted for at least in part by the fact that buyers expected to find extensive descriptions of lust and licentiousness in the work. Detailed exposés of sexual evils may well have provided a temporary respite from the rigid sexual controls imposed by conventional sexual ethics.

The large audience for erotic exposés of polygamy is suggestive of displaced lusts and desires, but what of the authors of this literature? Over half of the anti-Mormon novels were written by women, and women wrote all four of the novels published in the 1850s that provided the models for later anti-Mormon literature.[34] The fact that women were the authors of this explicit erotica raises some serious questions about Victorian attitudes towards female sexuality. According to the ideal, woman was innocent, dependent, good, and

32 For a discussion of nudity in nineteenth-century America, see David Brion Davis, *Homicide in American Fiction, 1798–1860* (Ithaca, 1957), 172–173.

33 Mrs. Mary Ettie V. Smith, *Fifteen Years with the Mormons*, in N. W. Green, *Mormonism: Its Rise, Progress and Present Condition* (Hartford, Conn., 1870), 49. In the same tone of moral indignation, Mrs. Smith described a series of attempted seductions at the hands of the Mormons that she had resisted. See *ibid.*, 280–303.

34 Arrington and Haupt, "Intolerable Zion," 244. Women wrote twenty of the thirty-six anti-Mormon novels published in the nineteeth century.

generous precisely because she was sexless.[35] Female authorship of this erotic material suggests that women were anything but sexless. The authors of the anti-polygamy literature and perhaps their readers, who were said to be mostly women,[36] appear to have been uneasy with the passive sexual role that had been laid out for them in the late nineteenth century.

The anti-polygamists may have been ambivalent in their attitude towards Mormon sensuality, but they were certain that the violation of moral law would be followed by predictable and visible results. Sexual indulgence would be followed by a loss of moral sense and an alienation from virtue. The anti-polygamists believed in a continuity between natural and moral law. By breaking the moral law of monogamy, Mormons had left themselves open to punishment; and this punishment was expected to take a physical or natural form. Sin against the moral law was expected to have social, spiritual, and physical consequences apparent to all. The people who practice polygamy "as in Utah," said Mrs. Jennie Froiseth, "will soon degenerate into mere brutes. Its effects are to destroy the moral and intellectual nature, and develop only the animal."[37]

It was to women that the anti-polygamists turned for evidence. Women were the first victims of the system: polygamy, according to Emily Austin, had seduced "many a virtuous and respectable woman into vices from which there is no redemption."[38] Polygamy was little more than legalized prostitution in the eyes of its critics. The stamp of oppression was visible in their faces, according to R. H. Seeley. Mormon women had a "subdued, dejected, disheartened appearance as if their will was broken, their courage lost, and they had fully accepted the position of hopeless inferiors."[39] The physical effects of sin were clear. Mrs. Jennie Froiseth argued that one

[35] For a description of the feminine ideal in the late nineteenth century, see David Kennedy, *Birth Control in America: The Career of Margaret Sanger* (New Haven, 1970), 50–57.

[36] For a discussion of the feminine audience for sentimental and reform literature, see Helen Waite Papashvily, *All the Happy Endings* (New York, 1956), xv and 35–45; and Herbert Ross Brown, *The Sentimental Novel in America, 1789–1860* (New York, 1959), 281–322, esp. 321–322.

[37] Froiseth, *Women of Mormonism*, 212.

[38] Emily M. Austin, *Mormonism: or Life Among the Mormons* (Madison, Wis., 1882), 216.

[39] R. H. Seeley, "The Mormons and Their Religion," *Scribner's Monthly*, III (Feb. 1872), 405.

need only look into the faces of Mormon women to see the mark that had been placed upon them as a consequence of their sin. "Especially do the first wives seem to carry the signs of care and sorrow —a mark of Cain, as it were, which separates them. . . ."[40]

More important than the physical results of polygamy on women, however, were the social consequences. Domestic institutions were threatened by the disruptive sexual passions of the Mormon polygamist. True womanhood was the only power that stood between man's destructive sexual impulse and the order of the home, and polygamy threatened to destroy that power.

If the home was the perfect republic in embryo for Victorian America, then the true woman was the philosopher-queen guiding that republic. Women represented cohesion, decency, and self-restraint; they were the bearers of poetry, purity, and domesticity.[41] Grover Cleveland, whose celebrated scandal over fathering an illegitimate child may have had some influence on his speeches defending conventional motherhood, declared that "the mothers of our land rule the nation as they mould the characters and guide the actions of their sons." It is important to note that women in Cleveland's time "ruled the nation" only within a carefully delineated sexual role. They did not rule directly, but only through their sons. The woman's place was firmly fixed in the home. The President went on to say that women shed the "warm light of true womanhood, unperverted and unpolluted, upon all within their pure and wholesome family circle." Addressing his remarks to the Mormons, he said: "These are not the cheerless, crushed and unwomanly mothers of polygamy."[42] Critics were unwilling to admit that true womanhood might survive under polygamy or that polygamy might multiply the feminine preserve in the home. True womanhood was in some unspecified way tied up with monogamy.

---

40 Froiseth, *Women of Mormonism*, 25.

41 For a discussion of the concept of "true womanhood," see Barbara Welter, "The Cult of True Womanhood: 1820–1860," *American Quarterly*, XVIII (1966), 151–174; and William R. Taylor and Christopher Lasch, "Two 'Kindred Spirits': Sorority and Family in New England, 1839–1846," *New England Quarterly*, XXXVI (1963), 23–41.

42 As quoted in Linn, *Story of the Mormons*, 588–589. There is little evidence that the women of the Utah Territory were "cheerless" and "crushed." For an examination of women's roles in Utah society, see Thomas G. Alexander, "An Experiment in Progressive Legislation: The Granting of Woman Suffrage in Utah in 1870," *Utah Historical Quarterly*, XXXVIII (1970), 20–30.

"True womanhood" was a virtue that was not automatically shared by all women. It involved a carefully defined social role. The "true woman" was the guiding force in the domestic enclave; she imparted decency and self-restraint to her mate and her children. Her contribution to society was made possible by her female nature which could subdue and control the disruptive lustfulness of her husband and sons. The power that sustained her in this lonely assignment and the power that made it possible was the affection that she shared with her husband. But affection between man and wife was impossible in the Mormon harem because attempts to live under polygamy could only produce an excess of woman's one possible vice: jealousy. Jealousy was the sourest heritage of polygamy. No one with the "slightest knowledge of the female heart" could believe that love could be divided among numerous wives. J. H. Beadle maintained that the system resulted in the "utter destruction of domestic love and harmony."[43] Even if a mother's love might endure the tensions of polygamy, the love she bore her husband became embittered, slowly hardened, and finally disappeared.[44]

The attitude toward women in the polemical literature is a curious mixture of veneration and doubt. The true woman performed a critical social function as the moral arbiter and sexual warden of the conjugal family, the structure which was designed to contain sexuality. Woman may have been less an object of veneration than an object of social necessity, but there is no question that her role was considered vital. Without the restraining influence of the conjugal family and true womanhood, there was no hope for social order. A fearful reign of lust, brutality, and barbarism would follow her demise. Despite the crucial role designed for the true woman, the critics had little confidence in her ability to perform in the face of sensual challenge. Thus, there was limited confidence in the ability of existing institutions to preserve the social order.

---

[43] Beadle, *Life in Utah*, 360–361. For a discussion of affection as the foundation of family relations, see Taylor and Lasch, "Sorority and Family," 33.

[44] Remy and Brenchley, *A Journey*, II, 92. Acting on this belief, the Anti-Polygamy Society prevailed upon Congress to appropriate funds for an Industrial Christian Home for Polygamous Wives in 1886. The structure was built to accommodate fifty of the thousands of wives who were said to be seeking shelter from polygamy, but no more than ten at a time ever took advantage of this opportunity to escape from the domestic nightmare of polygamy. Gustive O. Larsen, "An Industrial Home for Polygamous Wives," *Utah Historical Quarterly*, XXXVIII (1970), 263–273.

In addition to preventing women from serving as queens of the domestic enclave, polygamy was said to debase women in at least two other ways. Critics continually referred to the degraded social role of women under polygamy as mere slaves or property of tyrannical Mormon masters. Territorial Governor Eli H. Murray maintained that "polygamic slavery" was more debilitating than African slavery, and Harriet Beecher Stowe hoped that the time had come "to loose the bonds of a cruel slavery whose chains have cut into the very hearts of thousands of our sisters—a slavery which debases and degrades womanhood, motherhood, and family."[45] Senator Augustus Garland, arguing for the passage of the Edmunds Act in 1882, quoted a Professor Heeren who had studied the inner dynamics of the polygamous family. Polygamy produced domestic tyranny by "making woman a slave and man a tyrant." This arrangement produced a whole society rooted in tyranny.[46] Lustful husbands, blinded by sensuality and passion, were said to trade their wives as if they were cattle. An anonymous "victim" of polygamy described her reaction to her own father's attempt to sell her into polygamy's horror: "I was to be bartered, traded away for one of the loathsome old man's daughters." She realized that it was not love for another that motivated her father, but a "base, sensual desire to increase the inmates of his harem."[47] Many Mormon wives, however, saw their condition under polygamy not as slavery but as a form of liberation that allowed them to improve their own position and provide a better life for others in society.[48] Needless to say, the critics were not convinced by such arguments.

These arguments about women seem to suggest an incipient critique of existing social values along with the critique of polygamy. Were women already rebelling against the strict social role that had been defined for them in Victorian America? The frequent use of the language of liberation, often by female critics of polygamy,

---

45 Eli H. Murray, "The Crisis in Utah," *North American Review*, CXXXIV (April 1882), 342; preface by Harriet Beecher Stowe in T. B. H. Stenhouse, *"Tell It All"* (Hartford, Conn., 1874).

46 *Cong. Rec.*, 47 Cong., 1 sess. (1882), 1159.

47 "Saved from the Mormons," *The Galaxy*, XVI (Nov. 1872), 685.

48 Alexander, "Woman Suffrage in Utah," 23–24, 29. Martha Hughes Cannon, the first woman state senator in the United States and the fourth wife of a polygamist, argued that a plural wife was not as much a slave as a single girl. "If her husband has four wives, she has three weeks of freedom every single month." *San Francisco Examiner*, Nov. 8, 1896.

suggests that some critics may have projected their own desire for greater social and sexual freedom onto the anti-polygamy rhetoric. The complaints against a male-dominated society that treated women like cattle or property certainly had wider application than the Mormon community in the Utah Territory. Frances E. Willard made the connection between the degradation of women generally and the degradation of women under polygamy explicit in her introduction to Mrs. Jennie Froiseth's *Women of Mormonism.* "The degradation of man," she argued, "has always been the inseparable result of the subjection of women." The Mormons were simply the most flagrant practitioners of male dominance in America. Criticizing the exclusion of women from national politics and urging women to lead the endeavor against the Mormons until the "Book of Mormon is burned in the fierce blaze" of Christianity, Willard asserted that Jesus Christ had come into the world not only to redeem it, but to restore to woman her lost inheritance, "the equality of equals."[49]

The anti-polygamists held differing views on the role of women under polygamy, but they were certain that the continuity between the moral and natural law was nowhere more evident than among the offspring of polygamous union. The critics warned that to tamper with natural practices was to court disaster. Transgression of moral law (monogamy) was in this case said to be identical with the pollution of natural or biological law. Sexual sin, because it involved the pollution of the body, was expected to have bodily or physical consequences.

The alleged physical effects of polygamy on children were an obvious sign of degeneracy. Critics reported that the infant mortality rate for Utah far exceeded the rate for other regions of the country. This claim has been demonstrated to have been false, but the anti-polygamists apparently wanted to believe that it was true. They needed concrete evidence for their moral critique.[50] The children of polygamy, it was argued, exhibited all of the character-

[49] Frances Willard's introduction to Froiseth's *Women of Mormonism*, xv–xviii, is an extended essay that places Mormon polygamy in the context of the larger historical problem of the subjugation of women.

[50] Beadle, *Life in Utah*, 373–375. The infant mortality rate is examined in Stanley S. Ivins, "Notes on Mormon Polygamy," *Utah Historical Quarterly*, XXXV (1967), 309–321. This article is a good summary of the scope and character of polygamy in Utah Territory.

istics of a distinct, inferior race. One hostile doctor in Utah noted a "marked physiological inferiority" of the Mormons. "Feebleness and emaciation" were common, "while the countenances of almost all" were "stamped with a mingled air of imbecility and brutal ferocity."[51] Samuel Bowles felt that it was safe to predict that a few generations of polygamy would breed a physical, moral, and mental debasement of the Mormons. Indeed, he argued that the indications were already there.[52] Excessive sexual indulgence had produced biological evidence of the degenerate condition of Mormon polygamy for all the world to see.

These casual observations were supposedly validated by a "systematic" medical survey. Dr. Samuel A. Cartwright, an expert on the Negro's alleged inferiority, and Professor C. G. Forshey presented their hypothesis to the New Orleans Academy of Sciences in 1861. "The yellow, sunken, cadaverous visage," the report began, "the greenish-colored eye; the thick protuberant lips; the low forehead; the light, yellowish hair, and the lank angular person, constitute an appearance so characteristic of the new race, the production of polygamy, as to distinguish them at a glance. . . ."[53] With only minor alterations, this description of an inferior race could have been used to describe blacks. With thick protuberant lips and a low forehead, one only had to alter skin pigmentation to describe a Negro. Why did the anti-polygamists choose to identify the offspring of Mormon polygamy with the American Negro?

The analogy between Mormon polygamists and blacks was designed to deal with the problem of excessive sensuality. The inferior animal nature of the black man was already well established in the minds of Americans. By identifying the polygamist with the Negro, a critic simply placed the polygamist in the context of a role that had already been worked out for him. It was a simple matter to recognize the deterioration brought on by sexual indulgence of the

---

51 Handlin, *Race and Nationality*, 121.

52 Samuel Bowles, *Across the Continent* (Springfield, Mass., 1865), 124.

53 *DeBow's Review*, XXX (Feb. 1861) as quoted in Ivins, "Notes on Mormon Polygamy," 320. Samuel A. Cartwright was described as a "brutal Louisiana physician and publicist" by William Stanton in *The Leopard's Spots: Scientific Attitudes Toward Race in America, 1815–59* (Chicago, 1960), vii and 160. It is obvious that the theme of racial inferiority was more congenial to the South than to the North, but I have found three references to the theme of racial inferiority in the writings of northern critics.

black man, and the distinctive racial characteristics of the new Mormon "race" promised to be just as identifiable. The child of Mormon polygamy was simply a white Negro.

Once again, the moral law had found physical fulfillment. Polygamy not only destroyed the social order, it threatened to degrade the race. In order to convince their fellow Americans that the Mormons were dangerous, the anti-polygamists had to promise that the worst fate imaginable would follow the practice of polygamy. Unrestrained sexuality presented such a serious threat that there was almost no extreme to which the moral critics would not go in their attempts to condemn it. The critics promised the polygamist genetic suicide. The sin of his excessive indulgence would be visited upon the heads of his racially inferior children.

The moral critique was completely vindicated by bodily results. The moral nature of the "white or Adamic woman," according to Cartwright and Forshey, had been corrupted by polygamy to such a degree "as to render her incapable of breeding any other than abortive specimens of humanity." The new "race" was so degraded that if left to sustain itself it would "utterly perish from the earth."[54] Who could doubt that the sexual excesses of polygamy had produced these dire results? The self-indulgence of Mormon polygamy was nowhere more evident than in the faces of these mongrelized children.

If a high infant mortality rate and racial inferiority were not sufficient evidence to convince the public of the racial degeneracy of Mormons, the anti-polygamists went on to discuss the ratio of male to female births under polygamy. "As respects births," argued Remy and Brenchley, "a considerable inequality in favor of females indicates a degeneracy which the laws of physiology perfectly account for."[55] The self-proclaimed champions of true womanhood accepted the argument that an excess of female births over male births constituted a sign of inferiority. Obviously, the cult of true

---

[54] Cartwright and Forshey, "Report to the New Orleans Academy of Sciences," as quoted in Ivins, "Notes on Mormon Polygamy," 320. The Mormons were just as extreme in their predictions of the genetic benefits to be derived from polygamy as the anti-polygamists were in their predictions of genetic suicide. Parley Pratt proclaimed the regeneration of the race through polygamy. "Each succeeding generation, governed by the same principles, will still improve, till male and female may live and multiply for a hundred years upon the earth." *Key to Theology*, 179–180.

[55] Remy and Brenchley, *A Journey*, II, 171.

womanhood masked a belief that women were inferior to men. Woman might have a special role in society to fulfill, but a daughter was considered something less than a son. It was only through her son that a woman might make a meaningful contribution to society.

Despite the favored male role under polygamy, polygamists were almost always described as being without moral virtue. The widely known Mormon strictures against alcohol did not prevent the anti-polygamists from portraying the Mormon as a drunken, abusive husband.[56] The critics were unable to accept the possibility that one might yield to the self-indulgence they believed to be an inherent part of polygamy and still retain the ability to observe temperance. Apparently, sexual passion was closely associated with the blind passion of the drunkard.

The polygamous husband's debauchery was a perfect fulfillment of America's worst fears for this deviant family relationship. Deterioration was the fate of the polygamist. The obvious moral costs of polygamy were matched by a gradual physical and mental decay as man slid into beastliness. Seeley noted that in normal conversation a polygamist was sure to express himself in such a way as to demonstrate that his mind was decaying. "Even Brigham Young can hardly converse half an hour with lady visitors without some allusion to his amours. . . ."[57] Apparently, the social and spiritual consequences of polygamy were not convincing evidence of its wickedness without some physical confirmation. Americans needed reassurance that their sexual ethics were consistent with both nature and morality.

The polygamist's sexual opportunities that at first might have seemed inviting were invariably linked with fearful consequences that made them repugnant. Unrestrained sexual indulgence presented Americans with a cruel dilemma. Repressive sexual ethics called for abstinence and self-restraint. Conformity to this system led to tensions and frustrations that apparently called out for release. But to give in to sexual desire was to court moral disaster and physical decay. The American of good conscience was left with an ambivalence towards sexuality that could not be resolved.

56 For an analysis of the male image in the anti-Mormon literature, see Arrington and Haupt, "Intolerable Zion," 245–248.

57 Seeley, "The Mormons and Their Religion," 404–405.

One might give in to the desire to escape rigid sexual controls by dwelling at length on the sensual excesses of the Mormons, but this was only a temporary flight into sexual fantasy.[58] One then had to admit that there were "inevitable" consequences for polygamous self-indulgence. These consequences might take a social or a spiritual form, but they were most often expected to be physical results which would readily identify both the sinner and his sin. One might not be able to identify the precise nature of the penalty that would follow the violation of moral law, but one could be certain that an awful punishment awaited all transgressors.

In the polemics of the anti-polygamists, Mormon polygamy became an image of sexuality that was in large part fantasy. The power of sex was described with deep anxiety. Human will, by contrast, was seen as a fragile instrument of moral control that, having once yielded to sexual temptation, was not likely to function properly again. Maria Ward reported an innocent girl's confession of what had happened to her in the presence of Joseph Smith:

> He exerted a mystical magical influence over me—a sort of sorcery that deprived me of the unrestricted exercise of free will. It never entered into my brain that he could cherish impure motives; that one professing such sainted holiness could seek the gratification of lawless passions. No friendly voice was near to warn me, and I fell—[59]

The fragility of free will was contrasted to the corrupting power of sensuality. The passage obviously suggests that Americans had little confidence in the ability of their moral value system to withstand the pressures of overt sexual temptation, or of women to resist men's sexuality.

Because sex was perceived as a compelling force that might destroy the moral agency of men, it had to be completely controlled. If men were moral because they mastered sexual desire, then there was no room in a moral society for a people that allegedly encouraged unrestrained sensuality. When Harriet Beecher Stowe urged pastors to keep the subject of polygamy "in agitation until public

[58] "The literature of counter-subversion could thus serve the double purpose of vicariously fulfilling repressed desires, and of releasing the tension and guilt arising from rapid social change and conflicting values." David Brion Davis, "Some Themes of Counter-Subversion," 220.

[59] Ward, *Female Life*, 65.

sentiment shall force the enactment of such measures that will tend to the total abolition of the other twin relic of barbarism," she was not just campaigning against Mormon polygamy.[60] She was trying to reinforce public confidence in conventional sexual ethics. Intense moral indignation freed the anti-polygamist from the need to confront his own sexual frustrations directly. The campaign allowed Americans to express vicariously their repressed desires at the same time that they reinforced the rigid sexual values of the existing order.

---

[60] *Anti-Polygamy Standard*, June, 1880, p. 2.

SEXUALITY IN NINETEENTH-CENTURY AMERICA: BEHAVIOR, IDEOLOGY, AND POLITICS

Estelle B. Freedman

In the past decade, as historians have explored the "private side" of history, the subject of sexuality has attracted increasing scholarly attention. Well before Michel Foucault argued that the nineteenth century had witnessed an expansion of sexual discourse that created new categories of sexualities, social historians were reinterpreting not only the discourse on sexuality in nineteenth-century America, but changing patterns of sexual behavior as well. During the 1970s, when family historians identified changing rates of fertility and illegitimacy, they raised new questions about the frequency of marital intercourse and the possible use of contraceptives and abortion. When feminist historians explored the meanings of sexuality and reproduction in women's lives, they sparked lively debates about the relationship between ideology and behavior and about the regulation of female sexuality by the medical profession. Soon studies of prostitution, homosexuality, and sexual utopians expanded the scope of this historical inquiry. By the 1980s, public policy debates over abortion, adolescent sex, and homosexuality inspired a new interest in the origins of state regulation of sexuality.[1]

Within this growing literature, historians have focused for the most part on two broad subjects: sexual ideology and sexual behavior, or, as Carl Degler has summarized this distinction, "What Ought to Be and What Was."[2] Particularly for the nineteenth century, scholars have explored attitudes about proper sexual conduct, usually found in published advice literature, and the actual sexual practices that people engaged in, usually deduced from quantitative sources but also found in legal records and personal papers. Too often, however, historians have explained the relationship between ideology and behavior by asking whether or not ideas influenced individual sexual practice.

My reading of the literature on sexuality in nineteenth-century America has made me uneasy with the limitations of these two categories. By thinking only of ideas and behaviors, historians fail to recognize an important third category, one that might be labeled "sexual politics." The subject matter in this category includes political efforts to transform sexual thought or practice (for example, moral reform, antiprostitution, or birth control movements),

0048-7511/82/0104-0196 $01.00

while the interpretations take into account relationships of power, particularly those based on class or gender.

A second problem is the assumption that ideology precedes and then influences behavior, more or less effectively. The implied causality may be misleading. For example, by looking first at nineteenth-century sexual advice literature, which often advocated male self-control and female passionlessness, and then at the decline in white marital fertility rates, the latter can be seen as evidence that couples internalized these ideals, engaged less frequently in intercourse, and thus had fewer children. In contrast, by looking first at behavioral change, namely the means by which the decline in white, marital fertility was achieved, an alternative hypothesis emerges. For if the decline in fertility resulted from the separation of sexuality from its reproductive function—through the use of contraception and abortion, for example—then the main question for nineteenth-century sexual history is not whether repression was effective, but rather whether and how the growing importance of nonprocreative sexuality influenced sexual ideas and politics. Indeed, recent literature on sexual behavior, ideology, and politics reveals that the increasing visibility of erotic sexuality, separate from procreation, presented a central problem for nineteenth-century society.

Sexual Behavior

Historians who examine nineteenth-century sexual behavior take two demographic facts as starting points. One is the steady decline in white marital fertility rates, from 7.04 births in 1800 to 3.56 births in 1900.[3] The other is a two-phased shift in premarital pregnancy rates—first, a decline from a late eighteenth-century high of almost 30 percent of all births to a mid-nineteenth-century low of under 10 percent; and second, by the close of the century, an increase to approximately 20 percent of all births.[4]

The decline in marital fertility rates has important implications for the history of sexual behavior. Most explanations correlate this decline with urbanization, industrialization, or the availability of land.[5] These social and economic considerations undoubtedly influenced individual decisions to limit family size, but the question remains—*how* did couples achieve this reduction? According to Daniel Scott Smith, nineteenth-century women insisted on abstinence from intercourse within marriage in order to reduce the frequency of childbirth. Carl Degler agrees that women influenced the decision to control fertility, but he also provides extensive evidence that married, middle class white women might have used contraceptives or abortion, as well as abstinence, to do so. As James Mohr shows, increasing numbers of married, middle class women turned to abortion at mid-century. It is not clear whether the subsequent criminalization of abortion led to a reduction in its use, to greater reliance on contraceptives, or to both. From the work of Linda Gordon and others we know that information about contraceptive techniques, including douching, condoms, and withdrawal, was available in early nineteenth-century medical and popular health literature.[6] Women exchanged such information through their correspondence, and men no doubt learned of the techniques from visiting either prostitutes or doctors. Efforts to suppress birth control information, exemplified by the passage of the Comstock Law in 1873, may have been, in fact, a reaction to increased use. And despite Comstock's crusade, contraceptive information continued to circulate in medical if not popular texts.[7]

Fluctuations in premarital pregnancy rates have further implications for understanding the frequency of intercourse and use of contraceptives. Daniel Scott Smith and Michael Hindus argue that premarital pregnancy rates declined in the early nineteenth century when young people internalized an ideology of sexual continence and thus reduced the frequency of intercourse. By the late nineteenth century, increasingly autonomous young adults engaged in premarital sex and used contraceptive devices, indicating a new willingness to separate sexuality and reproduction.[8]

These studies of fertility, premarital pregnancy, and contraception pose a number of questions about sexual behavior. Did marital fertility decline not because married couples engaged in intercourse less frequently, but rather because they used contraception or abortion? Did doctors and druggists provide contraceptive information to married couples throughout the century? Did unmarried couples have greater access to contraceptives and abortion in the early nineteenth century, thus keeping the premarital pregnancy rates low, but less access in the latter part of the century, when such information may have gone "underground"? If the answers to these questions are positive, then the frequency of marital and premarital intercourse may have remained constant or even increased over the century, but the meaning of intercourse may have been changing as its reproductive function declined, thus allowing the erotic component of sexuality to emerge more clearly.

These questions, however, are based solely on evidence of the fertility of white, native-born Americans, particularly those living in the Northeast. The very few available studies of immigrants, southern whites, and blacks suggest that their fertility rates remained high during the nineteenth century, indicating either more frequent intercourse or less contraceptive use.[9] The most extensive research concerns slavery and focuses largely on whether it was masters or slaves who shaped sexual behavior on the plantation.[10] Most scholars agree that while older assumptions about black promiscuity are inaccurate, slaves did have a unique sexual system that drew upon certain African customs and resembled preindustrial sexual patterns elsewhere. They condoned premarital intercourse, accepted "illegitimate" births, and valued stable unions with frequent intercourse. It is not clear whether incentives for slave reproduction came from white masters or black slaves, but it is clear that reproduction was not the sole purpose of intercourse among blacks. As Genovese shows, slaves regarded love as a central motive for sex and marriage. Finally, most writers agree that sexual relations between masters and female slaves were less frequent than abolitionists claimed, in part because women resisted their masters and in part because of mutual interest in maintaining the integrity of the slave families.[11]

Although few investigations of working class sexual practices have appeared to date, several recent studies of prostitution provide clues that men engaged in pre- or extramarital intercourse. In mining and cattle towns, for example, working class, black and immigrant women (many of them Latin American or Asian) supported themselves as prostitutes for at least a few years of their lives. As families began to settle in these communities, the once-tolerated "red-light districts" came under attack, and prostitution went underground.[12] As in eastern cities, however, the opponents of prostitution remained conscious of its survival, and thus of the possibility of sexual experience that was entirely divorced from reproduction.

In addition to quantifying the frequency of marital and premarital intercourse, historians have begun to ask qualitative questions about how individuals experienced their sexuality and the personal identities they attached to it. Some of this research focuses on women in an attempt to discover whether they enjoyed or disliked marital intercourse. A small but growing literature investigates the meaning of same-sex love.

In answer to the question "Were women passionless?" historians such as Linda Gordon suggest that women may well have experienced an aversion to sex, not only because of powerful proscriptions on female passion but because women had good reason to fear the physical consequences of pregnancy and childbirth. And when men paid inadequate attention to female sexual pleasure, women had further reason to avoid intercourse. Carl Degler champions an alternative view. Drawing on the earliest available survey of female sexuality, he argues that married, middle class white women did exhibit sexual desire and that a significant proportion experienced orgasm. To further support his case Degler cites the private writings of nineteenth-century feminists who clearly expressed passionate desires. But the responses to the survey Degler uses can be calculated differently, as Carroll Smith-Rosenberg shows, to find that a majority of the respondents engaged in intercourse with their husbands more frequently than the women themselves wished. More importantly, the survey reveals that most of these women believed procreation, and not pleasure, was the purpose of intercourse.[13] Unfortunately, the study tells nothing about female sexual experience outside the white, middle classes.

Sexual experience, of course, is not confined to heterosexual intercourse. William Shade speculates that the decline in marital fertility may have been accompanied by an increase in masturbation and lesbianism. This view assumes a constant level of sexual activity that finds various forms of expression over time, an assumption that is difficult to support. Shade cites, for example, the shrill crusade against female masturbation in the nineteenth century.[14] (A similar attack upon masturbation by young men had originated at least a century earlier.) In the 1880s, many doctors condemned the widespread practice of masturbation by women of all classes, and some linked the practice to friendships among girls. At the same time, educators became suspicious of "smashing," or same-sex crushes, at women's schools. These public outcries do not in themselves indicate an increased level of masturbation or lesbianism, but there is some evidence to confirm that women engaged in both practices in the late nineteenth century. During the 1920s, Katharine B. Davis surveyed 2,200 women about their sex lives and found that a majority of those born after 1850 reported masturbating to orgasm, while one out of five college-educated women had some lesbian experiences.[15]

Intimate relationships between women friends had been considered acceptable since at least the eighteenth century. As Smith-Rosenberg explains, such "homosocial" relationships emerged naturally within the separate female sphere. In a recent examination of these intensely sensuous "romantic friendships," Lillian Faderman concludes that throughout the nineteenth century these attachments remained nonsexual. She argues that even those women who formed "Boston Marriages" (lifelong companionships in shared households) in the late nineteenth century had so internalized the ideal of passionlessness that they could not engage in genital sexuality. But Faderman repeatedly mistakes ideology for behavior, assuming, for instance, that fictional depictions of passionlessness provide an accurate guide to actual behavior. Whatever these couples may have done in private, Faderman argues convincingly that neither they nor the society termed these relationships "lesbian." At the beginning of the century, most legal and medical authorities could not imagine sexual relations between two women because female sexuality was, by definition, linked to reproduction. After 1900, however, these authorities recognized the possibility of female homosexuality and increasingly labeled it pathological.[16]

Same-sex love between men in nineteenth-century America has received less scholarly attention than has the subject of female relationships, but abundant documentary evidence confirms its existence. In his collection, *Gay American History*, Jonathan Katz published the records of both passionate male friendships and explicitly sexual relationships. The documents support the views of British writers such as Jeffrey Weeks that a distinct male homosexual identity and an urban gay subculture emerged toward the end of the nineteenth century.[17] At that time, as Faderman agrees, sexologists and medical authorities began to categorize homosexuality as a permanent, biological condition. As a result, they argue, those who engaged in homosexual acts increasingly took on homosexual identities. Though stigmatized, they could now find each other and begin to develop a unique sexual subculture.

Just as nineteenth-century writers identified women as "The Sex," most historians have limited their inquiries about sexual experience largely to the study of women. Aside from those men who visited brothels or left records of their homosexual activities, we have learned very little about either middle or working class men's sexuality. It is not yet clear whether sources such as medical records, divorce cases, diaries, and letters will provide sufficient evidence for generalizing about male sexual experience—a crucial task for understanding the separation of procreative and erotic sexuality.[18] Until historians investigate these sources, the most "private side" of history remains one-sided, and our understanding of nineteenth-century sexual behavior remains incomplete.

Sexual Ideology

The results of new research on sexual behavior—a decline in white marital fertility rates, evidence of contraceptive use, abortion, prostitution, and indications of both male and female homosexuality—provide an important background for understanding both dominant and alternate sexual ideologies of the nineteenth century. Despite wide variations in the content of published advice literature, a central tension runs throughout nineteenth-century sexual ideology—that is, whether sex "ought to be" a procreative or an erotic act. The evidence of behavioral change strongly suggests that the procreative function of sex declined over the century; but studies of sexual ideology reveal intensive efforts on the part of some to affirm that sex served reproductive ends and to contain the troubling potential of the erotic.

Before exploring this central tension, however, it is important to recognize the diversity of sexual advice found in the writings of clergy, doctors, and moral reformers from the late eighteenth to the late nineteenth centuries. Aimed at an audience of white, middle class women and men, this literature prescribed two basic virtues, male continence and female purity, which distinguished it from earlier texts. The former ideal required men to exert their will in order to control their natural lust; the latter ideal assumed an innate passionlessness on the part of women.[19] The principles of continence and purity, however, had a wide range of practical meanings. Some marriage manuals called for moderate conjugal intercourse, with female orgasm, while others called for abstinence for both sexes. Moreover, sexual ideals changed over the course of the century.[20]

Historians have arrived at divergent interpretations of male continence and female purity in part because they have read different authors, from different generations, and in different contexts. For example, the antebellum health reformer Sylvester Graham, the subject of a useful biography by Stephen Nissenbaum, represents an extreme case; Graham believed that any sensual excitement, including marital sex, depleted men's bodies. His prophylaxis for the "pathology of desire" included moderate diet, simple clothing, chaste reading, and minimal contact between the sexes.[21] In contrast, William Leach examines the writings of those he considers feminist reformers—an unspecified group of later nineteenth-century liberal women and men—and concludes that they did not repudiate sexual passion. Rather, authors such as Lester Ward and Elizabeth Cady Stanton "looked upon desire, passion, and feeling in both sexes within marriage as essentially beneficent and healthy forces."[22] Had Leach read the works of still other nineteenth-century feminists, such as advocates of social purity, he would have found abundant evidence that sexual restraint remained a powerful theme.

Discussions of female purity reveal similar distinctions. Nancy Cott identifies the cultural sources of an ideal of female passionlessness in texts on etiquette, morality, and religion published in the late eighteenth and early nineteenth centuries. Medical texts incorporated these views and many American doctors adopted the British physician William Acton's model of the asexual woman. Yet middle class women were also exposed to quite different sexual advice. As Carl Degler argues, many nineteenth-century authors, both male and female, encouraged women to experience physical pleasure in sex, and several doctors urged husbands to provide this pleasure. What these texts may indicate, however, is a change in the late nineteenth century rather than a contradiction of Cott's work on the earlier period. As Degler himself acknowledges, one can find almost any opinion in medical texts, including the ideal of passionlessness.[23]

Whether nineteenth-century authors viewed sexual desire as a disease or encouraged passionate sex for both spouses, during most of the century they agreed that procreation was the ultimate purpose of sexual activity. Thus, with the exception of a few radicals, they considered any means of birth control "unnatural." Even feminists, Linda Gordon shows, preferred to keep sexuality and reproduction linked; thus they rejected the use of artificial contraceptives that might separate the two. Similarly, any nonprocreative sexual act constituted an unnatural "abuse," and hence excessive marital sex, masturbation, and homosexual acts came to be seen as causes of physical and mental decline. For example, nineteenth-century authorities revived Tissot's notion that masturbation led to insanity, where earlier proscriptions had been based on the argument that masturbation interfered with conjugal sex; masturbation, along with sodomy (a term sometimes used to refer to all non-procreative sexual acts) changed from a sin to a disease that endangered both body and mind. Although this consensus on procreative sexuality began to break down at the end of the century, for most nineteenth-century Americans, to speak of sex was to speak of procreation.[24]

Recent work on utopian communities highlights the tension between procreation and eroticism that lay just beneath the surface of sexual thought. Both Lawrence Foster and Louis Kern show how the sexual ideals of Shakers, Oneidans, and Mormons elaborated upon the dominant sexual ideology at its most difficult oppositions: those of procreation versus erotic sexual activity and social versus individual control over sexuality.[25]

The struggle to incorporate both procreation and eroticism in utopian sexual life produced a variety of solutions. Shakers totally proscribed intercourse, thus rejecting procreation entirely, but they did allow for sensual expression through ritual dances, visions, and trances. At Oneida, procreation had a limited place, for in John Humphrey Noyes's regimen of "coitus reservatus," men preserved their semen by learning to avoid ejaculation during intercourse. Erotic pleasure, however, could be enjoyed by both men and women. The Mormons, in contrast, identified sex entirely with procreation.[26]

As in the larger society, the theme of self-control pervaded utopian sexual thought. According to Kern, male self-control served as an antidote to the "threat of the autonomous individual." But social control—the subordination of the individual to the community—played a large role in each utopian system. Shakers closely surveilled members' physical activity; Oneidans employed mutual criticism to enforce sexual norms and institutionalized a system of selective breeding known as stirpiculture. Mormons both elevated polygamy to a social duty and achieved some eugenic control by requiring church approval for men's choice of wives. Thus, despite the societal emphasis on the internalization of sexual restraint, utopians tried to keep sexuality a communal concern and emphasized the social benefits of both eroticism and procreation. In this sense they harked back to an earlier era of community control over sexuality. Their ideas suggest as well that Americans feared uncontrolled erotic sexuality as something that threatened to place the individual beyond the control of the community.[27]

In fact, many historical explanations of the ideal of male continence reinforce the conclusion that sexual control represented a means of assuaging fears of anarchy during a period when hierarchical restraints upon individual mobility were being removed. Both David Brion Davis and Ronald Walters use this argument, the former to explain the association of sex and death in American fiction, and the latter to explain the rhetoric of northern male abolitionists who attacked unrestrained lust among southern male slaveholders.[28] For abolitionists and others, control of the body offered a check upon individualism that would both reduce the threat of unrestrained use of power and insure the progress of civilization.

As in utopian communities, in the society at large sexuality provided an important link between self-control and social control. As Walters points out, when individuals channeled eroticism to serve reproductive ends, they contributed to the growth of a healthy, or eugenic, population. Perfectionist thought in the antebellum period originally fostered this view, and the introduction of Darwinism later in the century made the link between self-control and eugenic progress central in American sexual ideology.[29]

Toward the end of the century, one set of ideas—those of the Free Lovers—did challenge the dominant sexual ideology. Although these "sex radicals," who Hal Sears and Linda Gordon discuss, did oppose contraception and believe in the importance of self-control, they differed from most Victorians in two important ways. For one, writers such as Moses Harmon and Angela Heywood developed a critique of marriage that involved greater procreative and erotic choices for women. They believed women had the right to determine when to bear children *and* the right to experience erotic pleasure. Moreover, they insisted that the crucial, and often missing, element in sexual relations was love, which they saw as the only proper motivation for both procreation and pleasure. The sex radicals differed in a second important way when, as anarchists or libertarians, they stood firmly against state control of sexuality. Thus they opposed Anthony Comstock's notion of using the federal government to suppress information about sexuality and they rejected the goals of those eugenicists who advocated state intervention in mating and motherhood.[30]

Although recent histories have shown that nineteenth-century sexual ideology was not uniform, they do suggest that a set of common concerns about the meaning of nonprocreative sexuality prevailed. Procreation remained the most highly valued goal of sex, while erotic desire evoked ambivalence at best, and fear of disease and social anarchy at worst. Most Victorian authors emphasized the need to control eroticism, but their means for doing so ranged from abstinence to moderation to elaborate utopian designs for allowing individual pleasure within social boundaries.

What remains to be investigated is whether there were ideologies other than these white, middle class views that are so accessible through printed advice literature. Was there, for instance, a full-fledged defense of a sexual underground, or demimonde, such as that described for Victorian England? Or was there a distinct urban working class or ethnic view of sexuality? [31] By identifying such possible alternatives, it will become clearer whether there were in fact competing sexual ideologies in the nineteenth century or if, as we now tend to assume, a powerful middle class world view dominated sexual thought throughout American society.

Sexual Politics

It is difficult and somewhat artificial to draw a sharp line between ideology and politics, and much of the literature discussed here has as its purpose the interpretation of sexual ideas. But the subject of sexual politics differs from descriptions of the content of sexual thought because it asks basically political questions: Whose interests did ideas serve? By what means did notions of sexual propriety come to predominate? By which social groups were they enforced? In other words, what relationships of power were at stake? The answers to these questions generally involve class, age, and gender.

The role of class in determining Victorian sexual norms appears in the earliest literature on nineteenth-century sexual history, particularly but not exclusively in discussions of male sexuality. In his 1963 essay on sexual ideology and the social system in nineteenth-century England, Peter Cominos argued that Victorians associated economic success, or class mobility, with sexual sublimination. He identified the symbolic importance of sperm as a metaphor for accumulated capital and argued that sexual control came to be identified with the education of a gentleman. Not incidentally, this system rested upon a double standard that required the availability of working class women who, as prostitutes, safeguarded the ideal of purity in the middle class family.[32]

For the United States, G. J. Barker-Benfield uses similar arguments in characterizing antimasturbation literature and medical views of women as part of a "Spermatic Economy." In this closed energy system, each expenditure of sperm depleted the amount of energy a man had for productive economic tasks and capital accumulation. Thus, a man who wished to achieve upward class mobility within the competitive marketplace would have to preserve his resources through sexual self-control as well as control of female sexuality. The economic logic of this interpretation has been challenged, since consumption was also crucial to the developing market economy, but the symbolic power of the spending-saving metaphor, whether in Victorian pornography or in antimasturbation literature, cannot be dismissed.[33]

A more convincing analysis of the relationship between class and sexual ideology appears in the work of Charles Rosenberg. Sexual repression, he explains, supported particular class aspirations within a bureaucratizing society "by helping to create a social discipline appropriate to a middle class of managers, professionals and small entrepreneurs."[34] In addition, Rosenberg suggests that in America, as in England, middle class men differentiated themselves from the lower classes, and especially from domestic servants, by adopting the value of continence. The implication here is that the working class had a different set of sexual values, though it is not yet clear whether and how these views came in conflict with those of the middle class.

A few historians have looked at generational conflicts to explain changing sexual attitudes and practices. In their analysis of premarital pregnancy rates, for example, Smith and Hindus argue that during the late eighteenth century young people gained autonomy from parental controls by engaging in premarital intercourse; since marriage usually followed pregnancy, premarital sex could often assure them their own choice of mates. They also suggest that when young men no longer inherited land or crafts, they adopted sexual restraints, not only because self-control instilled habits of thrift and patterns of deferred gratification, but also because it helped young men avoid the economic burden of families. At the same time, young women could use their sexual purity as a bargaining point in the marriage market.[35]

Other historians have employed a less functionalist analysis to explain constraints on young people's sexuality. According to R. P. Neuman, the nineteenth-century association of masturbation with insanity should be seen as an aspect of parental struggles for control over adolescents who desired personal autonomy. Both Carroll Smith-Rosenberg and Mary Ryan have explored the symbolic meaning of autonomous young men in Jacksonian America. Smith-Rosenberg concentrates on male moral reformers who viewed the pubescent male as a symbol of uncontrolled individuality and used masturbation as a code for both autonomy and homosexuality. The male reformers, she argues, projected their fears of social change and sexual pollution upon the "loose" young urban men who were beyond the control of patriarchal fathers. As Ryan's study of a New York community reveals, class, age, and gender could converge in moral crusades; female moral reformers targeted young male clerks and college students as the source of licentiousness and attempted to place community controls over their sexual autonomy.[36]

The bulk of political interpretation of sexuality concentrates on gender and attempts to determine whether female purity, or passionlessness, served the interests of men (particularly doctors) or of women themselves. The strongest argument for the view that men attempted to control female sexuality in their own interests appears in studies of male medical authorities. Barker-Benfield, for instance, argues that doctors expressed a symbolic fear of women as absorbers of male sperm and thus employed radical obstetrics and gynecology (including ovariotomy, clitorodectomy, and uterine cauterization) to control unruly women.[37] Short of imputing conspiratorial motives to doctors, some historians who read the conservative medical literature have been struck by the projection of physical infirmity onto the female body. Michel Foucault explains this "hysterization" of women as one of several mechanisms by which sexual discourse spread throughout the society, but Smith-Rosenberg and Sarah Stage find a more precise meaning in the prevalent identification of women with their reproductive organs. For one, such biological determinism kept women securely in the home at a time when increasing numbers sought to enter the public sphere. In addition, the projection of sexual pathology onto women may have freed men to assume positions of strength.[38]

Critics of this point of view, such as Regina Morantz, argue that doctors did not single out women for treatment of the reproductive organs. Men, too, suffered from neurasthenia, worried about masturbation and seminal emissions, and occasionally had their genitals cauterized.[39] Still, men visited doctors of their own sex, something few women could do, and these doctors treated men's genitals almost entirely for sexual complaints such as venereal disease, masturbation, and impotence. For the most part, doctors prescribed individual will or self-control to cure men, while they prescribed medical and surgical interventions for a wide range of female complaints, whether or not the complaints were sexual in nature.

The recent studies of utopian communities contribute to the interpretation that men attempted to institutionalize control over female sexuality. Kern in particular argues that men used sex to maintain patriarchal power in the Shaker, Oneida, and Mormon communities. He detects a central fear of women's sexual and maternal power in Noyes's system: men had the power to select sexual partners, prevent ejaculation, and control breeding; women remained the weaker vessels, permitted to have orgasms that drained their vital energies, while denied the power derived from autonomous sexuality and motherhood.[40] But Kern's sweeping criticism of all three communities for subordinating women fails to explain the appeal these groups had for female members. And his interpretation does not rest on personal testimony that either men or women experienced a hierarchy of gender in these utopian communities.

Other historians, although not disputing the dominance of males, argue that Victorian sexual ideas could serve women's self-interest and at times provide leverage in their dealings with men. Several variations on this theme occur, ranging from the suggestion that women caricatured their sexual roles in order to escape from them, as in the case of hysteria, to the proposition that women achieved autonomy by denying their sexual desires.[41] In between lies the bulk of interpretation—that women attempted to utilize a repressive ideology in order to gain personal meaning and political influence.

A number of feminist historians argue that women who accepted the ideal of passionlessness may have done so in order to achieve greater personal freedom. Nancy Cott explains that passionlessness served to elevate women closer to moral equality with men. Others have reasoned that the physical consequences of intercourse, including potential venereal infection and debilitation from repeated childbearing, could make "prudery" a useful tool for women to gain freedom from reproduction or from unsatisfactory sexual relationships. And, as Linda Gordon shows, feminists emphasized women's right to say no to sex as a means of achieving female control over reproduction.[42]

Both Daniel Scott Smith and Carl Degler assume that women did in fact achieve such control within the context of the nineteenth-century family. Smith terms this control "domestic feminism" and believes it led to the decline of white marital fertility rates and ultimately to women's increased power in society. But Smith's reasoning about female sexual control, based solely on quantitative evidence, is suspect; it fails to ask whether women or men determined frequency of intercourse and whether the control of fertility has any implications for female independence in the public sphere. Degler attempts to provide documentation on both of these points with extensive qualitative evidence, some of which seems to contradict his earlier argument that women enjoyed sexual passion, now proving that they sought to avoid it. In the end, however, he concludes that women did limit sex in marriage, not from an aversion to sexual expression but as a means of gaining autonomy.[43] Thus sexual ideology and reproductive strategy may have converged to serve women's personal interests.

Although it is not clear whether middle class women did in fact refrain from intercourse except for the purpose of reproduction, many supported social movements that attacked men's ability to have sexual intercourse without taking responsibility for its reproductive consequences. In their campaigns against the double standard, women resisted the separation of sexuality and reproduction because they perceived it as antithetical to their interests. Thus, female moral reform associations in Jacksonian America attacked male licentiousness, waged a war on "seducers," and called for female control over the nation's sexual mores.[44] In the late nineteenth century, women left the home in the name of domesticity, proselytizing for a single sexual standard through the social purity movement and the Women's Christian Temperance Union. Degler calls these efforts "organizing to control sexuality"—especially men's nonreproductive sexuality. Through them women increasingly came to demand political power, as organizations such as the W.C.T.U. supported woman suffrage in the name of "Home Protection" and as a means of defending the single sexual standard.[45]

Most feminist historians interpret temperance and social purity as efforts to overturn women's subordinate domestic status, arguing that sexual control served women's interests. Barbara Epstein shares these views, but her recent book includes a criticism of reformers' insistence on a single sexual standard. Epstein argues that even if domesticity and purity did enhance women's power, it did so at the cost of their adhering to a "rigid and antisexual moral code" that required a loss of sexual self-assertion.[46] What Epstein does not consider is the possibility that those who attacked men's sexual behavior did not necessarily remain asexual themselves, either in marriage or with friends. She overlooks, for instance, W.C.T.U. President Frances Willard's passionate relationships with other women. Nonetheless, Epstein offers an important revision of the dominant interpretation of social purity and her book represents a significant step toward the integration of political and sexual history.

Nineteenth-century women's political response to the double standard has also been criticized for its role in encouraging state intervention in sexual matters. In the 1880s, both male and female purity crusaders supported legislation to raise the age of consent; moreover, some of them tolerated the antilibertarian tactics of moralists like Anthony Comstock. Both Mary Ryan and Judith Walkowitz have recently drawn parallels between women engaged in moral reform and antiprostitution in the nineteenth century and the current New Right efforts to achieve state regulation of sexual expression. The historical evidence for this parallel seems to be stronger for Britain, where, as Walkowitz shows, social purity took a decidedly antilibertarian turn after the 1880s.[47] Whether this holds for the United States has yet to be argued convincingly, but the question will undoubtedly influence future research on the politics of sexuality.

Conclusion

Recent investigations of sexuality in nineteenth-century America raise as many new questions about sexual behavior, ideology, and politics as they begin to answer. Because historians have focused largely on women's sexual behavior and on middle class sexual ideas, we have an incomplete and possibly distorted vision of how most people acted or thought. Because the analysis of sexual politics has been, for the most part, an implicit one, historians have not yet fully explored its possibilities. We need to know more about men, about the working class, and about the sexual underworld in nineteenth-century American cities; we need to explore the meaning of medical problems, such as venereal disease, for sexual thought; and we need to look more closely at the sexual experiences of those who articulated a politics of sexuality in the late-nineteenth century. Only after much imaginative research has uncovered a fuller historical record will it be wise to generalize about the direction and causes of change in nineteenth-century sexual history.

Nonetheless, the studies reviewed in this essay do point toward a hypothesis that bears further exploration. Over the course of the nineteenth century, as white American women bore fewer and fewer children, the reproductive function of sexuality became less central. Although some middle class Victorians may have heeded advice to limit sexual intercourse, others experienced sexuality as a nonprocreative act. The evidence of contraceptive use, abortion, and homosexuality, of a tension over eroticism within American sexual ideology, and of the political defense of a sexuality limited to reproduction all suggest that Americans struggled to come to terms with the potential of an erotic, nonprocreative sexuality. Thus, although the ideological support for the separation of sexuality and reproduction did not appear until the twentieth century, the process itself began much earlier.[48] The nineteenth-century conflict over nonreproductive sexuality provides an important context for understanding both the political campaigns to regulate sexuality at the end of the century and the preoccupation of modern sexual ideology with the erotic.

Most men and women living in nineteenth-century America were not conscious of the growing importance of nonreproductive sexuality, while many of those who were resisted the separation of reproduction and sexuality. White, middle class women, including feminists, may have feared that they would lose what limited social influence they had as mothers or that men would enjoy the benefits of erotic sexuality while women continued to take the reproductive risks. Some middle class men associated the erotic with the lower classes and sought to differentiate themselves by practicing sexual restraint. On the other hand, some utopians and radicals sought ways to incorporate the erotic within the sexual lives of both women and men; others attempted to control reproduction. Meanwhile, innumerable women and men—including couples who used contraception and abortion, some blacks and immigrants, prostitutes and their clients, homosexuals, and those who masturbated or had adulterous sexual relationships—unknowingly participated through their actions in the creation of new categories of sexuality.

By the 1880s, defenders of an older sexual order called for "reform"—criminalization of abortion, suppression of birth control information and of prostitution, condemnation of adultery, and, in general, the subordination of selfish (erotic) desires to a particular vision of the social good. Their voices still echo in contemporary America.[49] A thorough understanding of the historical circumstances that motivated these demands may contribute not only to a more accurate account of nineteenth-century society, but also to a more effective response to the sexual politics of our own time.

I am grateful to Peggy Pascoe for bibliographic assistance in the preparation of this essay, and to the following people for their helpful comments on earlier drafts: John D'Emilio, Susan Johnson, Susan Krieger, Sue Lynn, Elaine Tyler May, Diane Middlebrook, Peggy Pascoe, Elizabeth Pleck, Paul Robinson, Barbara Rosenblum, and Mary Ryan.

1. Michel Foucault, *The History of Sexuality: An Introduction*, vol. 1 (New York: Random House, Pantheon Books, 1978). For earlier surveys of historical literature on sexuality in America, see John C. Burnham, "American Historians and the Subject of Sex," *Societas* 2 (August 1972): 307–16; Ronald G. Walters, "Sexual Matters as Historical Problems: A Framework of Analysis," *Societas* 6 (Summer 1976): 157–75. On the interest in sexual history during the 1970s, see Stephen Nissenbaum, *Sex, Diet, and Debility in Jacksonian America: Sylvester Graham and Health Reform* (Westport, Conn.: Greenwood Press, 1980), p. xii. On the current interest in the politics of sexuality, see Ellen Ross and Rayna Rapp, "Sex and Society: A Research Note from Social History and Anthropology," *Comparative Studies in Society and History* 23 (January 1981): 72; "Sexuality in History," a special issue of the *Radical History Review* 20 (Spring-Summer 1979). On England, see Jeffrey Weeks, *Sex, Politics, and Society: The Regulation of Sexuality Since 1800* (London: Longman, 1981).

2. Carl N. Degler, "What Ought to Be and What Was: Women's Sexuality in the Nineteenth Century," *American Historical Review* 79 (December 1974): 1467–90.

3. Daniel Scott Smith, "Family Limitation, Sexual Control, and Domestic Feminism in Victorian America," in *Clio's Consciousness Raised*, eds., Mary S. Hartman and Lois Banner (New York: Harper and Row, 1974), p. 123.

4. Daniel Scott Smith and Michael S. Hindus, "Premarital Pregnancy in America, 1640–1971: An Overview and Interpretation," *Journal of Interdisciplinary History* 5 (Spring 1975): 537–70.

5. Summaries of historical interpretations of the decline in fertility rates appear in Carl N. Degler, *At Odds: Women and the Family in America from the Revolution to the Present* (New York: Oxford University Press, 1980), pp. 181–89; Michael B. Katz and Mark J. Stern, "Fertility, Class, and Industrial Capitalism: Erie County, New York, 1855–1915," *American Quarterly* 33 (Spring 1981): 63–70.

6. Smith, "Domestic Feminism"; Degler, *At Odds*, chs. 8–10; James C. Mohr, *Abortion in America: The Origins and Evolution of National Policy, 1800–1900* (New York: Oxford University Press, 1978), chs. 3–4; Linda Gordon, *Woman's Body, Woman's Right: A Social History of Birth Control in America* (New York: Grossman, 1976), chs. 2–3. Additional evidence of the use of abortion and contraception appears in John S. Haller, Jr. and Robin M. Haller, *The Physician and Sexuality in Victorian America* (Urbana: University of Illinois Press, 1974), esp. pp. 113–24; Michael A. LaSorte, "Nineteenth-Century Family Planning Practices," *Journal of Psychohistory* 4 (Fall 1976): 163–84. The increased use of birth control by English middle class couples is argued in Joseph A. Banks and Olive Banks, *Feminism and Family Planning in Victorian England* (New York: Schocken Books, 1964); Patricia Branca, *Silent Sisterhood: Middle-Class Women in the Victorian Home* (London: Croom and Helm, 1975); F. Barry Smith, "Sexuality in Britain, 1800–1900: Some Suggested Revisions," in *A Widening Sphere: Changing Roles of Victorian Women*, ed., Martha Vicinus (Bloomington: Indiana University Press, 1977), pp. 182–98.

7. According to Wilson Yates, there was a "continual flow of information from the medical profession to the public" between 1831 and 1900; even after 1873, medical journals provided a platform for discussing contraception. See Wilson Yates, "Birth Control Literature and the Medical Profession in Nineteenth-Century America," *Journal of the History of Medicine and Allied Sciences* 31 (January 1976): 44.

8. Smith and Hindus, "Premarital Pregnancy."

9. On immigrant rates, see Peter R. Shergold, "The Walker Thesis Revisited: Immigration and White American Fertility, 1800–1860," *Australian Economic History Review* 14 (September 1974): 168–89; Tamara K. Hareven and Maris A. Vinovskis, "Marital Fertility, Ethnicity, and Occupation in Urban Families: An Analysis of South Boston and the South End in 1880," *Journal of Social History* 8 (Spring 1975): 69–93; Degler, *At Odds*, pp. 220–22; Richard H. Steckel, "Antebellum Southern White Fertility: A Demographic and Economic Analysis," *Journal of Economic History* 40 (June 1980): 350; Michael R. Haines, "Fertility and Marriage in a Nineteenth-Century Industrial City: Philadelphia, 1850–1880," *Journal of Economic History* 40 (March 1980): 151–58. Katz and Stern, "Fertility," argue that class, rather than ethnicity, explains the differential rates in the New York county they studied. For differential rates of childbearing by black women, see Wilson H. Grabill, Clyde V. Kiser, and Pascal K. Whelpton, "A Long View," in *The American Family in Social-Historical Perspective*, ed. Michael Gordon (New York: St. Martins Press, 1973), pp. 389–91.

10. Robert Fogel and Stanley Engerman argue in *Time on the Cross: The Economics of American Negro Slavery* (Boston: Little, Brown, 1974) that slaves' sexual mores approximated those of white, middle class Victorians. Their critics on this point include Herbert G. Gutman, *Slavery and the Numbers Game: A Critique of Time on the Cross* (Urbana: University of Illinois Press, 1975), pp. 88–164; Herbert Gutman and Richard Sutch, "Victorians All? The Sexual Mores and Conduct of Slaves and Their Masters," in *Reckoning With Slavery: A Critical Study of the Quantitative History of American Negro Slavery*, eds. Paul A. David, Herbert G. Gutman, Richard Sutch, Peter Temin and Gavin Wright (New York: Oxford University Press, 1976), pp. 134–62; Eugene D. Genovese, *Roll, Jordan, Roll: The World the Slaves Made* (New York: Random House, Pantheon Books, 1974). Cheryll Cody's study of one plantation, "A Note on Changing Patterns of Slave Fertility in the South Carolina Rice District, 1735–1865," *Southern Studies* 16 (Winter 1977): 457–63, supports Fogel and Engerman's interpretation.

11. Genovese, *Roll, Jordan, Roll*, pp. 459–72; Gutman and Sutch, "Victorians All?," esp. pp. 136, 142. The possibilities for studying Native American sexuality are suggested in Martin B. Duberman, Fred Eggan, and Richard Clemmer, "Documents in Hopi Indian Sexuality: Imperialism, Culture, and Resistance," *Radical History Review* 20 (Spring-Summer 1979): 99–130.

12. Lucie Cheng Hirata, "Free, Indentured, and Enslaved: Chinese Prostitution in Nineteenth-Century America," *Signs* 5 (Autumn 1979): 3–29; Marion S. Goldman, *Gold Diggers and Silver Miners: Prostitution and Social Life on the Comstock Lode* (Ann Arbor: University of Michigan Press, 1981); George M. Blackburn and Sherman L. Ricards, "The Prostitutes and Gamblers of Virginia City, Nevada: 1870," *Pacific Historical Review* 48 (May 1979): 239–58; Carol Leonard and Isidor Wallimann, "Prostitution and the Changing Morality in the Frontier Cattle Towns of Kansas," *Kansas History* 2 (Spring 1979): 34–53. For a discussion of the treatment of prostitutes, see Estelle B. Freedman, *Their Sisters' Keepers: Women's Prison Reform in America, 1830–1930* (Ann Arbor: University of Michigan Press, 1981), chs. 1–2. On prostitution in England, see Judith R. Walkowitz, *Prostitution and Victorian Society: Women, Class, and the State* (New York: Cambridge University Press, 1980). For the Progressive era in the United States, see Mark Connelly, *The Response to Prostitution in the Progressive Era* (Chapel Hill: University of North Carolina Press, 1980); Ruth Rosen, *The Lost Sisterhood: Prostitution in America, 1900–1918* (Baltimore: Johns Hopkins University Press, 1982).

13. Gordon, *Woman's Body*, pp. 105–06; Degler, "What Ought to Be"; Degler, *At Odds*, ch. 11; Carroll Smith-Rosenberg, "A Richer and a Gentler Sex," paper presented at the Berkshire Conference on the History of Women, Bryn Mawr, Pennsylvania, June 1976.

14. William G. Shade, "'A Mental Passion': Female Sexuality in Victorian America," *International Journal of Women's Studies* 1 (January-February 1978): 15. On doctors' concerns about female masturbation, see James Reed, *From Private Vice to Public Virtue: The Birth Control Movement and American Society Since 1830* (New York: Basic Books, 1978), pp. 159–60; Hal D. Sears, *The Sex Radicals: Free Love in High Victorian America* (Lawrence: Regents Press of Kansas, 1977), pp. 188–89; Carroll Smith-Rosenberg, "Puberty to Menopause: The Cycle of Femininity in Nineteenth-Century America," in *Clio's Consciousness Raised*, eds. Hartman and Banner, pp. 23–37.

15. Shade, "Mental Passion," pp. 16–17; Vern L. Bullough and Martha Voght, "Homosexuality and Its Confusion with the Secret Sin in Pre-Freudian America," *Journal of the History of Medicine and Allied Sciences* 28 (April 1973): 150; Lillian Faderman, *Surpassing the Love of Men: Romantic Friendship and Love Between Women from the Renaissance to the Present* (New York: William Morrow, 1981), p. 291; Nancy Sahli, "Smashing: Women's Relationships Before the Fall," *Chrysalis* 8 (Summer 1979): 17–28.

16. Carroll Smith-Rosenberg, "The Female World of Love and Ritual: Relations Between Women in Nineteenth-Century America," *Signs* 1 (Autumn 1975): 1–29; Faderman, *Surpassing the Love of Men*, pp. 147–253. On the question of whether women's loving friendships were sexual, see Blanche Wiesen Cook, "Female Support Networks and Political Activism: Lillian Wald, Crystal Eastman, Emma Goldman," in *A Heritage of Her Own*, eds. Nancy F. Cott and Elizabeth H. Pleck (New York: Simon and Schuster, Touchstone, 1979), pp. 412–44; and "The Historical Denial of Lesbianism," *Radical History Review* 20 (Spring-Summer 1979): 60–65; Judith Schwarz, " 'Yellow Clover': Katharine Lee Bates and Katharine Coman," *Frontiers* 4 (Spring 1979): 59–67; Leila J. Rupp, " 'Imagine My Surprise': Women's Relationships in Historical Perspective," *Frontiers* 5 (Fall 1980): 61–70. On cross-dressing women who may have been lesbians, see Jonathan Katz, *Gay American History: Lesbians and Gay Men in the U.S.A.* (New York: Thomas Y. Crowell, 1976), pp. 209–79.

17. Katz, *Gay American History* (a second collection of documents is forthcoming from Harper and Row); Jeffrey Weeks, *Coming Out: Homosexual Politics in Britain from the Nineteenth Century to the Present* (London: Quartet Books, 1977), chs. 1-3; Kenneth Plummer, *The Making of the Modern Homosexual* (London: Hutchinson, 1981). On the emergence of homosexual subcultures in twentieth-century America, see John D'Emilio, "Gay Politics, Gay Community: San Francisco's Experience," *Socialist Review* 55 (January-February 1981): 77-104; and *Sexual Politics, Sexual Communities: The Making of a Homosexual Minority in the U.S., 1940–1970* (Chicago: University of Chicago Press, forthcoming).

18. Several recent studies suggest the possible uses of divorce records as evidence of adultery, sexual fantasies, and sexual complaints: Marion Goldman, "Sexual Commerce on the Comstock Lode," *Nevada Historical Society Quarterly* 21 (Summer 1978): 105; Robert L. Griswold, "Apart But Not Adrift: Wives, Divorce, and Independence in California, 1850–1890," *Pacific Historical Review* 49 (May 1980): 279–80; Elaine Tyler May, *Great Expectations: Marriage and Divorce in Post-Victorian America* (Chicago: University of Chicago Press, 1980), ch. 6.

19. The printed advice literature that stressed these themes, especially after 1830, is analyzed by Barbara Welter, "The Cult of True Womanhood, 1820–1860," *American Quarterly* 18 (Summer 1966): 150–74; Michael Gordon, "From an Unfortunate Necessity to a Cult of Mutual Orgasm: Sex in American Marital Education Literature, 1830–1940," in *Studies in the Sociology of Sex*, ed. James M. Henslin (New York: Appleton-Century-Crofts, 1971), pp. 53-77; Ronald G. Walters, *Primers for Prudery: Sexual Advice to Victorian America* (Englewood Cliffs, N.J.: Prentice Hall, 1974); Haller and Haller, *Physician and Sexuality*; Degler, "What Ought to Be"; Nissenbaum, *Sex, Diet, and Debility*.

20. On inconsistent and changing ideals, see Charles E. Rosenberg, "Sexuality, Class and Role in Nineteenth-Century America," *American Quarterly* 35 (May 1973): 131–53; R. P. Neuman, "Masturbation, Madness, and the Modern Concepts of Childhood and Adolescence," *Journal of Social History* 8 (Spring 1975): 1–27.

21. Nissenbaum, *Sex, Diet, and Debility*, esp. ch. 7.

22. William Leach, *True Love and Perfect Union: The Feminist Reform of Sex and Society* (New York: Basic Books, 1980), p. 95.

23. Nancy F. Cott, "Passionlessness: An Interpretation of Victorian Sexual Ideology, 1790–1850," *Signs* 4 (1978): 219–36; Haller and Haller, *Physician and Sexuality*, pp. 97–98; Degler, "What Ought to Be," and *At Odds*, ch. 11.

24. On the taboo against nonprocreative sex, see Louis J. Kern, *An Ordered Love: Sex Roles and Sexuality in Victorian Utopias* (Chapel Hill: University of North Carolina Press, 1981), pp. 32–33; Walters, *Primers for Prudery*, p. 44; Bullough and Voght, "Homosexuality," esp. p. 154; Gordon, *Woman's Body*, ch. 5; Peter L. Tyor, " 'Denied the Power to Choose the

Good': Sexuality and Mental Defect in American Medical Practice, 1850–1920," *Journal of Social History* 10 (June 1977): 473–75. New ideas about masturbation are discussed by Bullough and Voght, "Homosexuality"; Nissenbaum, *Sex, Diet, and Debility*, esp. pp. 30, 110; Robert H. MacDonald, "The Frightful Consequences of Onanism: Notes on the History of a Delusion," *Journal of the History of Ideas* 28 (July-September 1967): 423–31.

25. Lawrence Foster, *Religion and Sexuality: Three American Communal Experiments of the Nineteenth Century* (New York: Oxford University Press, 1981); Kern, *Ordered Love*.

26. Kern, *Ordered Love*, esp. pp. 41–46, 110, 146, 284; Foster, *Religion and Sexuality*, esp. pp. 47, 94, 227. For an interpretation of changing Mormon sexual ideas, see Klaus J. Hansen, "Mormon Sexuality and American Culture," *Dialogue* 10 (Autumn 1976): 45–56.

27. Kern, *Ordered Love*, esp. pp. 21–26, 78–79, 93–98, 133, 156, 288; Foster, *Religion and Sexuality*, esp. pp. 13, 47, 92, 98, 227, 235–37; Hansen, "Mormon Sexuality."

28. David Brion Davis, *Homicide in American Fiction, 1798–1860: A Study in Social Values* (Ithaca, N.Y.: Cornell University Press, 1957), pp. 153–56, 205; Ronald G. Walters, "The Erotic South: Civilization and Sexuality in American Abolitionism," *American Quarterly* 25 (May 1973): 180, 189, 198. On abolitionist sexual thought, see also Lewis Perry, " 'Progress, Not Pleasure, Is Our Aim': The Sexual Advice of an Antebellum Radical," *Journal of Social History* 12 (Spring 1979): 354–66.

29. Walters, "Erotic South," pp. 198–201; Kern, *Ordered Love*, pp. 299–300. Similarly, Foucault (*History of Sexuality*, pp. 104, 139–46) identifies population control as one means by which sexuality serves to regulate both the individual body and the social body. These analyses, however, do not distinguish between the relationship of men and that of women to reproduction, a crucial distinction for most nineteenth-century sexual theorists and for contemporary feminists.

30. Sears, *Sex Radicals*, esp. pp. 66, 120, 132, 175–79, 210, 234; Gordon, *Woman's Body*, ch. 5.

31. On the sexual underground and class-defined sexuality in England, see Steven Marcus, *The Other Victorians: A Study of Sexuality and Pornography in Mid-Nineteenth Century England* (New York: Basic Books, 1966); Ronald Pearsall, *The Worm in the Bud: The World of Victorian Sexuality* (Toronto: Macmillan, 1969); Fraser Harrison, *The Dark Angel: Aspects of Victorian Sexuality* (London: Sheldon Press, 1977); Leonore Davidoff, "Class and Gender in Victorian England: The Diaries of Arthur J. Munby and Hannah Cullwick," *Feminist Studies* 5 (Spring 1979): 87–141; Weeks, *Sex, Politics, and Society*, ch. 4.

32. Peter T. Cominos, "Late Victorian Sexual Respectability and the Social System," *International Review of Social History* (2 parts), 8 (1963): 18–48 and 216–50. Davidoff, "Class and Gender," explores the sexual relationships between upper class men and working class women, particularly servants.

33. Ben Barker-Benfield, "The Spermatic Economy: A Nineteenth-Century View of Sexuality," in *The American Family in Social-Historical Perspective*, ed. Michael Gordon (New York: St. Martins Press, 1973), pp. 336–72. Degler, *At Odds*, pp. 292–93, summarizes the criticisms of the economic logic. On pornography, see Marcus, *Other Victorians*.

34. Rosenberg, "Sexuality, Class, and Role," p. 132.

35. Smith and Hindus, "Premarital Pregnancy."

36. Neuman, "Masturbation"; Carroll Smith-Rosenberg, "Sex as Symbol in Victorian Purity: An Ethnohistorical Analysis of Jacksonian America," *American Journal of Sociology* 84 (Supplement 1978): S212–S247; Mary P. Ryan, "The Power of Women's Networks: A Case Study of Female Moral Reform in Antebellum America," *Feminist Studies* 5 (Spring 1979): 66–86.

37. G. J. Barker-Benfield, *The Horrors of the Half-Known Life: Male Attitudes Toward Women and Sexuality in Nineteenth-Century America* (New York: Harper and Row, 1976), part 2; Haller and Haller, *Physician and Sexuality*, pp. 38–40; Ann Douglas Wood, " 'The Fashionable Diseases': Women's Complaints and Their Treatment in Nineteenth-Century America," in *Clio's Consciousness Raised*, eds. Hartman and Banner, pp. 1–22.

38. Foucault, *History of Sexuality*, pp. 104, 146; Carroll Smith-Rosenberg, "Puberty to Menopause: The Cycle of Femininity in Nineteenth-Century America," in *Clio's Consciousness*

SMASHING: WOMEN'S RELATIONSHIPS BEFORE THE FALL

Nancy Sahli

Female sexuality has, within the context of the contemporary women's movement, become the focus of an increasing number of women's historians and feminist writers. Works as diverse as Susan Brownmiller's *Against Our Will* and Adrienne Rich's *Of Woman Born* are contributing to our understanding that sexual and emotional attitudes and behavior are culturally defined, nonempirical components of a continuum of time, power, belief, and circumstance.[1,2] Yet we are still confronted by the question of the degree to which these attitudes have been and will continue to be defined and determined by the prescriptions of a fundamentally patriarchal society.

Carroll Smith-Rosenberg has shown that a network of intimate, supportive relationships existed among American women during much of the eighteenth and nineteenth centuries.[3] This network was subjected to increasing stress after about 1875. Prescriptions for female behavior changed; indeed, a new definition of what constituted "normal" female relationships developed in both America and Europe. Middle-class women, specifically feminists and college-educated women, would logically be among the first either to be affected by or to initiate new types of relationships. Luckily, this class also provides readily accessible primary source material. However, the behavior and attitudes described in this article were not atypical and should not be regarded as such by historians trying to understand late nineteenth-century American women.

One of the problems encountered in writing about women's relationships is that of terminology. Words such as "lesbian" and "homosexual" did not come into use until the last decade of the nineteenth century, and even then there was much confusion about whether they referred to emotional or sexual behavior or both. This article uses the word "lesbian" in the same sense as it was used by Blanche Cook in her recent article on female support networks in the early twentieth century:

> *Women who love women, who choose women to nurture and support and to create a living environment in which to work creatively and independently, are lesbians.*[4]

Until about 1875,* intimate, supportive relationships with a high degree of emotional, sensual, and even sexual content existed freely among both single and married women in America.* One woman who participated in such a network was Anna E. Dickinson, orator, actress, and political activist. In her papers at the Library of Congress are numerous letters from female admirers written during the 1860's and early 1870's, when intense love relationships as well as strongly emotional language were still considered legitimate. Louise Brackett, the wife of a Boston artist, was typical in her enthusiasm:

*The point, of course, is not whether these relationships were sexual, even on an unconscious level; it is that women defined their parameters themselves.

Class gathering, Wellesley College, 1894.

How much I want to see you: as your letter gave me such exquisite pleasures indeed! I will marry you – run off any where with you, for you are such a darling – I can feel your soul – if not your body sweet Anna – do I offend your delicacy?[5(a)]

You are mine, and belong to me, until you get married – say it is true? . . . I have an irresistible desire all through this letter to make love to you.[5(b)]

Laura Curtis Bullard, editor of the suffragist-supported paper *Revolution*, was another correspondent:

Anna dear, you don't know how you have found your way to my heart, nor how ardently you are cherished there – Come soon *to see me – I kiss you a thousand times.*[6(a)]

Mr Bullard is still in Montreal. Virginia Townsend has his room, so you should have had your place in my bed had you come – & I am sorry you didnt . . . Sweet Anna, I shall hope to see you soon & kiss your soft, tender lips, either here or at Long Branch.[6(b)]

I am so glad *that I have* got *you for my darling that I can't find words to express my delight in my new love.*[6(c)]

A third woman who was close to Dickinson was suffrage leader Susan B. Anthony:

I mean always to keep beckoning you upward & onward till you speak right out in words the deep, rich, earnest love for your own sex that I know lies in the inner courts of your being. . . . So Anna as I love you & you love me – and we both love the right – I ask you to examine the "inner light" *– Lovingly yours, Susan B. Anthony.*[7(a)]

Now when are you coming to New York – do let it be soon – I have plain quarters *– at 44 Bond St –* double bed *– and big enough & good enough to take you* in *– . . . I do so long for the scolding & pinched ears & every thing I know awaits me – what worlds of experience since I last snuggled the wee child in my long arms. . . . Your loving friend* Susan[7(b)]

Dearly Loved Anna . . . How I have missed you & yet how I have longed to meet you – for more reasons than one – I shall try & meet you at Albany – the 16th – or at Rondout – unless you are going here right after – I must see you & can't put it on paper – My heart is full.[7(c)]

They parted company around 1874 because of political differences, but as late as 1895 Anthony wrote to Dickinson that her love had never abated for her first Anna.[7(d)]

After the early 1870's, however, this type of letter becomes increasingly scarce, and those that do exist convey the impression of being rhetorically self-conscious rather than innocently emotional in their language. Caution should be exercised, however, in interpreting this evidence as indicating any real change in Dickinson's own behavior, for during the 1880's Dickinson portrayed male roles on the commercial stage and was accom-

College Hall: student room, 1881.

panied on her tours by Betty Chatfield, a woman from whom Dickinson – according to her biographer, Giraud Chester – "seemed to get a satisfaction . . . that she had never sensed with her numerous suitors years before."[8]

During this same period, social change began to have an impact on women's relationships. One significant development was the entrance of women into coeducational universities such as Michigan and Boston, as well as the new women's colleges such as Wellesley. Founded by Henry Durant, an evangelical Bostonian, Wellesley had as its first president Ada L. Howard, a rigid authoritarian woman disliked by most of the faculty and students. Durant, along with his all-male board of trustees, was the real ruler of the kingdom and was parodied in an 1879 *Harvard Lampoon* sketch as "His Royal Highness, the Founder of Wellesley College."[9] It was a despotism. Faculty and students, as in other women's colleges, lived together in the same building; visitors were allowed only on Saturdays (and then only parents, brothers, and sisters, unless permission was secured for *others* from the President); and attendance was required at prayers, Bible classes, and chapel services on Sunday.[10,11] Not surprisingly, the *Lampoon* described the students as the "Grand Chorus of Unflirtables."

Asylums and other closed institutions develop internal definitions of acceptable behavior.[12] Wellesley was no exception. During Wellesley's first year of operation, 1875-1876, close relationships flourished between the students and some of the women faculty – an understandable phenomenon, since they were together under the same roof twenty-four hours a day, were nearly the same age, and felt a communion not only as innovators for women, but as opponents of the rigid rules by which the college was governed. We may never know exactly why three faculty members – Mary A. Burnham, Sarah Glazier, and Helen Stock – were fired at the end of the first year.* Ostensibly they presented too great a challenge to the authority of Durant and Howard; perhaps there were other reasons. What we can know, however, is how the Wellesley student community reacted to this event, as seen in the letters of Francis Robinson Johnson, one of the students, to her mother. On June 11, 1876, she wrote:

Oh mother what shall I do? I've been crying & I can't write straight. Ella & Emma rushed in a little while ago all worked up and said that Mr. Durant has publicly dismissed the three leading teachers in this college, the only ones who make it a college, the only ones who know anything and amount to anything. . . . the 3 have shown no signs that anything has happened except I have noticed that Miss Burnham has looked very sad & once I thought she had been crying. . . . This household has a gloom over it that it has never had before. The girls are fairly heartbroken. Miss Burnham looked so pityful and the tears came into her eyes very very often – . . . I never in my life saw such a beautiful, lovely & good woman as Miss B. – Miss Glazier was not at table. Jessie says she looks like a perfect ghost – all the reason Mr. D. gives them is that they conflict with the government *of the Coll. . . . I think the man must be crazy.*[13(a)]

Three days later, after writing several other letters describing other aspects of the situation, she continued:

We have been out boating. Such a pleasant time! The boats were all trimmed with daisies and the banners out. We took Miss Glazier the first time she has been out; . . . Miss Burnham went with her own boat; . . . Miss G. kept us laughing all the time. Poor woman, she little felt like it, I guess. We all sang and were as gay as possible. We escorted them up crowned them with daisys and certainly showed our love and respect for them. Each had a chain of daisies around her neck. Going up the stairs Miss G. says "How easy life would be if we had no harder yokes to bear than these children put upon us" – & Mother, it seems as if I could not bear the thought of coming back next year; to find those teachers gone; the only ones we loved and respected to

*Mary Burnham went to Northampton, Massachusetts, where she opened a school for girls.

be under the thumb of a man and woman that I despise.[13(b)]

Incidents such as this indicate the extent to which committed homo-emotional relationships among women had begun to take on a counter-cultural aspect.

New types of organizations, such as alumnae groups and sororities, resulted from the entrance of women into higher education. In 1881 the Association of Collegiate Alumnae – known today as the American Association of University Women – was formed, largely because of the alienation from the mainstream of social life which many women college graduates felt. The association's first research committee,* that on physical education, was organized after a paper on that topic was read at the first regular meeting, early in 1882, by Dr. Adaline S. Whitney.[14] The best-known result of this committee's activity was its 1885 report on *Health Statistics of Women College Graduates*, which disproved the contemporary theory that the rigors of academic life resulted in poor health among women students.[15]

Crews: left, 1889 class crew in "Tanager"; right, 1888 class crew in "Hesperus."

*Members of the committee included Alice Stone Blackwell, S. Alice Brown, Dr. Adaline S. Whitney, and Wellesley faculty members Lucy C. Andrews and Marion L. Pelton.

While the committee's chief objective was to challenge this viewpoint, initially set forth in Dr. E. H. Clarke's 1873 book *Sex in Education* (a work that ran into several editions during the following two decades), it is also possible that the committee was equally disturbed by Clarke's allegation that college-educated women were not "real women." His description, of course, applied not only to college women, but to feminists as well:

There are those who write and act as if their object were to assimilate woman as much as possible to man, by dropping all that is distinctively feminine out of her, and putting into her as large an amount of masculineness as possible. These persons tacitly admit the error just alluded to, that woman is inferior to man, and strive to get rid of the inferiority by making her a man. There may be some subtle physiological basis for such views; for many who hold and advocate them are of those, who, having passed middle life without the symmetry and development that maternity gives, have drifted into the hermaphroditic condition that sometimes accompanies spinsterism.

When arrested development of the reproductive system is nearly or quite complete it produces a change in the character, and a loss of power, which it is easy to recognize, but difficult to describe . . . In these cases, which are not of frequent occurrence at present, but which may be evolved by our methods of education more numerously in the future, the system tolerates the absence of the catamenia, and the consequent nonelimination of impurities from the blood. Acute or chronic disease, the ordinary result of this condition, is not set up, but, instead, there is a change in the character and development of the brain and nervous system. There are in individuals of this class less adipose and more muscular tissue than is commonly seen, a coarser skin, and, generally, a tougher and more angular makeup. There is a corresponding change in the intellectual and psychical condition, – a dropping out of maternal instincts, and an appearance of Amazonian coarseness and force. Such persons are analogous to the sexless class of termites.*[16]

Given the emphasis that the committee's report placed on physical health, it is interesting to note, especially in relation to the previous quotations, that a primary focus of the preliminary committee meetings was the emotional rather than the physical condition of women undergraduates, specifically something called "smashing." One description of this practice can be found in an 1873 letter to the *Yale Courant:*

There is a term in general use at Vassar, truly calculated to awaken within the ima penetralia *of our souls all that love for the noble and the aesthetic of which our natures are capable. The*

*Arrested development was one of the dire consequences Clarke predicted as the result of women's education, since presumably energy was deflected from the reproductive system to the brain.

term in question is "smashing." When a Vassar girl takes a shine to another, she straightway enters upon a regular course of bouquet sendings, interspersed with tinted notes, mysterious packages of "Ridley's Mixed Candies," locks of hair perhaps, and many other tender tokens, until at last the object of her attentions is captured, the two become inseparable, and the aggressor is considered by her circle of acquaintances as – smashed. *The mortality, so to speak, resulting from these smashups, is frightful to contemplate. One young lady, the "Irrepressible," rejoices in more than thirty. She keeps a list of them, in illuminated text, framed and hung up in her room like a Society poster. How . . . such a custom should have come into vogue, passes masculine comprehension. But the solemn fact remains, and Vassar numbers her smashes by the score.*[17]

Nor was this a recent development. For example, Frances Willard and her sister Mary** commented on the prevalence of smashing among themselves and their friends at the North Western Female College in the late 1850's and early 1860's. Mary wrote:

*Holland*** says that all girls have to pass through the "girl friendship" stage. And as they all have to do so did I, and I am not ashamed to tell of it. So when I first left home to attend a boarding school, I was willing in my loneliness to have a "little friendship." So I fell in love just like a boy, and wooed and won, as a friend and a good one, a sweet tempered, sweetfaced girl.*[18]

Her short-haired sister "Frank" fell in love with a girl named Maggie, the first of a long succession of close relationships she would have with women. In her autobiography she wrote:

Of the real romance of my life, unguessed save by a trio of close friends, these pages may not tell. When I have passed from sight I would be glad to have it known, for I believe it might contribute to a better understanding between good men and women.[20]

Willard's friends, however, never revealed the nature of this romance. In her copy of the book, *The Friendships of Women,*[21] now on the shelves of the Schlesinger Library, she wrote, "Someday I wish to write a book – a novel – with the Friendships of Women as its theme." That story too was never written.

M. Carey Thomas, president of Bryn Mawr College for nearly thirty years, mutually smashed with another student during her boarding-school days at the Howland Institute in the early 1870's, thereby causing extreme annoyance and jealousy on the part of Bessie King, one of her Baltimore friends who was also attending the school.

**For information on the Willards I have relied on reference 18, especially pages 75-83.

***Josiah Gilbert Holland, writer of such popular advice books as *Titcomb's Letters to Young People, Single and Married.*[19]

"Yes, they have no bananas." Left to right: back row, Mary Wheeler ('89), Martha MacFarland ('88); front row, Maud Bailey, Lena McMaster ('88).

Mary Whitall Thomas, while cautioning her daughter to tone down the intensity of her emotions, nevertheless acknowledged their validity: "I guess thy feeling is quite natural. I used to have the same romantic love for my friends. It is a real pleasure."[22(a)] She took a much dimmer view, however, of her daughter's playing male roles, dressed in men's clothes, at school functions: "It is repugnant to my taste. I do suppose it is great fun but I think it is not nice. It would be simply disgusting if any men were present and I don't like it anyhow."[22(b)]

One of the members of the Association of Collegiate Alumnae committee was Alice Stone Blackwell, daughter of pioneer women's rights leader Lucy Stone and in her own right a prominent leader in the women's movement. A graduate of Boston University in 1881, Blackwell commented on the committee discussions in an early 1882 letter: The committee

gave it as their strong opinion that one thing which damaged the health of the girls seriously was "smashes" – an extraordinary habit which they have of falling violently in love with each other, and suffering all the pangs of unrequited attachment, desperate jealousy &c &c, with as much energy as if one of them were a man. I could hardly have believed that the things they told were not exaggerations, if Maria Mitchell hadn't told me, when I was visiting at Vassar, what a pest the "smashing" was to the teachers there – how it kept the girls from studying, & sometimes made a girl drop behind her class year after year. Miss Brown, of our committee, told us her own experience, evidently not without some embarrassment, but for the general good; how she, at Smith, though not at all given to that sort of thing, had been a victim. "A veteran smasher" attacked her, & captured her, & soon deserted her for someone else; & she used to cry herself to sleep night after night, & wake up with a headache in the morning. And they write each other the wildest love-letters, & send presents, confectionery, all sorts of things, like a real courting of the Shakesperian style. If the "smash" is mutual, they monopolize each other & "spoon" continually, & sleep together & lie awake all night talking instead of going to sleep; & if it isn't mutual the unrequited one cries herself sick & endures pangs unspeakable. I listed with undisguised curiosity & amazement, for we had very little of that sort of thing at B.U. My theory is that it comes of massing hundreds of nervous young girls together, & shutting them up from the outside world. They are just at the romantic age, they see only each other, & so their sentimentality has no other outlet. The coeducational colleges don't suffer much from "smashes." . . . There are plenty of cases of "particular friends," but few or none of "smashes."[23]

Significantly, the committee's final report, published in 1885, contained no mention of smashing, although there were general references to such conditions as "weakness of the nervous system," "emotional strain," and "worriment . . . either over studies or personal affairs." The report also noted that "only a few of the students were so situated as to be able to enter into society other than the companionship of their fellow-students."[24]

Despite her comment that she "listened with undisguised curiosity and amazement," Alice Stone Blackwell was hardly without knowledge of either homosexual or lesbian behavior. Alice herself had been smashed in 1881 by Theodora, the adopted daughter of emigrant Norwegian feminist artist Aasta Hansteen (who had served as the model for the character of Lona Hessel in Ibsen's *The Pillars of Society*). Describing a visit to Hansteen's studio, Alice remarked on the daughter's behavior:

She did not squeeze me much this time, but held my hand & kissed it occasionally, which was much less objectionable. She told me how the children she played with at home used to call her "boy face," which I take to be equivalent to tomboy; & how when she was little she begged her father for a suit of boy's clothes. . . . When I came away she stood on the steps with the sun making her fair hair bright, & watched me away up the street. They are an odd couple, she & her mother.[25(a)]

Four months later Alice was still having her difficulties with Theodora:

The poor child has taken a liking to me – one of those wild unreasonable fancies which I used to take for older girls – and she comes to Dr. Clarke's on Sunday & sits by me & walks to the station with me afterward. I am sometimes a little at a loss how to deal with her, for she is uncouth in her ways – a sort of white bear's cub. As we walked up & down the platform waiting for the train one Sunday, I tried to make conversation by saying that it was a beautiful sunshiny day. In reply to this highly original observation, she summoned up her English & answered – "You are the first sunshine in my heart." And she dreamed about me at night, & tells me her dreams in extraordinary broken English . . . The mother is a bright woman, but odd. She is an artist. Papa does not like them; I fancy he has never quite got over his suspicion that that girl is a boy.[25(b)]

It is also interesting to note that Blackwell retained her self-consciousness regarding overt manifestations of her love for women. In 1884, for example, she wrote, "I fell in love with Mrs. P. like a schoolgirl, & feel rather ashamed of it, like that man in Hypatia: I had supposed I was past that."[25(c)]

One reason that Alice Stone Blackwell might have had for not regarding behavior of this sort as perfectly innocent was her knowledge that sexual expression could play a part in such relationships. During her first semester at Boston University, in 1877, Professor Buck, her Greek instructor, had explained the concept and practice of so-called Greek love to his class – an action interpreted by some members of the Blackwell family as an attempt to corrupt the morals of the students. Alice quickly pointed out that since Greek literature was

so full of references to that particular vice, an understanding of what it was is absolutely necessary, to understand what you read. . . . As for recommending such a vice to the class, he didn't . . . but he did say that the system had its good side to it, or to that effect.[25(d)]

One of the most interesting aspects of the history of sexuality is the development of psychiatric and other prescriptive literature on homosexuality and lesbianism, beginning in 1869 with the publication of Westphal's clinical description of two cases, one male and one female, in the *Archiv für Psychologie*, a German professional journal.[26] The published *Index-Catalogue of the Library of the Surgeon-General's Office, United States Army,*[27] gives an idea of the extent to which this question was being discussed by both European and American writers.

The first sixteen-volume series of the *Index-Catalogue* appeared between 1880 and 1895. The index category most closely related to the topic under discussion in this article was "sexual instinct." Under this general heading, 17 books and nine articles were listed. Its only subheading, "sexual instinct (perversion and disorders of)," included 30 books and 106 articles, the earliest of which was published in 1740. Generally, the term "inversion" was used to describe homosexuality and lesbianism, while "perversion" included these topics as well as such exotic variations as fetishism and necrophilia.

The second series of the catalog appeared between 1896 and 1916 and included entries primarily for materials published subsequent to the first series. The change between these two series, particularly as it related to women's sexual behavior, is startling. The category "women," for instance, which in the first series was simply that, was now broken down into a remarkably detailed set of subheadings and cross-references, including "masturbation in the female," "nymphomania," "sapphism," "sexual instinct (inversion of)," and "sexual instinct (perversion of)." A volume-by-volume, term-by-term comparison of both series' entries pertaining to women's health reveals no difference in the methods of indexing. Obviously, then, the late-nineteenth-century medical world was focusing more and more attention on sexuality. Now, in addition to the general category "sexual instinct," with 28 books and 38 articles, there were no fewer than 17 subheadings. The subheading "sexual instinct (inversion of)" listed 36 books and 228 articles. The other relevant category, "sexual instinct (perversion of)," contained 26 books and 300 articles.

Despite all this interest, few cases of female homosexuality ever came to the attention of researchers. For example, in their 1883 review article in *The Journal of Nervous and Mental Disease*,[28] New York psychiatrists J. C. Shaw and G. N. Ferris observed that out of a total of 19 homosexual case histories described in both European and American literature since 1869, only two were female. Those women who did come to the attention of professionals were likely to be labeled sexual perverts or inverts, not because they engaged in any variant sexual activities, but simply because they felt emotionally attracted to women or engaged in such suspicious practices as dressing in men's clothing. For example, a translation of Krafft-Ebing's 1884 article, "Perversion of the Sexual Instinct – Report of Cases," appeared in the *Alienist and Neurologist*, one of the United States' most influential psychiatric journals, in 1888.[29] The one female case cited reported that she enjoyed dressing in men's clothing because

Legenda Board of Editors, 1891.

it was "more convenient." Krafft-Ebing presented no evidence that she engaged in any sort of sexual activity with women, simply stating that "her friendship and self-sacrifices towards those she loved were boundless." The subject also disliked the idea of establishing relationships with men and "was carrying on a purely Platonic love affair with a young woman and wrote her tender love-letters." Is this really homosexual behavior? Or is it a pejorative labeling directed more at evidence of a woman's autonomy than at her sexual activity?

Perhaps the culmination of this tendency to define women's love relationships as perversions, regardless of the sexual activity involved, was in Havelock Ellis's 1897 book *Sexual Inversion.* Ellis's definition and descriptions are worth more than passing notice, particularly when they are placed in the context of both nineteenth-century feminism and the specific examples of behavior in this article. Ellis used the words "homosexuality" and "lesbianism" interchangeably to describe women's love relationships that did not necessarily include either physical involvement or actual genital contact. According to Ellis, women who loved women were abnormal, and they should more appropriately feel the pangs of guilt than the joy of innocence in contemplating their condition. Writing about his Case 29, for example, Ellis first let her talk about her own feelings:

"Love is with me a religion. The very nature of my affection for my friends precludes the possibility of any element entering into it which is not absolutely pure and sacred."

Ellis then commented:

Miss M. can see nothing wrong in her feelings; and, until a year ago, [when] she came across the translation of Krafft-Ebing's book, she had no idea "that feelings like mine" were "under the ban of society" as he puts it, or were considered unnatural and depraved. She is reticent regarding the details of her relationships, but it is evident that specific physical gratification plays no part in them.[30(a)]

Intense friendships among schoolgirls, or between them and their teachers, were particularly suspect: "conventional propriety recognizes a considerable degree of physical intimacy between girls, thus at once encouraging and cloaking the manifestations of homosexuality."[30(b)] What a contrast there is between this view and that of Frances Willard's favorite, W. R. Alger, who only 30 years before had written the following romantic lines on the same subject:

Keener agonies, more delicious passages, are nowhere else known than in the bosoms of innocent schoolgirls, in the lacerations or fruitions of their first consciously given affections. . . . Prob-

ably no chapter of sentiment in modern fashionable life is so intense and rich as that which covers the experience of budding maidens at school. In their mental caresses, spiritual nuptials, their thoughts kiss each other, and more than all the blessedness the world will ever give them is foreshadowed.[31]

For Ellis, however, the most suspect women of all were feminists:

It has been stated by many observers who are able to speak with some authority – in America, in France, in Germany, in England – that homosexuality is increasing among women. It seems probable that this is true. . . . The modern movement of emancipation . . . must be regarded as, on the whole, a wholesome and inevitable movement. But it carries with it certain disadvantages. . . . Marriage is decaying, and while men are allowed freedom, the sexual field of women is becoming restricted to trivial flirtation with the opposite sex, and to intimacy with their own sex; having been taught independence of men and disdain for the old theory which placed women in the moated grange of the home to sigh for a man who never comes, a tendency develops for women to carry this independence still further and to find love where they find work. I do not say that these unquestionable influences of modern movements can directly cause sexual inversion, though they may indirectly, in so far as they promote hereditary neurosis; but they develop the germs of it. and they probably cause a spurious imitation. This spurious imitation is due to the fact that the congenital anomaly occurs with special frequency in women of high intelligence who, voluntarily or involuntarily, influence others.[32]

In other words, lesbianism is a highly contagious disease to which feminists and other independent, autonomous women are particularly susceptible! In light of this, it should hardly seem remarkable that Henry James' classic novel about the feminist movement, *The Bostonians*, which was first published in book form in 1886,[33] was omitted from the twenty-six volume Scribner edition of his works published between 1907 and 1917.[34] This work was not reissued in the United States until 1945, when Philip Rahv in his preface described as its most disquieting feature its keen analysis of "the emotional economy of the Lesbian woman."[35] And yet nowhere in the novel can one find evidence of any variant sexual behavior whatsoever. Rahv's conclusion is drawn from the equation of autonomy and emotional commitment between women with actual lesbian sexual activity. The point is not whether these women really were lesbians; it is rather that they are called lesbians on the basis of their autonomous emotional behavior and not on the basis of their sexual behavior.

In the late nineteenth century a very definite change was occurring in definitions of normal patterns of women's relationships. There was a great deal of pressure against the intense, emotional, sensual, even sexual commitment between women that had existed without censure during the earlier part of the century, and we can reasonably expect that many women adjusted their behavior to conform to the new standards. Those who refused to conform, for whatever reason, were risking the disapproval, condemnation, and persecution of both society and their own potentially divided selves.

The question now is why. Why, during the first two-thirds of the nineteenth century, were relationships between women allowed to exist with the intensity that we have seen? Why was this a viable option? Why did this begin to change in the late nineteenth century, at a time when there was an active feminist movement, development of higher education for women, and a scientific-medical interest in the question of homoemotional and homosexual behavior?

One characteristic of the first generation of feminists, such as Susan B. Anthony and Anna E. Dickinson, was their intense religiosity – their internalization of Christian principles through either childhood training or later evangelical conversion. Whether one chooses to call it inner light, Garrisonian radical Christianity, or romantic evangelicalism, its essential features were the same:

emphasis upon the intuitive perception of truth through the feelings or emotions of the heart, emphasis upon a Christocentric theology in which "the personality of Jesus" became more important than the moral order of God, and upon a concomitant sentimental idealization of women, children, and parenthood as the most perfect embodiments if not the most efficient means of grace.[36]*

According to these principles, social relations should be based on love, not force. Therefore, restrictions – be they custom or "legally" enacted statutes – against love, in whatever form, were contrary to the spirit of Christ's example. As defined by the Bible, particularly the Gospel of St. John, the highest form of love was that of friend for friend. Hymns such as "I've Found a Friend, Oh, Such a Friend" and "Safe in the Arms of Jesus" reinforced this link between earthly relationships and the spiritually divine. Certainly it could be argued that if Jesus were the ultimate friend, then behavior acceptable in his presence should also be acceptable with one's earthly friends. Speculate on the implications of such hymn phrases as

Safe in the arms of Jesus, Safe on His gentle breast
There by His love O'ershaded, Sweetly my soul shall rest
Here let me wait in patience, Wait till the night is o'er
Wait till I see the morning Break on the golden shore.[38(a)]

*See also reference 37.

Or, "There are depths of love that I cannot know Till I cross the narrow sea, There are heights of joy that I may not reach Till I rest in peace with Thee."[38(b)] It is not insignificant that these lines were written by a woman, Fanny J. Crosby. Nor is it insignificant that Havelock Ellis's Case 29 described her feelings for other women in these terms: "'Love is with me a religion. The very nature of my affection for my friends precludes the possibility of any element entering into it which is not absolutely pure and sacred'."[39] By defining their love for other women as a spiritual force, women were, in many cases, able to sublimate any sexual feelings they may have had and make the intensity of their relationships acceptable to society.

In a sense, the feminist movement itself subverted the heightened emotional commitment which had typified women's relationships during most of the nineteenth century. As women began to be perceived by themselves and others as being capable of rational, intellectual thought, it seems evident that they would want to use this ability, rather than their emotions, to make decisions advancing their position *vis à vis* the male world, and, in their search for equality with men, that they would perceive this capacity as being on a higher status scale than that of the emotions. For example, in 1888, at an Association of Collegiate Alumnae meeting in Boston, Sarah L. Miner argued that among the qualities a woman gained by college training were

> *the ability to be controlled by correct judgment and sense of right instead of by impulse, the ability to plan for herself, a knowledge of relative values, a knowledge of the difference between means and ends, thoroughness, system, concentration, and power of reflection.*[39]

Another alumna commented that the college woman "learns to subordinate personal prejudice to impartial logic."[40]

This downplaying of emotion by the first generation of college women was observed by Jane Addams, herself a member of this group, who noted that they had

> *departed too suddenly from the active, emotional life led by their grandmothers and great-grandmothers. . . . somewhere in the process of "being educated" they had lost that simple and almost automatic response to the human appeal, that old healthful reaction resulting in activity from the mere presence of suffering or of helplessness.*[41(a)]

Likewise, Gail Parker says that Carrie Chapman Catt, one of the second generation of suffrage leaders, "never really believed in the inner light or the potential sublimity of women's souls."[41(b)]

At the same time, members of the growing professional scientific, medical, psychiatric, and social scientific communities assumed the roles of definers and arbiters of acceptable and desirable – i.e., normal – behavior. Female friendships now began to be seen not only as purely spiritual unions but as sexual ones as well, even if only on an unconscious level.

What constitutes normal behavior? Psychiatric historian Erwin Ackerknecht observed nearly twenty years ago that

what is psychologically normal depends to a high degree on the attitudes of different societies. . . . The criterion by which a person in any society is judged to be mentally ill is not primarily the presence of certain unvarying and universally occurring symptoms. It depends rather on whether the affected individual is capable of some minimum of adaptation and social functioning within his society, or whether the psychological change has progressed to such an extent that he has become a foreign body in his society.[42]

As long as women loved each other as they did for much of the nineteenth century, without threatening the system itself, their relationships either were simply ignored by men or were regarded as an acceptable part of the female sphere. Feminists, college graduates, and other independent women, however, were a real threat to the established order, and one way to control these sexless termites, hermaphroditic spinsters, or whatever one might call them, was to condemn their love relationships – the one aspect of their behavior which, regardless of their other social, political, or economic activities, posed a basic threat to a system where the fundamental expression of power was that of one sex over another.

Acknowledgments

My thanks for their comments, criticisms, suggestions about sources, and supportive good feelings to Blanche W. Cook, Carroll Smith-Rosenberg, Pat Haines, Bill Leach, and Wilma Slaight; and my appreciation to the many people who offered encouragement after hearing earlier versions of this paper at the Third Berkshire Conference on the History of Women, June 11, 1976, and the 1977 winter meeting of the Chesapeake Area Group of Women Historians.

References

1. Susan Brownmiller, *Against Our Will: Men, Women and Rape* (New York: Simon and Schuster, 1975).

2. Adrienne Rich, *Of Woman Born: Motherhood as Experience and Institution* (New York: W. W. Norton and Company, 1976).

3. Caroll Smith-Rosenberg, "The Female World of Love and Ritual: Relations Between Women in Nineteenth-Century America," *Signs* 1, No. 1 (Autumn 1975), pp. 1-30.

4. Blanche Wiesen Cook, "Female Support Networks and Political Activism: Lillian Wald, Crystal Eastman, Emma Goldman," *Chrysalis*, No. 3 (1977), p. 48.

5. Louise Brackett to Anna E. Dickinson, (a) June 15, 1863, and (b) March 8, 1865, Anna E. Dickinson Papers, Manuscript Division, Library of Congress.

6. Laura Curtis Bullard to Anna E. Dickinson, (a) April 2, (b) June 6, and (c) June 8, 1872, Anna E. Dickinson Papers, Manuscript Division, Library of Congress.

7. Susan B. Anthony to Anna E. Dickinson, (a) October 23, 1866, (b) March 18, 1868, (c) November 11, 1869, and (d) November 5, 1895, Anna E. Dickinson Papers, Manuscript Division, Library of Congress.

8. Giraud Chester, *Embattled Maiden: The Life of Anna Dickinson* (New York: Putnam, 1951), p. 217.

9. Handwritten transcription of "The Rose of Wellesley," from the *Harvard Lampoon*, 1879, Class of 1879 Papers, Wellesley College Archives.

10. Wellesley College, Regulations, 1876 and 1890, and "Legislation of Wellesley College," 1875-1888, Wellesley College Archives.

11. "Statutes of Wellesley College," in *Acts of Incorporation, Deeds of Gift, and Statutes of Wellesley College* (Boston: Frank Wood, 1885).

12. Erving Goffman, *Asylums* (New York: Doubleday-Anchor, 1961).

13. Frances Robinson Johnson to her mother, (a) June 11 and (b) June 14, 1876, Frances Robinson Johnson Papers, Wellesley College Archives.

14. Marion Talbot and Lois Kimball Mathews Rosenberry, *The History of the American Association of University Women, 1881-1931* (Boston: Houghton Mifflin, 1931), pp. 16, 115-117.

15. *Health Statistics of Women College Graduates*, Report of a Special Committee of the Association of Collegiate Alumnae, Annie G. Hawes, Chairman (Boston: Wright and Potter, 1885).

16. Edward H. Clarke, *Sex in Education; or, A Fair Chance for Girls* (Boston: James R. Osgood and Company, 1873), pp. 14, 92-93.

17. Letter to the *Yale Courant*, reprinted in *The Cornell Times*, March 15, 1873.*

18. Mary Earhart Dillon, *Frances Willard: From Prayers to Politics* (Chicago: University of Chicago Press, 1944)

19. Josiah Gilbert Holland, *Titcomb's Letters to Young People, Single and Married* (New York: C. Scribner, 1858).

20. Frances E. Willard, *Glimpses of Fifty Years, the Autobiography of an American Woman* (Chicago: Woman's Temperance Publishing Association, 1889).

21. William Rounseville Alger, *The Friendships of Women* (Boston: Roberts Brothers, 1868).

22. Edith Finch, *Carey Thomas of Bryn Mawr* (New York: Harper & Brothers, 1947), (a) p. 47 and (b) pp. 48-49.

23. Alice Stone Blackwell to Kitty Barry Blackwell, March 12, 1882, Blackwell Family Papers, Manuscript Division, Library of Congress.

24. *Health Statistics, passim.*

25. Alice Stone Blackwell to Kitty Barry Blackwell, (a) October 10, 1880, (b) February 20, 1881, (c) November 30, 1884, and (d) December 24, 25, and 31, 1877, and January 1, 1878, Blackwell Family Papers, Manuscript Division, Library of Congress.

26. "Die conträre Sexualempfindung, *Archiv für Psychologie*, Band II, Heft I, S. (1869), pp. 73-108. (Abstract in reference 25, pp. 187-189.)

27. *Index-Catalogue of the Library of the Surgeon-General's Office, United States Army*, 1st Series (Washington: Government Printing Office, 1880-1895) and 2nd Series (Washington: Government Printing Office, 1896-1916).

28. J. C. Shaw and G. N. Ferris, "Perverted Sexual Instinct," *The Journal of Nervous and Mental Disease* 10, No. 2 (April 1883).

29. Richard von Krafft-Ebing, "Perversion of the Sexual Instinct – Report of Cases," translated by A. M. Jewett, *Alienist and Neurologist* 9 (1888), pp. 565-581.

30. Havelock Ellis, *Sexual Inversion* (New York: Arno Press, 1975; reprint of the 1897 edition), (a) p. 89 and (b) pp. 84-85.

31. Alger, *op. cit.*, pp. 269-271.

32. Ellis, *op. cit.*, pp. 99-100.

33. Henry James, *The Bostonians* (London and New York: Macmillan and Co., 1886).

34. Henry James, *The Novels and Tales of Henry James*, 26 vols. (New York: C. Scribner's Sons, 1907-1917).

35. Cited in Jeannette Foster, *Sex Variant Women in Literature* (Baltimore: Diana Press, 1975; reprint of 1956 edition), pp. 95-96.

36. William G. McLoughlin, ed., *The American Evangelicals 1800-1900, An Anthology* (New York: Harper & Row, 1968), p. 14.

37. Aileen Kraditor, *Means and Ends in American Abolitionism* (New York: Random House, 1969), p. 83.

38. Fanny J. Crosby, (a) "Safe in the Arms of Jesus" and (b) "I Am Thine, O Lord," reprinted in *The Mission Hymnal* (Chicago: Biglow & Main, 1913), Nos. 41 and 13.

39. Ellis, *op. cit.*, p. 89.

40. Secretary's Report, April 28, 1888, Papers of the Association of Collegiate Alumnae, in American Association of University Women, Boston Branch Papers, Schlesinger Library, Radcliffe College.

41. Gail Parker, ed., *The Oven Birds* (Garden City, N.Y.: Doubleday, 1972), (a) p. 48 and (b) p. 12.

42. Erwin H. Ackerknecht, *A Short History of Psychiatry* (New York and London: Hafner Publishing Company, 1959), pp. 2-3.

*I am grateful to Patricia Foster Haines for providing me with this reference.

Nancy Sahli is on the staff of the National Historical Publications and Records Commission in Washington. She is currently working on a bibliography on women and sexuality in America, to be published by G.K. Hall.

THE MORBIDIFICATION OF LOVE BETWEEN WOMEN BY 19TH-CENTURY SEXOLOGISTS

Lillian Faderman, PhD

ABSTRACT: Twentieth-century attitudes toward love between women are very different from those of previous centuries. Fiction and personal correspondence that antedate the work of Krafft-Ebing and Havelock Ellis in the late 19th century indicate that a much broader spectrum of expression of love and affection between women had been acceptable than that to which we have become accustomed. Medical science and psychology for the past 100 years have morbidified intense love relationships between women by inventing a syndrome of ills that supposedly accompany such affection, and by denying the validity or seriousness of the affection where such ills are clearly not present. The result has been that (until the lesbian-feminist movement) 20th-century women were largely forced to deny their love for other women unless they were willing to acknowledge their concomitant morbidity.

Studies such as those by Carroll Smith-Rosenberg (1975) and by William Taylor and Christopher Lasch (1963) of early and mid-19th-century correspondence between women indicate that intense female same-sex emotional relationships were casually accepted at that time. Such relationships were considered within the bounds of legitimate, "normal" behavior according to these studies; they lead the reader to conclude that before the last decades of the 19th century there was virtually no stigma of morbidity or deviance attached to love between women. Much of the fiction that was written during the 19th century and earlier confirms Smith-Rosenberg's and Taylor and Lasch's findings. In Charles Brockden Brown's (1799–1937) *Ormond,* for example, the female narrator, who has just been reunited with a beloved woman friend, exclaims:

> *The appetite for sleep and for food were confounded and lost amidst the impetuousities of a master passion. To look and to talk to each other afforded enchanting occupation for every moment. I would not part from her side, but ate and slept, walked and mused and read, with my arm locked in hers, and with her breath fanning my cheek. . . . O precious inebriation of the heart! O pre-eminent love! what pleasure of reason or of sense can stand in competition with those attendant upon thee?*

Dr. Faderman is in the Department of English, California State University, Fresno, California 93721.

Journal of Homosexuality, Vol. 4(1), Fall 1978

At the conclusion of the novel, the two women vow to spend their lives together (that one has a husband is treated as being largely inconsequential), and here the narrator observes:

> *Henceforth, the stream of our existence was to mix; we were to act and to think in common. . . . Eyes and ears were to be eternally employed upon the conduct of each other: death, when it should come, was not to be deplored, because it was an unavoidable and brief privation to her that should survive.*

The two do not doubt that they will be forever united in "that state to which death is a passage."

Such intense love relationships between women were depicted in numerous novels of the subsequent century. In Louisa May Alcott's (1884) *Work: A Story of Experience* the female heroine, Christie, tells Rachel, "I must love somebody, and 'love them hard' as children say; so why can't you come and stay with me?" Christie's devotion to Rachel gives her life

> *the zest which it had lacked before. Now someone cared for [Christie], and, better still, she could make someone happy. . . . There was nothing in her possession that she did not offer Rachel, from the whole of her heart to the larger half of her little room. . . . [With Rachel, Christie] found happiness in the work that gave her better food than mere daily bread, and never thought of change; for love can make a home for itself anywhere.*

Although these fictional relationships are generally not specifically sexual, it must be remembered that neither are heterosexual relationships in novels of this period specifically sexual. But several novels do depict a sensual element (which is sometimes quite direct and sometimes rather coy) in the love between the female characters. For example, in Henry Wadsworth Longfellow's (1849/1965) novel *Kavanagh* Cecilia tells her woman friend, Alice, that she will send a carrier pigeon to Alice's bedroom to act as "a Iachimo in my Imogen's bed-chamber, to spy out its secrets. . . . He will see the book with the leaf turned down, and you asleep, and tell me all about you." In *A Mortal Antipathy* Oliver Wendell Holmes (1892) creates two female characters, Lurida and Euthymia, who have carried on a romantic friendship all through their school days and after graduation. At one point Lurida, who dabbles in art, tells her friend: "'It is a shame that you will not let your exquisitely molded form be portrayed in marble. . . .' She was startled to see what an effect her proposal had produced, for Euthymia was not only blushing but there was a flame in her eyes which she had hardly ever seen before." The women in these romantic novels are incapable of sinful behavior, and they are no more tainted or morbid than they are evil or corrupt.

That such relationships were not deemed improper is, as I have suggested elsewhere (Faderman, in press), evidenced by the fact that whereas men were persecuted for homosexual behavior throughout almost all of the Western world, women were generally ignored by the law.[1]

As late as 1896, Dr. Allan Hamilton, writing in the *American Journal of Insanity*, observed that "until within a comparatively recent period the mere insinuation that there could be anything improper in the intimate relations of two women would have drawn upon the head of the maker of such a suggestion a degree of censure of the most pronounced and enduring character." Hamilton went on to describe a "case" of lesbianism that had come to his attention a few years earlier and stated that "at that time her mental perversion was not of a recognized kind." Thus it is probable that the mid-19th-century reader would have been no more shocked in reading of Alice and Cecilia in *Kavanagh* (Longfellow, 1849/1965), that "in a word, they were in love with each other," than would the families of Sarah Butler Wister and Jeannie Field Musgrove had they read the letters that passed between these women in the 1860s:

> [Jeannie to Sarah] *Dear darling Sarah! How I love you and how happy I have been! You are the joy of my life. . . . I cannot tell you how much happiness you gave me, nor how constantly it is all in my thoughts. . . . My darling, how I long for the time when I shall see you. . . . I want you to tell me in your next letter, to assure me, that I am your dearest. . . . I do not doubt you, and I am not jealous but I long to hear you say it once more and it seems already a long time since your voice fell on my ear. So just fill a quarter page with caresses and expressions of endearment. . . . Goodbye my dearest, dearest lover—ever your Angelina.*
>
> [Sarah to Jeannie] *If the day should come when you failed me either through your fault or my own, I would forswear all human friendship, thenceforth. . . . I shall be entirely alone [this coming week]. I can give you no idea how desperately I shall want you.* (Smith-Rosenberg, 1975, pp. 4–5)

---

[1]*In America the only colonial law that seems to mention sexual relations between women was that passed in 1655 in the New Haven Colony; and even that law, based as it was on the ambiguous biblical injunction, is unclear and may be a reference to a woman practicing fellatio or permitting a man to perform anal intercourse on her: "If any woman change the natural use into that which is against nature, as Rom. I. 26. she shall be liable to . . . punishment." Throughout the 18th and most of the 19th century the law did not acknowledge lesbian relationships. There is some evidence that women in Europe who disguised as men were persecuted and even executed—for example, Catherina Margaretha Lincken in Germany in 1721 (Müller, 1891) and a woman in 16th-century France, described in Montaigne's (1889)* Journal du voyage en Italie en 1850 *(cited in Ellis 1897/1901, pp. 118–119). But these women seem to have been condemned not for loving other women but specifically for dressing in male attire and "using illicit inventions [i.e., dildos] to supply the defects of [their] sex" (Montaigne, 1889, p. 11).*

It is my contention that most 20th-century readers would greet these statements with a very different attitude, not simply because we know more about human sexual behavior in this century but primarily because medical science and psychology for the past 100 years have morbidified intense love relationships between women by inventing a syndrome of ills (which has changed from era to era) that supposedly accompany such affection, and by denying the validity or seriousness of the affection where such ills are clearly not present. My focus in this paper is on the work of Havelock Ellis and that of the predecessor by whom he was the most influenced, Richard von Krafft-Ebing. Both men believed that "true inversion," as Ellis (1897/1901, p. 133) called it, is congenital, that "antipathetic sexual instinct as an anomaly of sexual life (i.e., homosexuality) is only found in individuals who are tainted, as a rule, hereditarily" (Krafft-Ebing, 1882/1925, pp. 444–445).

CONGENITAL LESBIANISM

Although the theory of congenital lesbianism has been less widely accepted by psychiatrists and psychologists in the 20th century than those theories of Freud and his disciples who believed that homosexuality is "caused" by environmental factors,[2] nevertheless, Radclyffe Hall's (1928) *The Well of Loneliness*, with its preface by Havelock Ellis and its view of Stephen Gordon, the heroine, as a congenital invert, remains the one lesbian novel known to a wide public. Also, the congenital theory has of late been adopted by many gay militants because they believe (speciously) that it is politically expedient: that is, if homosexuality is an inherited condition, it can in no way be considered immoral; if people are born homosexual, then those not so born cannot "catch" homosexuality; therefore, there is no reason to make laws limiting the rights of homosexuals to teach, serve in the armed forces, and so forth. Significantly, the congenital theory has recently (1975) been used by Sergeant Leonard Matlovich's lawyers to argue that since his homosexuality is inherent it cannot be termed a vice and it cannot be spread to nonhomosexuals; therefore, it constitutes no cause for dismissing him from the air force. It would seem, then, that the congenital theory is far from dead, and we may expect it to be even further revived with the popularization of sociobiology.[3]

---

[2]*In "The Psychogenesis of a Case of Female Homosexuality" Freud (1920) explained that his patient had no congenital taint but suffered from penis envy as a result of rivalry with her brother. This caused her to change "into a man" in her thinking, and she "took her mother in place of her father as her love object"; therefore, she became a lesbian.*

[3]*See* Time, *August 1, 1977. John Addington Symonds (1896/1971) presented a much sounder argument in favor of social acceptance of homosexuality. Victorians by the late*

In the late 19th and early 20th centuries both Krafft-Ebing and Ellis pleaded, supported by their position that homosexuality was congenital, for the reform of antihomosexual laws (primarily for males, since lesbians were generally ignored by the law). But together with their sympathetic support for the rights of homosexuals, they invariably cast homosexual relationships in a morbid and violent light. Congenital homosexuality thus became inextricably linked with morbidity in popular perception. Ellis (1897/1901), for example, began his discussion of female homosexuals in the 19th century (in the chapter "Sexual Inversion in Women") with the story of Alice Mitchell, whom he called a "typical invert," who "cut [her lover's] throat." This he followed by two other cases of lesbian murder and attempted murder. Next he stated, "Homosexual relationships are also a cause of suicide among women" (p. 120)—with the apparent implication that heterosexual relationships are not. Although Ellis suggested throughout his study that many talented and gifted people have been homosexual and that (ostensibly disagreeing with Krafft-Ebing) homosexuality is not necessarily linked with morbidity, his emphases in all his case histories of women lead the reader to precisely the opposite conclusion.

The first 19th-century scientist to treat female homosexuality in any detail was Karl Westphal, who in 1870 reported in the *Archiv für Psychiatrie* a case of a woman who dressed in men's clothes and was amorously involved with women, and whom he identified as a congenital invert. Krafft-Ebing then expanded on Westphal's study and pointed out that lesbianism was due to "cerebral anomalies," that it was the sign of "an inherited diseased condition of the central nervous system" and a "functional sign of degeneration." This inherited condition he consistently referred to as "taint."[4] Although later writers such as Iwan Bloch,

---

19th century were becoming extremely concerned with the facts of the Malthusian theory: Food increased arithmetically; population increased geometrically. If the population continued to grow unchecked at the same rate the Victorians had witnessed, it would be only a matter of time before the food supply ran out. With reference to this alarming problem, Symonds suggested a powerful argument in defense of homosexuality: "In the present state of over-population, it is not to be apprehended that a small minority of men exercising sterile and abnormal sexual inclinations should seriously injure society by limiting the increase of the human race." Or, to put the point in terms that we have learned from 20th-century history, is it better for a society to check overpopulation through forced sterilization and wars waged for the real or imagined need for more Lebensraum *or through ceasing to discourage what is initially a natural human sexual inclination, through ceasing to attempt to socialize all its members into heterosexuality? If homosexuals today need any defensive argument in favor of homosexuality, Desmond Morris (1967) has presented a very good one. Homosexuals, he says, "provided they are well-adjusted and valuable members of the society outside the reproductive sphere... must now be considered as valuable non-contributers to the population explosion" (p. 101).*

[4]A year before his death, Krafft-Ebing (1901) wrote "Neue Studien auf dem Gebiete der

Magnus Hirschfeld, and John Addington Symonds agreed that homosexuality was congenital, they rejected Krafft-Ebing's views that the condition was also pathological. However, Havelock Ellis (and other writers such as Paul Moreaux, B. Tarnowsky, and Cesare Lombroso) largely accepted those views, as I have suggested and will further demonstrate, and it was Ellis' book on sexual inversion that remained for years one of the most influential treatises on homosexuality in English.[5] Hence, it was primarily through the work of Krafft-Ebing and Ellis that the stereotypes of lesbian morbidity were handed down from the late 19th century to the 20th century.

Krafft-Ebing and Ellis specifically distinguished between female homosexual behavior and female homosexuality. The former they saw as being common in particular situations. The latter they invested with a host of morbid symptoms which they deemed "typical" of the "true invert." Krafft-Ebing (1882/1925) recognized that it was not unusual for prepubescent children to engage in homosexual acts which, he believed, sprang from "hypersexuality, precocity, or some external influences" (p. 446). However, he insisted, such acts do not lead to inverted sexuality unless the individual has been born an invert. Krafft-Ebing also recognized a *faut de mieux* homosexuality—that is, the indulgence in homosexual acts in situations in which members of the opposite sex are not available, such as boarding schools, prisons, and garrisons. But in such

---

Homosexualität." In this article Krafft-Ebing reversed his lifelong stress on homosexual "degeneracy" and "taint" and conceded that although many deviants had mental disorders and were neuropathic, homosexuality was not a disease but rather a congenital anomaly that was not necessarily incompatible with mental health. But Psychopathia Sexualis *is, of course, a far better known work than this article. It is probably safe to guess that many readers who are familiar with his book and the theories promulgated there have no knowledge of the subsequent essay, and its impact on popular notions regarding homosexuals has been minimal.*

[5]*John Addington Symonds, the author of* A Problem in Modern Ethics, *collaborated with Ellis on* Sexual Inversion *but died before the work was published, and his family demanded that his name as coauthor be removed from the text. There are significant differences in the two works regarding the view of homosexuality as pathologically based. Symonds (1896/1971) argued in* A Problem in Modern Ethics *that ancient Greece, where homosexuality was a cultural custom and was even institutionalized, "offers insuperable difficulties to the theorists who treat sexual inversion exclusively from the point of view of neuropathy, tainted heredity, and masturbation" (pp. 36–37). He specifically criticized Krafft-Ebing, suggesting that at that moment in Europe there was probably not a single person who had inherited no neuropathic stain whatsoever. If that be true, Symonds argued, everybody is liable to sexual inversion, and so the principle of heredity becomes purely theoretical (pp. 48–49). Symonds did believe, however, that the true homosexual was a person born with sexual instincts improperly correlated to his/her sexual organs, and that no inherited or latent morbidity is (necessarily) involved. He granted that many homosexuals evince "nervous anomalies," but these, he said, are "not evidence of an originally tainted constitution, but the consequence of the unnatural conditions to which [they have] been exposed from the age of puberty" (p. 74).*

cases, he contended, there is an immediate return to normal sexual intercourse as soon as the obstacles to it are removed. In this way Krafft-Ebing (1882/1925) emphasized the distinction between "perversity" and "perversion" and concluded that "no case has yet been demonstrated in which perversity has been transformed into perversion—i.e., into an inversion of the sexual instinct" (p. 288). He further insisted that although an "untainted" female may be raised exactly like a male, she will not become homosexual, but rather "*the natural disposition is the determining condition; not education and other accidental circumstances, like seduction*" (italics are Krafft-Ebing's, 1882/1925, pp. 288n–289).[6] A homosexual, then, according to Krafft-Ebing, is, as a rule, not one who engages in homosexual behavior but rather one who is born in an inverted state.

Engaging in homosexual behavior by itself, Havelock Ellis (1897/1901) agreed, has no necessary relationship to true sexual inversion. Girl children may act out the "precocious play of the normal instinct" by mutual sexual touching and kissing; certain employments, such as hotel service, in which the women workers are kept in constant association with each other, day and night, and lace making, in which the women are confined for long hours in close contact to one another in heated rooms, may lead to "homosexual practices." But these practices constitute "a spurious kind of homosexuality" (pp. 127–127). Ellis argued that as soon as such females are given the opportunity to have relationships with men, the "normal instincts" will be brought "into permanent play" (p. 132).

Ellis, like his predecessor, largely ignored the role of social pressure in establishing this "normal instinct," although he occasionally hinted, without bringing the point to its obvious conclusion, that socialization and peer pressure or support might have something to do with what sexual feelings the 19th-century woman ultimately accepted as being appropriate for herself. With regard to the subsequent marriage of women who had regularly fallen in love with their female classmates when they had been students, Ellis observed that once they participated in "practical life" they learned to understand "the real nature of such feelings" and they developed a "subsequent distaste for them" (p. 132): Presumably, the women learned from the outside world that loving another female was considered perversion ("the real nature of such feelings") and thus realized that they must repress those emotions.

Ellis also understood, more or less, that the women's movement (which

---

[6]*Krafft-Ebing later in this work recognized, in apparent contradiction, the existence of "lasting acquired antipathetic sexual instinct." One may, he said, permanently acquire this abnormality through* faut de mieux *homosexuality: Where "no restoration occurs, the deep and lasting transformations of the physical personality may occur. . . . In this condition of deep and more lasting psycho-sexual transformation, the individual is like unto the (congenital) urning [homosexual] of high grade. The possibility of a restoration of the previous mental and sexual personality seems in such a case, precluded" (p. 297).*

toward the end of the century was experiencing considerable growth in America, France, Germany, and England) fostered love between women (pp. 147–148). (Ellis claimed here to support women's rights, but as with his support of homosexual rights, he was ambivalent at best. The women's movement, he said, has "involved an increase in feminine criminality and in feminine insanity. . . . In connection with these we can scarcely be surprised to find an increase in homosexuality, which has always been regarded as belonging to an allied, if not the same, group of phenomena.") The movement taught women to be independent of men and to disdain "the old theory which placed women in the moated grange of the home to sigh for a man who never comes," Ellis pointed out. But a corollary of such independence was homosexual behavior: Since women were still restricted in employment opportunities, and working women did not come in frequent contact with men but were segregated with other women, many working feminists, he observed, "find love where they find work." However, Ellis was quick to state in this regard that a woman who has been led to homosexuality through feminism is very likely not a real lesbian, but again only "a spurious imitation," unless she was born with the "germs" of inversion. In such a case, the women's movement might "promote hereditary neurosis."

How, according to Ellis, might one distinguish between the "spurious imitation" of the lesbian and the "true invert"? His case histories established the criteria: One common phenomenon which, he suggested, appears with almost uniform consistency in true inverts is the tendency of these women to have had girlhood crushes on other females. A second phenomenon, which *is* consistent in all his case histories, is congenital taint:

Case XXIX, Miss S.: *She belongs to a family in which there is a marked neuropathic element.*
Case XL, Miss M.: *There is a neurotic element in the family.*
Case XLI, Miss B.: *Among her brothers and sisters, one is of neurotic temperament and another is inverted.*
Case XLII, Miss H.: *Among her maternal relatives there is a tendency to eccentricity and to nervous disease.*

In insisting on the prevalence of congenital taint among homosexuals, Ellis seems to have ignored the common sense of his supposed collaborator, John Addington Symonds, who pointed out that at that moment in Europe there was probably not a single person who had inherited no neuropathic stain whatsoever (see Note 5 above). Ellis also seems to have ignored his own observation that "normal" girl children frequently indulged in same-sex crushes and erotic play.

A third phenomenon which, according to Ellis, distinguished "the actively inverted woman" from females who have schoolgirl crushes and *faut de mieux* lesbians is "a more or less distinct trace of masculinity" (pp. 133, 140). But, despite this assertion, where Ellis described the physical appearance of the subjects of his case histories, he often admitted that "the general conformation of the body is feminine" or that "her person and manners, though careless, are not conspicuously man-like" (pp. 136, 137). The seeming discrepancy is explained with the statement that such masculinity "may, in the least degree, consist only in the fact that she makes advances to the women to whom she is attracted" (p. 134). He did not deal with the corollary that at least one of the two partners in every homoerotic relationship between "schoolgirls" and between "lace makers" was by this reasoning a true invert.

Although most of his own case histories pointed in another direction, Ellis also repeatedly tried to associate lesbianism with transvestism, from the very beginning of his chapter "Sexual Inversion in Women," when he referred to 16th-and 17th-century women who were executed for dressing in male attire and using dildos. This association is emphasized by his report on the Countess Sarolta V. (which constitutes appendix E of his book), based on a medicolegal account published a few years earlier in Friedreich's *Blätter für Gerichtliche Medicin.* The totally bizarre case of Countess Sarolta is briefly referred to in the "Sexual Inversion in Women" chapter as being *"in most respects so typical"* (p. 140n, emphasis added) of true lesbians. Sarolta came from a family that had always been remarkable for eccentricity. One aunt was hysterical and somnambulistic; another aunt "lay in bed for seven years on account of an imaginary fatal illness," but at the same time gave balls; a third aunt believed that the console in her drawing room was bewitched; and a fourth aunt would not allow her room to be cleaned and would not wash or comb herself for 2 years. Her mother was "nervous and could not bear the moonshine." Her father's family "were generally regarded as rather crack-brained."

Sarolta's father educated her as a boy and his two sons as girls. The sons were dressed in women's clothing until they were 15. The father traveled extensively with Sarolta, insisting usually that she dress as a man. In 1888, at the age of 22 (Ellis observed that until that point her affairs had been typically brief—in conformity with the stereotype he wished to establish—with the exception of one previous relationship that had lasted for *3 years!*) she met a woman who believed her to be a man. The following year they were married. Sarolta deceived her bride's family by stuffing handkerchiefs or gloves into her trouser pocket to produce the appearance of sexual organs and by urinating in a standing position. When she was arrested, because of some financial difficulty with her father-in-law, one of her greatest concerns was having to give up her masculine garments in jail.

Ellis emphasized that Sarolta "recognized the morbidity of her sexual inclinations," that is, her love for other women. And he concluded by reiterating the expert opinion on her case that her "incriminated actions" were "due to her marked and irresistible sexual impulse." Through this incredible case, which he specifically called "typical," Ellis established the mystique of the "true lesbian"—a mystique that was subsequently accepted by many lesbians themselves who became transvestites and "butches" because such behavior demonstrated ipso facto that they were the genuine article, that they must be taken seriously and not be forced into heterosexual patterns. With the advent of the new women's movement in the 1960s, the butch and the female transvestite have largely disappeared, although the number of women who identify themselves as lesbians (and who have *chosen* to become lesbians after making a commitment to feminism) has multiplied, suggesting that one's sexual orientation generally has considerable references to one's immediate society, to "fashion" or to one's views regarding the appropriateness of a particular kind of sexual orientation.

FLAME RELATIONSHIPS

Whereas our contemporary climate permits relatively abundant opportunities for two adult women to make a permanent commitment to each other, such was obviously not the case in the Victorian era and earlier. If two young women of marriageable age wished to act on what was, even in Ellis' view, a fairly common attraction to one another,[7] they would have been beset with practical difficulties: How would they support themselves, since so few jobs were open to women? How, in an era when single women did not often leave their communities, would they resist pressure from family and peer group to marry? How, even if they were able to leave their communities, could they manage on the streets in the evening, in restaurants, theaters, anywhere, when it was generally assumed that a good woman seldom goes about unaccompanied? Perhaps one way of overcoming those difficulties was transvestism, which would have permitted two women to live together, one passing as a man. That such a solution was adopted and was successful with any frequency is doubtful. What must have happened much more often is that women commonly enjoyed "intimate attachments," in Ellis' phrase, to other women only until they received a suitable masculine proposal, which resulted in what Ellis saw as "the normal impulse" being brought "into permanent play" (p. 132).

---

[7]*Ellis said, "it frequently happens" that a young woman may experience "periods of intimate attachment to a friend of her own sex" (p. 132).*

Ellis denied that such premarital intimate attachments between women were lesbian. He did not take into account the social pressures I have outlined above which would guarantee that a woman marry if she could and when she could, usually regardless of the strengh of her homoerotic attachment. Although he devoted a section of his work (appendix D) to establishing how entirely common erotic love between young women was in his day, he pointedly invalidated the seriousness of such love relationships by describing them as "school-friendships of girls"—although some of the females included in this study were women in their 20s, and although he admitted that "these friendships are often found among girls who have left school" (p. 254) and thus cannot be considered "school-friendships" at all.

Ellis actually entitled appendix D "The School-Friendships of Girls." The appendix begins with an Italian study by two medical men, Obici and Marchesini, who observed female pupils between the ages of 12 and 20 in Italian normal schools in the late 19th century. They discovered that the "flame" ("rave," "spoon," "crush"—i.e., same-sex infatuation or love among young people) was in every college "regarded as a necessary institution," and that although it was often nongenital, "all the sexual manifestations of college youth circle around it," and "all the gradations of sexual sentiment" were expressed within it (p. 243).

Obici and Marchesini made clear that such a relationship was in no way simple friendship. Its beginning generally had the form of "a regular courtship": The one who was struck first would take frequent walks in the garden when the other was likely to be at her window; she would pause on the stairs to see her beloved pass; she was filled with "a mute adoration made up of glances and sighs"; she would send her beloved flowers, little messages, and finally "long and ardent letters of declaration" (p. 244).

The two doctors had read over 300 love letters which had been "carefully preserved by the receivers." From these letters they concluded that the "flame" generally arose from a "physical sympathy," an admiration for the physical form and style of the beloved. The letters themselves are "full of passion; they appear to be often written during periods of physical excitement and psychic erethism."

Obici and Marchesini specifically enumerated almost a dozen points that distinguished these relationships from ordinary friendships, such as: the frequent exchange of love letters; anxiety to be together, to embrace and kiss; persistent jealousy; exaltation of the beloved's qualities; determination to conquer all obstacles to the manifestation of the love; the pleasure of conquest (p. 245).

In addition to the Obici and Marchesini study, Ellis cited similar research from England and America. His English informant also distinguished between a friendship and—as it was commonly known in English girls' schools and women's colleges—a "rave": The young woman with a rave often had several intimate friends for whom she felt affection without the emotion, pleasurable excitement, and more or less erotic response that characterized a rave. Those who had afterwards been in love with men said that the emotions called forth in both cases were similar (pp. 250-256). The American study of such relationships was carried out at Clark University in Worcester, Massachusetts, by E. G. Lancaster, and published in *Pedagogical Seminary*, July 1897. Lancaster studied over 800 teachers and older pupils with regard to their emotional lives. Although his research questionnaires contained nothing about same-sex love, he reported that a large number of his respondents voluntarily offered information about their homosexual experiences, which led Lancaster to conclude that love of the same sex was very common, especially among young people, that such emotion was not in any way "mere friendship," but rather "the love is strong, real, and passionate" and contains "the same characteristics of intensity and devotion that are ordinarily associated with heterosexual love" (pp. 256—257).

Obici and Marchesini estimated the frequency of flames in normal schools at about 60%—to which a collaborator added the observation that of the remaining 40%, half of them did not indulge "because they are not sufficiently pleasing in appearance or because their characters do not inspire sympathy" (p. 244); that is, as much as 80% of all the females at the normal schools in Obici and Marchesini's study would have liked to or did experience romantic relationships with other females.

Since of these 80% none were specifically known to come from neuropathic families or to be "masculine" in any respect, how did Ellis explain the apparent frequency (i.e., "normality") of this phenomenon of same-sex love? He pointed out that although there is "an unquestionable sexual element in the flame relationship," such a relationship cannot be regarded as an absolute expression of "real congenital perversion of the sex-instinct" (p. 249). That it is a spurious imitation of homosexuality is evidenced not only by the fact that these females eventually slip into a heterosexual life-style but also by the fact that the phenomenon is so widespread. He seems to reason thus: If the majority of females experience this type of same-sex love, it cannot be "abnormal"; real abnormal sexual emotion is, therefore, something else—identifiable by characteristics that the majority of these young women do not ostensibly share. In this way, Ellis rejected as being "spurious imitations" all manifestations of homosexual love that proved it to be entirely common, and he characterized as being indicative of "true inversion" what was identifiable as morbid: a marked neuropathic heredity, a strain of violence, a penchant for transvestism.

His immediate disciples, such as Thoinot, who saw apparent flaws in

Ellis' theory, dealt with those flaws not by invalidating the theory, but rather by building on it. For example, how could one explain the phenomenon of a woman who had been married and had children but later became sexually involved with another woman? She suffered from congenital inversion that did not show itself until late in life, that is, "retarded inversion," as Thoinot called it in 1898. (See Karlen, 1971, p. 195. In fact, if Ellis' colleague, the English sex researcher J. A. Hadfield, can be believed, Ellis himself saw flaws in his congenital theory but adhered to it for political purposes alone. Hadfield, 1958, wrote: "Havelock Ellis maintained that homosexuality was of a constitutional type, but he admitted to me in person that he made this statement only because he wanted to emphasize that the individual could not help being what he was.")

Ellis' English contributor to appendix D hinted that raves among females were in some schools so much a "fashion" that "hardly anyone [was] free from it," and any student newly entering the school "would soon fall victim to the fashion." Occasionally there would be a "lull in the general raving," and after an interval it would appear again "in more or less of an epidemic form" (p. 252). Ellis once more did not draw this point to its logical conclusion: It would seem that homosexual passion or lack of it might often be dictated by what one's immediate environment admits as an appropriate passion, in the same way that large-breasted women are "in" with regard to male heterosexual interest in some eras and "out" in other eras. Erotic love has perhaps far less to do with innate instinct and far more to do with "fashion" than most sexual theorists have recognized.

20TH-CENTURY VIEWS

The "fashion" in the 20th century, as a result of the psychologists' attention to homosexuality, has generally been to regard same-sex love as morbid and accompanied by the various ills I have enumerated above. Thus the flame or rave usually does not run to "epidemic proportions" as it commonly did in 19th-century girls' schools and women's colleges. Females know today, as a result of the popularization of psychology, that such affectional behavior is generally considered queer and sick. When a female feels a particularly strong attraction to another female, she will undoubtedly try to hide it rather than "moon" openly as her counterpart in a more romantically inclined, less "psychologically knowledgeable" era would have. She is not able to regard herself as having a common emotional/erotic experience. As a result of our growing "sophistication" over the last hundred years, she will be given to understand that her love is morbid. The case of Miss M., which Ellis cited in his chapter "Sexual Inversion in Women," is a prototype in this respect. A year previous,

Ellis reported, Miss M. had come across a translation of Krafft-Ebing's book. From that book she learned "that feelings like mine were 'under the ban of society'" and that such feelings were "unnatural and depraved." Before reading Krafft-Ebing she had no notion that her feelings were anything other than a manifestation of love for a particular person (Ellis, 1897/1901, pp. 134–137).[8]

Such "wisdom" is reflected as well in the subsequent fiction. Before the lesbian-feminist movement that began in the late 1960s, almost all of the fiction that dealt with love between women took one of two positions: The woman who loved another female was either a villainous pervert or a pathetic invert. Love between women was no longer romanticized as it had been previous eras: At best, such love was a sorry, doomed thing; at worst it brought in its wake suicide, homicide, and a host of plagues. Clemence Dane's (1917) *Regiment of Women*, a novel about a destructive lesbian teacher in a girls' school, is an early example of the latter. The central character (whose last name is appropriately, Hartill—heart ill) is responsible for the suicide of a 14-year-old student who is infatuated with her (and whom she treats with incredible cruelty), for the seduction and near-ruin of an innocent young woman (who escapes because she is not a pervert like Clare Hartill but rather "as sound and sweet as an apple"), and for the great suffering of numerous other females who have the misfortune to come under her sway. At the conclusion the young woman is snatched from Clare's clutches by a heroic male, who understands that Clare is "abnormal," "perverse," "unpleasant," and generally evil. But the novel ends with the chilling suggestion that Clare will continue to kill and corrupt the innocent: "There were other fish in the sea. . . . That child in the Fourth." After the publication of this novel the schoolgirl crushes that Ellis described as being essentially "harmless" must certainly have been viewed (possibly for the first time?) with considerable alarm.

At the other extreme was Radclyffe Hall's (1928) *The Well of Loneliness*, with its introductory commentary by Havelock Ellis and its central character who is largely a composite of Ellis' case histories. Stephen Gordon, who is bright, generous, sensitive, and loyal ad nauseum, is a congenital invert, a member of the third sex, a man trapped in a wo-

[8]*Miss M., a "true invert," did not indulge in genital sexuality, like most of the "schoolgirls" Ellis described in appendix D. In fact one would be hard put to find significant differences in Ellis' description of Miss M.'s "inverted instinct" and the flame relationships that are cited in appendix D. If anything, she was* less *specifically sexual in her interests. Miss M. is quoted as saying: "I love few people . . . but in these instances when I have permitted my heart to go out to a friend I have always experienced most exalted feelings, and have been made better by them morally, mentally, and spiritually. Love is with me a religion. The very nature of my affection for my friends precludes the possibility of any element entering into it which is not absolutely sacred."*

man's body. Despite all her sterling qualities, she suffers because of her stigma throughout the novel, and she is consistently pathetic. At the conclusion she is alone, having given her lover up to a man for the other woman's greater happiness. The book ends with Stephen exhorting God to acknowledge the third sex "before the whole world."

These two novels, which have in common the view that love between women is necessarily doomed to be miserable, were perhaps the prototypes for the fiction of subsequent decades. Novels about love between women that did not take that view were, until the last few years, extremely rare. But more recently, the lesbian-feminist movement has opened the way for fiction such as Marge Piercy's *Small Changes* (1972). Bertha Harris' *Confessions of Cherubino* (1972), Rita Mae Brown's *Rubyfruit Jungle* (1973), and Elana Nachman's *Riverfinger Woman* (1974), which once again depicts love between women as being healthy and joyous. In this sense, the recent work has more in common (despite its explicit, "modern" focus on sex) with those novels of the 19th century and earlier that depicted love between women than with 20th-century fiction that showed the influence of the sexual theorists.

Lesbian-feminists have suggested that lesbianism is a political choice—that it has nothing to do with congenital propensities (or with, as Freud believed, early parent-child or sibling relationships), but rather that a woman becomes "woman-identified" and a lesbian when she understands the social and personal inequities between males and females. (See, for example, Abbott & Love, 1973; Johnston, 1973; Shelley, 1971, pp. 476–481.) And, in fact, not a few women in the contemporary feminist movement have, after years of identifying themselves as heterosexuals, chosen to become lesbians, sometimes in anger over what they perceive to be the nature of male-female relationships, sometimes as the result of having first learned through movement doctrine that antilesbianism is an antifeminist weapon and then (more positively) meeting other women whom they can love once the conditioned barriers to same-sex love are removed.

Alfred Kinsey (1965) observed in his work *Sexual Behavior in the Human Female* that there is an inherent physiological capacity in *all* animals to respond sexually to any sufficient stimulus. This, he said, is the *basic* explanation of the fact that some individuals respond to stimuli originating in other individuals of their own sex, and every individual could so respond if the opportunity were present and if one *were not conditioned against* making such responses. He found that the important factor that led one to identify or not identify oneself as a homosexual was "the indirect but powerful conditioning which *the opinions of other persons and the social codes* may have on an individual's decision to accept or reject this type of sexual contact" (p. 447, emphasis added). Exclusive preferences and patterns of behavior, Kinsey suggested, had nothing to do with inborn abnormalities or the lack of them, and not much to do with early trauma by itself, but rather those patterns developed "with experience or as *a result of social pressures*" (p. 450, emphasis added).

Of course, it is not social pressure by itself that keeps the majority of adults heterosexual. In their study "Bisexuality: Some Sociological Observations," Pepper Schwartz and Philip Blumstein (cited in Hite, 1976, "Lesbianism" section) pointed out that although we are all capable of both heterosexual and homosexual arousal, once we make a commitment to a particular kind of sexuality, for whatever reason, we generally "screen out" from our notice and our fantasy any potential partner of the other gender.[9] Thus a woman who has accepted a heterosexual identity will not think of other women in terms of potential sexual partners and will probably fail to notice the sexual attractiveness of another woman. The reverse may be said of a woman who has accepted a homosexual identity: She will screen out males as potential sexual partners and will generally fail to notice sexual attractiveness in males with whom she may come in contact.

Twentieth-century sophistication with regard to the "abnormality" of same-sex love has probably enforced a more efficient heterosexual screening out process in women. Before the 19th-century morbidification of love between women, females had no specific societal pressures to learn to screen out attractions toward other women, since those attractions were seen as virtually harmless—or in Henry Wadsworth Longfellow's (1849/1965) terms, "a rehearsal in girlhood of the great drama of woman's life" (p. 46)—because it was understood that a woman would, for economic reasons alone if nothing else, marry at the first suitable opportunity. With women's growing economic independence, particularly since World War I, it becomes possible for a woman to make a serious and permanent commitment to another woman, and thus female same-sex love is perceived, perhaps for the first time in history, as threatening to social mores. That, coupled with a ubiquitous knowledge of the existence of "sexual abnormality," has brought about societal pressures on females to censor any erotic impulses toward other women, and to be wary even of overly strong emotional (nongenital) involvements with other women. Those who have not screened out such impulses despite the mystique of lesbian morbidity which has been so well promulgated over the last 100 years have, in a sense, been less successfully

[9] *C. A. Tripp (1975, pp. 92–93) also develops this idea in* The Homosexual Matrix. *It is his hypothesis that a budding sexual value system (which takes its form by virtue of a large variety of factors) drowns out competing alternatives. Thus, as soon as a person begins to develop an interest in the qualities of one sex, s/he begins to view the analogous features of the other sex as dissonant. In Tripp's example, the man who has begun to respond to the muscularity or assertiveness of males will experience aversion reactions to "the female's roundness and submissive allure."*

socialized,[10] or their conventional socialization has been superseded by lesbian-feminism.

REFERENCES

Abbott, S., & Love, B. *Sappho was a right-on woman: A liberated view of lesbianism.* New York: Stein & Day, 1973.

Alcott, L. M. *Work: A story of experience.* Boston: Roberts Brothers, 1884.

Brown, C. B. *Ormond: Or the secret witness.* New York: American, 1937. (Originally published, 1799.)

Dane, C. *Regiment of women.* New York: Macmillan, 1917.

Ellis, H. *Studies in the psychology of sex: Sexual inversion.* Philadelphia: F. A. Davis, 1901. (Originally published, 1897.)

Faderman, L. Female same-sex relationships in novels by Henry Wadsworth Longfellow, Oliver Wendell Holmes, and Henry James. *New England Quarterly,* in press.

Freud, S. The psychogenesis of a case of female homosexuality. *Collected papers, 2.* London: 1949. (Originally published, 1920.)

Hadfield, J. A. The cure of homosexuality. *British Medical Journal,* 1958, *2,* 1323.

Hall, R. *The well of loneliness.* Garden City, N.Y.: Blue Ribbon Books, 1928.

Hamilton, A. M. The civil responsibility of sexual perverts. *American Journal of Insanity,* April 1896, *52*(4), 503–509.

Hite, S. *The Hite report.* New York: Dell, 1976.

Holmes, O. W. *A mortal antipathy.* New York: Houghton Mifflin, 1892.

Johnston, J. *Lesbian nation: The feminist solution.* New York: Simon & Schuster, 1973.

Karlen, A. *Sexuality and homosexuality: A new view.* New York: W. W. Norton, 1971.

Kinsey, A. *Sexual behavior in the human female.* New York: Pocket Books, 1965.

Krafft-Ebing, R. von. Neue Studien auf dem Gebiete der Homosexualität. *Jahrbuch für Sexuelle Zwischenstufen,* 1901, *3,* 1–36.

Krafft-Ebing, R. von. *Psychopathia sexualis.* New York: Surgeons, 1925. (Originally published, 1882.)

Longfellow, H. W. *Kavanagh.* New Haven, Conn.: College and University Press, 1965. (Originally published, 1849.)

Montaigne, M. E. de. *Journal du voyage en Italie en 1850* (d'Acona, Ed.). 1889. (Cited in Ellis, H. *Studies in the psychology of sex: Sexual inversion.* Philadelphia: F. A. Davis, 1901. Originally published, 1897.)

Morris, D. *The naked ape.* London: Jonathan Cape, 1967.

Müller, F. C. Ein weiterer Fall von conträrer Sexualempfindung. *Friedreich's Blätter,* H. 4, 1891.

Shelley, M. Women of lesbos. In E. Adams & M. L. Briscoe (Eds.), *Up against the wall, Mother.* Beverly Hills, Calif.: Glencoe Press, 1971.

Smith-Rosenberg, C. The female world of love and ritual: Relations between women in nineteenth century America. *Signs: Journal of Women in Culture and Society,* Autumn 1975, *1*(1), 1–24.

---

[10]Charlotte Wolff's (1971) statistical tables indicate that lesbians tend to be only children almost twice as often as heterosexual women. As only children they would have escaped sibling pressure toward proper socialization. I would also venture to guess that as only children, lacking the opportunity to develop within the family skills of getting along with other children, lesbians were less likely when young to be a part of a close-knit peer group. Being generally outside such cohesive groups, one may more easily reject peer pressure to conform to the prevailing sexual values.

Symonds, J. A. *A problem in modern ethics.* New York: Benjamin Blom, 1971. (Originally published, 1896.)
Taylor, W., & Lasch, C. Two kindred spirits: Sorority and family in New England, 1839-1846. *New England Quarterly*, March 1963, *36*(1), 23-41.
Tripp, C. A. *The homosexual matrix.* New York: McGraw-Hill, 1975.
Wolff, C. *Love between women.* New York: St. Martin's Press, 1971.

From Sexual Inversion To Homosexuality: Medicine And The Changing Conceptualization Of Female Deviance

BY GEORGE CHAUNCEY, JR.

Historians have recently identified the end of the nineteenth century as a crucial transitional period in the conceptualization and social experience of homosexual relations.[1] Jeffrey Weeks suggests that the "medical model of homosexuality" replaced the religious one during this period, characterizing homosexuality as the condition of certain, identifiable individuals rather than as a form of sinful behavior in which anyone might engage, while Lillian Faderman assigns the medical profession responsibility for the "morbidification" of relationships between women during these years. It was on the basis of the new medical models, they suggest, that individuals came to identify themselves — and distinguish themselves from others — as lesbians and gay men, members of a sexual minority.[2] The last years of the nineteenth

1 I would like to thank Lisa Biow, John Boswell, Jeanne Boydston, Nancy Cott, Mitchell Katz, Harry Scott, Chris Stansell, Tony Stellato and Jack Winkler for their comments on earlier drafts of this paper. Discussions with Jeanne Boydston were particularly helpful in developing some of the arguments presented in the third section.

2 Jeffrey Weeks, *Coming Out: Homosexual Politics in Britain from the Nineteenth Century to the Present* (London: Quartet Books, 1977); Lillian Faderman, "The Morbidification of Love Between Women by 19th-Century Sexologists," *Journal of Homosexuality* 4 (1978): 73-90; idem, "Lesbian Magazine Fiction in the Early Twentieth Century," *Journal of Popular Culture* II (1978): 700-17. Faderman's major work, *Surpassing the Love of Men* (New York: William Morrow, 1981), unfortunately appeared too late for me to incorporate its findings in this article.

century did witness a dramatic increase in medical interest in "deviant" sexual behavior. The first medical article on what was then termed sexual inversion was published in Germany in 1870 and was followed by American studies within the decade; by the mid-1910s, several U.S. journals devoted regular columns to sexology which frequently reported on the study of homosexuality.[3]

But it would be wrong to assume, I think, that doctors created and defined the identities of "inverts" and "homosexuals" at the turn of the century, that people uncritically internalized the new medical models, or even that homosexuality emerged as a fully defined category in the medical discourse itself in the 1870s. Such assumptions attribute inordinate power to ideology as an autonomous social force; they oversimplify the complex dialectic between social conditions, ideology, and consciousness which produced gay identities, and they belie the evidence of preexisting subcultures and identities contained in the literature itself. Although the literature is one of the sources most easily accessible to historians, we must guard against attributing to it a more central role in the formation of sexual identities than it actually may have played. It has not yet been adequately documented that medical models and homosexual identities appeared at the same time, even for the members of elite society who have been the subjects of existing studies. But even if we did know this to be the case, it would not necessarily indicate that one caused the other; both may have resulted from more fundamental historical processes. Only extensive and original research in more intimate records such as diaries and correspondence will enable us to measure the influence of the medical discourse on the emergence of gay identities and subcultures. (I use the plural

3 Nancy Sahli notes the increasing medical attention to sexual deviance as evidenced by the number of articles cited in the *Surgeon-General's Index Catalog* during these years in her article, "Smashing: Women's Relations Before the Fall," *Chrysalis* 8 (1979): 17-27. James Kiernan, one of the earliest writers on homosexuality, edited a "Sexology" column for the *Urologic and Cutaneous Review* from the early teens at least. It included abstracts of articles appearing in other medical journals, and short editorial comments, including three or four a year on homosexuality. *The Psychoanalytic Review*, begun in 1913 by William A. White and Smith Ely Jeliffe, included original articles, translations, and regular abstracts of articles published in major German-language psychoanalytic journals, including many on homosexuality. William J. Robinson established the short-lived *Journal of Sexology and Psychoanalysis* in 1923, to supercede the *American Journal of Urology and Sexology*, published from 1904 to 1922. The first issue of *JSP* carried an article by Stella Browne, "Studies in Feminine Inversion," 51-58. Thus by the early teens the number of articles or abstracts concerning homosexuality regularly available to the American medical profession had grown enormously.

deliberately, for the structure and social experience of sexuality and gender have varied along lines of class, race, and ethnicity.)

Nevertheless, analysis of the medical literature can make an important contribution to our study of the history of sexuality if we consider it, in the first instance, as a response to and reflection of the changes in the organization and ideology of sexuality which occurred in American culture at the turn of the century. As such, it can provide a key to our understanding of the transformation of the sex/gender system during that period, for the cultural definition of deviance indicates with particular clarity the parameters of the acceptable.[4]

It is highly significant in this light that the turn of the century witnessed the development not only of a new explanation of homosexual behavior, but also — and more centrally — of the very concept of homosexual desire as a discrete sexual phenomenon. Sexual inversion, the term used most commonly in the nineteenth century, did not denote the same conceptual phenomenon as homosexuality. "Sexual inversion" referred to a broad range of deviant gender behavior, of which homosexual desire was only a logical but indistinct aspect, while "homosexuality" focused on the narrower issue of sexual object choice. The differentiation of homosexual desire from "deviant" gender behavior at the turn of the century reflects a major reconceptualization of the nature of human sexuality, its relation to gender, and its role in one's social definition.

While the changing focus of medical inquiry into sexual deviance reflected a broad shift in conceptualization, each stage in that inquiry can be analyzed as a response to particular changes in and challenges to the Victorian sex/gender system such as the women's movement, the growing visibility of urban gay male subcultures, and the changing gender structure of the economy. Medical theories achieved general acceptance and influence because they reflected a much broader cultural uneasiness with and antipathy to these challenges, and because they took ideological forms commonly used to resist social change. Indeed, the early biological explanations offered for sexual deviance were an integral part of that nineteenth-century scientific discourse which sought to validate the existing social order by asserting its biological

4 Gayle Rubin introduced the term "sex/gender system" in her article, "The Traffic in Women: Notes on the 'Political Economy' of Sex," in Rayna R. Reiter, ed., *Toward an Anthropology of Women* (New York: Monthly Review Press, 1975), 157-210. Somewhat analogous to "political economy" in scope and purpose, "sex/gender system" is the general term for the many social systems by which sexuality, gender, and procreation are structured.

inevitability. Just as the contemporaneous theory of social Darwinism served to legitimate racism and colonialism by postulating a biologically-based racial hierarchy of social development, so the early sexology sought to justify the particular form of women's subordination to men during this period by asserting its biological determination.[5] Subsequent theories emphasized the psychic rather than biological "abnormalities" which resulted in sexual nonconformity, but accepted many of the premises of earlier work. In the process of debate, the literature developed many of the terms and categories which continue to structure our thinking about sexuality and gender.

The following pages, based on a review of approximately 85 medical books, articles, and reviews published in the United States between 1880 and 1930, examine the medical literature on inversion and homosexuality as a response to and reflection of changes in the sex/gender system at the turn of the century. After examining the changing focus of medical inquiry during these years, they analyze the assumptions about sexuality revealed by the explanations offered for sexual deviance, and then consider further the reasons for the emergence of medical concern about this subject.

The Changing Focus of Medical Inquiry

The Victorian assertion of male sexual aggressiveness and denial of female sexual interest established the logical framework for the earliest medical inquiry into sexual deviance, and determined the manner in which researchers defined it. The major current in Victorian sexual ideology declared that women were passionless and asexual, the passive objects of male sexual desire. In the 1880s and nineties, as Havelock Ellis noted in 1903, this belief was so deeply rooted a tendency in medical thought that many sexologists considered a woman's expresson of sexual

5 In recent years historians have written extensively on the role of medical arguments in the ideological struggles over gender roles in the late nineteenth century, and in some respects the discussion which follows should be seen as another aspect of the process they have described. See Ann Douglas Wood, "'The Fashionable Diseases': Women's Complaints and their Treatment in Nineteenth Century America," in Mary S.Hartman and Lois Banner, ed., *Clio's Consciousness Raised* (New York: Harper Colophon Books, 1974), 1-22; Carroll Smith-Rosenberg, "The Hysterical Woman: Sex Roles and Role Conflict in Nineteenth Century America," *Social Research* 39 (1972): 654-78; Charles Rosenberg and Carroll Smith-Rosenberg, "The Female Animal: Medical and Biological Views of Women," *Journal of American History* 60 (1973): 332-56.

desire even in her romantic life to be pathological.[6] Such an assessment of women's sexuality necessarily had fundamental implications for the medical conceptualization of lesbian relations. Indeed, in the context of female passionlessness, there was no place for lesbianism as it is currently understood: if women could not even respond with sexual enthusiasm to the advances of men, how could they possibly stimulate sexual excitement between themselves?

In the Victorian system, therefore, a complete inversion or reversal of a woman's sexual character was required for her to act as a lesbian; she had literally to become man-like in her sexual desire. That this logic governed early thinking about lesbianism is suggested by the descriptions of lesbians provided by early sexologists. In 1883, in one of the first articles on a "Case of Sexual Perversion," P.M. Wise described the behavior of a woman institutionalized after having been discovered passing as a man:

> In passing to the ward, she embraced the female attendant in a lewd manner and came near overpowering her before she received assistance. Her conduct on the ward was characterized by the same lascivious conduct, and she made efforts at various times to have sexual intercourse with her associates.[7]

This description, typical of the early literature, emphasizes the sexual aggressiveness of the female "pervert" in terms closely paralleling descriptions of male sexual lust prominent in nineteenth-century thought. At mid-century, for instance, the Female Moral Reform

6 See, e.g., the assertion by H. Fehling that "the appearance of the sexual side in the love of a young girl is pathological" (*Die Bestimmung der Frau*, 1892, p. 18), quoted in Havelock Ellis, *Studies in the Psychology of Sex*, 2d ed., rev. (1903, Philadelphia: F.A. Davis, Co., 1913): 3: 195. Ellis cited similar opinions by other major European sexologists who were influential in the United States, including Krafft-Ebing, Moll, Naecke, and Lombroso (pp. 194-96). Carl Degler's study of women's sexuality in the nineteenth century suggests that this ideology had begun to change earlier than historians previously thought ("What Ought to Be and What Was: Women's Sexuality in the Nineteenth Century," *American Historical Review* 79 (1974): 1467-90), but it relies for its evidence on sources published only in the last third of the century. My evidence suggests that the assertion of women's sexual subjectivity, which had become common by the 1920s, remained only a minority medical opinion in the closing years of the nineteenth century. For a reinterpretation of the origins and instrumentality of passionlessness, see Nancy F. Cott, "Passionlessness: A Reinterpretation of Victorian Sexual Ideology, 1790-1850," *Signs: A Journal of Women in Culture and Society* 4 (1978): 219-36.

7 P.M. Wise, "Case of Sexual Perversion," *Alienist and Neurologist* 4 (1883): 87-88.

Society thought the "male lecher . . . a creature controlled by base sexual drives which he neither could nor would control," according to Carroll Smith-Rosenberg; woman, "innocent and defenseless, gentle and passive," was just the opposite.[8] This polarization of masculine and feminine sexuality suggests that the perversion described by Wise was not so much in the object of the woman's sexual desire as in the masculine, aggressive form it took: the woman had inverted her whole sexual character.

Sexual inversion, the term used in most of the nineteenth century literature, thus had a much broader meaning than our present term, homosexuality, which denotes solely the sex of the person one sexually desires. Sexual inversion, rather, connoted a total reversal of one's sex role.

But in Victorian thought, people's sex roles were not limited to their behavioral roles in intimate sexual relations; rather, a woman's sexual passivity, for instance, was to serve as a paradigm for her complete gender role. In the thinking of many doctors, sexual inversion referred not only to sexual excesses or to non-procreative sexual activity, as some have argued,[9] but even more centrally to aberrations in one's sex-defined social role. As George Beard wrote in the 1880s, when "the sex is perverted, they hate the opposite sex and love their own; men become women and women men, in their tastes, conduct, character, feelings and behavior."[10] Richard von Krafft-Ebing explained that a person's thought, character and behavior "correspond with the peculiar sexual instinct [i.e., "the sexual role in which they feel themselves to be"], but not with the sex which the individual represents anatomically and physiologically."[11] Transvestism was therefore seen as characteristic of sexual inversion, and the case histories regularly observed that many inverts revealed their true nature as children by their queer behavior. "She was peculiar in girlhood," observed Wise, "in that she preferred masculine sports and labor; had an aversion to attentions from young

8 Carroll Smith-Rosenberg, "Beauty, the Beast, and the Militant Woman: A Case Study in Sex Role and Social Stress in Jacksonian America," *American Quarterly* 23 (1971): 571.

9 Vern Bullough, "Homosexuality and the Medical Model," *Journal of Homosexuality* 1 (1974): 99-110.

10 George M. Beard, *Sexual Neurasthenia*, ed. by A.D. Rockwell (New York: E.B. Treat, Co., 1884), 106.

11 Richard von Krafft-Ebing, *Psychopathia Sexualis, With Especial Reference to the Antipathic Sexual Instinct*, transl. by F.J. Rebman (Brooklyn: Physicians and Surgeons Book Co., 1908), 336.

men and sought the society of her own sex."[12] P.M. Lichtenstein's list of the "male characteristics" of female sex perverts in a conservative 1921 article included the fact that "they wear strictly tailor-made clothing, low shoes, and they seldom wear corsets. The hair is usually bobbed."[13] Another doctor observed with astonishment that "some of the women inverts can whistle admirably"; and Douglas McMurtrie characterized an invert by her drinking, smoking, and being "very independent in her ways."[14] W.C. Rivers, on the other hand, thought it significant that a male pervert "never smoked and never married; [and] was entirely averse to outdoor games," while two other researchers described as perverted a man who, among other things, was "fond of looking in the mirror . . . [and] talk[ed] in a squeaking, effeminate voice."[15]

Havelock Ellis provided perhaps the most comprehensive description of female sexual inversion. Although on the one hand claiming that transvestism was unrelated to homosexuality, Ellis nonetheless provided numerous examples of lesbian transvestites in his major work, *Sexual Inversion*, and noted that even those lesbians who wore female attire usually showed "some traits of masculine simplicity" in their dress. Furthermore,

> The brusque, energetic movements, the attitude of the arms, the direct speech, the inflexions of the voice, the masculine straightforwardness and sense of honor . . . will all suggest the underlying psychic abnormality to a keen observer. In the habits not only is there frequently a pronounced taste for smoking cigarettes, often found in quite feminine women, but also a decided taste and tolerance for cigars. There is also a dislike and

12 Wise, "Case of Sexual Perversion," 88; P. Leidy and C.K. Mills, "Reports of Cases of Insanity from the Insane Department of the Philadelphia Hospital," *Journal of Nervous and Mental Disease* 13 (1886): 712; Perry M. Lichtenstein, "The Fairy and the Lady Lover," *Medical Review of Reviews* 27 (1921): 370, 373-74; George F. Shrady, "Perverted Sexual Instinct," *Medical Record* 26 (1884): 70; Ralph Werther, "Studies in Androgynism," *Medical Life* 27 (1920): 243-45.

13 Lichtenstein, "The Fairy and the Lady Lover," 372.

14 K. "Review of Havelock Ellis' *Sexual Inversion*," *Alienist and Neurologist* 23 (1902): 111; Douglas C. McMurtrie, "Principles of Homosexuality and Sexual Inversion in the Female," *American Journal of Urology* 9 (1913): 147.

15 W.C. Rivers, "A New Male Homosexual Trait (?)," *Alienist and Neurologist* 41 (1920): 22; Leidy and Mills, "Reports of Cases of Insanity," 713.

> sometimes incapacity for needlework and other domestic occupations, while there is often some capacity for athletics.[16]

These examples suggest not only the paradigmatic nature of woman's sexual role for her social role, but also the polarization of masculine and feminine modes of behavior in Victorian thought. In their discussions of sexual behavior the doctors were unable to conceive of a single person simultaneously embodying both: a woman could not invert any aspect of her gender role without inverting her complete role.

The occasional medical accounts of the heterosexual relations of married inverts emphasize the importance of sexual role inversion rather than homosexual object choice in these discussions. Inverts were occasionally involved in heterosexual relations, if only because of social convention, but they were always attracted to someone whose sex role was opposite their own. Ellis thought that the man attracted to an inverted woman, for instance, must be exceptionally effeminate, and he cited the case of one such man he knew who was "of slight physique, . . . with a thin voice, . . . considerate to others to a feminine degree, . . . and very domesticated in his manner of living — in short, the man who might easily have been attracted to his own sex."[17] William Lee Howard, writing four years later, in 1900, warned that feminists and sexual perverts alike, both of whom he classed as "degenerates," married only men whom they could "rule, govern and cause to follow [them] in voice and action."[18] J.F.W. Meagher claimed in 1929 that

16 Havelock Ellis, *Sexual Inversion*, 3d rev. ed., Studies in the Psychology of Sex, vol. 2 (Philadelphia: F.A. Davis Co., 1915), 250. For other accounts which conceptualize inversion in these broad terms, rather than focusing exclusively on homosexual object choice, see William Lee Howard, "Effeminate Men and Masculine Women," *New York Medical Journal* 71 (1900): 686; Allan MacLane Hamilton, "The Civil Responsibility of Sexual Perverts," *American Journal of Insanity* 52 (1896): 505; Herbert J. Clairborne, "Hypertrichosis in Women: Its Relation to Bisexuality (Hermaphroditism): With remarks on Bisexuality in Animals, Especially Man," *New York Medical Journal* 99 (1914): 1181; J. Allen Gilbert, "Homosexuality and its Treatment," *Journal of Nervous and Mental Disease* 52 (1920): 297-322; James G. Kiernan, "Sexual Perversion and the Whitechapel Murders," *Medical Standard* 4 (1888): 170-72; Richard von Krafft-Ebing, "Perversions of the Sexual Instinct: Report of Cases," *Alienist and Neurologist* 9 (1888): 556-70, 579-81; Douglas C. McMurtrie, "Manifestations of Sexual Inversion in the Female: Conditions in a Convent School, Evidence of Transvestism, Unconscious Homosexuality, Sexuality of Masculine Women, Masturbation Under Homosexual Influences, Indeterminate Sexuality in Childhood," *Urologic and Cutaneous Review* 18 (1914): 444-46; idem, "Psychology of a Tribadistic Uxoricide: A Lombrosian Case Record," ibid., 18 (1914): 480; Shrady, "Perverted Sexual Instinct," 70-71.

17 Havelock Ellis, "Sexual Inversion in Women," *Alienist and Neurologist* 16 (1895): 154.

18 Howard, "Effeminate Men and Masculine Women," 687.

"a homosexual woman often wants to possess the male and not to be possessed by him. . . . With them," he added, "orgasm is often only possible in the superior position."[19] If a female behaved like a man, it seemed, she could only relate to a male who would be her "woman."

By 1900, however, a fundamental shift in conceptualization was underway, as medicine began to specify and narrow the definition of the sexual, and to distinguish and classify sexual deviations in ever more discrete categories, particularly in the case of men. While early investigators had maintained that male sexual inversion involved transvestism, effeminacy, and such unmasculine characteristics as the inability to whistle, as well as sexual desire for men instead of women,[20] Havelock Ellis and other writers tried at the turn of the century to redefine male sexual inversion in narrowly sexual terms. Ellis emphatically distinguished it from transvestism and other forms of gender inversion (initially called sexo-aesthetic inversion, and later Eonism), which he claimed were often practiced by heterosexual men. Sexual inversion, he told a meeting of the Chicago academy of Medicine in 1913, correctly referred "exclusively [to] such a change in a person's sexual impulses, . . . that the impulse is turned towards individuals of the same sex, while all the other impulses and tastes may remain those of the sex to which the person by anatomical configuration belongs."[21] He had already written that a man could invert his sexual object and behavior — becoming the "passive," "feminine" sexual partner to another man — while "remain[ing] masculine in his non-sexual habits."[22]

Sigmund Freud clarified this distinction by introducing the concepts of sexual object and aim in the first of his *Three Essays on the Theory of Sexuality* (1905). Sexual aim, in Freud's view, referred to a person's

19 J.F.W. Meagher, "Homosexuality: Its Psychobiological and Pathological Significance," *Urologic and Cutaneous Review* 33 (1929): 513.

20 One of the more bizarre — and late — examples of the literature which used this broad definition of male inversion was W.C. Rivers' article, "A New Male Homosexual Trait (?)." The newly discovered trait was cat-loving, and Rivers concluded that "If fondness for cats be entitled to a place among male homosexual traits, the reason will be that it is a woman's taste" (27).

21 Havelock Ellis, "Sexo-Aesthetic Inversion," *Alienist and Neurologist* 34 (1913): 156. In this speech, Ellis presented the case of a male heterosexual transvestite, and cited a case originally reported by Krafft-Ebing of what might now be termed male transsexualism. Magnus Hirschfeld's massive work, *Die Transvestiten*, which appeared in 1910 and made the same distinction between homosexuality and transvestism, obviously influenced Ellis a great deal, as he acknowledges.

22 Havelock Ellis, "Sexual Inversion in Men," *Alienist and Neurologist* 17 (1896): 142.

preferred mode of sexual behavior, such as genital or oral sex, or passive or active roles. Sexual object referred to the object of sexual desire; Freud classified children, animals, and persons of the same sex as "deviations in respect of the sexual object."[23]

The introduction of this distinction between aim and object, which may seem self-evident today, was a highly significant change at a particular moment in the intellectual history of sexuality, and reflects the changes which occurred in the sex/gender system around the turn of the century. In the late nineteenth century, as we have seen, the fact of active or passive sexual aim — seen as paradigmatic for one's complete gender role — was at least as important as sexual object in the social classification of sexuality. Investigators classified a woman as an invert because of her aggressive, "masculine" sexual and social behavior, and the fact that her sexual object was homosexual was only the logical corollary of this inversion; "men," whether biologically male or female, necessarily chose passive women as their sexual objects. By the turn of the century, however, researchers increasingly distinguished passive or aggressive sexual behavior from sexual object, and the latter became the more important element in the medical classification of sexuality.

Although discussions of both male and female sexuality reflect investigators' growing concern about sexual object choice, the change in focus occurred first and most decisively in the study of men. Ellis, as I have noted, distinguished men's homosexual object choice from their sexual and social behavior. Freud maintained that although the "secondary and tertiary characteristics" of one sex often appeared in the other, which he attributed to a kind of hermaphroditism, there was no correlation between their appearance and homosexual desire in the case of men. "The most complete mental masculinity," he observed, "can be combined with [male] inversion."[24] For many subsequent theorists, then, a man's sexual object choice, rather than his actual role in intimate sexual relations, was the primary determinant in the classification of his sexuality, and they no longer saw his sexual role as paradigmatic of his social role. Doctors postulated that he could be the passive partner to another man's sexual advances without necessarily being passive and effeminate in his social role, while creating the new category of heterosexual men whose deviance was embodied in their

23 Sigmund Freud, *Three Essays on the Theory of Sexuality*, trans. James Strachey, *et al.* (New York: Basic Books, 1962), 1-2.
24 Ibid., 8.

effeminacy. As Michel Foucault has argued, the varieties of perversion thus multiplied, as ever more discrete categories were labelled and distinguished — transvestism from homosexuality, effeminate behavior from taking the "passive" role in intercourse, and so forth.[25]

The growing differentiation of sexual object choice from sexual roles and gender characteristics, and the growing importance of object choice in the classification of sexuality, were reflected, albeit inconsistently, in the increasing frequency with which the term "homosexuality" was used in the place of sexual inversion after 1900. While "sexual inversion" referred to an inversion in the full range of gender characteristics, "homosexuality," precisely understood, referred only to the narrower issue of homosexual object choice, and did not necessarily imply gender or sexual role inversion. Although during the transition in medical thinking which I have described, some doctors, as one would expect, used the terms interchangeably, others distinguished them quite carefully, and in general the terminology of homosexuality achieved currency in the literature at the same time that concern about object choice was beginning to supercede concern about gender inversion.[26]

The change in the focus of sexual inquiry was slower and more complicated in the case of women. As with men, sexual object choice became relatively more important than character inversion, but doctors were less willing — perhaps culturally less able — to distinguish a woman's behavior in sexual relations from other aspects of her gender role. Doctors continued to characterize women who took the aggressive, "masculine" role in sexual relations as masculine in character and social role, even after they had determined that men who were "passive" sexually could engage in the social behavior which was masculine. The long statement by Havelock Ellis cited above, for instance, in which he characterized female inverts as masculine, appeared in the third edition of *Sexual Inversion*, which was published two years after his

25 Michel Foucault, *The History of Sexuality: An Introduction*, trans. Robert Hurley (New York: Pantheon Books, 1978).

26 Two additional points should be made. First, although "inversion" and "homosexuality" were the most common terms used, and reflect the changes in the conceptualization of sexuality which I have outlined, they were not the only terms used during this period to denote these concepts. Second, inversion has never entirely disappeared as a term or concept. A major study appearing in the mid-sixties, for instance, used the term in its title (J. Marmor, ed., *Sexual Inversion: The Multiple Roots of Homosexuality* [New York: Basic Books, 1965]), while individual researchers, particularly in periods of acute gender role distress such as postwar years, have attempted to revive the concept.

address to the Chicago Academy of Medicine. Freud, like Ellis and the whole of turn-of-the-century sexology, continued to assert that "character inversion" was a regular feature of *female* inversion, although no longer maintaining that this was true of male inverts.[27]

There were, however, changes in medical descriptions of women involved in lesbian relationships between 1880 and 1930 which paralleled the changes in ideas about male sexual deviance. Most of the early accounts of sexual inversion discussed only the invert, leaving her sexual partner anonymous and undefined. In the earliest accounts of this form of sexual deviance, those concerning women who dressed and passed as men, for instance, the women's "wives" received virtually no attention. In the nineteenth century accounts of passing women who married other women collected by Allan Berube and Jonathan Katz, the wives usually play only a minor role, and (when they are considered) are not labelled deviant in the same manner as their husbands. Many accounts simply treated them as normal wives, playing their proper feminine roles, as if it did not matter that their "husbands" were biologically female.[28] Further research would be required to substantiate this point, but it seems that many nineteenth-century doctors considered the truly serious offense to be the invert's assumption of the opposite gender role rather than either her or her "wife's" homosexual object choice.

Although later observers considered the role of the wifely partner in increasingly sexual and pathological terms, the nature of her relationship as wife to a female husband remained the fundamental paradigm which governed medical thought. In the Victorian context this might appropriately be termed the "heterosexual paradigm," for it represented conventional wisdom about the proper relation of husband to wife and man to woman. In a culture which polarized the acceptable behavioral and emotional characteristics of men and women, marriage was to represent a union of opposed but complementary characteristics, in which men were dominant and women submissive. This paradigm appears to have been so fundamental to Victorian concepts of marriage that when doctors began to scrutinize homosexual relationships — as well as individuals — around the turn of the century, they were unable to think of them in any other terms. No matter what

27 Freud, *Three Essays*, 8.

28 A few of the many accounts collected by Allan Berube are reported in his article, "Lesbian Masquerade," *Gay Community News* (17 November 1979). See also the documents reprinted in the chapter on "Passing Women, 1782-1920," in Jonathan Katz, *Gay American History* (New York: Avon, 1978), 317-423.

the anatomical sex of the two partners, they thought, one must play the man and the other the woman; one was an invert, and the other subject to homosexual tendencies.[29]

The "actively inverted woman," wrote Havelock Ellis in 1895, was distinguished from her partner by "one fairly essential character: a more or less distinct trace of masculinity." It was she who took the initiative in relations with other women. The second group of women were those "to whom the actively inverted woman is most attracted." Ellis described these women as "plain" in appearance and as almost asexual, with a "genuine, though not precisely sexual, preference for women over men"; they were "always womanly." He did not refer to these women as inverts, but rather as "a class in which homosexuality, while fairly distinct, is only slightly marked."[30] Allan MacLane Hamilton, writing in 1896, observed the same distinction between active and passive lesbians, emphasizing, like most writers, the correlation between inversion in sexual behavior and social role:

> The offender was usually of a masculine type, . . . [holding views which were] erratic, 'advanced,' and extreme, and she nearly always lacked the ordinary modesty and retirement of her sex. The passive agent was, as a rule, decidedly feminine, with little power of resistance, usually sentimental or unnecessarily prudish. . . . [T]he weak victim can be made the tool of the designing companion.[31]

Hamilton's description, like the one by Ellis, suggested that the passive, feminine woman was almost asexual, simply the recipient (or victim) of active lesbian advances, much as women might be considered the sexual victims of men. Her prudishness and sentimentality were also hallmarks of the Victorian lady's prescribed sexual consciousness — precisely the reverse of the invert's sexually aggressive, man-like character. As another writer later put it, one could imagine her

29 Only further research will reveal the actual organization and phenomenology of lesbian and gay male relationships during this period. In the mid-twentieth century, certainly, "butch-fem" relationships were the norm for many couples. For an important reappraisal of lesbian role-playing, see Joan Nestle, "Butch-Fem Relationships: Sexual Courage in the 1950s," *Heresies* 12 (1981): 21-24.

30 Ellis, "Sexual Inversion in Women," 147-48. Ellis used the same wording in the third edition of *Sexual Inversion* (1915), 222.

31 Hamilton, "Civil Responsibility of Sexual Perverts," 505.

remaining involved with inverts only until she came "under the influence of a man."

The passive homosexual woman thus occupied an ambiguous position in medical thinking, for though her deviation from social norms was qualitatively different from the more easily recognizable perversion of her seducer, the invert, she did respond to another woman's advances. By the end of the nineteenth century, however, the medical profession had begun expressing greater concern about such women. Hamilton himself complained about the lack of attention paid them in earlier years, citing the difficulties he had once faced in a case involving one, since "at that time her mental perversion was not of a recognized kind."[32] In explaining the difficulty — but urgency — of detecting female homosexuality, Ellis pointed out that "we are accustomed to a much greater familiarity and intimacy between women than between men, and we are less apt to suspect the existence of any abnormal passion."[33]

Doctors increasingly subjected to medical inquiry relations between women which they previously had considered properly asexual, and they sought to identify both active and passive lesbians. Doctors began to discern homosexual elements in such single-sex institutions as "convents, boarding schools, manufacturing establishments, etc.," and the "smashes" common to girls' schools — powerful emotional relationships between students — were studied by doctors in the United States and several European and Latin American countries.[34] The researchers viewed both active and passive lesbians as pathological because of their object choice. Douglas McMurtrie, for instance, who wrote prolifically on lesbianism in the mid-1910s, agreed that in "the relations of Lesbian couples we find that the sexuality of the two

32 Ibid., 507.

33 Ellis, "Sexual Inversion in Women," 142.

34 Douglas McMurtrie, "Sexual Inversion Among Women in Spain;" idem, "Principles of Homosexuality and Sexual Inversion in the Female;" Ellis, *Sexual Inversion*, 214-16. Ellis appended an essay on "The School Friendships of Girls" to *Sexual Inversion*, 368-84, which mentions studies in the United States, Italy, England, and Argentina. The U.S. study was by E.G. Lancaster, "The Psychology and Pedagogy of Adolescence," *Pedagogical Seminary* (July 1897). See also Nancy Sahli, "Smashing: Women's Relations Before the Fall," and Lillian Faderman, "Lesbian Magazine Fiction in the Early Twentieth Century." Faderman mentions several popular short stories which unselfconsciously describe intense, emotional relationships between girls and young women at school. For particularly charming examples, see Jeanette Lee, "The Cat and the King," *Ladies Home Journal* (October 1919), 10, 67-68, 71 — an unusually late example; and "The Evolution of Evangeline," in Josephine Dodge Daskam, *Smith College Stories* (New York: Scribners, 1900), 247-78.

individuals is comparative [i.e., 'complementary']." One would be the "more masculine" and "play the male part" both by courting the other and "play[ing] the active role in the sexual relations." But McMurtrie evinced none of the older nineteenth-century sympathy for the woman seduced. He even argued that these roles were reversible; the woman who played the masculine role in one relationship might be forced to play the woman to another, even more masculine partner.[35]

The role of the "wife" in lesbian relationships was increasingly sexualized in the medical literature, which saw her no longer as simply victimized by the invert's advances but as fully complicit in homosexual perversion. In later years the heterosexual paradigm itself seemed less satisfactory to doctors. In 1913, Margaret Otis published a study of interracial sexual relationships at a girls' reformatory ("A Perversion Not Commonly Noted"). Although keen to discover who "seemed the man" in the relationships, it was not obvious to her, and she defined the young women's perversion in terms of their homosexuality and interracialism rather than their role inversion.[36] It was only twenty years later, however, that researchers seriously disputed the heterosexual paradigm. Lura Beam and Robert Latou Dickinson carefully explained that every lesbian in their study who had been asked "whether she or the other person took the male part" answered that it was not she; "the typical reply was that they did not think of it in that way."[37] Beam emphasized that "no transposition to male feeling or manifestation of male sexuality" appeared in the case histories, and that the women alternately assumed various *female* roles such as child, equal, and mother in their relationships.[38] By refuting the paradigm, however, Beam's study highlighted the increasing importance attached to sexual object choice instead of gender characteristics in classifying women's sexual deviance.

The Explanation of the Perverse

Given the nature and purposes of the medical profession at the turn of the century, it is not surprising that so profound a redefinition of

35 McMurtrie, "Principles of Homosexuality and Sexual Inversion in the Female," 152. Elsewhere McMurtrie noted that "the authorities on this matter" believed all lesbians took on "active" or "passive" roles ("Manifestations of Sexual Inversion in the Female . . . ," 424).

36 Margaret Otis, "A Perversion Not Commonly Noted," *Journal of Abnormal Psychology* 8 (1913): 113-16.

37 Robert Latou Dickinson and Lura Beam, *The Single Woman: A Medical Study in Sex Education* (New York: Harper and Brothers, 1929), 212.

38 Ibid., 214, 203.

sexual deviance and the role of gender in sexual identity should have occurred. The medical profession's reconsideration of the nature of mental disease and disorder during this period also provided the context for the emergence of quickly changing and often contradictory explanations of inversion and homosexuality. Changes in theories concerning sexual deviance parallelled those concerning mental disease in general; doctors' growing conviction in the late nineteenth century that nervous disorders had a somatic (physical) basis and demonstrated somatic symptoms, for instance, profoundly influenced studies of inversion. Once sexual inversion had been successfully classified as a disease, therefore, its intellectual history was significantly influenced by broader trends in the history of medicine. Within this general context, the emergence of medical theories concerning inversion was related particularly closely to medical theories of women's and men's biological and social roles, physical ailments, and sexual disorders. Inversion theories were thus part of a logical system whose structure we can analyze in order to learn the medical profession's and society's basic assumptions about sexuality and gender.

Before the medical profession could explain inversion authoritatively, it had to demonstrate that inversion was symptomatic of a disease, and thus a matter properly in the domain of medicine, rather than of religion or the law. Numerous doctors in the 1880s and nineties had to argue that "conditions once considered criminal are really pathological, and come within the province of the physician."[39] As G. Frank Lydston wrote in 1889,

> The subject has been until a recent date studied solely from the standpoint of the moralist, and from the indisposition of the scientific physician to study the subject, the unfortunate class of individuals who are characterized by perverted sexuality have been viewed in the light of their moral responsibility rather than as the victims of a physical and incidentally of a mental defect.[40]

But although early medical theorists criticized the religious precept that sexual inversion represented a sinful act of will, for a short while

39 Shrady, "Perverted Sexual Instinct," 71; R.W. Shufeldt, "Dr. William Lee Howard on 'The Perverts'," *Pacific Medical Journal* 45 (1902): 143-50; Wise, "Case of Sexual Perversion," 91; William Lee Howard, "Sexual Perversion," *Alienist and Neurologist* 17 (1896): 6.

40 George Frank Lydston, "Sexual Perversion, Satyriasis and Nymphomania," *Medical and Surgical Reporter* 61 (1889): 253.

their theories gave willful anti-social behavior a central role in its etiology. The earliest medical model considered inversion to be an acquired disease, which the individual could avoid by refraining from improper activity. This is particularly evident in the role which Richard von Krafft-Ebing, George Beard, and others attributed to masturbation in inversion's etiology in the 1870s and eighties. Krafft-Ebing's concern about the effects of masturbation, for instance, resulted from his conviction that normal, "civilized" sexual relations could occur only in the emotional context of a loving, monogamous, heterosexual relationship, the result of "noble and ideal sentiments."[41] To masturbate was to seek the mere gratification of lust, and put one "at once on a level with the beast" thus "despoil[ing] the unfolded bud of perfume and beauty, and leav[ing] behind only the coarse, animal desire for sexual satisfaction."[42] The results could be ominous: a loss of interest in the other sex, preference for masturbation over "the natural mode of satisfaction," or even homosexual desire.[43] Self-abuse was thus a vice which one properly avoided, and inversion was only one of its worst consequences.[44]

New theories which emphasized inversion's congenital nature and biological basis superceded older concerns about environmental and volitional factors in the 1880s and nineties. This was simply one instance of the growing preeminence of somatically-based theories in the explanation of nervous disease, but the form taken by the somatic explanation of inversion highlights particularly sharply both the polarization of gender roles implicit in the broad definition given sexual inversion and the assertion by late Victorian medicine of the biological determination of the sex/gender system. Medical theory tied men and women's gender characteristics so closely to their respective biological sexes that a somatic explanation had to be found for those people who

41 Krafft-Ebing, *Psychopathia Sexualis*, 286.

42 Ibid., 1, 286.

43 The conviction that sexual relations were "healthy" only in the context of a romantic heterosexual relationship persisted. In 1929, Lura Beam noted that the famous gynecologist Robert Latou Dickinson considered "sex expression without avowed emotional interest in other persons" as well as homosexual desire to be "regress[ive]" (*Single Woman*, xiii).

44 Even after theories attributing a causal role to masturbation in the etiology of homosexuality were discarded, many medical observers continued to claim a correlation between the two. Wilhelm Stekel, *Bisexual Love*, transl. J.S. Teslaar (Boston: R.G. Badger, 1922), 13-15, e.g., while specifically criticizing Krafft-Ebing's reasoning, also asserted a correlation. See also William Lee Howard, "Psychical Hermaphroditism: A Few Notes on Sexual Perversion with Two Clinical Cases of Sexual Inversion," *Alienist and Neurologist* 17 (1897): 111-18; Ellis, *Sexual Inversion*, 276-77.

threatened to contradict the theory by appearing to be one sex while assuming the gender role of the other (the so-called "opposite" sex).

One of the most influential theories at the turn of the century proposed a radical solution to this dilemma, by asserting that inverts simply were not the sex they first appeared to be, but were hermaphrodites, incorporating biological elements of both sexes. For Herbert Clairborne, for instance, this provided the only possible explanation not only for lesbianism but also for the violent tactics of British suffragists in 1914, whose acts, he thought, "are certainly not in any sense feminine." The cause of both phenomena, he wrote in an article nomimally on hypertrichosis (excessive hair growth) in women, "lies in the possession by the individual of structural cellular elements of the opposite sex."[45] James Kiernan argued that the ancestors of the human race were "bisexual" (i.e., hermaphroditic), but that highly differentiated gender roles had evolved during the course of human civilization. Disease or congenital defects in a particular individual, however, could eliminate the "inhibitions" which prevented people from acting on their atavistic impulses.[46] Havelock Ellis incorporated a version of this theory in *Sexual Inversion* when he argued that each person contained male and female "germs" of varying strengths, arranged in a variety of configurations which determined the individual's physical and psychic states.[47] Thus masculine physical attributes could be a sign of psychic masculinity and perversion in women. "Bearded women approach the masculine type," Clairborne observed, and an exceptionally high percentage of them (68% in one 1881 survey he cited) were unmarried.[48]

Scientific concern about hermaphroditism has often resulted from challenges to the sex/gender system in Western history,[49] but it took

45 Clairborne, "Hypertrichosis in Women: Its Relation to Bisexuality (Hermaphroditism): With Remarks on Bisexuality in Animals, Especially Man," 1183, 1181.

46 Kiernan, "Sexual Perversion and the Whitechapel Murders," 129; Lydston, "Sexual Perversion, Satyriasis and Nymphomania," 254-55; George Frank Lydston, *The Disease of Society (The Vice and Crime Problem)* (Philadelphia: J.B. Lippincott, 1904).

47 Ellis, *Sexual Inversion*, 310-11.

48 Clairborne, "Hypertrichosis in Women . . . ," 1178. The survey cited by Clairborne was reported in Max Bartell, "Ueber abnorme Behaarung beim Menschen," *Zeitschrift fuer Ethnologie* 13 (1881). Of 146 women surveyed, 106 were single.

49 Hermaphroditism has long been associated with inversion and been a subject of medical inquiry. In 1836, for instance, a woman discovered passing as a married, male factory worker in Patterson, New Jersey, tried to persuade a court that she was an hermaphrodite. Although "surgical examination prove[d] her statement to be false," the newspaper account of the incident suggests the court might have considered this a reasonable excuse for her behavior (*The National Laborer*[New York], 25 August 1836; thanks to David Roediger for drawing my attention to this document). For

particular form in the scientific discourse of the late nineteenth century. Victorian medical conceptions of woman, for instance, centered on her reproductive role and organs, as Carroll Smith-Rosenberg has shown; puberty and menopause were the two great endpoints and crises of womanhood, and menstruation her fundamental identifying characteristic.[50] The early medical case histories of lesbians thus predictably paid enormous attention to their menstrual flow and the size of their sexual organs. Several doctors emphasized that their lesbian patients stopped menstruating at an early age, if they began at all, or had unusually difficult and irregular periods. They also inspected the women's sexual organs, often claiming that inverts had unusually large clitorises, which they said the inverts used in sexual intercourse as a man would his penis.[51] Underlying all such descriptions and inquiries was the assumption that persons who behaved as the female invert did simply could not be women.

As somatically-oriented psychological theories began to wane in the early years of this century, however, the theory of psychic hermaphroditism superceded that of the physical. The evidence against somatically-based theories of nervous and mental disease became overwhelming in the general scientific literature during this period, and this was the case in studies of inversion as well. For although scrupulous attention was paid to physical organs in the case histories, many investigators did after all have to report that there were no physical abnormalities.[52] Some doctors continued to argue, however, that even

49 Continued
discussion of earlier appearances of hermaphroditism as a subject of medical inquiry, see John Boswell, *Christianity, Social Tolerance, and Homosexuality: Gay People in Western Europe from the Beginning of the Christian Era to the Fourteenth Century* (Chicago: University of Chicago Press, 1980), and Michel Foucault, *Herculine Barbin: Being the Recently Discovered Memoirs of a Nineteenth-Century Hermaphrodite*, transl. Richard McDougall (New York: Pantheon Books, 1980).

50 Carroll Smith-Rosenberg, "Puberty to Menopause: The Cycle of Femininity in Nineteenth Century America," in *Clio's Consciousness Raised*, 23-37.

51 See, for example, Wise, "Case of Sexual Perversion," 90; Lichtenstein, "The Fairy and the Lady Lover," 372; J.C. Shaw and G.N. Ferris, "Perverted Sexual Instinct," *Journal of Nervous and Mental Disease* 10 (1883): 185-204, which summarizes the cases previously reported in the European literature; and James Kiernan's comment in 1916, when his opinion had changed, that although earlier doctors had usually looked for "an enlarged clitoris as a stigma of perversion," Havelock Ellis had since demonstrated that it was not characteristic of lesbians ("Increase of Sexual Perversion," *Urologic and Cutaneous Review* 20 (1916): 45).

52 Trignant Burrow, "The Genesis and Meaning of 'Homosexuality' and its Relation to the Problem of Introverted Mental States," *Psychoanalytic Review* 4 (1917): 272-84, and James Kiernan, "Comment on Burrows: The Genesis and Meaning of Homosexuality and its Relation to the Problem of Introverted Mental States," *Urologic and Cutaneous Review* 21 (1917): 467.

if the hermaphrodite's anatomical features were of its biological sex, its mind must surely be of the other sex. Karl Ulrichs, the first German writer (and for decades the only openly gay man) to discuss inversion in a public forum, had first characterized male inversion as representing a "woman's spirit in a man's body" in the 1860s. Many of the next generation of gay intellectuals, including Edward Carpenter and Magnus Hirschfeld, adopted a version of this theory at the turn of the century, claiming that they were best characterized as an "intermediate sex" (the loose but popular translation of *sexuelle Zwischenstufe*), hermaphroditically combining psychic qualities of both the male and female.[53]

Richard von Krafft-Ebing introduced degeneration theory as a means of explaining inversion in the early editions of his monumental work, *Psychopathia Sexualis*. His explanation quickly gained wide currency in the United States, for in the last years of the nineteenth century degeneration theory had come to dominate explanations of nervous and mental disease in general. The theory drew from those currents in late Victorian thought which postulated an organic relationship between the processes of evolution and civilization. The development of sexual morality and order, according to Krafft-Ebing, laid the "basis upon which social advancement is developed." Lust ran wild in primitive society, which tolerated acts which civilized society considered criminal, he argued, while the Victorian sexual order represented both the pinnacle and the necessary basis of the world's most advanced civilization. Maintaining such a society required that human sexual relations be based on love and monogamy; sexual relations outside of the heterosexual institution of marriage thus represented not only a degeneration to an earlier, lower state of evolution, but threatened civilization itself.[54]

Krafft-Ebing's theory led investigators to consider the relationship of social development to the evolution of sexual morality, and resulted in the publication of numerous anthropological studies of "primitive" sexual morality in medical journals. Several studies described the

53 For a brief statement of Edward Carpenter's views, see his essay, "The Intermediate Sex," in his *Love's Coming-of-Age* (London: George Allen and Unwin, Ltd., 1906; 12th enl. ed., 1923), 130-49. See also Florence Beery, "The Psyche of the Intermediate Sex," *Medico-Legal Journal* 41 (1924): 4-9.

54 Krafft-Ebing, *Psychopathia Sexualis*, 344-46. For background on degeneration theory, see Nathan Hale, Jr., *Freud and the Americans: The Beginnings of Psychoanalysis in the United States, 1876-1917* (New York and Oxford: Oxford University Press, 1971), 75-76.

institutionalization of homosexual relations or inversion in Native American and Asian societies (usually involving transvestism and mirroring the heterosexual paradigm), thus lending support to the argument that primitive cultures could be characterized by their tolerance of such practices.[55] Early gay scholars devoted much of their attention to the refutation of this argument, however, and the work of John Addington Symonds and others on the role of homosexuality in ancient Greek civilization was widely cited to that end. If homosexuality not only was tolerated but flourished in the culture which represented the epitome of Western civilization, they asked, how could it be associated with degeneration? Edward Carpenter argued that inverts had made special contributions to civilization as artists, spiritualists, and warriors in primitive societies.[56] Such arguments doubtless did not persuade the unconvinced, but they dominated the medical literature by the mid-teens.

Several theories, including that of degeneration, embodied middle class assumptions about the class nature of sexual morality as well as a concern about the standards of the 'civilized West.' For the medical profession grew out of the white middle class and reflected its values

55 C.G. Seligmann, "Sexual Inversion Among Primitive Races," *Alienist and Neurologist* 23 (1902): 580-83; William J. Robinson, "The Bote [abstract of an anthropologist's article]," *Journal of Sexology and Psychoanalysis* 1 (1923): 544-46; Ellis, *Sexual Inversion*, 205-9. One article, however, while making no comment on male homosexuality, described men's violent repression of lesbianism: Douglas McMurtrie, "Legend of Lesbian Love Among the North American Indians," *Urologic and Cutaneous Review* 18 (1914): 192.

56 Edward Carpenter, *Intermediate Types Among Primitive Folk* (London, 1914); John Addington Symonds, *A Problem in Greek Ethics: Being an Inquiry Into the Phenomenon of Sexual Inversion* (privately printed, 1883, 1901); M.H.E. Meier, "Paederastia," in J.S. Ersch and J.J. Gruber, *Algemeine Encyclopaedie der Wissenschaften und Kuensten* (Leipzig: Brockhaus, 1837), 3.9.149-88. Symond's privately printed treatise was "Addressed Especially to Medical Psychologists and Jurists" (title page). The work was to have been included as an Appendix to Ellis' *Sexual Inversion*, but Symonds' estate bought out the first English edition in 1897 and withdrew permission for its inclusion in subsequent editions (Weeks, *Coming Out*, 59-60). For examples of the utilization of the Greek evidence introduced by Symonds and others, see I.H. Coriat, "Homosexuality: Its Psychogenesis and Treatment," *New York Medical Journal* 97 (1913): 589-94; Ellis, *Sexual Inversion*, 197-98; Kiernan, "Homosexuality in Early Greek Poetry," *Urologic and Cutaneous Review* 24 (1920): 670; idem, "Sexual Inversion Among Greek Women," ibid.: 665-66; McMurtrie, "Principles of Homosexuality and Sexual Inversion in the Female," 145-46; Rivers, "A New Male Homosexual Trait (?)," 22. The wealth of information available did not prevent Freud from misrepresenting Aristophanes' legend of the hermaphrodites (Plato, *Symposium*, 189c-193d) in his *Three Essays*, 2. The original legend explained the creation of what might be called lesbians and gay men as well as heterosexuals, but Freud implied that it referred only to the latter.

and concerns in an extremely class-conscious manner; it perceived not only non-Europeans but also America's own lower classes as immoral. Doctors assumed that sexual license and sensuality characterized the poor and working classes, that only the middle and upper classes had "achieved" a sense of sexual propriety.[57] Degeneration theory explained the immorality of the poor — as well as their poverty — by asserting the degeneration of the class as a whole. Some nineteenth-century alienists maintained that sanity and morality alike were socially constructed and a function of class: behavior common to the "immoral" classes, when it appeared in a person from a higher class, could thus be a sign of insanity. Others maintained that the working class suffered from a high incidence of sexual disorders and disease because of its sexual excess.

Each of these tendencies is evident in the medical literature on homosexuality. A number of doctors who described inversion as a disease when it afflicted their middle class patients considered it to be an immoral, willfully chosen mode of behavior on the part of the poor. This distinction was sometimes expressed as the difference between congenital or disease-induced "perversion" and willfull, immoral "perversity"; the person suffering from perversion was to be pitied, while those who were simply perverse, perhaps responding to the pervert's advances, were "worse than the pervert and deserve no sympathy."[58] Furthermore, many doctors accused servants, the representatives of the working class in the middle class household, of introducing perversion into respectable homes. Highlighting one of the most frightful aspects of the Victorian "servant problem," doctors charged that servants showed children how to masturbate, which resulted in their becoming involved in homosexual activity.

Prostitutes, of whom Magnus Hirschfeld, Havelock Ellis, and other major sexologists asserted a quarter or more were lesbian, came under particular attack in this context. Female prostitutes (and even more emphatically their male counterparts) chose to respond to the perverse sexual demands of their diseased clients, in and of itself damnable behavior; many doctors maintained that in so doing the prostitutes further perverted their sexuality. In one widely accepted theory, the

57 Peter T. Cominos, "Late Victorian Sexual Respectability and the Social System," *International Review of Social History* 8 (1963): 33, 238-40; Smith-Rosenberg, "The Hysterical Woman," 667; Charles Rosenberg, "Sexuality, Class and Role in Nineteenth Century America," *American Quarterly* 25 (1973): 131-54.

58 Lichtenstein, "The Fairy and the Lady Lover," 374; Krafft-Ebing. "Perversion of the Sexual Instinct: Report of Cases," 565-66.

lesbianism of female prostitutes was but one of the sexual perversities resulting from their "satiation" with "normal" sex.[59] For others, however, prostitution necessarily indicated a partial, organic inversion, since the women were without "feminine honor." Havelock Ellis argued in this vein that the "prevalence of homosexuality among women in prison [presumably working class women] is connected with the close relationship between feminine criminality and prostitution."[60] To many doctors, prostitutes seem to have embodied the sensuality and sexual immorality of the working class, but doctors did not believe perversity was restricted to them. Female hotel servants and factory workers were also frequently accused of lesbian behavior. In part this seems to have reflected the growing concern about women in single-sex institutions such as boarding schools and convents, but the doctors' descriptions of autoeroticism, mutual masturbation, and other sexual activity amongst women workers were especially lurid and morbid. Even Havelock Ellis was shaken from his normal position to characterize factory-centered lesbianism as "homosexual *vice* . . . common and recognized."[61]

One of Havelock Ellis' major purposes was to establish the congenital basis of homosexuality; he considered this theory to be politically progressive, since it might remove homosexual behavior from the purview of the law.[62] By 1900, the medical profession had accepted the congenital theory in the explanation not only of inversion, but also of a wide range of other supposed mental diseases. Ellis and other sexologists also postulated the importance of heredity in its etiology, but how exactly it might have entered the hereditary chain continued to be disputed. The degenerationists themselves had claimed that, once acquired, sexual perversion was inheritable, each generation suffering an exacerbated form. Doctors such as George Beard, who associated inversion with a variety of other mental disorders, frequently noted the

59 Douglas McMurtrie, "Sexual Inversion Among Women in Spain"; Howard, "Sexual Perversion," 4; Ellis, "Sexual Inversion Among Women," 157.

60 Ellis, *Sexual Inversion*, 209-10.

61 Ibid., 214 (my emphasis; it is extremely uncharacteristic for Ellis to term homosexuality a vice); Douglas McMurtrie, "Record of a French Case of Sexual Inversion," *Maryland Medical Review* 57 (1914): 170-81; idem, "Sexual Inversion Among Women in Spain." Race also plays an important role in sexual ideology, and theories used to stigmatize homosexual relations were used similarly in the case of interracial relations. See, for instance, Charles E. Hughes, "Homo Sexual Complexion Perverts in St. Louis: Note on a Feature of Sexual Psychopathy," *Alienist and Neurologist* 28 (1907): 487-88, which seems to find the interracialism of Black and white men found dancing together as disturbing — and pathological — as their homosexuality.

62 Weeks, *Coming Out*, 57-67.

incidence of neurasthenia and other nervous disorders in the invert's family history.[63] Later theorists, such as Ellis, were careful to specify the incidence of inversion itself, though often in conjunction with other neuroses.[64] The hermaphroditic theory which Kiernan, Lydston, and others espoused was not wholly incompatible with the congenital theory, and thus continued as an important theoretical tendency even after the demise of other aspects of the degeneration theory.

But the new psychological theories of Freud and his American followers challenged the hegemony of the congenital theory in the early 1900s. In his most radical thought, Freud posed heterosexuality as problematic in the same sense as homosexuality, by arguing that the suppression of any aspect of the libido required explanation.[65] But although he maintained that many inverts neither desired nor needed treatment, his now familiar theory that the "aberration" of homosexuality resulted from the child's failure to resolve psychosexual relations with one or another parent presupposed a preferred, healthier course of development.[66] Freud's work reintroduced the acquired theory of homosexuality so forcibly that congenital theorists such as Ellis were compelled to devote much of their later work to its refutation.[67]

Nevertheless, Freud's American followers and other non-Freudian psychiatrists continued to mix his radically mental explanation of homosexuality with those which attributed the "disorder" to congenital defects and even to vice. C.P. Oberndorf, for instance, argued in 1919 that only the behavior of "objective," passive lesbians, or "subjective,"

63 Shardy, "Perverted Sexual Instinct," 70; James Kiernan, "Perverted Sexual Instinct," *The Chicago Medical Journal and Examiner* 48 (1884): 264; idem, "Insanity: Sexual Perversion," *Detroit Lancet* 7 (1884): 483.

64 Ellis claimed in 1915 that the frequency of inversion among the near relatives of inverts whose case histories appeared in the literature was "now indisputable" (*Sexual Inversion*, 308).

65 Freud, *Three Essays*, 11-12, note added in 1915.

66 Ibid., esp. pp. 114. Abraham Brill provided the first English translation of this text in 1910, and published an article summarizing the essay on inversion three years later, "The Conception of Homosexuality," *Journal of the American Medical Association* 61 (1913): 335-40. Isadore Coriat's article that year also essentially summarized Freud's essay, "Homosexuality: Its Psychogenesis and Treatment." The American Freudians, and Freud himself, treated male homosexuality almost exlusively in their early writings, as Trignant Burrow pointed out in 1917, "The Genesis and Meaning of 'Homosexuality' and its Relation to the Problem of Introverted Mental States." Freud finally devoted a full essay to the explanation of lesbianism in 1920, "The Psychogenesis of a Case of Homosexuality in a Woman," *The Standard Edition of the Complete Psychological Works of Sigmund Freud*, transl. James Strachey, *et al* (London: Hogarth Press, 1955), 18: 174-72. An extended analysis of Freudian theories is beyond the scope of this article.

67 Ellis, *Sexual Inversion*, 304-9.

aggressive gay men, could be explained by psychotraumatic processes. For an aggressive gay man behaved sexually as a man should, he argued, and the "abnormal" fact that he chose to initiate sexual relations with a man instead of a woman was explicable in terms of a traumatic heterosexual experience in childhood, and could be cured by psychoanalysis. But Oberndorf believed this theory was inadequate to explain the behavior of the "objective" gay man (i.e., the passive "object" of sexual activity), the man called an invert in the nineteenth-century literature. These men, he argued, represented "biological anomalies of development which are often coupled with unmistakable physical signs."[68] Not only was their sexual object abnormal, but also their sexual aim, and only with the older theories of hermaphroditism and sexual intermediacy could Oberndorf adequately account for so fundamental an inversion of the man's (or obverse woman's) role.

Oberndorf's interweaving of several traditions of conceptualization and explanation in his analysis of homosexuality accurately reflects the intellectual confusion and anachronism of the period under consideration. The very subject of the debate had narrowed from comprehensive gender inversion to homosexual desire, although the heterosexual paradigm continued to structure much medical thinking, as Oberndorf's article indicates. But while the shift in subject accounts for some of the theoretical fluctuation, the primary cause rests in the more general crisis of medical thought at the turn of the century. Speculation about the etiology of homosexuality was but an aspect of a more general reconsideration of the nature and etiology of nervous disease, and closely adhered to the more general pattern.

The Insrumentality of the Perverse

To note the relationship between theories of inversion and of other supposed mental disorders, however, does not explain why gender deviance and homosexual relations became the subject of medical inquiry when they did, nor does it account for the changing focus of the inquiry. To examine these questions we must assess the broader cultural context in which the medical inquiry emerged. Such analysis can only be tentative and suggestive at this stage in our research, although recent scholarship in women's history has made it possible to understand more deeply the social context of the study of female sexuality than of male. The analysis I suggest here focuses on the reasons for the study

68 C.P. Oberndorf, "Homosexuality," *Medical Record* 46 (1919): 841.

of lesbianism, although it also considers inquiry into male inversion and homosexuality. I think that three developments in American society during this period were particularly important in this context: the increasing visibility of urban gay male subcultures, the political and economic challenges posed to the Victorian sex/gender system by women in the late nineteenth century, and the related "resexualization" of women in mainstream sexual ideology in the first decades of the twentieth. The professionalization of medicine and its rise to ideological hegemony over religion and, in certain arenas, the state apparatus, were also crucial to the process, but I will only note those developments here.[69]

In the late nineteenth century, increasing numbers of women began to question and challenge the limits placed on their social role, both institutionally through the suffrage movement and more generally through their entrance into the wage-labor force and the efforts of many to achieve economic and social independence. The declining marriage and birth rates of the native-born middle class and the general movement of women into men's sphere alarmed many men. Joe L. Dubbert has argued that a "masculinity crisis" developed in the years 1880-1920 because of the challenge posed to masculine sex-role definitions by both the women's movement and men's perception that women exerted undue influence over key cultural and socializing institutions.[70] The declining autonomy of both working class men at the factory and middle class men at the office, due to the introduction of scientific management, the undermining of the crafts, and the rationalization of clerical work, also may have contributed to this crisis.[71] Men who had lost power at the workplace may have needed to reassert power and to redefine their masculinity in their marriages and families. Conservative medical pronouncements played a key role in the ideological reaction to these challenges, and as Carroll Smith-Rosenberg and Charles Rosenberg have argued, "would-be scientific arguments were used in the rationalization and legitimization of almost every aspect

69 Several useful essays on this process appear in Susan Reverby and David Rosner, ed., *Health Care in America: Essays in Social History* (Philadelphia: Temple University Press, 1979). See also Michel Foucault, *The History of Sexuality*, and the several essays by Carroll Smith-Rosenberg and Charles Rosenberg cited above.

70 Joe L. Dubbert, "Progressivism and the Masculinity Crisis," *The Psychoanalytic Review* 61 (1974): 443-55.

71 Harry Braverman, *Labor and Monopoly Capital: The Degradation of Work in the Twentieth Century* (New York: Monthly Review Press, 1974); David Montgomery, *Worker's Control in America* (Cambridge: Cambridge University Press, 1979).

of Victorian life, with particular vehemence in those areas in which social change implied stress in existing social arrangements.[72]

The sudden growth in the medical literature on sexual inversion, I would argue, was part of the general ideological reaction by the medical profession to women's challenge to the sex/gender system during this period. The designation of their challenge as the *disease* of sexual inversion allowed male doctors both to explain the phenomenon in a non-threatening way and to stigmatize it as deviant behavior which should be avoided by "healthy" women. Thus the observation by A.M. Hamilton in 1896, that "the views of such a person were erratic, 'advanced,' and extreme, and she nearly always lacked the normal modesty and retirement of her sex," was not simply a curious addendum to his description of her homosexuality, as some have assumed, but was central to his concept of women's sexuality and social place, and the nature of the "invert's" disorder.[73]

The implicit concern about challenges to the sex/gender system which pervades these medical accounts was made quite explicit in some, which linked the apparent rise in sexual inversion to the influence of the women's movement. Havelock Ellis, as Nancy Sahli has noted, asserted such a relationship:

> Having been taught independence of men and disdain for the old theory which placed women in the moated grange of the home to sigh for a man who never comes, a tendency develops for women to carry this independence still farther and to find love where they find work.[74]

Ellis had to qualify his argument by noting that the "unquestionable influences of modern movements cannot *directly* cause sexual inversion" (my emphasis), since otherwise it would contradict his congenital theory, but his point was clear. He quoted without qualification the opinion of "a well informed American correspondent" that one of the "obvious reasons" for the increase in sexual inversion was "the growing independence of the women, their lessening need for

72 Smith-Rosenberg and Rosenberg, "The Female Animal," 332; Aileen Kraditor, *The Ideas of the Woman Suffrage Movement, 1890-1920* (New York: Anchor Books, 1971), 12-37.

73 Hamilton, "The Civil Responsibility of Sexual Perverts," 505. "Advanced" was a common codeword for "feminist."

74 Ellis, *Sexual Inversion*, 262.

marriage." He also reported on the extensive debate within advanced German medical and feminist circles about this relationship.[75] Other doctors attributed the supposed increase in inversion to the repudiation of motherhood by women influenced by feminism. The progeny of the woman who "prefers the laboratory to the nursery," warned William Lee Howard in 1900, "are perverts, moral or psychical." By forsaking their proper social role, he claimed, these "emancipated" women produced effeminate sons and masculine daughters.[76]

While some doctors indicated their concern about the women's movement by warning that it led to an increase in sexual inversion, others were even more explicit in postulating a literally organic relationship between the two. James Kiernan's comments in 1914 on the Clairborne article on hermaphroditism are interesting in this light, for they suggest that such an association was often proposed. "As might be expected," Kiernan wrote, "Clairborne does not finish his paper [nominally on hypertrichosis] without touching upon the influence of defective sexuality in women upon political questions. While, of course, he does not think every suffragist an invert, yet he does believe that the very fact that women in general of today are more and more deeply invading man's sphere is indicative of a certain impelling force within them."[77] Other doctors were less restrained in their appraisal of the organic relationship between the women's movement and inversion. Howard warned in his article of 1900 that

> The female possessed of masculine ideas of independence; the viragint who would sit in the public highways and lift up her pseudo-virile voice, proclaiming her sole right to decide questions of war or religion, or the value of celibacy and the curse of women's impurity, and that disgusting anti-social being, the female sexual pervert, are simply different degrees of the same class — degenerates.[78]

The same historical processes which generated concern about female gender deviance contributed to social apprehension about male

75 Ibid., 261, n. 3, 262-63. For documents from the German debate, as well as contemporary lesbian literature, see Lillian Faderman and Brigitte Eriksson, ed., *Lesbian-Feminism in Turn-of-the-Century Germany* (Weatherby Lake, Mo.: Naiad Press, 1980).

76 Howard, "Effeminate Men and Masculine Women," 687.

77 James Kiernan, "Bisexuality," *Urologic and Cutaneous Review* 18 (1914): 375; Clairborne, "Hypertrichosis in Women," 1183.

78 Howard, "Effeminate Men and Masculine Women," 687.

inversion. Values under attack are likely to be reasserted with particular vigor, and, as Joe L. Dubbert has argued, many men reacted to the crisis in masculine role definition at the turn of the century by reasserting the traditional values of masculinity. In this context, any man who behaved as if he had rejected his masculinity must have generated considerable anxiety on the part of other men, since his behavior implicitly challenged the biological basis attributed to the prescribed male role. Indeed, much of the nineteenth-century literature on male inversion treats these men as veritable traitors to the sex, and the inverts' supposed fear of women was seen as one of their most damning unmasculine traits.

Concern about men who refused to conform to masculine gender norms was exacerbated by the increasing visibility of gay male subcultures, which many observers attributed to urbanization. That doctors were aware of these subcultures and considered them to be a crucial subject of their inquiry is evidenced in some of the earliest articles on male inversion. G. Frank Lydston observed in 1889 that there was "in every community of any size a colony of male sexual perverts; they are usually known to each other and are likely to congregate together."[79] The phenomenon seemed especially evident in New York; even in the early 1880s, George Beard thought that many male inverts lived there, while by 1913 A.A. Brill confidently estimated there were "many thousands of homosexuals in New York City among all classes of society." Three years later, James Kiernan noted that gay men were popularly called "fairies" in New York and "brownies" in Philadelphia; he also knew of interracial gay cafes in Chicago.[80] Furthermore, doctors realized that the subjects of their inquiry already identified themselves as part of a sexual underground; two articles reporting the case histories of male inverts in the 1880s noted that "these patients claim to be able to recognize each other."[81] The very existence of such subcultures motivated doctors' interest in male inversion and homosexuality; they considered it their proper domain — and responsibility — to map out the typology of the emerging sexual undergound, and to classify its inhabitants in ever more discrete

79 Lydston, "Sexual Perversion, Satyriasis and Nymphomania," 254.

80 Beard, *Sexual Neurasthenia*, 102; Brill, "The Conception of Homosexuality," 335; James Kiernan, "Classification of Homosexuality," *Urologic and Cutaneous Review* 20 (1916): 350.

81 James Kiernan, "Insanity: Sexual Perversion" *Detroit Lancet* 7 (1884): 482; G. Adler Blumer, "A Case of Perverted Sexual Instinct (Contraere Sexualempfindung)," *American Journal of Insanity* 39 (1882): 25. Krafft-Ebing made a similar observation of German "inverts" in "Perversions of the Sexual Instinct: Report of Cases," 570.

categories. They were investigating a subculture rather than creating one.

Despite the ideological attacks on feminist and wage-earning women, their challenge to the Victorian sex/gender system resulted in limited but significant changes. The number of employed women continued to increase; women secured new positions in the professions; and they won two major political campaigns, for suffrage and prohibition. Their economic and political advances led to changes in the cultural conception of middle class womanhood. The early decades of the century witnessed a "new freedom in manners and morals" for women, and the resexualization of women in mainstream sexual ideology. Although that ideology continued to postulate the greater sexual interest and aggressiveness of the male, it increasingly allowed women the capacity for sexual interest and initiative.[82] To a limited extent, gender norms changed to recognize the greater complexity of actual gender roles in the society. Particularly notable was the weakening of the holistic character of masculinity and femininity in the ideological system; doctors began to question whether one aspect of one's behavior — sexual passivity or aggressiveness — was paradigmatic for one's entire gender role, although more decisively in the case of men than of women. Thus the increasing differentiation of "perversions" in medical thought may itself have reflected the decline of the older holistic concepts of gender, and the increasing complexity of actual gender roles in American society.

But the liberalization of gender norms in the face of women's activism did not alter the fundamental power relations between men and women, and it was in this context that the "homosexual" replaced the "invert" as the subject of medical concern. For if it no longer was considered a deviation from the norm for a woman to initiate sexual relations, then it no longer needed to be considered an inversion of her sexual or social role to do so. But once all women were considered able to experience and act on sexual desire, medical concern shifted logically from the *fact* of women's sexual activity to their *choice* of sexual and

82 Michael Gordon, "From an Unfortunate Necessity to a Cult of Mutual Orgasm: Sex in American Marital Literature, 1830-1940," in James Henslin and Edward Sagarin, ed., *The Sociology of Sex* (New York: Schocken Books, 1978), 59-84; James McGovern, "The American Woman's Pre-World War I Freedom in Manners and Morals," *Journal of American History* 55 (1968): 315-33. The historical literature on women in this period is thoughtfully reviewed in Estelle B. Freedman, "The New Woman: Changing Views of Women in the 1920s," *Journal of American History* 61 (1974): 372-93.

social partners. The fact that some women chose other women rather than men as sexual partners thus became the primary fact to be explained and condemned, despite the narrowness of this issue compared to inversion; as we have seen, both the "active" and "passive" partners came under scrutiny. Indeed, the resexualization of women — in one sense a progressive development — was used to tie them to men, as the culture increasingly postulated the importance of women's sexual desire as a basis for their involvement in heterosexual institutions such as marriage, which their employment supposedly rendered less of an economic necessity than before. The new complexity — and restrictiveness — of sex/gender roles was epitomized by the flapper, who was at once both sexually precocious and profoundly heterosexual.

The new celebration of heterosexual bonding and the increasing hostility to homosexual relations between women evident in both the medical literature and the broader culture were central to the general subversion of women's culture and solidarity which Estelle Freedman and other historians have identified as instrumental in the decline of the women's movement after the attainment of suffrage in 1920. The growth of the movement, and the very ability of numerous activists and professional and working class women to work, had depended in part on the development in the nineteenth century of a women's culture of supportive friendships and networks.[83] The most striking indication of this development is that in the closing years of the century many feminist activists and professional women chose not to marry at all, but to be sustained by their relationships with other women. Heterosexual marriage and motherhood, as constituted in Victorian society — unlike relationships with women — would have left them little chance to pursue their chosen work.

In this context, the increasing denigration of single sex institutions and relations and the new urgency attached to the development of women's relations with men in the 1910s and twenties constituted — to modify a current phrase — a veritable "Heterosexual

83 Estelle Freedman, "Separatism as Strategy: Female Institution Building and American Feminism, 1870-1930," *Feminist Studies* 5 (1979): 512-29. The most important works contributing to this argument include Nancy F. Cott, *The Bonds of Womanhood* (New Haven: Yale University Press, 1977); Ellen DuBois, "The Radicalism of the Woman Suffrage Movement: Notes Toward the Reconstruction of Nineteenth-Century Feminism," *Feminist Studies* 3 (1975): 63-71; and Blance Weisen Cook, "Female Support Networks and Political Activism: Lillian Wald, Crystal Eastman, Emma Goldman," in Nancy F. Cott and Elizabeth H. Pleck, ed., *A Heritage of Her Own* (New York: Simon and Schuster, 1979), 412-44.

Counterrevolution." The available evidence suggests that this was a pervasive phenomenon in middle class culture; the newly burgeoning advertising industry did its part, and the marriage manuals of the 1920s and thirties, according to Christina Simmons, emphasized the need for men to develop "companionate marriages" in order to make marriage more attractive and satisfying to women. The results were also widely evident. Some observers noted that dyadic, heterosexual dating had replaced same-sex group activities as the dominant pattern of youth culture by the 1920s, while autobiographical material from the decade suggests that increasing numbers of professional women chose to marry, often to the detriment of their careers. A full explanation of the decline of the women's movement after 1920 would have to consider many factors, including outright political repression and more subtle processes such as the reconstitution of women as "consumers" upon the rapid expansion of the consumer economy during this period. But the increasing hostility to a women's culture of supportive relationships and networks was also crucial to the movement's decline,[84] and it is in this context that we may best understand the growing medical concern about homosexual desire. Scientific discourse reflected and was but one aspect of a much broader subversion of women's culture and reconstitution of sexual and gender relations in a manner which linked women to men.

Conclusion

Sexuality is socially structured in a complex relationship with gender, class, and other lines of social demarcation, in order to serve definite social purposes, and a recognition of how profoundly sexual categories and norms can change is essential to the development of a satisfactory conceptual framework for the historical and political analysis of sexuality. Examining the changing focus of sexological inquiry points out how important it is in our study of the history of homosexuality

84 Christina Simmons, "Companionate Marriage and the Lesbian Threat," *Frontiers* 4 (Fall 1979): 54-59. The observers of youth culture were Robert S. Lynd and Helen Merrell Lynd, *Middletown: A Study in American Culture* (New York: Harcourt, Brace & World, 1929), 110. Short autobiographies published in *The Nation* in the 1920s are collected in Elaine Showalter, ed., *These Modern Women* (Old Westbury, NY: The Feminist Press, 1978). See also J. Stanley Lemons, *The Woman Citizen: Social Feminism in the 1920s* (Urbana: University of Illinois Press, 1975) and Mary Ryan, *Womanhood in America* (New York: New Viewpoints, 1979, 2nd ed.), 151-82. Discussions in Nancy Cott's seminars at Yale in U.S. women's history also contributed substantially to my thinking on these issues.

to reconstruct the conceptual frameworks in which homoerotic desire and relations have been understood. As in the late nineteenth century, such conceptual schemas may not even have recognized homoeroticism as a discrete sexual phenomenon.

The medical literature on sexual deviance was not the central force in the transformation of popular attitudes and the social relations of sexuality between 1880 and 1930. But it does provide us with a key to understanding the politics of sexuality during that period. It developed in response to challenges to the Victorian sex/gender system and the emergence of sexual subcultures in the cities, and it changed in a manner which reflected changes in the actual organization of sex/gender roles in the society. The medical profession's increasing concern about homosexual desire, and its differentiation of homosexual object choice from deviant gender behavior, represent both a reorientation of gender norms and a continuing imperative to define and delimit the range of acceptable social relations.

"IMAGINE MY SURPRISE": WOMEN'S RELATIONSHIPS IN HISTORICAL PERSPECTIVE*

Leila J. Rupp

Leila Rupp teaches women's history and women's studies at Ohio State University in Columbus. She wrote this essay "in a burst of anger" after reading The Life of Lorena Hickok *and* The Making of a Feminist *while on fellowship at the Murray Research Center, and she is grateful to the Radcliffe Research Scholars Program for making possible her research at the Schlesinger Library. Rupp is currently writing a book on the American women's movement in the 1940's and 1950's and, with Verta Taylor, has received a grant from the National Endowment for the Humanities to interview women who were active in the movement at that time. They are hoping to learn, as preparation for the 1980's, how feminists survived the 1950's.*

When Carroll Smith-Rosenberg's article, "The Female World of Love and Ritual," appeared in the pages of *Signs* in 1975, it revolutionized the way in which women's historians look at nineteenth-century American society and even served notice on the historical profession at large that women's relationships would have to be taken into account in any consideration of Victorian society.[1] Since then we have learned more about relationships between women in the past, but we have not reached consensus on the issue of characterizing these relationships.[2] On the one hand, Smith-Rosenberg's work has increasingly been misused to deny the sexual aspect of relationships between prominent women in the past. On the other hand, feminist scholars have responded to such distortions by bestowing the label "lesbian" on women who would themselves not have used the term. The issue goes beyond labels, however, because the very nature of women's relationships is so complex. I would like to consider here the issue of women's relationships in historical perspective by reviewing the conflicting approaches, by presenting examples of different kinds of women's relationships from my own research on the American women's movement in the 1940's and 1950's, and finally, by suggesting a conceptual approach that recognizes the complexity of women's relationships without denying the common bond shared by all women who have committed their lives to other women in the past.

Looking first at what Blanche Cook proclaims "the historical denial of lesbianism," we find the most recent, most publicized, and most egregious example in Doris Faber's *The Life of Lorena Hickok: E.R.'s Friend*, the story of the relationship of Eleanor Roosevelt and reporter Lorena Hickok.[3]

The Hickok book would make fascinating material for a case study of homophobia. Author Doris Faber presents page after page of evidence that delineates the growth and development of a love affair between the two women, yet she steadfastly maintains that a woman of Eleanor Roosevelt's "stature" could not have *acted* on the love which she expressed for Hickok. This attitude forces Faber to go to great lengths with the evidence before her. For example, she quotes a letter Roosevelt wrote to Hickok and asserts that it is "particularly susceptible to misinterpretation." Roosevelt's wish to "lie down beside you tonight & take you in my arms," Faber claims represents maternal—"albeit rather extravagantly" maternal—solicitude. For Faber, "there can be little doubt that the final sentence of the above letter does not mean what it appears to mean."[4]

Faber's interpretation, unfortunately, is not an isolated one. She acknowledges an earlier "sensitive" and "fine" book, *Miss Marks and Miss Woolley*, for reinforcing her own views "regarding the unfairness of using contemporary standards to characterize the behavior of women brought up under almost inconceivably different standards."[5] Anna Mary Wells, the author of the Marks and Woolley book, set out originally to write a biography of Mary Woolley and almost abandoned the plan when she discovered the love letters of the two women. Ultimately Wells went ahead with a book about the relationship, but only after she decided, as she explains in the preface, that there was no physical relationship between them. Comforted by this conviction, Wells paints a detailed picture of the joys and sorrows of their life together, even acknowledging the role that hostility toward their relationship played in the careers of both women.

Another famous women's college president, M. Carey Thomas of Bryn Mawr, receives the same sort of treatment in a book that appeared at the same time as the Hickok book, but to less fanfare.[6] The discovery of the Woolley-Marks letters sparked a mild panic among Mount Holyoke alumnae and no doubt created apprehension about what might lurk in Thomas' papers, which were about to be microfilmed and opened to the public.[7] But Marjorie Dobkin, editor of *The Making of a Feminist: Early Journals and Letters of M. Carey Thomas*, insists that there is nothing to worry about. Thomas admittedly fell for women throughout her life. At fifteen, she wrote: "I think I must feel towards Anna for instance like a boy would, for I admire her so. Not any particular thing but just an undefined sense of admiration and then I like to touch her and the other morning I woke up and she was asleep and I admired her hair so much that I kissed it. I never felt so much with anybody else." And at twenty: "One night we had stopped reading later than usual and obeying a sudden impulse I turned to her and asked, 'Do you love me?' She threw her arms around me and whispered, 'I love you passionately.' She did not go home that night and we talked and talked." At twenty-three, Thomas wrote to her mother: "If it were only possible for women to elect women as well as men for a 'life's love!'... It *is* possible but if families would only regard it in that light!"[8]

Thomas did in fact choose women for her "life's loves," but Dobkin, who finds it "hard to understand why anyone should very much care" about personal and private behavior and considers the question of lesbianism "a relatively inconsequential matter," assures us that "physical contact" unquestionably played a part in Thomas' relationships with women, but "sexuality" just as unquestionably did not.[9] Along with this labored distinction between "physical contact" and "sexuality," Dobkin presents a battery of reasons why Thomas was not a lesbian: she never expressed the desire to be a man; she expressed a strong aversion to heterosexual intercourse when she learned the "facts of life" from a book at the age of twenty-one, an aversion, Dobkin insists, that would have applied even more strongly to homosexual sex; she was conventional in everything but her feminism; she once loved a man—or was at least unable to stop thinking about him—and considered marrying him (Dobkin, with evident relief, devotes the middle section of the book to this relationship); Thomas established mother-daughter relationships with the two women with whom she lived (one moved in when the first eloped with a man); the women known at the time to be lesbians whom Thomas included among her friends traveled with her only after Thomas was already approaching old age; and, finally, Thomas expressed negative attitudes toward homosexuality, including the fear that public discussion of it would make it difficult for women who lived together. Dobkin's ignorance about lesbianism is staggering; on no other topic would a scholar so unfamiliar with the relevant literature forge ahead with the sort of assumptions she reveals.

The authors of these three books are determined to give us an "acceptable" version of women's relationships in the past, and they seize gratefully on Smith-Rosenberg's work to do it. But even Doris Faber's feverish denials could not eliminate public speculation about Eleanor Roosevelt's "sexual orientation." An article about the Hickok book was even carried in the *National Enquirer* which, for a change, probably presented the material more accurately, if more leeringly, than the respectable press.[10] Arthur Schlesinger, Jr., in *The New York Times Book Review*, for example, notes that the big question in "some people's minds" will be whether Hickok and Roosevelt were "lovers in the physical sense."[11] Schlesinger, like Dobkin, finds this an "issue of stunning inconsequence," but he "reluctantly" supposes that it must be discussed. After devoting the rest of his review to a subject he evidently finds distasteful, he cites Smith-Rosenberg's work and concludes that the two women were "children of the Victorian age" which accepted celibate love between women; they were "wounded women, doomed by chaotic childhoods to the unceasing quest for unattainable emotional security." Schlesinger is emphasizing here the incompatibility of our modern heterosexual-homosexual dichotomy with the sensibility of an earlier age. As Blanche Cook points out in her review of Faber's book, however, it is absurd to pretend that the years 1932 to 1962 now belong to the nineteenth century.[12] Although it is vitally important not to impose modern concepts and standards on the past, I believe that we have gone entirely too far with the notion of an idyllic Victorian age in which chaste love between people of the same sex was possible and acceptable. A recent review in *The New York Times Book Review*, for example, discusses a biography of J. M. Barrie, the creator of Peter Pan, and almost congratulates Barrie for his "innocent, asexual, natural and dignified" love for the five boys who were both subjects and recipients of his stories. Despite the fact that Barrie was fond of photographing the boys, as the reviewer says, "*tout nu*, often bottoms up," he insists that there was nothing sexual about this love.[13] I think that we are naive to believe this.

It is not surprising, in light of such denials of sexuality, that many feminist scholars choose to claim as lesbians all women who have loved women in the past. Blanche Cook concludes firmly that "women who love women, who choose women to nurture and support and to create a living environment in which to work creatively and independently, are lesbians."[14] Cook names as lesbians Jane Addams, the founder of Hull House, who lived for forty years with Mary Rozet Smith; Lillian Wald, also a settlement house pioneer, who left evidence of a series of intense relationships with women; and Jeannette Marks and Mary Woolley. All, Cook says, were lesbians, and in the homophobic society in which we live must be claimed as such.

As it now stands, we are faced with a choice between, on the one hand, labeling women lesbians who might violently reject the label, or, on the other hand, glossing over the significance of women's relationships by labeling them Victorian, and therefore innocent of our post-Freudian sexual awareness. Although I understand and share the political perspective that leads Cook to claim women like Jane Addams as lesbians, I feel we need to see more precision in the use of the term. I would like to illustrate the diversity of women's relationships in the past—and the complexity of those relationships—with evidence from the American women's movement in the late 1940's and 1950's.

I have found evidence of a variety of relationships in collections of women's papers and in the records of women's organizations from this period. I do not have enough information about many of these relationships to characterize them in any definitive way, nor can I even offer much information about some of the women. But we cannot afford to overlook whatever evidence women have left us, however fragmentary. I believe that it is important simply to present some of these relationships, because they illustrate the complexity of women's relationships in the past and the problems that confront us if we attempt any simple categorization. Since my research focuses on feminist activities, the women I discuss here are by no means a representative group of women. All of them are white, educated, and middle- or upper-class. The women's movement in the period after the Second World War was composed primarily of white, middle-class women, in part because of the racism and classism of the movement, and in part because black women and working-class women involved in social movement activity most often organized around issues of race and class, respectively, not gender.

Within the women's movement were two distinct phenomena—couple relationships and intense devotion to a charismatic leader—that help clarify the problems that face us if we attempt to define these relationships in any cut-and-dried fashion. None of the women who lived in couple relationships and belonged to the women's movement in the postwar period would, as far as can be determined, have identified themselves as lesbians. They did, however, often live together in long-term committed relationships, which were accepted in the movement, and they did sometimes build a community with other women like themselves. Descriptions of a few relationships that come down to us in the sources provide some insight into their nature.

Jeannette Marks and Mary Woolley, subjects of the biography mentioned earlier, met at Wellesley College in 1895 when Marks began her college education and Woolley arrived at the college as a history instructor. Less than five years later they made "a mutual declaration of ardent and exclusive love" and "exchanged tokens, a ring and a jeweled pin, with pledges of lifelong fidelity."[15] They spent the rest of their lives together, including the many years at Mount Holyoke where Woolley served as president and Marks taught English. Mary Woolley worked in the American Association of University Women and the Women's International League for Peace and Freedom. Jeannette Marks committed herself to suffrage and, later, through the National Woman's Party, to the Equal Rights Amendment. It is clear from Marks' correspondence with women in the movement that their relationship was accepted as a primary commitment. Few letters to Marks in the 1940's fail to inquire about Woolley, whose serious illness clouded Marks' life and work. One married woman, who found herself forced to withdraw from Woman's Party work because of her husband's health, acknowledged in a letter to Marks the centrality of

Marks' and Woolley's commitment when she compared her own reasons for "pulling out" to "those that have bound you to Westport," the town in which the two women lived.[16] Mary Woolley died in 1947, and Jeannette Marks lived on until 1964, devoting herself to a biography of Woolley.

Lena Madesin Phillips, the founder of both the National and International Federations of Business and Professional Women's Clubs, lived for some thirty years with Marjory Lacey-Baker, an actress whom she first met in 1919. In an unpublished autobiography included in Phillips' papers, she straightforwardly wrote about her lack of interest in men and marriage. As a young girl, she wrote that she "cared little for boys," and at the age of seven she wrote a composition for school that explained: "There are so many little girls in the school and the thing i [sic] like about it there are no boys in school. i [sic] like that about it."[17] She noted that she had never taken seriously the idea of getting married. "Only the first of the half dozen proposals of marriage which came my way had any sense of reality to me. They made no impression because I was wholly without desire or even interest in the matter." Phillips seemed unperturbed by possible Freudian and/or homophobic explanations of her attitudes and behavior. She explained unabashedly that she wanted to be a boy and suffered severe disappointment when she learned that, contrary to her father's stories, there was no factory in Indiana that made girls into boys—and seemed impervious as well to the charges of lesbianism that her memories might provoke. She mentioned in her autobiography the "crushes" she had on girls at the Jessamine Female Institute—nothing out of the ordinary for a young woman of her generation, but perhaps a surprising piece of information chosen for inclusion in the autobiography of a woman who continued to devote her emotional energies to women.

In 1919, Phillips attended a pageant in which Lacey-Baker performed and she inquired about the identity of the woman who had "[t]he most beautiful voice I ever heard."[18] Phillips "lost her heart to the sound of that voice," and the two women moved in together in the 1920's. In 1924, according to notes that Lacey-Baker recorded for a biography of Phillips, the two women went different places for Easter; recording this caused Lacey-Baker to quote from *The Prophet*: "Love knows not its own depth until the hour of separation."[19] Phillips described Lacey-Baker in her voluminous correspondence as "my best friend," or noted that she "shares a home with me."[20] Phillips' friends and acquaintances regularly mentioned Lacey-Baker. One male correspondent, for example, commented that Phillips' "lady-friend" was "so lovely, and so devoted to you and cares for you."[21] Phillips happily described the tranquility of their life together to her many friends: "Marjory and I have had a lovely time, enjoying once more our home in summertime.... Marjory would join in the invitation of this letter and this loving greeting if she were around. Today she is busy with the cleaning woman, while I sit with the door closed working in my study."[22] "We have had a happy winter, with good health for both of us. We have a variety of interests and small obligations, but really enjoy most the quiet and comfort of Apple Acres."[23] "We read and talk and work."[24]

Madesin Phillips' papers suggest that she and Marjory Lacey-Baker lived in a world of politically active women friends. Phillips had devoted much of her energy to international work with women, and she kept in touch with European friends through her correspondence and through her regular trips to Europe accompanied by Lacey-Baker. Gordon Holmes, of the British Federation of Business and Professional Women, wrote regularly to "Madesin and Maggie." In a 1948 letter she teased Phillips by reporting that "two other of our oldest & closest Fed officers whom you know could get married but are refusing—as they are both more than middle-aged (never mind their looks) it suggests 50-60 is about the new dangerous age for women (look out for Maggie!)."[25] Phillips reported to Holmes on their social life: "With a new circle of friends around us here and a good many of our overseas members coming here for luncheon or tea with us the weeks slip by."[26] The integral relationship between Phillips' social life and her work in the movement is suggested by Lacey-Baker's analysis of Phillips' personal papers from the year 1924: "There is the usual crop of letters to LMP following the Convention [of the BPW] from newly-met members in hero-worshipping mood—most of whom went on to be her good friends over the years."[27] Lacey-Baker was a part of Phillips' movement world, and their relationship received acceptance and validation throughout the movement, both national and international.

The lifelong relationship between feminist biographer

Alma Lutz and Marguerite Smith began when they roomed together at Vassar in the early years of the twentieth century. From 1918 until Smith's death in 1959, they shared a Boston apartment and a summer home, Highmeadow, in the Berkshires. Lutz and Smith, a librarian at the Protestant Zion Research Library in Brookline, Massachusetts, worked together in the National Woman's Party. Like Madesin Phillips, Lutz wrote to friends in the movement of their lives together: "We are very happy here in the country—each busy with her work and digging in the garden."[28] They traveled together, visiting Europe several times in the 1950's. Letters to one of them about feminist work invariably sent greetings or love to the other. When Smith died in 1959, Lutz struggled with her grief. She wrote to her acquaintance Florence Kitchelt, in response to condolences: "I am at Highmeadow trying to get my bearings.... You will understand how hard it is.... It has been a very difficult anxious time for me."[29] She thanked another friend for her note and added: "It's a hard adjustment to make, but one we all have to face in one way or another and I am remembering that I have much to be grateful for."[30] In December she wrote to one of her regular correspondents that she was carrying on but it was very lonely for her.[31]

The fact that Lutz and Smith seemed to have many friends who lived in couple relationships with other women suggests that they had built a community of women within the women's movement. Every year Mabel Vernon, a suffragist and worker for peace, and her friend and companion Consuelo Reyes, whom Vernon had met through her work with the Inter-American Commission on Women, spent the summer at Highmeadow. Vernon, one of Alice Paul's closest associates during the suffrage struggle, had met Reyes two weeks after her arrival in the United States from Costa Rica in 1942. They began to work together in Vernon's organization, People's Mandate, in 1943, and they shared a Washington apartment from 1951 until Vernon's death in 1975.[32] Reyes received recognition in Vernon's obituaries as her "devoted companion" or "nurse-companion."[33] Two other women who also maintained a lifelong relationship, Alice Morgan Wright and Edith Goode, also kept in contact with Lutz, Smith, Vernon, and Reyes. Sometimes they visited Highmeadow in the summer.[34] Wright and Goode had met at Smith and were described as "always together" although they did not live together.[35] Like Lutz and Smith, they worked together in the National Woman's Party, traveled together and looked after each other as old age began to take its toll.[36]

These examples illustrate what the sources provide: the bare outlines of friendship networks made up of woman-committed women. Much of the evidence must be pieced together and it is even scantier when the women did not live together. Alma Lutz's papers, for example, do not include any personal correspondence from the postwar period, so what we know about her relationships with Marguerite Smith comes from the papers of her correspondents. Sometimes a relationship surfaces only upon the death of one of the women. For example, Agnes Wells, chairman of the National Woman's Party in the late 1940's, explained to an acquaintance in the Party that her "friend of forty-one years and house-companion for twenty-eight years" had just died.[37] When Mabel Griswold, executive secretary of the Woman's Party, died in 1955, a family member suggested that the Party send the telegram of sympathy to Elsie Wood, the woman with whom Griswold had lived.[38] This kind of reference tells us little about the nature of the relationship involved, but we do get a sense of the nature of couple relationships within the women's movement.

A second important phenomenon found in the women's movement—the charismatic leader who attracts intense devotion—also adds to our understanding of the complexity of women's relationships. Alice Paul, the founder and leading light of the National Woman's Party, inspired devotion that bordered on worship. One woman even addressed her as "My Beloved Deity."[39] But, contrary to both the ideal type of the charismatic leader and the portrait of Paul as it exists now in the historical scholarship, Paul maintained close relationships with a number of women she had first met in the suffrage struggle.[40] Paul's correspondence in the National Woman's Party papers does not reveal much about the nature of her relationships, but it does make it clear that her friendships provided love and support for her work.

It is true that many of the expressions of love, admiration, and devotion addressed to Paul seem to have been one-sided, from awe-struck followers, but this is not the only side of the story.

Paul maintained close friendships with a number of women discussed earlier who lived in couple relationships with other women. She had met Mabel Vernon when they attended Swarthmore College together, and they maintained contact throughout the years, despite Vernon's departure from the Woman's Party in the 1930's.[41] Of Alice Morgan Wright, she said that, when they first met, they "...just became sisters right away."[42] Jeannette Marks regularly sent her love to "dear Alice" until a conflict in the Woman's Party ruptured their relationship.[43] Other women, too, enjoyed a closer relationship than the formal work-related one for which Paul is so well known.

Paul obviously cared deeply, for example, for her old friend Nina Allender, the cartoonist of the suffrage movement. Allender, who lived alone in Chicago, wrote to Paul in 1947 of her memories of their long association: "No words can tell you what that [first] visit grew to mean to me & to my life.... I feel now as I did then—only more intensely—I have never changed or doubted—but have grown more inspired as the years have gone by.... There is no use going into words. I believe them to be unnecessary between us."[44] Paul wrote that she thought of Allender often and sent her "devoted love."[45] She worried about Allender's loneliness and gently encouraged her to come to Washington to live at Belmont House, the Woman's Party headquarters, where she would be surrounded by loving friends who appreciated the work she had done for the women's movement.[46] Paul failed to persuade her to move, however. Two years later Paul responded to a request from Allender's niece for help with the costs of a nursing home with a $100 check and a promise to contact others who might be able to help.[47] But Allender died, within a month, at the age of eighty-five.

Paul does not seem to have formed an intimate relationship with any one woman, but she did live and work within a close-knit female world. When in Washington, she lived, at least some of the time, at Belmont House; when away she lived either alone or with her sister, Helen Paul, in Vermont and later Connecticut. Helen Paul, through her relationship with Alice, often played a major role in Woman's Party work. It is clear that Alice Paul's ties—whether to her sister or to close friends or to admirers—served as a bond that knit the Woman's Party together. That Paul and her network could also tear the movement asunder is obvious from the stormy history of the Woman's Party.

Alice Paul is not the only example of a leader who inspired love and devotion among women in the movement. One senses from Marjory Lacey-Baker's comment, quoted above—that "newly-met members in hero-worshipping mood" wrote to Lena Madesin Phillips after every BPW convention—that Phillips too had a charismatic aura. But the best and most thoroughly documented example of a charismatic leader is Anna Lord Strauss of the League of Women Voters, an organization that opted out of the women's movement.

Strauss, the great-granddaughter of Lucretia Mott, came from an old and wealthy family; she was prominent and respected, a staunch liberal and an anti- or at best a nonfeminist. She never married and her papers leave no evidence of intimate relationships outside her family. Yet Strauss was the object of some very strong feelings on the part of the women with whom she worked. She, like Alice Paul and Madesin Phillips, received numerous hero-worshipping letters from awe-struck followers. But in her case we also have evidence that some of her coworkers fell deeply in love with her. It is hard to know how the following women would have interpreted their relationship with Strauss. The two women who expressed their feelings explicitly were both married women, and in one case Strauss obviously had a cordial relationship with the woman's husband and children. Yet there can be no question that this League officer fell in love with Strauss. She found Strauss "the finest human being I had ever known," and knowing her "the most beautiful and profound experience I have ever had."[48] Loving Strauss—she asked permission to say it—made the earth move and "the whole landscape of human affairs and nature" take on a new appearance.[49] Being with Strauss made "the tone and fiber" of her day different; although she could live without her, she could see no reason for having to prove it all the time.[50] She tried to "ration and control" her thoughts of Strauss, but it was small satisfaction.[51] When Strauss was recovering from an operation, this woman wrote: "I love you! I can't imagine the world without you.... I love you. I need you."[52]

Although our picture of this relationship is completely one-sided—for Strauss did not keep copies of most of her letters—it is clear that Strauss did not respond to such declarations of love. This woman urged Strauss to accept her and what she had to say without "the slightest sense of needing to be considerate of me because I feel as I do." She understood the "unilateral character" of her feelings, and insisted that she had more than she deserved by simply knowing Strauss at all.[53] But her hurt, and her growing suspicion that Strauss shunned intimacy, escaped on occasion. She asked: "And how would it hurt you to let someone tell you sometime how beautiful—how wonderful you are? Did you ever let anyone have a decent chance to try?"[54] She realized that loving someone did not always make things easier—that sometimes, in fact, it made life more of a struggle—but she believed that to withdraw from love was to withdraw from life. In what appears to have been a hastily written note, she expressed her understanding—an understanding that obviously gave her both pain and comfort—that Strauss was not perfect after all: "Way back there in the crow's nest (or at some such time) you decided not to become embroiled in any intimate human relationship, except those you were, by birth, committed to. I wonder.... There is something you haven't mastered. Something you've been afraid of after all."[55]

This woman's perception that Strauss avoided intimacy is confirmed elsewhere in Strauss' papers. One old friend was struck, in 1968, by Strauss' ability to "get your feelings out & down on paper!" She continued: "I know you so well that I consider this great progress in your own inner state of mental health. It is far from easy for you to express your feelings...."[56] This aspect of Strauss' personality fits with the ideal type of the charismatic leader. The other case of a woman falling in love with Strauss that emerges clearly from her papers reinforces this picture. This woman, also a League officer, wrote in circuitous fashion of her intense pleasure at receiving Strauss' picture. In what was certainly a reference to lesbianism, she wrote that she hoped Strauss would not think that she was "one of those who had never outgrown the emotional extravaganzas of the adolescent." Before she got down to League business, she added:

> But, Darling, as I softly close the door on all this—as I should and as I want to—and as I must since all our meetings are likely to be formal ones in a group—as I go

> back in the office correspondence to "Dear Miss Strauss" and "Sincerely yours,"...as I put myself as much as possible in the background at our March meeting in order to share you with the others who have not been with you as I have—as all these things happen, I want you to be very certain that what is merely under cover is still there—as it most surely will be—and that if all the hearts in the room could be exposed there'd be few, I'm certain, that would love you more than...[I].[57]

Apparently Strauss never responded to this letter, for a month later, this woman apologized for writing it: "I have had qualms, dear Anna, about that letter I wrote you. (You knew I would eventually of course!)." Continuing in a vein that reinforces the above quoted perception of Strauss' inability to be intimate, she wrote of imagining the "recoil...embarrassment, self-consciousness and general discomfort" her letter must have provoked in such a "reserved person." She admitted that the kind of admiration she had expressed, "at least in certain classes of relationships (of which mine to you is one)—becomes a bit of moral wrong-doing."[58] She felt ashamed and asked forgiveness. It is not at all clear what she meant by all of this, and I quote it here without speculating on the nature of their relationship.

What is clear is that this was a momentous and significant relationship to at least one of the parties. Almost twenty years later, this woman wrote of her deep disappointment in missing Strauss' visit to her city. She had allowed herself to dream that she could persuade Strauss to stay with her awhile, even though she knew that others would have prior claims on Strauss' time. She wrote:

> I have not seen you since that day in Atlantic City when you laid the gavel of the League of Women Voters down.... I do not look back on that moment of ending with any satisfaction for my own behavior, for I passed right by the platform on which you were still standing talking with one of the last persons left in the room and shyness at the thought of expressing my deep feeling about your going—*and* the fact that you were talking with someone else led me to pass on without even a glance in your direction as I remember though you made some move to speak to me!... But if I gave you a hurt it is now a very old one and forgotten, I'm sure—as well as understood.[59]

Whatever the interpretation these two women would have devised to explain their feelings for Strauss, it is clear that the widely shared devotion to this woman leader could sometimes grow into something more intense. Strauss' reserve, and her inability to express her feelings may or may not have had anything to do with her own attitude toward intimate relationships between women. One tantalizing letter from a friend about to be married suggests that Strauss' decision not to marry had been made early: "I remember so well your answer when I pressed you, once, on why you had never married. . . . Well, it is very true, one does not marry unless one can see no other life."[60] A further fragment, consisting of entries in the diary of Doris Stevens—a leading suffragist who took a sharp swing to the right in the postwar period—suggests that at least some individuals suspected Strauss of lesbianism. Stevens, by this time a serious redbaiter and, from the evidence quoted here, a "queerbaiter" as well, apparently called a government official in 1953 to report that Strauss was "not a bit interested in men."[61] She seemed to be trying to discredit Strauss, far too liberal for her tastes, with a charge of "unorthodox morals."[62]

Stevens had her suspicions about other women in the movement as well. She recorded in her diary a conversation with a National Woman's Party member about Jeannette Marks and Mary Woolley, noting that the member, who had attended Wellesley with Marks, "Discreetly indicated there was 'talk.'"[63] At another point she reported a conversation with a different Woman's Party member who had grown disillusioned about Alice Paul. Stevens noted that her informant related "weird goings on at Wash. hedquts wherein it was clear she thought Paul a devotee of Lesbos & afflicted with Jeanne d'Arc identification."[64]

Stevens' charges suggest that the intensity of women's relationships and the existence of woman-committed women in women's organizations had the potential, particularly during the McCarthy years, to attract ridicule or denunciation. Stevens wrote to the viciously right-wing and anti-Semitic columnist, Westbrook Pegler, to "thank you for knowing I'm not a queerie."[65] This would suggest that, at least in certain circles, participation in the women's movement was highly suspect.

What exactly should we make of all this? In one way it is terribly frustrating to have such tantalizingly ambiguous glimpses into women's lives. In another way, it is exciting to find out so much about women's lives in the past. I think it is enormously important *not* to read into these letters what we want to find, or what we think we should find. At the same time, we cannot dismiss what little evidence we have as insufficient when it is all we have; nor can we continue to contribute to the conspiracy of silence that urges us to ignore what is not perfectly straightforward. Thus, although it is tempting to try to speculate about the relationships I have described here in order to impose some analysis on them, I would rather simply lay them out, fragmentary as they are, in order to suggest a conceptual approach that recognizes the complexities of the issue.

It is clear, I think, that none of these relationships can be easily categorized. There were women who lived their entire adult lives in couple relationships with other women, and married women who fell in love with other women. Were they lesbians? Probably they would be shocked to be identified in that way. Alice Paul, for example, spoke scornfully of *Ms.* magazine as "all about homosexuality and so on."[66] Another woman who lives in a couple relationship distinguished between the (respectable) women involved in the ERA struggle in the old days and the "lesbians and bra-burners" of the contemporary movement.[67] Sasha Lewis, in *Sunday's Women,* reports an incident we would do well to remember here. One of her informants, a lesbian, went to Florida to work against Anita Bryant and stayed with an older cousin who had lived for years in a marriage-like relationship with another woman. When Lewis' informant saw the way the two women lived—sharing everything, including a bedroom—she said something to them about the danger of Bryant's campaign for their lives. They were aghast that she would think them lesbians, since, they said, they did not do anything sexual together.[68] If even women who lived with or maintained close attachments to other women would reject the label "lesbian," what about the married women, or the women who avoided intimate relationships?

The fact that the three recent historical studies discussed here misuse the concept of women's culture to proclaim that their subjects did not have sexual relationships with other women makes it imperative that historians pull back the veil that has too often shrouded love between women in the past. But it is equally important that we not obscure the enormous significance, from both an individual and historical perspective, of the formation of a lesbian identity. Recent research on the history of homosexuality shows that the concept of a homosexual identity or role only emerged in relatively recent times.[69] Paradoxically, as Smith-Rosenberg points out, the nineteenth century permitted a great deal of freedom in moving along the sexual and emotional continuum that ranges from heterosexuality to homosexuality. The twentieth century has not. What is important here is that we can begin to speak of a "lesbian identity" in American society by the twentieth century.[70] Passionate love between women has always existed, but it has not always been named. Since it *has* been named in the twentieth century, we need to distinguish between women who identify as lesbians and/or who are part of a lesbian culture, where one exists, and a broader category of woman-committed women who would not identify as lesbians but whose primary commitment, in emotional and practical terms, was to other women. It is especially important, in considering twentieth-century women, that we not sloppily apply the label "Victorian." In the 1950's there *was* such a thing as a lesbian culture—in local communities, in the bars, in the military. There is an important difference between women who put themselves in such a culture on the very fringes of society and women like Eleanor Roosevelt and the women whose relationships I have described here. Similarly, there is an important difference today between a politically active lesbian feminist and a "maiden aunt" who has lived her entire life with another woman but would reject any suggestions of lesbianism.

Identity, and not sexual behavior, is the crucial factor in the discussion.[71] There are lesbians who have never had a sexual relationship with another woman and there are women who have had sexual experiences with women but do not identify as lesbians. This is not to suggest that there is no difference between women who loved each other and lived together but did not make love (although even that can be difficult to define, since sensuality and sexuality, "physical contact" and "sexual contact" have no distinct boundaries) and those who did. But sexual behavior—something about which we rarely have historical evidence anyway—is only one of a number of relevant factors in a relationship. Blanche Cook has said everything that needs to be said about the inevitable question of evidence: "Genital 'proofs' to confirm lesbianism are never required to confirm the heterosexuality of men and women who live together for 20, or 50, years." Cook reminds us of the recently publicized relationship of General Eisenhower and Kay Summersby during the Second World War: they "were passionately involved with each other. They looked ardently into each others' eyes. They held hands. They cantered swiftly across England's countryside. They played golf and bridge and laughed. They were inseparable. But they never 'consummated' their love in the acceptable, traditional, sexual manner. Now does that fact render Kay Summersby and Dwight David Eisenhower somehow less in love? Were they not heterosexual?"[72]

Of course, emphasizing identity rather than proof of genital contact does not make everything simple. At this point, I think, the best we can do is to describe carefully and sensitively what we do know about a woman's relationships, keeping in mind both the historical development of a lesbian identity (Did such a thing as a lesbian identity exist? Was there a lesbian culture?), and the individual process that we now identify as "coming out" (Did a woman feel attachment to another woman or women? Did she act on this feeling in some positive way? Did she recognize the existence of other women with the same commitment? Did she express solidarity with those women?).[73] Using this approach allows us to make distinctions among women's relationships in the past—intimate friendships, supportive relationships growing out of common political work, couple relationships—without denying their significance or drawing fixed boundaries. We can recognize the importance of friendships among a group of women who, like Alma Lutz, Marguerite Smith, Mabel Vernon, Consuelo Reyes, Alice Morgan Wright, and Edith Goode, built a community of women but did not identify it as a lesbian community. We can do justice to both the woman-committed woman who would angrily reject any suggestion of lesbianism and the self-identified lesbian without distorting their common experiences.

This approach does not solve all the problems of dealing with women's relationships in the past, but it is a beginning. The greatest problem remains the weakness of sources. Not only have women who loved women in the past been wisely reluctant to leave evidence of their relationships for the prying eyes of a homophobic society, but what evidence they did leave was often suppressed or destroyed.[74] Furthermore, as the three books discussed above show, even the evidence saved and brought to light can be savagely misinterpreted.

How do we know if a woman felt attachment, acted on it, recognized the existence of other women like her, or expressed solidarity? There is no easy answer to this, but it is revealing, I think, that both Doris Faber and Anna Mary Wells are fairly certain that Lorena Hickok and Jeannette Marks, respectively, *did* have "homosexual tendencies" (although Faber insists that even Hickok cannot fairly be placed in the "contemporary gay category"), even if the admirable figures in each book, Eleanor Roosevelt and Mary Woolley, certainly did not. That is, both of these authors, as hard as they try to deny lesbianism, find evidence that forces them to discuss it, and both cope by pinning the "blame" on the women they paint as unpleasant—fat, ugly, pathetic Lorena Hickok and nasty, tortured, arrogant Jeannette Marks.

And, of course, despite censorship, we do know about women in the past who acted on their feelings for other women and who created lesbian communities. Consider the French lesbian culture of the late nineteenth-early twentieth century, the world depicted in Radclyffe Hall's *The Well of Loneliness*.[75] And we are beginning to learn more about working-class and middle-class lesbian communities in the 1950's as well—in the closet, in the bars, and in the military.[76]

Using this approach, then, allows us to make distinctions among different sorts of women's relationships in the past without denying their significance or assigning fixed categories. Returning to the relationships described in this paper, we can differentiate between the intimate and supportive friendships, the couple relationships with other women that some women formed, and the feelings of falling in love that others expressed. I think it is important to state here that these relationships, whatever their nature, are not simply a side issue for the history of feminism and the women's movement. Blanche Cook has argued that the existence of female support networks has been vital to women's political activism; Smith-Rosenberg and others have shown how nineteenth-century "women's culture" both led to, and ultimately limited, organizing and public activity among middle-class women.[77] I believe that women's relationships have been absolutely central to the success of feminist activity throughout history. Woman-committed women have had the emotional commitment, the support, and often the time to devote their lives to a cause, as did many of the women I have discussed.

It is important that nineteenth-century American women sought and found emotional support in a homosocial world. It is also important that throughout history there have been women who chose other women for the primary relationship in their lives. It is important that some of these women would have been shocked to be labeled lesbians, and it is important that some of them claimed their lesbianism and built a culture and community around it with other lesbians. It is imperative that we not deny the reality of any of these women's historical experiences by blurring the distinctions among them. At the same time, recognition of the common bond of commitment to women shared by diverse women throughout history strengthens our struggle against those who attempt to divide and defeat us.

NOTES

*Holly Near's song, "Imagine My Surprise," celebrates the discovery of women's relationships in the past. The song is recorded on the album, *Imagine My Surprise*, Redwood Records. I am grateful to Holly Near and Redwood Records for their permission to use the title here.

1. Carroll Smith-Rosenberg, "The Female World of Love and Ritual: Relations between Women in Nineteenth-Century America," *Signs*, 1, 1 (1975), 1-29.

2. Nancy F. Cott, *The Bonds of Womanhood* (New Haven: Yale Univ. Press, 1977), Ch. 5; Nancy Sahli, "Smashing: Women's Relationships Before the Fall," *Chrysalis*, No. 8 (1979), pp. 17-27; Blanche Wiesen Cook, "Female Support Networks and Political Activism: Lillian Wald, Crystal Eastman and Emma Goldman," *Chrysalis*, No. 3 (1977), pp. 43-61; and Blanche W. Cook, "The Historical Denial of Lesbianism," *Radical History Review*, 20 (1979), 60-65. See especially the Lesbian History issue of FRONTIERS, Vol. 4, No. 3 (Fall 1979); see also, Judith Schwarz, "*Yellow Clover*: Katharine Lee Bates and Katharine Coman," FRONTIERS, 4, 1 (Spring 1979), 59-67.

3. Doris Faber, *The Life of Lorena Hickok: E.R.'s Friend* (New York: William Morrow and Co., 1980).

4. Faber, p. 176.

5. Anna Mary Wells, *Miss Marks and Miss Woolley* (Boston: Houghton Mifflin, 1978); Faber, p. 354. Cook, "Historical Denial," is a review of the Wells book.

6. Marjorie Housepian Dobkin, *The Making of a Feminist: Early Journals and Letters of M. Carey Thomas* (Kent, Ohio: Kent State

Univ. Press, 1980). See the review by Helen Vendler, "Carey Thomas of Bryn Mawr," *The New York Times Book Review*, February 24, 1980, pp. 24-25. Vendler accuses Dobkin of psychological naivete in her portrait of Thomas.

7. *The New York Times*, August 21, 1976, p. 22.

8. Dobkin, p. 72; p. 118; p. 229.

9. Dobkin, pp. 79, 86.

10. Edward Sigall, "Eleanor Roosevelt's Secret Romance—the Untold Story," *National Enquirer*, November 13, 1979, pp. 20-21.

11. Arthur Schlesinger, Jr., "Interesting Women," *The New York Times Book Review*, February 17, 1980, p. 31.

12. Blanche Wiesen Cook, review of *The Life of Lorena Hickok*, *Feminist Studies*, 6 (1980), 511-16.

13. Morton N. Cohen, "Love Story, Victorian-Style" (review of Andrew Birkin's *J. M. Barrie and the Lost Boys*), *The New York Times Book Review*, January 13, 1980, p. 3.

14. Cook, "Female Support Networks," p. 48.

15. Wells, p. 56.

16. Caroline Babcock to Jeannette Marks, February 12, 1947, Babcock papers, box 8 (105), Schlesinger Library, Cambridge, Massachusetts. I am grateful to the Schlesinger Library for permission to use the material quoted here.

17. "The Unfinished Autobiography of Lena Madesin Phillips," Phillips papers, Schlesinger Library.

18. "Chronological Record of Events and Activities for the Biography of Lena Madesin Phillips, 1881-1955," Phillips papers, Schlesinger Library.

19. "Chronological Record of Events and Activities for the Biography of Lena Madesin Phillips, 1881-1955," Phillips papers, Schlesinger Library.

20. Lena Madesin Phillips to Audrey Turner, January 21, 1948, Phillips papers, Schlesinger Library; Lena Madesin Phillips to Olivia Rossetti Agresti, April 26, 1948, Phillips papers, Schlesinger Library.

21. Robert Heller to Lena Madesin Phillips, September 26, 1948, Phillips papers, Schlesinger Library.

22. Lena Madesin Phillips to Mary C. Kennedy, August 20, 1948, Phillips papers, Schlesinger Library.

23. Lena Madesin Phillips to Gordon Holmes, March 28, 1949, Phillips papers, Schlesinger Library.

24. Lena Madesin Phillips to [Ida Spitz], November 13, 1950, Phillips papers, Schlesinger Library.

25. Gordon Holmes to Madesin & Maggie, December 15, 1948, Phillips papers, Schlesinger Library.

26. Lena Madesin Phillips to Gordon Holmes, March 28, 1949, Phillips papers, Schlesinger Library.

27. "Chronological Record of Events and Activities for the Biography of Lena Madesin Phillips, 1881-1955," Phillips papers, Schlesinger Library.

28. Alma Lutz to Florence Kitchelt, July 1, 1948, Kitchelt papers, box 6 (177), Schlesinger Library.

29. Alma Lutz to Florence Kitchelt, July 29, 1959, Kitchelt papers, box 7 (178), Schlesinger Library.

30. Alma Lutz to Florence Armstrong, August 26, 1959, Armstrong papers, box 1 (17), Schlesinger Library.

31. Alma Lutz to Rose Arnold Powell, December 14, 1959, Powell papers, box 3 (43), Schlesinger Library.

32. Mabel Vernon, "Speaker for Suffrage and Petitioner for

Peace," an oral history conducted in 1972 and 1973 by Amelia R. Fry, Regional Oral History Office, University of California, 1976.

33. Press release from Mabel Vernon Memorial Committee, Vernon, "Speaker for Suffrage"; obituary in the *Wilmington Morning News*, September 3, 1975, Vernon, "Speaker for Suffrage."

34. Alice Morgan Wright to Anita Pollitzer, July 9, 1946, National Woman's Party papers, reel 89. The National Woman's Party papers have been microfilmed and are distributed by the Microfilming Corporation of America. I am grateful to the National Woman's Party for permission to quote the material used here.

35. Alice Paul, "Conversations with Alice Paul: Woman Suffrage and the Equal Rights Amendment," an oral history conducted in 1972 and 1973 by Amelia R. Fry, Regional Oral History Office, University of California, 1976, p. 614. Courtesy, the Bancroft Library. Nora Stanton Barney to Alice Paul, n.d. (received May 10, 1945), National Woman's Party papers, reel 86.

36. Alice Morgan Wright to Caroline Babcock, June 28, 1945, National Woman's Party papers, reel 86; Edith Goode to Caroline Babcock, July 10, 1946, Babcock papers, box 7 (98), Schlesinger Library; Edith Goode to Emma Guffey Miller, December 23, 1963, National Woman's Party papers, reel 108; Edith Goode to Jacques Sichel, March 22, 1967, National Woman's Party papers, reel 110; Paul, "Conversations," p. 614.

37. Agnes Wells to Anita Pollitzer, August 24, 1946, National Woman's Party papers, reel 89.

38. Alice Paul to Dorothy Griswold, February 2, 1955, National Woman's Party papers, reel 101.

39. Lavinia Dock to Alice Paul, May 9, 1945, National Woman's Party papers, reel 86.

40. See, for example, Susan D. Becker, "An Intellectual History of the National Woman's Party, 1920-1941," Diss. Case Western Reserve University 1975.

41. Vernon, "Speaker for Suffrage."

42. Paul, "Conversations," p. 197.

43. Jeannette Marks to Alice Paul, March 25, 1945, National Woman's Party papers, reel 85; Jeannette Marks to Alice Paul, March 30, 1945, National Woman's Party papers, reel 85; Jeannette Marks to Alice Paul, April 27, 1945, National Woman's Party papers, reel 85.

44. Nina Allender to Alice Paul, January 5, 1947, National Woman's Party papers, reel 90.

45. Alice Paul to Nina Allender, March 9, 1950, National Woman's Party papers, reel 96.

46. Alice Paul to Nina Allender, November 20, 1954, National Woman's Party papers, reel 100; Kay Boyle to Alice Paul, December 5, 1954, National Woman's Party papers, reel 100; Alice Paul to Nina Allender, December 6, 1954, National Woman's Party papers, reel 100.

47. Kay Boyle to Alice Paul, February 13, 1957, National Woman's Party papers, reel 103; Alice Paul to Kay Boyle, March 5, 1957, National Woman's Party papers, reel 103.

48. Letter to Anna Lord Strauss, December 22, 1945, Strauss papers, box 6 (118), Schlesinger Library. Because of the possibly sensitive nature of the material reported here, I am not using the names of the women involved.

49. Letter to Anna Lord Strauss, September 19, 1946, Strauss papers, box 6 (119), Schlesinger Library.

50. Letter to Anna Lord Strauss, May 9, 1947, Strauss papers, box

6 (121), Schlesinger Library.

51. Letter to Anna Lord Strauss, June 28, 1948, Strauss papers, box 6 (124), Schlesinger Library.

52. Letter to Anna Lord Strauss, February 26, 1951, Strauss papers, box 1 (15), Schlesinger Library.

53. Letter to Anna Lord Strauss, December 22, 1945, Strauss papers, box 6 (118), Schlesinger Library.

54. Letter to Anna Lord Strauss, May 9, 1947, Strauss papers, box 6 (121), Schlesinger Library.

55. "Stream of consciousness," March 10, 1948, Strauss papers, box 6 (124), Schlesinger Library.

56. Augusta Street to Anna Lord Strauss, n.d. [1968], Strauss papers, box 7 (135), Schlesinger Library.

57. Letter to Anna Lord Strauss, February 11, 1949, Strauss papers, box 6 (125), Schlesinger Library.

58. Letter to Anna Lord Strauss, March 3, 1949, Strauss papers, box 6 (125), Schlesinger Library.

59. Letter to Anna Lord Strauss, March 8, 1968, Strauss papers, box 7 (135), Schlesinger Library.

60. Lilian Lyndon to Anna Lord Strauss, April 23, 1950, Strauss papers, box 1 (14), Schlesinger Library.

61. Diary entries, August 30, 1953 and September 1, 1953, Doris Stevens papers, Schlesinger Library.

62. Diary entry, August 24, 1953, Doris Stevens papers, Schlesinger Library.

63. Diary entry, February 4, 1946, Doris Stevens papers, Schlesinger Library.

64. Diary entry, December 1, 1945, Doris Stevens papers, Schlesinger Library.

65. Doris Stevens to Westbrook Pegler, May 3, 1946, Stevens papers, Schlesinger Library.

66. Paul, "Conversations," pp. 195-96.

67. Interview conducted by Verta Taylor and Leila Rupp, December 10, 1979.

68. Sasha Gregory Lewis, *Sunday's Women: A Report on Lesbian Life Today* (Boston: Beacon Press, 1979), p. 94.

69. Mary McIntosh, "The Homosexual Role," *Social Problems*, 16, 2 (1968), 182-91; Jeffrey Weeks, *Coming Out: Homosexual Politics in Britain, from the Nineteenth Century to the Present* (London: Quartet Books, 1977); Bert Hansen, "The Historical Construction of Homosexuality," *Radical History Review*, 20 (1979), 66-73.

70. See Vern Bullough and Bonnie Bullough, "Lesbianism in the 1920s and 1930s: A Newfound Study," *Signs*, 2, 4 (1977), 895-904; Lewis; and Madeline Davis, Liz Kennedy, and Avra Michelson, "Aspects of the Buffalo Lesbian Community in the Fifties," Buffalo Women's Oral History Project, paper presented at the National Women's Studies Association Conference, Bloomington, Indiana, May 1980. Local research projects are beginning to explore the history of gay and lesbian culture in the pre-gay liberation and women's movement years in a number of cities in addition to Buffalo. Such projects currently exist in Boston, Chicago, New York, Philadelphia, and San Francisco.

71. Much of the recent literature on lesbianism emphasizes this crucial distinction between identity and experience. See, for example, Barbara Ponse, *Identities in the Lesbian World: The Social Construction of Self* (Westport, Conn.: Greenwood Press, 1978); and E. M. Ettore, *Lesbians, Women and Society* (London: Routledge & Kegan Paul, 1980).

72. Cook, "Historical Denial," p. 64.

73. On coming out as a process, see Ponse; Ettore; Julia Penelope Stanley and Susan J. Wolfe, *The Coming Out Stories* (Watertown, Mass.: Persephone Press, 1980); and Margaret Cruikshank, *The Lesbian Path* (Monterey, Ca.: Angel Press, 1980).

74. The Mount Holyoke administration closed the Marks-Woolley papers when Wells discovered the love letters, and the papers are only open to researchers now because an American Historical Association committee, including Blanche Cook as one of its members, applied pressure to keep the papers open after Wells, to her credit, contacted them. Faber describes her unsuccessful attempts to persuade the archivists at the FDR Library to close the Lorena Hickok papers.

75. See Dolores Klaich, *Woman + Woman* (1974; rpt. New York: Morrow-Quill, 1979), pp. 129-215; and Barbara Grier and Coletta Reid, *Lesbian Lives: Biographies of Women from the Ladder* (Baltimore: Diana Press, 1976).

76. Lewis; Davis, Kennedy, and Michelson.

77. Cook, "Female Support Networks"; Smith-Rosenberg; Cott; Mary P. Ryan, "The Power of Women's Networks: A Case Study of Female Moral Reform in Antebellum America," *Feminist Studies*, 5 (1979), 66-85; Carroll Smith-Rosenberg, "Beauty, the Beast and the Militant Woman: A Case Study of Sex Roles and Social Stress in Jacksonian America," *American Quarterly*, 23, 4 (1971), 562-84. See Ellen DuBois et al., "Politics and Culture in Women's History," *Feminist Studies*, 6 (1980), 26-64.

The American Woman's Pre-World War I Freedom in Manners and Morals

JAMES R. MCGOVERN

THE Twenties have been alternately praised or blamed for almost everything and its opposite;[1] but most historians hold, whether to praise or to condemn, that this decade launched the revolution in manners and morals through which we are still moving today. This judgment seems to be part of an even more inclusive one in American historiography to exceptionalize the Twenties. No other decade has invited such titles of historical caricature as *The Jazz Age, This Was Normalcy, Fantastic Interim,* or *The Perils of Prosperity*. Richard Hofstadter's classic, *The Age of Reform*, subtly reinforces this view by seeing the Twenties as "Entr'acte," an interim between two periods of reform, the Progressive era and the New Deal, which themselves display discontinuity.[2]

Revisionism, in the form of a developmental interpretation of the relationship between the Progressive era and the Twenties, has been gaining strong support in recent years. De-emphasizing the disruptive impact of World War I, Henry F. May asked whether the 1920s could be understood fully "without giving more attention to the old regime."[3] He declared that "Immediately prewar America must be newly explored," especially "its inarticulate assumptions—assumptions in such areas as morality, politics, class and race relations, popular art and literature, and family life."[4] May pursued his inquiry in *The End of American Innocence* and showed that for the purposes of intellectual history, at least, the Twenties

Mr. McGovern is professor of history in Newton College of the Sacred Heart.

[1] Henry F. May, "Shifting Perspectives on the 1920's," *Mississippi Valley Historical Review*, XLIII (Dec. 1956), 405-27.

[2] Richard Hofstadter, *The Age of Reform: From Bryan to F. D. R.* (New York, 1955), 282-301.

[3] May, "Shifting Perspectives on the 1920's," 426. See also Henry F. May, "The Rebellion of the Intellectuals, 1912-1917," *American Quarterly*, VIII (Summer 1956), 115, wherein May describes 1912-1917 as a "pre-revolutionary or early revolutionary period."

[4] May, "Shifting Perspectives on the 1920's," 427.

were not as significant as the preceding decade.[5] Political historians have been reassessing the relationship of the Progressive era to the Twenties as well. Arthur Link has demonstrated that progressivism survived World War I,[6] and J. Joseph Huthmacher has established continuity between progressivism and the New Deal in the immigrant's steadfast devotion to the ameliorative powers of the government.[7] Together with May's analysis, their writings suggest that the 1920s are much more the result of earlier intrinsic social changes than either the sudden, supposedly traumatic experiences of the war or unique developments in the Twenties. Since this assertion is certain to encounter the formidable claims that the 1920s, at least in manners and morals, amounted to a revolution, its viability can be tested by questioning if the American woman's "emancipation" in manners and morals occurred even earlier than World War I.

Even a casual exploration of the popular literature of the Progressive era reveals that Americans then described and understood themselves to be undergoing significant changes in morals. "Sex o'clock in America" struck in 1913,[8] about the same time as "The Repeal of Reticence."[9] One contemporary writer saw Americans as liberated from the strictures of "Victorianism," now an epithet deserving criticism, and exulted, "Heaven defend us from a return to the prudery of the Victorian regime!"[10] Conditions were

[5] Henry F. May, *The End of American Innocence: A Study of the First Years of Our Own Time, 1912-1917* (New York, 1959).

[6] Arthur S. Link, "What Happened to the Progressive Movement in the 1920's?" *American Historical Review*, LXIV (July 1959), 833-51.

[7] J. Joseph Huthmacher, "Urban Liberalism and the Age of Reform," *Mississippi Valley Historical Review*, XLIX (Sept. 1962), 231-41. Other political and economic historians concur on a developmental interpretation. Gerald D. Nash, *State Government and Economic Development: A History of Administrative Policies in California, 1849-1933* (Berkeley, 1964), 250, 291, 326, views the period 1900-1933 as a unit because it was characterized by notable coordination and centralization of authority by agencies of state government in California. Donald C. Swain, *Federal Conservation Policy, 1921-1933* (Berkeley, 1963), 6, sees the national conservation program making continuous advances through the 1920s based upon beginnings in the Progressive period.

[8] "Sex O'clock in America," *Current Opinion*, LV (Aug. 1913), 113-14. The anonymous author borrowed the phrase from William M. Reedy, editor of the St. Louis *Mirror*.

[9] Agnes Repplier, "The Repeal of Reticence," *Atlantic Monthly*, CXIII (March 1914), 297-304, objected to the "obsession of sex which has set us all a-babbling about matters once excluded from the amenities of conversation" (p. 298). Articles on birth control, prostitution, divorce, and sexual morals between 1910 and 1914 were cumulatively more numerous per thousand among articles indexed in the *Reader's Guide to Periodical Literature* than for either 1919 to 1924 or 1925 to 1928. Hornell Hart, "Changing Social Attitudes and Interests," *Recent Social Trends in the United States: Report of the President's Research Committe on Social Trends* (2 vols., New York, 1933), I, 414.

[10] H. W. Boynton, "Ideas, Sex, and the Novel," *Dial*, LX (April 13, 1916), 361. In Robert W. Chambers, *The Restless Sex* (New York, 1918), 143, the heroine remarks, "What was all wrong in our Victorian mothers' days is all right now."

such that another commentator asked self-consciously, "Are We Immoral?"[11] And still another feared that the present "vice not often matched since [the time of] the Protestant Reformation" might invite a return to Puritanism.[12] Yet, historians have not carefully investigated the possibility that the true beginnings of America's "New Freedom" in morals occurred prior to 1920.[13] The most extensive, analytical writing on the subject of changing manners and morals is found in Frederick L. Allen's *Only Yesterday* (1931), William Leuchtenburg's *The Perils of Prosperity* (1958), May's *The End of American Innocence* (1959), and George Mowry's *The Urban Nation* (1965).

Allen and Leuchtenburg apply almost identical sharp-break interpretations, respectively entitling chapters "The Revolution in Manners and Morals" and "The Revolution in Morals."[14] Both catalogue the same types of criteria for judgment. The flapper, as the "new woman" was called, was a creature of the 1920s. She smoked, drank, worked, and played side by side with men. She became preoccupied with sex—shocking and simultaneously unshockable. She danced close, became freer with her favors, kept her own latchkey, wore scantier attire which emphasized her boyish, athletic form, just as she used makeup and bobbed and dyed her hair. She and her comradely beau tried to abolish time and succeeded, at least to the extent that the elders asked to join the revelry. Although there were occasional "advance signals" of "rebellion" before the war, it was not until the 1920s that the code of woman's innocence and ignorance crumbled.

May, who comes closest to an understanding of the moral permissiveness before the 1920s, describes in general terms such phenomena of the Progressive era as the "Dance Craze," birth control, the impact of the movies, and the "white-slave panic."[15] He focuses on the intellectuals, how-

[11] Arthur Pollock, "Are We Immoral?" *Forum*, LI (Jan. 1914), 52. Pollock remarks that "in our literature and in our life to-day sex is paramount."

[12] "Will Puritanism Return?" *Independent*, 77 (March 23, 1914), 397.

[13] Mark Sullivan, *Our Times: The War Begins* (New York, 1932), 165-93, states in colorful and impressionistic terms that significant changes in moral attitudes had taken place in the Progressive era. He attributes much of this to the influence of Freud, Shaw, and Omar Khayyám. Preston William Slosson, *The Great Crusade and After: 1914-1928* (New York, 1930), describes the period 1914-1928 as a unit, but his material dealing with morals centers on the 1920s. For example, there are only five footnotes based on materials written between 1914 and 1919 in his chapter, "The American Woman Wins Equality," 130-61. Samuel Eliot Morison makes brief mention of a "revolution in sexual morals" before 1920 in *The Oxford History of the American People* (New York, 1965), 906-08.

[14] Frederick Lewis Allen, *Only Yesterday: An Informal History of the Nineteen-Twenties* (New York, 1931), 88-122; William E. Leuchtenburg, *The Perils of Prosperity: 1914-32* (Chicago, 1958), 158-77.

[15] May, *The End of American Innocence*, 334-47, is lightly documented; there are only twelve footnotes to support his discussion of these and similar developments.

ever, and therefore overlooks the depth of these and similar social movements. This causes him to view them as mere "Cracks in the Surface" of an essentially conservative society. He quotes approvingly of the distinction made by the *Nation* "between the fluttering tastes of the half-baked intellectuals, attracted by all these things, and the surviving soundness of the great majority."[16] His treatment also ignores one of the most significant areas of changing manners and morals as they affected the American woman: the decided shift in her sex role and identification in the direction of more masculine norms. Again, *The End of American Innocence* does not convincingly relate these changes to the growth of the cities. Perhaps these limitations explain Mowry's preference for a "sharp-break" interpretation, although he wrote seven years after May.

Mowry, who acknowledges especial indebtedness to Leuchtenburg,[17] is emphatic about the "startling" changes in manners and morals in the 1920s.[18] He highlights "the new woman of the twenties"[19] whose "modern feminine morality and attitudes toward the institution of marriage date from the twenties."[20] Mowry concedes to the libidos of progressives only the exceptional goings-on in Greenwich Village society.

These hypotheses, excluding May's, hold that the flapper appeared in the postwar period mainly because American women en masse then first enjoyed considerable social and economic freedom. They also emphasize the effect of World War I on morals.[21] By inference, of course, the Progressive era did not provide a suitable matrix. But an investigation of this period establishes that women had become sufficiently active and socially independent to prefigure the "emancipation" of the 1920s.

A significant deterioration of external controls over morality had occurred before 1920. One of the consequences of working and living conditions in the cities, especially as these affected women, was that Americans of the period 1900-1920 had experienced a vast dissolution of moral authority, which formerly had centered in the family and the small commu-

[16] *Ibid.*, 347. May's view of women's changing attitudes is contradicted by Margaret Deland: "Of course there were women a generation ago, as in all generations, who asserted themselves; but they were practically 'sports.' Now, the simple, honest woman . . . the good wife, the good mother—is evolving ideals which are changing her life, and the lives of those people about her." Margaret Deland, "The Change in the Feminine Ideal," *Atlantic Monthly*, CV (March 1910), 291.

[17] George E. Mowry, *The Urban Nation: 1920-1960* (New York, 1965), 250.

[18] *Ibid.*, 23.

[19] *Ibid.*

[20] *Ibid.*, 24.

[21] "By 1930 more than ten million women held jobs. Nothing did more to emancipate them." Leuchtenburg, *Perils of Prosperity*, 160. See also Allen, *Only Yesterday*, 95-98. For estimates of the effects of World War I on morals, see Leuchtenburg, *Perils of Prosperity*, 172-73; Allen, *Only Yesterday*, 94; Mowry, *Urban Nation*, 24.

nity. The traditional "straight and narrow" could not serve the choices and opportunities of city life.[22] As against primary controls and contacts based on face-to-face association where the norms of family, church, and small community, usually reinforcing each other, could be internalized, the city made for a type of "individualization" through its distant, casual, specialized, and transient clusters of secondary associations.[23] The individual came to determine his own behavioral norms.

The "home is in peril" became a fact of sociological literature as early as 1904.[24] One of the most serious signs of its peril was the increasing inability of parents to influence their children in the delicate areas of propriety and morals.[25] The car, already numerous enough to affect dating and premarital patterns,[26] the phone coming to be used for purposes of romantic accommodation,[27] and the variety of partners at the office or the factory,[28] all together assured unparalleled privacy and permissiveness between the sexes.

[22] Population in urban territory comprised only about 28 percent of the total American population in 1880; but by 1920, approximately 52 percent were living there. Department of Commerce, Bureau of the Census, *Historical Statistics of the United States, Colonial Times to 1957* (Washington, 1960), 14.

[23] Scott Nearing and Nellie M. S. Nearing, *Woman and Social Progress* (New York, 1912), 137-41. The Nearings wrote: "The freedom which American Women have gained through recent social changes and the significance of their consequent choice, constitutes one of the profoundest and at the same time one of the most inscrutable problems in American life" (p. 138). William I. Thomas, *The Unadjusted Girl: With Cases and Standpoint for Behavior Analysis* (Boston, 1923), 86. Ernest R. Mowrer, *Family Disorganization* (Chicago, 1927), 6-8. Mowrer attributes "Family Disorganization" to the "conditions of city life" which resulted in a "rebellion against the old ideals of family life. . . ."

[24] George Elliott Howard, "Social Control and the Functions of the Family," Howard J. Rogers, ed., *Congress of Arts and Sciences: Universal Exposition, St. Louis, 1904* (8 vols., Boston, 1906), VII, 702.

[25] Louise Collier Willcox, "Our Supervised Morals," *North American Review*, CXCVIII (Nov. 1913), 708, observes: "The time is past when parents supervised the morals of their children. . . ."

[26] There was a surprisingly large number of cars sold and used in America between 1910 and 1920. Approximately 40 percent as many cars were produced each year between 1915 and 1917 as were manufactured between 1925 and 1927. *Facts and Figures of the Automobile Industry* (New York, 1929), 6, 22. There were approximately 7,500,000 cars registered in 1919. "Existing Surfaced Mileage Total" on a scale of 1,000 miles was 204 in 1910, 332 in 1918, 521 in 1925, and 694 in 1930. *Historical Statistics of the United States*, 458. Newspapers reported the impact of the automobile on dating and elopements. For a moralistic reaction to the phenomenon, see Dorothy Dix, Boston *American*, Sept. 5, 1912. For an enthusiast of "mobile privacy" in this period, see F. Scott Fitzgerald, "Echoes of the Jazz Age," *Scribner's Magazine*, XC (Nov. 1931), 460. Fitzgerald wrote: "As far back as 1915 the unchaperoned young people of the smaller cities had discovered the mobile privacy of that automobile given to young Bill at sixteen to make him 'self-reliant.'"

[27] Dorothy Dix, "A Modern Diana," Boston *American*, April 7, 1910.

[28] Beatrice Fairfax, *ibid.*, May 28, 1908; Dorothy Dix, *ibid.*, Sept. 9, 1912.

Individualization of members served to disrupt confidence between generations of the family, if not to threaten parents with the role of anachronistic irrelevance. Dorothy Dix observed in 1913 that there had been "so many changes in the conditions of life and point of view in the last twenty years that the parent of today is absolutely unfitted to decide the problems of life for the young man and woman of today. This is particularly the case with women because the whole economic and social position of women has been revolutionized since mother was a girl."[29] Magazine articles lamented "The Passing of the Home Daughter" who preferred the blessed anonymity of the city to "dying of asphyxiation at home!"[30] The same phenomenon helps to explain the popularity in this period of such standardized mothers as Dorothy Dix, Beatrice Fairfax, and Emily Post, each of whom was besieged with queries on the respective rights of mothers and daughters.

Woman's individualization resulted mainly because, whether single or married, gainfully employed or not, she spent more time outside her home. Evidence demonstrates that the so-called job and kitchen revolutions were already in advanced stages by 1910. The great leap forward in women's participation in economic life came between 1900 and 1910; the percentage of women who were employed changed only slightly from 1910 to 1930. A comparison of the percentages of gainfully employed women aged 16 to 44 between 1890 and 1930 shows that they comprised 21.7 percent of Americans employed in 1890, 23.5 percent in 1900, 28.1 percent in 1910, 28.3 percent in 1920, and 29.7 percent in 1930.[31] While occupational activity for women appears to stagnate from 1910 to 1920, in reality a considerable restructuring occurred with women leaving roles as domestics and assuming positions affording more personal independence as clerks and stenographers.[32]

Married women, especially those in the upper and middle classes, enjoyed commensurate opportunities. Experts in household management advised women to rid themselves of the maid and turn to appliances as the "maid of all service."[33] Statistics on money expended on those industries

[29] *Ibid.*, Aug. 21, 1913.

[30] Marion Harland, "The Passing of the Home Daughter," *Independent*, LXXI (July 13, 1911), 90.

[31] Sophonisba P. Breckinridge, *Women in the Twentieth Century: A Study of Their Political, Social and Economic Activities* (New York, 1933), 112. Overall percentages of women gainfully employed rose from 19 percent of the total work force in 1890 to 20.6 percent in 1900, 24.3 percent in 1910, 24 percent in 1920, and 25.3 percent in 1930. *Ibid.*, 108.

[32] While the number of women who worked as domestics declined after 1910, large numbers of women were employed for the first time as clerks and stenographers. In fact, more women were employed in both these occupations between 1910 and 1920 than between 1920 and 1930. *Ibid.*, 129, 177.

which reduced home labor for the wife suggest that women in middle-income families gained considerable leisure after 1914.[34] This idea is also corroborated from other sources,[35] especially from the tone and content of advertising in popular magazines when they are compared with advertising at the turn of the century. Generally speaking, women depicted in advertising in or about 1900 are well rounded, have gentle, motherly expressions, soft billowy hair, and delicate hands. They are either sitting down or standing motionless; their facial expressions are immobile as are their corseted figures.[36] After 1910, they are depicted as more active figures with more of their activity taking place outside their homes.[37] One woman tells another over the phone: "Yes[,] drive over right away—I'll be ready. My housework! Oh that's all done. How do I do it? I just let electricity do my work nowadays."[38] Vacuum cleaners permitted the housewife to "Push the Button—and Enjoy the Springtime!"[39] Van Camp's "Pork and Beans" prom-

[33] Martha Bensley Bruere and Robert W. Bruere, *Increasing Home Efficiency* (New York, 1914), 236-41.

[34]

Item	Total Amount Expended in Millions of Dollars				
	1909	1914	1919	1923	1929
(a) canned fruits and vegetables	162	254	575	625	930
(b) cleaning and polishing preparations	6	9	27	35	46
(c) electricity in household operation	83	132	265	389	615.5
(d) mechanical appliances (refrigerators, sewing machines, washers, cooking)	152	175	419	535	804.1
Percentage of expenditures on household equipment to total expenditures	9.9%	9.2%	10.3%	11.6%	13.2%

(a-b) is found in William H. Lough, *High-Level Consumption: Its Behavior; Its Consequences* (New York, 1935), 236, 241. These figures are tabulated in millions of dollars for 1935. Items (c-d) and the percentage of expenditure on household equipment to total expenditures were taken from James Dewhurst, *America's Needs and Resources: A New Survey* (New York, 1955), 702, 704, 180.

[35] Realistic novelists note the leisure of the middle-class women. David Graham Phillips, *The Hungry Heart* (New York, 1909) and *Old Wives for New* (New York, 1908); Robert Herrick, *Together* (New York, 1908), especially 515-17.

[36] For example, see *Cosmopolitan*, XXXV (May-Oct. 1903); *Ladies Home Journal*, XXI (Dec. 1903-May 1904). A notable exception showing a woman riding a bicycle may be found in *ibid.* (April 1904), 39.

[37] *Ladies Home Journal*, XXXIV (May 1917), for example, shows a woman entertaining stylish women friends (34, 89, 92), driving the car or on an automobile trip (36-37, 74), economizing on time spent in housework (42), the object of "outdoor girl" ads (78), beautifying at a social affair or appearing very chic (102, 106). Perhaps the best illustration for woman's activity in advertisements was employed in *Ladies Home Journal* by Williams Talc Powder. It read, "After the game, the ride, the swim, the brisk walk, or a day at the sea-shore, turn for comfort to Williams Talc Powder." *Ibid.*, XXXIV (July 1917), 74.

[38] *Collier's*, 56 (Nov. 27, 1915), 4.

[39] *Cosmopolitan*, LIX (June 1915), advertising section, 50.

ised to save her "100 hours yearly,"[40] and Campbell's soups encouraged, "Get some fun out of life," since it was unnecessary to let the "three-meals-a-day problem tie you down to constant drudgery."[41] Wizard Polish, Minute Tapioca, and Minute Gelatine also offered the same promise. The advertising image of women became more natural, even nonchalant. A lady entertaining a friend remarks: "I don't have to hurry nowadays. I have a Florence Automatic Oil Stove in my kitchen."[42] It had become "so *very* easy" to wax the floors that well-dressed women could manage them.[43] And they enjoyed a round of social activities driving the family car.[44]

It was in this setting that the flapper appeared along with her older married sister who sought to imitate her. No one at the office or in the next block cared much about their morals as long as the one was efficient and the other paid her bills on time. And given the fact that both these women had more leisure and wished "to participate in what men call 'the game of life' " rather than accept "the mere humdrum of household duties,"[45] it is little wonder that contemporaries rightly assessed the danger of the situation for traditional morals by 1910.

The ensuing decade was marked by the development of a revolution in manners and morals; its chief embodiment was the flapper who was urban based and came primarily from the middle and upper classes. Young—whether in fact or fancy—assertive, and independent, she experimented with intimate dancing, permissive favors, and casual courtships or affairs. She joined men as comrades, and the differences in behavior of the sexes were narrowed. She became in fact in some degree desexualized. She might ask herself, "Am I Not a Boy? Yes, I Am—Not."[46] Her speech, her interest in thrills and excitement, her dress and hair, her more aggressive sexuality, even perhaps her elaborate beautification, which was a statement of intentions, all point to this. Women, whether single or married, became at once more attractive and freer in their morals and paradoxically less feminine. Indeed, the term sexual revolution as applied to the Progressive era means reversal in the traditional role of women just as it describes a pronounced familiarity of the sexes.

[40] *Collier's*, 56 (Sept. 25, 1915), 22.
[41] *Ibid.* (Nov. 27, 1915), 25.
[42] *Ladies Home Journal*, XXXV (April 1918), 58.
[43] *Ibid.*, 57.
[44] *Ibid.*, XXXIII (Jan. 1916), 46-47. Women drove their friends and families about in their cars. *Ibid.*, XXXII (July 1915), 34-35; (Aug. 1915), 38-39; (Oct. 1915), 86; XXXIII (Nov. 1916), 71.
[45] Susanne Wilcox, "The Unrest of Modern Women," *Independent*, LXVII (July 8, 1909), 63.
[46] Nell Brinkley, a nationally syndicated cartoonist and commentator on women's activities, asked this question of one of her young women. Boston *American*, July 14, 1913.

The unmarried woman after 1910 was living in the "Day of the Girl."[47] Dorothy Dix described "the type of girl that the modern young man falls for" in 1915 as a "husky young woman who can play golf all day and dance all night, and drive a motor car, and give first aid to the injured if anybody gets hurt, and who is in no more danger of swooning than he is."[48] Little wonder she was celebrated in song as "A Dangerous Girl"; the lyrics of one of the popular songs for 1916 read, "You dare me, you scare me, and still I like you more each day. But you're the kind that will charm; and then do harm; you've got a dangerous way."[49] The "most popular art print . . . ever issued" by *Puck* depicts a made-up young lady puckering her lips and saying "Take It From Me!"[50] The American girl of 1900 was not described in similar terms. The lovely and gracious Gibson Girl was too idealized to be real.[51] And when young lovers trysted in advertising, they met at Horlick's Malted Milk Bar; he with his guitar, and she with her parasol.[52] Beatrice Fairfax could still reply archaically about the need for "maidenly reserve" to such queries as those on the proprieties of men staring at women on the streets.[53] And the *Wellesley College News* in 1902 reported that students were not permitted to have a Junior Prom because it would be an occasion for meeting "promiscuous men," although the college sanctioned "girl dances."[54]

The girls, however, dispensed with "maidenly reserve." In 1910, Margaret Deland, the novelist, could announce a "Change in the Feminine Ideal."

> This young person . . . with surprisingly bad manners—has gone to college, and when she graduates she is going to earn her own living . . . she won't go to church; she has views upon marriage and the birth-rate, and she utters them calmly, while her mother blushes with embarrassment; she occupies herself, passionately, with everything except the things that used to occupy the minds of girls.[55]

Many young women carried their own latchkeys.[56] Meanwhile, as Doro-

[47] Nell Brinkley coined the phrase. *Ibid.*, Nov. 14, 1916.

[48] *Ibid.*, May 4, 1915. See also *Ladies Home Journal*, XXXII (July 1915), which depicts a young woman driving a speedboat while her boyfriend sits next to her.

[49] Boston *American*, Oct. 1, 1916.

[50] *Collier's*, 56 (March 4, 1916), 38.

[51] Emma B. Kaufman, "The Education of a Debutante," *Cosmopolitan*, XXXV (Sept. 1903), 499-508.

[52] *Cosmopolitan*, XXXIX (Oct. 1905).

[53] "Girls, Don't Allow Men to be Familiar," Boston *American*, June 17, 1904; *ibid.*, July 15, 1905.

[54] *Wellesley College News*, Feb. 20, 1902. Wellesley relented on "men dances" in 1913.

[55] Deland, "The Change in the Feminine Ideal," 291.

[56] *Ibid.*, 289.

thy Dix noted, it had become "literally true that the average father does not know, by name or sight, the young man who visits his daughter and who takes her out to places of amusement."[57] She was distressed over the widespread use by young people of the car which she called the "devil's wagon."[58] Another writer asked: "Where Is Your Danghter This Afternoon?" "Are you sure that she is not being drawn into the whirling vortex of afternoon 'trots' . . . ?"[59] Polly, Cliff Sterrett's remarkable comic-strip, modern girl from *Polly and Her Pals*, washed dishes under the shower and dried them with an electric fan; and while her mother tried hard to domesticate her, Polly wondered, "Gee Whiz! I wish I knew what made my nose shine!"[60]

Since young women were working side by side with men and recreating more freely and intimately with them, it was inevitable that they behave like men. Older people sometimes carped that growing familiarity meant that romance was dead[61] or that "nowadays brides hardly blush, much less faint."[62] And Beatrice Fairfax asked, "Has Sweet Sixteen Vanished?"[63] But some observers were encouraged to note that as girls' ways approximated men's, the sexes were, at least, more comradely.[64] The modern unmarried woman had become a "Diana, Hunting in the Open."[65] Dorothy Dix reported that "nice girls, good girls, girls in good positions in society—frankly take the initiative in furthering an acquaintance with any man who happens to strike their fancy." The new ideal in feminine figure, dress, and hair styles was all semi-masculine. The "1914 Girl" with her "slim hips and boy-carriage" was a "slim, boylike creature."[66] The "new figure is Amazonian, rather than Miloan. It is boyish rather than womanly. It is strong rather than soft."[67] Her dress styles, meanwhile, de-emphasized both

[57] Boston *American*, May 6, 1910.
[58] *Ibid.*, Sept. 5, 1912.
[59] Ethel Watts Mumford, "Where Is Your Daughter This Afternoon?" *Harper's Weekly*, LVIII (Jan. 17, 1914), 28.
[60] Boston *American*, Sept. 5, 1916; *ibid.*, Jan. 4, 1914.
[61] Alice Duer Miller, "The New Dances and the Younger Generation," *Harper's Bazaar*, XLVI (May 1912), 250.
[62] Deland, "Change in the Feminine Ideal," 293.
[63] Boston *American*, March 24, 1916. In a letter to the editor of the New York *Times*, one critic of the "women of New York" complained that they seemed to be part of a "new race" or even a "super-sex." He waxed poetic: "Sweet seventeen is rouge-pot mad, And hobbles to her tasks blase, . . . Where are the girls of yesterday?" New York *Times*, July 20, 1914.
[64] Miller, "New Dances and the Younger Generation," 250. According to Helen Rowland, the woman was "no longer Man's plaything, but his playmate. . . ." Helen Rowland, "The Emancipation of 'the Rib,'" *Delineator*, LXXVII (March 1911), 233.
[65] Boston *American*, April 7, 1910.
[66] *Ibid.*, March 20, 1914.
[67] *Ibid.*, June 11, 1916.

hips and bust while they permitted the large waist. The boyish coiffure began in 1912 when young women began to tuck-under their hair with a ribbon;[68] and by 1913-1914, Newport ladies, actresses like Pauline Frederick, then said to be the prettiest girl in America, and the willowy, popular dancer Irene Castle were wearing short hair.[69] By 1915, the *Ladies Home Journal* featured women with short hair on its covers, and even the pure type of woman who advertised Ivory Soap appeared to be shorn.[70]

The unmarried flapper was a determined pleasure-seeker whom novelist Owen Johnson described collectively as "determined to liberate their lives and claim the same rights of judgment as their brothers."[71] The product of a "feminine revolution startling in the shock of its abruptness," she was living in the city independently of her family. Johnson noted: "She is sure of one life only and that one she passionately desires. She wants to live that life to its fullest. . . . She wants adventure. She wants excitement and mystery. She wants to see, to know, to experience. . . ." She expressed both a "passionate revolt against the commonplace" and a "scorn of conventions." Johnson's heroine in *The Salamander*, Doré Baxter, embodied his views. Her carefree motto is reminiscent of Fitzgerald's flappers of the Twenties: " 'How do I know what I'll do to-morrow?' "[72] Her nightly prayer, the modest " 'O Lord! give me everything I want!' "[73] Love was her "supreme law of conduct,"[74] and she, like the literary flappers of the Twenties, feared "thirty as a sort of sepulcher, an end of all things!"[75] Johnson believed that all young women in all sections of the country had "a little touch of the Salamander," each alike being impelled by "an impetuous frenzy . . . to sample each new excitement," both the "safe and the dangerous."[76] Girls "seemed determined to have their fling like men," the novelist Gertrude Atherton noted in *Current Opinion*, "and some of the stories [about them] made even my sophisticated hair crackle at the roots. . . ."[77] Beatrice Fairfax deplored

[68] *Ibid.*, Nov. 27, Dec. 8, 1912.

[69] On Newport and Boston society women see *ibid.*, July 6, 27, Aug. 10, 24, 1913. Pauline Frederick's picture may be found in *ibid.*, Aug. 2, 1913. For Irene Castle, see Mr. and Mrs. Vernon Castle, *Modern Dancing* (New York, 1914), 98, 105.

[70] *Ladies Home Journal*, XXXII (July and Sept. 1915); *ibid.* (Nov. 1915), 8.

[71] Owen Johnson, *The Salamander* (Indianapolis, 1914), Foreword, n.p.

[72] *Ibid.*, 9.

[73] *Ibid.*, 129.

[74] *Ibid.*, 66.

[75] *Ibid.*, 61.

[76] *Ibid.*, Foreword, n.p. Chamber's young heroine Stephanie Cleland in *The Restless Sex*, 191, practiced trial marriage in order to learn by experience. See also Phillips, *Hungry Heart*, 166-80; Terry Ramsaye, *A Million And One Nights: A History of the Motion Picture* (2 vols., New York, 1926), II, 702-04.

[77] "Mrs. Atherton Tells of Her 'Perch of the Devil,' " *Current Opinion*, LVII (Nov. 1914), 349.

the trends, especially the fact that "Making love lightly, boldly and promiscuously seems to be part of our social structure."[78] Young men and women kissed though they did not intend to marry.[79] And kissing was shading into spooning (" 'To Spoon' or 'Not to Spoon' Seems to Be the Burning Question with Modern Young America")[80] and even "petting," which was modish among the collegiate set.[81] In fact, excerpts from the diary of a co-ed written before World War I suggest that experimentation was virtually complete within her peer group. She discussed her "adventures" with other college girls. "We were healthy animals and we were demanding our rights to spring's awakening." As for men, she wrote, "I played square with the men. I always told them I was not out to pin them down to marriage, but that this intimacy was pleasant and I wanted it as much as they did. We indulged in sex talk, birth control. . . . We thought too much about it."[82]

One of the most interesting developments in changing sexual behavior which characterized these years was the blurring of age lines between young and middle-aged women in silhouette, dress, and cosmetics.[83] A fashion commentator warned matrons, "This is the day of the figure. . . . The face alone, no matter how pretty, counts for nothing unless the body is as straight and yielding as every young girl's."[84] With only slight variations, the optimum style for women's dress between 1908 and 1918 was a modified sheath, straight up and down and clinging.[85] How different from the styles of the high-busted, broad-hipped mother of the race of 1904 for whom Ella Wheeler Wilcox, the journalist and poet, advised the use of veils because "the slightest approach to masculinity in woman's attire is always unlovely and disappointing."[86]

The sloughing off of numerous undergarments and loosening of others underscored women's quickening activity and increasingly self-reliant mor-

[78] Boston *American*, Feb. 8, 1917.

[79] The "kiss of friendship" criticized by Fairfax had become a major issue of her mail by 1913. See, for example, *ibid.*, July 5, 1913. Girls shocked her with inquiries as to whether it was permissible to "soul kiss" on a first date. *Ibid.*, Feb. 13, 1914. An engaged girl asked whether it would be all right to kiss men other than her fiance. *Ibid.*, May 2, 1916.

[80] *Ibid.*, Feb. 8, 1917.

[81] Fitzgerald, "Echoes of the Jazz Age," 460.

[82] Thomas, *Unadjusted Girl*, 95.

[83] "Today in the world of fashion, all women are young, and they grow more so all the time." Doeuilet, "When All The World Looks Young," *Delineator*, LXXXIII (Aug. 1913), 20. Advertisements used flattery or played up the value of youth for women and warned that they might age unless certain products were used. *Cosmopolitan*, LIX (Nov. 1915), 112; *ibid.* (July 1915), 81; *Ladies Home Journal*, XXXII (Nov. 1915), 65; *Cosmopolitan*, LIX (Oct. 1915), 57.

[84] Eleanor Chalmers, "Facts and Figures," *Delineator*, LXXXIV (April 1914), 38.

[85] Boston *American*, March 20, 1910; *Delineator*, LXXXIX (Oct. 1916), 66.

[86] Boston *American*, March 28, 1904.

als. Clinging dresses and their "accompanying lack of undergarments" eliminated, according to the president of the New York Cotton Exchange, "at least twelve yards of finished goods for each adult female inhabitant."[87] Corset makers were forced to make adjustments too and use more supple materials.[88] Nevertheless, their sales declined.[89]

The American woman of 1910, in contrast with her sister of 1900, avidly cultivated beauty of face and form. In fact, the first American woman whose photographs and advertising image we can clearly recognize as belonging to our times lived between 1910 and 1920. "Nowadays," the speaker for a woman's club declared in 1916, "only the very poor or the extremely careless are old or ugly. You can go to a beauty shop and choose the kind of beauty you will have."[90] Beautification included the use of powder, rouge, lipstick, eyelash and eyebrow stain. Advertising was now manipulating such images for face powder as "Mother tried it and decided to keep it for herself,"[91] or "You can have beautiful Eyebrows and Eyelashes . . . . Society women and actresses get them by using Lash-Brow-Ine."[92] Nearly every one of the numerous advertisements for cosmetics promised some variation of "How to Become Beautiful, Fascinating, Attractive."[93]

In her dress as well as her use of cosmetics, the American woman gave evidence that she had abandoned passivity. An unprecedented public display of the female figure characterized the period.[94] Limbs now became legs and more of them showed after 1910, although they were less revealing than the promising hosiery advertisements. Rolled down hose first appeared in 1917.[95] Dresses for opera and restaurant were deeply cut in front and back, and not even the rumor that Mrs. John Jacob Astor had suffered a chest cold as a result of wearing deep decolleté[96] deterred their wearers.

[87] New York *Tribune*, April 4, 1912; Eleanor Chalmers, "You and Your Sewing," *Delineator*, LXXXIII (Aug. 1913), 33.

[88] Eleanor Chalmers, *Delineator*, LXXXIV (April 1914), 38. The sense of relief these changes brought is amusingly described in Dorothy A. Plum, comp., *The Magnificent Enterprise: A Chronicle of Vassar College* (Poughkeepsie, 1961), 43-44.

[89] Percival White, "Figuring Us Out," *North American Review*, CCXXVII (Jan. 1929), 69.

[90] Boston *American*, Dec. 10, 1916.

[91] *Delineator*, LXXXV (July 1914), 55.

[92] Boston *American*, Sept. 3, 1916.

[93] *Cosmopolitan*, LIX (July 1915).

[94] An editorial declared that women's dresses in 1913 had approached "the danger line of indecency about as closely as they could." New York *Times*, July 6, 1914.

[95] *Ladies Home Journal*, XXXIV (Oct. 1917), 98.

[96] Boston *American*, June 8, 1907. "The conventions of evening dress have changed radically in the last four or five years. Not so very long ago a high-necked gown was considered *au fait* for all evening functions except formal dinners and the opera. Nowadays, well-dressed women wear decolleté dresses even for home dinners, and semi-decolleté gowns for restaurants and theaters." *Delineator*, LXXV (Jan. 1910), 60.

As for gowns, "Fashion says—Evening gowns must be sleeveless. . . . afternoon gowns are made with semi-transparent yokes and sleeves."[97] Undoubtedly, this vogue for transparent blouses and dresses[98] caused the editor of the *Unpopular Review* to declare: "At no time and place under Christianity, except the most corrupt periods in France. . . . certainly never before in America, has woman's form been so freely displayed in society and on the street."[99]

In addition to following the example of young women in dress and beautification, middle-aged women, especially those from the middle and upper classes, were espousing their permissive manners and morals.[100] Smoking and, to a lesser extent, drinking in public were becoming fashionable for married women of the upper class and were making headway at other class levels.[101] As early as 1910, a prominent clubwoman stated: "It has become a well-established habit for women to drink cocktails. It is thought the smart thing to do."[102] Even before Gertrude Atherton described in the novel *Black Oxen* the phenomenon of the middle-aged women who sought to be attractive to younger men, supposedly typifying the 1920s,[103] it was evident in the play "Years of Discretion." Written by Frederic Hatton and Fanny Locke Hatton, and staged by Belasco, the play was "welcomed cordially both in New York and Chicago" in 1912. It featured a widowed mother forty-eight years of age, who announces, "I intend to look under forty—lots under. I have never attracted men, but I know I can."[104] Again, "I mean to have a wonderful time. To have all sorts and kinds of experience. I intend to love and be loved, to lie and cheat."[105] Dorothy Dix was dismayed over "the interest that women . . . have in what we are pleased to euphoniously term the 'erotic.' " She continued, "I'll bet there are not ten thousand women in the whole United States who couldn't

[97] *Cosmopolitan*, LIX (July 1915).

[98] *Ladies Home Journal*, XXXII (Oct. 1915), 108; *ibid.*, XXXIII (Oct. 1916), 82; *ibid.*, XXXIII (Nov. 1916), 78-79; *ibid.*, XXXIV (Jan. 1917), 53.

[99] "The Cult of St. Vitus," *Unpopular Review*, III (Jan.-March 1915), 94.

[100] Boston *American*, July 6, 1912. Dix noted "flirtatious" middle-aged women were "aping the airs and graces of the debutante" and "trying to act kittenish" with men.

[101] *Ibid.*, Dec. 6, 10, 1912. Anita Stewart, a movie star who wrote "Talks to Girls," though personally opposed to smoking, admitted that "lots of my friends smoke" and "they are nice girls too." *Ibid.*, Dec. 14, 1915. In 1916, the Boston *American* titled a column on a page devoted to women's interests "To Smoke or Not to Smoke." *Ibid.*, April 12, 1916. The *Harvard Lampoon*, LXXI (June 20, 1916), 376, spoofed women smoking: it carried a heading "Roman Society Women Agree to Give Up Smoking" and a commentary below, "Oh, Nero, how times have changed!"

[102] Boston *American*, March 7, 1910.

[103] Leuchtenburg, *Perils of Prosperity*, 174-75.

[104] " 'Years of Discretion'—A Play of Cupid at Fifty," *Current Opinion*, LIV (Feb. 1913), 116.

[105] *Ibid.*, 117.

get one hundred in an examination of the life and habits of Evelyn Nesbitt and Harry Thaw. . . ."[106] Married women among the fashionable set held the great parties, at times scandalous ones which made the 1920s seem staid by comparison.[107] They hired the Negro orchestras at Newport and performed and sometimes invented the daring dances.[108] They conscientiously practiced birth control, as did women of other classes.[109] And they initiated divorce proceedings, secure in the knowledge that many of their best friends had done the same thing.

Perhaps the best insights on the mores and morals of this group are to be found in the writings of the contemporary, realistic novelist, Robert Herrick.[110] Herrick derived his heroines from "the higher income groups, the wealthy, upper middle, and professional classes among which he preferred to move."[111] His heroines resemble literary flappers of the 1920s in their repudiation of childbearing. "It takes a year out of a woman's life, of course, no matter how she is situated," they say, or, "Cows do that."[112] Since their lives were seldom more than a meaningless round of social experiences, relieved principally by romantic literature, many of them either contemplated or consented to infidelity. Thus Margaret Pole confesses to her friend, Conny Woodyard, " 'I'd like to lie out on the beach and forget children and servants and husbands, and stop wondering what life is. Yes, I'd like a vacation—in the Windward Islands, with somebody who understood.' 'To wit, a man!' added Conny. 'Yes, a man! But only for the trip.' "[113] They came finally to live for love in a manner that is startlingly reminiscent of some of the famous literary women of the Twenties.[114]

[106] Boston *American*, April 10, 1908. Evelyn Nesbitt, the wife of Harry Thaw, was romantically involved with architect Stanford White, whom Thaw shot to death.

[107] *Ibid.*, Aug. 25, Sept. 1, 1912.

[108] Most of the dances which became very popular after 1910, such as the Turkey Trot, the Bunny Hug, and the Grizzly Bear, afforded a maximum of motion in a minimum of space. The Chicken Flip was invented by a Boston society woman. *Ibid.*, Nov. 11, 1912. See also "New Reflections on the Dancing Mania," *Current Opinion*, LV (Oct. 1913), 262.

[109] Louis I. Dublin, "Birth Control," *Social Hygiene*, VI (Jan. 1920), 6.

[110] Alfred Kazin, "Three Pioneer Realists," *Saturday Review of Literature*, XX (July 8, 1939), 15. Herrick's biographer, Blake Nevius, declares, "It can be argued that Herrick is the most comprehensive and reliable social historian in American fiction to appear in the interregnum between Howells and the writers of the Twenties. . . ." Blake Nevius, *Robert Herrick: The Development of a Novelist* (Berkeley, 1962), Preface.

[111] Nevius, *Robert Herrick*, 177.

[112] Herrick, *Together*, 91, 392.

[113] *Ibid.*, 263, 250-51, 320-24.

[114] Herrick describes the temperament of the modern woman as one of "mistress rather than the wife. . . . 'I shall be a person with a soul of my own. To have me man must win me not once, but daily.' " *Ibid.*, 516. The last sentence above nearly duplicates Rosalind's statement to her beau in *This Side of Paradise*, "I have to be won all over again

Insights regarding the attitudes of married women from the urban lower middle class can be found in the diary of Ruth Vail Randall, who lived in Chicago from 1911 to the date of her suicide, March 6, 1920.[115] A document of urban sociology, the diary transcends mere personal experience and becomes a commentary on group behavior of the times. Mrs. Randall was reared in a family that owned a grocery store, was graduated from high school in Chicago, and was married at twenty to Norman B. Randall, then twenty-one. She worked after marriage in a department store and later for a brief period as a model. She looked to marriage, especially its romance, as the supreme fulfillment of her life and was bitterly disappointed with her husband. She began to turn to other men whom she met at work or places of recreation, and her husband left her. Fearing that her lover would leave her eventually as well, she killed him and herself.

The diary focuses on those conditions which made the revolution in morals a reality. The young couple lived anonymously in a highly mobile neighborhood where their morals were of their own making. Mrs. Randall did not want children; she aborted their only child.[116] She was also averse to the reserved "womanly" role, which her husband insisted that she assume.[117] She complained, "Why cannot a woman do all man does?"[118] She wished that men and women were more alike in their social roles.[119] She repudiated involvement in her home, resolved to exploit equally every privilege which her husband assumed, drank, flirted, and lived promiscuously. Telephones and cars made her extramarital liaisons possible. Even before her divorce, she found another companion; flouting convention, she wrote, "He and I have entered a marriage pact according to our own ideas."[120] Throughout her diary she entertained enormous, almost magical, expectations of love. She complained that her lovers no more than her husband provided what she craved—tenderness and companionship. Disillusionment with one of them caused her to cry out, "I am miserable. I have the utmost contempt for myself. But the lake is near and soon it will be warm. Oh, God to rest in your arms. To rest—and to have peace."[121]

That America was experiencing a major upheaval in morals during the Progressive era is nowhere better ascertained than in the comprehensive ef-

every time you see me." F. Scott Fitzgerald, *This Side of Paradise* (New York, 1920), 194.

[115] Chicago *Herald and Examiner*, March 10-17, 1920.

[116] *Ibid.*, March 10, 1920.

[117] *Ibid.*, March 11, 1920.

[118] *Ibid.*

[119] *Ibid.*, March 11, 12, 1920.

[120] *Ibid.*, March 13, 14, 1920.

[121] *Ibid.*, March 15, 1920.

forts by civic officials and censorial citizens to control them. Disapproval extended not only to such well-known staples as alcohol, divorce, and prostitution, but also to dancing, woman's dress, cabarets, theaters and movies, and birth control. "Mrs. Warren's Profession" was withdrawn from the New York stage in 1905 after a one night performance, the manager of the theater later being charged with offending public decency.[122] When a grand jury in New York condemned the "turkey trot and kindred dances" as "indecent," the judge who accepted the presentment noted that "Rome's downfall was due to the degenerate nature of its dancers, and I only hope that we will not suffer the same result."[123] Public dancing was henceforth to be licensed. Mayor John Fitzgerald personally assisted the morals campaign in Boston by ordering the removal from a store of an objectionable picture which portrayed a "show-girl" with her legs crossed.[124] Meanwhile, the "X-Ray Skirt" was outlawed in Portland, Oregon, and Los Angeles;[125] and the police chief of Louisville, Kentucky, ordered the arrest of a number of women appearing on the streets with slit skirts.[126] Witnessing to a general fear that the spreading knowledge of contraception might bring on sexual license, the federal and several state governments enacted sumptuary legislation.[127] And in two celebrated incidents, the offenders, Van K. Allison (1916) in Boston and Margaret Sanger (1917) in New York, were prosecuted and sent to jail.[128]

Public officials were apprehensive about the sweeping influence of the movies on the masses, "at once their book, their drama, their art. To some it has become society, school, and even church."[129] They proceeded to set up boards of censorship with powers to review and condemn movies in four states: Pennsylvania (1911), Ohio (1913), Maryland (1916), and Kansas (1917), and in numerous cities beginning with Chicago in 1907.[130] The Pennsylvania board, for example, prohibited pictures which displayed nudity, prolonged passion, women drinking and smoking, and infidelity. It protected Pennsylvanians from such films produced between 1915 and

[122] New York *Tribune*, Nov. 1, 1905.

[123] New York *Times*, May 28, 1913.

[124] *Ibid.*, Dec. 20, 1912.

[125] *Ibid.*, Aug. 20, 23, 1913.

[126] *Ibid.*, June 29, 1913.

[127] Carol Flora Brooks, "The Early History of the Anti-Contraceptive Laws in Massachusetts and Connecticut," *American Quarterly*, XVIII (Spring 1966), 3-23; George E. Worthington, "Statutory Restrictions on Birth Control," *Journal of Social Hygiene*, IX (Nov. 1923), 458-65.

[128] Boston *American*, July 14, 21, 1916; New York *Times*, Feb. 6, 1917.

[129] *Report of the Pennsylvania Board of Censors*, June 1, 1915 to Dec. 1, 1915 (Harrisburg, 1916), 6.

[130] Ellis Paxson Oberholtzer, *The Morals of the Movie* (Philadelphia, 1922), 115-23.

1918 as "What Every Girl Should Know," "A Factory Magdalene," and "Damaged Goodness."[131]

Such determination proved unavailing, however, even as the regulatory strictures were being applied. According to one critic the "sex drama" using "plain, blunt language" had become "a commonplace" of the theater after 1910 and gave the "tender passion rather the worst for it in recent years."[132] Vice films packed them in every night, especially after the smashing success of "Traffic in Souls," which reportedly grossed $450,000.[133] In Boston the anti-vice campaign itself languished because there was no means of controlling "the kitchenette-apartment section." "In these apartment houses, there are hundreds of women who live as they please and who entertain as they will."[134] Mayor Fitzgerald's "show-girl," evicted from her saucy perch, gained more notoriety when she appeared in a Boston newspaper the following day.[135] Even Anthony Comstock, that indefatigable guardian of public morals, had probably come to look a bit like a comic character living beyond his times.[136]

When Mrs. Sanger was arrested for propagating birth control information in 1917, she confidently stated, "I have nothing to fear. . . . Regardless of the outcome I shall continue my work, supported by thousands of men and women throughout the country."[137] Her assurance was well founded. Three years earlier her supporters had founded a National Birth Control League; and in 1919, this organization opened its first public clinic.[138] But most encouraging for Mrs. Sanger was the impressive testimony that many Americans were now practicing or interested in birth control.[139] When Paul B. Blanchard, pastor of the Maverick Congregational Church in East Boston, protested the arrest of Van K. Allison, he charged, "If the truth were made public and the laws which prevent the spreading of even oral information about birth control were strictly enforced how very few of the married society leaders, judges, doctors, ministers, and businessmen would be outside the prison dock!"[140]

[131] *Report of the Pennsylvania State Board of Censors*, 1915, pp. 14-15; *ibid.*, 1916, pp. 24-25; *ibid.*, 1917, pp. 8-9.

[132] Boston *American*, Aug. 10, 1913.

[133] Ramsaye, *A Million and One Nights*, II, 617.

[134] Boston *American*, July 7, 1917.

[135] *Ibid.*, Dec. 20, 1912.

[136] Heywood Broun, *Anthony Comstock: Roundsman of the Lord* (New York, 1927); Mary Alden Hopkins, "Birth Control and Public Morals: An Interview with Anthony Comstock," *Harper's Weekly*, LX (May 22, 1915), 489-90.

[137] Boston *American*, Jan. 4, 1917.

[138] Norman E. Himes, "Birth Control in Historical and Clinical Perspective," *Annals of the American Academy of Political and Social Sciences*, 160 (March 1932), 53.

[139] Dublin, "Birth Control," 6.

[140] Boston *American*, July 16, 1916. According to International News Service, "Mrs.

The foregoing demonstrates that a major shift in American manners and morals occurred in the Progressive era, especially after 1910. Changes at this time, though developing out of still earlier conditions, represented such visible departures from the past and were so commonly practiced as to warrant calling them revolutionary. Too often scholars have emphasized the Twenties as the period of significant transition and World War I as a major cause of the phenomenon. Americans of the 1920s, fresh from the innovative wartime atmosphere, undoubtedly quickened and deepened the revolution. Women from smaller cities and towns contested what was familiar terrain to an already seasoned cadre of urban women and a formidable group of defectors. Both in their rhetoric and their practices, apparent even before the war, the earlier group had provided the shibboleths for the 1920s; they first asked, "What are Patterns for?" The revolution in manners and morals was, of course, but an integral part of numerous, contemporary, political and social movements to free the individual by reordering society. Obviously, the Progressive era, more than the 1920s, represents the substantial beginnings of contemporary American civilization.

The revolution in manners and morals, particularly as it affected women, took the twofold form of more permissive sexuality and diminished femininity. Women from the upper classes participated earlier, as is evidenced by their introductory exhibition of fashions, hair styles, dances, cosmetics, smoking, and drinking. Realistic novels concerned with marriage suggest that they entertained ideas of promiscuity and even infidelity before women of the lower classes. Yet the cardinal condition of change was not sophistication but urban living and the freedom it conferred. As technology and economic progress narrowed the gap between the classes, middle-class women and even those below were free to do many of the same things almost at the same time. Above all, the revolution in manners and morals after 1910 demonstrates that sexual freedom and the twentieth-century American city go together.

Rose Pastor Stokes was literally mobbed by an eager crowd in Carnegie Hall when she offered, in defiance of the police, to distribute printed slips bearing a formula for birth control." *Ibid.*, May 6, 1916.

LESBIAN MAGAZINE FICTION IN THE EARLY TWENTIETH CENTURY

By Lillian Faderman

To Carol
My love has a forehead broad and fair,
And the breeze-blown curls of her chestnut hair
Fall over it softly, the gold and the red
A shining aureole round her head.
Her clear eyes gleam with an amber light
For sunbeams dance in them swift and bright!
And over those eyes so golden brown,
Long, shadowy lashes droop gently down...
Oh, pale with envy the rose doth grow
That my lady lifts to her cheeks' warm glow!...
But for joy its blushes would come again
If my lady to kiss the rose should deign.

Jean Lennox

from "The Lass of the Silver Sword"
St. Nicholas: An Illustrated Magazine For Young Folks, 1908

If the above poem had been written by one female character to another in magazine fiction after 1920, the poetess of the story would no doubt have been rushed off to a psychoanalyst to undergo treatment for her mental malady, or she would have ended her fictional existence broken in half by a tree, justly punished by nature (with a little help from a right-thinking heterosexual) for her transgression. Much more likely, such a poem would not have been written by a fictional female to another after the first two decades of the twentieth century, because most popular magazines by that time considered the explicit discussion of same-sex love taboo. In the early twentieth century, however, and throughout the nineteenth century, popular stories often treated the subject totally without self-consciousness and without awareness that such relationships were "unhealthy" or "immoral."[1]

I am not suggesting that before our era women were permitted rampant sexual expression with each other, but rather that homoaffectional expression between women was far less restricted in the past, that permissible behavior included caressing, holding, exchanges of endearments, and expressions of intense emotional commitment to each other. While it is unlikely that many of these relationships would have included genital contact, it was barely more likely that a love relationship between a man and a woman before marriage would have included genital contact. And just as the male-female relationship is nevertheless characterized as heterosexual, the female-female relationship of similar intensity may be characterized as homosexual.

Such homosexual relationships were not considered threatening in previous centuries for two reasons. First of all, it was clearly understood that a woman would give up her female love with the advent of a suitable male who could (a) support her, in an era when almost no work opportunities were available for women outside of the lower class, (b) provide her with status in the community—which was generally closer-knit and more dictatorial with regard to life-styles than it is today, and (c) provide her with a family, the sine qua non of her existence in the days before the contemporary women's movement and fears of over-population. This tacit understanding is suggested by novelists such as Henry Wadsworth Longfellow and Oliver Wendell Holmes who were reflecting their society's calm acknowledgement of homoaffectional ties and the confidence that those ties would not be destructive to the fabric of society when they characterized love relationships between women as a "rehearsal in girlhood of the great drama of woman's life"[2] and observed "the friendships of young girls prefigure the closer relations which will one day come in and dissolve their earlier intimacies."[3]

Secondly, "the lesbian" as a sexual category was until recently virtually non-existent. One might in fact say that "lesbianism" and the familiar contemporary attitudes toward female homosexuality are for the most part an invention of our times. It was, in fact, not until the 1880's and the work of scientists such as Richard von Krafft-Ebing, Magnus Hirschfeld, and Havelock Ellis that "lesbianism" became a medical problem. As late as 1894 Dr. Allan Hamilton wrote in the *American Journal of Insanity*, a professional journal for alienists and neurologists, that "until within a comparatively recent period the mere insinuation that there could be anything improper in the intimate relations of two women would have drawn upon the head of the maker of such a suggestion a degree of censure of the most pronounced and enduring character." He attributes recognition by his contemporaries of the existence of such variance to "romances from the pens of French and German writers" of the last thirty years, such as Theophile Gautier's *Mademoiselle de Maupin*. But apparently recognition was not particularly widespread, since Hamilton speaks in the same article of a "case" of lesbianism that came to his attention a few years earlier, "at that time her mental perversion was not of a recognized kind."[4]

Legal persecution for homosexuality seems to have focused almost exclusively on males in pre-twentieth century America and England. In his collection of historical documents, *Gay American History: Lesbians and Gay Men in the U.S.A.*, Jonathan Katz includes evidence of a half dozen executions and other forms of punishment of gay men in America.[5] But suggestions that women were similarly persecuted are scant.[6] Even once the medical professions and the law became aware–whether through French and German novels or the writings of Krafft-Ebing, Havelock Ellis, Magnus Hirschfeld and others–that female homosexuality existed, most same-sex female relationships would have been permitted to continue undisturbed because it was believed that "true" lesbians were rare and were readily identifiable. According to Havelock Ellis, writing in an American medical journal in 1895, sexual inversion in women was generally accompanied by exhaustion, hysteria and epilepsy.[7] According to Allan Hamilton, the female homosexual "was usually of a masculine type, or if she presented none of the 'characteristics' of the male, was a subject of pelvic disorders, with scanty menstruation, and was more or less hysterial or insane."[8] Thus if a woman appeared reasonably feminine and in good health, by definition she was not an invert and her love for another woman was not suspect.

In short, before the 1920's women were permitted a broader spectrum of expressions of love for their own sex,[9] primarily for two reasons: (1) love relationships between women were not threatening, since it was understood that women would marry if they could, for economic and social reasons, despite such affectional ties; (2) it was generally believed that women, being for the most part non-sexual outside of procreative activity, were entirely unlikely to engage in "improper. . .intimate relations" with other females, and that those few who did transgress were easily identifiable through external characteristics. Although, as Hamilton points out, by mid-nineteenth century there were a number of French and German novels which dealt with love between women in a manner which suggested decadence and corruption, those novels–and even the late nineteenth century "discoveries" of medical men–were unfamiliar to the mass of the population. Thus it was that popular magazine fiction, well into the twentieth century, could depict female-female love relationships with an openness that later became, as I shall discuss, impossible.

Early twentieth century "lesbian"[10] fiction appeared in England and America in magazines such as *Ladies' Home Journal, Century, Harper's, Strand,* and even magazines for children such as *St. Nicholas*. Frequently the setting is a girls' school or a women's college, and the love relationship centers around a freshman and an older student, or just as often, a younger woman and an older woman who serves as her mentor, whether inside of an academic situation or out. It is possible that these two types of relationships became the focus of so many homoaffectional stories after the popularity of Josephine Dodge Daskam's *Smith College Stories*[11] (which was first published in 1900 and reissued a number of times in the following decades) and Mary MacLane's *The Story of Mary MacLane,*[12] an autobiographic confessional (which was published in 1902 and was followed by two sequels and a number of reprints). At least two of Daskam's stories appear to reflect the ordinariness of emotional involvements between women, "A Case of Interference" and "The Evolution of Evangeline." In the latter story for example, the older girls invite the younger to dances and customarily ask, "What color is your gown? I should like to send you some flowers." When one older girl, Biscuits, is obliged to invite Evangeline, who is not attractive to her, "visions of the pretty little freshman she had in mind on filling out her [dance] programme flashed before her with irritating clearness." When another freshman is disappointed in her hope of being escorted to the dance by her favorite sophomore, the narrator observes, "the little freshman cried herself to sleep, for she had dreamed for nights of going with Suzanne, whom she admired to stupefaction."

The Story of Mary MacLane is particularly straightforward about the narrator's love for a former teacher, Fannie Corbin (whom she affectionately calls the anemone lady), who is twelve or thirteen years older than Mary. Mary speaks of her passion for Fannie "burn[ing] with a vivid fire of its own." Fannie is "my first love–my only dear one," and "the thought of her fills me with a multitude of feelings, passionate yet wonderfully tender." With her, Mary experiences "a convulsion and a melting within." Mary believes that if she could live with Fanny "in some little out-of-the-world place high up on the side of a mountain for the rest of my life–what more would I desire?" Lest the reader think that platonic love alone is being described here, Mary says "I feel in the anemone lady a strange attraction of sex... Do you think a man is the only creature with whom one may fall in love?"

Modern critics have been wont to explain such statements by attributing the description of what appears to be same-sex love to the rhetoric and sentimentality of the age,[13] and thus denying the validity of the speaker's feelings. But such criticism skirts the issue. If a female character is conceived to have cried all night over her disappointment about not being taken to a dance by another female, or if she claims that all her desire would be fulfilled if she could live with her beloved for the rest of her life, surely the author intended the reader to believe that the character feels a certain powerful emotion (which her age has permitted her to express and which another age might force her to deny). Whether or not that emotion is described in extravagant terms and phrases such as "stupefaction" or "a convulsion and a melting within" is irrelevant in this respect. What is relevant is that it has been communicated to the reader that the female character was emotionally touched by another female.

The language in "The Cat and the King," which appeared in *Ladies' Home Journal* in October 1919, is similarly extravagant.[14] The characters here too are students at a women's college. When the freshman Flora sees her idol, the senior Annette, the narrator observes:

> To the freshman gazing from her walk, it was as if a goddess, high-enshrined and touched by the rising sun, stood revealed. She gave a gasp of pleasure.

Perhaps it is easy to dismiss such a description as rhetoric and sentimentality of the age. But it is less easy to dismiss the *fact* of the character's emotion and the *action* of the story: Flora has a crush on Annette, a senior and the captain of the college ball team. When Annette hurts her ankle and is hospitalized in the school infirmary, Flora decides the best way to meet her idol is to feign a strange illness and to be hospitalized too. But on Flora's first day in the infirmary, Annette is released. A kindly woman doctor discerns what has been happening and helpfully devises two ways to get the girls together: she employs Flora in her lab where Annette also works, and she had Flora placed on the ball team. The doctor exits from the story, telling Flora happily, "You are to report at once to the captain–in her room."

It is inconceivable that such a story would have been printed in a magazine such as *Ladies' Home Journal* a decade or even a few years later. In a more psychoanalytically sophisticated society the rapture that Flora expresses over her beloved would generally be considered appropriate only if that beloved were of the opposite sex. When Flora's roommate assures her, "You can live if you don't make the team [and thus lose the opportunity to be near Annette]. Other folks do," Flora responds, *"I can't!"*[italics not mine.] When, in the infirmary, the doctor says, as she is taking Flora's pulse, that Flora will have a bed near Annette, the pulse speeds up so that the doctor "started and glanced sharply down at the wrist under her fingers." When Flora is in Annette's presence she is described as looking at Annette "adoringly," watching her "with devoted happy eyes," and gazing "at the beloved face." When Annette is released from the infirmary sooner than Flora expected, Flora "subsided, a bundle of sobs, under the tumbled clothes."

Even more inconceivable today is a story of this nature in a children's magazine. "The Lass of the Silver Sword," which was published serially in *St. Nicholas: A Magazine for Young People* during 1908-1909,[15] opens at a girls' boarding school in the midst of a basketball game. As in "The Cat and the King," the older girl, Carol Armstrong, eighteen, is loved by the younger Jean Lennox: the narrator states that "Jean had fallen in love with [Carol] at first sight." Again, the description of her involvement is one that the reader might expect to find in contemporary popular magazines only if the subject were male and female:

> Alas! the course of true love never did run smooth! Jean had not dared to confess her admiration to anyone but Cecily Brook, whom she had pledged to keep her secret. Now and then she made offerings of candy and flowers anonymously, leaving them on Carol's desk, and so far all Carol's attempts to play detective had failed, and it looked as if her admirer would remain forever unknown.

But, as a prank, two other girls steal Jean's notebook, which contains "poems and stories, and *odes*" to Carol, and having discovered "She's dead in love with her," they send the notebook to Carol. Carol is delighted by the discovery, as she tells Jean: "To think I might have gone on to the end of school, and never found you out, you dear!"

Although there is some vague suggestion of heterosexual interests in the story, the real emotional center is the relationship between Jean and Carol–and frequently when it appears to have shifted slightly, in fact it has remained the same. For example: Jean has written a novel in which Carol is the protagonist. A scene from the work is cited in which Carol is happily awaiting the approach of a handsome young man with the knightly name of Arthur de Lancy. But just previous to the discussion of this fantasy, Jean has talked about forming with her other school friends an order of knights, The Silver Sword, of which she is to become the leader. Thus it is likely that the author is suggesting Jean fantasizes herself as a King Arthur or a Lancelot, and that she herself is Carol's love interest in her seemingly heterosexual fictions.

The physical affection that Jean and Carol exchange is totally without the self-consciousness that would be inevitable in a post-Freudian era. For example, at one point in the story "Carol came in, caught Jean, whirled her around, pulled her down on a cot, and gave her a warm kiss." At a later point Carol pulled Jean "in to her lap and hugged her tight. 'You precious little Jeanie Queen! I never saw anything so dear as you in all my life.'" Most significantly, there is nothing covert in their relationship. All the other characters understand that these two are devoted to each other–and their popularity does not suffer: Jean is elected to head the Order of the Silver Sword, and Jean and Carol together organize a girls' camp which their classmates are eager to attend.

It must be emphasized at this point that most of these stories do *not* deal with pre-pubescent friendships or the kinds of relationships that Freudians such as Helene Deutsch and Clara Thompson have described as being necessary to a young girl's psychosexual development but dangerous if they are permitted to continue into adolescence or post-adolescence. The characters generally are young adults and sometimes even mature women. For example, O. Henry's short story "The Last Leaf," which was first published in *Strand Magazine* in 1906,[16] concerns two women, Sue from Maine and Joanna from California, who met in New York and now live together and support themselves as artists. They are liberated women even to the extent that they have dropped their feminine names: Joanna is called Johnsy and Sue is called Sudie.

Johnsy is severely ill with pneumonia. The doctor informs Sue that her friend's chances of recovery are one in ten, and that she will live only if she has a strong desire to fight for her life. In the dialogue that follows between Sue and the doctor, O. Henry seems to validate the women's independent lifestyle, and even their relationship. The doctor comes off as being pompous and insensitive. He tells Sue:

"Your little lady has made up her mind that she's not going to get well. Has she anything on her mind?"
"She–she wanted to paint the Bay of Naples some day," said Sue.
"Paint?–bosh! Has she anything on her mind worth thinking about twice–a man, for

instance?"
"A man?" said Sue, with a jew's-harp twang in her voice. "Is a man-worth-but, no, doctor, there is nothing of the kind."

O. Henry suggests not only that for these women men are not of amorous interest, but also that the two are almost everything to each other. And when Sue fears that Johnsy is dying, she implores her, "Dear, dear!...Think of me if you won't think of yourself. What would I do?" The only other area of importance in their lives is their art. When Johnsy recovers she tells her mate with serious conviction, "Sudie, some day I hope to paint the Bay of Naples." There is no hint in this early twentieth century piece of popular magazine fiction that the two women will be distracted from their interest in each other and their profession by what in the doctor's unimaginative terms is something "worth thinking about twice–a man, for instance."

Perhaps a popular writer such as O. Henry could afford to be so sympathetic in his view of these characters because women had not achieved independence in significant numbers by 1906: it was not yet socially threatening if occasional independent women–those who, for example, could eek out a living as artists and were bohemian enough to ignore convention–chose to devote themselves to one another. Most women still had no means of becoming independent; they must and would marry, regardless of their youthful emotional ties.

The general inevitability of marriage for those ordinary women who had no extraordinary calling is suggested in a story which appeared in *Harper's Magazine* in 1912, "The Beautiful House."[17] The author is apparently very sympathetic to the extraordinary character, Mary Hastings, who remains unmarried, and to her love for Sylvia Brunton (who leaves her for a man); but the lack of permanence in such relationships is emphasized not only in the action of the story, but even in the somewhat heavy-handed symbolism. Sylvia and Mary find a beautiful house, which they both love and hope to inhabit together. The caretaker explains that the house is called "Love o' Women" because "it won't last long." And, in fact, the house burns to the ground as Mary loses Sylvia to her handsome male cousin, Evan Hardie.

Mary, a thirty-five year old woman, is consistently described in positive terms: she is "handsome" and has a "dignity of carriage that went beyond her years." She suffers from none of the characteristics that popular literature has so often attributed to the "old maid":

> Spinsterhood suited her temperament and had not faded her vitality in the slightest degree; indeed, her independence and the passage of time had marked her only with a finer gravity of bearing. Her occupation gave her abiding content, she was an able and even distinguished landscape painter, and her sufficient income was increased by the sale of her sketches that she liked least. Her best work she either kept or gave away.

Like the two women in O. Henry's story, she is a committed artist. Sylvia, on the other hand, is not committed to her art; and, as far as the reader can see, she is not economically independent. She is described as "one of the time-markers," who thinks she wants to be an artist because she has an "overpowering sense of the responsibility of life that comes to the serious young [we are told that she is between twenty and thirty], a trust of years and opportunity which must be met, it seemed to her, and met instantly, and which she had all too hastily supposed was an obligation to paint pictures." Sylvia attended an art school where "Mary Hastings saw her, and in a manner fell in love with her." On her own level, Sylvia seems to return the affection, and they continue for a while in perfect intimacy; "and then to intensify their communion they found the House, which gathered together the threads of their love, and held it as a body should its soul." At this point Sylvia seems as involved in the relationship as Mary. It is she who convinces Mary that they must have the "beautiful house':

"We could come here together," Sylvia went on. "Just whenever we wanted to. Just you and I, Mary beloved," she almost whispered, "wouldn't you like it?" Her slender hands lay out along the table, palms turned up. Mary gathered them in her own hands and kissed them. "I should like it!" she said, whimsically insistent on the moderate word.

But despite her "adoration" of Mary, and her insistence that she "can't possibly do without seeing" Mary frequently, Sylvia is after all only a "time-marker" who seems to be waiting to pass on to something else, while Mary, "although she did not perceive it," soon permits herself to "picture their relationship to each other...crystalized and enduring."

The relationship is not without an erotic element, at least in Mary's mind: for example, as Sylvia admires an old bust in the garden of the beautiful house, "Mary thought of nothing else but how adorable Sylvia looked there, with the transparent pink of her skin against the old gray stone head." Mary's love is certainly what would be called "homosexual" in more recent times, but since-coming from a less sophisticated time–the author did not avail herself of terms which would have suggested "perversity" or "abnormality," Mary is the most sympathetic character, while Sylvia appears to be a flibberty-gibbet; and Evan is silly and insensitive–looking at the beautiful old ivy in the garden, for example, "he stopped and became serious. 'If you were to strip down that ivy,' he said with animation, 'you could have a fives-court here.'"

Sylvia goes off with him in perfect contentment, with "the happy security of a bird that drops upon its nest," while Mary mourns. However, the author's point is clearly not that all women need and want a heterosexual relationship, but rather that most women do not have Mary's resources: her strength, her commitment to her art, and not the least of these–her ability to support herself. Because women such as Mary are rare, it is likely that the "love o' women" will be impermanent: not because it is inherently flawed, but because most women require the "happy security" of a "nest," i.e., marriage and family.

In Helen Hull's "The Fire," which appeared in *Century Magazine* in

1917,[18] the older character, Miss Egert, is again a self-supporting artist, an unmarried woman who is perfectly happy with her lot, despite the fact that she must battle her brother's "attempts to make [her] see reason" and the community's suspicion of her independence. The author is completely sympathetic to her and makes us admire her strength, her gentleness, and her joy in beautiful things.

Cynthia Bates, her young art student, loves her. Cynthia's mother becomes suspicious of the relationship, believing that it causes Cynthia to "drift away from us, your head full of silly notions," and she forbids Cynthia to continue her art lessons and even her visits to Miss Egert. Her opposition is complex: she fears that Cynthia will develop under Miss Egert's influence values that will make her unsatisfied with the unimaginative, staid, routine-ridden lives of her parents, that she will lose hold over Cynthia, who begins to worship art and beauty, which are alien to Mrs. Bates. But by 1917, towards the close of the War which was largely responsible for the beginning of women's changing status in our society, late nineteenth century theories such as those of Hirschfeld and Ellis (which had for long been confined to medical journals and books for professional men) were gradually filtering down into popular consciousness. Perhaps by this time affection between women was becoming slightly suspect. There are hints in Hull's story that Mrs. Bates fears not only Miss Egert's artistic influence on her daughter, but the possibility of an erotic relationship between them as well. "What were you doing when I found you?" she yells at her daughter. "Holding hands! Is that the right thing for you? She's turning your head." When Cynthia protests that they were talking about beauty, her mother is outraged:

> Beauty! You disobey your mother, hurt her, to talk about beauty at night with an old maid!...Pretending to be an artist...to get young girls who are foolish enough to listen to her sentimentalizing...I've always trusted you, depended on you; now I can't even trust you.

And there does in fact seem to be an erotic element which is here inextricably mixed with the women's roles as mentor of beauty and courage and devoted pupil, as their farewell scene suggests:

> Cynthia's fingers unclasped, and one hand closed desperately around Miss Egert's. Her heart fluttered in her temples, her throat, her breast. She clung to the fingers, pulling herself slowly up from an inarticulte abyss. "Miss Egert,"–she stumbled into words,–"I can't bear it, not coming here! Nobody else cares except about sensible things. You do, beautiful, wonderful things.
>
> "You'd have to find them for yourself, Cynthia." Miss Egert's fingers moved under the girl's grasp. Then she bent towards Cynthia and kissed her with soft, pale lips that trembled against the girl's mouth. "Cynthia, don't let anyone stop you! Keep searching!" She drew back, poised for a moment in the shadow before she rose. Through Cynthia ran the swift feet of white ecstasy. She was pledging herself to some tremendous mystery, which trembled all about her.

And although Cynthia bows to her mother's pressure to the extent that she gives up Miss Egert, it is made clear that she will not give up Miss Egert's influence, which is seen as being entirely positive and constructive in contrast to the pathetically narrow ideals that Cynthia's parents try to impose on their daughter.

However, such distinctly positive views of same-sex relationships seem to have disappeared from popular literature shortly after this point. The change in attitude came about primarily for the reasons I have hinted at above. First of all, women on a large scale were gaining a modicum of economic freedom, their helping roles in World War I having liberated them from traditional stereotypes and given them some semblance of independence. This meant that, perhaps for the first time in history, love relationships between women could conceivably be permanent, and need not be only "a rehearsal in girlhood for the great drama of woman's life." Not only could women support themselves, but they were also mobile–they could move out of the community in which they were raised and thereby free themselves of the social dictates that would have demanded that they eventually form a heterosexual relationship "and dissolve their earlier intimacies." A society which could not yet come to terms with women as sexual beings outside of their procreative functions, and which had no fears of the evils of over-population, would find such female liberation truly threatening. In addition to these circumstances, the change in attitude towards female-female relationships may also be attributed to the popularization of psychology and particularly Freudianism, as evinced by mass circulation magazine articles which appeared about this time with titles such as "How it Feels to be Psychoanalyzed," "Freud and Our Frailties," and "A New Diagnosis for Hidden Mental Taint." Everyone who read now became "wise" about the existence of "perversion," and relationships that could have been carried on without self-consciousness earlier would from this point on be scrutinized for "taint." Labels were now available, and to thus label would categorize a same-sex relationship, limit and define it, and emphasize the erotic (*viz.* homo*sexual*), even if that were a minor or incidental aspect of the love relationship.

Popular magazines such as *Ladies Home Journal* and *St. Nicholas* no longer printed fiction that dealt with same-sex love. Magazines with a more sophisticated readership, such as *Harper's, Dial,* and *Vanity Fair,* did occasionally print such stories, but only if they presented same-sex love in a fairly negative light or if the treatment of the subject was so veiled that it was barely discernible. "Art" magazines alone were likely to publish occasional stories in which same-sex love was treated openly and with some sympathy.

One indication of the rapidly changing attitudes towards love between women after World War I is suggested by a comparison of "The Beautiful House" which was published in *Harper's* in 1912 and a serialized novel, *Julie Cane,* which appeared in the same magazine twelve years later.[19] The wide-spread Freudian consciousness which had overtaken the pages of popular magazines at this time is suggested by a poem by Elias Lieberman, which (only incidentally) immediately preceded the first installment of

Julie Cane in the February 1924 issue: "Our lives would not be so complex/Without suppressed desires and sex." *Julie Cane* is rife with suppressed desires and sex. Here too, as in the stories discussed above, there is a relationship between an older woman, Martha, and a younger, Julie Cane; but in contrast to the earlier stories, the "spinster" is unhappy and neurotic rather than productive, content, and dignified. She develops her "fixation" on Julie (who is somewhat tom-boyish because of her odd upbringing) as a manifestation of a neurosis that has grown and gotten out of hand–and this fixation is a desperate, pathetic thing to witness:

> "Do you love me?" she would whisper. Julie, blushing and awkward would answer "Yes" in an abrupt, strained voice, like a boy. And Martha would murmur tearfully, "You're so sweet."

As her "sickness" progresses she "puts herself to sleep at night imagining Julie was in her arms." She is obsessive about seeing Julie every day. In the evening she locks herself in the sewing room to sew clothes for the girl: "She kissed the undergarments that were to touch the beloved young body, and when she had made a dress for Julie she caressed it with her hands and hugged it to her breast so that it might, by proxy, be her arms around Julie whenever Julie wore it." When she has the opportunity actually to try clothes on her beloved, "her hands shook, her heart suffocated, and she turned Julie away from her and wept." After the girl leaves the room Martha "sat with her face in her hands, her cheeks burning against her cold fingers, her mouth aching, seeing still the dimples in Julie's shoulders, kissing them in her imagination and crying weakly, starved." When she thinks that Julie is leaving her to go away to college, she finally has a "nervous breakdown."

Unlike the noble artist in "The Fire," who teaches her pupil about beauty and courage, the woman here is fatuous. "She was determined to make Julie over in her own image, not only externally but in the inward graces," and she foists on her unwilling pupil Victorian philosophies and attitudes which the roaring twenties would have found laughable. "She endeavored to convert her pupil to the gospel of young ladyhood according To Ruskin and Tennyson, giving Julie copies of *Sesame and Lilies* and Tennyson's *Princess* as a Sunday-school teacher might give a prize Bible." While the older woman in the earlier story is completely admirable, poor Martha is simply pitiable. At best, she becomes a reconciled old maid once she accepts Julie's forthcoming marriage. She then has a complete recovery from her "invalidism."

Thus, in the few magazine stories dealing with the subject that were published in the 1920's, love between women was generally treated as a morbidity–a stage of illness that must be gotten over if one was to be wholesome again. D. H. Lawrence's *The Fox,* which was serialized in *Dial Magazine* in 1922, presents, as later observers have pointed out, a "clinical" study of this "morbidity": Edmund Bergler, for example, in his essay "D.H. Lawrence's 'The Fox' and the Psychoanalytic Theory of Lesbianism," believes that "The effectiveness of 'The Fox' derives from Lawrence's predominantly correct...observations of a series of clinically verifiable facts on Lesbianism."[20] Commentators such as Bergler neglect to see beyond their own Freudian assumptions to the fearful concerns of the novelist with regard to the growing independence of women in the second decade of the twentieth century.[21] *The Fox* is less a "clinically correct" study of lesbianism[22] than a study of Lawrence's worry that women have taken their pursuit for independence too far.

The Fox is set on a farm in the year 1918, right after the War which taught English women that they could fend for themselves in the world if need be, and even do the world some good, that they need not be stuck in petticoats and tight corset, that there was a world outside of their insulated communities to which they could even travel alone if they liked. The two women of *The Fox* decide to live on a farm together and work it by themselves. One learns carpentry and joinery and goes about in breeches and puttees, belted coat and loose cap. To a reactionary such as Lawrence, their notions–which were characteristic of many of the English and American feminists of his day–were certainly disturbing.

By comparing Lawrence's first version of "The Fox"[23] with the novel length version that was published four years later in *Dial* (1922) one sees something of his mounting hostility, which appears to be a response to his worry that men are more and more losing hold over women, who are becoming "self-important." In version I, Henry and March marry "although to Banford it seemed utterly impossible," but Banford is permitted to live. In the *Dial* version Henry kills her. As her body quivers with little convulsions he knows that she is really dead, or will be soon, "He knew it, that it was so. He knew it in his soul and his blood. The inner necessity of his life was fulfilling itself, it was he who was to live. The thorn was drawn out of his bowels." This mounting hostility is also evident in passages such as those in which Henry decides to make March his wife. Lawrence added to the *Dial* version a long description in which Henry's pursuit of March is likened to a hunter's stalking a deer. "It is a subtle, profound battle of wills, which takes place in the invisible. And it is a battle never finished till your bullet goes home." Lawrence concludes this description with Henry's realization that "it was as a young hunter that he wanted to bring down March as his quarry."

That two women could be a great deal to each other while they awaited men to lead them to marriage and the real business of life is negligible; that they could believe that the real business of life is in their being a great deal to each other and that men are only incidental to their lives--as women could now, for the first time in history, believe–is, of course, frightening to a society which prefers to conserve old social patterns. It is probably for this reason that a magazine of the 1920's would publish a story such as *The Fox,* which teaches that lesbians must either be killed or captured–and not stories such as those of the earlier period which focus on a woman's love for another woman and her personal growth through that love. There were very few lesbian stories published in magazines after the War that did not carry a moral such as Lawrence's: women could not find satisfaction with each other, and some terrible disaster would befall those who tested this truth.

The few lesbian stories that did not emphasize this moral appeared only in "art" magazines such as *The Little Review* (which was, in fact, run by two lesbians, Margaret Anderson and Jane Heap) or their subject matter was disguised in what amounted to a code language. An example of the latter is Gertrude Stein's "Miss Furr and Miss Skeene," which appeared in *Vanity Fair* in 1922. The story is a play on the word "gay," which was not yet widely understood to mean homosexual—but those who had become a part of what was by this time a flourishing lesbian subculture would have discerned what Stein meant by her description of Georgine Skeene and Helen Furr:

> They were regular in being gay, they learned little things that are things in being gay, they learned many little things that are things in being gay, they were gay every day, they were regular, they were gay, they were gay the same length of time every day, they were gay, they were quite regularly gay.

Those *Vanity Fair* readers who were not familiar with the language of the sub-culture would no doubt have thought this a story in the notorious, wacky Stein style about two happy women.

The lesbian stories which appeared in *The Little Review* never suggested that two women could live together happily ever after, but they are noteworthy because, unlike the stories of the twenties which appeared in magazines such as *Harper's* and *Dial,* they presented in a sympathetic manner lesbian characters who were not sick. For example, Os-Anders' story, "Karen: A Novel," which appeared in *The Little Review* in Spring 1922,[24] is concerned with a middle-aged Norwegian immigrant woman, Karen, who loves from a distance Dorothea, a woman of her age but not of her class: "She wished she had the courage to go to her, to die for her." When she sees Dorothea she cannot "take her eyes away"; her love for Dorothea is to Karen one of the most important things in her life: "Each person has only one or two thoughts–one of hers had been Dorothea." When Dorothea dies her husband Andreas asks Karen to marry him because he cannot run the farm by himself. She accepts only because she wants to be near what will remind her of Dorothea, and the marriage is apparently never consummated. With Andreas' death one of Dorothea's daughters is anxious to claim the farm for herself and threatens Karen, "I will go to the church and tell them why you were never my father's wife," referring, of course, to Karen's lesbian love for Dorothea. But it is the daughter here who, in her cruelty and pettiness, is seen as being sick, not the lesbian character. The story ends with Karen bedridden after an accident. The author pointedly attempts to maintain the reader's sympathy for Karen through the conclusion:

> She was helpless now. She could not be going any more in the night, as she had gone in all the years since Dorothea died, with bucket and soap to wash Dorothea's

tombstone: to keep it white. Walking the long miles to the graveyard, in the night, to do this for Dorothea. She was old and helpless now–there was nothing–nothing.

It is illuminating to compare this story particularly to *Julie Cane* which was published in *Harper's* about the same time (i.e., early 1920's). The *Harper's* story, intended of course for a wider reading audience, insists on the morbidity of Martha, a middle-aged woman who falls in love with another female, and her attachment is laughable. Karen's love for Dorothea in the "art" magazine story is sad because it is never satisfied, but it is seen as being neither morbid not laughable. The author of "Karen" and the editors of *The Little Review* seem to have been so concerned with not reflecting the societal fears towards same-sex love of the 1920's that they reached for another extreme in a totally noble and selfless character who would claim all of the reader's sympathy.

However, outside of "art" magazine fiction and stories in code such as Stein's "Miss Furr and Miss Skeene" lesbianism, by this time was seldom dealt with in magazines, and where it was treated the author invariably showed lesbian love to be sick. Only in the last few years has the image begun to change in periodicals other than those devoted to an exclusively lesbian readership. The feminist movement, with its interest in viewing same-sex relationships in a new and positive way, accounts for much of this change, as is reflected in popular feminist journals such as *Ms.* But magazines such as *Ladies' Home Journal* and contemporary equivalents of *St. Nicholas,* which are tuned in to the fears of the most conservative elements of the population, still do not publish stories that sympathetically portray same-sex love as did *Ladies' Home Journal's* "The Cat and the King" and *St. Nicholas'* "The Lass of the Silver Sword" in the early decades of this century.

Same-sex relationships, although the nature of the emotions involved may not have changed over the last sixty or seventy years, are no longer seen in the same light: in our sex-conscious era readers are not likely to believe in the possibility of an intense sentimental love between two women which is entirely devoid of an erotic component. But, more pertinently, because of the growth of women's social and economic independence it may no longer be assumed that love between women is merely transitional to heterosexuality, and because of the popularization of "medical" views (from Krafft-Ebing to Freud and his disciples) such relationships have been defined by labels that suggest they are morbid, perverse, and generally unpleasant.

NOTES

[1]See, for example, nineteenth century novels such as Henry Wadsworth Longfellow's *Kavanagh* (1849) and Oliver Wendell Holmes' *A Mortal Antipathy* (1885); in both these novels the central female characters form powerful love attachments with other females. Longfellow says of his two

female characters, "in a word, they were in love with each other." Holmes' Lurida says to her beloved female friend, "I want you!. . . *I want to look at you* [italics are Holmes'] . . . I want to wander in the woods with you, to float in the lake, to share your life."

[2]*Kavanagh*

[3]*A Mortal Antipathy*

[4]Allan McLane Hamilton, "The Civil Responsibility of Sexual Perverts," *American Journal of Insanity*, vol. 52, no. 4 (April 1896), 503-509.

[5]Jonathan Katz, *Gay American History: Lesbians and Gay Men in the U.S.A.*, New York: Thomas Y. Crowell Company, 1976.

[6]In 1638 John Cotton proposed that the Massachusetts Bay Colony penal code place sexual relations between women on a par with those between men for legal purposes. His proposal was rejected. Twenty years later the New Haven Colony enacted a statute which was perhaps unique among colonial laws because it seems to refer to lesbian acts: "If any woman change the natural use into that which is against nature, as Rom. I, 26, she shall be liable to . . . punishment"–but we cannot be certain that this statute (and, for that matter, Rom. I, 26) does indeed refer to lesbian acts and not to fellatio or permitting anal intercourse. The only apparent prosecution for lesbian activities in seventeenth century America occurred in Plymouth colony in 1649: two women were charged with "lewd conduct" and one of them was found guilty (*Records of the Colony of New Plymouth in New England*, ed. Nathaniel B. Shurtleff, Boston: William White, 1855-1861, 2:137). While there is abundant evidence of the persecution of male homosexuals in the eighteenth century, American historians have been able to find no information relevant to the legal or even social persecution of female-female relations. Katz includes a document relating to a women who was amorously involved with at least three other women and served in male attire as a soldier in the American revolution. When her sex was discovered in 1783 she was honorably discharged, and at her death in 1827 the United States Congress passed an "Act for the relief of the heirs of Deborah Gannett, a soldier of the Revolution." There is also no record of significant persecution of women throughout most of the nineteenth century, until the last two decades of that century. Nor have American laws and attitudes been peculiar in this regard, as many observers have pointed out. For example, D.S. Bailey concludes his survey of attitudes towards male and female homosexuality, *Homosexuality and the Western Christian Tradition*, London: Longmans, Green and Co., 1955, with the point that throughout western history laws and public opinion have "almost completely disregarded sexual acts committed by women with one another."

[7]Katz, p. 139. It is revealing to note that while Ellis maintained that such ailments were typical of the lesbian the subjects of several of his case histories were free of them. In his book devoted to homosexuality, *Studies in the Psychology of Sex: Sexual Inversion* (1897), Ellis attempted to distinguish between the "true" lesbian and women who have "crushes" on other women only until the right man comes along (See "Sexual Inversion

in Women" chapter and appendix D, "The School-Friendships of Girls"); however his distinctions are often contradicted by his own evidence: the "school girl crushes" are sometimes experienced by women in their twenties and older, the "true" invert is often masculine in no discernible way, the nature of the love that a "true invert" feels for another woman is often less sexual than that experienced by the "school girl"—for example, Ellis quoted Miss M., whom he called a "true invert" as saying "I love few people... but in these instances when I have permitted my heart to go out to a friend I have always experienced most exalted feelings, and have been made better by them morally, mentally, and spiritually. Love is with me a religion. The very nature of my affection for my friends precludes the possiblity of any element entering into it which is not absolutely sacred." A similar statement of the non-genital aspect of "lesbian" love in the late nineteenth and early twentieth centuries may be found in Ruth F. Claus, "Confronting Homosexuality: A Letter from Frances Wilder," *Signs* II, 4 (Summer 1977), 932. It would seem then that the primary distinction between a "true" lesbian and a woman who loves another woman only until she is able to marry is that the "true" lesbian has made a commitment in time to other women. In this sense, there were few "true" lesbians in other eras because, as I have suggested above, women generally had to marry before they became too old, for practical reasons if nothing else.

[8]Hamilton, op. cit.

[9]See also Carroll Smith-Rosenberg, "The Female World of Love and Ritual: Relations Between Women in Nineteenth Century America," *Signs: Journal of Women in Culture and Society,* I, 1 (Autumn 1975), 1-24; and William Taylor and Christopher Lasch, "Two Kindred Spirits: Sorority and Family in New England, 1839-1846," *New England Quarterly,* XXXVI,1 no. 1 (March 1963), 23-41. Both articles study the correspondence between nineteenth century women and conclude that intense female-female love relationships were entirely common in the nineteenth century.

[10]The word lesbian would not, of course, have been used in such fiction--or for that matter, anywhere outside of a few medical texts. The 1903 edition of the *OED* defines "lesbian" only as meaning "of or pertaining to the Land of Lesbos, in the northern part of the Grecian archipelago."

[11]*Smith College Stories,* New York: Scribners, 1900; rpt. 1921.

[12]*The Story of Mary MacLane,* Chicago: Herbert Stone and Co., 1902.

[13]See, for example, two reviews attacking a study which suggests that Emily Dickinson had homoaffectional attachments: John Ciardi (*New England Quarterly,* vol. 25, 1952, 93-98) says that the language of Dickinson's ostensible love poems and love letters to other women "came out of the sentimental extravagance of the Romantic and Gothic novel." Grace B. Sherrer (*American Literature,* vol. 24, 1952, 255-258) observes, "We need to remember that Emily breathed the air of Victorian sentimentality. Even though she rebelled against doctrine, her vocabulary was formed by her heritage and her time. The passionate intensity of the poems equally pervades the letters. It is a character of writing not derived from any one experience in the writer's life."

[14]Jeanette Lee, "The Cat and the King," *Ladies Home Journal,* October 1919, pp. 10, 67-68, 71.

[15]Margaret Constance Dubois, "The Lass of the Silver Sword," *St. Nicholas,* December 1908-October 1909. Dubois was the author of a number of girls' books, including *Elinor Arden, Royalist* (1904), *The League of the Signet Ring* (1910), and *The Girls of Old Glory* (1918).

[16]Reprinted in William Sidney Porter, *The Trimmed Lamp,* New York: Doubleday, Page and Co., 1914.

[17]Catherine Wells, "The Beautiful House," *Harper's Magazine,* vol. 124 (1912), 503, 511.

[18]Helen Hull, "The Fire," *Century Magazine,* vol. 95 (November 1917), 105-114. Hull was also the author of two novels which dealt with homoaffectional relationships between women, *Quest* (1922) and *Labryinth* (1923).

[19]Harvey O'Higgins, *Julie Cane, Harper's Magazine,* vol. 148, serial begins February 1924. O'Higgins was a prolific author who produced more than a dozen books before he was forty, including army novels, detective novels, and studies of Mormonism.

[20]In Harry T. Moore, *D.H. Lawrence: A Critical Survey* (London: Forum House, 1969), pp. 49-55; originally published in *Journal of Nervous and Mental Disease* (Baltimore, Maryland), 1958. Bergler enumerates these observations in scientific tones–"1. Lawrence describes the typical husband-wife camouflage of Lesbians, and at the same time stresses the psychic-masochistic substructure of the camouflage...2. Lawrence correctly describes March's constant 'injustice collecting,' hence her hidden psychic-masochism...3. Lawrence accurately depicts the two sets of identification in March: the 'leading' masochistic identification with the victim, and the 'misleading' masculine identification, deposited in the Oedipal camouflage of her relationship with Banford...4. Lawrence ingeniously hints that the fox, the devourer of chickens, symbolizes the 'devouring' mother; we know that the fear of being devoured has priority in the 'septet of baby fears'...5. Lawrence describes the unvarying inner defense of his masochistic heroine: the search for love, which these sick women can find neither in the Lesbian nor in the connubial bed since 'injustice collecting' is the real aim...6. Finally, Lawrence presents with clinical correctness the defensive pseudo-aggression so predominant in Lesbians."

[21]As Frank Kermode (D.H. Lawrence, New York: The Viking Press, 1973, p. 116) observes, Lawrence began his "career of male chauvinism" in his "Preface" to *Sons and Lovers,* written in 1913, and such chauvinism appears consistently in all his later works. However, in the years immediately following World War I he seems to have reached a sort of apogee, perhaps because it was becoming shockingly clear to him that women were moving in the direction of freedom–a direction opposite to what he saw as necessary if the world was to right itself–more rapidly than ever at this time. His letters of this particular period suggest his hostility to "self-important" and "bullying" females, both in his own life and in the world in general. For example, writing to his Russian translator friend, S.S.

Koteliansky on March 14, 1919, I Lawrence complains of his wife, "She really is a devil–and I feel as if I would part with her forever–let her go alone to Germany, while I take another road. For it is true, I have been bullied by her long enough. I really could leave her now, without a pang, I believe. The time comes, to make an end, one way or another." (*The Collected Letters of D.H. Lawrence*, ed. Harry T. Moore, New York: The Viking Press, 1962, vol. I, 581). A couple of months later (May 7, 1919) he complained to Koteliansky of Margaret Radford, a writer and casual acquaintance, "I wish one could exterminate all her sort under a heap of Keating's powder. I feel utterly 'off' the soulful of clever or witty type of female–in fact, the self-important female of any sort." (*Collected Letters*, I, 585.) His work at this time is full of assertions that women must concern themselves not with "thinking" and "abstracting," but with their womanly activities, "the immediate personal life" ("Education of the People," 1918, in *Phoenix: The Posthumous Papers of D.H. Lawrence*,New York: T. Seltzer, 1921) and that the "intelligent" woman is a perversion of the "true" woman, whose business is at night. During the day she must remain "half in fear" of the male. Always she must submit to a purpose which is "beyond her" (*Fantasia of the Unconscious*, New York: T. Seltzer, 1922).

[22]See contemporary discussions of lesbianism which very effectively take issue with Freudian biases: e.g., Bettie Wysor, *The Lesbian Myth*, New York: Random House, 1974; Jane Rule, *Lesbian Images*, Garden City, N.Y.: Doubleday, 1975; Martha Shelley, "Notes of a Radical Lesbian," in *Sisterhood is Powerful*, ed. Robin Morgan, New York: Vintage Books, 1970; Shere Hite, *The Hite Report, New York: Dell, 1976 ("Lesbianism" chapter).*

[23]In *D.H. Lawrence: A Critical Survey*, pp. 28-48.

[24]pp. 22-28. I have been unable to ascertain definitely the identity of Os-Anders, but I believe the name to have been a pseudonym for Margaret Anderson who infrequently wrote fiction. It is likely that Anderson would have used some pseudonym if "Karen" is her story, not only because of the subject matter but also because she would have been sensitive to accusations of vanity she might have received for publishing her own fiction.

Lillian Faderman is a professor of English at California State University, Fresno. She is co-editor of Speaking for Ourselves: American Ethnic Writing *(1969; second ed. 1975) and* From the Barrio: A Chicano Anthology *(1973). She has published several articles on female same-sex relationships in literature.*

The Crime of Precocious Sexuality: Female Juvenile Delinquency in the Progressive Era

STEVEN SCHLOSSMAN
Radcliffe Institute, Harvard University

STEPHANIE WALLACH
Simmons College

The juvenile justice system's discrimination against poor and minority children has been well documented, but the system's discrimination on the basis of gender has been less widely recognized. Drawing on neglected court records and secondary sources, Steven Schlossman and Stephanie Wallach show how girls bore a disproportionate share of the burden of juvenile justice in the Progressive era. The authors note that during the Progressive era female juvenile delinquents often received more severe punishments than males, even though boys usually were charged with more serious crimes. Schlossman and Wallach conclude that the discriminatory treatment of female delinquents in the early twentieth century resulted from racial prejudice, new theories of adolescence, and Progressive-era movements to purify society.

This essay is an historical inquiry into the practice of sexual discrimination against female juvenile delinquents. Although American public policy toward girl offenders first took shape in the middle decades of the nineteenth century—the Victorian era—we have decided to focus on the Progressive era of the early twentieth century. During this latter period scientific and popular literature on female delinquency expanded enormously, and most states adopted the main components

The authors would like to thank Nancy Pottishman Weiss, Merle Borrowman, Geraldine Joncich Clifford, and Sheldon Messinger for their helpful suggestions on earlier drafts of this essay. A portion of the research for this essay was supported by the Spencer Foundation, to which we extend our sincere thanks. Responsibility for errors in fact or interpretation is, of course, our own.

Harvard Educational Review, Vol. 48, No. 1, February 1978.

0017-8055/78/0200-0065$02.35/0

of modern correctional machinery. Our essay spotlights the differences between stated intentions, revealed preferences, and actual outcomes.[1] Although we attempt to develop a broad interpretation, we must emphasize the selectivity of our historical research. We do not pretend to have exhausted available sources, to have explored all possible interpretations of our evidence, or, certainly, to have written the definitive account. Instead, we offer a preliminary synthesis of untapped sources in an effort to call attention to a neglected subject, to encourage additional research on it, and to suggest ways of integrating the topic of female delinquency into the rapidly growing fields of women's history and the history of corrections.

Our essay speaks only indirectly to modern-day issues in juvenile justice. Continuities between past and present will often be apparent, to be sure, but we dare not draw them too explicitly for the simple reason that social scientists know very little about the theory and practice of female juvenile justice between the 1920s and the 1960s.[2] Nonetheless, we do believe it is possible to use history as a force for social change by laying bare the roots and assumptions of anachronistic policies—policies, in this instance, that lag behind our current attitudes toward female sexuality and equal justice for women. Given our reformist goals, it may be useful to explain in advance why we focus on sexual discrimination as opposed to other equally blatant injustices in the correctional system.

Like other critics of American juvenile justice, we decry practices that lead to unwarranted labeling and incarceration of children and that discriminate against poor, minority youth, regardless of sex.[3] We consider it indisputable that, from the early nineteenth century to the present, the juvenile justice system has systematically singled out lower-class children for punishment and ignored middle- and upper-class youth.[4] In this essay, however, our main concern is not with class, ethnic, racial, or age bias, for we believe those themes have been adequately treated elsewhere. Rather, what most interests us now is how, in a correctional system that discriminates consistently against poor, minority children as a whole, females carry a disproportionate share of the burden of injustice.

Discussion of female delinquency is conspicuously absent from most scholarly writing on criminal justice. Despite a persistent hue and cry during the last decade

1 See Lawrence Cremin, "Foreword," in *American Education and Vocationalism*, eds. Marvin Lazerson and W. Norton Grubb (New York: Teachers College Press, 1974), p. ix.

2 One reason for the lack of scholarly attention to girl offenders in this period was the emphasis on gang delinquency, in which girls participated very little. There is, however, Paul Tappan's classic *Delinquent Girls in Court* (Montclair, N.J.: Patterson Smith, 1969), originally published in 1947.

3 See, for example, Lois Forer, *"No One Will Lissen"* (New York: Grosset and Dunlap, 1970); Patrick Murphy, *Our Kindly Parent . . . The State* (New York: Viking, 1974); Lisa Richette, *The Throwaway Children* (New York: Dell, 1969); and Ken Wooden, *Weeping in the Playtime of Others* (New York: McGraw-Hill, 1976).

4 See, for example, Michael Katz, *The Irony of Early School Reform* (Cambridge, Mass.: Harvard University Press, 1968); Anthony Platt, *The Child Savers* (Chicago: University of Chicago Press, 1969); Alexander Liazos, "Class Oppression: The Functions of Juvenile Justice," *The Insurgent Sociologist*, Fall 1974, 1, 2–24; and Steven Schlossman, *Love and the American Delinquent* (Chicago: University of Chicago Press, 1977).

about spiraling rates of delinquency, despite mounting evidence demonstrating the ineffectiveness of correctional programs, and despite the women's rights movement, girl offenders are largely ignored. Even as the number of females processed through the juvenile courts climbs steadily, an implicit consensus remains that the male teenager defines the delinquency problem in modern America and suffers most egregiously from correctional injustices.[5]

We suggest two main reasons why girl delinquents receive so little attention. First, girls are accused primarily of so-called victimless crimes, that is, offenses that do not involve clear-cut damage to persons or property. If committed by adults, these actions would not be legally punishable; if committed by boys, the same acts would be interpreted less seriously and punished less severely. Thus, rather ironically, the plight of female delinquents receives little scrutiny because they are accused of committing less flagrant violations of legal codes. Second, traditional stereotypes of women as the weaker and more dependent sex rationalize, indeed even legitimate, discriminatory correctional practices in the name of humanitarianism. As the half-century struggle to enact the Equal Rights Amendment makes abundantly clear, one of the most tenacious beliefs in our society is that women require more comprehensive legal protection than do men. Society justifies "preventive" intervention into the lives of antisocial girls under the rationale that they are especially vulnerable to evil forces and temptations. This so-called chivalrous attitude leads to earlier intervention and longer periods of supervision for delinquent girls than delinquent boys.

The sparse historical writing about female delinquency concentrates on reformatories, especially the pioneering nineteenth-century institutions, rather than on the juvenile justice system as a whole.[6] Furthermore, several of the studies are uncritical and Whiggish in their interpretations, seeing a benign humanitarian spirit

[5] For exceptions see Don Gibbons, *Delinquent Behavior* (Englewood Cliffs, N.J.: Prentice-Hall, 1976), 2nd ed., pp. 169–189; William Sanders, *Juvenile Delinquency* (New York: Praeger, 1976), pp. 64–83; Rose Giallombardo, *The Social World of Delinquent Girls* (New York: Wiley, 1974); Meda Chesney-Lind, "Juvenile Delinquency: The Sexualization of Female Crime," *Psychology Today*, July 1974, 8, 43–46; Meda Chesney-Lind, "Judicial Enforcement of the Female Sex Role: The Family Court and the Female Delinquent," *Issues in Criminology*, Fall 1973, 8, 51–69; Kristine Rogers, "'For Her Own Protection . . .': Conditions of Incarceration for Female Juvenile Offenders in the State of Connecticut," *Law and Society Review*, 1972, 7, 223–246; Sarah Gold, "Equal Protection for Juvenile Girls in Need of Supervision in New York State," *New York Law Forum*, 1971, 17, 570–598; Robert Terry, "Discrimination in the Handling of Juvenile Offenders by Social Control Agencies," in *Becoming Delinquent*, eds. Peter Garabedian and Don Gibbons (Chicago: Aldine, 1970), pp. 78–92; Freda Adler, *Sisters in Crime* (New York: McGraw-Hill, 1975), chap. 4; *Crime and Delinquency*, 1977, 23 (issue theme: "Criminal Justice to Women: Not Fair!"); and Paul Katzeff, "Equal Crime," *Boston Magazine*, December 1977, 107–108, 206, 208-210. For an estimate that girls now form nearly one-quarter of the juvenile court clientele, see Rosemary Sarri and Robert Vintner, "Justice for Whom? Varieties of Correctional Approaches," in *The Juvenile Justice System*, ed. Malcolm Klein, v (New York: Russell Sage, 1975), p. 171.

[6] See the pioneering studies by Barbara Brenzel, "Lancaster Industrial School for Girls: A Social Portrait of a Nineteenth Century Reform School for Girls," *Feminist Studies*, Fall 1975, 3, 40–53; and by Estelle Freedman, "Their Sisters' Keepers: The Origins of Female Corrections in America," Dissertation, Columbia University, 1976.

behind early twentieth-century correctional innovations for girls. Margaret Reeves, for example, conducted an exhaustive survey of girls' reformatory programs in the 1920s and concluded, with few reservations, that they embodied the triumph of social conscience in America and the onward march of correctional science.[7] Recently, Robert Mennel, in his ambitious survey of juvenile correctional history, described Progressive-era policies as "the first sign of a more sympathetic attitude toward female delinquents."[8]

On the basis of our research, we consider the traditional interpretation to be lacking in four principal respects: it offers little empirical evidence of benign or effective treatment of girl offenders; it generally blurs the distinction between the stated intentions of correctional reformers and the actual outcomes of their efforts; it deals inadequately with the fears and prejudices underlying benevolent programs for poor, immigrant children; and it does little to illuminate, even obliquely, the practice of sexual discrimination in the juvenile justice system today. We do not quarrel with historians who emphasize the humanitarian spirit that guided such famous juvenile reformers as Jane Addams, Sophonisba Breckinridge, and Edith Abbott, or such lesser figures as Augusta Bronner, Mabel Elliott, Emma Lundberg, and Edith Burleigh.[9] But we do believe that the humanitarian schemes were often quite repressive in design and even more so in outcome.

Our main arguments can be sketched as follows. Although public response to female delinquency emerged in the Victorian era, not until the Progressive period was female delinquency widely perceived as a social problem requiring extensive governmental intervention. In the Progressive period the abundant literature on delinquency was riddled with stereotypical assumptions about women and, in particular, about immigrant women. These stereotypes laid a basis for more punitive treatment of delinquent girls than delinquent boys. Girls were prosecuted almost exclusively for "immoral" conduct, a very broad category that defined all sexual exploration as fundamentally perverse and predictive of future promiscuity, perhaps even prostitution. But while girls, unlike boys, were almost never accused of violating criminal statutes, they received stiffer legal penalties.

Discriminatory treatment of female delinquents was consistent with racial prejudices in the Progressive period. Ethnic girls—immigrants or daughters of immigrants—were seen as inherently more predisposed to immoral conduct than Yankee girls—daughters of native-born parents. Discriminatory correctional practices also embodied the new wisdom of the behavioral sciences, particularly the theories of adolescence generated by such pioneer psychologists as G. Stanley Hall. Finally, the practice of female juvenile justice reflected the quasi-utopian, but ultimately repressive, pursuit of Progressive-era reformers for a more "pure" society, as revealed in the eugenics, antiprostitution, and sex-education campaigns.

7 Margaret Reeves, *Training Schools for Delinquent Girls* (New York: Russell Sage, 1929).

8 Robert Mennel, *Thorns and Thistles* (Hanover, N.H.: University Press of New England, 1973), p. 172.

9 See especially Robert Bremner, *From the Depths* (New York: New York University Press, 1956); and Walter Trattner, *Crusade for the Children* (Chicago: Quadrangle, 1970).

Female Delinquency: The Emergence of a Social Problem

Public response to female delinquency can be traced at least as far back as the Jacksonian period, although the traditional date of origin is 1856, when Massachusetts opened the nation's first reform school for girls. Well known in the latter half of the century, the Massachusetts example inspired emulation by diverse philanthropic organizations in the East and Midwest. Several state governments responded to the wishes of these organizations and built reformatories for girls. Compared to the huge reformatories for boys erected in the nineteenth century—by the 1850s the New York House of Refuge held over one thousand inmates—the institutions for girls were generally small and makeshift, often consisting of two or three converted farmhouses. Several of the girls' facilities were little more than receiving stations; their primary purpose was to facilitate the smooth operation of boys' reformatories after attempts to house both sexes in the same buildings had proved embarrassing failures.[10]

The female reformatories incorporated the evangelical spirit of Victorian religious revivalism. Until the end of the nineteenth century the image of the female delinquent remained mainly that of the individual "fallen woman."[11] This image contrasted sharply with that of the male delinquent, who was described less as a sinner than as a carefully nurtured young criminal.[12] To be sure, boys' delinquencies were roundly condemned but were rarely, as was often the case with girls', regarded as indications of innate moral perversity.

Nineteenth-century authors of crime literature wrote endlessly about delinquency—the classic presentation being Charles Loring Brace's *The Dangerous Classes of New York and Twenty Years' Work among Them*[13]—but they paid very little attention to female delinquents. The "dangerous classes" against whom the reformers warned and about whom newspapers printed sensational stories were overwhelmingly male.[14] When the girl offender did appear in the literature, she was treated mainly as a footnote to the problem of boy delinquency. But early in the twentieth century—especially in the decade preceding the First World War—female delinquency began to attract increasing attention as a separate and pressing social problem.

The heightened public awareness of and growing governmental response to female delinquency in the Progressive era are well documented. Articles on girl

10 Brenzel, "Lancaster"; Mennel, *Thorns and Thistles*, chap. 4; Freedman, "Their Sisters' Keepers," chaps. 3 and 4.

11 On the image of the "fallen woman,' see Freedman, "Their Sisters' Keepers," chap. 2; for the emphasis on environmental causes behind male criminality, see David Rothman, *The Discovery of the Asylum* (Boston: Little, Brown, 1971).

12 Schlossman, *Love*, chaps. 2, 3, and 5.

13 Charles Loring Brace, *The Dangerous Classes of New York and Twenty Years' Work among Them* (New York: Wynkoop and Hallenbeck, 1872).

14 Miriam Langsam, *Children West* (Madison, Wis.: State Historical Society of Wisconsin, 1964); Thomas Bender, *Toward an Urban Vision* (Lexington, Ky.: University Press of Kentucky, 1975); and Steven Schlossman, "The 'Culture of Poverty' in Ante-Bellum Social Thought," *Science and Society*, 1974, 38, 150–166.

offenders appeared in a wide range of popular and scholarly journals. The prestigious philanthropic organization, the National Conference of Charities and Correction, began to discuss female delinquency regularly for the first time since the organization's founding in the early 1870s. Several books were devoted in whole or in part to female criminality. While the mass media continued to emphasize the "boy problem," many civic groups began giving equal attention to the "girl problem." Local organizations such as PTAs, juvenile protective associations, women's clubs, and settlement houses sponsored lectures and discussions on the causes and cures of girls' delinquency; they also led campaigns to garner funds for such innovations as girls' clubs, YWCA summer camps, and, to a lesser extent, Girl Scouts.[15]

Governmental investment in the custody and treatment of female delinquents increased dramatically in the Progressive era. The decade between 1910 and 1920 was an especially prolific period for the creation of publicly sponsored reformatories for girls. Whereas between 1850 and 1910 an average of fewer than five new reformatories were created per decade, twenty-three new facilities opened between 1910 and 1920. Furthermore, older ninteenth-century reformatories were expanded in size, staff, and clientele in this decade. Equally important, a number of states took over private girls' reformatories.[16] In short, the involvement of government with female delinquency grew sharply in the Progressive period, reflecting the expanded discussion of the subject in the literature on juvenile crime.

The Practice of Sexual Discrimination

Before trying to explain the rising interest in female delinquency in the Progressive era, it is necessary to demonstrate that girls received discriminatory treatment in juvenile courts and reformatories. The historical sources for such an empirical study are vast but have never been tapped. We have examined the sources selectively and have chosen for close analysis those we believe are representative of three bodies of evidence.

First, we briefly analyze scattered statistical data to demonstrate that juvenile courts treated female delinquents more harshly than male delinquents. Second, we present an overview of cases in a single juvenile court to evoke the actual decision-making process and thereby show that sentimental notions of the "good girl" and conventional ideals of domesticity prefigured punitive treatment for girl delinquents. Third, we look synoptically at the rehabilitative goals and methods of female reformatories to illuminate further the discriminatory nature of treatment. Our goal is to provide empirical evidence for the contention, developed later in

15 These observations draw upon Schlossman's study of social-reform groups in Milwaukee and of parent-education organizations throughout the country. See Schlossman, *Love*, chap. 7, and "Before Home Start: Notes Toward a History of Parent Education in America, 1897–1929," *Harvard Educational Review*, 1976, 46, 436–467. Also useful is David McLeod, "Good Boys Made Better: The Boy Scouts of America, Boys' Brigades, and YMCA Boys' Work, 1880–1920," Dissertation, University of Wisconsin, 1973.

16 Reeves, *Training Schools*, pp. 39ff; and Mennel, *Thorns and Thistles*, pp. 171–179.

this essay, that the practice of female juvenile justice coincided with the ideology of treatment. Discrimination on the basis of sex was no accident, we believe, but rather was integral to both the theory and practice of Progressive-era juvenile justice.

The first body of evidence was derived from court records in Chicago, San Francisco, Milwaukee, and New Haven. Several points stand out most prominently from these data: the vast majority of delinquents, boys and girls alike, were poor, ghetto-dwelling children of recent immigrants; however, unlike males, females were brought to court almost exclusively for alleged early sexual exploration; and female offenders were treated more punitively than males.

The ethnic origins of both boy and girl delinquents are revealing. In Milwaukee, for example, more than 90 percent of the children brought into court were the offspring of European immigrants. Of these, three out of four were either German or Polish. In Chicago, San Francisco, and New Haven the ethnic background of delinquents was similar, although southeastern European countries were more frequently represented, reflecting the different patterns of immigrant settlement in these cities.[17]

That the delinquents were predominantly poor is evident in a number of ways. Although it is impossible to compare the incomes of families of delinquent and nondelinquent children or to assess the contributions of different family members to total income, we do have periodic salary data for the fathers of delinquent youth in Milwaukee. These data suggest the truth of the popular impression that delinquents were primarily from the working class. Their fathers' salaries were low, generally reported to be less than ten dollars per week. Moreover, the salaries were highly irregular: many fathers moved frequently from job to job; many were unemployed for long periods because of seasonal hiring, debilitating illnesses (particularly tuberculosis), and drinking bouts. In addition, an analysis of the occupations of delinquents' fathers, using city directories and addresses supplied in court to distinguish individuals with the same names, indicates that the majority were working class or lower on the economic scale, the single largest category being that of "laborer."[18] A further indication that delinquents came mainly from poor, ghetto families is their residence patterns. The majority of Milwaukee delinquents lived in the poorest immigrant neighborhoods surrounding the city's scattered railway network.

Although similar in their social and cultural backgrounds, girl and boy delinquents were treated very differently in court. Consider the types of crimes for which boys and girls made their first courtroom appearances. The majority of boys were charged with offenses that fell under the adult criminal code. In Chicago, for

[17] For data on Milwaukee see Schlossman, *Love*, appendix 2, table 6. Our main source for Chicago is Sophonisba Breckinridge and Edith Abbott, *The Delinquent Child and the Home* (New York: Russell Sage, 1912); for San Francisco, Emily Huntington, Leona Jones, Donna Moses, and Ruth Turner, "The Juvenile Court," Bachelor of Arts Thesis, University of California at Berkeley, 1917; and for New Haven, Mabel Wiley, *A Study of the Problem of Girl Delinquency in New Haven* (New Haven, Conn.: Civic Federation of New Haven, 1915).

[18] Schlossman, *Love*, pp. 143–144.

example, stealing accounted for more than half of the reported crimes.[19] The charges against girls were of an entirely different nature. The majority were charged under the loose heading of "immorality";[20] however, a charge of "immorality" did not mean that a girl had had intercourse or performed some other mature sexual act. Rather, a girl only had to show "signs" in her appearance, conversation, and bearing that she had probably had intercourse in the past or might do so in the near future. These criteria naturally opened the way to invidious judgments, especially because the delinquents were mainly daughters of immigrants, who were, according to contemporary racial mythology, instinctively emotional and lacking in self-restraint. Thus judges and probation officers would see precocious sexual activity where it did not exist, would prematurely regard unfamiliar cultural patterns of behavior and expression as signs of advanced sexual experience, and would be more pessimistic about the implications of sexual exploration by ethnic than by Yankee girls.

In practice, an extraordinarily wide range of conduct was included under the label of immorality: staying away from home, associating with persons of dubious character, going to dance houses, fornicating, coming home late at night, masturbating, using obscene language, riding at night in automobiles without a chaperone, strutting about in a lascivious manner, and so forth. To the courts, being "on the road to ruin" was but one short step from being "ruined"; hence, so-called predelinquents were treated much like those who actually engaged in mature sexual relations. The ostensible purposes behind such a loose definition of crime were to root out the underlying causes of misconduct as soon as they became evident and to instruct ethnic girls that their Yankee counterparts upheld higher standards of sexual propriety than their own parents practiced or condoned.[21]

The different treatment of boy and girl delinquents was even more apparent in the disposition of cases. Far more frequently than girls, boys received the relatively noncoercive sanction of probation—supervision in the child's own home or in a surrogate home approved by the court. In Chicago, for instance, 59 percent of the boys who appeared in court between 1899 and 1909 were placed on probation, as compared to only 37 percent of the girls. Conversely, significantly higher proportions of girls than boys were incarcerated in reformatories for sentences that could last several years. In Milwaukee twice as many girls as boys were committed, and in Chicago one-half of the girl delinquents, as contrasted with one-fifth of the

19 Breckinridge and Abbott, *The Delinquent Child,* pp. 28–35. See also Huntington et al., "The Juvenile Court," appendix.

20 Breckinridge and Abbott, *The Delinquent Child,* pp. 38–40; Huntington et al., "The Juvenile Court," appendix; Alida Bowler, "A Study of Seventy-Five Delinquent Girls," *Journal of Delinquency,* 1917, 2, 157; Mabel Elliott, *Correctional Education and the Delinquent Girl* (Harrisburg, Pa.: Commonwealth of Pennsylvania Department of Welfare, 1928), pp. 34–35; Louise Ordahl and George Ordahl, "A Study of Delinquent and Dependent Girls," *Journal of Delinquency,* 1918, 3, 34–35; and Wiley, *A Study of the Problem,* p. 11.

21 Bowler, "A Study of Seventy-Five Delinquent Girls," p. 159; Breckinridge and Abbott, *The Delinquent Child,* pp. 35–39; Elliott, *Correctional Education,* pp. 34–35; Ordahl and Ordahl, "A Study of Delinquent and Dependent Girls," pp. 55–59; and Wiley, *A Study of the Problem,* p. 9.

boy delinquents, were sent to reformatories.[22] In sum, girls appeared in juvenile court on noncriminal charges far more frequently than boys; nonetheless, girls received more punitive dispositions.[23]

We turn now to another body of evidence: the day-to-day experiences of girls in juvenile court. From the archival records of the Milwaukee Children's Court we have chosen several cases from between 1901 and 1920 for examination. Transcripts from actual hearings, we believe, provide the most vivid and dramatic demonstration of the assumptions that shaped the definition and treatment of female delinquency in the Progressive era.[24]

Alleged girl delinquents in Milwaukee had their private lives probed in fine detail so that judges and probation officers could assess the underlying causes of misbehavior. Whenever it could be demonstrated that a girl had used vile language, masturbated, or indulged in lascivious thoughts, the court freely employed some type of intervention, usually probation. Consider the case of Annagret Schmitt. Neither the hearing transcript nor the accompanying records provides a precise reason why Annagret was brought into court—a common occurrence, since it was assumed that some form of aberrant sexual expression was behind any specific accusation. Thus Annagret, like every girl who appeared in court, was subjected to a vaginal examination. The only proof of virginity was an intact hymen. To his own surprise the examing doctor concluded that Annagret was still a virgin, but he informed the court that irritation in her clitoral area indicated she was a regular masturbator. The probation officer, a woman, analyzed the situation as follows: "She masturbates, and she has somewhat injured herself in that way, and probably this is the cause of her conduct at home, and says things [sic] that are not true. . . . [Annagret] most likely is trying to imagine things, and then believes everything is true." Thus, according to the court, Annagret's masturbatory habits explained her penchant for fantasy and justified labeling her a delinquent and placing her under supervision.

In cases of advanced sexual misconduct, the court usually explored the circumstances in excruciating detail. The ostensible goals were to procure evidence

22 Breckinridge and Abbott, *The Delinquent Child*, p. 41; and Schlossman, *Love*, appendix 2, table 3.

23 In arguing that girls received more punitive treatment, we assume that incarceration is, by its very nature, a harsher form of punishment than probation. We are *not* saying, however, that the treatment of girls in reformatories was harsher than that of boys in reformatories.

24 These cases derive from Schlossman's sample of 1,200 cases in Milwaukee (10 percent of the total heard in this period). To the best of our knowledge, the Milwaukee court is the only one to have opened its early records for historical investigation; it is consequently impossible to say whether they are strictly representative of experiences in courts elsewhere. Although selected with an eye toward the exemplary and archetypal, each case was necessarily idiosyncratic because, obviously, no two children or their parents were exactly alike. The cases that follow should be appreciated much like opera highlights, as suggestive of a larger drama and of characteristic patterns of interaction among protagonists. To protect client anonymity we have changed the names of children and parents who appeared in court, although we have tried to retain their particular ethnic origins. For the same reason we have not cited the specific dates or docket numbers of individual cases.

against the male or males involved and to evaluate the girls' attitudes toward men and sex. At times, though, the immediate goal seemed to be nothing other than sheer titillation, much like the famous vice reports in this period. Such reports offered, in the names of science and social reform, pornographic scenes that would have been censored in the commercial media. In court, girls were required to recount, with some attempt to recreate the atmosphere, the steps that led to their sexual encounters, their physical experiences ("How far did he go into you; what did you feel; did you bleed?"), and their later subjective reactions. In pursuing this line of questioning the court's assumptions were transparent; it presumed that a girl's moral condition and potential for rehabilitation depended on just how much of her biological purity had been preserved and on how morally revolted she was by her experiences.

At the same time that the court avidly investigated the girls' sex lives, it preached a conventional code of Victorian morality, highlighting especially the virtues of chastity and the joys of marriage. With all good intentions the court lectured sexually precocious girls on how their behavior was endangering their later salability as wives. Without doubt many of the sexually active girls who appeared in juvenile court were immature and would have benefited from intelligent advice about sex. But the advice the court proffered must have struck these girls as naive and irrelevant to their current needs and past experiences. Consider, for example, one judge's advice to a girl who had contracted venereal disease:

> By and by, three or four years from now, some nice fellow will come along, and you love him, and he will love you, and you will get married, and live right. That ought to be the aim of a girl like you, to look forward to the time you have a good home and a good man.

Quaint moral admonitions like these were the court's main antidote to sexual precocity among girls and, if nothing else, reveal the cultural stereotypes that shaped the legal processing of female delinquents.

As observed earlier, juvenile courts did not distinguish between actual delinquency and predelinquency because they saw their mission as the treatment of underlying causes. The courts aimed to "save" girls once it became apparent they were "on the road to ruin." Consider the case of Sara Wadrewski. Sara's father had brought her into court on a charge of disobedience, alleging that she had refused to work, stayed out late, and gone to parties where the girls dressed like boys. As often happened, a probation officer was on hand to supplement the parents' charges by relating neighborhood gossip. Sara, he intimated, probably had had intercourse with several boys because she was seen lying on the grass with them in a local park. A group of neighbors made similar accusations. To the judge's question, "In what way is she a bad girl?" one neighbor responded, "Why, for the reason that she bums around and doesn't work, and doesn't bring no money home, and runs to parties, and then calls names, calls her brother names, he is a cripple." Sara roundly denied most of the allegations, particularly the charges that she had had group sex, or indeed, that she had ever had "connection." But her protestations of virginity were to no avail; shortly after the initial hearing she was committed to the local Catholic reformatory.

Juvenile court sessions were often like scenes from a Kafka novel. One could never be sure that the disposition of a case would be on the basis of the accusations or on the quality of evidence. Despite these uncertainties it was almost guaranteed that a girl would be sent to a reformatory if either she or her parents, especially her mother, were not blushingly contrite about the girl's sexual adventures. A classic case is that of fifteen-year-old Deborah Horwitz, who freely admitted staying out late at night with many boys and who casually flaunted her sexual desires. In addition to Deborah's self-incriminating testimony, efficient snooping by a probation officer into Deborah's bedroom bureau turned up even more incriminating evidence: five self-photos that the court considered racy (although Deborah got no more racy than opening the top button of her high-necked blouse and removing her hat); and a remarkably candid series of letters to a sailor friend that left no doubt about her initiation into the joys of sex.

In such cases the court's custom was to blame the mother for her daughter's actions. Mrs. Horwitz, however, would not stand for it: "I got lots of trouble with the other girl, she needs an operation, and I got lots of trouble with the other children." Nor would Deborah accept the court's harsh evaluation of her behavior. Thus the judge intoned:

> Well, Deborah, this is a very serious matter. If you would live a good life you would be a good woman, and be useful to society, but you have started out very bad. There is only one way to reform you and this is to send you to an institution. I cannot let you go home to your parents. . . . How is it, can't you stop?

Deborah responded, "I can stop, of course I can." "Why don't you behave yourself, then?" the judge rejoined. "These boys tell me that you just coax them." "I never coaxed anybody," Deborah maintained. But to no effect. Precocious sexuality in a girl who would not at least feign repentance and whose parents would not at least feign shock was intolerable to the court. Deborah was committed forthwith to the state reformatory for girls.

As these excerpts reveal, the court defined female delinquency wholly in sexual terms and responded to girls on the basis of Victorian views of women's social role and sexuality. We shall have more to say later about the persistence of these Victorian assumptions in the Progressive period. For the present we will extend our study of actual treatment by examining the female reformatories, which, as noted earlier, expanded rapidly in the early twentieth century. Like the juvenile courts, the reformatories operationalized prevailing cultural stereotypes about women and transformed these stereotypes into tools for punishment and rehabilitation.

Female reformatories in the Progressive era had four principal goals. The basic one was the isolation from males of sexually precocious females, preferably in bucolic settings. Elaborate efforts were made to keep all men away from the institutions or, indeed, from anywhere near the girls. In California, for example, sponsors of the female reformatory concluded that the mile separating the male from the female institution was inadequate. A new facility far removed from males was essential to eliminate "the influences that mysteriously emanate from the proximity of the sexes."[25] The mere act of isolating delinquent girls came to be seen as a rehabilitative tool. As such, it served an important, latent economic function by rationalizing a minimal public investment in other, more positive, methods of treatment.

Not only were the institutions situated so as to eliminate sexual temptation, but they were also designed to serve a second long-range function. Safe custody was considered a spur to later marriage. By incarcerating delinquent girls the reformatories removed them from the unregulated sexual marketplace of ghetto streets and forced them to save their sexual favors, moral reputations, and health until they were of marriageable age. Most inmates of female reformatories were fifteen or sixteen years old, too young to marry in most states. A minimal stay of two to three years was therefore considered essential; upon release the girls would be of marriageable age and could seek legitimate gratification for their pent-up sexual energies. The institutions further promoted marriageability by placing the girls, after release, in new social settings where their moral improprieties were not common knowledge and where they could search anew for companionship.[26] Like the isolation of inmates from all contacts with men, the assumption that custodial care could have long-term therapeutic value underlay the marital goals of the reformatories. Thus, it could seriously be argued that custody in female reformatories was itself a form of treatment.[27]

25 Adina Mitchell, *Special Report on the Whittier State School* (Sacramento, Calif.: State Printing Office, 1896), p. 11. See also Mary Berry, "The State's Duty to the Delinquent Girl," National Conference on the Education of Truant, Backward, Dependent and Delinquent Children, *Proceedings* (1918), pp. 82–83; Mrs. Jennie Griffith, "The Training of Delinquent Girls," Conference of the National Committee on Prisons and Prison Labor, *Proceedings* (1919), pp. 15, 17; Miriam Van Waters, "Where Girls Go Right," *Survey Graphic*, 1922, 1, 365; and Maine Industrial School for Girls, *Annual Report* (Waterville, Me.: Sentinel Publishing Co., 1909), pp. 7–8.

26 Breckinridge and Abbott, *The Delinquent Child*, p. 8; Huntington et al., "The Juvenile Court," appendix; Olga Bridgman, "An Experimental Study of Abnormal Children, with Special Reference to the Problems of Dependency and Delinquency," University of California, *Publications in Psychology*, 1918, 3, 8; Berry, "The State's Duty," p. 87; Edith Burleigh and Frances Harris, *The Delinquent Girl* (New York: New York School of Social Work, 1923), pp. 32, 38–43; Mary Dewson, "Probation and Institutional Care of Girls," in *The Child in the City*, ed. Sophonisba Breckinridge (Chicago: Chicago School of Civics and Philanthropy, 1912), pp. 360–362; Martha Falconer, "Work of the Girls' Department, House of Refuge, Philadelphia," National Conference of Charities and Correction, *Proceedings* (1908), p. 393; and National Conference of Charities and Correction, *Proceedings* (1903), p. 517. Elliott's *Correctional Education*, a follow-up study of ex-inmates from the Sleighton Farms reformatory in Pennsylvania, left no doubt that marriage was the most important variable in explaining postrelease behavior.

27 This argument was rarely advanced about the boys' reformatories. In fact, although historians have yet to provide adequate documentation, male reformatories apparently experimented with a variety of new correctional ideas in the Progressive era and participated tangentially in the "progressive education" movement. Elaborate vocational-training programs at a few of the larger reformatories became the envy of "progressive" educators such as David Snedden. In addition, many public reformatories experimented with self-government programs designed loosely along the lines suggested by William George in his famous Junior Republics; many adopted new forms of recreational and military training to improve health and discipline and upgraded their academic

Female reformatories did employ nominally rehabilitative programs, if only to give the girls something to do while their virtue was being protected. These programs embodied traditional stereotypes about women. The institutions attempted to instill in inmates the ideology of domesticity and the minimal skills necessary for its practice. According to correctional administrators, a girl's delinquency alone revealed that she had not learned to revere domestic pursuits. Instruction in domesticity was allied with the reformatories' marital goals: inmates would become so devoted to and skillful at domestic chores that they would easily attract husbands. It was as if, in the moral calculus of the juvenile reformers, a rigorous pursuit of domesticity would compensate for the girls' previous immoralities. Moreover, even if the girls failed to find mates shortly after release, they would at least be trained as domestics and so could support themselves while working in upright, middle-class households.[28]

Inmates were expected to take care of their reformatory cottages with the same pride that middle-class women lavished on their homes. Ideally, the girls would assimilate middle-class domestic values and lower-class domestic skills.[29] In each reformatory cottage, the matron served as the domestic educator, teaching girls both proper attitudes and skills. To increase public regard for the vocational-training programs, reformatory superintendents described them as if they were part of the larger home-economics movement that swept the country in the Progressive era.[30] Actually, the training rarely went beyond the chores necessary for personal hygiene and cottage upkeep, with a cooking class or two added for good measure. As one superintendent blithely argued,

---

offerings for older inmates. Of course we do not believe that these newer correctional programs necessarily rehabilitated inmates. Our point is simply that levels of interest and public investment in rehabilitative programs were greater in boys' than girls' reformatories. For background on the relation between "progressive education" and juvenile corrections, see Walter Drost, *David Snedden* (Madison, Wis.: University of Wisconsin Press, 1967); and Jack Holl, *Juvenile Reform in the Progressive Era* (Ithaca, N.Y.: Cornell University Press, 1971).

28 A widely discussed social "problem" in the Progressive era was the declining availability of trained domestic help; hence it can be argued that the reformatories' emphasis on domestic training was economically functional for the girls. It was also recognized, though, that domestics received wages so low that some were tempted to turn to prostitution for supplementary income.

29 Mary Berry, "Co-Ordination of Industrial and Vocational Work with Parole Administration," National Conference on the Education of Truant, Backward, Dependent and Delinquent Children, *Proceedings* (1920), pp. 52–60; Bowler, "A Study of Seventy-Five Delinquent Girls," pp. 156–157; Burleigh and Harris, *The Delinquent Child*, pp. 8–9; William Fairbanks, "Girls' Reformatories and Their Inherent Characteristics," National Conference of Charities and Correction, *Proceedings* (1901), pp. 254–262; Miss Mary Hinkley, "Problems of Administration: The Responsibilities of a School Toward Its Girls," National Conference on the Education of Truant, Backward, Dependent and Delinquent Children, *Proceedings* (1920), pp. 20–23; Maine Industrial School for Girls, *Annual Report* (1909), p. 15; Griffith, "The Training of Delinquent Girls," p. 17; and Miss Elizabeth Mansell, "An Institution Program for Delinquent Girls," National Conference on the Education of Truant, Backward, Dependent and Delinquent Children, *Proceedings* (1917), p. 35.

30 See Emma Weigley, "It Might Have Been Euthenics: The Lake Placid Conference and the Home Economics Movement," *American Quarterly*, 1974, 26, 79–96; and Barbara Ehrenreich and Deidre English, "The Manufacture of Housework," *Socialist Revolution*, October–December, 1975, 5, 5–40.

> We never have taught typewriting and stenography. I find that in our community you can get about a dozen girls, who want to use a typewriter to one that wants to use a scrubbing brush. It seems to me that if you can get girls to understand that to be a homemaker is about the best thing that can come into the life of a woman, this is almost the best education they can have at the present time.[31]

Another superintendent was candid enough to admit what must often have been true in other reformatories that boasted "scientific" courses in home economics: "We teach the girls in practical cooking, as few are mentally capable of appreciating food values as taught in regular domestic science courses."[32]

The fourth and final goal of the female reformatories, surely their most ambitious, is implicit in the previous remark on inmates' mental limitations. The female reformatories were expected to play a central role in fulfilling the objectives of the eugenics movement, which achieved its greatest popularity at precisely the same time that governmental investment in female corrections significantly expanded.[33]

Eugenicists in the Progressive era sought to improve the "genetic fund" of the American population by discouraging and, if possible, forcibly preventing propagation by individuals considered innately inferior in culture and intellect. Almost by definition, the eugenicists identified recent immigrants from southeastern Europe as inferior. Relying on the rediscovery of Mendelian genetic theory in 1900, the eugenicists presented several key arguments: social conditions, such as poverty, and personality traits, such as laziness and courage, were discrete "unit characters" transmitted through heredity; unit characters were immutable; race was the primary determinant of human capacities; in some races socially undesirable unit characters predominated; and social legislation was necessary to encourage breeding of the racially fit and discourage breeding of the unfit. According to the eugenicists, persistent immorality among children was a sign of their genetic inferiority or racial degeneracy. To keep these degenerates from further diluting the nation's "genetic fund" and to prevent the nation from committing "race suicide," eugenicists insisted that permanent institutionalization and, if possible, sterilization were essential. The hereditarily degenerate threatened the eugenicists' vision of a more perfect and efficient world devoid of crime, poverty, and disease—a world quite consistent with the vision of many well-known reformers who outwardly were not eugenicists themselves.

Male and female reformatories were to play a special role in the larger eugenics campaign, as early detectors of innate criminality. In this role, however, the reformatories faced a unique problem: from a clientele composed mainly of chil-

[31] National Conference of Charities and Correction, *Proceedings* (1901), p. 258.

[32] California School for Girls, *Biennial Report* (Sacramento, Calif.: State Printing Office, 1918), p. 9.

[33] For background on the eugenics movement we have relied especially on Mark Haller, *Eugenics* (New Brunswick, N.J.: Rutgers University Press, 1963); Donald Pickens, *Eugenics and the Progressive Era* (Nashville, Tenn.: Vanderbilt University Press, 1968); Rudolph Vecoli, "Sterilization: A Progressive Measure?" *Wisconsin Magazine of History*, 1960, 48, 190–203; Peter Tyor, "Segregation or Surgery: The Mentally Retarded in America, 1850–1920," Dissertation, Northwestern University, 1972; and Allan Chase, *The Legacy of Malthus* (New York: Knopf, 1976).

dren of racially inferior immigrants, how were they to identify those whose inheritance was so inferior as to warrant permanent incarceration or sterilization? By the 1910s the principal method of detection became mental testing, which rapidly evolved through a bewildering variety of forms, culminating in the 1916 Stanford revision of the Binet test—the intelligence quotient (IQ) test. With a seemingly precise instrument like the Stanford-Binet test in hand, psychologists and their helpers administered mental tests with virtual abandon to captive inmate populations. The tests were purported to identify those delinquents whose innate intelligence was so low that, in the judgment of the psychologists, they could never learn to control their instincts and become civilized members of society. These defective delinquents, as they were commonly called, were to be transferred from the reformatories and incarcerated, if facilities permitted, in homes for feeble-minded children— institutions that proliferated in the Progressive era. In sum, the newly devised mental test legitimated eugenic goals by providing a scientific instrument for weeding out from the delinquent population those children whose antisocial behavior was inbred.[34]

Eugenic goals, as we noted, applied equally to male and female reformatories, and IQ and other mental tests were freely administered in both. But the literature on delinquency discussed feeble-mindedness among girls with a special urgency. In part this was because delinquent girls appeared at first to test at somewhat lower levels than delinquent boys.[35] More important, though, were the two widely held beliefs that women bore the primary moral responsibility for determining whether to have children and that women lacked the sexual drives of men. From

[34] *The Journal of Delinquency*, published in California, provided the principal forum for discussing this use of mental tests. Its articles were written mainly by psychologists, physicians, psychiatrists, and correctional workers. The *Journal* came especially under the influence of Lewis Terman and several of his students at Stanford, although other prominent members of its editorial board included William Healy, founder of the Juvenile Psychopathic Clinic in Chicago, and Arnold Gesell, the developmental psychologist from Yale.

[35] See, for example, C. S. Bluemel, "Binet Tests on Two Hundred Juvenile Delinquents," *Training School Bulletin*, 1915, 12, 191. Of all the drawbacks of the early IQ tests administered to delinquents, the most basic one was the leeway given to the examiner. The tests left much room for interpretation; often there was no clear-cut right or wrong answer. In such instances the examiners frequently came to dubious conclusions about inmates' mental ages. Consider the following example from Bluemel (p. 187), in which the examiner asked:

> "What is the difference between pride and pretension?" The first replies: "If you have too much pride, you go to certain places—cafes and dance halls. Some pretend to be proud but are poor." The second replies: "Pride means to be proud, and pretension means to pretend to be something that you are not." The third replies: "Pride is something in you that makes you—if you have enough of it—hold yourself a little above people that are without pride. Pretension is false pride." Obviously, these answers indicate that the three girls are at different mental levels. This fact is also attested by their answers to the other questions; and the answers in their totality permit one to make a fair estimate of their mental ages.

See also Ordahl and Ordahl, "A Study of Delinquent and Dependent Girls," pp. 41–73; and Jean Walker, "Factors Contributing to the Delinquency of Defective Girls," University of California, *Publications in Psychology*, 1925, 3, 147–207.

this perspective, sexually precocious girls were morally and biologically perverse. When this view was joined with the belief that delinquent girls' intelligence was so far below normal that they could never learn to control their instincts, it becomes clear why the specter of female delinquency haunted the eugenics movement and why delinquent girls were more frequently incarcerated than delinquent boys.

Sexual Precocity and the Social Order in the Progressive Era

Having sketched the main elements of female juvenile justice in the Progressive era, we return to our earlier questions: why did public interest and investment in female delinquency burgeon so noticeably in this period, and why were girls treated more punitively than boys?

Perhaps the most obvious explanation of the rising interest in female delinquency in the Progressive period would be that the incidence of female delinquency grew until it simply could not be ignored. Much evidence could be marshaled to sustain this argument. One could turn, for example, to the remarkable data on family breakdown, cultural disintegration, and crime in urban immigrant communities documented in Thomas and Znaniecki's 1927 classic, *The Polish Peasant in America.*[36] Equally familiar are Jane Addams's poignant commentaries on the tensions and communication gulfs between mothers and daughters in *Democracy and Social Ethics* and *The Spirit of Youth and the City Streets.*[37] Similarly, one could assess the moral consequences of growing female participation in the work force. Did the increasingly familiar, "promiscuous" social relations of young men and women at work, mainly in the factory, encourage early sexual experimentation, as many contemporaries feared?[38] Finally, one could point to the pervasive image of the white-slave trade, as embodied in the work of the Chicago Vice Commission or Jane Addams's *A New Conscience and an Ancient Evil.*[39] The image of the white-slave trader fueled the era's antiprostitution campaigns and expressed metaphorically the common view that impoverished women were vulnerable to unscrupulous entrepreneurs. In short, the rising public investment in and sensitivity to female delinquency could be seen as a pragmatic response to a real and growing social problem.

Although this argument is appealing, two serious limitations, one methodological and the other conceptual, persuade us, while not ignoring or denying it, to focus our attention elsewhere. First, the argument encounters the methodological difficulties common to all attempts to calculate the actual incidence of crime, whether in the present or, especially, in the past. We agree with modern-day sociologists and criminologists that official crime data and popular impressions of

36 William Thomas and Florian Znaniecki, *The Polish Peasant in America*, 2 vols. (New York: Knopf, 1927).

37 Jane Addams, *Democracy and Social Ethics* (New York: Macmillan, 1902); and *The Spirit of Youth and the City Streets* (New York: Macmillan, 1909).

38 For example, see "Are Low Wages Responsible for Women's Immorality?," *Current Opinion*, May 1913, 54, 402.

39 Jane Addams, *A New Conscience and an Ancient Evil* (New York: Macmillan, 1913).

crime waves are unreliable indices of illegal activity in any period.[40] Second, as Edwin Schur and others have argued, the traditional foci in criminological research on the incidence of crime and the personal characteristics of offenders have often obscured the fact that crime is a social and legal artifact.[41] Crime does not exist in the abstract; certain activities become illegal only when so labeled. This holds true particularly for juvenile delinquency because, as we have seen, its legal definition is extremely broad and imprecise.

To reiterate, we do not deny the possibility that rates of female delinquency were actually on the rise in the Progressive era, although it would be nearly impossible, given the broad definition of delinquency, to determine how to measure its incidence. Rather, our point is simply that the public agencies responsible for defining, prosecuting, and punishing antisocial behavior invariably shape a society's awareness of criminal conduct at any moment. Therefore, whatever the actual incidence of delinquency, it is essential to examine the cultural context in which delinquency was defined and the legal and penal context in which codes were enforced.[42]

We believe the heightened sensitivity to female delinquency and the growing governmental investment in correctional institutions can be best understood in relation to three developments that directly and indirectly affected social policies —eugenic solutions to social problems, increasing popularity of theories of adolescence, and the movement for "social purity." We have already dealt with the first development, the pervasive appeal of eugenics,[43] and so will proceed to the second development, the growing popularity of theories of adolescence.

[40] The previously cited texts of Gibbons and Sanders (see footnote 5) are especially sensitive to this difficulty. See also the essays collected under the heading, "The Data of Delinquency: Problems of Definition and Measurement," in *Juvenile Delinquency*, ed. Rose Giallombardo (New York: Wiley, 1966).

[41] Edwin Schur, *Radical Non-Intervention* (Englewood Cliffs, N.J.: Prentice-Hall, 1973).

[42] See especially Platt, *The Child Savers;* and Leon Radzinowicz, *Ideology and Crime* (New York: Columbia University Press, 1966).

[43] The theories and policies proposed in the eugenics movement drew upon several long-term preoccupations of American social reformers. Hereditarian thinking and racial mythologies were staples of American social thought throughout the nineteenth century, existing before the influence of Social Darwinism. Similarly, anti-immigrant hostility was common from the early nineteenth century onward, particularly in the large cities of the Northeast. We believe, nonetheless, that racial mythologies and anti-immigrant prejudice attained, in tandem, a new degree of legitimacy after the rediscovery in 1900 of Mendel's ideas, especially after these were popularized, and distorted, by social scientists whose influence on social policy grew enormously in the Progressive period. For example, Henry Goddard, one of the leading applied social scientists in the country and the first person to translate and adapt the Binet-Simon intelligence tests to American needs, wrote the best-selling bible of the eugenics movement, *The Kallikak Family* (New York: Macmillan, 1912) and led campaigns for literacy tests, restrictive marriage covenants, sterilization laws, and immigration restrictions. Even Jane Addams, a quintessential environmentalist, could endorse "the new science of eugenics" and "its recently appointed university professors" (*A New Conscience*, pp. 130–131). See Charles Rosenberg, "The Bitter Fruit: Heredity, Disease, and Social Thought," *Perspectives in American History*, 1974, 8, 189–235; Ray Billington, *The Protestant Crusade, 1800–1860* (New York: Macmillan, 1938); and Oscar Handlin, *Boston's*

Differential treatment of boy and girl delinquents did not represent a failure in implementation, we believe, but rather was an inevitable outcome of the sexually biased social-science theories of adolescence that matured in the Progressive era.[44] These theories gave the imprimatur of science to traditional Victorian views of women as weak, impressionable, emotional, and yet erotically impassive.[45] Moreover, these theories helped shape juvenile justice in two major ways: they invalidated the most optimistic features of the juvenile court movement as applied to girls, and they legitimated the creation of new reformatories for girls just when institutional care for boys was being widely challenged.

The central role of Clark University president G. Stanley Hall in developing and popularizing new ideas about adolescence has been well documented.[46] Following Hall's lead, reformers of various hues portrayed adolescence as at once the most malleable and the most problematic time of development. Adolescence represented a new stage of life: anything was possible, for better or for worse. Most important, during adolescence a child's permanent character took shape. Jane Addams captured the common viewpoint most poignantly in her paean to the "spirit of youth": in adolescence the human spirit bursts forth anew in unsuspecting children, enthralling them with the enchantment of life, confusing them with the rush of passion and idealism.[47] During this stage of life, the reformers admonished, children required especially solicitous parental care and creative social planning to help them cope safely with the potentials of adolescence.

Not surprisingly, most commentators believed that the female youngsters of poor immigrant families were particularly vulnerable. They grew up in slums, came from inferior racial stock, and were scarred by cultural norms that sanctioned the open display of male sexual interest. However, this concern for the vulnerability of ethnic girls did not lead to extensive social programs for them. The many organizations developed for children in the Progressive era, such as day and evening clubs, scouts, and summer camps, were promoted much less vigorously

---

Immigrants (Cambridge, Mass.: Harvard University Press, 1941). On the growing role of social scientists, see Julius Weinberg, *Edward Alsworth Ross and the Sociology of Progressivism* (Madison, Wis.: State Historical Society of Wisconsin, 1972); Barry Karl, *Charles E. Merriam and the Study of Politics* (Chicago: University of Chicago Press, 1974); Julia and Herman Schwendinger, *Sociologists of the Chair* (New York: Basic Books, 1974); and Chase, *The Legacy of Malthus*, pt. 2.

[44] Although such theories were not nearly as new as their proponents claimed, they did exert considerable influence on Progressive-era social reformers. See Joseph Kett, *Rites of Passage* (New York: Basic Books, 1977), chap. 8; and Steven Schlossman, "G. Stanley Hall and the Boys' Club: Conservative Applications of Recapitulation Theory," *Journal of the History of the Behavioral Sciences*, 1973, 9, 140–147.

[45] Two articles that advance the same argument as it applies to formal criminological theory are Doris Klein, "The Etiology of Female Crime: A Review of the Literature," *Issues in Criminology*, Fall 1973, 8, 3–30; and Dale Hoffman-Bustamante, "The Nature of Female Criminality," *Issues in Criminology*, Fall 1973, 8, 117–136.

[46] See Dorothy Ross, *G. Stanley Hall* (Chicago: University of Chicago Press, 1972); Kett, *Rites of Passage*, chap. 8; and Schlossman, "G. Stanley Hall and the Boys' Club."

[47] Addams, *The Spirit of Youth*.

for girls than for boys.[48] This resulted, in part, because boys were a much more immediate social threat: their delinquencies posed a clear and present danger, whereas girls' delinquencies engendered more long-term fears. But the best explanation, we believe, lies in the fact that adolescent girls were considered much less malleable than adolescent boys. Institutions like girls' clubs and Girl Scouts received less support than their male counterparts because adolescence in girls, as a life stage, was regarded as a much less promising period for reshaping character. Rather than a new beginning, adolescence in girls was the time when character traits instilled earlier were put to the test. Most writers assumed that by the time girls reached puberty the most promising time for shaping their character had long since passed.[49] Thus, while the psychological theories of adolescence provided a new source of "scientific" optimism for preventing delinquency among boys, they gave no such hope for aiding girls.[50]

For similar reasons, we believe, the promise of the juvenile court movement was less widely acclaimed for girls than for boys. As Schlossman argues in his history of

48 On boys' clubs, see Schlossman, "G. Stanley Hall and the Boys' Club"; on camps, see McLeod, "Good Boys Made Better"; on Boy Scouts, see Jeffrey Hantover, "Sex Role, Sexuality, and Social Status: The Early Years of the Boy Scouts of America," Dissertation, University of Chicago, 1976; and Peter Schmitt, *Back to Nature* (New York: Oxford University Press, 1969), chap. 10. For a more comprehensive synthesis of these and other organizations aimed at youth, see Kett, *Rites of Passage*, chaps. 7 and 8.

49 In reaching this conclusion we have relied especially upon: Augusta Bronner, "Effect of Adolescent Instability on Conduct," *Psychological Clinic*, 1915, 7, 249–265; Burleigh and Harris, *The Delinquent Girl*; Mary Paddon, "A Study of Fifty Feeble-Minded Prostitutes," *Journal of Delinquency*, 1918, 3, 1–11; Maude Miner, "The Woman Delinquent," New York City Conference of Charities and Correction, *Proceedings* (1911), pp. 152–165; Rheta Dorr, "Reclaiming the Wayward Girl," *Hampton's Magazine*, January 1911, 26, 67–78; Bridgman, "An Experimental Study of Abnormal Children"; Mary Moxcey, *Girlhood and Character* (New York: Abingdon, 1916); Winifred Richmond, *The Adolescent Girl* (New York: Macmillan, 1926); Ruth True, "The Neglected Girl," in *West Side Studies*, ed. Pauline Goldmark (New York: Survey Associates, 1914), pp. 1–134; Emily Lamb, "A Study of Thirty-Five Delinquent Girls," *Journal of Delinquency*, 1919, 4, 75–85; Ordahl and Ordahl, "A Study of Delinquent and Dependent Girls"; Merritt Pinkney, "The Delinquent Girl and the Juvenile Court," in *The Child in the City*, ed. Breckinridge, pp. 349–354; Breckinridge and Abbott, *The Delinquent Child;* Wiley, *A Study of the Problem;* William Thomas, *The Unadjusted Girl* (Boston: Little, Brown, 1923); Miriam Van Waters, "Causes and Cure" and "The True Value of Correctional Education," in the Miriam Van Waters Papers, Box 11, Schlesinger Library, Radcliffe College; Falconer, "Work of the Girls' Department"; Elliott, *Correctional Education*; Huntington et al., "The Juvenile Court"; Walker, "Factors Contributing to the Delinquency of Defective Girls"; Miss Vida Francis, "The Delinquent Girl," National Conference of Charities and Correction, *Proceedings* (1906), pp. 138–145; and Jane Rippin, "Social Readjustment as the Function of the Judge," Conference of the National Committee on Prisons and Prison Labor, *Proceedings* (1919), pp. 25–31.

50 We quote from Kett, *Rites of Passage*, p. 224; "Hall, moreover, had written very little about girls, a bias fully reflected in both the literature on boys-work after 1900 and in the masculine orientation and sexual segregation of scouting. . . . It was a boy's world, not a girl's and not a man's, a fact which prompted H. W. Gibson, a YMCA tractarian and boys-worker, to reduce all of adolescent psychology to something called 'boyology.' " A very useful compendium which nicely captures the differences in the theories is *Boy Training*, ed. John Alexander (New York: Association Press, 1915).

"progressive" juvenile corrections, the main rehabilitative tool of the court movement was probation.[51] Ideally, probation was to be a means of family education. Probation officers were to function less as agents of law enforcement than as visiting teachers who would instruct parents and children on how to eliminate family stress and how to use community resources to increase economic security and recreational enjoyment. The theory of probation was built firmly on the assumptions that most children became delinquent during their adolescent years, that adolescents were especially malleable, and that the successful rechanneling of youthful energies into lawful pursuits would motivate parents to modify their behavior toward their children and eliminate delinquency-producing conditions in the home. Probation epitomized the belief that adolescents merited several chances to become upright citizens.

Not so—or at least markedly less so—with erring adolescent girls.[52] Writers on female delinquency argued that, while a female's delinquencies were less criminally culpable, they were also less amenable to change through a relatively informal means of supervision like probation. Girls also received probation less frequently than boys because of the greater tendency to blame parents of delinquent girls. Unlike boys, it was argued, girls did not have places other than their homes in which to spend free time safely. Although writers on delinquency recognized that immigrant mothers and youth entered the work force because of poverty, they nonetheless held that rearing a girl imposed special moral responsibilities. Thus all mothers, regardless of economic circumstances, were obliged to keep their girls at home, when not in school or church, and to transform homes into refuges for protecting female virtue. This tendency to hold mothers more directly responsible for the behavior of girl delinquents than of boy delinquents further diminished the likelihood of probation for girls. If the female delinquent was considered less redeemable than her male counterpart, so too was her mother.

As probation was devalued for girl offenders, incarceration was judged more suitable. Earlier we examined the main rationales for female reformatories; here we will present additional justifications that illuminate why girl and boy delinquents were treated differently. One was the belief that girl delinquents, unlike boys, were not at all childlike in their behavior. By usurping the ultimate adult prerogative—sexual intercourse—female delinquents forfeited their right to be regarded merely as innocent, curious children. Moreover, precocious sexual exploration by girls threatened society's attempt to keep children innocent, chaste, and dependent until marriageable age. Female delinquents thereby subverted family government and had to be removed from their natural homes for the protection of neighborhood youth. Finally, imprisonment was seen as a boon to rehabilitation because of the speed with which neighborhood grapevines disseminated the repu-

51 Schlossman, *Love*, chap. 4.

52 The citations in note 49 are all relevant here, especially Breckinridge and Abbott, *The Delinquent Child*, pp. 35–38, 72–73, 169; Ordahl and Ordahl, "A Study of Delinquent and Dependent Girls," pp. 60–61; Van Waters, "Causes and Cure," p. 5; Paddon, "A Study of Fifty Feeble-Minded Prostitutes," p. 10; and True, "The Neglected Girl," p. 19.

tations of "bad girls." One writer summed up these diverse rationales for more frequent incarceration of delinquent girls:

> And suppose a boy does bolt? He can try again. Suppose he "goes bad" a second or a third time, either through animal spirits or bad companions? He can begin all over again. Suppose he even stays out nights, and goes into lower forms of degradation? Even then if he can pull himself together physically and morally, he has not lost the chance for a decent manhood and a square deal. But is it so with any delinquent girl? No, a thousand times no! By the publicity of even the appearance in Court her reputation is tarnished, and with her reputation in question, her chance to retrieve herself in the same environment is very small. And in that eighty percent of crimes against the person, does my girl get a fair chance to "try again?" No, the world is against her, evil men are ready to tempt her further, the industrial situation helps to put her at their mercy, and even nature herself gives a last push towards the downward path when she physically handicaps herself. No! My girl who has once become delinquent finds it a 1000 times more difficult to straighten herself than the boy. The delinquent girl must be preserved against the *opportunities* of temptation which are inevitably more fatal to her than to the boy.[53]

Clearly, then, the juvenile reformatory was the best possible place to treat delinquent girls—to protect society from them and them from society.

The third and final development behind growing awareness of female delinquency in the Progressive era was the movement for "social purity." More particularly, we want to analyze the relation of the purity ideal to what several historians have described as the "sexual revolution" of the Progressive era or the beginnings of "the modernization of sex." We believe that changes in sexual mores provided the cultural foundation for the burgeoning interest in female delinquency, the expansion of female reformatories, and the differential treatment of boy and girl delinquents. To explicate our position, we will first examine changing sexual mores in the Progressive era and then point up how they shaped new policies toward female delinquents.[54]

[53] Francis, "The Delinquent Girl," p. 140.

[54] In the 1950s and 1960s the most common historical approach to the subject of morals and sex in the Progressive era was to emphasize its puritanical features. This approach flowed from the interpretation of social-reform movements epitomized by the work of Richard Hofstadter, especially *The Age of Reform* (New York: Knopf, 1955). In the past few years a different historical interpretation has emerged that stresses the loosening grip of Victorian morality on sexual attitudes and holds that "modern" attitudes toward sex first emerged in the Progressive era rather than, as is more commonly thought, in the 1920s. This view rests on several sources of evidence: the work of historical demographers, who argue that rates of premarital pregnancy rose markedly in this period; self-report studies, which indicate that dramatic increases in premarital intercourse occurred; and reexamination of literary sources, which suggests that social discourse in the Progressive era was a good deal less prudish than had been thought. As examples, see Linda Gordon, *Woman's Body, Woman's Right* (New York: Grossman, 1976), pt. 2; Paul Robinson, *The Modernization of Sex* (New York: Harper & Row, 1976); John Burnham, "The Progressive-Era Revolution in American Attitudes Toward Sex," *Journal of American History*, 1973, 59, 885–908; James McGovern, "The American Woman's Pre-World War I Freedom in Manners and Morals," *Journal of American History*, 1968, 55, 315–333; and Carl Degler, "What Ought To Be and

Increasing investment in reformatories for sexually precocious girls reflected a widespread revulsion against the growing frequency and legitimacy of sex as an everyday topic of discussion.[55] The expansion of the government's capacity to punish sexual promiscuity formed one phase of what we term a "sexual counter-revolution." The men and women who led this counterrevolution were, by and large, the same types of middle-class, nonethnic individuals who participated in the better-known political and social reforms of the period. For these men and women, the sexual counterrevolution represented a moral analogue to the cleansing of corruption in the political and economic arenas.[56]

To the counterrevolutionists the public's fascination with sex was inherently dangerous because it threatened the maintenance of conventional family life. They were particularly troubled by many recent changes: the flagrant commercialization of sex in the press; the demystification of sex by doctors, psychologists, and intellectuals; the increasingly open propaganda for dissemination of birth-control devices; and the moral dangers inherent in the discovery of new medical remedies for venereal disease. The counterrevolutionists urged that new strategies were essential to revitalize older sexual ideals, neutralize overstimulated sexual appetites, and purify social discourse on sex. If reticence was no longer possible, purity was.[57]

The counterrevolutionists engaged in three major "reform" campaigns: the wholesale destruction of prostitution; the widespread dissemination of sex educa-

---

What Was: Women's Sexuality in the Nineteenth Century," *American Historical Review*, 1974, 79, 1467–1490.

While we agree with the historians who argue that the early twentieth century witnessed a marked increase in the public's willingness to discuss sex openly, we are uneasy about the tendency to locate the origins of sexual modernity in the Progressive era. This approach, we feel, exaggerates indications of the new morality and plays down evidence of older Victorian thinking. Most important for the history of female juvenile justice, this interpretation shifts attention away from major efforts in this period to reaffirm Victorian moral and sexual standards as well as to recast older religious commands into new secular, scientific language. Thus we both agree and disagree with the new interpretation.

55 On the scholarly side, the psychologist Helen Thompson Woolley noted that between 1910 and 1914 "the number of experimental investigations in the field [psychology of sex] has increased to such an extent that whereas it was difficult at that time [1910] to find anything to review, it is now impossible to review all that I could find" ("The Psychology of Sex," *The Psychological Bulletin*, 1914, 11, 353). If scholars were having a field day with sex, so was the American public: "A wave of sex hysteria seems to have invaded this country," wrote the anonymous author of a piece which has since become an historical classic. "Our former reticence on matters of sex is giving way to a frankness that would even startle Paris." ("Sex O'Clock in America," *Current Opinion*, August 1913, 55, 113).

56 This is our impression from reading the literature; we have not conducted empirical research on the social origins of the counterrevolutionists. Certainly Theodore Roosevelt was the most prominent of the individuals who engaged as fervidly in moral as in political reform. Roosevelt popularized the notion of "race suicide" and boasted that one of his greatest achievements was to have exercised enough will power to remain a virgin until marriage (William Harbaugh, *The Life and Times of Theodore Roosevelt* [New York: Oxford University Press, 1975], p. 15).

57 For general background see David Pivar, *Purity Crusade* (Westport, Conn.: Greenwood, 1973); and David Kennedy, *Birth Control in America* (New Haven, Conn.: Yale University Press, 1970).

tion; and, our main subject, the punishment of sexually precocious girls. Each campaign had a number of concrete, functional goals, but each needs to be seen symbolically as well. Together, the campaigns represented a ritualistic protest against cultural change, a spirited reaffirmation of older moral ideals, and an urgent call for creative new strategies to realize them.

The campaign against prostitution was, ironically, both a contribution to and a sharp reaction against what one author wittily called the arrival of "sex o'clock" in America.[58] Prostitution had been a widespread and fairly well-accepted part of American urban life. To be sure, moralists of many kinds had periodically remonstrated against the easy acceptance of prostitution and were probably responsible for insuring that only one brief effort was made, in St. Louis, to experiment with European methods of regulation.[59] By and large, though, prostitutes sold their services with little interference, and, all evidence indicates, remarkably large percentages of American males used them.[60]

In the Victorian years prostitution was silently tolerated for three principal reasons. For one, prostitutes thrived mainly in the poorer, immigrant neighborhoods, and the feeling was, then as now, that as long as prostitutes remained in the slums, more respectable communities need not worry unduly about them. Second, nineteenth-century popular opinion sanctioned the view that men possessed superabundant sexual energies that required frequent release for mental and physical health. We must be careful not to exaggerate here; for opposite beliefs on male sexuality were also held in the Victorian period. Several reformers argued, for example, that sexual indulgence destroyed men's bodies and minds and that men should be continent in their sexual expression.[61] In retrospect, though, what is remarkable is how easily these contradictory sentiments coexisted—the latter as ideology for public consumption, the former as an "underground" precept guiding actual behavior.[62]

[58] "Sex O'Clock in America."

[59] John Burnham, "Medical Inspection of Prostitutes in Nineteenth Century America—The St. Louis Experiment and Its Sequel," *Bulletin of the History of Medicine,* 1971, 45, 203–218.

[60] See Roy Lubove, "The Progressives and the Prostitute," *Historian,* 1962, 24, 308–330; Robert Riegel, "Changing American Attitudes toward Prostitution (1800–1920)," *Journal of the History of Ideas,* 1968, 29, 437–452; Keith Thomas, "The Double Standard," *Journal of the History of Ideas,* 1959, 20, 195–216; Egal Feldman, "Prostitution, the Alien Woman and the Progressive Imagination, 1910–1915," *American Quarterly,* 1967, 19, 192–206; Eric Anderson, "Prostitution and Social Justice: Chicago, 1910–15," *Social Service Review,* 1974, 48, 203–228; Claudia Johnson, "That Guilty Third Tier: Prostitution in Nineteenth-Century American Theaters," in *Victorian America,* ed. Daniel Howe (Philadelphia: University of Pennsylvania Press, 1976), pp. 111–120; and James Wunsch, "Prostitution and Public Policy: From Regulation to Suppression, 1858–1920," Dissertation, University of Chicago, 1976.

[61] A very useful introduction to the ideals and practices of sex in the Victorian period is *Primers for Prudery,* ed. Ronald Walters (Englewood Cliffs, N.J.: Prentice-Hall, 1974). See also Gordon, *Woman's Body,* chaps. 4 and 8; and Patricia Vertinsky, "Education for Sexual Morality: Moral Reform and the Regulation of American Sexual Behavior in the Nineteenth Century," Dissertation, University of British Columbia, 1974, sect. 2.

[62] We borrow the term "underground" from Bryan Strong, who writes of the attempt in the early twentieth century "to counteract the underground belief in what was called the 'sexual

The third reason for toleration of prostitution was the Victorian sentimentalization of womanhood.[63] "Respectable" women—the only kind men dared marry—were placed gingerly upon a pedestal and viewed as rarefied creatures without sexual motivation. By nature they were so innocent and gentle that it would have been cruel for husbands to impose their sexual lusts upon them. This viewpoint obviously facilitated public acceptance of prostitution: the practice was rationalized as a protection of the home and domestic life through the absorption of men's excess sexual energies.

In the reform campaigns of the Progressive era, the ambivalences and contradictions of Victorian sexual thinking gave way to the unyielding pursuit of purity and innocence. Under the leadership of the counterrevolutionists, city after city conducted elaborate studies of prostitution, revealing how openly prostitution flourished. Estimates varied, but it was conservatively calculated that well over half of American males from all social classes used or had used prostitutes and that many had contracted some form of venereal disease. Using these facts to support their position, the counterrevolutionists attacked regulation or even the toleration of prostitution as blasphemy. The wholesale destruction of prostitution became their goal, and, to a remarkable extent, they succeeded in wiping out many of the nation's most famous red-light districts in the years before the First World War.[64]

The metaphor of the white-slave trade fueled the antiprostitution campaign, but the extent to which prostitution was centrally organized was always uncertain.[65] Two other well-publicized arguments, though, helped sustain the fight against prostitution. The first resulted from several major scientific advances in detection and treatment of venereal disease. The counterrevolutionists drew grave moral implications from these scientific developments. On the one hand, they insisted, the physical devastation and easy communicability of venereal disease demanded rapid elimination of prostitution to safeguard family health. On the other hand, they asserted, the discovery of effective cures for venereal disease required quick destruction of prostitution, lest men be tempted to greater vice by the knowledge that they need not fear infection.[66]

The second rationale for destroying prostitution also drew upon medical opin-

---

necessity,' which declared that men must exercise their sexual power lest their organs weaken or atrophy for want of use. Belief in a 'sexual necessity,' of course, was inconsistent with the ideal of chastity and continence" ("Ideas of the Early Sex Education Movement in America, 1890–1920," *History of Education Quarterly*, 1972, 12, 145).

[63] See, for example, Anne Scott, *The Southern Lady* (Chicago: University of Chicago Press, 1970); and Barbara Welter, "The Cult of True Womanhood: 1820–1860," *American Quarterly*, 1966, 18, 151–174.

[64] See Gordon, *Woman's Body*, p. 204. While we find her argument intriguing, we do not believe there is sufficient evidence to support Gordon's cause-effect contention that "the basis for the weakening of prostitution between 1910 and 1920 was not the conversion of men to purity; it was the conversion of women to 'indulgence' " (p. 192).

[65] For example, see Clifford Roe, *The Prodigal Daughter: The White Slave Evil and the Remedy* (Chicago: L. W. Walter, 1911); and *War on the White Slave Trade*, ed. Ernest Bell (Chicago: Charles C. Thompson, 1909).

[66] The principal medical spokesperson and organizational leader of the counterrevolutionists

ion, although in this instance it was more a medical assertion than a demonstrable advance in scientific knowledge. The counterrevolutionists contended that a single standard of sexual behavior—that of continence—should prevail for men and women.[67] This ideal, as we observed, also had its supporters in the Victorian era. The twentieth-century proponents of continence did little to challenge the underground Victorian view that men's sexual appetites were ravenous. Instead, they emphatically urged continence as part of the larger Progressive-era moral revival, which included such other popular displays of conscience as the prohibition movement and the campaigns against child labor, dime novels, cheap movies, and the easy availability of narcotic drugs. Furthermore, the counterrevolutionists now gained the concerted support of powerful medical organizations against the underground doctrine of "sexual necessity." Three hundred of the nation's leading physicians, for example, issued a much-publicized manifesto in favor of male continence, which declared in part:

> In view of the individual and social dangers which spring from the widespread belief that continence may be detrimental to health, and of the fact that municipal toleration of prostitution is sometimes defended on the ground that sexual indulgence is necessary, we, the undersigned, members of the medical profession, testify to our belief that continence has not been shown to be detrimental to health or virility; that there is no evidence of its being inconsistent with the highest physical, mental, and moral efficiency; and that it offers the only sure reliance for sexual health outside of marriage.[68]

In sum, the counterrevolutionists, who led the antiprostitution campaign, relied heavily on medical opinion to persuade the American public that Victorian sexual liberties were sinful and unhealthy and that continence was possible through moral exertion and the removal of temptation. Paradoxically, then, at the very time when sex was becoming an accepted part of social discourse, a surprisingly effective campaign was led to eliminate one of the most common figures of nineteenth-century society, the prostitute.

Like the antiprostitution crusade, the sex-education movement drew heavily on medical science. Proponents of sex education saw themselves as progressive, fearlessly attacking the Victorian "conspiracy of silence" about sex. On closer inspection, though, sex education appears to have been anything but a modernizing influence. The sex educators fought mainly against imaginary adversaries, for sex was already an everyday topic of conversation. Moreover, the movement's rhetoric was largely puritanical, revealing deep fears about the moral impact of cultural change.[69]

---

was Dr. Prince Morrow, whose activities are well treated in Burnham, "The Progressive Era Revolution."

[67] See especially Thomas, *The Unadjusted Girl;* and Strong, "Ideas of the Early Sex Education Movement."

[68] Quoted in Maurice Bigelow, *Sex-Education* (New York: Macmillan, 1918), p. 161.

[69] We are especially indebted to the works of Pivar, Strong, and Vertinsky, "Education for Sexual Morality." The best primary sources, in our estimation, are *The Social Emergency*, ed. William

The main goals of sex education were to purify discourse on sex, particularly in the popular press and among children, and to instill moral inhibitions against sexual gratification now that effective birth control and cures for venereal disease were becoming widely available. The sex educators were moral crusaders marching under the banners of medical and pedagogical science. They sought to develop instructional techniques for innocently conveying new medical knowledge about sex to children and, at the same time, imbuing sex with older spiritual meanings. Sex education was a means of pedagogical warfare against the purveyors of sexual titillation. Far from encouraging freer discussion of sex, the sex educators wanted to discipline lust and channel it to conventional moral ends.[70]

While the sex educators claimed to bring discussion of sex into the open, their pedagogical approach was so indirect as to be obscurantist. About the only form of open sexual discussion they could tolerate, in fact, involved the mating of plants. The copulation of pistils and stamens served as a model for teaching children acceptable sexual emotion and was much preferred to analogies between human and animal sexuality.[71] To the extent that sex educators actually discussed human sex, it was always as a form of spiritual communion; intercourse was mainly a melding of chaste minds. The sex-education movement, then, is best conceived as part of a new strategy for realizing Victorian moral ideals in an era growing increasingly comfortable with sex. If adults in the Progressive period had become unduly attracted to sex, their children need not be.[72]

How is the sexual counterrevolution related to our main subject—female juvenile justice in the Progressive era? We believe the sentiments that motivated the antiprostitution and sex-education campaigns also inspired punitive treatment of female delinquents. The expansion of female reformatories was especially significant, for they played important instrumental and symbolic roles in the sexual counterrevolution. First, and most pragmatically, the female reformatories

---

Foster (Boston: Houghton-Mifflin, 1914); Bigelow, *Sex-Education*; and National Society for the Scientific Study of Education, *Education with Reference to Sex* (Chicago: University of Chicago Press, 1909).

[70] Although the sex educators, by and large, wanted nothing to do with Freud, they were advocating a form of creative repression akin to the goals of the early conservative champions of Freud in America. See Nathan Hale, *Freud and the Americans* (New York: Oxford University Press, 1971).

[71] For example, Bigelow writes in *Sex-Education*: "Like eating, [sex] is a necessary function inherited from animals; but there has been an evolution of greater significance. In the animal world, sexual activity has only one function, reproduction; but human life at its highest has superadded psychical and social meaning to sexual relationships, and the result has been affection and the human family. If we reject this higher view of the double significance of sexuality in human life, and insist that only the necessary propagative function is worthy of recognition, it is almost inevitable that most people will continue to accept the hopeless view that human sexuality is on the same vulgar plane as that of the animals; in short, that it is only an animal function. This, I insist, is a depressing interpretation that will never help overcome the prevailing vulgar attitude toward sex" (p. 74).

[72] For assessments of the influence of the sex-education movement, see Strong, "Ideas of the Early Sex Education Movement," pp. 152–153; and Vertinsky, "Education for Sexual Morality," chap. 9.

assisted in the medical effort to eliminate venereal disease. They isolated those girls who were assumed most likely to become disease carriers. If the girls were already carriers, the reformatories prevented them from spreading disease and made treatment possible. Second, and most presumptuously, the incarceration of sexually promiscuous girls was thought to facilitate the moral ideal of male continence. By removing from view a prime source of sexual temptation, the reformatories, it was earnestly hoped, would also eliminate a stimulant of sexual desire in ghetto communities, especially for teenage boys. Third, and most urgently, the reformatories took sexually active girls off the street during the age range when prostitutes were most commonly recruited.[73] Hence reformatories, aided by the juvenile courts' punitive attitude toward sexual precocity among girls, would contribute to the attack on prostitution by cutting off a likely supply of new recruits.

Finally, and most idealistically, the reformatories assumed a special symbolic role in the sexual counterrevolution. In an era becoming increasingly fascinated by all things sexual, reformatories offered a warning that society would still not tolerate girls who showed the same interest in sex as boys and reinforced the traditional belief that "normal" girls were sexually impassive. These sentiments seem to us to have represented, to a large extent, a rearguard defense against emerging modern views on the reality of female sexual desire. But if, in fact, the counterrevolutionists lost the war, they were a powerful enough force in the Progressive era to win important battles. We should not gauge their significance in the early twentieth century by their long-term defeat in the battle for sexual liberation.

In sum, we believe that female juvenile justice in the Progressive era was closely tied to the evolution of sexual mores. In an era of shifting cultural norms, new social policies emerged to defend older moral ideals. As we noted earlier, we do not deny the possibility that there may have been a real increase in female delinquency in the early twentieth century. But we insist that, whether the increase was real or imagined, the public response to female delinquency formed part of a larger cultural reaction, an attempt to revitalize Victorian morality and to punish women —prostitutes and sexually precocious girls alike—who impeded attainment of that goal.

Conclusion

We promised earlier not to draw glib comparisons between past and present because of the incomplete nature of our historical research. But our research unequivocally demonstrates that the roots of sexual discrimination in juvenile

[73] According to Jane Addams, "it has been estimated that at any given moment the majority of girls utilized by the trade are under twenty years of age and that most of them were procured when younger . . . the average age of recruits to prostitution is between sixteen and eighteen years. . . . All the recent investigations have certainly made clear that the bulk of the entire traffic is conducted with the youth of the community, and that the social evil, ancient though it may be, must be renewed in our generation through its younger members. The knowledge of the youth of its victims doubtless in a measure accounts for the new sense of compunction which fills the community." *A New Conscience*, pp. 52, 142.

justice are deep indeed. Despite radically different attitudes today toward the social role and sexual desires of women, our correctional policies share many of the assumptions common in the nineteenth and early twentieth centuries.[74] Perhaps mainstream ideas about the proper role of women and of female sexuality have not changed as much as some may think;[75] perhaps correctional policies always lag behind changes in cultural perception; perhaps we as a society are trying unconsciously to relieve guilt about the passing of older moral standards by continuing to punish the most vulnerable group of females—poor, minority children who today, as in the past, predominate among incarcerated girls. We do not have a ready answer, but we do believe that there is an intimate relation between a society's correctional system and its deepest values and beliefs. And without doubt the values and beliefs that shaped a discriminatory system of juvenile justice in the Victorian and Progressive eras still dominate the administration of female juvenile justice today.

[74] Richard Flaste, "Is Juvenile Justice Tougher on Girls Than on Boys?" *New York Times*, 6 September 1977, p. 48, cols. 1–4.

[75] The classic argument, of course, is presented in Betty Friedan, *The Feminine Mystique* (New York: Norton, 1963). In addition to previously cited books and articles, the following historical works shed much light on continuities between past and present: Charles Rosenberg, "Sexuality, Class, and Role," *American Quarterly*, 1973, 25, 131–153; Charles Rosenberg and Carroll Smith-Rosenberg, "The Female Animal: Medical and Biological Views of Women," *Journal of American History*, 1973, 60, 332–356; Rosalind Rosenberg, "The Dissent from Darwin, 1890–1930: The New View of Woman among American Social Scientists," Dissertation, Stanford University, 1974; and Paula Fass, *The Damned and the Beautiful* (New York: Oxford University Press, 1977).

A Guide to Additional Primary-Source Materials on Female Juvenile Delinquency in the Early Twentieth Century

Bowen, Mrs. Joseph. "The Delinquent Child of Immigrant Parents." National Conference of Charities and Correction, *Proceedings* (1909), pp. 255–261.

Bridgman, Olga. "An Experimental Study of Abnormal Children, with Special Reference to the Problems of Dependency and Delinquency." University of California, *Publications in Psychology*, 1918, 3, 2–59.

Bronner, Augusta. *A Comparative Study of the Intelligence of Girls*. New York: Teachers College Press, 1914.

Burleigh, Edith. "The Advantage of Parole Under a Separate Superintendent." National Conference on the Education of Truant, Backward, Dependent and Delinquent Children, *Proceedings* (1916), pp. 80–83.

Burleigh, Edith. "Some Principles for Parole for Girls." National Conference of Charities and Correction, *Proceedings* (1918), pp. 147–154.

DeBolt, Mrs. L. N. "Industrial Employment as a Factor in the Reformation of Girls." National Conference of Charities and Correction, *Proceedings* (1900), pp. 214–220.

Dummer, Mrs. W. F. "Introduction to Roundtable Discussion on the Delinquent Girl." The American Sociological Society, *Publications*, 1921, 16, 185–186.

Dye, Charlotte. "The Defective Delinquent." National Conference on the Education of Truant, Backward, Dependent and Delinquent Children, *Proceedings* (1917), pp. 78–82.

Falconer, Martha. "The Culture of Family Life Versus Reformatory Treatment." National Conference of Charities and Correction, *Proceedings* (1914), pp. 108–110.

Falconer, Martha. "Reformatory Treatment for Women." National Conference of Charities and Correction, *Proceedings* (1914), pp. 253–256.

Goddard, Henry. "The Treatment of the Mental Defective Who Is Also Delinquent." National Conference of Charities and Correction, *Proceedings* (1911), pp. 64–65.

Hamilton, Dr. Alice. "Venereal Disease in Institutions for Women and Girls." National Conference of Charities and Correction, *Proceedings* (1910), pp. 53–56.

Harris, Dr. Mary. "Preparing Delinquent Women for the New Citizenship." Conference of the National Committee on Prisons and Prison Labor, *Proceedings* (1919), pp. 6–14.

Harris, Dr. Mary. *I Knew Them in Prison*. New York: Viking, 1936.

Hoag, Dr. Ernest, and Dr. Edward Williams. *Crime, Abnormal Minds and the Law*. Indianapolis, Ind.: Bobbs-Merrill, 1923.

Hodder, Jessie. "The Next Step in the Treatment of Girls and Women Offenders." National Conference of Charities and Correction, *Proceedings* (1918), pp. 117–121.

Holsopple, Francis. "Social Non-Conformity: An Analysis of 420 Delinquent Girls and Women." Dissertation, University of Pennsylvania, 1919.

Kauffman, Reginald. *The Girl That Goes Wrong*. New York: Macaulay, 1911.

Kenworthy, Dr. Marion. "The Logic of Delinquency." The American Sociological Society, *Publications*, 1921, 16, 197–204.

Lundberg, Emma. "The Child-Mother as a Delinquency Problem." National Conference of Charities and Correction, *Proceedings* (1920), pp. 167–168.

Miner, Maude. *Slavery of Prostitution*. New York: Macmillan, 1916.

Miner, Maude. "The Individual Method of Dealing with Girls and Women Awaiting Court Action." Congress of the American Prison Association, *Proceedings* (1921), pp. 8–12.

Montgomery, Miss Sarah. "Discipline and Training of Girls in Industrial Schools." National Conference of Charities and Correction, *Proceedings* (1908), pp. 198–201.

Morrow, Dr. Louis, and Dr. Olga Bridgman. "Delinquent Girls Tested by the Binet Scale." *Training School Bulletin*, 1912, 9, 33–36.

Morse, Mrs. Frannie. "The Methods Most Helpful to Girls." National Conference of Charities and Correction, *Proceedings* (1904), pp. 306–311.

Murray, Virginia. "The Runaway Girl and the Stranded Girl." National Conference of Charities and Correction, *Proceedings* (1920), pp. 175–180.

National Conference on the Education of Truant, Backward, Dependent and Delinquent Children, *Proceedings* (1915), pp. 49–53, and (1917), pp. 36–41, 82–90.

Renz, Emile. "The Intelligence of Delinquents and the Eugenic Significance of Mental Defect." *Training School Bulletin*, 1914, 11, 37–39.

Rippin, Jane. "Municipal Detention for Women." National Conference of Charities and Correction, *Proceedings* (1918), pp. 132–139.

Sessions, Dr. Kenosha. "Some Deductions from the Wasserman Test." National Conference on the Education of Truant, Backward, Dependent and Delinquent Children, *Proceedings* (1915), pp. 47–49.

Sessions, Dr. Kenosha. "The Delinquent Girls as a Community Problem." National Conference on the Education of Truant, Backward, Dependent and Delinquent Children, *Proceedings* (1918), pp. 76–78.

Smith, Dr. Carrie. "The Unadjusted Girl." National Conference of Charities and Correction, *Proceedings* (1920), pp. 180–183.

Taft, Jessie. "Some Problems in Delinquency—Where Do They Belong?" The American Sociological Society, *Publications*, 1921, 16, 186–196.

Van Waters, Miriam. "Juvenile Court Procedure as a Factor in Diagnosis." The American Sociological Society, *Publications*, 1921, 16, 209–217.

Wald, Mrs. Lillian. "The Immigrant Young Girl." National Conference of Charities and Correction, *Proceedings* (1909), pp. 261–266.

Wilson, Otto. *Fifty Years' Work with Girls, 1883–1933*. Alexandria, Va.: National Florence Crittendon Mission, 1933.

Worthington, George, and Ruth Topping. *Specialized Courts Dealing with Sex Delinquency*. New York: Frederick H. Hitchcock, 1925.

The Canadian Review of American Studies, Volume IX, Number 1, Spring, 1978

Nineteenth-Century Sexuality and the "Sexual Revolution" of the Progressive Era

Howard I. Kushner

This essay is an attempt to investigate the present state of our historical understanding of sexuality in the United States in the nineteenth and early twentieth centuries. In the pages that follow, I make no claim to present new *evidence* about sexuality during this period; rather, my essay does argue that if some of our present assumptions are probed, many of our conclusions about the history of sexual attitudes and practice will be called into question.

I propose to suggest that our view of nineteenth-century sexuality has been at least partly distorted. One reason for this is that the vocal demands of physicians and moral reformers for a more rigid sexual ideology have often been used as descriptions of the actual sexual habits and practices of the general population. The assumption that most nineteenth-century Americans were puritanical about sex has led, in turn, to a second confusion: that the increased public discussion of sexual matters in the early twentieth century signalled a "sexual revolution."

I propose that what often is referred to as the sexual revolution of the Progressive era can be viewed instead as an attempt by some groups and individuals to institutionalize the values of earlier moral reformers. This essay will consequently concentrate upon two aspects of sexual reform: first, it will investigate the evidence which is frequently employed to portray nineteenth-century Americans as sexually repressed; second, it will analyze those reforms of the first two decades of the twentieth century usually described by the term "sexual revolution," among these being sex education, divorce reform, antiprostitution movements and the birth control movement. The conclusion will suggest new directions for future work in this field.

I

While there is some evidence available concerning the childhood experiences and sexual attitudes of the elite and middle classes in the nineteenth century, there is little about anyone else. Nevertheless, many studies impute a single sexual morality to all classes. Of course, such a view may neglect the notion that there was much variation of sexual attitudes and habits within the middle class itself.[1] Thus the term "middle class morality" is employed here in Peter Cominos' sense of "respectable sexual ideology."[2]

The allegation that nineteenth-century Americans were sexually repressed relies upon three circumstantial sources about attitudes: first, the great volume of sexual-advice books for parents and children;[3] second, the conclusions of many physicians about sexuality;[4] and third, the writings of those who, in the first two decades of the twentieth century, allegedly assailed repression (though not always sexual)—especially the widely read works (among upper-middle-class reformers) of William James, Havelock Ellis, Maria Montessori, John Dewey and Sigmund Freud.[5]

Victorian advice manuals were quite explicit in their warnings. Readers were told that if the young were taught anything at all about sexual matters, sensuality should be deemphasized and emphasis should be placed upon the moral and reproductive functions of sex. Masturbation was presented as a vile practice, and children were to be prevented from masturbating, even if physical restraints were required.[6] Premarital sex was presented not only as sinful, but also as the road to somatic and psychic disorders. Prostitution was even worse: it was one of the greatest evils of civilization. The manuals advocated its prohibition and the punishment of all prostitutes. Those who refused to heed the warnings against premarital sex and prostitution ran the risk of contracting venereal disease. Even in marriage, some writers warned, sexual intercourse was to be limited solely to the purposes of procreation.[7]

Diet, warned the manuals, was one of the prominent causes of sexual desire, and therefore the moral person should avoid exotic and stimulating foods which were alleged to lead to sexual excesses. Instead, exercise and other forms of physical sublimation were suggested as the surest way to control one's mind and one's passions.[8] In short, promiscuity could lead only to physical decay and madness. The authors of advice books couched their arguments with impressive medical and historical "evidence" which proved that sensuality was among the greatest dangers to health in America.

Such an outpouring of warning of the dangers of sexuality in children and adults, however, does not necessarily prove that most Americans led sexually repressed lives in the nineteenth century. In fact, it may be proof of just the opposite. After all, one would not continually warn the nation of the dangers of sexual excesses if no one were being sexually excessive. There is no pressing need to call for the passage of laws against crimes which are not being committed. As Carl Degler recently pointed out, most historians view sexual-advice literature to middle-class women in the late nineteenth century as "descriptive of the sexual ideology of the time when in fact they were part of an effort by some other medical writers to establish an ideology, not to delineate an already accepted one." Perhaps the reason that we find so many advice books on sexuality all during the nineteenth century is precisely because so many Americans adhered to a different set of sexual standards.[9]

Another possibility is found in Linda Gordon's argument that some feminists supported the social purity movement as a self-protective device for "enforcing men's responsibility for their sexual behavior." Consequently, the work of Gordon and others may lead us to the conclusion that for some nineteenth-century women sexual self-restraint was self-conscious rather than unconscious.[10] In the area of feminine sexuality as well, several recent works have presented evidence that Victorian physicians saw sexual desires among their female patients as symptoms of severe disorder.[11] Again, however, the frequency of the physicians' complaints about their female patients' sexual desires could as easily be further evidence that many nineteenth-century women did not accept a repressive sexual ideology (see Degler, pp. 1471-77).

Those works which, relying heavily on statistical methodology, have investigated sexual habits rather than attitudes are also beginning to call into question the notion that nineteenth-century Americans were sexually repressed. Degler, while admittedly relying on a limited sample, provides evidence which leads him to suggest that it is not true that middle-class women in the nineteenth century were "inhibited from acknowledging their sexual feelings" (p. 1469). Daniel Scott Smith has found that in the nineteenth century the premarital-pregnancy rate was surprisingly high. Even more interesting is the fact that Smith's findings lead him to conclude that this rate was higher among the working classes. Women of middle- and upper-class backgrounds, he finds, "maintained conservative sexual standards longer than the remainder of the population" ("Dating," p. 239).[12] Smith, of course, assumes that puritanical sexual standards were breaking down. Yet there is increasing evidence that just the opposite is true—that what we call a puritanical ideology was quite new to the nineteenth century.[13] For, as new evidence has demonstrated, in the eighteenth century high premarital-pregnancy rates can be shown.[14]

II

An assumption which has become accepted by many historians of American sexuality is that the first two decades of the twentieth century witnessed a fundamental revolution in sexual habits and attitudes in the United States.[15] Some historians are now debating whether this revolution took place before, during or after World War I.[16] One scholar who supports the proposition of a sexual revolution alleges that "nineteenth century Anglo-

Americans were stricter about sexual morality than their puritan ancestors." These puritanical attitudes, such a view suggests, were successfully attacked by some progressive reformers, as well as challenged by the changing role of women in America.[17] The net result is argued to have been a general change in attitude and practice among Americans from accepting sex only as a means of procreation to pursuing sexuality as a source of pleasure.[18]

Yet, if as I have suggested, nineteenth-century Americans prove less repressed than we generally have been taught, what values and habits were changed by the "sexual revolution" of the Progressive era? Logically—and it is often presented as such—one would expect that the sexual revolution overthrew older, more puritanical sexual values. Scholars of the "sexual revolution" begin by suggesting that the writings of Freud, Ellis and others had a profound effect upon the intellectuals of the first two decades of the century, and indeed they had.[19] The implications of such allegations is that sexual reformers discussed and accepted the more liberated notions of Freud and Ellis, and pushed for programs aimed at freeing American libidos. Curiously, this was not so. In fact, as John Burnham concludes, the sexual revolution came down to two things: ending the conspiracy of silence about sexuality (within the middle class) and attacking the middle class double standard. Neither movement, however, aimed at sexual liberation. Instead, the net result of this so-called revolution was to replace religious reasons for repression with more scientific ones.[20] Thus, while the sexual reformers did discuss sexuality more openly, their goals, in almost every case, were not liberation, but scientific and intellectual rationales for continued and expanded sexual regulation.

The Progressive reformers' calls for sex education in the schools seems to support this view. G. Stanley Hall's crusade for sex education in American secondary schools is often cited as evidence for the sexual revolution thesis. Hall, for instance, attacked the scare tactics used to frighten adolescents into sexual chastity until marriage. Hall's objection, however, was to the tactics, not the goal of adolescent chastity. He suggested that through proper schooling adolescent sexuality could be channelled into socially and morally uplifting endeavors. In arguing for such tactical changes, Hall insisted that "the ideals of chastity are perhaps the highest that can be held up to youth...." He claimed that his conclusions about chastity were based upon the best scientific evidence concerning proper adolescent physical development: "Yielding to mere and gross sensual pleasure shortens the growth period and the only way to prolong it and attain an even higher and fuller maturity for the race is by the plain old virtue of self-restraint."[21]

In his study of the sex education movement of the Progressive period, Bryan Strong concludes that its primary aim was "to sustain an old morality that demanded the repression of all sexual activities except those desired for procreation."[22] Certainly advice-book authors like Dr. Kellogg had asked for no more in the 1870's. While the nineteenth-century guide-book authors hoped that sex education at home would inculcate sexual control in the young, Progressive reformers attempted to institutionalize those values for the masses as part of the curriculum of American public education.[23]

The issue of divorce as a Progressive reform seems quite confusing. William O'Neill discovers that "the changing outlook on the legitimacy of divorce" in the Progressive era manifested itself in contradictory ways. At one point O'Neill notes that this changing attitude toward divorce was "very much a part of the cultural revolution" in which "the whole of American society and culture was undergoing a change...[for] the Victorian synthesis was fragmenting, and new modes of thought and behavior... were coming into being." Yet earlier he sums up the phenomenon quite differently: "Instead of the cultural transformation its prophets had anticipated, the new morality led merely to the establishment of divorce as a valid (and perhaps necessary) part of the family system."[24]

Within O'Neill's contradictions lies a synthesis. Divorce was legal long before the Progressive period. In states like North and South Dakota easily obtained divorces had become a small industry by the 1890's. The major legislative and reform movements which concentrated on divorce in the early twentieth century aimed at restricting divorce, not at making it more liberal. The main thrust of this divorce reform was the attempt to pass a national uniform marriage and divorce law. This movement began in the 1890's and continued through the 1920's. When such a bill was introduced in the Senate for the first time, its sponsor, Senator James H. Kyle of South Dakota, listed among his reasons for introducing such legislation that it would eliminate divorce colonies like South Dakota where quick divorces were available due to minimal residency requirements. Moreover, Kyle argued that his bill "would preserve the family and the home, and thus lay a broad foundation for the perpetuity of the nation." As O'Neill shows, the supporters of the movement for a uniform marriage and divorce law saw such legislation as the best method for restraining divorce.[25] President Theodore Roosevelt, a supporter of the uniform law, summed up the point of view of many of its advocates in his 1905 message to Congress calling for this legislation: "The institution of marriage is, of course, at the very foundation of our social organization.... There is a widespread conviction that the divorce laws are dangerously lax and indifferently administered in some of our states, resulting in a diminishing regard for the sanctity of the marriage relations." Senator George W. Norris of Nebraska upheld Roosevelt's views, arguing that since divorces could not be completely eliminated, a uniform law could at least reduce their number.[26]

Even if some supporters of liberalized divorce genuinely desired easier access to the divorce court, that is not necessarily evidence of a call for sexual liberation. Nor is the increasing divorce rate by the 1920's proof of greatly changed sexual habits. Instead, the crusade for divorce reform affirmed, rather than denied, that the proper partner for sexual relations was one's legally approved spouse.[27]

Not surprisingly, while in the nineteenth century most divorces took place within the elite classes, in the Progressive period divorce regulations were increasingly aimed at the rest of society.[28] Of course, this does not prove that working class marriages break up less frequently in the nineteenth than in the twentieth century.[29] Instead, the Progressive divorce reforms merely attempted to extend middle-class morality to the lower classes. The law could now intervene in working-class marriage and divorce with greater frequency than it had before.

Clearly, whether one advocated more restrictive or more liberalized divorce laws, divorce in Progressive terms was a scientific solution to a social problem. By the early twentieth century the debate over divorce had moved from the realm of Christian morality into arguments between social scientists and politicians over the social effects of divorce. We must not forget, nevertheless, that the ultimate solution divorce offered was the reaffirmation of the institution of marriage as the sole recognized and legitimate sphere for sexual intercourse. Certainly nineteenth-century guide books had asked for no more. The limitation of sexual intercourse to marriage was now not only additionally sanctified, it had also gained the potential force of law.

Implicit in the early twentieth-century demand by physicians that the "conspiracy of silence" about venereal disease be ended, was a warning to the public of the great danger of sexual intercourse outside the traditional bonds of marriage. Both the Chicago Vice Commission's and Dr. Prince A. Marrow's New York crusades against prostitution included the argument that prostitution was a health hazard to the frequenters' families.[30] Such arguments, even if based on some truth, confirmed in the public consciousness the same message conveyed by the nineteenth-century advice books: sexual relations outside marriage could lead to permanent physical and psychic damage.

To this the Progressive reformers added their voices. While during most of the nineteenth century prostitution was tolerated as an inevitable, if detestable institution,[31] Progressive reformers, in demanding an end to the "conspiracy of silence" about prostitution, also demanded that prostitution be made a crime.[32] Of course, as early as the 1830's and continuing to the 1890's various moral reform and feminist groups did attempt both to reform prostitutes and to coerce their patrons into discontinuing their clientele.[33] There were also various calls for the legal punishment of prostitutes; yet such calls went unheeded and were regarded by many reformers as unrealistic. Instead, the existence of prostitution was denied in polite society by a general refusal even to discuss it. Police arrests of prostitutes had to be made under the guise of violations of laws against the keeping of disorderly houses, vagrancy or indecent exposure. Moreover, the general attitude of the police, as opposed to that of feminist reformers, was that prostitution should be regulated rather than outlawed.[34] In any case, prostitution itself was not illegal.

To Progressive reformers, however, as in the case of divorce, prostitution was a social disease that demanded scientific cures. All solutions pointed toward legislation. The most famous of these laws, which made it a crime to working-class marriages break up less frequently in the nineteenth than in the transport a woman across state lines for immoral purposes, was the Mann Act of 1910.[35] Influential in demanding the criminalization of prostitution was the American Vigilance Association, founded in 1912 and led by David Starr Jordon and Jane Addams. In 1916 this group joined other anti-prostitution organizations and formed the American Federation for Social Hygiene.[36]

Pressures from such organizations and physicians' groups led various states and localities to set up commissions to investigate the extent of prostitution. The result was an almost unanimous call by these commissions for the elimination of prostitution. By World War I prostitution had been declared illegal in most jurisdictions in the United States, and increasing numbers of prostitutes were forced to turn to organized crime for protection.[37] As in the cases of sex education and divorce, what had been a matter of private conscience in the nineteenth century became in the twentieth a public problem regulated by law.

Both in terms of enforcement and intent, the Progressive reforms of prostitution were aimed at the lower class.[38] That prostitutes were mainly of the lower class during these periods is hardly to be doubted.[39] In any case, given the loose definition of prostitution itself, many working-class and immigrant women were legally defined as prostitutes for simply being less sexually puritanical than middle-class women.[40] What is as important was the belief among the reformers like Jane Addams and Abraham Flexner that prostitutes invariably came from the poorer and immigrant classes.[41] In this sense, the reformers' attitudes and beliefs were acted upon, and their movement concentrated as much upon controlling working-class behavior as upon ridding it of prostitution.

Clearly, in the Progressive era as in the nineteenth century, prostitution was a degrading and exploitative occupation for many women. Yet one does not have to defend the institution in order to point out that some working-class prostitutes remained more ambivalent about the profession than the reformers were. In his famous 1858 survey of prostitution in New York City, William Sanger found, much to his surprise, that more than one quarter of the prostitutes interviewed said that they had voluntarily chosen prostitution "in order to gratify the sexual passions." In fact, Sanger was hard-pressed to produce any evidence that more than a small minority of prostitutes saw anything morally wrong with the way in which they earned a living.[42] While Victorian reformers rejected, as Sanger had, his evidence about women's sexual desires, they did accept the notion that some women actually chose prostitution. "Low wages and poor working conditions," argued feminist reformers, "practically forced women into prostitution." These assumptions, however, were challenged by Progressive reformers' studies, one of which concluded that while women who entered prostitution were mainly from the working classes, those with higher paying positions were more likely to become prostitutes than those lower down. Whether these statistics were accurate or not, such information led Progressive reformers to the conclusion that prostitution was a complex phenomenon that could be eradicated only by a whole range of social legislation.[43]

In many ways Margaret Sanger's crusade for birth control is a microcosm of the general argument that I have been making. Until the notorious Comstock laws of the 1870's, there was no clear attitude toward contraception even within the middle class.[44] Indeed, two important works on contraceptive methods appeared in the 1830's: Robert Dale Owen's *Moral Physiology* (1830), and Charles Knowlton's *Fruits of Philosophy* (1832). Both of these works were quite explicit and were available to many middle-class Americans.[45] More important is the fact of declining birth rates all during the nineteenth century. This decline suggests that some form of birth control was practiced on a wide scale, especially by the middle class.[46] Again, what had been a private practice became a public matter—except that in the case of contraception the change occurred in the late nineteenth rather than in the early twentieth century.

In that context Margaret Sanger's birth-control movement was truly the one whose goals initially involved both sexual liberation and freedom from repression for the working classes.[47] Herein lies its importance: it is the exception which proves the rule. Unlike the other reforms of the so-called sexual revolution, the birth-control movement was forcibly suppressed, and precisely because in its final aims it was authentically revolutionary. In 1914, when she began her crusade, Sanger explicitly tied the dissemination of birth-control information to the uplifting of the working class. By denying to the working class control over their own reproductive systems, she argued, the capitalist class maintained its power. It is crucial to remember that Sanger was first indicted, in August 1914, for the publication of anarchistic material in the March issue of her *Woman Rebel*. It was not until November 1916 that she was indicted under section 1142 of the New York State Penal Code which made it illegal to disseminate information or devices for the "prevention of conception."[48] The Progressive leadership's response to the birth-control issue says much about the concept of a sexual revolution at the time.

Not until the 1920's, when Sanger gave up her class analysis of American society, her concentration on the dissemination of birth-control information to the working classes, and her anarchist associates, did she gain the kind of national social and political support that would eventually lead to the repeal of the Comstock laws. By 1920 she had changed her emphasis from birth control to control of population.[49] Moreover, her new upper-middle-class and professional allies supported her movement, not to free the working classes, but to limit their threat to society. In the twenties, many of those who now supported Sanger saw her movement as an answer to the problems posed by eugenics theory: birth control could be used to prevent the less pure and less intelligent immigrant and lower classes from over-populating the United States. It is, consequently, not surprising that once contraception could be employed as an argument for protecting the purer national stock, it gained more favor from the ruling classes than it had when it was tied to political revolt. Perhaps this also helps to explain why the immigrant and working classes proved increasingly resistant to population control by the 1920's.[50] Ironically, Sanger's movement, which began as a revolt against middle-class morality, ended as one of its staunchest allies.

The Progressive period's sexual revolution was a middle-class movement because it met middle-class needs. It especially met the requirements of middle-class reformers who—as the career of Jane Addams amply demonstrates—could no longer accept traditional religious reasons for sexual repression. As "modern" men and women of the intellectual class, they required modern and intellectual rationales for the repression of sexuality. Yet their arguments in the end reached the same conclusions as the nineteenth-century advice books that they claimed to reject. As Christopher Lasch has shown, these intellectual reformers had scarcely rid themselves of sexual guilt; at best, they had merely displaced it upon others.[51]

Nor should this be surprising. While the nineteenth-century advice books tried to persuade Americans to adopt sexually puritanical attitudes and habits of self denial, the Progressive reformers passed legislation which attempted to make promiscuity illegal. In this sense, the Progressive sexual revolution was an attempt to institutionalize the very goal of the nineteenth-century moral reformers: a uniformly shared sexual consciousness.

III

If it is possible that the sexual revolution of the Progressive period resulted in a repressive rather than a liberative sexual ideology, then we should question further our assumptions concerning nineteenth-century American sexuality. We find that we have learned some things about the sexual attitudes and habits of a limited number of persons. We know very little in this area about the vast majority of Americans. And what little we do know suggests that the current wisdom concerning the dominance of the puritanical attitude may be misleading.

Before we are able to reach additional conclusions, we must ask some different questions: first, we must decide what use child-rearing manuals and physicians' reports have for the historian of sexuality;[52] second, we should realize that any questions concerning sexual attitudes and habits may have very different answers, not only for differing classes, but also within those classes. Thus, as a very minimum, we must be class specific in our research. Most important, we must concentrate both upon the sexual habits of Americans as well as upon the sexual attitudes of those who desired to form the habits and attitudes of others. One thing seems evident: historians of American sexuality must revise not only the questions that they ask, but also the methodologies they employ, if we are to learn anything more about sexual attitudes and habits. Those works which have concentrated upon sexual practice, as opposed to sexual attitudes, demonstrate the utility of quantitative methodology for the study of sexuality. While we should never go so far as to assume that the data uncovered with the aid of quantification are objective or self-explanatory, the quantitative work of Smith, Karlen and others has helped to lead us away from unproved assertions about the pervasiveness of sexual repression in nineteenth-century America.[53]

Another aid may be found in the use of the psychoanalytic theory of projection.[54] From the time of the earliest settlement of North America until the present, the lower classes have been described by their social "betters" as licentious.[55] Such fears of lower-class sexuality are evident in the moral reform movements of the 1830's and 1840's and in the sexual-advice literature of the late nineteenth century. Early nineteenth-century moral reformers often claimed to desire to uplift the poor and working classes from drunkenness, sexuality and prostitution.[56] To the extent that these reformers and their late nineteenth-century followers may have been projecting their own sexual fantasies and ambivalences upon the poor and working classes, we can learn much about the sexual tensions inherent in middle-class reform movements. At the very least we are compelled to ask questions about the sex lives of the reformers. This is not to suggest that we should dismiss or try to explain away sexual reform as a result of middle-class neurosis or as the response of some reformers to fears of their own sexuality. It would be just as foolish, nevertheless, to ignore the clinical notion that in trying to deny sexuality to others, moral reformers were unconsciously affirming their own fears and desires.[57]

Nor should we dismiss the reformers' descriptions of the sexual habits of the poor and the working classes simply as snobbish rantings. Some historians have passed off such descriptions as symptoms of class prejudice or as valid for only a few unfortunates or for a minority of deviants in the lower classes.[58] Since many scholars view the imputation of sexual promiscuity as slanderous, it rarely occurs to us to see promiscuity as evidence of a different value structure. Yet, as recent studies of the American working class are beginning to demonstrate, different classes in nineteenth-century America held to very different sets of moral values, tied in part to class function.[59] The notion of referring to non-middle-class (non-puritanical) moral standards as licentious says more about a writer's values than it does about the life of the poor and working classes.

Finally, we must not deny the suggestion of truth that lies within every stereotype. In any case, once we cease clinging to the assumption that sexual liberty is proof of degradation, we might begin to ask the kinds of questions that may lead us to new answers concerning nineteenth-century American sexual habits and values.[60]

Notes

[1]See, for instance, R. S. Neale, "'Middle Class' Morality and the Systematic Colonizers," in his *Class and Ideology in the Nineteenth Century* (London, 1972), pp. 121-25.

[2]See Peter Cominos, "Late Victorian Sexual Respectability and the Social System," *International Review of Social History*, 8 (1963), 18; and Steven Marcus, *The Other Victorians: A Study of*

Sexuality and Pornography in Mid-Nineteenth Century England (New York, 1964).

[3]Various works deal at great length with these guide books and sex-advice manuals: See Bernard Wishy, *The Child and the Republic: The Dawn of Modern Child Nurture in America* (Philadelphia, 1968), esp. pp. 136-57; Joseph Kett, *Rites of Passage: Adolescence and Youth in America, 1790 to Present* (New York, 1977), esp. pp. 125-26, 168-72; Kett, "Adolescence and Youth in Nineteenth Century America," *Journal of Interdisciplinary History*, II (Autumn, 1971), 283-98 (esp. pp. 287-88); David J. Pivar, *Purity Crusade: Sexual Morality and Social Control, 1868-1900* (Westport, Conn., 1973); Ronald G. Walters, ed., *Primers for Prudery: Sexual Advice to Victorian America* (Englewood Cliffs, N.J., 1974); Jay Mechling, "Advice to Historians on Advice to Mothers," *Journal of Social History*, 9 (Fall, 1975), 44-63. See also Michael Gordon, "From an Unfortunate Necessity to a Cult of Mutual Orgasm: Sex in American Marital Education Literature, 1830-1940," in *Studies in the Sociology of Sex*, ed. James Henslin (New York, 1971), pp. 53-60; and Nathan G. Hale, *Freud and the Americans, The Beginnings of Psychoanalysis in the United States, 1876-1917* (New York, 1971), pp. 35-38.

[4]Various recent secondary works have dealt with nineteenth-century physicians' attitudes toward sexuality: see John S. Haller, Jr., and Robin M. Haller, *The Physician and Sexuality in Victorian America* (Urbana, Ill., 1974); Charles E. Rosenberg, "Sexuality, Class and Role in 19th-Century America," *American Quarterly*, 25 (May, 1973), 131-54; Carroll Smith-Rosenberg and Charles Rosenberg, "The Female Animal: Medical and Biological Views of Woman and Her Role in Nineteenth-Century America," *Journal of American History*, LX (Sept., 1973), 332-56; Carroll Smith-Rosenberg, "The Hysterical Woman: Sex Roles and Role Conflict in 19th Century America," *Social Research*, 39 (Winter, 1973), 652-78; Ann Douglas Wood, "'The Fashionable Diseases': Women's Complaints and Their Treatment in Nineteenth-Century America," *Journal Of Interdisciplinary History*, 4 (Summer, 1973), 25-52.

[5]David M. Kennedy, *Birth Control in America: The Career of Margaret Sanger* (New Haven, 1970), pp. 67-68.

[6]John Harvey Kellogg, M.D., *Plain Facts for Old and Young* (Burlington, Iowa, 1882), pp. 17-21, 320-21, 377, 428-34; Joseph W. Howe, M.D., *Excessive Venery, Masturbation, and Continence* (New York, 1883), pp. 17-22; Walters, *Primers*, pp. 20-28; Bryan Strong, "Ideas of the Early Sex Education Movement, 1890-1920," *History of Education Quarterly*, 12 (Summer, 1972), 134-35; Kett, "Adolescence," pp. 286-87, 297. An essay which relates this sexual ideology to the nature of the American economy in the nineteenth century is Ben Barker-Benfield, "The Spermatic Economy: A Nineteenth Century View of Sexuality," in Michael Gordon, ed., *The American Family in Social-Historical Perspective* (New York, 1973), pp. 336-72; see also Rosenberg, "Sexuality, Class and Role," pp. 131-33, 151-52. The most comprehensive work on the subject of masturbation is R. P. Neuman, "Masturbation, Madness, and the Modern Concepts of Childhood and Adolescence," *Journal of Social History*, 8 (Spring, 1975), 1-27.

[7]Kellogg, *Plain Facts*, pp. 170-89, 205-09, 236-37, 248, 284-85, 302-04, 308-09; William W. Sanger, *The History of Prostitution* (New York, 1858); Walters, *Primers*, pp. 34, 42, 44, 49-50, 69-71, 76-92, 129-30; Robert E. Riegel, "Changing Attitudes Toward Prostitution, 1800-1920," *Journal of the History of Ideas*, 29 (July-Sept., 1968), 438-39.

[8] Kellogg, *Plain Facts*, pp. 76-77, 183-84, 192, 210-14, 391-93; Walters, *Primers*, pp. 7, 12-13, 60-63, 110-18; Richard Shryock, "Sylvester Graham and the Health Reform Movement, 1830-1870," *Mississippi Valley Historical Review*, 18 (Sept., 1931), 172-73; Stephen Nissenbaum, "Careful Love: Sylvester Graham and the Emergence of Victorian Sexual Theory in America, 1830-1840," (Ph.D. diss., University of Wisconsin, 1968); Dio Lewis, *In a Nutshell: Suggestions to American College Students* (New York, 1883).

[9]Carl N. Degler, "What Ought to Be and What Was: Women's Sexuality in the Nineteenth Century," *American Historial Review*, 79 (Dec., 1974), 1477. One writer suggests that the strident moral tone of advice books and the passage of the Comstock laws (outlawing the sale and dissemination of birth control materials) during the last third of the nineteenth century "is consistent with the hypothesis that Victorian moral order was already in crisis before 1900.... The official responses to what was considered sexual deviancy resulted from an objective increase in 'deviant' behavior." See Daniel Scott Smith, "Dating the American Sexual Revolution: Evidence and Interpretation," in Gordon, ed., *The American Family*, pp. 330-31. See also Rosenberg, "Sexuality, Class and Role," pp. 135-40.

[10]Linda Gordon, *Woman's Body, Woman's Right: A Social History of Birth Control in America* (New York, 1976), pp. xiii, 95-115. See also Carroll Smith-Rosenberg, "Beauty, the Beast, and the Militant Woman: A Case Study in Sex Roles and Social Stress in Jacksonian America,"

American Quarterly, 23 (Oct., 1971), 562-84; Linda Gordon, "Voluntary Motherhood: The Beginnings of Feminist Birth Control Ideas in the United States," in Mary Hartman and Lois Banner, eds., *Clio's Consciousness Raised: New Perspectives on the History of Women* (New York, 1974), pp. 54-71; Daniel Scott Smith, "Family Limitation, Sexual Control, and Domestic Feminism in Victorian America," *ibid.*, pp. 119-36.

[11]Barker-Benfield, "The Spermatic Economy," pp. 347-61; Smith-Rosenberg and Rosenberg, "The Female Animal," pp. 343-50; Smith-Rosenberg, "The Hysterical Woman," pp. 669-71; for a view critical of these conclusions, see Regina Morantz, "The Lady and Her Physician," in Hartman and Banner, pp. 38-53.

[12]Smith, "Dating," p. 239. For a complete discussion of the relation between premarital pregnancy and nonmarital sexual behavior, as well as of the limits of this type of data, see Edward Shorter, "Illegitimacy, Sexual Revolution, and Social Change in Modern Europe," *Journal of Interdisciplinary History*, II (Autumn, 1971), 237-72.

[13]Kathryn Kish Sklar, "Sex and the Sage Victorian," *Reviews in American History*, 2 (Dec., 1974), 541-43; Walters, *Primers*, pp. 10-11; Pivar, *Purity Crusade*, pp. 3-12. A recent essay suggests that the ideology of sexual purity resulted from a conscious policy of nineteenth-century women who wanted to gain control over their own bodies. See Gordon, "Voluntary Motherhood," pp. 54-71; and Smith, "Family Limitation," pp. 119-36.

[14]Demos found that between 1740 and 1760 the premarital pregnancy rate was 49%, and between 1760 and 1780 it was 44% in Bristol, Rhode Island. See John Demos, "Families in Colonial Bristol, Rhode Island: An Exercise in Historical Demography," *William and Mary Quarterly*, 25 (3rd ser., 1968), 56, table 10. See also Demos, "Notes on Life in Plymouth Colony," *William and Mary Quarterly*, 22 (3rd ser., 1965), 273-74. Additional evidence for a high premarital pregnancy rate in eighteenth-century America may be found in Daniel Scott Smith and Michael S. Hindus, "Premarital Pregnancy in America, 1640-1971: An Overview and Interpretation," *Journal of Interdisciplinary History*, 5 (Spring, 1975), 537-70, esp. 561-65.

[15]James R. McGovern argues that "a major shift in American manners and morals occurred in the Progressive era...[which] represented such visible departures from the past and were so commonly practiced as to warrant calling them revolutionary." See his essay, "The American Woman's Pre-World War I Freedom in Manners and Morals," *Journal of American History*, 55 (Sept., 1968), 333. While asserting that "sexual repression increased through the nineteenth century, then declined in the twentieth," William L. O'Neill suggests that the new sexual freedom was limited in the pre-World War I years "chiefly to upper middle class women." See his *The American Sexual Dilemma* (New York, 1972), p. 2. See also Kennedy, *Birth Control*, who calls this a "revolution in morals" (p. 67). Bryan Strong alleges that "Toward the end of the nineteenth century American sexual attitudes were beginning to undergo a fundamental alteration... [because] the dominant sexual ideology of sex as restraint was being challenged increasingly by the hitherto radical doctrine of sex as pleasure" ("Ideas," p. 129). John C. Burnham, who essentially supports these views, adds that "despite the avowedly conservative goals of the reformers, change in middle-class standards of sexual behavior was revolutionary." See his "The Progressive Era Revolution in American Attitudes Toward Sex," *Journal of American History*, 59 (March, 1973), 885. In one of the few studies to discuss American sexual habits in the 1910's and 1920's, Arno Karlen concludes that "there was no vast revolution in behavior," but adds that "The greatest revolution in the twenties was in attitudes, expectations, and values." See his *Sexuality and Homosexuality: A New View* (New York, 1971), pp. 274-75. Daniel Scott Smith, another historian who emphasizes habits rather than attitudes, discovers that in terms of premarital pregnancies and illegitimate births (indicators of premarital coitus), the rates in the first two decades of the twentieth century were not significantly different from the last three decades of the nineteenth ("Dating," pp. 321-35).

[16]See McGovern, who in "The American Woman's Freedom" (p. 333) argues that the revolution took place before World War I, but after 1910. On the other hand, Daniel Scott Smith who, in tying the revolution to premarital pregnancies produces evidence that demonstrates in terms of practice the "take-off stage" of the sexual revolution took place in "the last third of the nineteenth century." Yet Smith's data lead him to the conclusion that "Change in sexual behavior has probably not been linear and continuous." For Smith, the "'revolutionary' character of the sexual revolution can be easily overstated" ("Dating," pp. 321-35). Earlier statistical studies of sexual habits seem to demonstrate increased premarital coitus for white women born after 1890, thus giving some credence to McGovern's assertion. See Katherine B. Davis, *Factors in the Sex Lives of Twenty-Two Hundred* (New York, 1929), p. 19; Lewis M. Terman, *Psychological Factors in*

Marital Happiness (New York, 1938), p. 321; and Ira L. Reiss, "Standards of Sexual Behavior" (unpublished material from Kinsey and associates), in Albert Ellis and Albert Abarnel, *The Encyclopedia of Sexual Behavior* (New York, 1961), II, 99. Nevertheless, as Smith correctly points out, these studies concentrated upon a small minority of college-educated women: "Furthermore, it is not clear *which* college educated women appear in these studies; it is possible that the older women interviewed by Kinsey and associates were drawn more heavily from religious groups instead of universities and clubs" ("Dating," p. 328).

[17]Henry F. May, *The End of American Innocence* (New York, 1959), pp. 340-47. The puritanical nature of the Puritans has been seriously challenged. See Edmund S. Morgan, "The Puritans and Sex," *New England Quarterly*, 15 (Dec., 1942), 591-607; John Demos, *A Little Commonwealth: Family Life in Plymouth Colony* (New York, 1970). See also Kennedy, *Birth Control*, pp. 65-67; Burnham, "The Progressive Era Revolution," pp. 896-907; McGovern, "American Woman's Freedom," p. 333.

[18]Strong, "Ideas," p. 129. More skeptical than many, Linda Gordon accepts the concept of a sexual revolt for a small number of the elite: "Whether these changes in sexual behavior and attitudes constituted a revolution or not, they created a new concept of birth control. Birth control now meant reproductive self-examination along with unlimited sexual indulgence. This new definition—quite different from that of voluntary motherhood—understood sexual activity and reproduction as two separately justified human activities." But, she concludes, "Freedom of sexual expression was allowed only if it did not challenge the essential family structure; premarital sex and adultery were tolerated because they offered no challenge and even temporarily shored up the rotting timbers of housewifery. The sexual revolution certainly offered no liberation to working class and middle class housewives" (*Woman's Body*, pp. 189-90, 202-03).

[19]Karlen, for instance, argues that there was a revolutionary change in attitudes, but only among the middle classes (*Sexuality*, p. 275). See also Pivar, *Purity Crusade*, p. 4; and Kennedy, *Birth Control*, pp. 67-69.

[20]Burnham, "The Progressive Era Revolution," p. 907. See also Neuman, "Masturbation," p. 9. Barbara Sicherman has recently presented a similar argument about the origins of the mental health movement in "The Paradox of Prudence: Mental Health in the Gilded Age," *Journal of American History*, 62 (March, 1976), 890-912, esp. 892-93; Norman H. Clark has done the same in relation to Prohibition in *Deliver Us from Evil: An Interpretation of American Prohibition* (New York, 1976).

[21]The fullest statement of this view is found in Kett, *Rites*, pp. 216-24. See also Neuman, "Masturbation," pp. 14-16. For more on Hall's view of schooling, see Dorothy Ross, *G. Stanley Hall: The Psychologist as Prophet* (Chicago, 1972), pp. 279-340. See also G. Stanley Hall, *Adolescence* (New York, 1905), 2 vols., I, 453, 438-39.

[22]Strong, "Ideas," p. 136; see also Hale, *Freud*, pp. 258-59.

[23]For more on this point see Joel Spring, *Education and the Rise of the Corporate State* (Boston, 1972), esp. pp. 62-107.

[24]O'Neill, *Divorce*, pp. 255-58, 163-64; see also pp. 30-32, 89.

[25]Nelson Manfred Blake, *The Road to Reno: A History of Divorce* (New York, 1962), pp. 123-29, 136-37, 140-48; O'Neill, *Divorce*, pp. 231-46; *U.S. Congressional Record*, 52nd Cong., 1st sess. (Feb. 3, 1892), p. 792.

[26]Theodore Roosevelt (Jan. 30, 1905), *Messages and Papers of the President* (Washington, 1907), X, 850-51; O'Neill, *Divorce*, p. 246.

[27]Paul H. Jacobson, *American Marriage and Divorce* (New York, 1959), p. 90; Blake, *Road to Reno*, pp. 226-28; O'Neill, *Divorce*, pp. 20, 12, 89, 164-65; Karlen, *Sexuality*, p. 275.

[28]William J. Goode, *The Family* (Englewood Cliffs, N.J., 1964), pp. 81-82. O'Neill, *Divorce*, p. 23.

[29]For more on this point see Bernard Farber, *Guardians of Virtue: Salem Families in 1800* (New York, 1972), pp. 142, 147-48; Richard Sennett, "Middle Class Families and Urban Violence: The Experience of a Chicago Community in the Nineteenth Century," in Gordon, *The American Family*, pp. 124-25.

[30]Hale, *Freud*, pp. 254, 258; Pivar, *Purity Crusade*, pp. 243-45; *The Social Evil in Chicago: A Study of Existing Conditions with Recommendations by the Vice Commission of Chicago* (Chicago, 1911), pp. 25-26; see also Roy Lubove, "The Progressive and the Prostitute," *Historian*, 24 (May, 1962), 319; Hale, *Freud*, p. 254; Burnham, "The Progressive Era Revolution," pp. 890-901.

[31]Howard B. Woolston, *Prostitution in the United States* (New York, 1921; rptd. 1969), pp. 26-31; Vern L. Bullough, *The History of Prostitution* (New Hyde Park, N.Y., 1964), pp. 187-95; Riegel, "Changing Attitudes," p. 437.; Pivar, *Purity Crusade*, pp. 24-34.

[32]Woolston, *Prostitution*, pp. 31-36; Bullough, *History of Prostitution*, pp. 194-95; Hale, *Freud*, pp. 254-55; Haller and Haller, *The Physician and Sexuality*, pp. 248-51; Lubove, "The Progressive and the Prostitute," pp. 326-28.

[33]The fullest recent treatment of the reformers' attitudes toward prostitution is presented in Pivar's *Purity Crusade*. Woolston, *Prostitution*, pp. 26-31; Bullough, *History of Prostitution*, pp. 187-95; Pivar, *Purity Crusade*, pp. 24-28; Hale, *Freud*, pp. 252-54; see also Smith-Rosenberg, "Beauty, the Beast, and the Militant Woman," pp. 568-70.

[34]Pivar, *Purity Crusade*, pp. 32-33, pp. 28-30; Riegel, "Changing Attitudes," p. 445. Late nineteenth-century attempts to license prostitutes met with strong opposition from both the feminist groups and the social purity movement. See John C. Burnham, "The Social Evil Ordinance—A Social Experiment in Nineteenth Century St. Louis," *Missouri Historical Society Bulletin*, 27 (April, 1971), 203-17; as well as his "Medical Inspection of Prostitutes in America in the Nineteenth Century: The St. Louis Experiment and its Sequel," *Bulletin of the History of Medicine*, 65 (1971), 203-18.

[35]Woolston, *Prostitution*, pp. 31-33; Riegel, "Changing Attitudes," p. 449; Lubove, "Progressive and Prostitute," pp. 324-28. For the legislative background leading to the passage of the Mann Act see, U. S. Senate, *Reports of the Immigration Commission: Importation and Harboring of Women for Immoral Purposes* (Doc. no. 753, 61st Cong., 3rd sess.).

[36]Jane Addams also published a book entitled *A New Conscience and an Ancient Evil* (New York, 1912), calling for an end to the toleration of prostitution. She opposed all efforts at regulation and urged the abolition of prostitution. For more on Addams' crusade see, Allen F. Davis, *American Heroine: The Life and Legend of Jane Addams* (New York, 1973), pp. 176-84. See also Riegel, "Changing Attitudes," p. 452.

[37]Woolston, *Prostitution*, pp. 119-22; Bullough, *History of Prostitution*, pp. 195, 198; Lubove, "The Progressive and the Prostitute," pp. 318-19, 328; Hale, *Freud*, pp. 254-55; Haller and Haller, *The Physician and Sexuality*, pp. 248-51; Riegel, "Changing Attitudes," p. 452; Gordon, *Woman's Body*, p. 204.

[38]See Davis, *American Heroine*, pp. 178-84; Woolston, *Prostitution*, pp. 47-51, 61. For an interesting study concerning anti-prostitution laws in England which concludes that the effect of such laws was to separate prostitutes from the lower classes, see Judith R. Walkowitz and Daniel J. Walkowitz, "'We Are Not Beasts of the Field': Prostitution and the Poor in Plymouth and Southampton under the Contagious Diseases Acts," in Hartman, *Clio's Consciousness Raised*, pp. 192-225. See also Hale, *Freud*, pp. 254-56.

[39]In Sanger's 1858 study of New York City prostitution he found that 1,488 out of 2,000 (78%) prostitutes interviewed listed their occupations previous to prostitution as working-class jobs. The working-class background percentage was probably higher, since 499 others listed their previous occupations as "living with parents." Surely not all of this latter group were from middle-class or elite backgrounds. See Sanger, *The History of Prostitution*, p. 524. Woolston's 1917 study of prostitution in the United States supported Sanger's findings. "In most of the cases studied the parents were rather simple working people.... While it cannot be said that all prostitutes were poor girls, it is very near the truth to assert that most of them came from poor homes" (*Prostitution*, p. 61; see also pp. 60-64). See also, Haller and Haller, *The Physician and Sexuality*, pp. 244-47.

[40]See Walkowitz and Walkowitz, "'We Are Not Beasts of the Field,'" pp. 206-07; R. P. Neuman, "Industrialization and Sexual Behavior; Some Aspects of Working Class Life in Imperial Germany," in Robert J. Bezucha, ed., *Modern European Social History* (New York, 1972), pp. 285-87.

[41]See Addams, *A New Conscience*, pp. 17-52; Egal Feldman, "Prostitution, the Alien Woman and the Progressive Imagination, 1910-1915," *American Quarterly*, 19 (Summer, 1967), 192-94.

[42]Sanger, *History of Prostitution*, pp. 488-94. Sanger was horrified and believed that such an explanation must have other reasons, for as he noted, "In itself such an answer would imply innate depravity, a want of true womanly feeling, which is actually incredible."

[43]Riegel, "Changing Attitudes," pp. 447, 449-51; The Committee of Fourteen in New York, *Department Store Investigation of the Sub-Committee* (New York, 1915), pp. 1-15; see also U. S. Senate (Exec. doc. 645, 61st Cong., 2nd sess.), "Report on the Condition of Women and Child Wage Earners in the United States," 19 vols. (Washington, 1910-12), 5, 28-36; see Addams, *A New Conscience*, pp. 151-57; Woolston, *Prostitution*, pp. 58-69.

[44]Walters, *Primers*, pp. 123-28; Kennedy, *Birth Control*, pp. 30-31; Gordon, *Woman's Body*, pp. 17-25.

[45]Norman Himes, *The Medical History of Contraception* (Baltimore, 1936; rptd. New York, 1970), pp. 224-30. The reception given Knowlton's work was mixed. He was fined for violation of Massachusetts law and briefly jailed. Nevertheless, his books continued to circulate freely in other jurisdictions. From 1834 to 1876, 40,000 copies of *Fruits of Philosophy* were sold in England. See also Walters, *Primers*, p. 127.

[46]*Historical Statistics of the United States* (Washington, 1961), pp. 23-24, 180-81; Himes, *Medical History*, pp. 210-11; Walters, *Primers*, p. 141; Kennedy, *Birth Control*, p. 42.

[47]I would like to thank Carol R. Kushner of SUNY, Buffalo for clearing up my many misimpressions about Margaret Sanger. The best work on Sanger and the Birth Control Movement is Gordon's *Woman's Body, Woman's Right*. The section on Sanger (pp. 205-36) is particularly enlightening. See also Kennedy, *Birth Control*, p. 22. The role of radical politics in the modern American birth control movement has often been neglected. Sanger's introduction to birth control came from her experience as an IWW organizer, beginning in 1912. She gained early support and encouragement from Emma Goldman, Big Bill Haywood, Elizabeth Gurley Flynn and Benjamin Reitman. In fact, Goldman and Reitman had publicly advocated birth control before Sanger herself became committed to it. See Gordon, *Woman's Body*, pp. 213-20. For more on Goldman's role as a pioneer in this cause see Richard Drinnon, *Rebel in Paradise: A Biography of Emma Goldman* (Chicago, 1961), pp. 164-72.

[48]Margaret Sanger, *An Autobiography* (New York, 1938; rptd. 1971), pp. 85-89, 106-12, 219-33; Gordon, *Woman's Body*, pp. 221-23; Kennedy, *Birth Control*, pp. 22-24, 83-84. See also Linda Gordon, "The Politics of Population: Birth Control and the Eugenics Movement," *Radical America*, 8 (July-Aug., 1974), 63-65.

[49]Sanger, *Autobiography*, pp. 260-61; Kennedy, *Birth Control*, pp. 75-76, 92-94; Gordon, "Politics of Population," pp. 65-66, 74-75. As Gordon has recently explained, "Politically, population control has almost nothing in common with birth control. The former applies norms of ideal family size without respect for cultural, social, or political self-determination. The fact that both rely on contraception as a tool... has led to an understandable popular association of the two" (*Woman's Body*, pp. xiv-xv, 136-58).

[50]Kennedy, *Birth Control*, pp. 118-19, 120-25; Gordon, "Politics of Population," pp. 74-78; Gordon *Woman's Body*, pp. 157-58, 224-25. For more on the eugenics movement see Mark Haller, *Eugenics: Hereditarian Attitudes in American Thought* (New Brunswick, N.J., 1963).

[51]See Christopher Lasch, *The New Radicalism in America, 1889-1963: The Intellectual as a Social Type* (New York, 1965), pp. 3-37. See also his chapter, "Mabel Dodge Luhan: Sex as Politics," pp. 104-40.

[52]One recent article which deals in depth with this problem in Mechling, "Advice," pp. 44-63.

[53]See notes 16 to 19 for more on this point.

[54]Freud's theory of projection may be found in his *Inhibitions, Symptoms, and Anxiety*, in the *Complete Works of Freud*, Standard Edition, 20 (1926).

[55]For example, see G. J. Barker-Benfield, *The Horrors of the Half-Known Life: Male Attitudes Towards Women and Sexuality in Nineteenth Century America* (New York, 1976). Another study which employs projection theory is Joel Kovel's *White Racism: A Psychohistory* (New York, 1970).

[56]See Smith-Rosenberg, "Beauty, the Beast, and the Militant Woman," pp. 562-84; Pivar, *Purity Crusade*, pp. 13-49.

[57]The danger of reducing history to individual psychopathological complexes is discussed in my "Pathology and Adjustment in Psycho-history: A Critique of the Erikson Model," *The Psychocultural Review*, I (Fall, 1977), 493-506.

[58]For instance, see Robert W. Fogel and Stanley L. Engerman, *Time on the Cross: The Economics of American Slavery* (Boston, 1974), pp. 131-37. Fogel and Engerman assume that the reader accepts the notion that if slaves can be shown to have been less promiscuous than is often assumed, the institution of slavery will be shown to have been less harsh than generally acknowledged (pp. 136-37). They assume that only when people are degraded will they act "promiscously." It never occurs to Fogel and Engerman to view the non-acceptance of middle-class white morality as a form of rebellion. If the data in *Time on the Cross* are correct, the real horror of slavery may prove to have been the slaves' adoption of middle-class morality and their concomitant rejection of sexual freedom (or promiscuity). See also Rosenberg, "Sexuality, Class and Role," p. 144.

[59]Among the best of these recent works is Bruce Laurie, "'Nothing on Impulse': Life Styles of Philadelphia Artisans, 1820-1850," *Labor History*, 15 (Summer, 1974), 337-66, esp. 344-52;

Herbert Gutman, "Work, Culture, and Society in Industrializing America, 1818-1919," *American Historical Review*, 78 (June, 1973), 531-88. See also Farber, *Guardians*, pp. 141-45.

[60]Both Gutman's and Laurie's studies cited in the previous note are excellent insofar as they attempt to deal with working-class ideology and attitudes toward work. Both, however, seem to shrink from discussing in depth working-class sexuality. A study which deals with nineteenth-century working-class sexuality, unfortunately for our purposes, concentrates upon German workers. See R. P. Neumann, "Industrialization," pp. 270-98.

An earlier version of this essay was presented at the Pacific Coast Branch Meeting of the American Historical Association in August 1975 at the University of California at Berkeley. I would like to thank Professor Robert P. Neuman of Amherst College for his suggestions.

"A NEW GENERATION OF WOMEN": PROGRESSIVE PSYCHIATRISTS AND THE HYPERSEXUAL FEMALE

ELIZABETH LUNBECK

In the early years of the twentieth century, a number of prominent American psychiatrists identified the hypersexual female, the willfully passionate woman who could not control her desires for sexual pleasure, as an issue of pressing medical concern. Psychiatrists diagnosed women whose sexuality they deemed abnormally aggressive as "psychopaths"; these women, they explained, suffered from an inborn condition for which there was no remedy save institutionalization. Borrowing the term "psychopathic" from the nosologies of their German counterparts, who began using it in the late nineteenth century to classify male deviants (including vagabonds, criminals, anarchists, revolutionaries, and reformers), American psychiatrists employed it to account for what many agreed was the problem of women's sexual excess. Psychiatrists early identified prostitutes and female juvenile delinquents, most of whom had been charged with immoral behavior, as psychopaths; soon, a variety of other young women whose sexuality violated medical and social conceptions of proper female deportment swelled their ranks. "New women" of the working class, these hypersexual psychopaths sought a sexual freedom unknown to their mothers. "A new generation of women has arrived," proclaimed one of them, Ethel Hancock, a twenty-one-year-old waitress, "and the wrong of Grandma's day is the right of today."[1]

Confronted by a revolution in sexual mores among working-class youth, psychiatrists, like other social investigators – sociologists, social workers, criminologists – turned to the problem of female immorality. Psychiatrists, like many others, ascribed the lax sexual etiquette of the time to the deterioration of women's

Feminist Studies 13, no. 3 (Fall 1987).

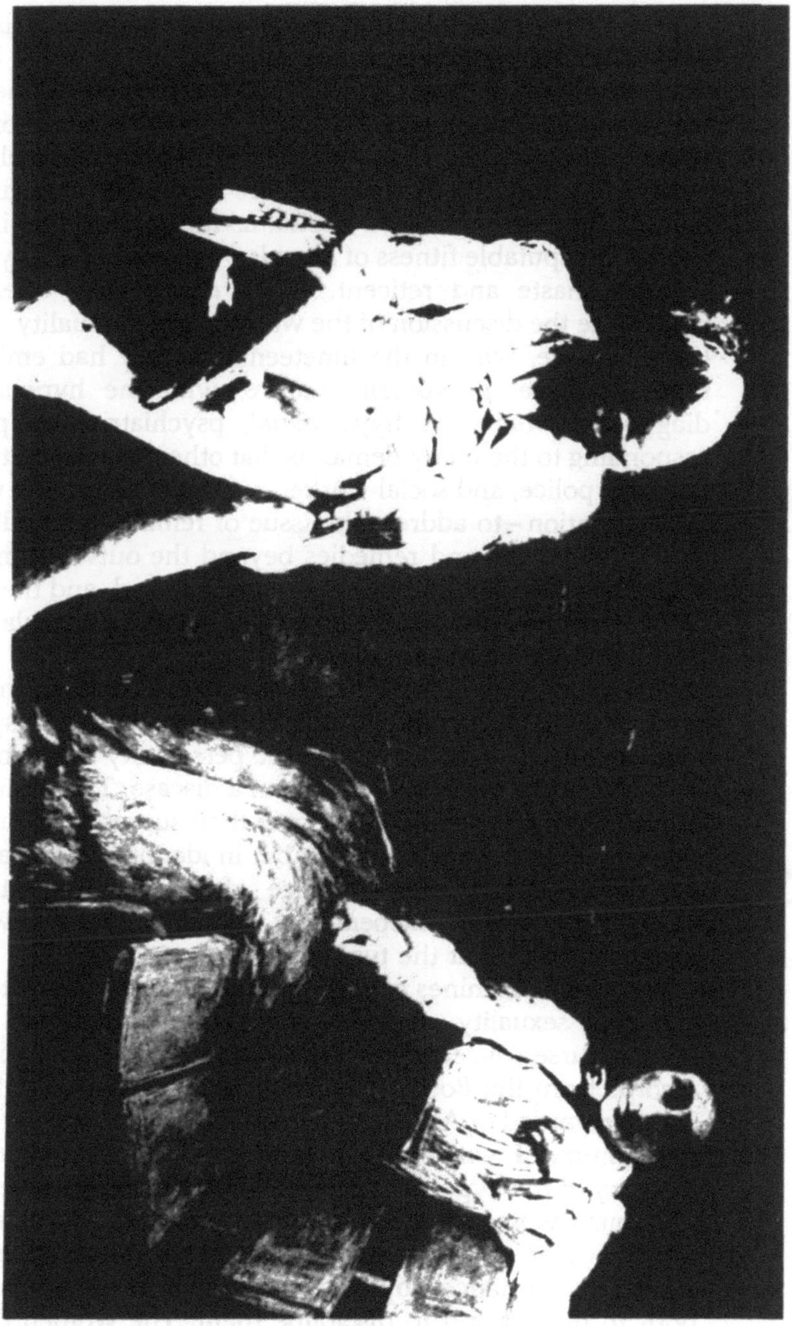

Forming the Fifth International, 1985. Acrylic on canvas, 78 x 120 inches. Collection of the artist. Photo by David Heinlein.

morals.[2] They explained that psychopathic hypersexuals, women who could not restrain their boundless desires, were to blame for slack sexual mores; men were at best the passive recipients or, at worst, the unwitting victims of their unwanted attentions.

In constructing the category of the female hypersexual, psychiatrists proclaimed themselves arbiters of rapidly changing sexual mores. They drew on their capital as medical experts in arguing for the indisputable fitness of an older Victorian morality that held women chaste and reticent. In so doing, they attempted to medicalize the discussion of the working girl's sexuality, to replace the prostitute, who in the nineteenth century had embodied all that was base in women's nature, with the hypersexual. In diagnosing women as hypersexual, psychiatrists in part were responding to the many demands that others placed on them – the families, police, and social workers who brought young women to their attention – to address the issue of female immorality and to find explanations and remedies beyond the outworn moral categories that saw the promiscuous woman as bad, and the sociological theory that cast her as a victim. Yet the particular solution psychiatrists chose – to diagnose these women as incurable psychopaths – was problematic. For these women manifested none of the usual symptoms of mental disorder, and psychiatrists readily conceded that psychopathic personality might be thought of as a conduct disorder rather than a disease. The significance of psychiatrists' intervention lies not in their success in controlling, or even defining, female sexuality, but in identifying and attempting to comprehend a social change of singular importance: the emergence of the independent, sexually assertive woman in American society at the turn of the century.

This essay examines a moment in the largely unwritten history of female sexuality when psychiatrists first attempted to control the discourse concerning women's erotic nature. Drawing on case records from the Boston Psychopathic Hospital, one of the most highly regarded of American mental hospitals in the early years of the century, I will examine how psychiatrists constructed the category of the hypersexual psychopath and explore the worlds of the young women they considered oversexed.[3] Psychiatrists saw these women as sick; middle-class social workers, bonded by gender but distanced by class, saw them as victims and sought both to protect and to discipline them. The women themselves fashioned their own interpretations of their predicaments from elements of both perspectives; they sometimes admitted, when pressed, to fears that they were not normal, that they were sick or bad, that they needed help and supervision. But they could also reject psychiatrists' and social workers' concerns altogether and argue for an end to the double standard of sexual morality that marked them as diseased. From this welter of confused perspectives a female voice emerged to challenge the strictures governing sexual conduct. This working-class voice was often halting and unsure. At times, however, it spoke with a strength and clarity rare in the annals of the historically invisible.

A RIGHTFUL ADOLESCENCE

Psychiatrists argued that the sexual natures and needs of young women and men differed fundamentally. A woman was by nature wholly sexual, her life colored by barely controllable sexual impulses that first surfaced at adolescence. Adolescence was a time of rapid physical and mental growth, of strong, conflicting emotions, of storm and stress for both sexes; if difficult for boys, it was treacherous for girls. Subject to the caprice of her developing physique, a growing girl was ever in danger of straying from the narrow path of respectability into promiscuity; indeed, the slightest sign of interest in boys or sex might set her on the road to ruin. The growing boy's course was less hazardous. Not burdened like a girl by the efflorescence of strong sexual impulses, he could celebrate their acquisition with ardor and evoke only the bemused tolerance of psychiatrists; the curiosity, experimentation, and satiation of desire that was symptomatic of gross defect in a girl was but the commendable manifestation of the boy's natural drive for self-expression and mastery. Psychiatrists held that social convention, which tolerated and even encouraged the fulfillment of male desire, only mirrored the immutable dictates of human nature. If it was for a girl once soiled, forever spoiled, while a boy could "sow an unusually large crop of wild oats," straighten up, and become a good citizen thereafter, this was the natural order of things. Men, unlike women, could weather a phase of intense sexual activity without breaking down under it; among men, psychiatrists agreed, "a separate standard of moral and sexual life" could and did prevail.[4]

In its recognition of female desire the double standard that psychiatrists championed differed from that of the Victorian era. Middle-class Victorian sexual ideology had set the passionlessness of women against the lustfulness of men, elevating the former and excusing the latter, with tacit tolerance of prostitution as a necessary social evil. Although they paid a high price in their renunciation of passion, Victorian women managed to turn this ideology to their advantage; trapped in a society that offered them little outside marriage, they fell back on their supposed passionlessness to gain a measure of control over sexual relations with their husbands and thus over the timing and number of their pregnancies.[5] Progressive psychiatrists, as they ceded some ground to women by recognizing their capacity for passion, stripped away from them all the protections Victorian ideology had offered. They not only overturned sexual Victorianism, but they reversed its equation of desire as well, casting women as sexual predators, men as sexual victims. If women wanted passion, they would give it to them with a vengeance.

Psychiatrists' recasting of the Victorian sexual drama is most starkly evident in their elaboration of the category of the hypersexual. Hypersexuality, like its elusive counterpoint, normal sexuality, first became apparent at adolescence. It was then that overdeveloped girls, girls who prematurely developed the womanly contours that so enfeebled male resolve, first began to constitute a real social menace. Upstanding men were absolutely unable to resist these young women. As psychiatrists related it, particularly attractive young women seduced many a hapless man over telephone lines, in automobiles, on public conveyances, and even in church; young temptresses led countless sailors astray. Invigorated by overwhelming desire, a young woman could haul a man through the windows of her residence or accost an innocent on the street and force him to submit, against his will, to intercourse on the spot! The city's abundant public places teemed with hypersexuals, ready to lure unsuspecting men into questionable establishments, to hire rooms for immoral purposes, to plague men with the demands of their insatiable immorality.[6]

Psychiatrists elaborated this theory of female desire as they confronted the sexual mores of a generation of working-class new women. These women, born between 1890 and 1905, were among the first to achieve for themselves some limited freedom from family obligations, some limited freedom to earn and spend, and some limited freedom to associate with whom they pleased – all freedoms we now see as the prerogatives of late adolescence. Juvenile experts, the psychologist G. Stanley Hall and the physician William Healy foremost among them, had only recently delineated adolescence as a socially and biologically constructed interlude between childhood and adulthood. Working-class boys, however, had been enjoying the privileges of adolescence for decades. For them, adolescence was a time to taste the pleasures of adulthood – independence, mastery, sexuality – without having to assume all its burdens. Parents who loosed boys from the bonds of the family economy as soon as they entered the workplace, together with juvenile authorities who tolerated the lapses of boys who went too far – who smoked, drank, or associated with fast companions – on the conviction that they could later go straight, smoothed the way for widespread acceptance of adolescent boyhood as an admittedly difficult but indisputably normal stage of life.[7] Adolescent girlhood was, by contrast, nearly unthinkable, the very phrase so oxymoronic in its coupling of the female sex with what was so essentially male that juvenile experts could barely imagine its contours. Female adolescence appears only fitfully in the works of Hall. On the one hand, he argues that women are by nature forever adolescent – dependent, childish, without ambition – and on the other hand, he advocates, in prose thick with sexual innuendo, that they forever teeter on the brink of knowledge and sexual maturity. In many other works, including Healy's, considerations of what might have been the pleasures of adolescent girlhood – growing independence, pride in a maturing body – are so conflated with the problem of juvenile delinquency as to make them one and the same; indeed, the girl who sought the independence that was a boy's by birthright was by her very desire delinquent. As parents and juvenile authorities conceived it, the years of a girl's life that corresponded to those of the boy's adolescence were filled with danger, not possibility. They were years in which she was to submerge, rather than to free, her yearnings for independence, years in which she was to reconcile herself to her dependence on men and the inevitability of marriage. They were years best avoided altogether; ideally, a girl would progress from childhood directly to the exalted state of motherhood.[8]

These young women of the early twentieth century were the

first to live in large numbers on their own in cities. They challenged, if only for a few precious years, the familiar, patriarchal paradigm that saw them moving from their fathers' to their husbands' homes. The rapid entrance of young women into the urban work force – into the new pink-collar clerical occupations, into factory work like candymaking, in which they had long predominated, and, to a lesser extent, into occupations like printing that had been the exclusive preserve of men – provided the context in which some of them staked their claim to a rightful adolescence. Living alone or in boardinghouses with others like themselves, working for meager wages, skimping on food to buy the fine clothing that conferred status and an air of sophistication, these young women, many country-bred, chose to participate fully in the life of the city. With little cash, without family obligations, and with few concerns for the future, they worked by day and pursued pleasure by night through the exciting commercial amusements – movies, dance halls, and theaters – that were just appearing on the urban scene. In these public, anonymous establishments, young women and their men, as they carried on the courtships formerly overseen by watchful parental and neighborly eyes, rewrote the code that governed their mutual relations. This code had long sanctioned sexual play – passionate kissing, petting, even intercourse – between young women and men who intended to marry.[9] After the turn of the century, some young women sought, with varying degrees of self-consciousness, to engage in the same sorts of intimacies with men they did not intend to marry.

SEXUAL ETHICS

Participating in the sexual sphere was no easy task. With no construction of respectability available to her, the working girl struggling to define a morality that would enable her to do more than sit alone in her room at night was frustrated at every turn by the seeming timeless equation of the working girl and the prostitute. Codified in countless late-nineteenth and early-twentieth-century investigations that found her virtue wanting, this equation was assuming new and damning resonances as reformers campaigning to eradicate the necessary evil once and for all transformed the prostitute from a pitiable yet redeemable fallen woman into a hardened predator, a spreader of vicious disease.[10] It was as well an equation to whose strictures she might be subject in her day-today dealings with men. Too often the working girl was taken for an easy mark, complained one woman who, because she had worn silk stockings to work one day, had suffered the taunts of her male workmates. Surely only a kept woman could afford such luxuries, they teased: "No one has anything on me," she shot back.[11]

The working girl seeking a good time and respectability was frustrated, too, by the restrictions of poverty. Many girls worked long hours to earn between six and eight dollars a week, barely enough to cover room, board, and carfare. To gain entrance to the movies, shows, and dances that were the stuff of working-class leisure, some of them who claimed respectable status – who did not, that is, consider themselves prostitutes – chose to bargain with sexual favors, ranging from flirtation to intercourse, exchanged for men's "treats" to entertainments. Others thought such exchanges unworthy of a self-respecting young woman. Yet the urban working-class view of sex as a commodity shaped the heterosexual relations of even those working girls who thought "treating" beneath them. The woman who did not want to give herself to a man knew she must refuse any favors or money he might proffer; as one woman, pregnant, out of work, and desperate, explained, "I never approved of taking money from men. It places you in their obligations." The nature of those obligations was well understood by all; they were nakedly manifest in the many cases where men paid women one or two dollars in exchange for intercourse. The implicit bargain that structured such exchanges – that sex came at a price, for men as well as women – allowed women some leverage in their dealings with the opposite sex, enabling them to extract something of value, whether cash or charity, in return for their favors. But the bargain also put the working girl at a disadvantage in her relations with men, for men knew women had little in the way of capital besides sex and taunted them with this knowledge. As one young woman, desperate for money, told social workers, "Time and time again I have had chances to go astray, large sums of money and flattering remarks." She offered as an example of such the fellow who wanted to give her fifteen dollars "to go to a room with him, but I told him money could not buy me, he had the wrong girl." She continued, "Then he asked me, 'would I go as a gift,' and I said no and not for charity either."[12]

If sex, or its promise, was the working girl's capital, to middle-class eyes it was capital she too readily squandered. It is hardly surprising that middle-class observers of the working-class sexual economy saw girls' behavior as promiscuous. Nor is it surprising that they focused on the dangers to which the young working woman was daily exposed: on her own in the anonymous metropolis, bereft of male protection, underpaid and overworked, the working girl was all too easy prey for male seducers, schemers, and white slavers. There was much that was true in this construction. Women in the case records I examined were often subject to exploitation at the hands of dishonest men; at least one woman was raped, by a man claiming to be an employment agent, as she looked for work in the city, and women regularly complained of having to rebuff unwanted advances.

Why, then, did psychiatrists and social workers absolve men of all blame? Why did women become the dangerous characters? And why did the sexual prowess of the young woman on her own assume such mythic proportions? When social workers reported that young women hauled men through windows, waylaid grocery boys, and tried to force unwilling, respectable young men to "sexual connection," they may have been reporting the facts as they were. It is more likely, however, that attraction, seduction, and conquest were reciprocal, if not, as some young women insisted, solely the work of men. The evolving conventions of working-class courtship celebrated easy familiarity between the sexes on the streets and in theaters and dance halls. The sexual behavior of working-class men was of little concern to social workers, who saw that women bore all the untoward consequences of their new sexual freedom. Ignorant of any means of birth control other than abortion (to which they often resorted), women faced the prospect of pregnancy with each encounter. Additionally, a man, free of the constraints of custom, family, and neighborhood, might renege on his promises, explicit or not, to support or marry a woman he impregnated. As one pregnant twenty-one-year-old domestic servant, abandoned by the man she had hoped would marry her, put it, "it is pretty mean of a fellow to get a girl into trouble and not to stand by her." Her only recourse was her vow "to make it hard for him," uttered "rather vindictively" in the social workers' estimation. This woman's predicament pointedly illustrates that an urban revolution in sexual mores might render women vulnerable to new forms of exploitation.[13]

Still, this concern for young women's vulnerability does not fully account for the fact that psychiatrists and social workers blamed girls, not boys; women, not men. Nor does it explain why they cast the problem in terms of the "uncontrolled sex impulses" of one sex and not the other. Psychiatrists could understand the girl from a bad home who got into trouble. Her upbringing poor and her material pleasures few, this girl – the classic delinquent – traded favors for money. Material need, not passion, motivated her; most likely she felt no passion at all, like the sexually active young woman whom psychiatrists judged merely delinquent, not psychopathic, because, as she told them, she was "entirely without sexual feeling." The woman who did *not* receive money in exchange for her favors, who was "attracted to such acts by sexual passion alone," psychiatrists were at a loss to explain. Men were expected to seek sexual pleasure; indeed, a man's *failure* to do so might earn for him the designation psychopathic. It was, on the other hand, unseemly but increasingly all too common for a woman forthrightly to pursue sexual fulfillment. Women, according to conventional wisdom, properly relied on intrigue and feminine wile to attain their ends; men, on a "direct and open procedure," as one commentator put it. Women should be sly and devious, should seduce and tease. A woman who openly avowed passion, who could observe of her sexual exploits, like one putative psychopath, that "life is too short to worry. If you don't enjoy this life you might as well be dead," was, in psychiatrists' eyes, altogether without moral sensibility, altogether inexplicable, altogether pathological.[14]

The psychopath's forthright sexuality was the most visible and disturbing manifestation of her social autonomy; the right to actively seek sexual fulfillment was but the most salient of male prerogatives she assumed. She wanted the freedom to earn and spend, like a man, free of supervision; she wanted to enjoy the pleasures of the city without having her character impugned; she wanted to make her own choices and live independently. Her independence of what many held were the proper and fitting constraints of family and home was nearly as troubling as her hypersexuality. Many hypersexuals had nothing to do with their families. Employed in factories or as domestic servants they enjoyed a freedom from adult supervision that many social commentators agreed was the source of their troubles. Others, in their twenties or thirties, eschewed marriage and chose instead to work and to live singly or with other women. To be sure, some of the young women psychiatrists diagnosed psychopathic looked forward to becoming respectable wives and mothers. One unmarried mother, for example, told psychiatrists she was "not worried about the morality of her act as many other young women have gotten into the same trouble and they have turned out alright and later established good homes."[15] But others rejected the conventional female lifeprint that saw a woman passing from her father to her husband.

The concern over female autonomy that was implicit in the category of hypersexuality helps explain why psychiatrists considered failure to engage in heterosexual courtship – whether simple lack of interest or overtly lesbian behavior – just as psychopathic as a woman's too vigorous exercise of her seductive powers. The "spark of womanliness," for example, glowed but feebly in one psychopathic woman who lacked "ordinary feminine charm and appeal." Wrote one of the hospital's psychiatrists: "It would be difficult to imagine . . . even the most accomplished Lothario successfully drawing her into a flirtation or being able to keep a sustained interest in the pursuit." A more explicit rejection of heterosexuality, like that of a woman who lived with a female companion and questioned the institution of marriage, might mark a woman psychopathic as well. This twenty-year-old, who claimed that she had "never cared for boys" and had "never had anything to do with them," informed psychiatrists she did not intend to marry. Asked to account for this, she explained: "You don't know what you are getting into. It is just as well to live single and be happy. From what I have seen, they don't always get along in marriage." Twenty-eight-year-old Rose Butler, too, preferred "single blessedness." She did not lack offers; indeed, it seemed to her that men were "like flies around a sugar bowl, when they see a girl." Troubled by her indifference to men, one psychiatrist confronted her: "On the whole you have not much use for men?" Smiling slyly, she replied: "As much as I have for women." Butler turned the tables on psychiatrists, asserting cheekily that "Adam made woman sin. They say it was Eve who gave him the apple, but he did not have to bite into it."[16]

The psychopath's disturbing assumption of male prerogative was carried to its literal extreme in the case of Julia Brown, alias Alfred Mansfield, a lesbian cross-dresser who for twelve years had lived as a man – smoking a pipe, drinking whiskey regularly, sporting men's suits, working as a printer, and, most puzzling to psychiatrists, escorting young women to dances, suppers, and shows. Brown originally adopted male attire expecting "to find it easier to get work and better pay as a man." But, she admitted to social workers, "I think I really did it because I was so crazy about the girls." She "got more pleasure in making love to women than she ever did in having men make love to her," she told psychiatrists. To their puzzled query as to how she avoided the problem of matrimony, she voiced their worst fears, averring that "all women cared for was a good time, they did not want to get married." The sexual activities of these women who refused to seduce men were of little interest to psychiatrists, who focused instead on their gender-inappropriate independence. Before the mid-twenties, psychiatrists focused on the lesbian's supposed masculinity, not her sexual object choice; the lesbian's refusal to court men, not her preference for women, marked her as a sexual deviant.[17]

A MEDICAL DIAGNOSIS FOR IMMORALITY

It was in this context of growing concern over female independence and sexual deviance that psychiatrists settled on psychopathic personality as an explanation for female immorality. Many correctional and psychiatric experts had earlier assumed that defective intelligence would prove responsible for immorality. Psychiatrists first considered a diagnosis of feebleminded, which could be established with certainty and precision, when faced with immoral behavior, and reformers cited feeblemindedness as the cause of prostitution until it became clear that the scientific tests that were to have proven prostitutes defective instead demonstrated they were normal. Many sexual delinquents, like prostitutes, scored too high on mental tests to be considered feebleminded, and they, too, rarely manifested any of the usual signs of mental disease. Psychiatrists observed that in contrast to the many feebleminded people they saw, the majority of psychopathic girls "rated high from an intellectual point of view." But if immoral women were too intelligent to be feebleminded, they were still too defective to be normal. Psychiatrists argued that they belonged to a group of subnormal individuals that intelligence tests were powerless to identify. The diagnosis of psychopathic personality satisfied their search for a medical diagnosis for immorality.[18]

The women whom psychiatrists diagnosed as psychopaths at the Boston Psychopathic Hospital were overwhelmingly young (75 percent were younger than twenty-one), single, native-born whites. One-half were Protestant, one-third were Catholic, and the rest were Jewish. Although a few worked at middle-class occupations, such as teaching or office work, most, if employed at all, worked in factories or as domestic servants. Families, police, or courts committed one-half of them to the Boston Psychopathic Hospital for a variety of reasons; state social workers, or visitors, committed the rest.

Twenty-two-year-old Lillian Thomas's background, sexual behavior, and path to the hospital are typical. Thomas lived on her own in a home for young working girls. Her ties to her family had been severed long before; at age ten she had come under the care of the city as a neglected child. Court workers placed her with a woman who "looked after her very carefully and would not allow young men to call on her regularly." In her eighteenth year Thomas began living on her own, working as a waitress and "discouraging advances from young men for fear they might lead her into temptations." Within the year, however, she fell in love with a man she judged honorable and agreed to "illicit relations" with him. Finding herself pregnant, she considered his proposal of marriage. But she discovered he drank and, she told psychiatrists, she "preferred the alternative of living single and fighting out her own battle rather than being the wife of a drunkard." Thomas entered a home for expectant single women; one month after her boy's birth the matron of the home had her committed to the hospital to determine whether she was capable of caring for him. Social workers noted that Thomas's reputation was less than exemplary. At her previous lodgings she had been accused of entertaining men in her room at night; she "went often to dances and came home very late"; one man told them that she "could make up to men quicker than any girl he knew"; and, the case record notes portentously, "it is said she was discharged from one restaurant for underchecking accounts to men."[19]

Thomas was a single working woman who adhered to a standard of sexual morality that many working-class women and men lived by, a standard that sanctioned sexual relations between those who intended to marry. Her only mistake, and the chief evidence of her hypersexuality, lay in withdrawing from the impending compact. Many of the other women committed to the hospital by their families, police, or courts, had, like Thomas, long been on their own. Some had run away from intolerable family situations, others had been orphaned, and still others, in their late twenties and early thirties, had chosen not to marry. Many lived in boardinghouses; in some cases the matrons of these homes, observing behavior they judged either bizarre or promiscuous, petitioned to have them committed to the hospital. The failed suicide attempts of lonely and despondent young women brought a few others under psychiatrists' purview; family members, deeming the behavior of a daughter or sister inappropriate, committed still other women.

The other group of women diagnosed as psychopathic were "state charges" brought to the Boston Psychopathic Hospital for observation as to their sanity. Courts had already found these girls delinquent, primarily on the basis of their sexual behavior, and had committed them to the care of the State Industrial School at Lancaster, Massachusetts. Many of their parents, underemployed and alcoholic, burdened with large families (many of these girls had six or seven siblings) they could barely support, had originally petitioned for their commitment because they could not control them. Their daughters, they complained, went with undesirable companions, were on the streets at all hours, had immoral relations with boys, and, in general, ran wild. Some of this behavior, like taking to the streets, was a form of protest against overly strict parental control. Many widowed fathers, for example, expected their young daughters to keep house for them, prepare their meals, and wait on them as their wives had; many mothers expected daughters to perform heavy household labor – laundry, scrubbing, cleaning – as well as to care for younger siblings. Some of it, too, was textbook delinquent behavior; more than a few girls had consented to intercourse in exchange for various sums of cash, ranging from twenty-five cents for sex among the barrels at a beach resort to fifteen dollars – a substantial sum – for six episodes in a cheap hotel. But the relatively innocuous driving in automobiles with immoral persons; the frequenting of pool halls, dance halls, and saloons; the carousing with evil-minded girls and boys; and the casual sexual play that figured so prominently in parental and professional accounts of girls gone wrong point to the larger battle being waged between parents and daughters, between middle-class professionals and working-class girls, over the nature of working-class adolescent girlhood. Could a girl make her own life the same as a boy? To parents who expected their adolescent daughters to refrain from any sort of sexual activity, to hand over their wages without protest, and to assume the household duties of a wife, the girl who strayed undermined not only her own reputation but the fragile family economy, which depended on her services, as well. Her transgressions, then, provided sufficient cause for commitment to reform school.

At Lancaster, delinquent girls were subjected to a heavy dose of domestic service – cooking, cleaning, sewing – designed to inculcate industrious habits in the slack and shiftless while exposing them to the pleasures of true domesticity. These pleasures, though, would forever remain beyond the reach of girls for whom domesticity was, and would always be, sheer drudgery. Further, the conditions under which they were paroled from Lancaster, as domestic servants in private homes, were sufficiently loathsome to quell any faintly felt domestic yearnings. State social workers justified the placement of young girls as domestic servants by arguing that only in private homes could troublesome girls be constantly supervised. Occupations other than housework were too fraught with peril for young women already convicted of immorality, they argued; such occupations as waitressing or factory work afforded too many enticing opportunities. As a visitor said authoritatively, discussing one girl's placement: "I do not think she should wait on table. It would lead to prostitution."[20]

As domestic servants, many girls began anew with their employers the sorts of battles that had landed them in reform school in the first place. The city's pleasure palaces beckoned, and lonely, underpaid, and overworked girls saw little reason to resist their allure. Many ran away from their employers for short periods during which they roamed the streets and indulged their cravings for music, dancing, and male companionship. Still worse, the private homes in which they were placed could themselves be problematic, for they offered ample opportunities for secret assignations with employers' husbands and sons. The matron of one home, for example, found her nineteen-year-old domestic servant clad, only in a kimono, perched on the lap of her son, a Harvard student. Another woman dismissed her state charge after she heard her husband suggest they have sex. And the girl who became pregnant after two years of sexual relations with her employer's thirty-five-year-old son was but one of many young women whose behavior mocked social workers' earnest efforts to ensconce them within the confines of a safe domesticity.[21]

The state social workers who committed these "Burleigh girls" – girls supervised by Edith Burleigh, superintendent of the Girls' Parole Department, and her staff of twelve visitors – deemed them bad tempered, irritable, untruthful, and saucy and complained of their waywardness and petty thievery.[22] Yet psychiatrists, charmed yet baffled by their good-natured, pleasant, and essentially normal dispositions, could find nothing remarkable in the mental examinations of most of them. As a psychiatrist observed in one case, "the contrast between the impression gained by the examination of the girl, and the report as given by the Parole Department is rather striking." Remarked another: "It does not seem possible that everyone who goes to Lancaster can be surly, sullen, have outbursts of temper, etc. etc. Certainly we never see a case whose description doesn't have nearly all those adjectives. On the whole when they come here they behave pretty well." Judging them "perfectly attractive sorts of girls," psychiatrists nevertheless diagnosed them as psychopathic, noting that this was "the group to which most of Miss Burleigh's girls belong."[23]

The case history of eighteen-year-old Gertrude Blackstone is similar to those of the most troublesome and impulsive state girls psychiatrists considered psychopathic. Social workers noted that from earliest childhood, Blackstone had been a persistent liar who stole repeatedly, went with bad companions, and, in general, ran wild. Unable to control her, her widowed father had her committed to the care of the state. She proved unsatisfactory in each of the five homes to which state workers sent her. "Lazy, slack, and shiftless about her work," she also told vulgar stories to the children in these homes and continued to steal. Committed to Lancaster after confessing to immoral relations with two men, Blackstone, although "bad tempered and saucy at times," proved "not a difficult girl." She was paroled at home and allowed to study shorthand and typewriting. But she soon became "saucy, lazy and independent" and was placed out to do housework. At this point Blackstone's real trouble began. She paid visits to disreputable families, was immoral on several occasions, and stole from her employer. Next, she married a man whom social workers judged "poor stuff," quickly left him, began to work as a waitress and go out with other men. Eventually she was returned to reform school. Noting that she was "good natured, pleasant company, but deceitful and unreliable," Burleigh had her committed to the Boston Psychopathic Hospital for observation. She "seems very much fascinated by the life of prostitutes," Burleigh noted. "Enjoys and seeks the attention of men whom she knows to be not good and voluntarily talks about the 'white slave traffic.'" Burleigh closed her report with the observation that Blackstone "says she cannot see the use of living unless you can live as you wish."[24]

For girls like Gertrude Blackstone, the widely shared desire to live life as they wished was well-nigh unattainable. Once identified as delinquent and enmeshed in the state's agencies of social and moral reform, they enjoyed few opportunities and had few choices. Confronted with the bleak reality of these girls' lives – the isolation, the meager wages, the endless round of domestic duties – psychiatrists worried that "a great many of these people don't have enough decent amusement." But the "sport, basketball and such things" they hoped to substitute for the moving pictures, automobiles, and dance halls that they saw as sources of the girls' immorality would hardly have appealed to psychopaths, like one Violet, whose recreational tastes ran to "noisy, frolicking times with jazz music, dancing and loud laughter," or to those like the fifteen-year-old who preferred "dancing and nice clothes and amusements of rather low character" to "interest in the healthy pursuits of life." The wholesome entertainments social workers advocated – the church concerts, choir rehearsals, and chaperoned dances – elicited only the disdain of girls who frequented dance halls, palm gardens, and moving picture shows. The much-vaunted young man of good reputation, who would carry on a courtship "by bi-weekly letters and semi-yearly visits," stood little chance of engaging their interest.[25]

COMPETING IMMORALITIES

Psychiatrists and social workers did not distinguish among the many varieties of female sexual activity they subsumed under the rubric of immorality. In diagnosing women whose behavior appeared to violate accepted moral standards – girls who rode unchaperoned in automobiles with young men or who engaged them in lewd telephone conversations, as well as those who accepted money in exchange for intercourse – psychiatrists pointed to the prostitute, the archetypal sexually active woman, with whose sordid activities and fallen state they identified all sexual activity outside marriage. So resonant with associations of voracious sexuality and irredeemable immorality was the prostitute that psychiatrists had only to invoke her for a young woman's sexual expression to be transformed into hypersexuality. The distinction between the young woman who received indecent letters from men and the prostitute who received money was of little consequence; psychiatrists assumed that reception of the former led inexorably to reception of the latter.

Girls and women who readily admitted to their uncontrollable sexual desires conformed to psychiatric notions of hypersexuality. Theresa Beauvais, for example, confessed "that she could not control herself with respect to sex relations." Bessie Dunston "seemed thoroughly ashamed" of the activities that had resulted in her pregnancy "but said she could not seem to help it, the desire was so strong." Other young women admitted the "temptations of sex were too much" for them, that they "did not have the strength to decline," and that they were "powerless to resist" themselves. One girl's declaration that she would choose to be shut up in an institution could she not "live the life" exemplified the defiantly immoral sexuality psychiatrists considered psychopathic.[26]

These women, however emblematic their declarations, comprised a minority. More commonly, women asserted they were not hypersexual and objected that the psychiatrists and social workers examining them assumed only the worst. Nineteen-year-old Ethel Townson, for example, admitted to a social worker that she had "acted very foolishly" but argued she had "not gone to the extremes as perhaps you and a good many others think." Never had she been, she protested, "so overwhelming with joy to devote my time to such indiscriminate lewdness." "I am no– – –," she added, "for if I had ever been why should I ever be in want of money? I would have lots of clothes and an apartment." She was instead a girl having difficulty finding work. Psychiatrists argued to nineteen-year-old Alice Lawson that her difficulties resulted from her bad temper and sexual activities. She disagreed, telling them all her "troubles started with the social workers. They imagine a whole lot." "They say you are fond of boys," a psychiatrist teasingly challenged her. "I like boys but I am not crazy about them," she replied. "It is only nature" to be fond of men, contended another girl. "Are you so fond of them that you cannot get along without them?" a doctor queried. "No," she conceded, "I could get along without them." These girls argued that their activities were normal. A young girl naturally would, as one said, want "to be on the go, i.e. to see life, movies, young men and dances." But in the girls' activities, however limited, social workers saw only nascent immorality.[27]

Psychiatrists' and social workers' conceptions of respectable, moral behavior rigidly divided good from bad women. The specter of the prostitute informed their prescriptions about girls' proper dress and deportment. To social workers, working girls who spent their meager incomes on frivolous ribbons and silk stockings and who purchased clothing on installment plans were no better than the "dolled-up" psychopathic prostitutes who found satisfaction in lavish personal adornment, plucking and penciling their eyebrows, and flaunting their wares as they strutted about in striking, cheap-rich styles of dress. But flashy dress, so tellingly tawdry to middle-class eyes, was the norm among working girls. Fine clothing compensated for the daily drudgery of work; it could bolster self-esteem flagging under the double burden of overwork and underpay; it could also enhance a young woman's desirability in the marketplace of pleasures. Social workers held that the working girl's meager wages were best allotted to the necessities, not the frivolities, of life; the claim of room and board on a young woman's wages, according to their calculus of economic rationality, was prior to that of clothing. Social workers might complain that working girls had "no idea of the value of money," but working girls knew better; money invested in clothes was money well spent, capable of yielding ample returns.[28]

Many observers agreed that girls' sartorial desires and recreational tastes exposed them to moral dangers. Young women may have made light of these concerns, but they were not necessarily inappropriate. As young women moved more visibly into the public sphere, they confronted new dangers as well as new opportunities. Many knew nothing of sex – its mechanics, its pleasures – until knowledge was forced on them. As one twenty-five-year-old woman who became pregnant after her first experience with men, automobiles, and drink ruefully noted, "I thought a few cigarettes, one or two cocktails were harmless, that a girl could always take care of herself, and there I was mistaken." Women did, however, rightfully object to the narrow construction of respectability that rigidly separated good from bad women, that blurred the distinction between prostitution and sexual activity outside marriage, and that saw in this woman's pregnancy – even though, as she emphasized, "I never had anything to do with men except that once" – the "start of a new career."[29]

It was the readiness of psychiatrists and social workers to forever consign them, on the slightest of evidence, to the ranks of the promiscuous that young women found so irksome. Psychiatrists measured them against a middle-class moral code, a code that ensured that the middle-class woman would not squander her virtue, her most marketable of assets. But the strict morality they advocated held little appeal for working girls for whom a willingness to play fast was of equal value to the middle-class girl's chastity. A number of putative psychopaths struggled to define standards of sexual morality appropriate to the circumstances of their lives. Psychiatrists were puzzled that they could entertain any real self-respect – testified to in some cases by girls' refusal to accept money for their irregularities – while engaging in relations the psychiatrists judged promiscuous.[30] Yet this distinction was central to these women who were trying to forge another standard of sexual morality. They objected to the double standard that marked them defective. "Do you think there will ever be equality of sex, one moral standard for both?" Ethel Hancock, the "immoral" woman who heralded the arrival of a new generation of women, demanded of Mary C. Jarrett, the head of the Social Service at the hospital. "If so, I hope it comes in my day, I would be as good as a bad man, which is twice as good as a virtuous woman. Wouldn't it be great to do just as one pleased?" In response, psychiatrists warned that for women "a little knowledge is dangerous thing" and urged them not to question the dictates of conventional morality. Jarrett had warned Hancock not to "read or discuss on any subject, especially sex, that [she] did not understand and had not the education and intelligence to grasp in just the manner the author intended." Yet young women did think about sex in spite of experts' warnings. Hancock's declaration that she would "simply love it, revel in it" could she indulge her desires and maintain respectability at the same time only highlighted how weakened were the foundations of conventional morality. Though she added that her revelry would be "not as a pig wallows in swill – because I'd surely have some good desires," her intentions were clear. And Rose Talbot's admission that she had "read Casqueline's (I think it is spelled) *Truth about Woman* and Havelock Ellis' *Psychology of Sex* which," she wrote, "quite knocked all my good resolutions to smash," only underlined the dangers of free thinking. "So you see it is not wicked to have sexual intercourse with other men than your husband. It is simply not the fashion."[31]

Even as they decried the injustices of the double standard, these women fell back on its very distinctions as they assessed their own behavior. Many lived by moral codes structured, like those of the largely female social workers, around considerations of good and bad. But they defined good behavior far more broadly than social workers; and their respectability was a complex thing, a measure not of chastity but of self-respect.

Social workers and their charges, for example, agreed that a woman could "go wrong" or "to the bad." While these phrases signified to social workers a debased state from which a girl could never recover, to the young women they denoted a process that could be reversed at any point. A girl could start to go to the bad and stop; one, for example, jilted by the lover whom she had hoped to marry, thought of herself as a now-respectable woman who had once "started to go wrong."[32] "Going wrong" had as much to do with a woman's attitude as with her activities; it was not the social fact of her surrender to temptation, whether occasioned by need or passion, that signified a woman's descent into debasement but, rather, the discouraged state of mind that ofttimes preceded it. Although she might stray, a respectable young woman only became truly bad, in the idiom of the working class, when she succumbed to despondency and thought of herself as bad.

From this female working-class perspective, material need was a familiar culprit. Young women implored social workers to confront this, but the latter were indifferent to economic arguments.

Rose Butler, a highly paid compositor, emphasized that she was not fast nor did she wish to be. She pointed out, however, familiar as she was with the privations of single womanhood, that need could sorely tempt a girl: "Why is it girls get discouraged? Why do girls get tired of trying? Why should a girl be befriended and then scorned and snubbed and squashed when she does try? I have come to the point where I don't blame a girl to get discouraged." Similarly, a twenty-year-old tried to impress upon social workers that desperate circumstances like hers – for the past two years she had owned barely any clothes – "would drive anyone to the bad, no work, no money, and nothing to wear."[33] The road to ruin, then, could begin with discouragement and end with self-respect and reputation lost.

At the same time, a woman could salvage her self-respect by dint of determined hard work. Self-respect regained, she could reclaim respectability, which pulled powerfully even on those women who most brazenly flouted its strictures. Ethel Townson, whose breezy nonchalance appeared the embodiment of the hypersexual's disdain for morality, responded to its call. After leaving home at age fifteen, Townson settled into a life of visiting cafes, going with men, tangling with police, and working but irregularly. Social workers judged her sullen, uncommunicative, and defiant. On one occasion she informed them ominously that she had "learned a great deal in the past few days"; on another she announced her intention to secure an abortion, claiming "quite calmly" that "lots of girls get in the same box and take the same way out." Yet Townson, for all her bravado, admitted something was wrong. "I can't control myself when I am once started," she wrote. "I do my self really know there is something the matter with me and I do want to grow and be a respectful young woman." Ethel Hancock, too, sought respectability. Sexual relations with her first husband disgusted her, she confided to social workers; it was only with her next husband, with whom she was not much in love, that she had experienced "strong sexual desires." Separated from him by a bitter quarrel, Hancock began living as a single woman, working as a waitress in a restaurant with a "fast crowd of girls." She quickly and deliberately went to the bad, she told social workers. On one occasion she went with her workmates to a sporty place but left, intoxicated and disgusted, when their unspecified sexual debauches began, and on another she was found with a man in her room in the early hours of the morning by the matron of the home in which she lived. It seemed to psychiatrists that Hancock did not take her many transgressions very seriously. But, over the course of her five-year epistolary relationship with social worker Mary Jarrett, Hancock struggled to make good. "It seems as if I'm always doing some fool thing and the harder I try the more of a muddle I get in," she observed. "I have not yet learned self control, not even a wee bit. Goodness knows I try hard enough." She wrote triumphantly to another social worker: "Oh, my dear, you can't imagine how proud I am to be able to write that I've actually been good for two whole weeks." Hancock desperately sought respectability. Her lament – "I've been so dreadfully bad and I will truly do something big if I can make something proud of out of my comparatively wretched life" – was echoed in those of the otherwise confident young women who found it difficult to manage the psychic conflicts their unconventional behavior engendered.[34]

Hancock did make good, although, as she put it, only "by force of circumstance." Working as a telegrapher at Western Union, she could find "no time at all for mere masculine sex." She derived some satisfaction from the knowledge, gained through experience, that she could "start out at anytime and make a good living" for herself. Yet she still wished – "when I am up to devilry," she added, "mischief is too mild" – she could "give rein to all [her] evil desires" without incurring the wrath of social workers.[35] Hancock's repentance redeemed her in social workers' eyes. As they told her tale – her fall, her struggle, her triumph – they cast her as both offender and victim. Both were familiar roles; the prostitute had played the two well. Need, bad fortune, poor company – all led women astray, all fit neatly within social workers' moral universe. True, this construction of Hancock's story overlooked her willful sexual experimentation, her professions of desire, and her own interpretation of her successful struggle for respectability as one in which she had paid an almost unacceptably high price; but the final, favorable outcome allowed social workers to mold it to fit the conventions of a familiar genre, that of the fallen woman redeemed through the timely, though lengthy, intervention of middle-class female rescuers. In casting hypersexuals as prostitutes, then, social workers were not just relegating them to the nether reaches of the moral spectrum but rendering them familiar as well.

The prostitute, though deplorable, was at least a known quantity. The young women who celebrated the pleasures of sex free of the moderating influence of moral concerns or social context–who, that is, perfectly exemplified the psychiatric notion of the hypersexual–were, by contrast, women wholly outside social workers' and psychiatrists' moral universe. Simple declarations of erotic desire unmediated by morality stunned them into silence. Prudence Walker, for example, a nineteen-year-old with a long history of sexual exploits, followed her desires even as they led her into trouble. "I must have someone all the time to love me," she told social workers. Sometimes, she confessed, "I get so excited that I don't know what to do–and it's then I consent to the things I do and have done." She had no excuse to offer "except the old one–that we don't know what we do–in that condition." In a similar vein, eighteen-year-old Helen Perkins wrote to a friend of her latest adventure: "The old saying is go as far as you like the Sky is the limit But Jee I think we have gone our limit. don't you?" She had "fallen in love" with a man who had come to repair the furnace in the house she occupied. "Of course you know what that means. I was so God Dam hot that I didn't know weather I was going home or to hell. I suppose you got yours from Fred," she added generously. "I hope so anyway." Psychiatrists and social workers focused on sexual practice, not pleasure. They were uncharacteristically reticent when confronted with evidence of the latter, tacit recognition, perhaps, that these declarations of female desire were, indeed, an altogether new thing.[36]

If white immorality was a symptom of disease, black immorality, on the other hand, was entirely normal. "On the whole I have been very chary in making the diagnosis of psychopathic personality in these colored girls," one psychiatrist explained. "The level of the negro regarding conduct, using that term in the broad sense, is decidedly different [from] the conduct of the white." Psychiatrists contended that the fooling with boys that was a definite symptom of psychopathy in white girls was in blacks only the expression of the natural immorality of the race. A "normal negress" was unintelligent but high spirited, and her immorality could be shrugged off with the assurance that there was "nothing abnormal about her delinquencies. Some of us get caught, some do not."[37] Adding a psychiatric twist to a very old set of beliefs concerning the sexual nature of black women, psychiatrists diagnosed as normal those with histories every bit as flamboyant as the supposedly psychopathic whites. Only black women whose immorality was of such proportions that it offended even the low standards of their race were psychopathic. Thus, the psychiatrist had to determine first of all whether a woman was "normal for her race." The sexual ethics of blacks, for example, "for thousands of years [had] been other and peculiar"; it was questionable whether they could "get on under the marriage conventions of the Aryan race." One psychiatrist's cautionary admonition that immoderate sexual behavior could not be "merely racial" because "not every member of the race does this sort of thing" fell on deaf ears.[38]

It was a strange disease indeed that so respected social convention. Yet psychiatrists were firm in their conviction that psychopathic personality was an inborn and incurable condition. Unlike "simple" delinquents, who were "perfectly able to do otherwise if they wish" and who could learn from experience, the inborn defects of the psychopath rendered her unable to refrain from misdeeds. Some psychopaths thought differently, acknowledging their delinquent behavior but attributing it to poor upbringing, not inborn taint. Their mothers had been unable to care for them properly, several girls told psychiatrists; no one had taught them right living. Others, like Alice Lawson, insisted there was nothing at all wrong with them. As Lawson emphasized: "There is not a thing the matter with me. I eat and sleep well. I am perfectly normal. I have no hallucinations, illusions or delusions." She implored doctors to release her. "I am sure shutting a girl up – shutting her away from civilization does not help the girl any."[39]

Some young women rejected not only psychiatrists' etiologies but their pessimistic prognoses as well. They promised they would make good if psychiatrists would give them their freedom. But the policies of the parole department and social workers' distrust of the world of work ensured they would be trained for little. "There are a number of things I should like to do," one young woman told the psychiatrists "but there is only one thing I will be able to do, and that is to go back to housework. I am very fond of study, and I should like to study more." Another said that she "wanted to do something different from housework, such as in an office of some kind," but added, "I don't think I am educated enough." Alice Lawson, too, did not want to do housework. "What else can you do?" one psychiatrist queried. "There are lots of things a girl can do besides housework," Lawson countered, but to the psychiatrist's challenge, "What else can you do?" she could only reply, "Can't I wait on table?" "What else?" he demanded. "I have not thought of anything else," she feebly replied.[40]

Psychiatrists ridiculed these women's aspirations and made light of their resolve to go straight. The endeavors of Yvette Gagnon, a newspaper editor who had "many extreme ideas as to women's rights" and who was writing a book entitled "Daughters of Tomorrow," only testified, psychiatrists asserted, to "her delusional insanity re her mental genius in the art of book writing." Psychiatrists consigned these women, endowed with boundless sexual desire and limited occupational skills, to futures circumscribed by their sexuality. As a psychiatrist confidently predicted of one young woman, "I can see her becoming a manic-depressive or a prostitute."[41]

Although psychiatrists proposed that all psychopaths be segregated in rural colonies, they realized that this was easier proclaimed than accomplished. First, they would never be able to ensnare the many psychopaths running wild in their communities. Large numbers of defectives, "stunningly asocial in conduct," would "never see an institution." Second, the psychopaths that psychiatrists were able to supervise temporarily they could not commit as insane; a diagnosis of psychopathic personality was insufficient grounds for long-term commitment to a mental hospital. Psychiatrists duly released most of the women they diagnosed as psychopaths. They returned Miss Burleigh's girls to her; most of them continued to work as domestics until age twenty-one, when they gained their freedom. The rest gained their freedom immediately.[42]

In the twenties, as the sexual revolution reached the ranks of the middle class, and as behavior that psychiatrists labeled hypersexual became more prevalent and less easily ascribed to a deviant working-class minority, psychiatrists' interest in hypersexuality flagged. The sexual psychopath of the late twenties and beyond was male and most often homosexual; rapists, child molesters, and other sex offenders displaced working-class women as objects of psychiatric attention. As psychiatrists adjusted their theories to new sexual mores, they championed a sanitized heterosexuality that could be safely contained within marriage. Indeed, psychiatrists transformed the passion that had been such a mark of deviance into the very criterion of normality. Frigidity, not its obverse, marked the deviant woman; the lesbian, the all-too-independent woman who rejected men and patriarchy altogther, inherited the mantle of sexual deviance from the hypersexual who, however worthy of contempt, at least had played the game. As the hypersexual faded, the lesbian became the exemplar of female sexuality gone awry.[43]

It is possible to see in psychiatrists' rendering of the hypersexual an exemplary instance of Michel Foucault's suggestive observation that the science of sexuality has functioned as the *ars erotica* of the Western world. In the guise of a decent positivism, Foucault argues, the late-nineteenth-century psychiatrists—Richard Krafft-Ebing, Auguste Tardieu, Havelock Ellis—who recorded and classified the manifold forms human sexual desire assumed, inadvertently created "a great archive of the pleasures of sex." There was pleasure to be derived from the very creating of this archive, Foucault goes on; the "obligatory and exhaustive confessions" psychiatrists elicited, and, we might add, the subjects from whom they were drawn, could themselves stimulate and titillate.[44]

The confrontations between psychiatrists and the young women they deemed hypersexual partook, at times, of the erotic. On at least one occasion a psychiatrist, dismayed at seeing his colleagues succumb to the blandishments of a particularly attractive young woman, burst out: "You all say give her a chance. To say 'Give her a chance' is an emotional way of putting it. The question," he reminded them, "is whether this girl is hypersexual." An attractive girl who assumed the pose of injured innocence, she was, he argued, all the more dangerous in her ability to "get the sympathy of men."[45] Uncomfortable with their own vulnerability to young women's charms—which were considerable relative to those of the rest of the mental hospital population—psychiatrists, eager perhaps to establish the collective innocence of the male half of the species, fell into blaming women for seducing them. The overdrawn sexuality of the adolescent girl in psychiatric discourse is in part, by this interpretation, but the projection of these psychiatrists' own barely acknowledged desires.

But there was more to the hypersexual than this. Proclaiming women wholly sexual creatures, psychiatrists fixed on their sexuality in attempting to comprehend a larger process of social change that saw women moving out of the home and more visibly into the world of work. The psychopathic hypersexual was in part a product of psychiatric imagination; the confident hedonist who seduced men left and right was the working-class new woman, the woman with a little cash and a lot of savvy, seen through middle-class, mostly male, eyes. But the sexually assertive woman, the woman endowed with passion equal to that of a man, was real, and psychiatrists, however exaggerated their notions of her sexual prowess, were alone in recognizing her passion as dicey. For the moment, psychiatrists stood back, a bit awed perhaps, and attempted to comprehend this new phenomenon, the passionate woman. Reflexively, they turned to the familiar categories of the pure woman and the prostitute. At the same time they recognized this old dichotomy would not do. The uneasiness of the construct of the female hypersexual embodied their confusion and ambivalence toward women and their sexuality. With it they enjoined women to be at once chaste and seductive, to tease but not to conquer. The psychopathic hypersexual was at times a pathological deviant in psychiatrists' discourse. More often, however, she was Everywoman. If, as one authority proposed, "a clean and protected moron was not far from corresponding to the ideal woman of the Victorian age," the psychopathic hypersexual was her redoubtable twentieth-century counterpart.[46]

NOTES

I am grateful to Elizabeth Pleck, Molly Nolan, Barbara Rosenkrantz, Sherrill Cohen, Lorraine Daston, Peter Mandler, Estelle Freedman, Nancy Cott, Theodore Brown, Christopher Lasch, and Gary Gerstle for comments on earlier versions of this essay.

From a book to be published by Oxford University Press.

1. Case 6867, 1917, letter from Ethel Hancock to Mary C. Jarrett, head of the Social Service at the Boston Psychopathic Hospital. All cases cited are from this hospital; all case numbers and patient names have been altered. Original punctuation and spelling have been retained in all quotations. The essay is based on analysis of data drawn from a simple random sample of 1,290 cases drawn from a total of 17,000 admissions to the Boston Psychopathic Hospital from 1912 to 1921, as well as on examination of more than 100 cases (not included in the sample) of women diagnosed as psychopathic. Psychiatrists diagnosed 5 percent of all patients as psychopathic; three-quarters of these were women. I have also drawn on an extensive published psychiatric and correctional literature, some of which is cited below.

2. The literature on the post-Victorian sexual revolution is incomplete and largely inconclusive. Most historians agree that there was a middle-class revolution in mores. See, for example, James R. McGovern, "The American Woman's Pre-World War I Freedom in Manners and Morals," *Journal of American History* 55 (September 1968): 315-33. Several historians, however, have questioned our notions of sexual Victorianism; for example, see Carl Degler, "What Ought to Have Been and What Was: Women's Sexuality in the Nineteenth Century" *American Historical Review*, 79 (December 1974): 1467-90; and, most recently, Peter Gay, *Education of the Senses*, Vol. 1, *The Bourgeois Experience, Victoria to Freud* (New York: Oxford University Press, 1984). For a thoughtful critique of these attempts to rehabilitate Victorian sexuality, see Carol Zisowitz Stearns and Peter N. Stearns, "Victorian Sexuality: Can Historians Do It Better?" *Journal of Social History* 18 (Summer 1985): 625-34. Historians have focused too little on working-class sexuality; the problem of working-class sexual revolution has been even less adequately explored. For exceptions to this general neglect, see Christine Stansell, *City of Women: Sex and Class in New York, 1789-1860* (New York: Alfred A. Knopf, 1986) on nineteenth-century working-class sexuality; and Kathy Peiss, "'Charity Girls' and City Pleasures: Historical Notes on Working-Class Sexuality," in *Powers of Desire: The Politics of Sexuality*, ed. Ann Snitow, Christine Stansell, and Sharon Thompson (New York: Monthly Review Press, 1983): 74-88.

3. The Boston Psychopathic Hospital was established in 1912 to diagnose and treat acute and curable mental disease; as used in the hospital's name 'psychopathic' denoted mental disease without neurological basis.

4. Case 7025, 1916, case conference. On adolescent male sexuality, see William Healy, *The Individual Delinquent: A Text-Book of Diagnosis and Prognosis for All Concerned in Understanding Offenders* (Boston: Little, Brown, and Company, 1915): 255-56, 588-89 esp.

5. Daniel Scott Smith, "Family Limitation, Sexual Control, and Domestic Feminism in Victorian America, *Feminist Studies* 1 (Winter-Spring 1973): 40-57; reprinted in *A Heritage of Her Own: Toward a New Social History of American Women*, ed. Nancy F. Cott and Elizabeth Pleck (New York: Simon and Schuster, 1979): 222-45.

6. On the relationship between overdevelopment and sexual precocity, see Healy, 244-54, 402-4. The extraordinary nature of his claim that "the overwhelmingly attraction which negro men occasionally have for white girls and women. . .is to be explained by the hypersexualism of the female attracted" (p. 403) can best be appreciated when set against the racism that pervades the literature of the time.

7. See Leslie Woodcock Tentler, *Wage-Earning Women: Industrial Work and Family Life in the United States, 1900-1930* (New York: Oxford University Press, 1979), chap. 4, for a discussion of the boy's relationship to the family economy. Both female and male criminologists considered the delinquencies of boys far less serious than those of girls. See, for one example among many, Mary W. Dewson, *Conditions That Make Wayward Girls: A Study Based on Last Year's Commitments to the Massachusetts State Industrial School for Girls* (Lancaster, Mass., 1910), 1: "The boy often gets into trouble because of an excess of animal spirits, because of energy which, rightly utilized, should be his greatest asset."

8. In 1922, years after the appearance of his two-volume *Adolescence: Its Psychology and Its Relation to Physiology, Anthropology, Sociology, Sex, Crime, Religion, and Education* (New York: D. Appleton and Company, 1904), G. Stanley Hall noted that "of all the stages of human life [the adolescent girl's] was *terra incognita*." The pubescent boy was, by contrast, an open book. See "Flapper Americana Novissima," *Atlantic Monthly* 129 (June 1922): 771. I found Carol Dyhouse's perceptive discussion of adolescent girlhood, although primarily concerned with middle-class girls, very useful in thinking about working-class adolescent girls. Dyhouse notes Hall's "leery" tone when writing of

adolescent girls. See her *Girls Growing Up in Late Victorian and Edwardian England* (London: Routledge & Kegan Paul, 1981), 115-22.

9. On the growth of commercial amusements, see Kathy Peiss, *Cheap Amusements: Working Women and Leisure in Turn-of-the-Century New York* (Philadelphia: Temple University Press, 1986). Tentler, 109-13, also discusses the appeal of commercial amusements. On small-town courtship, see the essay by Ernest W. Burgess, "Sociological Aspects of the Sex Life of the Unmarried Adult," in *The Sex Life of the Unmarried Adult: An Inquiry into and an Interpretation of Current Sex Practices*, ed. Ira S. Wile (New York: Garden City Publishing Company, 1934): 116-54.

10. Most noteworthy among the investigations are Carroll D. Wright, *The Working Girls of Boston* (Boston, 1889), 118-26 esp., where Wright attempts to counter what he considers the prevailing view that working girls are immoral; Robert A. Woods and Albert J. Kennedy, *Young Working Girls: A Summary of Evidence from Two Thousand Social Workers* (Boston, 1913), 84-100; and William I. Thomas, *The Unadjusted Girl: With Cases and Standpoint for Behavior Analysis* (1923; Montclair, N.J.: Patterson Smith, 1969), 98-150. On changing views of the prostitute, see Ruth Rosen, *The Lost Sisterhood: Prostitution in America, 1900-1918* (Baltimore: Johns Hopkins University Press, 1982); and Allan M. Brandt, *No Magic Bullet: A Social History of Venereal Disease in the United States Since 1880* (New York: Oxford University Press, 1985).

11. Case 6062, 1917, letter to social worker.

12. See Peiss, "'Charity Girls' and City Pleasures," for a discussion of "treating." Quotations are from case 10397, 1917, case report and case 6062, 1916, letter to social worker. My understanding of the working-class sexual milieu owes much to Stansell's *City of Women*, 76-101, 171-92. See Thomas, *Unadjusted Girl*, 98-150, for a contemporary's analysis of this same milieu.

13. Case 8196, 1916, case record.

14. Elizabeth G. Evans and Mary W. Dewson, *Feeble-Mindedness and Juvenile Delinquency* (Boston, 1909), 1; case 11046, 1918, case conference; case 8184, 1916, case conference; W.I. Thomas, *Sex and Society: Studies in the Social Psychology of Sex* (Chicago, 1907), 313; case 5602, 1915, letter to social worker.

15. Case 3735, 1914, case record.

16. Martin W. Peck, "Psychopathic Personality: Report of a Case," *Journal of Abnormal and Social Psychology* 17 (July-September, 1922): 192; case 5634, 1915, case conference; case 6062, 1915, case conference.

17. Case 5943, 1915, case conference. In their published account of Brown's case, E.E. Southard and Mary C. Jarrett wrote that they had minimized the issue of her sexual preference and had "purposely laid little stress upon the sex delinquencies, heterosexual and homosexual, which are suspected or implicit in some parts of" her case. See *The Kingdom of Evils: Psychiatric Social Work Presented in One Hundred Case Histories Together With a Classification of Social Divisions of Evil* (New York: Macmillan, 1922), 137. Southard was director of the Boston Psychopathic Hospital from 1912 until he died in 1919. For an analysis of the stress on gender deviance, see George Chauncey, Jr., "From Sexual Inversion to Homosexuality: Medicine and the Changing Conceptualization of Female Deviance," *Salmagundi* 58-59 (Fall 1982-Winter 1983): 114-46.

18. Rosen points out that prostitutes were among the first populations tested for feeblemindedness. She cites contemporary investigations of prostitution that found high proportions – around 30 percent – of prostitutes to be feebleminded (pp. 21-22). But the fact that the majority of prostitutes proved to be *not* feebleminded shocked and troubled reformers who quickly turned to psychopathy to account for prostitutes' immorality. See, for example, Mabel Ruth Fernald, Mary Holmes Stevens Hayes, and Almena Dawley, *A Study of Women Delinquents in New York State* (New York: The Century Co., 1920). The authors concluded that their data failed "absolutely to justify the

view expressed recently by certain propagandists that delinquency and defective intelligence are practically synonymous, and that, accordingly, solving the problem of mental deficiency will solve the problem of delinquency" (p. 434). Steven Schlossman and Stephanie Wallach argue that Progressive courts began to define female delinquency almost entirely in sexual terms; see "The Crime of Precocious Sexuality: Female Juvenile Delinquency in the Progressive Era," *Harvard Educational Review* 48 (February 1978): 65-94.. The quotation on psychopathic girls is from case 8487, 1917, case conference.

19. Case 3735, 1914, case record.

20. See Barbara M. Brenzel, *Daughters of the State: A Social Portrait of the First Reform School for Girls in North America, 1856-1905* (Cambridge: MIT Press, 1983), for a history of the Lancaster state school; case 6187, 1915, case conference. The visitor may have been right. Frances Donovan noted that the games waitresses played with men bordered "on prostitution, although not actual prostitution because the waitresses earn the necessaries of life for themselves." See her *The Woman Who Waits* (Boston: R.G. Badger, 1920), 211-12.

21. Case 6286, 1915, case report; case 10284, 1917, case record; case 10545, 1918, visitor's report.

22. One girl told psychiatrists "they call it saucy if you turn round up there." Case 10869, 1918, case conference.

23. Ibid.; case 8184, 1916, case conference; case 7763, 1916, case conference.

24. Case 7853, 1916, Girl's Parole Department visitor's report.

25. Case 7643, 1917, case conference; Peck, 190; case 15784, n.d., case history; case 4760, 1915; case 10469, 1917, visitor's report.

26. Southard and Jarrett, 354; case 4760, 1915, visitor's report; case 7693, 1916, case report; case 8184, 1916, case conference; case 10869, 1918, case conference; case 5664, 1915, case conference.

27. Case 5844, 1915-19, letters to social workers; case 6187, 1915, case conference; case 10264, 1918, case conference; case 10701, 1919, case record.

28. See Augusta Scott, "Three Hundred Psychiatric Examinations Made at the Women's Day Court, New York City," *Mental Hygiene* 6 (April 1922), 362-64, on dolled-up prostitutes; quotation is from case 11046, 1918, visitor's report. Many contemporaries called attention to the working-class girl's near-obsession with clothes. See Thomas, *Unadjusted Girl*, 109ff. for one account. Stansell, 92-101, 187-88; and Peiss, *Cheap Amusements*, 62-67, discuss the significance of clothing in working-class culture.

29. Case 10397, 1917, autobiography and case report.

30. Southard and Jarrett, 60, 70.

31. Case 6867, 1917, letter from Hancock to Jarrett; case 1272, 1913, case conference; letter from Hancock to Jarrett; Southard and Jarrett, 55. The book Talbot read was C. Gasquoine Hartley, *The Truth about Woman* (New York, 1914).

32. Case 6062, 1916, letter to social worker.

33. Ibid; Case 2202, 1916, letter to social worker.

34. Case 5844, 1915, letters and case record; case 6867, 1916-17, letters to social workers.

35. Ibid.

36. Case 5602, 1915, letter to social worker; case 2366, 1913, letter to friend.

37. Case 10264, 1918, case conference.

38. Case 10666, 1918, case conference.

39. Case 8184, 1916, case conference; case 6187, 1915, case conference.

40. Case 7763, 1916, case conference; case 8563, 1917, case conference; case 6187, 1915, case conference.

41. Case 10397, 1917, case conference; case 1272, 1913, case conference.

42. Case 10264, 1918, case conference.
43. Estelle B. Freedman, "'Uncontrolled Desires': The Response to the Sexual Psychopath," *Journal of American History* 74 (July 1987): 83-106; Christina Simmons, "Companionate Marriage and the Lesbian Threat," *Frontiers* 4 (Fall 1979): 54-59; Michael Gordon, "From an Unfortunate Necessity to a Cult of Mutual Orgasm: Sex in American Marital Education Literature, 1830-1940," in *Studies in the Sociology of Sex*, ed. James M. Henslin (New York: Appleton-Century-Crofts, 1971): 53-77.
44. Michel Foucault, *The History of Sexuality*, vol. 1, *An Introduction*, trans. Robert Hurley (New York: Random House, 1978), 53-73.
45. Case 6187, 1915, case conference.
46. Thomas, *Unadjusted Girl*, 166.

COMPANIONATE MARRIAGE AND THE LESBIAN THREAT

Christina Simmons

Christina Simmons writes, "I was born in 1948 and grew up in Indianapolis, Indiana. I work in women's history and am a graduate student in American Civilization at Brown University. I am currently writing a dissertation on the place of sexuality in courtship and marriage in the United States, 1912-1941. Involvement in the women's movement from 1971 on led me to the study of women's history in order to understand the roots of women's subordination in our culture and thus how it can be changed. I participated for six years in the Women's Liberation Union of Rhode Island while I was living in Providence. I live now in Halifax, Nova Scotia, where I am writing my dissertation and working with the Nova Scotia Women's Action Committee."

> Back in the dim ages when I was a schoolgirl we were not so well informed about the proper names for things . . . . If, now, Miss Barnes' school is representative at all, we have indications of a growth in half-knowledge which makes all girlish fondnesses suspect, so that the door is shut on these minor "innocent" outlets which have done so much to preserve woman's purity, or else it is opened wide on the horrendous and fascinating.
>
> Lorine Pruette, "The Flapper"[1]

Citing Carman Barnes' story about a girls' boarding school, psychologist Lorine Pruette reflected in 1930 that sharpened public awareness of sexuality was creating a new kind of moral rigidity in American culture. Affection and friendship between young women which had seemed innocent in the nineteenth century might arouse disapproval in the twentieth.[2] A girl might either be pushed ever earlier into "the frankness of a heterosexual relation" or be exposed to homosexual possibilities newly made "horrendous and fascinating" by the flapper's modish but superficial sexual knowledge.[3] Pruette commented that the older women in Katharine B. Davis' famous study had moved easily "between homosexual and heterosexual relations without necessarily evil consequences," but they had been raised "before our present era of frankness was well under way."[4] Pruette's reflection raises an important historical question—why fear of lesbianism constituted such a significant problem in the dominant heterosexual ideology of the 1920's and 1930's.

As much of the "sexual revolution" of the 1920's took place in words as in actions.[5] A spate of literature outlining the new "companionate" marriage, one based on friendship and sexual satisfaction, appeared in the 1920's, followed by more technical marriage manuals and popular medical advice in the next decade.[6] These works represented the cultural definition of changes in gender relations which had been stirring in social life since the late nineteenth century.[7] Those who wrote books and articles on sex were educators, social workers, psychologists, physicians, and others in a rising class of trained professional people, mostly male. In the 1910's and 1920's radical voices among them spoke for feminism and/or for sexual liberation.[8] Many more, however, acknowledged social changes but feared conflict between the sexes might result. They sought harmony between the sexes by reforming what seemed the most oppressive elements of Victorian marriage. This latter group articulated a new sexual ideology which achieved cultural hegemony by the 1930's and which represented a morality more suited to the social needs of the corporate liberal state than its Victorian predecessor.[9]

Proponents of the new companionate marriage gave great attention to women because they attributed the need for sexual reform primarily to historical changes in women's lives. The nineteenth-century sex-segregation of leisure among the respectable classes began dissolving in the 1890's; by the 1910's a small but noticeable group of elite urban women were going to restaurants and cabarets in male company. Middle-class couples joined working-class men and women at the new movie theatres. Already in the 1910's a few women adopted boyish "flapper" clothing and male habits like smoking and drinking in public. They turned against styles which emphasized women's distance and differentiation from men.[10] The expansion of women's education and of their paid employment in the higher social classes by 1900 generated a less exclusively domestic image of women in the culture. The professional work of some college women, the political activity of the suffrage movement, even the social and charitable activity of club women gave women a more salient presence outside the home.[11] Women of the upper-middle and upper classes were the implicit concern because they were the most immediate subjects of the dominant sexual morality and were expected to exemplify it to the women of other classes.[12]

As women discarded Victorian delicacy they seemed more like men, that is, as individuals with a right to personal fulfillment rather than a duty to sacrifice self for men and children. For example, in one 1919 novel an aspiring young social researcher exclaims, when asked if she would disobey her father, "Certainly! First of all I am a human being. That is what Ibsen's Nora said."[13] Being drawn into the public sphere made them more sexual, too: "By the very act of working, something has happened to her . . . she has become in important psychological elements, a man . . . most significantly they absorb, with their jobs, the masculine attitude toward sex."[14] Recognition of women's individuality and sexuality was a way of acknowledging a new kind of energy and social power, which pertained to more than reproduction and the domestic sphere. Companionate marriage represented the attempt of mainstream marriage ideology to adapt to women's perceived new social and sexual power.

This power was manifested, as one man observed, in "the increasing subordination of . . . maternity to sexuality . . . of love to passion, of procreation to recreation." The "vast reservoirs of erotic energy resident in women," freed from purely domestic and reproductive activities, were overflowing.[15] Many sexual reformers cited Freudian concepts to justify belief in the strength and universality of sexual drives. They argued that suppressing sexual desire was psychologically and even physically unhealthy.

Companionate marriage directed female sexual energies toward men and marriage. Judge Ben Lindsey popularized the essential elements in his 1927 book *Companionate Marriage:* 1) easier divorce, especially for childless marriages; 2) legalization of birth control; 3) provision of sex education for youth. These concrete reforms relied on two assumptions: that intense psychological companionship, or friendship, should characterize relations between husband and wife and that the sexual aspect of this intimacy was particularly important.[16] This form of marriage was said to provide the equality women deserved and to be a bond of "creative companionship and interdependent cooperation." "Does the husband really want a mere permanent housekeeper, a faithful drudge, an unpaid servant, or does he desire a real life companion and a friend . . .?"[17] The wife was to be included in the budget planning and was to have access to money without asking for it; the husband might help a little with dishes and housework. Women were to receive their rights to sexual pleasure as well; sexual literature warned men to abandon the stereotypical Victorian sexual aggression in favor of sensitivity, gentleness, and a slower pace.[18] Divorce, birth control, and sex education all helped women to exercise greater control over the conditions of the marital bond.

The new model compared favorably with reformers' exaggerated image of Victorian marriage—its duty-bound separate male and female spheres and its emotional and sexual repression. One sociologist concluded "there is every reason to suppose that asceticism has received in this generation a death blow from which it can never recover. It has passed forever from the category of ideals into that of mental abnormalities, and its morbid significance is being generally recognized."[19] By deprecating nineteenth-century marriage, advocates of companionate marriage in effect showed how enlightened and fair the new form was.

But what happened if women did not wholly reject Victorian gender relations but rather kept their distance from men and preferred each other's company? The ponderous traditions and social structures separating and differentiating the sexes now appeared as obstacles to heterosexual comradeship and romance. And conversely, women's segregation and solidarity with each other took on a menacing aspect unknown in earlier generations.[20] If women's sexual desires exhibited the urgency long attributed to men's, and if an intense love relationship seemed vital for personal happiness, then lesbian relationships were the logical result of the absence or failure of heterosexuality. "We do not blame anyone for seeking normal affection and love; we all need it to be happy. How can we blame a woman, who, through no fault of her own, has been deprived of such affection from a man, and turns to another woman for it?''[21] In these writings the specter of lesbianism arose in association with perceptions of the persisting differences and distance between men and women. But as is so clear in racial segregation, such separation meant inequality as well and consequently resistance from the oppressed group. Whether female resistance to heterosexual relationships actually occurred or not, the recognition of sexual inequality engendered in the culture a male *fear* of resistance, often expressed as a fear of lesbianism.

Within the voluminous literature of this new sexual ideology a conception of homosexuality was developing which made it into a very significant, if not the major, ''deviation'' from the dominant heterosexual pattern, especially for women. Historian Carroll Smith-Rosenberg has argued that early nineteenth-century American culture did not define lesbianism as a distinct sexual pattern.[22] Such innocence was gone by 1920. Accompanying the reformulation of heterosexual ideology during this period was a surprisingly extensive commentary on female homosexuality. The critical point about this literature is that it treated homosexuality as a condition which developed in specific relation to heterosexuality, namely through the failure or deprivation or rejection of the latter. Consequently, such writings denigrated not only exclusive lesbians but also women who might once have moved easily between homosexuality and heterosexuality and women experiencing conflict in relationships with men.[23]

By the 1920's discussion of homosexuality was expanding a little beyond strictly medical and scientific circles and was using popular Freudian concepts.

Older theories of homosexuality as a congenital abnormality still appeared, and some researchers pursued hormone theories, but environmental explanations were taking precedence.[24] The ascendancy of psychodynamic explanations focused attention on the process whereby young people ''acquired'' homosexuality and strengthened efforts to control it by changing the predisposing environmental factors. Both lay and medical writers loosely included factors from social as well as from family life among possible causes.

Whether homosexuality was actually increasing or not, some commentators said that is it was, owing to the disruptions of the Great War and the changing sexual morality of the 1920's. "The rhythm of the jazz age has infected our sex life. . . . The modern mad quest for stimulation is driving men and women into the arms of abnormality."[25] Such beliefs can be understood as expressions of cultural anxiety about the supposed social sources of homosexuality, as discussions of the "social" causes of homosexuality were a constituent element of the dominant heterosexual ideology. Often, homosexuality was turned into a threatening, oppositional alternative to the heterosexual pattern, especially in the case of women, thus presenting a cultural meaning that homosexuality had not carried in the nineteenth century.

Inherited rules governing social interaction between the sexes were premised on a fear of heterosexual contact for respectable women outside of marriage. But some marriage reformers began to feel that the spirit of the rules was so directed against heterosexuality that to some women romantic involvement with other women appeared socially safer than involvement with men: "Paradoxically many women believe, long after they have grown up, that an emotional relationship with a member of their own sex is no such breach of the conventions as an intimate relationship with a man."[26] Several authors noted that the hazards of adolescent heterosexual adventures were much exaggerated compared to the failure of heterosexuality altogether: "The anxious parental and social attempts to insure against such accidents, by repression and segregation, can produce homosexuality, perversions of all sorts, and sexual and emotional incapacities which can in the long run produce more individual unhappiness and more social ills than a boy's gonorrhea or a girl's illegitimate baby."[27]

Sex-segregated institutions, particularly schools, were said to be keeping young women and men from learning to know and live with each other. Sexual theorists' emphasis on individual fulfillment and romantic intimacy made marriage an arena for compromise and adjustment between two personalities. As the marriage manifestoes of the 1920's faded into the more technical advice works of the 1930's, problems of psychological adjustment within marriage received much attention.[28] Concerned about sources of marital instability, reformers scrutinized single-sex education: "the unwholesome fashionable practice of sex-segregated schools brings young people into a homosexual atmosphere." Deprived of male contact, young girls might not learn to love men. They would develop an "unconscious homosexuality" which would operate "to make mating so difficult as to be almost impossible, and to make matings unsatisfactory and unstable when they . . . [were] formally achieved."[29]

Failure to "achieve" heterosexual union was labeled immaturity. Critical of women's "emotional debauchery," one pair of researchers said of a lesbian college student: "she was so much of a child that she needed the complete understanding which only a person of her own sex could give her."[30] From another perspective, one might say the defenders of marriage were afraid that if psychological compatibility had become a major criterion for good relationships, then two women might sometimes find happiness more easily than a woman and a man.

The many single graduates of the women's colleges as well as independent young reformers and professional women, made notorious when Theodore Roosevelt accused them of causing race suicide, were widely known to live with other women when they did not live with their families. [31] Suspicion accumulated that these relationships were "unhealthy" at least. The mother of a young statistician portrayed in one novel asked, " 'Have you never met a man you fancied?' . . . 'I shall never love romantically,' was the forcible answer. 'What time have I for love?' " Yet the daughter "spoke with more enthusiasm" of her roommate: " 'She is studying to be a librarian. We met each other last year and we've been rooming together since this fall; she means everything to me, mummy.' " The novelist judges the daughter's bohemian existence unnatural, the result of feminist disdain for domesticity and absorption in work and social causes.[32]

Despite overwhelming male economic advantages and social and political power, some women, especially in the higher social classes, were better able than their mothers and grandmothers had been to decline marriage if they chose.[33] One psychologist attributed female homosexuality in part to a feminist desire for life work besides motherhood and an unwillingness to marry the average man.[34] Another author speculated, not unreasonably, that women's ability not to marry had raised public awareness of lesbianism: "For thousands of years moralists and legalists have denounced homosexuality between men, but no code has ever forbidden physical relationship between women . . . since it did not necessarily prevent child-bearing, or cause children to be born illegitimately. . . . When feminism . . . increased, and women began to be increasingly celibate, the question of 'mannish' women began finding its way into popular novels *(The Well of Loneliness)* into plays *(The Children's Hour)* and into parlor conversations."[35]

Suspicions of lesbianism often centered on women of higher status because they were perceived to have significant power. One critic noted that employment made all women more sexually receptive but that working-class women became heterosexually promiscuous while professional women became lesbians.[36] Upper-middle-class and upper-class women were the ones who worked for suffrage and Progressive reforms and lived in social settlements, but they were still needed to support, comfort, and provide children for men of their class. Roosevelt had criticized their childlessness, but dominant-class ideologues of the 1920's and 1930's showed fear and disapproval of these women's independence by insinuating their lesbianism.[37] What marriage reformers were doing in effect was to perceive women's autonomy and resistance to male domination in sexual terms and to deprecate the legitimacy of their social and economic aspirations.

Remnants of Victorian gender relations, then, acted as social causes of homosexuality according to many architects of the new marriage. Influenced by rules of propriety and sex-segregated institutions, women with education and financial resources established domestic arrangements that were free of male support or control and which were possibly lesbian.[38] Some critics found lesbianism an unfortunate but understandable result of such conditions, to be pitied, even tolerated. As companionate marriage gained legitimacy, however, others began to see a "psychologically sick" lesbianism as the cause rather than the effect of women's resistance to heterosexuality. They became defensive, trying to reduce women's protests to narrowly sexual motiviation: "The driving force in many agitators and militant women who are always after their rights, is often an unsatisfied sex impulse, with a homosexual aim. Married women with a completely satisifed libido rarely take an active interest in militant movements."[39] Such a reversal occurred among reformers concerned about the persistence of sexual conflict even in the new marriage. Claiming that companionate marriage had ended Victorian inequities, they found in lesbianism an "irrational" psychological cause for behavior which subtly challenged male sexual dominance within marriage.

Lesbianism was blamed for both aggressive and inhibited female sexuality. Despite the alleged equality of partners in companionate marriage, male sexual leadership remained the norm. Women who flouted feminine decorum in intercourse drew harsh disapproval. The male superior position in coitus, for example, symbolized the man's dominance in the relationship, and a woman who wished to usurp it risked censure. One physician claimed, "A homosexual woman often wants to possess the male and not to be possessed by him. . . . With them orgasm is often only possible in the superior position."[40] He associated lesbianism with a rejection of women's natural, subordinate role within heterosexual activity.

The complete absence of female sexual participation, however, also indicated lesbianism to these modern defenders of marriage. Women had to walk a fine line between appropriate modesty and neurotic prudery. The latter became problematic when women internalized sexual conventions so thoroughly as to resist heterosexuality in disgust or fear. Because sexual harmony was so sought after in companionate marriage, too much female naivete or embarrassment was counterproductive and seemed old-fashioned by the 1920's.[41] Purity, too, began to arouse suspicions of lesbianism. An upbringing of "excessive repressions" or "morbid or silly warnings against the opposite sex" might encourage lesbian tendencies. Alternatively, a person characterized by " 'prudishness' and 'stiffness,' or more favorably . . . . 'unapproachable purity' or 'high ideals,' " might be influenced by "unconscious homosexuality."[42]

More specifically, prudery caused frigidity, the leading female problem in marital adjustment according to most proponents of companionate marriage. Many writers expressed sympathy for women with the problem and saw them as victims of a sexually repressive socialization. In that sense frigidity provided an argument for sex education and women's sexual rights in companionate marriage.[43] At the same time, certain reformers, including some who also expressed sympathy, feared or resented female frigidity. They interpreted it as a sign of "man-hating," or rejection of the female role.

Mixed with words of encouragement to women to accept and express their sexuality were warnings of what might happen if they did not: "women will have to be bluntly reminded that one main source of prostitution and unfaithfulness is the selfish and unsurrendered wife."[44] Losing a husband was what women risked when they failed in heterosexual "adjustment."

As the cultural definition of marriage shifted to include greater emphasis on mutual sexual pleasure, women's dissatisfaction grew proportionately more alarming. "The woman who gets no pleasure at all in coitus cannot truly love her husband. Love demands more than respect or admiration." Respect or admiration might have been sufficient for the Victorians, but no more. Defensive sexual advisers turned to attack. "Some married women thought to dislike coitus only because of a superior modesty, in reality are deceiving themselves and others. Their frigidity is on a homosexual basis, all their real interests being feminine."[45] Another man described the "nightmare" of marriage to a lesbian: After intercourse, "they feel cold, and do not experience the normal glow; they talk *as though nothing important had hap-*

pened. These women often despise their husbands in various ways'' (my italics).[46] In normal heterosexual intercourse ''something important'' did happen—when a woman expressed or feigned love and desire for a man in spite of the socially determined inequality between them, she symbolized some acceptance of her position, whether from having achieved an individually satisfactory relationship or from the need to please him. Overt sexual coldness destroyed the illusion of harmony.

Thus in cultural terms lesbianism represented women's autonomy in various forms—feminism, careers, refusal to marry, failure to adjust to marital sexuality.[47] It became a symbol in a cultural context of increased expectation and evaluation of sexual activity for women as well as for men in the new form of companionate marriage. How well this new ideology of marriage described the typical patterns of people's sexual lives requires investigation, but no one could have remained totally isolated from its power. Directives about gender relations were expressed not only in articles and books of advice but directly by health care and social work professionals, clergy, radio, movies, advertising, and government policies.[48] We cannot know how many people were influenced by arguments for co-education, earlier dating and marriage, and breaking up friendships between adolescent girls. The intention was clear—''to train young people for—we need not hesitate to use the phrase—living happily ever after in heterosexual matehood.''[49]

The ebullient atmosphere of sexual liberation which characterized the 1910's and 1920's allowed room for more open discussion of lesbianism than had ever existed in the United States before. Trying to explain what most of them could not accept as legitimate, sexual theorists found social causes of lesbianism in clashes between an anachronistic morality and a perceived new female power in social and sexual life. As the ideology of companionate marriage became established, however, attitudes toward female resistance, and thus toward lesbianism, hardened among many marriage theorists and counselors. Creators of the new ideology had hoped to modify some extreme features of male dominance but were far from ready to institute what feminists would have defined as equality. The decline of organized feminism after 1920 must certainly have been one factor allowing dissemination of such an intensely heterosexual vision of personal life. In the absence of a powerful feminist voice, exponents of companionate marriage tempered the liberating potential of new sexual ideas and judged women's sexuality acceptable only insofar as its energy was channeled into marriage and the service of men.

NOTES

Thanks to Linda Kealey and Bruce Tucker for their comments on this essay.

1. Lorine Pruette, "The Flapper," in V. F. Calverton and S.D. Schmalhausen, *The New Generation: The Intimate Problems of Modern Parents and Children* (New York: Macaulay, 1930), pp. 574-75.

2. Diana Frederics [pseud.], *Diana: A Strange Autobiography* (1939; rpt. New York: Arno, 1975), p. 222.

3. Pruette, p. 577.

4. Ibid., p. 585. Katharine B. Davis did one of the earliest sociological studies of sexual behavior. She used written questionnaires to survey college graduate and club women in the early 1920's and published the results in 1929 in *Factors in the Sex Life of Twenty-Two Hundred Women* (New York: Harper & Bros.).

5. Maurice A. Bigelow, *Sex-Education: A Series of Lectures Concerning Knowledge of Sex in Its Relation to Human Life* (New York: Macmillan, 1916), p. 254; Ernest R. Groves, *The Marriage Crisis* (New York: Longmans, Green, 1928), pp. 165-68.

6. For example, Ben Lindsey and Wainwright Evans, *The Companionate Marriage* (New York: Boni and Liveright, 1927); Floyd Dell, *Love in the Machine Age: A Psychological Study of the Transition from Patriarchal Society* (New York: Farrar, 1930); LeMon Clark, *Emotional Adjustment in Marriage* (St. Louis: C.V. Mosby, 1937); *Sexology*, 1933+; *Popular Medicine*, 1934+.

7. Christopher Lasch, *Haven in a Heartless World: The Family Besieged* (New York: Basic Books, 1977), p. 9; V. F. Calverton, *The Bankruptcy of Marriage* (New York: Macaulay, 1928), p. 146.

8. Grete Meisel-Hess, *The Sexual Crisis: A Critique of Our Sex Life*, trans. Eden and Cedar Paul (New York: Critic and Guide, 1917), pp. 20-24, 74; V. F. Calverton, "Sex and Social Struggle," in *Sex in Civilization*, ed. V. F. Calverton and S. D. Schmalhusen (New York: Macaulay, 1929), p. 271; J. William Lloyd, "Sex Jealousy and Civilization," in *Sex in Civilization*, pp. 233-46; Calverton, *Bankruptcy*, p. 215.

9. Dell, p. 68; Stuart Ewen, *Captains of Consciousness: Advertising and the Social Roots of the Consumer Culture* (New York: McGraw-Hill, 1976), especially Part III, chapters 1, 5, 6

10. Lewis Allan Erenberg, "Urban Night Life and the Decline of Victorianism: New York City's Restaurants and Cabarets, 1890-1918," Diss. University of Michigan 1974, p. 131; Lary Linden May, "Reforming Leisure: The Birth of Mass Culture and the Motion Picture Industry, 1896-1920," Diss. University of California, Los Angeles 1977, p. 110; James R. McGovern, "The American Woman's Pre-World War I Freedom in Manners and Morals," *Journal of American History*, 55 (1968), 322; Floyd Dell, *Looking at Life* (New York: Knopf, 1924), pp. 23-24.

11. Phyllis Blanchard and Carlyn Manasses, *New Girls for Old* (New York: Macaulay, 1930), pp. 231, 235, 241-46; C. Gasquoine Hartley, *Women's Wild Oats: Essays on the Re-Fixing of Moral Standards* (New York: Stokes, 1920), pp. 38, 43; S.D. Schmalhausen, "The Sexual Revolution," in *Sex in Civilization*, p. 359-60.

12. Daniel Scott Smith has argued that working-class sexual behavior was beginning to leave behind Victorian styles after 1875 and that the "sexual revolution" of the 1920's was middle-class, "The Dating of the American Sexual Revolution: Evidence and Interpretation," in *The American Family in Social-Historical Perspective*, ed. Michael Gordon (New York: St. Martin's, 1973), pp. 321-35. Floyd Dell also explicitly proclaims sexual changes as a "middle-class revolution," *Love in the Machine Age*, p. 201.

13. Nalbro Bartley, *A Woman's Woman* (Boston: Small, Maynard, 1919), p. 46.

14. Horace Coon, *Coquetry for Men* (New York: Amour Press, 1932), pp. 110-11; Clark, p. 51.

15. Schmalhuasen, "The Sexual Revolution," pp. 379, 402. Younger feminists of the period differed from their predecessors in embracing sexuality more enthusiastically. See Elaine Showalter, ed., *These Modern Women: Autobiographical Essays from the Twenties* (Old Westbury, N.Y.: Feminist Press, 1978), p. 15.

16. Lindsey and Evans, pp. 175-76; Coon, pp. 184-88; Ira S. Wile and Mary Day Winn, *Marriage in the Modern Manner* (New York: Century, 1929), pp. 12-13, 263-64.

17. Sherwood Eddy, *Sex and Youth* (Garden City, N.Y.: Doubleday, Doran, 1929), pp. 140, 149; Wile and Winn, p. 178; Beatrice Forbes-Robertson Hale, "Women in Transition," in *Sex in Civilization*, p. 75.

18. Eddy, pp. 151, 154; Margaret Sanger, *Happiness in Marriage* (New York: Blue Ribbon, 1926), pp. 122-24, 225; Groves, p. 100.

19. Groves, p. 214.

20. Carroll Smith-Rosenberg, "The Female World of Love and Ritual: Relations between Women in Nineteenth-Century America," *Signs*, 1, 1 (Autumn 1975), 27.

21. Ralph Hay, "Mannish Women or Old Maids?" *Know Yourself*, 1 (July 1938), 78; also, Lindsey and Evans, p. 187; Eleanor Bertine, M.D., "Health and Morality in the Light of the New Psychology," *Proceedings of the International Conference of Women Physicians* (New York: The Womans Press, 1919), IV, pp. 10, 11.

22. Smith-Rosenberg, 8, 27; Jonathan Katz, *Gay American History* (New York: Thomas Y. Crowell, 1976), p. 449.

23. Katz includes a good example of such doubt in excerpts from the diary of Dorothy Thompson, 1932, p. 558.

24. Arno Karlen, *Sexuality and Homosexuality: A New View* (New York: Norton, 1971), pp. 324, 330; John F. W. Meagher, M.D., "Homosexuality: Its Psychobiological and Psychopathological Significance," *The Urologic and Cutaneous Review*, 33 (1929), 510.

25. S. D. Schmalhausen, "The Freudian Emphasis on Sex," in *The Sex Problem in Modern Society*, ed. John Francis McDermott (New York: Modern Library, 1931), p. 64; also, Olga Knopf, *Women on Their Own* (Boston: Little, Brown, 1935), p. 157.

26. Dorothy Dunbar Bromley and Florence Haxton Britten, *Youth and Sex: A Study of 1300 College Students* (New York: Harper, 1938), p. 129; also Hay, 77; Noah E. Aronstam, M. D., "*The Well of Loneliness*—An Impression," *The Urologic and Cutaneous Review*, 33 (1929), 543.

27. Floyd Dell, "Sex in Adolescence," in *Sex Education: Facts and Attitudes* (New York: Child Study Association of America, 1934), p. 49; Norman Himes, *Your Marriage: A Guide to Happiness* (New York: Farrar & Rinehart, 1940), p. 24. One of the authors more tolerant of homosexuality argued that homosexuality was indeed less serious than illegitimacy or venereal disease and that people should not be so upset about it. Aaron J. Rosanoff, M.D., "Human Sexuality, Normal and Abnormal, From a Psychiatric Standpoint," *Urologic and Cutaneous Review*, 33 (1929), 530. The novel *A Woman's Woman* (above, note 13) contrasts a celibate sister who lives with another woman and the other sister in the family, a flirtatious girl who falls for a worthless man. The latter's failings are much better accepted by the family.

28. For example, Blanchard and Manasses, pp. 186-87; Clark, p. 7.

29. Dell, *Love in the Machine Age*, pp. 238, 308; also Bromley and Britten, p. 118. The proportion of American colleges confined to one sex or the other declined continuously from 1870 on, mostly because the majority of new schools were co-educational. Very few women's colleges opened after 1930; I have not discovered whether fears of lesbianism played any direct role in this phenomenon. See Mabel Newcomer, *A Century of Higher Education for American Women* (New York: Harper, 1959), pp. 37-40.

30. Bromley and Britten, p. 129; also, Himes, p. 22.

31. Linda Gordon, *Woman's Body, Woman's Right* (New York: Grossman, 1976), p. 136; Eleanor Rowland Wembridge, "The Professional Education of Women and the Family Problem," *Social Hygiene*, 6 (1920), 183.

32. Bartley, pp. 27-29.

33. Peter Filene, *Him/Her/Self: Sex Roles in Modern America* (New York: Harcourt, Brace, Jovanovich, 1974), pp. 29-30. Filene cites figures showing that in 1915, for instance, only 39 percent of all living alumnae of eight women's colleges and Cornell were married, p. 27. Actually the proportion of ever-married people in the population was rising, and the age of marriage was declining, from 1890 on. Because the reality differed from reformers' impressions, it seems even more likely that the more visible single women of higher classes were the primary

concern. See Donald J. Bogue, *The Population of the United States* (Glencoe, Ill.: The Free Press, 1959), p. 216.

34. Phyllis Blanchard, *The Adolescent Girl: A Study From the Psychoanalytic Viewpoint* (New York: Moffat, Yard, 1920), pp. 170-71.

35. Hay, 77.

36. Coon, pp. 112-15; also Maurice Chideckel, M.D., *Female Sex Perversion* (New York: Eugenics, 1935), p. vii. In practice, accusations were not restricted by class. In the film, *With Babies and Banners: Story of the Women's Emergency Brigade*, Women's Labor History Film Project, 1978, about women's participation in the 1937 autoworkers' strike in Flint Michigan, one participant recalls that male unionists called women "queers" when they wanted to do more than traditional support work for the union.

37. Blanche Wiesen Cook has described these women's relationships with each other and with men in "Female Support Networks and Political Activism: Lillian Wald, Crystal Eastman, Emma Goldman," *Chrysalis*, No. 3 (1977), pp. 43-61.

38. Katz, p. 449. Katz notes the historical change from the assumption of asexual friendships to "vulgarizations of Freudianism" which found sex everywhere.

39. Meagher, 511.

40. Meagher, 513; see also George K. Pratt, M.D., "Accepting One's Sexual Role," in *Sex Education: Facts and Attitudes*, p. 39; Ernest R. Groves, Gladys Hoagland Groves, and Catherine Groves, *Sex Fulfillment in Marriage* (New York: Emerson, 1942) suggested for instance, that other positions were useful in exceptional circumstances such as when the man was weak or lacking in sexual control, pp. 163, 179-80.

41. Eddy, p. 127; Dell, *Love in the Machine Age*, p. 311; Sanger, p. 100.

42. In order, Meagher, 508; Edward Podolsky, M.D., " 'Homosexual Love' in Women," *Popular Medicine*, 1 (February 1935), 375; Dell, *Love in the Machine Age*, p. 308. See also Blanchard, p. 169.

43. Groves, *Marriage Crisis*, p. 100; Wile and Winn, p. 54; Clark, p. 96; Joseph Collins, M.D., *The Doctor Looks at Love and Life* (Garden City, N.Y.: Doubleday, Doran, 1926), pp. 36, 43.

44. Eddy, p. 316; also Clark, pp. 31, 97; Lindsey and Evans, pp. 119, 199; Groves et al., *Sex Fulfillment*, p. 186.

45. Meagher, 512.

46. Podolsky, 375.

47. Blanche Wiesen Cook has argued similarly in her essay, " 'Women Alone Stir My Imagination': Lesbianism and the Cultural Tradition," *Signs*, 4, 4 (Summer 1979), 739.

48. Robert S. Lynd and Helen Merrell Lynd, *Middletown: A Study in Modern American Culture* (New York: Harcourt, Brace, and World, 1929), pp. 266-71; May, pp. 212-31; Ewen; Lasch, pp. 20-21; U.S. Public Health Service, *Sex Education: A Symposium for Educators* (Washington, D.C., 1927), pp. v-vi.

49. Dell, *Love in the Machine Age*, p. 364; also Himes, p. 26; Lindsey and Evans, p. 134; Edwood L. Fantis, M.D., "Homosexuality in Growing Girls," *Sexology*, 2 (February 1935), 349.

Lesbianism in the 1920s and 1930s: A Newfound Study

Vern Bullough and Bonnie Bullough

Because lesbianism has been much less studied than male homosexuality, much less is known about the female homosexual than the male. There are many reasons for the paucity of studies. One of the most obvious is that most past researchers in sexuality have been men, in no position to research the topic fully. Another explanation is that lesbians, never the object of the same type of legal persecution as their male counterparts, have been less likely to interest authorities. Most of the laws against variant sexual behavior were concerned with penetration and only incidentally with oral-genital contacts or other forms of non-procreative sex. Though two women who allegedly engaged in lesbian activities in Plymouth colony in 1649 were charged with lewd conduct and one of them was found guilty,[1] this seems to have been the only prosecution in American history for lesbian activities;[2] a similar lack of prosecutorial zeal is noted in England. Still another reason for the existence of comparatively few studies is that the female homosexuals apparently have made considerable effort to remain as unobtrusive as possible.

1. *Records of the Colony of New Plymouth in New England,* ed. Nathaniel B. Shurtleff (Boston: William White, 1855–61), 2:137.

2. We rely upon the researches of Alfred C. Kinsey and his associates for this statement, although our own independent researches tend to validate them. See Alfred C. Kinsey, Wardell B. Pomeroy, Clyde E. Martin, and Paul H. Gebhard, *Sexual Behavior in the Human Female* (Philadelphia: W. B. Saunders Co., 1953), p. 48.

[*Signs: Journal of Women in Culture and Society* 1977, vol. 2, no. 4]

Much of the source material about lesbianism that does exist —bondage and discipline literature, for example—is obviously suspect.[3] A more reliable source of the late nineteenth and early twentieth centuries can be found in case histories collected by psychiatrists, psychologists, and similar interested professionals. However, they are used to illustrate the pathological nature of lesbianism rather than to examine actual lesbian behavior or to allow us to understand the nature of the lesbian relationship.[4]

Obviously the situation has begun to change today. New attitudes toward both women and homosexuality have encouraged women to write up their own experiences and give us descriptions of lesbian relationships.[5] Biographies and autobiographies have also become more frank.[6] Still these do not picture the life of ordinary women who happened to be lesbian, far from centers of literary attention, unsuspected even by their neighbors. Undoubtedly material exists, hidden away in records, but finding it is a problem, even more than finding descriptions of what the average nonlesbian women of the past did and thought.

However, we were recently willed an unfinished manuscript dealing with lesbianism in a middle-sized American city during the 1920s and 1930s. Included in the materials were data about twenty-five lesbian women, based for the most part on interviews. In many ways they were no different from a similar respectable nonlesbian group, except for their fear of exposure. Perhaps this was enhanced because the community was located in Salt Lake City, a city not then or now as tolerant of homosexuality as the larger metropolitan cities. The manuscript dates from 1938. The author, then about forty, attempted to put down a scholarly description of her own life and those of her partners and twenty-three of her lesbian friends. She also included data on some eight male homosexuals who were on the fringe of this particular community or active in a bohemian literary club with which many of the homosexu-

3. There are numerous titles along with summaries of these works in Pisanus Fraxi, *Bibliography of Prohibited Books*, 3 vols. (vol. 1, 1877; vol. 2, 1879; vol. 3, 1885; reprint ed., London: Jack Brussell, 1962).

4. For a rather comprehensive listing of these studies, see Vern L. Bullough, Dorr Legg, Barry Elcano, and James Kepner, *A Bibliography of Homosexuality* (New York: Garland Publishing, in press). For a discussion of women who may or may not have been lesbian, but who acted as men, and of the pertinent literature, see Vern L. Bullough, *Sexual Variance in Society and History* (New York: Wiley Interscience, 1976), pp. 595–602.

5. See, e.g., Jane Rule, *Lesbian Images* (New York: Doubleday & Co., 1975); Del Martin and Phyllis Lyon, *Lesbian/Woman* (San Francisco: Glide Publications, 1972); Sidney Abbot and Barbara Love, *Sappho Was a Right-on Woman* (New York: Simon & Schuster, 1973); Dolores Klaich, *Woman Plus Woman* (New York: William Morrow & Co., 1975). For a change in attitudes, compare these studies with an earlier one, that of Ann Aldrich: *We, Too, Must Love* (New York: Fawcett Publications, 1958).

6. For some of these, see Jeannette H. Foster, *Sex Variant Women in Literature* (New York: Vantage Press, 1956), passim; Bullough et al., passim; and Kate Millett, *Flying* (New York: Alfred A. Knopf, 1974).

als in the city, male and female, had some affiliation. The author of the manuscript, M. B., had been gathering data for some twenty years. She had started the project as an honor's thesis while in college, had been discouraged from pursuing it by her adviser, but nonetheless had continued to gather data. The study was never finished.

Upon examining the manuscript, the reasons for this failure seem to be due to her ambivalence about her own sex preference and lifestyle. On the one hand, she desperately wanted to understand and justify her own homosexuality and in the process add to the scientific literature on the topic. On the other hand, she had an overwhelming fear of exposure and wanted to protect her sisters from the scrutiny of others. Some indication of this fear of publicity appears in the reaction that she and her friends had to the publication of *The Well of Loneliness* in 1928.[7] Instead of applauding the fact that lesbianism was being brought out in the open and discussed publicly, almost to a woman they decried its publication. One woman, seemingly typical, felt that the novel caused people who before had never heard of lesbianism to try to classify as a lesbian every woman who wore a suit (with a skirt) and was seen more than once in the company of another woman. They also feared that such fictional works put homosexuality in the wrong light, if it did not do actual harm to their cause.

At the time of M. B.'s final attempt to write up her findings, she was living with a young social worker. They had what was described as an "ideal home" and were "socially accepted," a fact that meant a great deal to her. In a sense, the two women adopted traditional marriage patterns; M. B. explained that she "managed" the "male part of the household," while her companion "delighted" in being a "happy wife at home." Most close friends of the couple were lesbians, but they also numbered some male homosexuals among their acquaintances as well as several middle-aged married couples.

To explain how we received the manuscript, it is necessary to give some additional personal information about M. B. In spite of her apparent happiness with her partner, the relationship later broke up. At the outbreak of World War II, M. B. left her job as a photographer to become a machine-shop worker in a war-related industry. There she met the mother of one of the authors of this present paper (B. B.). The two women joined their households. After the war the couple moved to a small town outside Salt Lake City, where they used their skills to set up a shop for the manufacture of jewelry and plastic products. At home M. B. continued to act the husbandly role, while her new partner accepted the more traditional housewife role. We often visited the two women, and M. B. frequently mentioned her manuscript, considering it her most

7. Radclyffe Hall, *The Well of Loneliness* (London: Jonathan Cape, 1928). The American edition was published by Covici, Friede in 1929.

precious possession, although she made no further move to finish it. Inevitably, when M. B. died (at the age of seventy-two), the manuscript arrived in our mail, complete with summaries of her interviews, most of them over forty years old. In willing us the precious manuscript, her plan and the hope of our mother was that we would publish the findings of the empirical study and thus help M. B. achieve her lifelong goal of making a contribution to the literature of lesbianism without endangering her privacy or the anonymity of her informants.

Unfortunately, the interview schedules for each individual have not been preserved. What have survived are detailed summaries of each interview in a case-history format. We do, however, have a copy of the questions which were asked as part of the interview schedule. The author's adoption of the case-history method to summarize her study is indicative of the medical model of sexuality then in existence.[8] As far as homosexuality was concerned, this model was heavily influenced by Richard von Krafft-Ebing's *Psychopathia-sexualis*. Krafft-Ebing believed that a natural predisposition to homosexuality was a functional sign of degeneration. Certain kinds of activities increased the likelihood of one becoming homosexual. A major causal factor was masturbation. Krafft-Ebing, however, did not find much evidence of homosexuality in women, in large part because most of his cases had been drawn from court records. He explained this lack as due to the fact that women did not come forward for treatment. In any case, they were neither as sensual nor as aggressive as men.[9]

By the time M. B. began compiling her data, the theories of Krafft-Ebing about the pathological nature of homosexuality had been challenged by Magnus Hirschfeld, who insisted that homosexuality was a biological phenomenon, not pathological;[10] and by Havelock Ellis, who had also argued for the nonpathological basis of homosexuality.[11] M. B. was inclined to accept the notions of Hirschfeld and Ellis. She amplified upon the argument that genetic predisposition, which she believed to be a causal factor in homosexuality, would also make lesbian women have many masculine features. Many of the questions she asked in her survey reveal her conviction about the existence of such masculine features.

Unfortunately, the existing case histories do not always include the complete answers to questions on the interview schedule, and we know that additional information must have been gathered through personal interviews. This lack of consistently reported data makes it difficult to

8. Vern L. Bullough, "Homosexuality and the Medical Model," *Journal of Homosexuality* 1 (1974): 99–110, and *Sex, Society and History* (New York: Neale Watson, 1976).

9. See Richard von Krafft-Ebing, *Psychopathia-sexualis*, translated from the seventh enlarged and revised edition by C. Chaddock (Philadelphia: F. A. Davis, 1894).

10. See Magnus Hirschfeld, *Die Homosexualität* (Berlin: L. Marcus, 1920).

11. Havelock Ellis, *Studies in the Psychology of Sex*, vol. 2, *Sexual Inversion* (reprint ed., New York: Random House, 1936).

determine whether data are actually missing on a particular case history, whether the question was answered in the negative, or whether for some reason the information was not sought. In spite of this inconsistency, the survey is the earliest we know that exists of a lesbian community. This makes it invaluable.

At the time the interviews are gathered, the ages of the women ranged from nineteen to fifty-six, with a median age of approximately twenty-nine. A variety of occupational identities were reported, including six teachers (both high school and college), two nurses, two waitresses, two secretaries, one mining engineer, one beauty operator, one barber, one concession operator, one farm laborer, three housewives (married to men), two housewife partners of lesbian women, and one temporarily unemployed drifter. Our author and her partner, as indicated, were a photographer and a social worker, respectively. With the exception of the mining engineer, the barber, the farm laborer, the concession operator, and perhaps the photographer, the women were in what might be regarded as traditional women's occupations. The most obvious difference from any random group of twenty-five women picked at that time is the significance of working women. Though three of the women were married to men at the time of the interview, they were regarded by the group and by themselves as lesbians. Unfortunately, we are not sure how their husbands viewed them, although in at least one case the lesbian was married to a male homosexual.

All of the sample were Caucasian, all from what would be called middle-class backgrounds. On this question M. B. showed considerable bias. In describing her respondents' backgrounds, she used such terms as "good respectable pioneer stock," "American descent," "New England Quaker stock," or even the superlative, "good untainted middle class genteel people." Her concern appears to have been to emphasize that there was no hereditary taint of degeneracy, as Krafft-Ebing implied, as well as to emphasize the respectability of her respondents. While the case histories do not mention much involvement in religious activities, most of the women (not all) seem to have been born into Latter-Day Saint (Mormon) homes, probably a reflection of the dominant Utah pattern rather than any significant incidence of lesbianism among Mormons. Two of the women, however, were from large, polygamous families, which may well have given them second thoughts about participating in the institution of marriage.

Generally M. B. and her respondents did not adhere to any Freudian notion about causality, but they were not ignorant of Freudian assumptions. The most obvious attempt to apply Freud by M. B. is in her consideration of childhood tragedies among her respondents. She herself had lost her mother as an infant and had been reared by her father and older brothers. Among her respondents, two had been reared by a single parent because of the death of the other; two came from families broken by divorce; three had alcoholic parents; and two of the women reported being seduced by men at young ages. The significance of such information is questionable, since more than half of the group were not reported to have any significant tragedy during their childhood. The educational level of the group, like the employment rate, was higher than that for comparable groups of women in the 1920s and 1930s. Two of the respondents had earned master's degrees, six had bachelor's degrees, and the two nurses were still in training at the time of the interview. Most of the remaining repondents had finished high school, although the educational level of four persons was not indicated.

M. B. took great pains to collect data about the body build of her subjects because of her belief that, if there was a biological basis for homosexuality, it would be evident through obvious masculine characteristics. The data she gathered to support her predispositions has serious limitations, and even with the existence of her bias it fails to back up her hypothesis. Most accurate of these data are probably those dealing with height and weight. The median height was five feet, seven inches, while the median weight was 145 pounds. She described half of her group as being somewhat masculine in build, which she equated with broad shoulders, small breasts, and narrow hips. Only two persons are described as big breasted and broad hipped. The rest are simply not described. It may be that M. B. felt that an ordinary feminine appearance was unworthy of note, while masculine or ultrafeminine builds were significant.

She was much more meticulous in identifying what she called the "psychology" of each individual. For her, psychology included a role identification in terms of orientation and behavior of either a masculine or feminine type, as well as a preference for sexual partners who were more masculine or feminine. Thus an individual who enjoyed vigorous outdoor sports and preferred feminine women as love objects was classified by her as having as masculine psychology. The reverse was also true. She classified ten subjects as having a masculine psychology, eight as having a feminine one, and five as fluctuating from time to time. She did not classify her partner. She herself was a very small woman, with very noticeable feminine contours, and from our acquaintance would be classified as "fluctuating" in her own terminology. However, she viewed herself as having a masculine psychology.

Six of the group indicated that they realized they were homosexual at a very early age and had made no attempt to orient themselves toward men as love objects. The rest of the group had not accepted a homosexual identity until much later, although some admitted early inclinations toward lesbianism which they had tried to suppress. Six had actually married, and three of these, as indicated above, were still married at the time they were interviewed. Four others had become engaged but had never been married, while four others had experimented with heterosexual intercourse. In addition, two of the group had been seduced as girls, and one of these seductions had resulted in a pregnancy. This woman had firmly refused marriage and was rearing her illegitimate child herself. Except for the three presently married women (about whom the other members of the group felt ambivalent) all of the respondents felt they would never try marriage in the future.

Social theories of the time which conceptualized homosexuality as a psychopathology suggested that such groups would also have other signs of maladjustment. Such a supposition could not have been demonstrated by this sample, although there are two indications that the group did exist under some strain. Two of the twenty-five had attempted to commit suicide before being interviewed, although how serious such attempts were is not clear. We do know that one person later succeeded in a suicide attempt. Another indication of the difficulties of a stigmatized status was the recurring theme in the individual case histories of an attempt to escape the bounds of societal respectability through alcohol. Periodically members of the group were reported as having drinking bouts.

However, it is not these failures to conform which dominate the material but, rather, the drive for respectability which all of the women, except perhaps the "drifter," shared. They were always conscious of the need to keep their lesbian identities hidden except from their most trusted friends or associates. In this sense the Salt Lake lesbians were a success.

In our minds, it is doubtful that the Utah citizenry were ever aware of the existence of lesbian groups in their midst. The Mormon church, which publicly excommunicates homosexuals in a psychologically devastating trial procedure, never moved against any of the Mormon members of the group or, to our knowledge, any of the other lesbians at that time. Most of the women held responsible and respectable jobs. In fact their very success in disguising their sexual orientation to the outside world leads us to hypothesize that lesbianism in the past was more prevalent than the sources might indicate, since society was so unsuspecting. Part of the success of the lesbians in disguising their sexual orientation might well have been due to the masculine bias in reporting or observing women's activities, although the women's desire for a respectable facade was also important.

This facade undoubtedly affected the outlook of the individuals. One of the contradicitions that appear to us in the case histories is an often reported belief in sexual repression and abhorrence of all bodily functions. For example, there was a consensus among the group that menstruation was a disgusting function, although no respondent reported having an extraordinary amount of discomfort during her menses, compared with other women. Masturbation, perhaps because Krafft-Ebing regarded it as a possible causal factor in homosexuality, was frowned upon, and the respondents uniformly denied that they had ever practiced it when it was brought up in the interview. In fact they tended to describe such practices as repulsive. How much this reflects the bias of the interviewer and how much that of interviewee is uncertain, but the subject had been discussed by various members of the group. One of the teachers in the sample is described in the following passage: "She is considered one of the best physical education instructors in the system and has a very high moral influence on her pupils who respect and admire her. She demands strict obedience and never allows any evidence of delinquency to go uninvestigated. She has a horror of masturbation and watches for evidence of it among her pupils closely. She has done a great deal of good in correcting this abominable habit among her students. She also has done a good deal in stamping out unwholesome sex relationships among the pupils." Their self-image of themselves as respectable women might well have helped them to be more rigid and conforming than other women. How much this need to conform was due to the Salt Lake City environment and how much it was a common trait in lesbian groups is uncertain. Most of their social life, whether by choice or necessity, took place in their homes. This tended to reinforce the caution they exhibited toward the outside world and in the process helped make their lives more confining and restrictive than might otherwise have been the case. Several of them, for example, regarded San Francisco as a kind of mecca and, when they could afford to, visited that city, where they were apparently somewhat bolder in their social activities, including bar hopping.

Superficially the lesbians as a group and particularly M. B. tended to downgrade many of the so-called feminine virtues. How much this had to do to the general societal attitudes subordinating feminine virtues to the male ones and how much to their interpretation of their sexual orientation is uncertain. Probably both factors were involved. When M. B. wanted to present a favorable synopsis of a particular woman, she usually described her in masculine terms or quoted her as describing herself in masculine terms. An interviewee would be described as having a "deep rooted masculine psychology" or as being "practical and hard-headed with no emotional instability." Another was said to show "the masculine trait of being able to keep her emotional life and business life in separate parts." On the other hand, what M. B. found most unsatisfying and unattractive in some of the male homosexuals she met, including several in her study, were their "attempts at femininity." She described one male homosexual in a rather hostile fashion, as walking "with a mincing gait"; being "hypersensitive to criticism"; having a "suicidal mania"; liking to "sew, cook, and keep house" and all "the things which delight the feminine heart." Another male homosexual was described as being "emotionally unstable and vacillating in his affections," traits which she frowned upon but regarded as "characteristics of many cases of male homosexuals."

A consistent theme throughout the manuscript and in the histories is a denial of a societal image of themselves as "perverts" or "pathological cases." They consistently denied that they were sick, pathological, or disturbed, although they were very much aware that a society tended to regard all homosexuals in this light. As indicated above, in all respects except sexual behavior, the women as a group were probably far less alienated from society than the average contemporary woman, if only because of better education and their jobs, which threw them more into the societal mainstream than the traditional married women. Though general psychoanalytic theory might hold that homosexuals should be unhappy, lonely, and guilt ridden, and undoubtedly some of the individuals in this study had periods when they displayed all of these symptoms, they generally did not regard such descriptions as applying to themselves. As a group they seem hostile to others who noticeably deviated from societal norms, perhaps conscious of the efforts that it cost them to keep the facade of respectability. What appears consistently throughout the questionnaire is what Evelyn Hooker later found in her study of a similar small sample of male homosexuals, that except for sex preference the group seem remarkably well-adjusted to society.[12] Recently Henry T. Heald and Mary K. Finley found this was also true for their lesbian sample.[13]

What kind of conclusions can be drawn from this previously unpublished study? The most obvious to our mind is the existence of significant unreported and unobserved lesbian groups. This fact gives new validity to some of the fictional portraits of women in which many have read hidden accounts of lesbianism. Many such portraits now seem to have been basic insights of the creative writers who probably had greater insight into the existence of lesbianism than the medical investigators. As far as we know, none of the women in the study ever became a case study for a psychiatrist, emphasizing further the possible distortion present in such studies, which included only the most maladjusted of lesbians. Another remarkable aspect is the desire in such a "deviant" social group to conform and be respectable, even though the need to conform may well have worked against their own emancipation. Finally, the manuscript shows how much assumptions about a "deviant" group, even when

12. E. Hooker, "The Adjustment of the Male Overt Homosexual," *Journal of Projective Techniques* 21 (1957): 18–31.

13. Henry T. Heald and Mary K. Finley, "Alienation and Sexuality: A Comparison of Homosexual and Heterosexual Women" (paper presented at the seventieth annual meeting of the American Sociological Association, San Francisco, August 25–29, 1975).

these assumptions are rejected by the group, have considerable influence on the self-image of its members. The consistent attempt to reject their condition as pathological is indicative of the anxieties that society had imposed upon them. But while they rejected this particular assumption, they did tend to believe that they were different from other women, and these differences they saw in terms of their qualities of masculinity.

Department of History
California State University, Northridge (V. Bullough)

Department of Nursing
California State University, Long Beach (B. Bullough)

ORAL HISTORY AND THE STUDY OF SEXUALITY IN THE LESBIAN COMMUNITY: BUFFALO, NEW YORK, 1940-1960

MADELINE DAVIS AND
ELIZABETH LAPOVSKY KENNEDY

We began a study of the history of the Buffalo lesbian community, 1930-1960, to determine that community's contribution to the emergence of the gay liberation movement of the 1960s.[1] Because this community centered around bars and was highly role defined, its members often have been stereotyped as low-life societal discards and pathetic imitators of heterosexuality. We suspected instead that these women were heroines who had shaped the development of gay pride in the twentieth century by forging a culture for survival and resistance under prejudicial conditions and by passing this sense of community on to newcomers; in our minds, these are indications of a movement in its pre-political stages.[2] Our original research plan assumed the conceptual division between the public (social life and politics) and the private (intimate life and sex), which is deeply rooted in modern consciousness and which feminism has only begun to question. Thus we began our study by looking at gay and lesbian bars – the public manifestations of gay life at the time – and relegated sex to a position of less importance, viewing it as only incidentally relevant. As our research progressed we came to question the accuracy of this division. This article records the transformation in our thinking and explores the role of sexuality in the cultural and political development of the Buffalo lesbian community.

At first, our use of the traditional framework that separates the public and private spheres was fruitful.[3] Because the women who patronized the lesbian and gay bars of the past were predominantly working class and left no written records, we chose oral history as our method of study. Through the life stories of over forty nar-

Feminist Studies 12, no. 1 (Spring 1986). © by Feminist Studies, Inc.

rators, we found that there were more bars in Buffalo during the forties and fifties than there are in that city today. Lesbians living all over the city came to socialize in these bars, which were located primarily in the downtown area. Some of these women were born and raised in Buffalo; others had migrated there in search of their kind. In addition, women from nearby cities, Rochester and Toronto, came to Buffalo bars on weekends. Most of the women who frequented these bars had full-time jobs. Many were factory workers, taxi drivers, bartenders, clerical workers, hospital technicians; a few were teachers or women who owned their own businesses.[4]

Our narrators documented, beyond our greatest expectations, the truth of our original hypothesis that this public bar community was a formative predecessor to the modern gay liberation movement. These bars not only were essential meeting places with distinctive cultures and mores, but they were also the central arena for the lesbian confrontation with a hostile world. Participants in bar life were engaged in constant, often violent, struggle for public space. Their dress code announced them as lesbians to their neighbors, to strangers on the streets, and of course to all who entered the bars. Although confrontation with the straight world was a constant during this period, its nature changed over time. In the forties, women braved ridicule and verbal abuse, but rarely physical conflict. One narrator of the forties conveys the tone: "There was a great difference in looks between a lesbian and her girl. You had to take a streetcar – very few people had cars. And people would stare and such."[5] In the fifties, with the increased visibility of the established gay community, the concomitant postwar rigidification of sex roles, and the political repression of the McCarthy era, the street dyke emerged. She was a full-time "queer," who frequented the bars even on week nights and was ready at any time to fight for her space and dignity. Many of our fifties' narrators were both aware and proud that their fighting contributed to a safer, more comfortable environment for lesbians today.

> Things back then were horrible, and I think that because I fought like a man to survive I made it somehow easier for the kids coming out today. I did all their fighting for them. I'm not a rich person; I don't even have a lot of money; I don't even have a little money. I would have nothing to leave anybody in this world, but I have that that I can leave to the kids who are coming out now,

who will come out into the future, that I left them a better place to come out into. And that's all I have to offer, to leave them. But I wouldn't deny it; even though I was getting my brains beaten up I would never stand up and say, "No, don't hit me, I'm not gay, I'm not gay." I wouldn't do that.

When we initially gathered this material on the growth and development of community life, we placed little emphasis on sexuality. In part we were swept away by the excitement of the material on bars, dress, and the creation of public space for lesbians. In addition, we were part of a lesbian feminist movement that opposed a definition of lesbianism based primarily on sex. Moreover, we were influenced by the popular assumption that sexuality is natural and unchanging and the related sexist assumption of women's sexual passivity—both of which imply that sexuality is not a valid subject for historical study. Only recently have historians turned their attention to sexuality, a topic that used to be of interest mainly to psychologists and the medical profession. Feminists have added impetus to this study by suggesting that women can desire and shape sexual experience. Finally, we were inhibited by the widespread social reluctance to converse frankly about sexual matters. Thus for various reasons, all stemming, at least indirectly, from modern society's powerful ideological division between the public and the private, we were indisposed to consider how important sexuality might have been to the women we were studying.

The strength of the oral history method is that it enables narrators to shape their history, even when their views contradict the assumptions of historians. As our work progressed, narrators volunteered information about their sexual and emotional lives, and often a shyly asked question would inspire lengthy, absorbing discourse. By proceeding in the direction in which these women steered us, we came to realize that sexuality and sexual identity were not incidental but were central to their lives and their community. Our narrators taught us that although securing public space was indeed important, it was strongly motivated by the need to provide a setting for the formation of intimate relationships. It is the nature of this community that it created public space for lesbians and gay men, while at the same time it organized sexuality and emotional relationships. Appreciation of this dynamic interconnection requires new ways of thinking about lesbian history.

What is an appropriate framework for studying the sexual component of a lesbian community's history and for revealing the role of sexuality in the evolution of twentieth-century lesbian and gay politics? So little research has been done in this area, that our work is still exploratory and tentative. At present, we seek primarily to understand forms of lesbian sexual expression and to identify changes in sexual norms, experiences, and ideas during the 1940s and 1950s. We also look for the forces behind these changes in the evolving culture and politics of the lesbian community. Our goal has been to ascertain what part, if any, sexuality played in the developing politics of gay liberation. As an introduction to this discussion, we shall present our method of research because it has been crucial in our move to study sexuality, and so little has been written on the use of oral history for research on this topic.

USING ORAL HISTORY TO CONSTRUCT THE HISTORY OF THE BUFFALO LESBIAN COMMUNITY

The memories of our narrators are colorful, illuminating, and very moving. Our purpose, however, was not only to collect individual life stories, but also to use these as a basis for constructing the history of the community. To create from individual memories a historically valid analysis of this community presented a difficult challenge. The method we developed was slow and painstaking.[6] We treated each oral history as a historical document, taking into account the particular social position of each narrator and how that might affect her memories. We also considered how our own point of view influenced the kind of information we received and the way in which we interpreted a narrator's story. We juxtaposed all interviews with one another to identify patterns and contradictions and checked our developing understanding with other sources, such as newspaper accounts, legal cases, and labor statistics.

As mentioned earlier, we first focused on understanding and documenting lesbian bar life. From the many vibrant and humorous stories about adventures in bars and from the mountains of seemingly unrelated detail about how people spent their time, we began to identify a chronology of bars and to recognize distinctive social mores and forms of lesbian consciousness that were associated with different time periods and even with different bars. We checked and supplemented our analysis by research into newspaper accounts of bar raids and closings and actions of the State Liquor Authority. Contradictions frequently emerged in our material on bars, but, as we pursued them, we found they were rarely due to idiosyncratic or faulty memory on the part of our narrators but to the complexity of bar life. Often the differences could be resolved by taking into account the different social positions of our narrators or the kinds of questions we had asked to elicit the information we received. If conflicting views persisted we tried to return to our narrators for clarification. Usually, we found that we had misunderstood our narrators or that contradictions indeed existed in the community at the time. For instance, narrators consistently told us about the wonderful times in bars as well as how terrible they were. We came to understand that both of these conditions were part of the real experience of bar life.

When we turned our attention to sexuality and romance in this community, we were at first concerned that our method would not be adequate. Using memories to trace the evolution of sexual norms and expression is, at least superficially, more problematic than using them to document social life in bars. There are no concrete public events or institutions to which the memories can be linked. Thus, when a narrator talks about butch-fem sexuality in the forties, we must bear in mind the likelihood that she has modified her view and her practice of butch-fem sexuality in the fifties, sixties, seventies, and eighties. In contrast, when a narrator tells about bars in the forties, even though social life in bars might have changed over the last forty years, she can tie her memories to a concrete place like Ralph Martin's bar, which existed during a specific time period. Although not enough is known about historical memory to fully evaluate data derived from either type of narrative, our guess is, that at least for lesbian communities, they are equally valid.[7] The vividness of our narrators' stories suggests that the potential of oral history to generate full and rich documents about women's sexuality might be especially rich in the lesbian community. Perhaps lesbian memories about sexual ideals and experiences are not separated from the rest of life because the building of public communities is closely connected with the pursuit of intimate relationships. In addition, during this period, when gay oppression marked most lesbians' lives with fear of punishment and lack of acceptance, sexuality was one of the few areas in which many lesbians found satisfaction and pleasure. This was reinforced by the fact that, for lesbians, sexuality was not directly linked with the pain and/or danger of women's responsibility for childbearing and women's economic dependence on men. Therefore, memories of sexual experience might be more positive and more easily shared. But these ideas are tentative. An understanding of the nature of memory about sexuality must await further research.

The difficulty of tying memories about sexual or emotional life to public events does present special problems. We cannot identify specific dates for changes in sexual and emotional life, such as when sex became a public topic of conversation or when role-appropriate sex became a community concern. We can talk only of trends within the framework of decades. In addition, we are unable to find supplementary material to verify and spark our narrators' memories. There are no government documents or newspaper reports on lesbian sexuality. The best one can find are memoirs or fiction written about or by residents in other cities, and even these don't exist for participants in working-class communities of the forties.[8] In general, we have not found these problems to require significant revision of our method.

Our experience indicates that the number of people interviewed is critical to the success of our method, whether we are concerned with analyzing the history of bar life or of emotional and sexual life. We feel that between five and ten narrators' stories need to be juxtaposed in order to develop an analysis that is not changed dramatically by each new story. At the present time, our analysis of the white lesbian community of the fifties is based on oral histories from over fifteen narrators. In contrast, we have only five narrators who participated in the white community of the forties, four for the black community of the fifties, and one from the black community of the forties. Therefore, we emphasize the fifties in this article and have the greatest confidence in our analysis of that decade. Our discussion of the forties must be viewed as only tentative. Our material on the black community is not yet sufficient for separate treatment; so black and white narrators' memories are interspersed throughout the article. Ultimately, we hope to be able to write a history of each community.

SEXUALITY AS PART OF THE CULTURAL POLITICAL DEVELOPMENT OF THE BUFFALO LESBIAN COMMUNITY

Three features of lesbian sexuality during the forties and fifties suggest its integral connection with the lesbian community's cultural-political development. First, butch-fem roles created an authentic lesbian sexuality appropriate to the flourishing of an independent lesbian culture. Second, lesbians actively pursued rich and fulfilling sexual lives at a time when sexual subjectivity was not the norm for women. This behavior was not only consistent with the creation of a separate lesbian culture, but it also represented the roots of a personal and political feminism that characterized the gay liberation movement of the sixties. Third, although butch-fem roles and the pursuit of sexual autonomy remained constant throughout this period, sexual mores changed in relation to the evolving forms of resistance to oppression.

Most commentators on lesbian bar life in the forties and fifties have noted the prominence of butch-fem roles.[9] Our research corroborates this; we found that roles constituted a powerful code of behavior that shaped the way individuals handled themselves in daily life, including sexual expression. In addition, roles were the primary organizer for the lesbian stance toward the straight world as well as for building love relationships and for making friends.[10] To understand butch-fem roles in their full complexity is a fundamental issue for students of lesbian history; the particular concern of this article is the intricate connection between roles and sexuality. Members of the community, when explaining how one recognized a person's role, regularly referred to two underlying determinants, image, including dress and mannerism, and sexuality.[11] Some people went so far as to say that one never really knew a woman's role identity until one went to bed with her. "You can't tell butch-fem by people's dress. You couldn't even really tell in the fifties. I knew women with long hair, fem clothes, and found out they were butches. Actually I even knew one who wore men's clothes, haircuts and ties, who was a fem."

Today, butch-fem roles elicit deep emotional reactions from many heterosexuals and lesbians. The former are affronted by women assuming male prerogatives; the latter by lesbians adopting male-defined role models. The hostility is exemplified by the prevalent ugly stereotype of the butch-fem sexual dyad: the butch with her dildo or penis substitute, trying to imitate a man, and the simpering passive fem who is kept in her place by ignorance. This representation evokes pity for lesbians because women who so interact must certainly be sexually unfulfilled; one partner cannot achieve satisfaction because she lacks the "true" organ of pleasure, and the other is cheated because she is denied the complete experience of the "real thing." Our research counters the view that butch-fem roles are solely an imitation of sexist heterosexual society.

Inherent to butch-fem relationships was the presumption that the butch is the physically active partner and the leader in lovemaking. As one butch narrator explains, "I treat a woman as a woman, down to the basic fact it'd have to be my side doin' most of the doin'." Insofar as the butch was the doer and the fem was the desired one, butch-fem roles did indeed parallel the male/female roles in heterosexuality. Yet unlike the dynamics of many heterosexual relationships, the butch's foremost objective was to give sexual pleasure to a fem; it was in satisfying her fem that the butch received fulfillment. "If I could give her satisfaction to the highest, that's what gave me satisfaction." As for the fem, she not only knew what would give her physical pleasure, but she also knew that she was neither object of nor receptacle for someone else's gratification. The essence of this emotional/sexual dynamic is captured by the ideal of the "stone butch," or untouchable butch, that prevailed during this period. A "stone butch" does all the "doin'" and does not ever allow her lover to reciprocate in kind. To be untouchable meant to gain pleasure from giving pleasure. Thus, although these women did draw on models in heterosexual society, they transformed those models into an authentically lesbian interaction. Through role-playing they developed distinctive and fulfilling expressions of women's sexual love for women.

The archetypal lesbian couple of the 1940s and 1950s, the "stone butch" and the fem, poses one of the most tantalizing puzzles of lesbian history and possibly of the history of sexuality in general.[12] In a culture that viewed women as sexually passive, butches developed a position as sexual aggressor, a major component of which was untouchability. However, the active or "masculine" partner was associated with the giving of sexual pleasure, a service usually assumed to be "feminine." Conversely, the fem, although the more passive partner, demanded and received sexual pleasure and in this sense might be considered the more self-concerned or even more "selfish" partner. These attributes of butch-fem sexual identity remove sexuality from the realm of the "natural," challenging the notion that sexual performance is a function of biology and affirming the view that sexual gratification is socially constructed.

Within this framework of butch-fem roles, individual lesbians actively pursued sexual pleasure. On the one hand, butch-fem roles limited sexual expression by imposing a definite structure. On the other hand, this structure ordered and gave a determinant shape to lesbian desire, which allowed individuals to know and find what they wanted. The restrictions of butch-fem sexuality, as well as the pathways it provided for satisfaction, are best captured and explored by examining what it meant for both butch and fem that the butch was the doer; how much leeway was there before the butch became fem, or the fem became butch?

Although there was complete agreement in the community that the butch was the leader in lovemaking, there was a great deal of controversy over the feasibility or necessity of being a "stone butch." In the forties, most butches lived up to the *ideal* of "the untouchable." One fem, who was in a relationship with an untouchable butch at that time, had tried to challenge her partner's behavior but met only with resistance. Her butch's whole group—those who hung out at Ralph Martin's—were the same. "Because I asked her one time, I said, 'Do you think that you might be just the only one?' 'Oh no,' she said. 'I know I'm not, you know, that I've discussed with. . .different people.' [There were] no exceptions, which I thought was ODD, but, I thought, well, you know. This is how it is."

In the fifties, the "stone butch" became a publicly discussed model for appropriate sexual behavior, and it was a standard that young butches felt they had to achieve to be a "real" or "true" butch. In contrast to the forties, a fifties' fem, who was out in the community, would not have had to ask her butch friend why she was untouchable, and if there were others like her. She would have known it was the expected behavior for butches. Today our narrators disagree over whether it was, in fact, possible to maintain the ideal and they are unclear about the degree of latitude allowed in the forties or fifties before a butch harmed her reputation. Some butches claim that they were absolutely untouchable; that was how they were, and that's how they enjoyed sex. When we confronted one of our narrators, who referred to herself as an "untouchable," with the opinion of another narrator, who maintained that "stone butches" had never really existed, she replied, "No, that's not true. I'm an 'untouchable.' I've tried to have my lover make love to me, but I just couldn't stand it. . . . I really think there's something physical about that." Like many of our butch narrators, this woman has always been spontaneously orgasmic; that is, her excitement level peaks to orgasm while making love to another woman. Another "stone butch" explains: "I wanted to satisfy them [women], and I wanted to make love – I love to make love. I still think that's the greatest thing in life. But I don't want them to touch me. I feel like that spoils the whole thing – I am the way I am. And I figure if a girl is attracted to me, she's attracted to me because of what I am."

Other butches who consider themselves, and had the reputation of being, untouchable claim that it is, as a general matter, impossible to be completely untouchable. One, when asked if she were really untouchable replied, "Of course not. How would any woman stay with me if I was? It doesn't make any sense. . . . I don't believe there was ever such a class – other than what they told each other." This woman preferred not to be touched, but she did allow mutual lovemaking from time to time during her long-term relationships. A first time in bed, however:

> There's no way in hell that you would touch me. . .if you mean untouchable like that. But if I'm living with a woman, I'd have to be a liar if I said that she hadn't touched me. But I can say that I don't care for it to happen. And the only reason it does happen is because she wants it. It's not like something I desire or want. But there's no such thing as an untouchable butch – and I'm the finest in Buffalo and I'm telling you straight – and don't let them jive you around it – no way.

This narrator's distinction between her behavior on a first night and her behavior in long-term relationships appeared to be accepted practice. The fact that some – albeit little – mutuality was allowed over the period of a long relationship did not affect one's reputation as an untouchable butch, nor did it counter the presumption of the butch as the doer.

This standard of untouchability was so powerful in shaping the behavior of fifties' butches that many never experienced their fems making love to them. By the seventies, however, when we began our interviewing, norms had changed enough so that our butch narrators had had opportunities to experience various forms of sexual expression. Still, many of them – in fact all of those quoted above on "stone butches" – remained untouchable. It was their personal style long after community standards changed. Today these women offer explanations for their preference that provide valuable clues about both the personal importance and the social "rightness" of untouchability as a community norm in the forties and fifties. Some women, as indicated in one of the above quotes, continue to view their discomfort with being touched as physical or biological. Others feel that if a fem were allowed the physical liberties usually associated with the butch role, distinctions would blur and the relationship would become confusing. "I feel that if we're in bed and she does the same thing to me that I do to her, we're the same thing." Another narrator, reflecting on the fact that she always went to bed with her clothes on, suggests that "what it came to was being uncomfortable with the female body. You didn't want people you were with to realize the likeness between the two." Still other butches are hesitant about the vulnerability implicit in mutual lovemaking. "When the first girl wanted to make a mutual exchange sexually, . . .I didn't want to be in the position of being at somebody's disposal, or at their command that much – maybe that's still inside me. Maybe I never let loose enough."

But many untouchables of the fifties did try mutual lovemaking later on, and it came as a pleasant surprise when they found they enjoyed being touched. "For some reason. . .I used to get enough mental satisfaction by satisfying a woman. . .then it got to the point where this one woman said, 'Well, I'm just not gonna accept that,' and she started venturing, and at first I said, 'No, no,' and then I said, 'Well, why not?' and I got to enjoy it." This change was not easy for a woman who had spent many years as an "untouchable." At first she was very nervous and uncomfortable about mutual sex, but "after I started reaching physical climaxes instead of just mental, it went, that little restlessness about it. It just mellowed me right out, y'know." The social pressure of the times prevented some women from experiencing expanded forms of sexual expression they might have enjoyed, and it also put constraints upon some women who had learned mutual sex outside of a structured community. One of our narrators had begun her sex life with mutual relations and enjoyed it immensely, but in order to conform to the community standard for butches, adopted untouchability as her sexual posture. She acceded to this behavioral change willingly and saw it as a logical component of her role during this period.

How was a community able to monitor the sexual activities of its members, and how might people come to know if a butch "rolled over"—the community lingo for a butch who allowed fems to make love to her? The answer was simple; fems talked! A butch's reputation was based on her performance with fems.

Despite the fact that sexual performance could build or destroy a butch's reputation, some butches of the fifties completely ignored the standard of untouchability. Our narrators give two reasons for this. One reason is the opinion that a long-term relationship requires some degree of mutuality to survive. One butch, a respected leader of the community because of her principles, her affability, and her organizational skills, was not only "touchable" but also suspects that most of the butches she knew in the fifties were not "stone butches." "Once you get in bed or in your bedroom and the lights go out, when you get in between those sheets, I don't think there's any male or there's any female or butch or fem, and it's a fifty-fifty thing. And I think that any relationship. . .any true relationship that's gonna survive has got to be that way. You can't be a giver and can't be a taker. You've gotta both be givers and both gotta be takers." The second reason is the pleasure of being touched. Some women experienced this in the fifties and continued to follow the practice.

> When it came to sex [in the fifties] butches were untouchable, so to speak. They did all the lovemaking, but love was not made back to them. And after I found out how different it was, and how great it was, I said, "What was I missing?" I remember a friend of mine, that I had, who dressed like a man all her life. . .and I remember talking to [her] and saying to her, you know you've got to stop being an untouchable butch, and she just couldn't agree. And I remember one time reaching over and pinching her and I said, "Did you feel that?" and she said, "Yes," and I said, "It hurt, didn't it? Well, why aren't you willing to feel something that's good?"

We do not know if in the forties, as in the fifties, butches who preferred a degree of mutuality in lovemaking existed side by side with the ideal of untouchability because we have considerably less information on that decade. Therefore, we cannot judge whether there was in fact a development toward mutual sexuality, the dominant form of lesbian lovemaking of the sixties and seventies, or whether the "stone butch" prescribed ideal and mutual love-making couples existed side by side consistently throughout the forties and fifties.

Our information on fem sexuality is not as extensive as that on butch sexuality because we have been able to contact fewer fem narrators. Nevertheless, from the fems we have interviewed and from comments by butches who sought them out and loved them, we do have an indication that fems were not passive receivers of pleasure, but for the most part, knew what they wanted and pursued it.[13] Many butches attributed their knowledge of sex to fems, who educated them by their sexual responsiveness as well as by their explicit directions in lovemaking.

As implied by our discussion of butch sexuality, many fems had difficulty accepting "untouchability." One fem narrator of the forties had a ten-year relationship with an untouchable butch, and the sexual restrictions were a source of discomfort for her. "It was very one-sided, you know, and. . .you never really got a chance to express your love. And I think this kind of suppressed. . .your feelings, your emotions. And I don't know whether that's healthy. I don't think so." But at the same time the majority of these fems appreciated being the center of attention; they derived a strong sense of self-fulfillment from seeking their own satisfaction and giving pleasure – by responding to their butches. "I've had some that I couldn't touch no parts of their bodies. It was all about me. Course I didn't mind! But every once in a while I felt like, well, hey, let me do something to you. I could NEVER understand that. 'Cause I lived with a girl. I couldn't touch any part of her, no part. But boy, did she make me feel good, so I said. . .All right with me. . .I don't mind laying down."

What emerges from our narrators words is in fact a range of sexual desires that were built into the framework of role-defined sexuality. For butches of the period, we found those who preferred untouchability; those who learned it and liked it; those who learned it and adjusted to it for a time; those who preferred it, but sensed the need for some mutuality; and those who practiced mutuality regularly. For fems, we found those who accepted pleasure, thereby giving pleasure to their lovers; usually such women would aggressively seek what they wanted and instruct their lovers with both verbal and nonverbal cues. Some fems actively sought to make love to their butches and were successful. And finally, we found some women who were not consistent in their roles, changing according to their partners. In the varied sex lives of these role-identified women of the past, we can find the roots of "personal-political" feminism. Women's concern with the ultimate satisfaction of other women is part of a strong sense of female and potentially feminist agency and may be the wellspring for the confidence, the goals, and the needs that shaped the later gay and lesbian feminist movement. Thus, when we develop our understanding of this community as a predecessor to the gay liberation movement, our analysis must include sexuality. For these lesbians actively sought, expanded, and shaped their sexual experience, a radical undertaking for women in the 1940s and 1950s.

Although butch-fem roles were the consistent framework for sexual expression, sexual mores changed and developed throughout this period; two contradictory trends emerged. First, the community became more open to the acceptance of new sexual practices, the discussion of sexual matters, and the learning about sex from friends as well as lovers. Second, the rules of butch-fem sexuality became more rigid, in that community concern for role-appropriate behavior increased.

In the forties there were at least two social groups, focused in two prominent bars, Ralph Martin's and Winters. According to our narrators, the sexual mores of these two groups differed: the former group was somewhat conservative; the latter group was more experimental, presaging what were to become the accepted norms of the fifties. The lesbian patrons of Ralph Martin's did not discuss sex openly, and oral sex was disdained. "People didn't talk about sex. There was no intimate conversation. It was kind of hush, hush. . .I didn't know there were different ways." By way of contrast, this narrator recalls a visit to Winters, where other women were laughing about "sixty-nine." "I didn't get it. I went to [my partner] and said, 'Somebody says "sixty-nine" and everybody gets hysterical.'" Finally her partner learned what the laughter was all about. At that time our narrator would have mentioned such intimacies only with a lover. It wasn't until later that she got into bull sessions about such topics. Not surprisingly, this narrator does not recall having been taught about sex. She remembers being scared during her first lesbian experience, then found that she knew what to do "naturally." She had no early affairs with partners older than herself.

The Winters' patrons had a more open, experimental attitude toward sex; they discussed it unreservedly and accepted the practice of oral sex. These women threw parties in which women tried threesomes and daisy chains. "People would try it and see how it worked out. But nothing really happened. One person would always get angry and leave, and they would end up with two." Even if their sexual adventures did not always turn out as planned, these women were unquestionably innovative for their time. Our narrator from the Winters' crowd reminisced that it was always a contrast to go home to the serene life of her religious family. She also raved about two fems who were her instructors in sexual matters, adding, "I was an apt pupil."

During the fifties the picture changed, and the mores of the Ralph Martin's group virtually disappeared. Sex came to be a conversation topic among all social groups. Oral sex became an accepted form of lovemaking, so that an individual who did not practice it was acting on personal preference rather than on ignorance or social proscription. In addition, most of our fifties' butch narrators recall having been teachers or students of sex. As in the Winters' group in the forties, an important teacher for the butch was the fem. "I had one girl who had been around who told me. I guess I really frustrated the hell out of her. And she took a piece of paper and drew me a picture and she said, 'Now you get this spot right here.' I felt like a jerk. I was embarrassed that she had to tell me this." According to our narrator, the lesson helped, and she explains that, "I went on to greater and better things."

The fifties also saw the advent of a completely new practice – experienced butches teaching novice butches about sex. One narrator remembers that younger women frequently approached her with questions about sex: "There must be an X on my back. They just pick me out. . . ." She recalls one young butch who "had to know every single detail. She drove me crazy. Jesus Christ, y'know, just get down there and do it – y'get so aggravated." The woman who aggravated her gives the following account of learning about sex:

> And I finally talked to a butch buddy of mine. . . . She was a real tough one. I asked her "What do you do when you make love to a woman?" And we sat up for hours and hours at a time. . . . "I feel sexually aroused by this woman, but if I take her to bed, what am I gonna do?" And she says, "Well, what do you feel like doing?" and I says "Well, the only thing I can think of doing is. . .all I want to do is touch her, but what is the full thing of it. . .you know." So when [she]

> told me I says, "Really," well there was this one thing in there, uh. . .I don't know if you want me to state it. Maybe I can. . .well, I won't. . .I'll put in terms that you can understand. Amongst other things, the oral gratification. Well, that kind of floored me because I never expected something like that and I thought, well, who knows, I might like it.

She later describes her first sexual experience in which she was so scared that her friend had to shove her into the bedroom where the girl was waiting.

At the same time that attitudes toward discussions of and teachings about sexuality relaxed, the fifties' lesbian community became stricter in enforcing role-appropriate sexuality. Those who deviated from the pattern in the forties might have identified themselves as "lavender butch" and might have been labeled by others as "comme ci, comme ça." Although their divergence from the social norm would have been noticed and discussed, such women were not stigmatized. But the community of the fifties left little room to deviate. Those who did not consistently follow one role in bed were considered "ki-ki" (neither-nor), or more infrequently "AC/DC," both pejorative terms imposed by the community. Such women were viewed as disruptive of the social order and not to be trusted. They not only elicited negative comments, but they also were often ostracized from social groups. From the perspective of the 1980s, in which mutuality in lovemaking is emphasized as a positive quality, it is important to clarify that "ki-ki" did not refer to an abandonment of role-defined sex but rather to a shifting of sexual posture depending upon one's bed partner. Therefore, it was grounded absolutely in role playing. One of our narrators in fact defined "ki-ki" as "double role playing."[14]

These contradictory trends in attitudes and norms of lesbian sexuality parallel changes in the heterosexual world. Movement toward open discussion of sex, the acceptance of oral sex, and the teaching about sex took place in the society at large, as exemplified by the publication of and the material contained in the Kinsey reports.[15] Similarly, the lesbian community's stringent enforcement of role-defined behavior in the fifties occurred in the context of straight society's postwar move toward a stricter sexual division of labor and the ideology that accompanied it.[16] These parallels indicate a close connection between the evolution of heterosexual and homosexual cultures, a topic that requires further research.[17] At this point, we wish to stress that drawing parallels with heterosexuality can only partially illuminate changes in lesbian sexual mores. As an integral part of lesbian life, lesbian sexuality undergoes transformations that correspond with changing forms of the community's resistance to oppression.

Two developments occurred in this prepolitical period that are fundamental for the later emergence of the lesbian and gay liberation movement of the sixties. The first development was the flourishing of a lesbian culture; the second was the evolving stance of public defiance. The community of the forties was just beginning to support places for public gatherings and socializing, and during this period lesbians were to be found in bars only on weekends. Narrators of the forties do not remember having role models or anyone willing to instruct them in the ways of gay life. The prevalent feeling was that gay life was hard, and if people wanted it, they had to find it for themselves. In the fifties, the number of lesbian bars increased, and lesbians could be found socializing there every night of the week. As bar culture became more elaborate and open, lesbians more freely exchanged information about all aspects of their social lives, including sexuality. Discussion of sex was one of many dimensions of an increasingly complex culture. The strengthening of lesbian culture and the concomitant repression of gays in the fifties led the community to take a more public stance. This shift toward public confrontation subsequently generated enough sense of pride to counter the acknowledged detriments of gay life so that members of the community were willing to instruct newcomers both socially and sexually. Almost all our narrators who came out in the fifties remember a butch who served as a role model or remember acting as a role model themselves. Instruction about sexuality was part of a general education to community life that developed in the context of expanding community pride.

However, the community's growing public defiance was also related to its increased concern for enforcing role-appropriate behavior in the fifties. Butches were key in this process of fighting back. The butches alone, or the butch-fem couple, were always publicly visible as they walked down the street, announcing themselves to the world. To deal effectively with the hostility of the straight world, and to support one another in physical confrontations, the community developed, for butches in particular, rules of appropriate behavior and forms of organization and exerted pressure on butches to live up to these standards. Because roles organized intimate life, as well as the community's resistance to oppression, sexual performance was a vital part of these fifties' standards.

From the vantage point of the 1980s and twenty more years of lesbian and gay history, we know that just as evolving community politics created this tension between open discussion and teaching about sex and strict enforcement of role-appropriate sexual behavior, it also effected the resolution. Our research suggests that in the late sixties in Buffalo, with the development of the political activities of gay liberation, explicitly political organizations and tactics replaced butch-fem roles in leading the resistance to gay oppression. Because butch-fem roles were no longer the primary means for organizing the community's stance toward the straight world, the community no longer needed to enforce role-appropriate behavior.[18] This did not mean that butch-fem roles disappeared. As part of a long tradition of creating an authentic lesbian culture in an oppressive society, butch-fem roles remain, for many lesbians, an important code of personal behavior in matters of either appearance, sexuality, or both.

NOTES

This article is a revision of a paper originally presented at the "International Conference on Women's History and Oral History," Columbia University, New York, 18 November 1983. We want to thank Michael Frisch, Ellen DuBois, and Bobbi Prebis for reading the original version and offering us helpful comments. We also want to thank Rayna Rapp and Ronald Grele for their patience throughout the revision process.

1. This research is part of the work of the Buffalo Women's Oral History Project, which was founded in 1978 with three goals: (1) to produce a comprehensive, written history of the lesbian community in Buffalo, New York, using as the major source, oral histories of lesbians who came out prior to 1970; (2) to create and index an archive of oral history tapes, written interviews, and relevant supplementary materials; and (3) to give this history back to the community from which it derives. Madeline Davis and Elizabeth (Liz) Kennedy are the directors of the project. Avra Michelson was an active member from 1978 to 1981 and had a very important influence on the development of the project. Wanda Edwards has been an active member of the project since 1981, particularly in regard to research on the black lesbian community and on racism in the white lesbian community.
2. This hypothesis was shaped by our personal contact with Buffalo lesbians who came out in the 1940s and 1950s, and by discussion with grass roots gay and lesbian history projects around the country, in particular, the San Francisco Lesbian and Gay History Project, the Boston Area Gay and Lesbian History Project, and the Lesbian Herstory Ar-

chives. Our approach is close to and has been influenced by the social constructionist tendency of lesbian and gay history. See in particular, Jonathan Katz, *Gay American History, Lesbians and Gay Men in the U.S.A.* (New York: Thomas Y. Crowell Co., 1976); Gayle Rubin, Introduction to *A Woman Appeared to Me* by Renée Vivien (Nevada: Naiad Press, 1976), iii-xxxvii; Jeffrey Weeks, *Coming Out: Homosexual Politics in Britain from the Nineteenth Century to the Present* (London: Quartet Books, 1977). We want to thank all these sources which have been inspirational to our work.

3. The Buffalo Women's Oral History Project has written two papers on bar life, both by Madeline Davis, Elizabeth (Liz) Kennedy, and Avra Michelson: "Buffalo Lesbian Bars in the Fifties," presented at the National Women's Studies Association, Bloomington, Indiana, May 1980, and "Buffalo Lesbian Bars: 1930-1960," presented at the Fifth Berkshire Conference on the History of Women, Vassar College, Poughkeepsie, N.Y., June 1981. Both papers are on file at the Lesbian Herstory Archives, P.O. Box 1258, New York, New York 10116.

4. We think that this community could accurately be designated as a working-class lesbian community, but this is not a concept many members of this community would use; therefore, we have decided to call it a public bar community.

5. All quotes are taken from the interviews conducted for this project between 1978 and 1984. The use of the phrase "lesbian and her girl" in this quote reflects some of our butch narrators' belief that the butch member of a couple was the lesbian and the fem member's identity was less clear.

6. A variety of sources were helpful for learning about issues and problems of oral history research. They include the Special Issue on Women's Oral History, *Frontiers* 2 (Summer 1977); Willa K. Baum, *Oral History for the Local Historical Society* (Nashville, Tenn.: American Association for State and Local History, 1974); Michael Frisch, "Oral History and *Hard Times*: A Review Essay," *Oral History Review* (1979): 70-80; Ronald Grele, ed., *Envelopes of Sound: Six Practitioners Discuss the Method, Theory, and Practice of Oral History and Oral Tradition* (Chicago: Precedent Publishing, 1975); Ronald Grele, "Can Anyone over Thirty Be Trusted: A Friendly Critique of Oral History," *Oral History Review* (1978): 36-44; "Generations: Women in the South," *Southern Exposure* 4 (Winter 1977); "No More Moanin'," *Southern Exposure* 1 (Winter 1974); Peter Friedlander, *The Emergence of a UAW Local, 1936-1939* (Pittsburgh: University of Pittsburgh Press, 1975); William Lynwood Montell, *The Saga of Coe Ridge: A Study in Oral History* (Knoxville: University of Tennessee Press, 1970); Studs Terkel, *Hard Times: An Oral History of the Great Depression* (New York: Pantheon Books, 1970); Martin B. Duberman, *Black Mountain: An Exploration in Community* (Garden City, N.J.: Doubleday, 1972); Sherna Gluck, ed., *From Parlor to Prison: Five American Suffragists Talk about Their Lives* (New York: Vintage, 1976); and Kathy Kahn, *Hillbilly Women* (New York: Doubleday, 1972).

7. For a helpful discussion of memory, see John A. Neuenschwander, "Rememberance of Things Past: Oral Historians and Long-Term Memory," *Oral History Review* (1978): 46-53; many sources cited in the previous note also have relevant discussions of memory; in particular, see Frisch; Grele, *Envelopes of Sound;* Friedlander; and Montell.

8. See for instance, Joan Nestle, "Esther's Story: 1960," *Common Lives/Lesbian Lives* 1 (Fall 1981): 5-9; Joan Nestle, "Butch-Fem Relationships, Sexual Courage in the 1950s," *Heresies* 12 (1981): 21-24; Audre Lorde, "Tar Beach," *Conditions*, no. 5 (1979): 34-47; and Audre Lorde, "The Beginning," in *Lesbian Fiction*, ed. Elly Bulkin (Watertown, Mass.: Persephone Press, 1981), 255-74. Lesbian pulp fiction can also provide insight into the emotional and sexual life of this period; see for instance, Ann Bannon's *I Am a Woman* (Greenwich, Conn.: Fawcett Publications, 1959) and *Beebo Brinker* (Greenwich, Conn.: Fawcett Publications, 1962).

9. See, for instance, Nestle, "Butch-Fem Relationships"; Lorde, "Tar Beach"; Del Martin and Phyllis Lyon, *Lesbian/Woman* (New York: Bantam Books, 1972); John D'Emilio, *Sexual Politics, Sexual Communities: The Making of a Homosexual Minority in the United*

States, 1940-1970 (Chicago: University of Chicago Press, 1983).

10. For a full discussion of our research on butch-fem roles, see Madeline Davis and Elizabeth (Liz) Kennedy, "Butch-Fem Roles in the Buffalo Lesbian Community, 1940-1960" (paper presented at the Gay Academic Union Conference, Chicago, October 1982). This paper is on file at the Lesbian Herstory Archives.

11. These two main determinants of roles are quite different from what would usually be considered as indicators of sex roles in straight society; they do not include the sexual division of labor.

12. The origins of the "stone butch" and fem couple are beyond the scope of this paper. For an article that begins to approach these issues, see Esther Newton, "The Mythic Mannish Lesbian: Radclyffe Hall and the New Woman," *Signs* 9 (Summer 1984): 557-75.

13. Our understanding of the fem role has been enhanced by the following: Nestle's "Butch-Fem Relationships" and "Esther's Story"; Amber Hollibaugh and Cherrie Moraga, "What We're Rolling Around in Bed With: Sexual Silences in Feminism: A Conversation toward Ending Them," *Heresies* 12 (1981): 58-62.

14. For indications that "ki-ki" was used nationally in the lesbian subculture, see Jonathan Katz, *Gay/Lesbian Almanac, A New Documentary* (New York: Harper & Row, 1983), 15, 626.

15. Alfred C. Kinsey, Wardell B. Pomeroy, and Clyde E. Martin, *Sexual Behavior in the Human Male* (Philadelphia: W.B. Saunders Co., 1948); and Alfred Kinsey et al., *Sexual Behavior in the Human Female* (Philadelphia: W.B. Saunders Co., 1953). Numerous sources document this trend; see, for instance, Ann Snitow, Christine Stansell, and Sharon Thompson, eds, *Powers of Desire: The Politics of Sexuality* (New York: Monthly Review Press, 1983), in particular, Introduction, sec. 2, "Sexual Revolutions," and sec. 3, "The Institution of Heterosexuality," pp. 9-47, 115-71, 173-275; and Katz, *Gay/Lesbian Almanac*.

16. See Mary P. Ryan, *Womanhood in America: From Colonial Times to the Present* (New York: Franklin Watts, 1975).

17. A logical result of the social constructionist school of gay history is to consider that heterosexuality is also a social construction. Katz, in *Gay/Lesbian Almanac*, begins to explore this idea.

18. Although national homophile organizations began in the fifties, no such organizations developed in Buffalo until the formation of the Mattachine Society of the Niagara Frontier in 1969. But we do not think that the lack of early homophile organizations in this city made the bar community's use of roles as an organizer of its stance toward the straight world different from that of cities where homophile organizations existed. In general, these organizations, whether mixed or all women, did not draw from or affect bar communities. Martin and Lyon in chap. 8, "Lesbians United," *Lesbian/Woman* (238-79), present Daughters of Bilitis (DOB) as an alternative for those dissatisfied with bar life, not as an organization to coalesce the forces and strengths of the bar community. Gay liberation combined the political organization of DOB and the defiance and pride of bar life and therefore affected and involved both communities.

Copyright Information

Smith, Daniel Scott, and Michael S. Hindus. "Premarital Pregnancy in America 1640-1971: An Overview and Interpretation." *The Journal of Interdisciplinary History* 5:4 (Spring 1975): 537-570. "Reprinted from *The Journal of Interdisciplinary History*, V:4 (1975), 537-570, with permission of the editors of *The Journal of Interdisciplinary History* and the MIT Press, Cambridge, Massachusetts (USA). ©1975 by the Massachusetts Institute of Technology and the editors of *The Journal of Interdisciplinary History*."

Cott, Nancy F. "Passionlessness: An Interpretation of Victorian Sexual Ideology, 1790-1850." *Signs: Journal of Women in Culture and Society* 4:2 (Winter 1978): 219-236. "©1978 by The University of Chicago. All rights reserved." Chicago, Illinois, USA.

Smith-Rosenberg, Carroll. "The Female World of Love and Ritual: Relations between Women in Nineteenth-Century America." *Signs: Journal of Women in Culture and Society* 1:1 (Autumn 1975): 1-29. "©1975 by The University of Chicago. All rights reserved." Chicago, Illinois, USA.

Degler, Carl N. "What Ought to Be and What Was: Women's Sexuality in the Nineteenth Century." *American Historical Review* 79 (December 1974): 1467-1490. ©Professor Carl Degler, Margaret Byrne Professor of American History, Stanford University, Stanford, California, USA.

Gadlin, Howard. "Private Lives and Public Order: A Critical View of the History of Intimate Relations in the U.S." *The Massachusetts Review* 17:2 (1976): 304-330. "Reprinted from *The Massachusetts Review*, ©1977, The Massachusetts Review, Inc.," Amherst, Massachusetts, USA.

Campbell, D'Ann. "Women's Life in Utopia: The Shaker Experiment in Sexual Equality Reappraised—1810 to 1860." *The New England Quarterly* 51:1 (March 1978): 23-38. ©The New England Quarterly, Inc., The Colonial Society of Massachusetts, Northeastern University, Boston, Massachusetts, USA.

Rothman, Ellen K. "Sex and Self-Control: Middle-Class Courtship in America, 1770-1870." *Journal of Social History* 15:3 (1981): 409-425. ©Carnegie-Mellon University Press, Pittsburgh, Pennsylvania, USA.

DuBois, Ellen Carol, and Linda Gordon. "Seeking Ecstasy on the Battlefield: Danger and Pleasure in Nineteenth-Century Feminist Sexual Thought." *Feminist Studies* 9:1 (Spring 1983): 7-25. ©by Feminist Studies, Inc., Women's Studies Program, University of Maryland, College Park, Maryland, USA.

Dunfey, Julie. "'Living the Principle' of Plural Marriage: Mormon Women, Utopia, and Female Sexuality in the Nineteenth Century." *Feminist Studies* 10:3 (Fall 1984): 523-536. ©by Feminist Studies, Inc., Women's Studies Program, University of Maryland, College Park, Maryland, USA.

Ruggles, Steven. "Fallen Women: The Inmates of the Magdalen Society Asylum of Philadelphia, 1836-1908." *Journal of Social History* 16 (Summer 1983): 65-82. ©*Journal of Social History*, Carnegie-Mellon University Press, Pittsburgh, Pennsylvania, USA.

Brumberg, Joan Jacobs. "'Ruined' Girls: Changing Community Responses to Illegitimacy in Upstate New York, 1890-1920." *Journal of Social History* 18 (Winter 1984): 247-272. ©*Journal of Social History*, Carnegie-Mellon University Press, Pittsburgh, Pennsylvania, USA.

Cannon, Charles A. "The Awesome Power of Sex: The Polemical Campaign against Mormon Polygamy." *Pacific Historical Review* 43 (February 1974): 61-82. "©by the Pacific Coast Branch, American Historical Association. Reprinted from *Pacific Historical Review*, Vol. 43 (February 1974): pp. 61-82 by permission" of the Association and the author.

Freedman, Estelle B. "Sexuality in Nineteenth-Century America: Behavior, Ideology, and Politics." *Reviews in American History* 10 (December 1982): 196-215. ©1982 by The Johns Hopkins University Press, Baltimore, Maryland, USA.

Sahli, Nancy. "Smashing: Women's Relationships before the Fall." *Chrysalis* 6 (1979): 17-27. ©Nancy Sahli, Silver Spring, Maryland, USA.

Faderman, Lillian, PhD. "The Morbidification of Love between Women by 19th-Century Sexologists." *Journal of Homosexuality* 4:1 (Fall 1978): 73-90. ©1978 by The Haworth Press, Inc. All rights reserved, Binghamton, New York, USA.

Chauncey, Jr., George. "From Sexual Inversion to Homosexuality: Medicine and the Changing Conceptualization of Female Deviance." *Salmagundi* 58/59 (Fall 1982-Winter 1983): 114-146. *Salmagundi, A Quarterly Journal of the Humanities and Social Sciences*, ©1982 Skidmore College, Saratoga Springs, New York, USA.

Rupp, Leila J. "'Imagine My Surprise': Women's Relationships in Historical Perspective." *Frontiers* 5:3 (1981): 61-70. ©Professor Leila J. Rupp, Ohio State University, Columbus, Ohio, USA.

McGovern, James R. "The American Woman's Pre-World War I Freedom in Manners and Morals." *The Journal of American History* 50:2 (September 1968): 315-333. ©Organization of American Historians, Indiana University, Bloomington, Indiana, USA.

Faderman, Lillian. "Lesbian Magazine Fiction in the Early Twentieth Century." *Journal of Popular Culture* 11:4 (Spring 1978): 800-817. ©1978 by Ray B. Browne and the *Journal of Popular Culture*, Bowling Green State University, Bowling Green, Ohio, USA.

Schlossman, Steven, and Stephanie Wallach. "The Crime of Precocious Sexuality: Female Juvenile Delinquency in the Progressive Era." *Harvard Educational Review* 48:1 (February 1978): 65-94. "Copyright ©1980 by the President and Fellows of Harvard College. All rights reserved." Cambridge, Massachusetts, USA.

Kushner, Howard I. "Nineteenth-Century Sexuality and the 'Sexual Revolution' of the Progressive Era." *The Canadian Review of American Studies* 9:1 (Spring 1978): 34-49. ©*The Canadian Review of American Studies*, Social Science Centre, The University of Western Ontario, London, Ontario, Canada.

Lunbeck, Elizabeth. "'A New Generation of Women': Progressive Psychiatrists and the Hypersexual Female." *Feminist Studies* 13:3 (Fall 1987): 512-543. ©1987 by Elizabeth Lunbeck, Princeton, New Jersey, USA.

Simmons, Christina. "Companionate Marriage and the Lesbian Threat." *Frontiers* 4:3 (Fall 1979): 54-59. ©1979 Frontiers Editorial Collective, Women's Studies Program, University of Colorado at Boulder, Boulder, Colorado, USA. Reprinted with permission of the Journal and the author.

Bullough, Vern and Bullough, Bonnie. "Lesbianism in the 1920s and 1930s: A Newfound Study." *Signs: Journal of Women in Culture and Society* 2:4 (1977): 895-904. "©1977 by The University of Chicago. All rights reserved." Chicago, Illinois, USA.

Davis, Madeline, and Elizabeth Lapovsky Kennedy. "Oral History and the Study of Sexuality in the Lesbian Community: Buffalo, New York, 1940-1960." *Feminist Studies* 12:1 (Spring 1986): 7-26. ©by Feminist Studies, Inc, Women's Studies Program, University of Maryland, College Park, Maryland, USA.

Index

Bei Fragen zur Produktsicherheit wenden Sie sich bitte an:
If you have any questions regarding product safety,
please contact:

Walter de Gruyter GmbH
Genthiner Straße 13
10785 Berlin
productsafety@degruyterbrill.com